THE STREETS OF LONDON

The Booth Notebooks –South East

Editors:
Jess Steele
Mike Steele

2019

Deptford Forum Publishing, 2 Osberton Road, London SE12 8AH

The Booth Inquiry archive, of which these notebooks form a part, is held at the British Library of Political and Economic Science at the London School of Economics.

Edited by Jess Steele and Mike Steele
Design and layout by Nixx and Ed Fredenburgh
Cover design and title page graphic by Lionel Openshaw
Sketch maps by Nixx and Community Desktop Publishing
Original illustrations by Godfrey Jones
Original publication printed by Biddles Ltd, Guildford, Surrey

This is not a facsimile edition. We have tried to reproduce the text in a format that can satisfy both academic and general interest. This has meant making some minor changes for the sake of consistency and readability.

Second edition 2019 recreated from original and printed by Short Run Press, Exeter

Second edition dedicated to Peter Hill RIP

ISBN 978-1-898536-31-4
British Library Cataloguing in Publication Data
A catalogue record for this book is available from the British Library

Special thanks to:

Karen, who sat in the Coal Hole pub in the Strand on a freezing day early in 1994 and first gave me faith that other Londoners would be fascinated by Booth's streets. She followed that up with three years of active involvement. This is a result for her as much as for anyone.

Mike Steele for checking the fate of every Booth street in the modern A to Z to discover what happened to Booth's London.

I am grateful for the help and encouragement of David Englander & Rosemary O'Day from the Charles Booth Centre for Social Investigation at the Open University, Dr Angela Raspin and Sue Donnelly from BLPES Archives, and Carlos and Carl from LSE Photography Unit.

I would also like to thank Richard, Ed, Peter, Lionel and most of all Nixx for their usual level of hard work, commitment and support.

Photographs courtesy of Lewisham Local Studies Library, Greenwich Local History Centre, Southwark Local Studies Library and Lambeth Local Studies Library.

The Borough of Deptford sponsored by Malcolm Edwards
The Borough of Lewisham sponsored by Lewisham Libraries

Lambeth sponsored by Lambeth College
Bermondsey sponsored by Harry & Edna Bowling
Brockley & Deptford sponsored by Lewisham College
Charlton sponsored by Viscount Gough
Crofton Park sponsored by Rossy and Nancy Bailey and Juliet Desailly
Eastcombe sponsored by Diana Rimel

Amersham Vale sponsored by Chief Superintendant Ken Chapman (Retired)
Blackhorse Road sponsored by Richard White
Breakspears Road sponsored by Roy Bourne
Bronze Street sponsored by Margaret Sandra
Chipley Street sponsored by the Walden Family
Creekside sponsored by Jani Llewellyn
The Cut sponsored by Southwark College
Czar Street sponsored by Tsarevich Paul (The Unsung)
Deptford Green sponsored by Richard Walker
Deptford High Street sponsored by Revival Cafe
Edward Street sponsored by Vincent s Hodgson
Embleton Road sponsored by Julian & Marion Watson
Erlanger Road sponsored by Des Malone
Frankham Street sponsored by Dr Nick McAdoo
Idonia Street sponsored by Nixx
Laurie Grove sponsored by Centre for Continuing & Community Education, Goldsmiths College
McMillan Street sponsored by Jill Goddard
Mill Lane sponsored by Callum Sheridan Lee
Montford Place sponsored by Laura Hastings-Smith
New Cross Road sponsored by Jess Steele to thank George Hunt
Rolt Street sponsored by Mrs G Braybrook in memory of Charles Braybrook
Rutland Gate sponsored by Mrs W S H Paul
Rye Lane sponsored by Alan Bailey
Selbourne Road sponsored by Adrian Goodall (for Dad)
Strickland Street sponsored by Ray Wheeler
The Stowage sponsored by Ed Fredenburgh
Upland Road sponsored by Karen Bray
Warwick Street sponsored by George Hunt
Woodlands sponsored by Godfrey Smith

We are extremely grateful for the continuing support given to us by the Booth family. They enabled us to publish the original version of the Streets of London: South East in 1998 and now have made this reprint possible.

Jess and Mike Steele
Deptford Forum Publishing

Jess first found the Booth Inquiry archive when researching a local history of Deptford in the early 1990s. Sitting in the chilly archive room she found herself writing out in pencil the full text of the walks from the so-called 'police notebooks'. She knew then that she wanted to publish these fascinating snapshots.

With much help in transcribing we were pleased to publish this volume of South East London walks in 1998 and had at that time high hopes of producing the other volumes in rapid succession. However, constraints of time and money delayed us by a mere 20 years!

In the meantime LSE have digitised the original notebooks and made them available at www.booth.lse.ac.uk. We feel a physical book offers a more useable format. It's certainly much easier to read than the longhand and being organised into chapters, it is possible to browse through these neighbourhoods, aided by sketch maps, contemporary photographs and new illustrations, or to use the index to gain a sense of what your street was like 120 years ago.

There are 392 notebooks in the Booth archive which cover three research collections: Poverty; Industry; and Religious Influences. Around 30 of these are the handwritten notes of 300 walks across the whole of London, while others record over 1,000 interviews with businessmen, workers and trades union representatives, school board visitors, publicans and vicars. The original project had begun by collecting detailed information about individual households. Later they chose to focus on whole streets as it became too time-consuming.

These neighbourhoods were dynamic: "the rich and poor both leave but the middle class are coming in". Since the research aimed to update their own earlier material these notebooks not only describe the neighbourhoods at the end of the century but also how they had changed in the previous ten years.

Despite the impressive scale and fascinating detail of these walks, it has to be said that Booth's researchers and their policemen companions are often obnoxious and patronising. They make outrageous assumptions and blatant generalisations which readers may find disturbing. The notebooks reveal as much about the researchers as they do about the poor of Southwark, Deptford or Woolwich. Their views are, of course not those of myself or Deptford Forum Publishing.

We hope that this volume, and the East London one, will contribute to the debates on London's history and its future, its problems and their solutions. We want it to be used in many different ways: as a source for history and the social sciences, as a resource for school projects, as a guide for Sunday strolling, as a spur to comparison and compassion for those who live in London's poverty 120 years after these walks. Most of all we want readers to enjoy the exploration of their own neighbourhoods, whether out on the streets or from the comfort of an armchair.

Jess Steele, June 2019

POLICE AND SOCIAL INQUIRY IN LATE-VICTORIAN LONDON

Charles Booth has never wanted for an audience. The seventeen-volume survey *Life and Labour of the People in London*, which he published between 1889 and 1903, provided the first scientific estimates of poverty and has been the starting point for all serious discussion of the subject ever since. It is rightly regarded as one of the high points in the British tradition of empirical social research. Employing a subsistence definition of poverty Booth found, contrary to his expectations, that nearly 31 per cent of those surveyed were in poverty. His researches showed too that, apart from inefficient expenditure, the principal sources of poverty were due to low wages, unemployment and old age.

Social inquiry, for Booth, was not an academic pursuit but a guide to social action. His suggestions for the creation of an effective policy on employment ranged from the reform and rationalisation of the labour market to the provision of non-contributory old age pensions. His contribution in respect of the latter, first introduced in 1908, was indeed every bit as important as his work on the conceptualisation and measurement of poverty.

Booth's Life and Motivations

Charles James Booth was born in Liverpool on 30th March 1840 into a public-spirited commercial family that was Liberal in politics and Unitarian in religion. Booth was involved in communal controversies from an early age. Earnest, serious and civic-minded, he combined the development of his shipping line with an active commitment to franchise reform, popular education and social betterment. Booth, though, was no ordinary philanthropist. He rejected charity as a cure and Christianity as a creed. Positivism, the Religion of Humanity, presented a more satisfying foundation for a rational faith. Positive Philosophy offered the young, the intellectually curious and those of unsettled faith a humanist religion and a new ethic of personal social obligation. The crisis of authority had a material as well as a spiritual dimension and Positivists were as much preoccupied with the 'social question' as with any other. Booth, like so many of his generation, was repelled by the crass materialism of the age and the selfishness it encouraged. "The race for wealth is run by a few only and the prizes fall to those who are already rich", he wrote.

"The leaders in this fatal competition, blind to all else, are willing to sacrifice everything to the production of wealth and even talk of the laws which govern this struggle as though they were the only guides to human life...I would not undervalue the motive of this race, or the effect it has had in developing the resources of the world and the power of the workers, nor do I say that it can be dispensed with. But I do say that it now needs checking and that it is only in its subordination to public welfare that we can look for that social improvement which we need."

Positivism had its share of drawing-room radicals, idealists and dreamers. But it also had a hard edge. Booth's close cousin, the able and engaging lawyer Henry Crompton, was among that group of reform-minded intellectuals who enjoyed a special relationship with the trade union movement during the 1860s and '70s. As a large employer of port labour, Booth was hardly unaware of working people and their wants. His attempts to interest trade unionists in arbitration and conciliation procedures, though they proved unavailing, served to enlarge his experience of labour and labour questions as did the Trades Hall which he helped to found. The sectarianism that destroyed his attempts to introduce free secular education into Liverpool's schools convinced him that Humanity could be better served by means other than politics. The social crisis of the 1880s gave a clear focus to his brooding intellect and expanding moral imagination.

By this time Booth had moved from Liverpool to London where family wealth and connections gave ready access to that band of moralists, philanthropists and members of the professional classes who dominated public debate on the social question. As a Positivist believing that social action should be grounded in the scientific study of the laws of society, Booth found himself both moved and fascinated by the lives of the working poor. The fixing of his interest upon the East End of London, however, may well have reflected the influence of his wife Mary.

Mary Booth was the daughter of Charles Zachary Macaulay, a disting-uished public servant. Her mother's father established the *Manchester Guardian*. It was Mary Booth who, on a visit to the East End in 1878, told her husband that she was stirred "to help in all this misery". Her cousins Kate, Teresa and Beatrice Potter, who were engaged in voluntary social work in Whitechapel, no doubt contributed to that quickening of interest which led Booth to take lodgings in the East End and to invite workmen to his home in the West End in order to extend his knowledge of working class life.

The onset of economic depression, mass unemployment, socialism and social unrest gave these interests a new urgency. Such anxieties as he possessed, however, found release in social inquiry rather than in social work. Impatient with the glacial pace of conventional philanthropy, critical of the a priori assumptions of political economy and

Mary Booth, wife of Charles, in 1880

disturbed by the challenge of socialism, Booth gave primacy to the collection of facts and an accurate description of the condition of the people throughout London as the basis for social diagnosis and public policy. For all the scope, precision and arresting detail of the Life and Labour Inquiry, begun in 1886 and completed 17 years later, it was not a simple compendium or statistical cyclopaedia but a major contribution to social economy and social action. The work of a team of researchers who were co-ordinated and financed by Booth himself, it was probably the largest private inquiry ever undertaken.

Life and Labour and the Poverty Maps

Life and Labour of the People in London was divided into three series. The four-volume Poverty Series related degrees of comfort and wellbeing to the ways in which people lived. The Industry Series examined in five volumes how people worked, what they produced and what they received. The remaining seven volumes were devoted to the Religious Influences Series which, in spite of its title, said little about the spiritual life of the people and much about the distinctive character of the religious life and activities in the various districts of London. A striking feature of the project was the inclusion of a series of thematic maps to show the distribution of degrees of comfort and wellbeing and the spatial relationships between the classes. These maps, reproduced here in full colour, have not received the attention they deserve.

The extent to which Booth's poverty maps consciously belonged to an existing tradition is uncertain. Social mapping developed during the 19th century in response to commercial and municipal requirements and also to satisfy Victorian concerns about the physical and moral health of the urban masses. Gradation shading, developed by the Belgian statistician Adolphe Quetelet in the 1820s to display the distribution of crimes against people and property, had been translated in 1842, making the technique familiar to an English audience. The Census of Ireland in the previous year had also made innovative use of shaded maps to illustrate population density and certain other social characteristics. Colour-coded maps of social conditions to plot the spread of cholera and insanitary housing likewise gave evidence of the growth of a more sociologically-informed cartography around the mid-century. What Booth knew of all of this remains to be established. That he could have worked independently of his predecessors seems improbable but cannot be ruled out. A tendency to re-invent the wheel appears to be a distinctive feature in the history of empirical social research. What is clear is that, from its inception, the diagrammatic representation of poverty was regarded as an integral feature of Booth's Inquiry.

Booth's Descriptive Map of Poverty was first presented to the public in the form of a pilot study of East London delivered to the Royal Statistical Society in 1887. An extended version was included with the first two-volume edition of Life and Labour of the People in London published in 1889-91. The map represented the predominant social class and character of each of the streets of the Metropolis, classified according to a seven-point colour scheme based largely on the impressions of the School Board Visitors (subsequently known as school attendance officers) as told to Booth's research staff. These impressions were then transferred by hand onto a twenty-five inch base map that was subsequently reduced and reprinted by the celebrated map-maker and publisher Edward Stanford. The maps reproduced here have been photographed from the hand-painted 25-inch originals held at BLPES.

The importance of the Descriptive Map of Poverty may be gauged from the considerable resources that Booth invested in its revision in 1897/8 in order to incorporate the changes caused by urban redevelopment and the movement of population in the previous ten years. This time, however, Booth relied upon the impressions of Metropolitan Police officers rather than upon those of the School Board Visitors as his principal source of information. It was a role for which the police were by no means ill prepared.

Police Evidence

Police duties, then as now, extended well beyond the suppression of crime. Britain, though not a police state, often cast the police as a social agency, a kind of substitute civil service, collecting evidence on social problems, asserting a certain expertise in selected areas and offering counsel and advice – sometimes unsolicited – to policy makers. The requirements of public order gave the police considerable latitude in the demarcation of their interests. Questions of poverty, crowding and insanitary conditions, crime, immigration and industrial displacement defined the scope of police observation. Policemen gave evidence to all the principal parliamentary and governmental inquiries of the period: on the housing of the working classes, the sweating system, labour, foreign immigration and the operation of the Sunday Trading laws.

The recognition of police evidence as a significant source of social observation extended beyond the corridors of Whitehall and Westminster. Charles Booth, like Charles Dickens before him, valued the police not only for their protection but also for their opinions and local expertise. With the consent of Police Commissioner Sir Edward Bradford "experienced members of the police force, chosen for their local knowledge" were assigned to the Booth Inquiry in connection with the revision of the Descriptive Map of London Poverty. The Metropolis was parceled out into a number of beats each patrolled together by interviewer and policeman. The bulk of these walks were undertaken by Booth's companionable associate George Herbert Duckworth, the half-brother of Virginia Woolf, who subsequently enjoyed a distinguished career in the public service. Nearly every street in the Metropolitan Police District of London was visited and its social composition recorded. Not only were policemen required to identify the social class and ethnic make-up of individual streets, they also presented much incidental information about the character of the community. "During these walks", wrote Booth, "almost every social influence was discussed, and especially those bearing upon vice and crime, drunkenness and disorder."

How representative are such sources? Bobbies on the beat have left few records. Station records, too, are rare and incomplete. Recent studies of the social composition of the police labour force do, however, suggest that, in terms of class origins, the Metropolitan Police were close to those whom they policed. Policemen were drawn overwhelmingly from the unskilled and semi-skilled working class. With police recruitment (at least up to divisional level) based on a single-tier entry system, lines of authority did not follow social class divisions, as in the military. Serving officers had a close understanding of the everyday experiences and practices – legal and otherwise – of the people in London's streets. Booth's investigators, though sceptical of much that was said, had no grounds for thinking that police observation was rank-related or distorted by social class. And neither have we. The information given to the Booth Inquiry is probably as representative of police attitudes and opinion as we are likely to obtain.

The police were asked to accompany the Booth team on their perambulations and give their views on the changes that had taken place on their 'patch' or 'manor' over the course of the previous ten years but the commentaries to the walks are also a prime source for information about the police themselves, their lifestyle and opinions. Such information varies enormously. The policemen themselves seem to leap from the page as Duckworth and his colleagues sum up their appearance and biography. "Sergeant Vanstone is a fresh-coloured young man; a native of Deptford and far away the best officer I have met so far as local knowledge is concerned. In nearly every street he knew personally some of the people."

Duckworth often noted their attitude to the task at hand. "Sergeant Nunn is a burly, awkward rather heavy man but a good fellow and a very willing guide." Some police were in a better position than others to judge the areas. "O'Dell is a fat man, very fat. He is not now on active outdoor duty but is employed in the clerks' office. He is intelligent and knows a good deal more about the different parts of the Division in their criminal aspects than most of the policemen who have been round with me. All charges from every quarter pass through his hands every day."

It Takes All Sorts

The types of crime and disorder which characterised each area are summarised in a few words by the policemen. In Milan Place near Waterloo Sergeant Saltmarshe explained that "fathers fight their sons of a Saturday night". In nearby Cornwall Road "last Saturday...a woman threw a lighted lamp at her husband and both were burned to death". In Brockley the "bucolic, beefy and provincial" PC Moss told Ernest Aves that the charges were mostly "drunk and disorderly". In Lewisham "the typical local misdemeanour appears to be afternoon house-breaking, houses being entered while the occupiers are away. In such a district as this, this crime is difficult to prevent or even to detect and Lloyds was amusing in describing the effrontery of the invader – how, having forced the lock, often a very simple operation, he deceives any chance onlooking neighbour that there may be, by greeting and shaking hands with an imaginary person, entering as he does so and closing the door. On leaving the same thing may be repeated, and no suspicions are aroused until it is too late."

The police faced some substantial dangers in particular areas. In the notorious Dust Hole in Woolwich Duckworth learnt from his guide that "the police only come when there is a bad row and they are summoned. No man would go alone. When called he waits for at least one other. Missiles are showered on them from every window when they interfere. It is out of bounds for soldiers and the military patrol can capture and confine any soldier found there. But nevertheless the low class soldier goes there. The police know and see them but have no right to arrest them." Another very specific problem was discussed in Brockley when Ernest Aves and PC Moss arrived at One Tree Hill in November 1899. "The road leads by the bank and fence of the Hill round which the attack during the 'battles of One Tree Hill' of a year or so ago chiefly waged. Moss was on duty but was stationed at a point where no attack was made. It appears that on the first Sunday the few police on duty were a good deal mauled, but on the second they were in strong force, with a large hidden reserve, and the arrests made with the subsequent punishments of imprisonment without the option of a fine, speedily put an end to the trouble."

The very respectability of a street might be dependent upon and defined by the fact that police lived upon it. In Mercy Terrace near Ladywell Road, Aves noted that "a policeman lives in one of them rent-free and acts as a kind of agent. It was his business to get the houses into good and quiet order and, according to Lloyds, he has succeeded." Ormside Street in Hatcham "used to be rough but better now. Got two policemen to live here; these men are privileged to report themselves to the sergeant on the beat instead of at the station. Always quiets a street if they get a policeman in."

There were clearly debates within the police force and beyond about the best ways of tackling street crime. No less a mortal than the Metropolitan Police Commissioner debated appropriate policing with George Duckworth. "Met Sir E. Bradford on my way to the station. He on horseback making one of his surprise visits. He stopped & talked for some time in the street – said that he hoped I found the police had a good knowledge of the inhabitants in each street 'for that I believe is the real way in which they should do their work'...In rough streets he liked them to know the names & occupations of every inhabitant. The difficulty, he said, lay in preventing the people feeling they were watched...To be always in the background except when there was real need & then to come down like a thunderbolt was he believed the real policy of the police, ending with 'Don't you think so?'."

Despite all this incidental detail, the purpose of the walks was not to reveal the attitudes of the police nor yet to inform the reader of their working lives and practices. Rather it was to use the policeman's knowledge of the various districts to facilitate an informed revision of the 1889 maps. How well did the police know the community in which they worked? How did the nature of their work determine the help which they were able to offer Duckworth?

On the face of it, they were very knowledgeable and well able to give the researchers the assistance they needed. There were, however, limits to the police knowledge of the streets and their people. They knew most about the people who caused trouble. This had important implications. If a community did not have a high profile in terms of public disorder or criminality, the police knew relatively little about its life. If a street was well known for charges this was reflected in the police estimate of its colour. Booth and his associates were aiming to use the map to describe the levels of poverty and comfort but they used as guides men for whom criminality and disorder, or their absence, were the defining characteristics of the population. George Arkell walked around the poorest parts of Deptford with Inspector Gummer and Sergeant Goddard but "both officers agree that it is better than it was: not so much crime or violence. To me, little or no improvement is apparent in the poor streets and I have grave doubts as to the knowledge of the police of the social condition of the people. They measure the streets mainly by the proportion of offences against the law and diminution of these is an improvement which they attribute to increasing social position."

Black and Blue

'BLACK' and 'DARK BLUE' became associated less with degrees of poverty than with degrees and kinds of criminality, roughness and disorderliness. In the map key BLACK was defined as "vicious and semi-criminal". In two Kennington streets, tucked away by themselves, "there are so many charges for assaults and drunkenness that the BLACK line of the map might remain". The police were excellent barometers in these respects: they proved a less sensitive instrument in others. They accepted that there could be respectable poor but they were generally defined by the absence of criminality. There was little detailed comment about these poor people – other than the fact that their worst excesses were getting drunk on a Saturday night and their greatest virtues working hard and keeping inside their houses.

Duckworth, Arkell, Aves and the police used the external appearance of buildings, streets and people as the criteria by which they measured the accuracy of the map of 1889, so that the reader is oftentimes bemused, wondering precisely what was being assessed. The term 'poverty' is not frequently used (if at all) in the notebooks. Rather the pages are littered with references to 'rough', 'respectable', 'vicious', 'quiet', 'disreputable', 'poor', 'well-to-do' and so on. The BLACK and DARK BLUE areas are defined not by income but by their criminal characteristics. Baildon Street was considered one of the worst streets in Deptford: "'Better than it was' says the sergeant, 'fewer cases come from here'. Used to have to send 20 men to make arrests. He would hardly call it criminal now. To me the street looks worse than it did 10 years ago. If any men and women have the criminal brand on their faces, these seem on my two visits unmistakenly to bear it. DARK BLUE with BLACK line as map."

Often the description was based on the researcher's impression of a whole scene. In Mason's Buildings in Southwark "The exit into Borough High St is down a passage under a house, not a yard wide. The inhabitants of the houses and common lodging houses are prostitutes and ponces and thieves. Youths and middle-aged men of the lowest casual class loafing; undergrown men; women slouching with draggled skirts, hatless but hidden under long shawls; a deformed boy with naked half-formed leg turned in the wrong direction, made up the scene."

Sometimes the researcher would challenge a police description as in Borough's Bell Court, "a dreary well of a place. "'Paint it as BLACK as you can' said my guide, 'it is a little hell upon earth', but when I pressed for a diagnosis it appeared to resolve itself into the common Bermondsey charge of drunkenness and resulting disorders. DARK BLUE as map." In other cases, such as Woolwich's Rope Yard Rails, they accepted the gauge of criminality "This street is a fair BLACK all through, not for poverty but for vice."

The context of the houses could also cause problems with assessing their proper colour. In Shardeloes Road there were some houses "of a kind that in Peckham or Hoxton would be put down as PINK with little hesitation. In Brockley, however, with a much larger proportion of houses taken on lease, with rents paid quarterly and a different class often found in occupation, the right colour becomes more doubtful. Here I am told that the tenancies are yearly and that there are servants in many of the houses. Perhaps from RED of map, to PINK-barred. The alternative, PINK." After a while the colour scheme became so natural a descriptive method for both researcher and policeman that they would talk of "a RED house" or even "a PINK man".

Changing neighbourhoods

The police knowledge of the various districts led Duckworth and the others to an understanding of the changes going on in the capital's various neighbourhoods. Changes in the physical environment accounted for changes in the population. In his general remarks to the walk around St Saviour's near London Bridge, Duckworth concluded: "The same change is going on in Southwark that in years past took place in the City. As site values rise those who can most afford to pay for them leave, ie the rich leave first. After them go the fairly comfortable and last of all the poor and very poor. Hence those who properly can the least afford to pay high rents are the last to leave. The rich were the first of the residents to leave the City, the poor have only just left. In Southwark the rich have already left; the fairly comfortable are leaving; the poor and the very poor remain and will remain until they are evicted."

Changes in rents, extensions to the railways and slum clearance of various types resulted in pushing round London the former inhabitants of BLACK and DARK BLUE areas. Often they did not go far. "The old tenants of Kings Bench Walk etc, though dispossessed, have yet found houseroom close to their own haunts and...others displaced by railway extension...have found their way in. The inhabitants are all South Londoners. None have come from the north side of the Thames. They are the dregs of the population and not scum that has floated off from distant places and infected new areas as in Notting Dale." In Deptford the phrase "people from Mill Lane have come in" was bound to mean costers, prostitutes and nightly fights.

The Researchers

We should remember that the records of the London walks were not kept by the police themselves but by George Duckworth, George Arkell and Ernest Aves. The views of the police are, therefore, mediated and to them are added those of the researcher. Sometimes there is direct quotation from the police, more often there is a summary of the results of the conversation between the two about the neighbourhood. Often we are presented with the researcher's own impressions. In Watergate Street Arkell noted: "Faint foetid smell prevails, overpowered in places by disgusting stench. Rough women, one with head bandaged; others with black eyes; one old harridan sitting on doorstep with dirty clay pipe; shoeless children. Costers, street-sellers, gut cleaners." Risdon Street, Rotherhithe was "full of children, mess of paper, no bread. Children out at knees and elbow but all well fed, no sore eyes, faces very dirty, boots bad, dancing to a barrel organ. Women with sack or dirty white aprons and bare arms. Struggling pots and tins of flowers at the windows." The researchers were learning, with police help, to read the code of the streets.

These walks are not a tourist guide to London. There is much here of local interest so that the modern reader can form a picture of the physical environment, even to the extent of the width of the streets, the height of the buildings, and the existence of courts uncharted on any contemporary map. But the perspective of the walks is heavily influenced by the policeman's working environment. As a result one has to accept that the level of detail is variable and the reliability of the information likewise.

Yet, for Booth's purposes, the police served to underline the purpose of his Inquiry, to describe the lives of Londoners in response to the perceived social crisis of the 1880s. They, like few others, were in a position to pinpoint troublespots and troublemakers. They were prepared to reinforce their assessment of the vicious inhabitants of one neighbourhood by a graphic description of hundreds of rats infesting a cargo of fatty ham. They had views, which they readily recounted to the researchers about the 'problems' of the age – prostitution, gambling, drink, immorality, immigration, marriage, theft, housing, overcrowding, environment. They were always willing to generalise.

"He has never seen a girl brought in drunk under 20 years of age. It is when they get older that women take to gin & ale & become regular soakers." "The worst men as a class for drink are carmen & dockers. They can stand a deal more than ordinary men whose work is not in the open air but even so they take more than they can stand." Coalies were also said to be hard drinkers and easy spenders.

The Drama of the Age

Of all the pre-occupations of the late-Victorian period, prostitution ranks highly. Vigilance committees were trying to clear out the brothels but many police felt it was "better to have them where you can put your finger on them than in places where you don't know of their existence until they are firmly established". St Gabriel Street was defined as "Poor and vicious, thieves and prostitutes. Used to be all brothels at the north east end but cleared out two years ago with the help of the Vigilance Association. Some prostitutes still remain but no brothels. The infamous 'Girdle' gang came from here. When the brothels were turned out they migrated and were discovered in a coffee house at the east end of Graham St in Hackney. Other prostitutes went to Deptford". The researchers sometimes offer us a smile at police methods as when "Sales has had men out dressed as females to convict the brothels but has never succeeded. 'They always know'."

Prostitution was often associated with the common lodging houses such as those in the vicinity of Redcross Place. "Last year there were over 4,000 charges from this block of streets." The Borough prostitutes were mainly Irish women. "Their gains are made far more by robbery than by prostitution...Bullies live on their earnings. They are English or Irish cockneys, not foreigners. The foreign bully has nearly deserted London since the law of last October and foreign women come no further south than Stamford St. The police have tried to run in the English bully from the High St courts but had a failure in their first case and are fearful of trying again. The man they charged was notorious as a ponce but was able to prove that he had earned some money by himself and therefore the charge fell to the ground."

Woolwich was another notorious area. "They cling to the neighbourhood of the Barracks, 'Flies round the honey pot'. Clyne says their usual charge to soldiers is 9d or 1/- and soldiers are allowed to go on tick and pay when their money comes in. The male inhabitants are bullies, dock and waterside labourers, costers, hawkers and tramps. The women are prostitutes...The clean white apron and the frizzed hair and earrings is the mark of this class. Clyne says the majority of young and old, male and female are Irish...If the man is known to have money or jewels on him he is made to hire a room and robbed, 'always cleaned out'. If he has only enough to pay the woman then the street is used. There is no regular charge, each man pays as much as the woman can get from him...Those who suffer most from the Dust Hole are the recruits. Woolwich is a depot with drafts constantly coming and going. These are the young flies that are caught and may be ruined for life."

Engaging and alarming, inexhaustible and compulsive, these Booth Notebooks present a townscape of crowded streets and bustling thoroughfares, of claustrophobic courts and dark back alleys, a fluid, fast-changing environment in which commerce and people vie for space and amenity, industry and identity. They evoke the sight and sounds, indeed almost the smell, of the congested capital a century ago. George Duckworth, with his acute powers of observation and novelist's eye for detail, ushers us into unseemly enclosures and unmapped passageways, through run-down neighbourhoods and the more fashionable quarters, recording land-use changes and population movements with care and precision. Included, too, was much incidental information on house rents and local prices and, where access could be secured, on home work and individual family circumstances.

The streets of London, as presented here, are defined not only by charters and legal regulations, but also by popular culture and popular usage. The information gathered, though selective, is extraordinarily rich. Duckworth was attentive both to the diversity of the built environment and to variations in local architecture. The general condition of the inhabitants, their occupations, dress and bearing, were of equal interest. All were captured by his running pen. The modern reader who wishes to understand Victorian London will find Duckworth an indispensable guide. His observations, for all their absorbing and irresistible qualities, however, are not a simple mirror-image of London at its imperial zenith. Perambulations with the police supplied a stock of knowledge that was shot through with a whole range of personal and professional concerns. It embodied the beliefs, attitudes and opinions of policemen both as public servants and as self-conscious members of the independent working classes.

Apart from the occupational and class biases of police informants, there was the particular viewpoint of the Life and Labour Inquiry itself. The observations, recorded in these Booth Notebooks, were passed through an evaluative filter by which the moral and material were re-combined to create a body of information that was always something more than a descriptive map of poverty. The colour coding of a particular location was a multiple of discrete assessments based on environment, appearance, spatial relationships, trades, dress, clatter and clamour, ethnicity and crime. It also included a large number of surrogate measures of respectability and deviance ranging from clean curtains and a well-scrubbed doorstep to a neat window-box or strategically-placed flower display. These caveats, though, do not diminish the importance of the Booth Notebooks either as source or text. These Notebooks not only impress us by their vividness, immediacy and precision, but also by their idiosyncracy and humanity. As a guide to the preoccupations of the age they have few rivals.

DAVID ENGLANDER & ROSEMARY O'DAY
David Englander and Rosemary O'Day are Directors of the Charles Booth Centre at the Open University. Their numerous books include *Mr Charles Booth's Inquiry, Life and Labour of the People in London Reconsidered* (Hambledon Press, 1993) and *Retrieved Riches, Social Investigation in Britain, 1840-1914* (Scolar Press, 1995).

Each walk has a reference code (eg. B363). This is the method used at the British Library of Political and Economic Science to archive all the the Booth material. They are reproduced here to enable readers to find the original notebooks.

Both on the colour maps reproduced in this book and within the text each street is colour-coded to indicate the level of poverty or comfort of the people who lived there.

YELLOW	-	Upper-middle and Upper classes. Wealthy
RED	-	Middle class. Well-to-do.
PINK	-	Fairly comfortable. Good ordinary earnings.
PURPLE	-	Mixed. Some comfortable, others poor.
LIGHT BLUE	-	Poor. 18s. to 21s. a week for a moderate family.
DARK BLUE	-	Very poor, casual. Chronic want.
BLACK	-	Lowest class. Vicious, semi-criminal.

A combination of colours – as DARK BLUE and BLACK, or PINK and RED – indicates that the street contains a fair proportion of each of the classes represented by the respective colours. Occasionally a researcher lapses and describes a street as VIOLET!
A bookmark with this colour key is included within this publication.

Booth divided London into 48 numbered districts. The following districts appear in this volume:

31	Lambeth, St Saviour's, Southwark
32	Trinity Newington, St Mary Bermondsey
33	St James' Bermondsey, Rotherhithe
34	Lambeth, Kennington
40	Streatham, Norwood and Dulwich
41	St Peter's Walworth, St Mary Newington
42	St George's Camberwell
43	Camberwell
44	Peckham
45	Deptford
46	Greenwich
47	Sydenham, Lewisham, Eltham, Lee
48	Woolwich

The maps at the start of each area show the boundaries of each walk. They are similar to the rough sketches which the researchers drew in the notebooks at the start of each walk.

The researchers only wrote on the right hand pages and they often used the left hand page for detailed sketches to show the exact layout and colouring of a block of streets. These are sometimes referred to in the text.

The name of each street visited was underlined within the text and an assessment made of its colour according to Booth's code. When all the books were complete one of the secretaries went through them and made a decision whether or not to accept recommended changes in the map colours. These changes were recorded in neat handwriting on the right hand pages. Eventually, the maps were revised in line with these decisions. Charles Booth used the records of the walks when he wrote up his Religious Influences Series.

Compass points given as a single capital letter at the start of each street (ie. N, E, S, W) indicate the direction of the walk. When used descriptively for a part of a street or area the full description is given (ie. north, east, south, west).

The reader should bear in mind that we have transcribed notes written in long hand and cannot guarantee 100% accuracy. Where the handwriting proved impossible to decipher we have tried to make the best guess.

There are some common phrases which may be initially confusing:
"bread in street" – in an age before throw-away packaging, the main litter was bread
"bricks rubbed" – this was a sign of people leaning against them, loafing
"model Buildings or Dwellings" - homes for the Victorian working classes built by companies receiving a competitive return on investment. The principle of philanthropic intention with capitalist return was known as "five per cent philanthropy"
"bullies" – pimps
Gates – the South London millionaire who built a lot of property, particularly in the Nunhead area. See p211 for his details

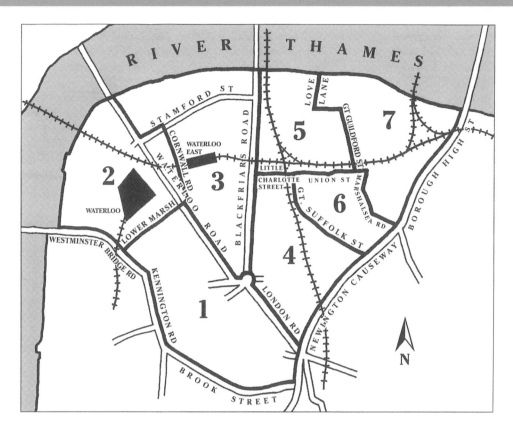

Walk 1

Tuesday 25 April 1899.
George Duckworth with Reserve Inspector Albert Green.
Inspector Green is a fat man rather over middle height, jovial rubicund face, fair moustache, has been 26 years in the Force and seen service in the Drury Lane District and Notting Dale (three years). He has been in this Division over six years.

Starting at St George's Circus.
W along Westminster Bridge Rd. N up **Dodson Street** (late Duke St). 3-st and 2½-st. Some very poor at the south west end and in the centre of the east side. Most of the east side already down and all to come down when leases fall in. Windows and curtains broken, patched, dirty. Bread in street. Costers' barrows and two mattresses lying in the muddy road. A few thieves and prostitutes. "One of the worst places in the Division but not to be compared with Bangor St in the matter of vice." LIGHT BLUE-barred rather than BLACK of the map. At the N corner of Webber St and Dodson St are **Quinn's Buildings**. 6-st. Look poor, well kept inside. LIGHT BLUE to PURPLE, in map PURPLE. On the west side, opposite Quinn's Buildings, Dodson St is very poor.
E along Webber St. N up **Falka Place** (late Ann Place). Houses on east side closed. The west side is Quinn's Buildings. DARK BLUE of map goes.
W along **Tower Street**. 3-st. Many small shops. Better than Duke St. Labouring class above. Many windows broken and patched. Doors open but all with a bit of floor cloth or

matting. Rough-looking, hatless Irishwomen about but many fairly comfortable. Bread in street. 4lb loaf selling in one of the shops for 4d. LIGHT BLUE, in map DARK BLUE.

Out of the E end N side is **Gilbert's Court**. Eight 2-st houses. Very poor costers. DARK BLUE to LIGHT BLUE, not shown in map.

W along Tower St. S down **Gerridge Street** (late Charles St). Jubilee Buildings make the north east side. A large block, courtyard and well-kept trees. That part facing Webber St looks poorer than the rest. Children clean, well dressed. PINK to PURPLE, in map PINK. Gerridge St itself is LIGHT BLUE and 2-st on north west. Unmarked in map. The east side, south of Webber St, is markedly better, 3-st. PURPLE as map. At the corner of the Westminster Bridge Rd are 4½-st buildings, working class. PURPLE to LIGHT BLUE, in map RED. The west side of Webber St is taken up by School except one very poor house. DARK BLUE if marked.

E & W along **Webber Street**. Poor, like Tower St. LIGHT BLUE to PURPLE, in map LIGHT BLUE. Not LIGHT BLUE now east of Jubilee Buildings on north side.

N into Gerridge St. W along Tower St. Out of its NW end is **Short Street**. 3-st. LIGHT BLUE as map but inhabited on east side only.

N into **Pearman Street**. Respectable mechanics. Dull 3-st yellow-brick houses. Many police from 'A' and 'L' Divisions. It is now continued as a street eastwards to the south east of map. The continuation is like the rest and PINK. The south east now better, 2-st, some fairly comfortable at north and one or two still very poor. Altogether LIGHT BLUE.

N up **Mary's Buildings**. 2-st. LIGHT BLUE. Cement paved, clean. One family to a house. LIGHT BLUE to PURPLE, in map PURPLE.

Transwell Street (late Isabella St). 2-st, some with basement. Better than Mary's Buildings. PURPLE as map.

Out of the NW end of Transwell St is **Robert's Place**. Six 2-st houses, flowers at windows, costers. LIGHT BLUE to PURPLE, in map PURPLE.

E along **Thomas' Place**. Four houses on north and two on south. 3-st. Poor. LIGHT BLUE, in map PINK. It is continued east of Coral St with five houses on south side only. LIGHT BLUE, in map PINK.

S down **Little Thomas' Street**. Narrow flagged passage, only 9 ft between house and house. Old inhabitants at north end, very poor at south end. North end is still PURPLE, south is LIGHT BLUE to DARK BLUE. Children clean and well dressed except stockings and knickerbockers of the boys ragged. Mark the whole LIGHT BLUE?

E along Whitinor St and N up **Coral Street**. Built 1820. 2-st and some with basement. PURPLE as map.

W along **Oakley Street**. "Has a bad reputation for roughness and prostitutes" but Green has never been able to understand why. PINK and PURPLE as map. It is a 3-st wood-paved street. There have been brothels in it.

S down **Johanna Street**. Cul de sac. Mud, puddles, children playing in them. 2-st plus attic. Many windows broken but oil cloth in all the passages. Most doors open. LIGHT BLUE to PURPLE, in map PURPLE. North of Oakley St Johanna St is poorer. LIGHT BLUE to DARK BLUE.

W along **Grindal Street** (late Harriet St). Rough, low class, Irish. Like Duke St. All doors open, bread etc. Street full of women and children. Though this is a poor district all the children are remarkable for their clean faces. DARK BLUE, in map LIGHT BLUE.

N into **Lower Marsh**. Very busy shopping street, barrows all along the north side. Groves large clothing establishment on south side. 3-st. PINK-barred to RED, in map PINK-barred.

S down Frazier St. Out of its E side is a small court (north of Gloucester St) called

Corsham Place (late Paved Place). Eight houses, four on north and four on south. Only 4 ft between the houses. Very poor, old people. DARK BLUE, not shown in map.

Frazier Street itself has small, poor shops. LIGHT BLUE, in map PURPLE.

W along **Murphy Street** (late Charles St). Working class. 2-st with 4-st Buildings at north west end. Crowds of children, hatless, clean faces. LIGHT BLUE to DARK BLUE, in map LIGHT BLUE.

Out of the **SW** end is a court called **James' Place**. Seven 2-st houses, only two rooms to a house. Rents 5/- for old tenants and 5/6 for new. LIGHT BLUE to DARK BLUE, in map LIGHT BLUE.

At its **W** end **Murphy Street** turns south. W Hawn's, the great theatrical scene painter's studio, is on the west side and north of it are two houses. LIGHT BLUE, not shown in map.

S into Oakley St, **W** to Westminster Bridge Rd, **N** to Lower Marsh. **E & S** into **Lambeth Square**. 3½-st. Small neglected square, grass and trees, no flowers in the centre. One takes the house and lets off. Tallyman going his rounds. PINK as map.

W into Westminster Bridge Rd and **S**, turning **E** at **Burdett Road**. Burdett Buildings on north side, 6-st. PURPLE. Buildings on south side rather poorer. LIGHT BLUE. Both go up to the corner of the Westminster Bridge Rd. On south side of buildings are two very poor and rough houses. DARK BLUE.

S to **Lanfranc Street**. 3-st and 2-st. At the east corner of Burdett Rd and Lanfranc St is a beerhouse for all the world like a dwelling house except for small letters over door. This street is poor. Many women home workers, sound of machines, but LIGHT BLUE rather than DARK BLUE of map.

E along Westminster Bridge Rd and **S** down **King Edward Street**. Quiet, semi-detached on west side, front gardens, apartments. PINK to PINK-barred. One or two servants.

S into **Lambeth Road**. The houses on the north side are called Barkham Terrace. 3½-st, dingy outside, some servants. Superintendent of 'A' Police Division lives here. In the centre is the Upton Baptist Chapel. PINK-barred to RED, in map RED.

N up **St George's Road**. Wood paved. 3½-st on west side. Roman Catholic Cathedral on east with a house for resident priests north of it. PINK-barred to RED.

E & S down **Barbel Street** (late Joiner St). 3-st houses on both sides. The "worst street about here". No common lodging houses but thieves and prostitutes. Windows broken, patched, stuffed, all doors open, no oilcloth or matting in the passages. Irish cockneys the majority. Prostitutes go out to Clapham Common, don't bring men home. "No strong feeling against them in a street like this." Some flowers in windows. Children with dirty faces, sore eyes, torn frocks, hatless. Compares with Bangor St except for the absence of common lodging houses and the rows here are family rows and not against the exercise of authority, police rarely hurt. 6-roomed houses, rents 12/- and 10/-. BLACK as map.

E along **Lambeth Road**. Many without servants. PINK-barred, in map RED.

W along Westminster Bridge Rd. Out of **S** side is **Whitehorse Yard**. Now a private stable yard. Foreman and washers living above on south west side and south east side only. PURPLE, in map DARK BLUE.

E & S down **London Road**. Busy shopping street, costers. PINK-barred to RED, in map RED.

W at **Gladstone Street**. 2½-st. Clerks, no servants, some mechanics, "all go to their work over the water". Six rooms plus scullery, rent £36 to £40 plus rates and takes subletting by one and two rooms. Rents 6/- to 8/- for two rooms. A large family of children would not be allowed in these houses. The schools of Notre Dame have taken in the west end up to the point where the street turns abruptly south. PINK as map.

E & N up **Colnbrook Street** (late Richmond St). Like Gladstone St. PINK as map.

S down **Garden Row**. Many poor. New 3-st flats on west side are PINK, but the whole street is PURPLE to LIGHT BLUE. "A little better than Tower St." In map PINK.

E & N up **Burman Street**. Poor and very poor on east side. New houses but poor on north west. Most of west side taken up by new bus yard which runs through into Garden Row. LIGHT BLUE to DARK BLUE, in map BLACK. It is a 2-st street, inhabited by costers, rough, low, not vicious. The old houses on the east side let four rooms for 10/- to 12/-. The new on the north west let four rooms for 15/-.

E & S down **Marshall Street**. 2-st and 2½-st. Quiet. Labourers working in Maudslays. PURPLE to LIGHT BLUE, in map PINK.

E & N up **Gaywood Street**. 3½-st. Sublet. Dull, dark, rather narrow. A few poor. Rents £36 to £38. Two top floor rooms rent for 6/6, first floor for 7/-, ground floor for 7/- (these are more convenient than the others to get at but the passage has to come out of their size so the rent is the same as for the first floor). The house tenant lives in the basement. Each floor's back room is fitted with a range for cooking. Washing is done in the copper in the basement which is common to all. Washing days are by mutual arrangement by floors. PINK to PURPLE, in map PINK.

E & S down **Princess Street**. Like Gaywood St. Cobble paved. PINK to PURPLE, in map PINK. The passage out of the east side has one poor (LIGHT BLUE) house on north side only.

W along St George's Rd and S down **Ely Place**. A few houses, 2-st, on south side only. PINK, in map PINK-barred.

E into **West Square**. 3½-st and 4½-st. The east side keeps a few servants and is PINK-barred as map. The rest rather PINK. Messy square, great deal of loose paper.

Out of the S side is **Austral Street**. Girls' home on west side. PINK, in map PURPLE.

Out of the SE side of the Square is **Orient Street**. Rather rough, mixed. Badly-mended road. PURPLE to LIGHT BLUE, in map PINK. That part which runs due east is also PURPLE to LIGHT BLUE, in map PINK. The LIGHT BLUE shown in the passage leading to Hayles St has gone.

N up **West Square**. The houses standing back on the north east side are PINK as map.

N up **West Street**. No houses except one cottage, a public house, on the west side. PINK.

E along St George's Rd and S down **Hayles Street**. 2-st and 3-st. Good proportion of poor. "Some ladies here who work the Elephant." Some new PINK houses on the north east side but the whole is PURPLE, in map PINK.

E along **Lamlash Street** (late John St). Some police. Two very poor houses on north side. These should be DARK BLUE and the rest PINK or the whole PURPLE. Houses on both sides, PINK in map.

N up **Elliott's Row**. LIGHT BLUE to DARK BLUE as map south east but less of it. Above on the east side are new buildings, Hayles' Buildings, 5-st, PINK. The west side is not so good.

E & S down **Oswin Street** (late Temple St). 4-st, quiet, fairly comfortable. PINK to PURPLE, in map PINK. The south east end should be LIGHT BLUE, in map PURPLE. This and the preceding streets belong to a Mr Geats who started life as a labourer and now runs a great deal of property here and in Dulwich.

E along **St George's Road**. The corner is all taken by Rabbit's factory, only a caretaker sleeps. There is no PINK behind.

General Remarks

Green said that the change of the last ten years had been from bad to better and from best to less good. The bad streets are not quite so bad as they were, the good streets are not nearly so good. Thus the BLACK streets (Duke St and Burman St) are LIGHT BLUE or LIGHT BLUE-barred and Tower St, formerly DARK BLUE, is now LIGHT BLUE. But the PINK streets on the west side of the London Rd are fast becoming PURPLE. Green ascribed the change to the effect of neighbouring demolitions. "The fairly comfortable are the first to move, the poor refuse to and have not the money to go far away even if they wished to do so."

Men, women and children seem to live in the street more than they do north of the Thames. Courts swarm with children and the main streets with working men and women going to and from their work. More loafers here at the street corners. Top hats rarely seen; bowlers, soft felt hats and caps the usual head gear.

Walk 2   B363

Friday 28th April 1899.
George Duckworth with Sergeant Saltmarshe.
Sergeant Saltmarshe has a round, fat face and brown moustache, middle height, 21 years service, 11 years in this Division. Inspector Green confessed to not knowing much about the streets east of the Westminster Bridge Rd and Supt Wren accordingly recommended Saltmarshe.

Starting at the corner of Lower Marsh and Waterloo Road.
N up Waterloo Rd and E at **Pear Tree Street**. Cul de sac, quiet. Fourteen 2-st houses. Rents 7/6 to 9/- for four rooms plus scullery. Not coloured in map, PURPLE to PINK.
N & E at Holmes Terrace. 3-st houses on north side only. Very poor. Many prostitutes living in the street, work the Strand and Waterloo Rd. All doors open. DARK BLUE, in map PURPLE. West of Chartley Place, Holmes Terrace is 2-st, poor but respectable. LIGHT BLUE. Costers' barrows. The south side is down and the City & Waterloo Electric Railway works take up the west end.
N & W along **Aubin Street**. Mixed, some fairly comfortable. Many railway porters. "Railway porters are known for the amount they drink, earnings not precarious but varying largely in amount from day to day." PURPLE all through rather than PINK and PURPLE of map. The west end is largely stables and a break has been made in the centre leading to Launcelot St.
Out of the **SW** end is **Granby Gardens**. Windows very bad, mess, fowls. Built 1851. The west side is coming down for railway extension. Woman with baby, dirty, bare-armed, bare-headed. Pays 4/- for one room. It is LIGHT BLUE and DARK BLUE, in map LIGHT BLUE.
W into **Granby Place**. North east coming down, one house still occupied. West side and south east are poor, messy, labourers, bad windows. Look rough but Saltmarshe said they were no trouble to the police. DARK BLUE to LIGHT BLUE, in map PURPLE.
E along Aubin St. **S** into **Launcelot Street**. Mixed, 2-st, many poor. East end taken up by Railway Electric Works. PURPLE to LIGHT BLUE, in map PURPLE.
S into Lower Marsh. E then N up **Chartley Place** and **Grove Place**. LIGHT BLUE. Public library takes up east side south of Holmes Terrace. Well appointed as seen through windows but very few using it (hour 11.30).
E along Lower Marsh, N up Waterloo Rd, under the railway bridge. W along **Vine Street**. PINK to PURPLE, in map PURPLE. Railwaymen. This and the following streets are all PINK to PURPLE.

Out of the S side is **Robert Street**. PINK as map. Railway foremen and firemen. Very few living.

N & E along **Francis Street**. 2½-st. Fairly comfortable. PINK as map.

N & W along **James Street**. Like it. PINK as map.

Anne Street. PINK as map. All these streets are alike and PINK to PURPLE in character. 6-roomed houses, letting at 12/- or 14/- per week and sublet. Streets themselves badly kept and want mending.

N up Waterloo Rd, turning W at the York Public House into **York Road**. "Poverty Junction and Out At Elbows Corner", the corner where the poorer Music Hall artistes loaf in hope of a job. York Rd itself is full of Variety Agents. "The demand for 'pros' increases every year."

N to York Rd. W & N up **Tenison Street**. 3½-st, respectable, very few prostitutes. Apartments for musical profession. PINK as map.

E & S down **Howley Place**. 2-st on west, 5-st on east, that is the backs of the houses which face on the much higher level of the Waterloo Rd. The two bottom storeys are used as cellars and stores except a few at north east end which are lived in. Messy. PURPLE as map.

W along Belvedere Rd and S down **Sutton Street**. PINK as map.

E along **Howley Street**. 2-st. Narrow, no thoroughfare for vehicles. PINK as map. Comfortable, quiet.

N to **Belvedere Road**. Mixed street. North side all factories, wharves. Brewery with foremen's houses attached. South side many poor but many fairly comfortable. PURPLE to PINK, in map PINK.

W & S down **Belvedere Crescent**. Rather better east than west. 3-st and 2-st. PURPLE to PINK, in map PINK.

S down **Vine Street**. 2½-st and 3½-st. PINK as map.

Out of the SE side is **Manners Street**. 2½-st flush with pavement. Narrow, no thoroughfare for vehicles. PINK as map.

S then W along York Rd and into **Princes Buildings**. 2-st houses. Flagged court crammed with children, clean, well dressed and fed. Four rooms for 9/- and 9/6. Only 9 ft between the housefronts. PURPLE as map.

W along York Rd and N up **Chichely Street** (called in map Edward St). 3-st. Not so many houses lived in on east side as formerly. Mixed. PURPLE as map.

N & W along Belvedere Rd. Out of its S side is **Cox's Buildings**. 3-st. Children well fed and dressed. Cats crowding round cats' meat men, three sticks of meat taken in at one house, 2d a stick. PURPLE to LIGHT BLUE. Houses are on both sides (north and south) of the court and come over the arch under which the court is entered. Map shows houses on south only.

E along Belvedere Rd, N at **College Street**. Mixed. Two houses on the west side given up to prostitutes. Saltmarshe called them prostitutes' "homes" and explained himself to mean that only some houses would board prostitutes and those that did so were called "homes" by the police. "They must live somewhere and don't bring men home to them. Those who work the same road like to live together". PURPLE as map.

S then W along the **York Road**. Variety agents, warehouses, hotels, prostitutes. Many hotels little else than brothels, "girls live there and bring men home". Some servants. PINK-barred as map.

S down **Addington Street**. PINK as map. 3-st.

Out of the W side is **Addington Crescent**. Flagged court, clean, comfortable. PINK. Note: That there are one or two houses lived in on the east side, south of the Board School as well as the turning north of it.

S & E & N up **York Street**. Old fashioned. Small 2-st cottages with front gardens. PURPLE as map.

At the back on the W side is **Sapphire Place**. 2-st. Five rooms plus scullery for 10/- in the northernmost houses, the rest 7/6 to 9/-. Houses on east side only and at north side of north end. PURPLE as map.

E along York Rd. N then turning E at Bazon St. S down **Commercial Buildings**. Now a cement passage, clean, no-one living. LIGHT BLUE at north west end goes.

E into **Bazon Street** (late Bond St). 2-st plus basement. Flush with pavement. Rough mixture, many prostitutes. PURPLE to LIGHT BLUE, in map PURPLE.

E along **Cage Place** (late Cottage Place). 2-st. Washing hanging across. Some houses very poor. Children fairly clean and well dressed. LIGHT BLUE to DARK BLUE, in map DARK BLUE. Rents: four rooms 7/6 for new tenants, 5/6 for old.

S & E along **Bond Place**. Very poor. 2-st. Children and girls, dirty, boots bad, pink and black toes showing through boots. Mess of paper, cellars with open doors full of mess, pickings from the dustyard in Commercial Rd where most of the women work. Windows patched and broken, bare and untidy rooms seen through open doors. Washing day, washing being done in a tub outside front doors. Redraining to houses at east end. Rents: two rooms 5/6 and four rooms 7/6. It is a flagged court. DARK BLUE as map.

N & E along **Doon Street**. Mixed, many poor. PURPLE as map.

Out of S side is **Milan Place**. Eight cottages with a tap in centre to supply houses, defective and water running to waste by gallons. (This is a common sight in the South London courts seen hitherto). Looks quiet and clean, great array of flowers under wire netting at one house, but Saltmarshe said it was noted for family rows, "fathers fight their sons of a Saturday night". Birdcages. Not very poor. Two very dirty well-fed children seen. Two and three rooms for 6/-. LIGHT BLUE to DARK BLUE, in map DARK BLUE.

Opposite on the N side of Doon St is **Elizabeth Place**. 2-st. Two rooms plus wash-house 5/6. Geraniums. LIGHT BLUE as map.

E to Cornwall Rd and N. On the W side is **Henry Place**. Four 2-st cottages. Two rooms 5/6, four rooms 9/-. DARK BLUE to LIGHT BLUE, in map LIGHT BLUE.

Opposite on E side of Cornwall Rd is **Druce's Place**. Two 2-st houses, one DARK BLUE, the other LIGHT BLUE, in map PINK.

Opposite on W side of Cornwall Rd, S of Doon St is **Perry's Place**. Houses on east and west sides. Children dirty with bad boots, well fed. DARK BLUE to LIGHT BLUE, in map LIGHT BLUE.

Into the **Cornwall Road**. 3-st. Many poor and rough at this north end. "Last Saturday in one of these houses a woman threw a lighted lamp at her husband and both were burnt to death." LIGHT BLUE to PURPLE, in map PURPLE.

General Remarks

The demolitions in the neighbourhood of Lower Marsh owing to railway extension (London & South Western Railway) and the Waterloo and City Electric Railway engine station; the fairly comfortable round Waterloo Station; prostitutes and brothels in the York Rd and the very poor and rough off the north east corner of the Waterloo Rd; are the features of this round. Railway disturbance has only displaced some 'PURPLE' and not much of that. Otherwise the district is much as it was ten years ago. Prostitutes crowd round Waterloo as they do round St Pancras and King's Cross and the York Rd has much the same reputation as the Euston Rd. Rents run between 2/- and 3/- per room.

Walk 3

Monday 1st May 1899.
George Duckworth with Sergeant P S Waters.

Starting at the corner of Exton Street and the Waterloo Road.
E along **Exton Street**. 3½-st. Two and three families to a house. PINK as map.
N up **Secker Street**. 3-st. Rather poorer. St Patrick's Catholic schools on south east side.
PINK to PURPLE, in map PINK.
N & W at **Cornwall Place**. Flagged, fairly clean court. Front gardens now cemented over,
"but they used to be fine some years ago". Used to be Irish but fewer of them now. Windows
and curtains fairly clean. Doors open, fairly well-furnished rooms to be seen inside. Many
old tenants, since 18 and 20 years. Waterside labourers. The extreme west end is the poorest.
At the back of the north side is a large woodyard with piles of wood stacked alongside of the
chimneys, nearly overlapping. There has never been a fire but it is hard to imagine anything
that looks more dangerous. Rents 6/- for two rooms, no copper, kettle has to be boiled and
washing done in tub in front yard. WCs in front. LIGHT BLUE, leave DARK BLUE at west
end, in map all is DARK BLUE.
N past **Cornwall Mews**. A woodyard, no-one living. The thoroughfare into Waterloo Rd
has been closed.
On the E side of Cornwall Rd is **Salutation Place**. 3-st houses. Rents for three rooms 7/-,
7/6 and 8/-. No wash-house nor copper. WCs in black wooden sheds in front. Houses on north
side only. "He should give us coppers. It lays us all up with bronchitis being without them."
GEA says that the Prince of Wales is landlord. At the east end Salutation Place turns abruptly
southward, becomes 2-st and much poorer. East end not shown in map, DARK BLUE. West
end DARK BLUE in map, to LIGHT BLUE. Costers' streets, hawkers, old inhabitants.
S of Salutation Place out of Cornwall Rd is **Peer's Cooperage**. 3-st. Poor, flowers in
windows, costers. LIGHT BLUE, in map DARK BLUE.
N into Stamford St, E, then N up **Coin Street** (late Princes St). 3½-st. Clean,
comfortable, some prostitutes. PINK as map.
E along Commercial Rd. S down **Duke Street**. 3-st, old-fashioned. Small panes to
occasional small shops. PURPLE as map.
E & S into **Cory Square** (late Princes Square). 3-st houses. Court in course of being well
laid with cement. Children very dirty but well fed. Poor and very poor and a few fairly
comfortable. All doors open. Some bread about. A few Irish. West side poorer than the east.
five-roomed houses let at 10/-, all the east side at this price. Small glass bottle factory out of
the east side. Old tenants, one had been 26 years in the court and another boy of about 16
had lived at various times with his family in every one of the various houses in the court.
DARK BLUE as map.
E & S down **Broad Wall**. 3-st buildings called 'Parish Garden Dwellings' on the west side.
Rough, poor and very poor. LIGHT BLUE to DARK BLUE. The 2-st houses on the east side
are in good repair, also poor. LIGHT BLUE as map.
E along **Old Barge House**. Warehouses on south side.
S down **Hatfield Street**. Working class. PINK as map.
E & S down **Boddy's Bridge**. East side is warehouse (or school?) wall. LIGHT BLUE in
map. Very poor on west side. DARK BLUE to LIGHT BLUE, in map LIGHT BLUE. The
southern court (**called Upper Ground Place**) is more respectable (in map PURPLE). East

side not so good as west, rather LIGHT BLUE than PURPLE. One woman who had been there 16 years pays 14/- for her house of six rooms (three floors) and wash-house. She lets off at 6/- per floor or 4/- for a single room.

E & S down **Bennett Street**. 3½-st on east side. Old, built for a servant-keeping class. Poor. LIGHT BLUE, in map PINK. Cooks, the draper in St Paul's Churchyard, has the whole of the west side as a residence for his employees. PINK as map. The houses at the north east end of Bennett St are smaller, poorer, should be DARK BLUE.

E & S down **King's Arms Court**. Twelve 3-st houses. Six on east and west sides. Ropes across for hanging clothes. Windows broken and patched. Lowest class of prostitutes and thieves. One barefoot child. Rough women with hair in metal curlers, men with faces of criminal type at the windows. Rows on Saturday nights. Children, boys and girls, playing tipcat; dirty, ragged but all well fed and of good colour. "Like Joiner St." BLACK, in map DARK BLUE.

S down Blackfriars Rd and W along **Stamford Street**. 3½-st plus attic. "Great many prostitutes living here. The hotels are places of accommodation, some are little else than brothels. The girls live in them, walk out and bring men home to them. There have not been so many foreign prostitutes since the passing of the Act against bullies." The most disreputable hotels are west of the Waterloo Rd but there are some almost as bad east of it. PINK as map but PINK-barred as map west of Cornwall Rd where there is a greater proportion of servant-keeping hotels.

W & S down Cornwall Rd. E at **Palmer Street**. North side is factories, south side is back gardens of the houses in Whittlesey St.

S down **Theed Street**. Railwaymen. PINK as map.

W along **Whittlesey Street** (late Richard St). 2-st, clean. Railwaymen. PINK as map.

W across Cornwall Rd. Along **Alaska Street**. West end blocked by operations for widening railway bridge. 2-st. PINK to PURPLE, in map PINK.

S down Cornwall Rd. W along **Sandell Road**. Houses on south only. PINK, not coloured in map.

W into Waterloo Rd. S past a beer stores which used to be a Wesleyan Chapel. E along **Morpeth Place**. 2-st. "Four rooms plus wash-house let for 10/-, let off rooms at 4/- each" said one man. Windows bad, children hatless. LIGHT BLUE as map.

S & E at **Peartree Street**. 3-st and 2-st. Small shops, sweep etc. PURPLE, in map PINK.

N up Cornwall Rd. On the W side is **Hammond Place**. Five houses. Quiet, poor. One house at the west end is double-fronted. Four rooms upstairs let at 6/6, three rooms down at 6/9. The other houses are 2-roomed, let at 6/6, "you pay a little more to have the place to yourself" said one woman. LIGHT BLUE to DARK BLUE, in map DARK BLUE.

N up Cornwall Rd. E along **Roupell Street**. Quiet, comfortable, like Whittlesey St and Theed St except at the south east end which is markedly poorer and should be LIGHT BLUE. There are no houses in the court at the back which only leads to the backs of the Brad St houses.

N up **Broad Wall**. Poor. 3-st and 2½-st. Some old red tile-roofed and wooden-sided houses. The block of LIGHT BLUE which was common lodging houses at the south east end is now all warehouses. The rest LIGHT BLUE as map.

W & S down **Duke Street**. Some small shops mixed with poor and very poor. LIGHT BLUE, in map PURPLE. The main entrance to the Peabody Dwellings is here, many poor. PURPLE to PINK, in map PINK.

W along **Aquinas Street**. 2½-st. Flush with pavement, quiet. PURPLE as map.

Off the N side is a small court of two houses called **Thomas' Cottages**. Entered down steps.

Two rooms in each let for 5/6 a week.

W into **Coin Street** (late Prince St). Very poor at south west. LIGHT BLUE. The rest is PINK as map.

Out of the **NE** side is **Prince's Mews**. Cabyard, carts etc. Only one tenanted. In map PURPLE, now not worth marking but it is either PINK or LIGHT BLUE.

W along Stamford St, **S** down Cornwall Rd, E along **Brad Street**. Houses at east end only. Those (eight) on south side to come down for the railway. Notices to quit when wanted being served. One woman on taking hers said "well, I shan't quit till they come to turn us out". Poor, scavengers, costers and labourers. LIGHT BLUE as map, but less of it on south side.

S down Eaton St and W along **Wootton Street**. North side (in map PURPLE with two courts, LIGHT BLUE and DARK BLUE off it) down for railway extension. South side is mixed, poor and comfortable. 2-st. Many windows broken. PURPLE as map.

Out of the **SW** end is **Wootton Court**. Eighteen 3-st houses. Flagged passage. One room up and one down plus small back yard. Very poor, curtains dirty and windows bad. DARK BLUE as map. Two landlords and one landlady to this block. The landlady lives in one of the houses herself. Rents 6/- and 7/- for two rooms plus kitchen. 7/- for new tenants.

E into Windmill St and **E & W** along **Ethelm Street**. Poorer east than west of Windmill St. 2½-st. Two or three very poor at extreme north west. PURPLE as map west of Windmill St, LIGHT BLUE east of it. The east corner of Windmill St also LIGHT BLUE. It looks as though the poorer of those off the north side of Wootton St had come in here.

S down **Eaton Street**. LIGHT BLUE to DARK BLUE, in map DARK BLUE.

W along **Little Windmill Street**. 5-st Waldeck Buildings on the north side. PINK as map. Stables on south side not lived in (LIGHT BLUE in map) except a few houses, very poor, at south west end. These should be DARK BLUE. The DARK BLUE court on the west side of Windmill St is closed and seems to have moved across the road. "Waldeck Buildings are rather better than the Peabody's."

N & W along **St Andrew's Place**. Twelve houses, 2-st, on south side only. Clean flagged passage. Very poor. Dustyard scavengers. Young wives, dirty children but all enough to eat, ragged. Houses let for 5/9 for two rooms and a very small yard behind.

E along Ethelm St. **S** down Eaton St and E at **Victoria Place**. Six houses on north side, three on south and three on the east side of turning south out of it. Bare passage, flagged. Fretful, dirty children, hair matted, hatless, dirty faces. Windows dirty and broken and stuffed. Women rough, bare-armed. All doors open. Half-witted loafer standing at corner. Bare passages seen through open doors. Children and girls throwing bread at one another. Plaster peeling off the house walls. Inhabitants thieves and prostitutes. There seemed to be one respectable family at the west end house north side. "Like Kings Arms Court and Joiner St." BLACK as map but less of it because there are no houses on the west side of the cul de sac which runs south out of the Place.

N up Broad Wall. Out of **W** side is **Sidwell Place**. Twelve houses on north, south and west sides. Newly cement paved. All doors open. Poor, women with sack aprons. Houses 2-st, four-roomed, letting at 10/6 and 11/- for the whole house. When sublet they fetch 4/- for upstairs front, 3/6 for downstairs front, back rooms 3/- each. There is to each a kitchen and copper. DARK BLUE as map.

N past **Mitre Place**. A private yard, none living. In map LIGHT BLUE.

N up **Hatfield Street**. 2½-st and 3½-st mixed. North better than south. Asphalt paved, well-kept road. Some poor. PURPLE to PINK, in map PINK.

Along Stamford St. **S** down **Bennett Street**. Sainsbury the provision merchants' warehouses take up all east side (in map PINK). On the west is a public house, some dwelling houses and Cooksey's (the hat makers) offices. PINK as map.

W along **Stamford Street**. Common lodging house on the south side between Bennett St and Brunswick St. PURPLE rather than PINK of map.

S down **Brunswick Street**. Mixed, asphalted, clean, birdcages at windows. PURPLE as map.

E into **Brunswick Place**. Fourteen 2-st houses, clean flagged passage. Poor. LIGHT BLUE to PURPLE, in map PINK.

E along **Collingwood Street**. Old-fashioned 2-st wooden houses with dormer windows and red-tiled roofs on south side. PINK as map but it should be PURPLE where it runs north and south, many poor, instead of PINK of map.

Off the W side of Brunswick St is **Brunswick Court**. 2-st, very poor. In map it is PURPLE and LIGHT BLUE. The houses at the north east rather less poor than the rest, 2-st. DARK BLUE.

S down **Hatfield Place** which is a flagged passage. Nineteen 2-st houses on the east side, five at south west side. Hatless children, most doors open. A few fairly comfortable families remaining but they are the exceptions, the majority are poor and very poor. LIGHT BLUE to DARK BLUE, in map PURPLE.

E along **Meymott Street** (late Cross Street). Wood-paved, narrow shopping street, not very busy but much wheel traffic as it is the short cut from Blackfriars Rd to Waterloo Station. PINK as map.

E into Blackfriars Rd. On the W side N of Meymott St is **Runninghorse Yard**. Only two still occupied at west end. "Used to be very rough when the houses on the south side were tenanted, now they are stable lofts", said a fat man who had lived there 46 years. Mark LIGHT BLUE, all the DARK BLUE shown in the map has gone.

W & S down Collingwood St. W along **Jane Street**. 2-st. South side not so good as north. Street up for cement paving. PURPLE to PINK, in map PINK.

S down Broad Wall and E at **Isabella Street**. 2-st. North side down for railway extension. Many poor. PURPLE, in map PINK.

Out of the S side is **Norfolk Street**. 2-st. PURPLE to PINK, in map PURPLE. Elwood's hat and helmet factory is at the south east corner.

S into **Great Charlotte Street**. Broad. Shops on north side. Large common lodging house on the south side, Great Surrey Chambers, 5½-st. Separate rooms 8d a night or 3/- a week. Good accommodation 6d a night or 2/6 a week. PINK on north, PURPLE on south, as map.

S down Marlborough St. E along **John Street West**. 2-st. Houses on south side. PURPLE as map.

N up **Burrows Mews**. A few living above stables on north east, south east and south west. In map LIGHT BLUE but in the wrong places.

W to **Gray Street**. 2-st. Many poor. PURPLE to LIGHT BLUE, in map LIGHT BLUE.

N up Short St, out of whose W side run **Ufford Street** (late Queen St), **Mitre Street** and **Caffyn Street** (late New St). All 2-st. Poorer than they used to be, a few fairly comfortable remaining but the majority poor and very poor. Caffyn St is the poorest. Map marks Ufford St and Mitre St PURPLE and Caffyn St DARK BLUE, now there is more of a dead level of LIGHT BLUE. A boy in a fit in Caffyn St with the whole neighbourhood out of window and in the street to look at him.

W to **Webber Street**. Poor. The best parts are the small shops south of the Victoria at the north west end and again between Webber Row and Barons' Place (both sides of street). These might remain PINK, all the rest is LIGHT BLUE to PURPLE. Marshall's Buildings out of the east side north of Valentine Place distinctly LIGHT BLUE. In map the whole is PINK.

Out of the W side N of Gray St is **Asa Place**. Six houses. Small court but 12 children playing in it. Very poor and very rough, the children's clothes all holes. There is a copper in

the court common to all the houses. Two rooms 5/- and 5/6. DARK BLUE, not shown in map.
W along **Gray Street**. Common lodging house on south side, beds 4d and 6d, but not near
so bad as it used to be. Some prostitutes but majority have been cleared out. LIGHT BLUE to
DARK BLUE, in map DARK BLUE.
S down Waterloo Rd and E at **Baron's Place**. 2-st. Very poor costers living here. DARK
BLUE to LIGHT BLUE, in map DARK BLUE and on north side only.
E along **Valentine Place**. Pascall's sweet factory takes up a large part of the north side east
end. LIGHT BLUE as map.
S down **Angel Place**. Passage with 2-st houses on either side. Labourers. "Like Caffyn,
Mitre and Ufford Streets." Not rough. LIGHT BLUE as map.
Into **Valentine Row**. 2-st. Old inhabitants. Rents 9/- for four rooms plus kitchen. Single
rooms let off for 3/6 and 4/-.
W into **Webber Row**. North side down except a few houses. "They propose building model
dwellings here." The south side is poor. LIGHT BLUE not PURPLE.
Out of the **SE** end is **William's Place**. Poor 2-st cottages, shored up to prevent falling in.
Children clean and well fed. Stable yard at south end. One woman who had been there two
years pays 4/6 for two rooms plus wash-house. DARK BLUE as map.
W of it out of Webber Row is **Bennett's Yard**. Two 2½-st houses. LIGHT BLUE to
PURPLE, not shown in map. The DARK BLUE shown in map now disappears. It is merely a
rambling ramshackle stable yard with no-one living over.
E into Blackfriars Rd and S. On the E side are Peabody Dwellings, **Blackfriars Square**.
Large prison-like buildings, asphalt square in centre, fair open space planted with trees.
Eagerly tenanted. Some poor but as a whole PINK as map.

General Remarks

The poorest places in the wedge between the Thames on the north, Blackfriars Rd on the
east and Waterloo Rd on the west are: Bond Place out of Bazon St; Perry's Place out of
Cornwall Rd; Cornwall Place out of Cornwall Rd; Salutation Place out of Cornwall Rd;
Cory Square out of Commercial Rd; Regent's Court out of Ground St; Brunswick Court
out of Brunswick St; Hatfield Place, Meymott St; Wootton Court out of Wootton St; St
Andrew's Place out of Windmill St; Sidwell Place out of Broad Wall; Little Windmill St
south west end; Asa Place out of Webber St; Baron's Place out of Webber St; William's
Place out of Webber Row. All these are DARK BLUE or between DARK BLUE and LIGHT
BLUE. Two of them are BLACK in Regent's Court and Victoria Place. Victoria Place was
BLACK 10 years ago and is still BLACK. Regent's Court now becomes BLACK and was
DARK BLUE. As a whole there has been no increase of the DARK BLUE in this district but
at the same time no decrease. But there has been a large increase in the amount of LIGHT
BLUE and a marked decrease in the amount of PINK. The tone of the whole is today more of
a uniform LIGHT BLUE though a LIGHT BLUE dotted with patches of DARK BLUE.
Railway clearances and increased facilities have driven out the DARK BLUE and carried
off the PINK. The DARK BLUE has sought refuge in the streets nearest to those from which
they were driven while the PINK has found house-room further afield. The district therefore
is getting poorer. It is probable that the streets as marked this year show their minimum of
poverty owing to the goodness of the times and trade and the mildness of the winter.
Except in the few streets north of Stamford St the bulk of the inhabitants both work and
sleep in the district. In this respect the place differs from most of the districts already seen
north of the Thames. The inhabitants make one vast, poor family whose lives are well known
to one another. There is more street life than even in the East End, more children in the

street and more women gossiping at the doors.

The New Cut and Lambeth Lower Marsh is the common meeting place and market street, always busy though busiest on Friday and Saturday nights and Sunday mornings. The prices as I passed were 4d for a 4lb loaf. Meat-scraps from 2d to 3½lb, pork chops (first rate) 6½d each, half a cooked chicken 8d and 9d (not appetising to look at). Sheep heads, uncooked, 5d each. Best eggs, three for 2½d. Eggs 'special line' 24 for 1/-. Four duck's eggs 3d. Whole skinned rabbit 6½d, three bunches of radishes 1d, lemons three a penny. Good cucumbers in the shops 2d and 4d and the same in appearance on the barrows 1d and 1½d. The largest crowd was round a fish barrow where cod or whiting pollock and plaice were being sold, the buyers all women. No excitement, Dutch auction, each fish was cut in half and shown, the seller fixed the price and lowered it until it was bought. Most of it went at the price he first named. A large plaice was to be bought for 4d, cod's head and perhaps 1½lbs of meat cut off with it for 3d, the rest of the fish (4 or 5 lbs at a guess) went for 4d, a whole fish for 6d. Only once had he to lower his outset price; a plaice, fair size, offered for 3½d found no buyer until 2½d was reached. The flesh of all the fish was white and looked fairly fresh. Rump steaks, good, ran from 9d to 11d in the shops and mutton chops 8d and 9d.

The costers' barrows are on the north side only – by arrangement with the Vestry? Besides fish and fruit there are barrows of flowers, fuschias, geraniums and small bedding plants in wooden boxes, barrows of old keys and ironwork, haberdashery etc, but the glory of the Lower Marsh is by night. It is shy and quiet by day.

Walk 4

B363

Thursday 11th May 1899.
George Duckworth with Sergeant F J O'Dell.
O'Dell is a fat man, very fat. He is not now on active outdoor duty but is employed in the clerks' office. He is intelligent and knows a good deal more about the different parts of the Division in their criminal aspects than most of the policemen who have been round with me. All charges, from every quarter, pass through his hands every day.

Starting at the corner of Earl Street and London Street.
E along **Earl Street**. 2-st. Poor, quiet, careful. Many rag pickers at Joseph's great warehouse. LIGHT BLUE to PURPLE, in map PURPLE and LIGHT BLUE.
N up **Mansfield Street**. A few 2-st 6-roomed houses on west side only, letting at 14/- a week. PURPLE as map. Hoe's large printing machine works take up the whole of the east side.
E & S down **Kell Street**. Houses at north east and south west only. The rest on the west side are down and the east closed. "No good doing up property of this kind. Owners find it better worth their while to pull the whole thing down and rebuild for a different class." A drunken and disorderly class here, some ex-convicts. Windows very bad. DARK BLUE to LIGHT BLUE-barred as map but less of it.
W & N up **Dantzig Street** (late Market St). Houses on east only, Hoe's printing machine work on west. Drunks, like Kell St. 2-st, windows and curtains bad, all doors open. "A class that has money enough for drink and amusement but nothing for their homes." DARK BLUE to LIGHT BLUE-barred, in map LIGHT BLUE. It would seem as though the inhabitants of demolished Kell St had turned in here.
E & S down Kell St, across Earl's St. Out of the S side is **Earl's Place**. Six 2-st houses. Children dirty, well fed, fairly clothed. 5/6 for two rooms. Women very rough, "very poor

and very bad". DARK BLUE-barred to BLACK, in map LIGHT BLUE and DARK BLUE.

S to **St George's Place**. 2-st, well asphalted. One fairly comfortable house, the rest very poor. DARK BLUE to LIGHT BLUE-barred, in map LIGHT BLUE.

W across Dantzig St and along **Butcher Row**. Cement passage. Small 1-st houses on the south side which once were the booths of a busy market. The market consists now of stables and a few orange and potato merchants. The houses on the north side are poor, rough, 3-st or 4-st. Windows broken, patched, all doors open. Ice cream vendors. Children dirty and ragged, sore eyes but well fed. Costers' barrows in evidence. DARK BLUE to LIGHT BLUE, in map LIGHT BLUE. The cul de sac turning north looks less poor, LIGHT BLUE. The block opposite the mews also less poor, LIGHT BLUE to DARK BLUE, and behind this are a few tack cottages apparently tenanted, DARK BLUE. The Mews has only one family living over at the north east. All the tenants here are rough poor, plenty of money at times and none at others. Women sitting about on doorsteps. A few thieves and prostitutes and betting roughs, men who regularly snatch the tickets from those who come with their slips after a race to be paid. They are in league with the smaller bookmakers. Perhaps the colouring of the whole should be LIGHT BLUE-barred.

S along **W** end of the market and **E** along **Parliament Street**. 3-st. Same class as Butcher Row. LIGHT BLUE-barred or DARK BLUE. The market has gone to the east side of London Rd which every day of the week is lined with barrows.

SW down **Ontario Street** (late London St). 3-st and 2-st. "Rather better than Earl St, nearly on a par with Mansfield St." Shirt and tailoring homeworkers. Some evident effort at cleanliness in the matter of windows and curtains. Rather poorer west than east of Dantzig St. Bread and potato parings in the street. PURPLE to LIGHT BLUE, in map PURPLE.

A row of butchers shops, one slaughtering on the premises, in London Road.

S & N up **Skipton Street** (late York St). "Like Ontario St." Tenement houses above shops. Built to be a shopping street but is a business failure, shops of struggling class, barely make ends meet. PURPLE, in map PINK.

S to Newington Causeway. **S & N up London Road**. Very busy. The market part of the street stretches from Newington Causeway to a little north of Ontario St. Many Jews from the Lane sell here with "women's finery". Trams, omnibuses and cabs crowd in here from Waterloo Rd, Blackfriars Rd and Westminster Bridge Rd – the neck of a bottle.

E along **Bath Street**. Poor at north west end. Rents 12/- to 14/-. 2-st. Peculiar "People's Chapel" on south side, "not much favoured, 12 to 15 on Sunday morning". Most doors open. PURPLE to LIGHT BLUE, in map PURPLE.

N & E along Earl St to **Lancaster Street**. Broad, formerly a tram route, now discontinued, lines remain. PINK as map.

S & N up **Southwark Bridge Road**. Hardly a servant. PINK, in map PINK-barred.

Out of the W side is **Stanhope Place**. On south side only. PURPLE, in map PINK.

N & W to **Borough Road**. The north side is RED in map but now very few shopkeepers live over and the shops are of a poor class. PINK rather than RED. The LIGHT BLUE of map west of Warwick St is now down and a new public library in its place.

The street immediately W of the library is called **Library Street** (late New St). 2-st. Quiet, poor labourers. Public library takes up the east side. LIGHT BLUE, in map PINK. Round the corner at No.8 lives a London City Missionary. On the north side are new buildings of Faulkner's tobacco works (PINK in map). "Do a large public house trade in cheap tobaccos, cigars and cigarettes", employ 400 to 500.

S down **Warwick Street**. 3-st on east side north of King James St. PURPLE to LIGHT BLUE, but LIGHT BLUE on both sides south of King James St and 2-st. In map PINK.

E along **King James Street** (late James St). Houses on north side only, until east of Minor Place. Rebuilding at south west end. St Alphege's on south side. Father Edwardes, "the costers' parson", women flock to him. Windows of street bad, bread and mess. Borough market porters and costers. LIGHT BLUE as map.

At SE end is **Minor Place** (in map Mina Place). 3-st tenement houses, seven rooms to a house. Two rooms 6/-. Great mess of paper, children dirty. LIGHT BLUE to PURPLE, in map LIGHT BLUE.

Out of the N side of King James St starting at the east end runs **Upper Green Street**. Asphalted passage, washing across. 2-st. Very poor. DARK BLUE to LIGHT BLUE, in map LIGHT BLUE.

W & S down **Bean Street**. 2-st. Cement paved, every door open, washing across. Noisy rough class, "do a good deal of singing before they go to bed". Children well fed and a little cleaner than in the other streets but houses poorer, less furniture to be seen through the doors. DARK BLUE, in map LIGHT BLUE.

W & N up **Tupman Place** (late Francis Place). Labourers, poor, mess, doors open. LIGHT BLUE to DARK BLUE, in map PURPLE.

W & S down **Flint Street**. Has only a few very poor houses of its own at the north west end. The lower blocks are the backs of the Gun St dwellings. DARK BLUE at north west, not shown in map.

W & S down **Gun Street**. The southern half of the road up for redraining. The northern half has been up and very badly re-laid. Loose stones and brickbats lying about the dwellings. On either side at the south end are very rough crowds of children, girls and women and hooligan boys loafing about. North of the dwellings are County Council buildings, Clandon Buildings etc. 3-st, less poor but poor, LIGHT BLUE. Gun St should be LIGHT BLUE and

DARK BLUE and the whole should have a line of BLACK.

W & N up **Miniver Street** (late Martain St). Road up, strong smell of gas. LCC Dwellings. Gun St buildings run through at south east. Children very dirty and inhabitants very poor looking. LIGHT BLUE to DARK BLUE, in map LIGHT BLUE.

W & S down **Lancaster Street**. 3-st and 2-st. 15/- for 3-st houses. Mixture of factory labourers, mechanics and city warehousemen, many poor. St Alphege's Mission at north east. PURPLE as map.

W & N up **Little Surrey Street**. 2-st. Very poor, nearly every door open. Heavy bloated-faced women, middle aged and old, not young mothers. Birdcages at windows. Houses in fair outward repair. Fearful mess of bread, meat, paper and sacking in the street. "Same class as Joiner St." Gas lamps from wall brackets. Children sore-eyed, hatless, some clean. Many cats. Organ playing but only one child dancing. DARK BLUE-barred rather than LIGHT BLUE-barred of map.

E along **Friar Place**. Houses on north side only. DARK BLUE as map.

W & S down **Warwick Street**. 3-st. Narrow dark street. Tenements, family to each floor. Many builder's labourers. Small turning off west side rather poorer. Bread, paper, mess. Mark the street PURPLE and the turning LIGHT BLUE, all in map is PINK.

N to **Friar Street**. The Hope Mission Hall has taken place of DARK BLUE court shown in map on north east side. Wicks rotary type machine factory on north side, only a few now living on north side. North side between Green St and Board School down. South side is shops with poor living over. PURPLE as map but less of it.

W & N up **Great Suffolk Street**. East side poor, fairly comfortable on west. Old inhabitants. Should be PINK and PURPLE and LIGHT BLUE, in map PURPLE.

W & S down **Hill Street**. Drapers Almshouses still remain but Rowland Hill's Almshouses are now Parnwell's Cooperage. The LIGHT BLUE on south west of map is now down.

W & S down **Belvedere Buildings**. Houses on west only. PURPLE as map. 3-st and 3½-st. Factories on east.

N up **Green Street**. Some DARK BLUE remains but there are some fairly comfortable on either side north of Kings Bench Walk and wedged close by some very poor. On the east side are Merrow and Ripley Buildings, LCC red-brick, which run through to Kings Bench Walk. North of them there are some very poor. In the west side all the courts are down and replaced by Salsbury's lamp works and Harrison & Barkers' horse slaughtering establishment (the same people have a large place in Belle Isle).

Bird Court. Remains. Houses on north side. Cardboard box homework. DARK BLUE.

E along **Kings Bench Walk**. "Used to be a nest of criminals", now few remain but the old houses are still very poor. DARK BLUE, LIGHT BLUE where the LCC building come through from Green St. In map DARK BLUE-barred.

N & W along **Pocock Street**. East end north side is PINK but some poor in the street. PURPLE as a whole as map.

W & S down **Wellington Place**. 2-st. Very poor, criminal. Tops of cardboard hatboxes drying at the windows. Children well fed. DARK BLUE to LIGHT BLUE, perhaps LIGHT BLUE-barred, in map LIGHT BLUE.

N up Blackfriars Rd and E at **Surrey Row**. Better than it used to be, very poor only at the north east and north west. Some PINK on the south side. Many printing office labs. LIGHT BLUE, in map DARK BLUE (leave DARK BLUE at the north east and north west) and take off the RED from the south side.

Out of the **NE** end is **Caran Terrace**. Nine houses. 2-st. 5/- for two rooms, no wash-house. LIGHT BLUE to DARK BLUE, in map DARK BLUE.

N up **Great Suffolk Street**. Common lodging house and public houses on west side. PURPLE to LIGHT BLUE, in map LIGHT BLUE.

W along **Charlotte Street**. 3-st and 4-st. Old-fashioned houses, shops with small window panes, asphalt paved. Lincoln Bennett's hat factory on south side by Nelson Square, "less hat business done now in London, fewer top hats worn". PURPLE to PINK, in map PURPLE.

S down Blackfriars Rd and E into **Nelson Square**. Old-fashioned, balconied, 4½-st and 5½-st houses. Good trees but barely-kept square. Women's University Settlement on the south side and one good private house on the north but many let in tenements and servants only occasional. PINK-barred, in map RED.

Out at the NE corner by Lincoln Bennett's factory. E along Charlotte St. S down Great Suffolk St. W at Southwark Bridge Rd. S down **Collinson Street**. 6-st. Queen's Buildings on the east side. "Rough, respectable poor, don't get looked up like Bean and Miniver streets." With a few exceptions the tenants work for their living, several police. Rents, four rooms for 8/6 to 9/-, three rooms 6/-, 7/- and 7/6, two rooms 5/-. The greater number in 3-roomed holdings. PURPLE as map. The back blocks are less good than the front and should be LIGHT BLUE.

Out of the E side is **Bittern Street**. Mixed. PURPLE, in map PINK.

S of it is **Toulmin Street**. Also mixed. PURPLE, in map PINK. The north east and south east ends of Collinson St are rather better than the rest and might remain PINK as map.

S & W along **Montague Street**. None living. Back entrances to the police court and to two public houses on either side of it.

N up **Scouell Street**. Great mess in street. High, forbidding, 6-st Queen's Building on either side. PURPLE as map.

General Remarks

The block of streets on either side of Friar St between Pocock St on the north, the railway on the east, Borough Rd on the south and Blackfriars Rd on the west have the reputation of being as poor and as rough as any place in the Division. They only just yield premier place to the courts between High St Borough and Redcross St in that they are not quite so vicious and there is no single place quite so bad as Redcross Place. O'Dell spoke of these two and a block off the east side of Great Dover St as being as bad as any district in London. Drunk and disorderly cases, juvenile thieves, van draggers and race course roughs and a few prostitutes come from the Friar St area. The courts between Redcross St and Borough High St have all these and a good proportion of ponces and prostitutes of the lowest class as well.

Juvenile thieving and betting O'Dell spoke of as the most serious increases on the charge sheet. Drunkenness does not decrease but roughness does. The population is easier to deal with from a police point of view than it used to be.

The departure of the fairly comfortable from the district he also said was most marked. Concurrently there is the displacement of the very poor by demolition for new warehouses and railway extension. The very poor crowd in as close as they can to their old haunts and in many cases replace the fairly comfortable. The nett result is that the very poor are slightly better off than before but the district as a whole loses because every year the proportion of the very poor to the fairly comfortable becomes larger.

Betting the police try to stop but fail. Lately their efforts have had a check. At the north end of Wellington Place is a beerhouse where money is paid over by the bookie's agents to those who have won. On this ground the police ran the offenders in but the magistrates held that although betting was illegal the mere receiving of money from bets already made was not so.

Walk 5

B363

Sunday 13th May 1899.
George Duckworth with H Barton.

Starting at the corner of Charlotte Street (late Little Charlotte Street) and
Blackfriars Road.
Charlotte Street. PURPLE as map. At north east end the Surrey Chapel is now a factory
of garden implements.
N up Blackfriars Rd and E at **Scoresby Street** (late York St). 3-st. Working class,
printers, harness makers. Whole house taken and sublet. Three rooms 7/-. South side is
railway arches. PURPLE to LIGHT BLUE, in map LIGHT BLUE.
E & S down **Gambia Street** (late William St). Factory on south east (in place of LIGHT
BLUE on map). Industrial Dwellings on south west, built 1880. 3-st. Children fairly dressed.
PURPLE to LIGHT BLUE, in map PURPLE.
W along **George Street.** Asphalt. 3-st. Like Scoresby St. Gillett's lodging houses at south
west end. Beds 6d a night, 2/6 a week. Regular tenants. Birdcages at house window. PURPLE
to PINK, in map PURPLE. There should be houses also at the east end north side just west of
the railway, not shown in map.
E & N up **Bear Lane.** Mixed. Armstrong Whitworth's ordnance factory at south east and
Isles Artesian Well works on west side. Christchurch parochial schools now in place of
Henley Square. DARK BLUE in map.
N of the schools Bear Lane is called **Henley Terrace** and this might be PURPLE, in map
LIGHT BLUE.
W along **Edward Street.** 2-st, poor houses, east of railway. LIGHT BLUE, in map PURPLE.
West of railway is PURPLE as map. On the south side are the 5-st Ponsonby Buildings.
Mixed class, hatters, carmen, printers. They run through to Charles St.
S & E along **Charles Street.** 3-st on south, 5-st Ponsonby Buildings on north. PURPLE to
PINK, in map PINK.
E into **Chancel Street** (late Robert St). Albert Institute and free library takes up the east
side.
N & W along **Burrell Street.** On the south side are Edward's Almshouses, founded 1753,
rebuilt 1891. Where Burrell St turns north to Southwark Bridge Rd one very poor house
on the east side. Child with dirty head thrust through broken pane of window. LIGHT BLUE.
S down Bear Lane and E at **Price's Street.** Old-fashioned, narrow, improving with a
different class of house at east end south side. LIGHT BLUE to PURPLE, in map PURPLE.
Mechanics and brewery men at east end.
S down Gravel Lane. Out of W side is **Paved Place.** 2-st. All doors open. One barefoot,
rags, faces fairly clean. Three rooms for 8/-. No wash-house but yard behind. Windows bad.
Women with sack aprons, "not vicious, only school board cases". Mostly one family to a
house. DARK BLUE to LIGHT BLUE, in map LIGHT BLUE.
Out of E side of Gravel Lane is **Farnham Place.** Nine houses, 2-st on north side. South
side monopolised by Measure's yard for steel building joists. LIGHT BLUE on south side goes.
S to **Lavington Street.** All offices and warehouses. The LIGHT BLUE court goes (called
Dyer's Buildings).
E & S down **Ewer Street.** Baths and wash-houses at north east. As map.
E to **Great Guildford Street.** Only three houses remain on the east side north of Keppel

St. Small shops. PINK and a few on west also PINK, in map PURPLE. On the west side is the Grove Mission, the rest is factories.

Out of the E side is **Keppel Street**. In map LIGHT BLUE. Now a paved passage between factories.

S of it is **America Street**. In map DARK BLUE, now factories on north side and railway extension on south.

N up **Great Guildford Street**. Fairly comfortable houses on north west. PINK as map.

W along **Sumner Street**. Small shops, some poor live over. Old-fashioned. PINK to PURPLE, in map PINK. Note: The LIGHT BLUE courts and west side of Sumner St (south west end) are down and not yet replaced.

S down **Canvey Street** (late Essex St). Buildings. LIGHT BLUE to PURPLE at north west, in map LIGHT BLUE.

E along **Corliss Place** (late Pleasant Row). No houses. Great mess at east end, bread, rags, bones, etc.

Where it turns N it is called **Wagstaffs Buildings**. Old, wooden, 2-st houses, nearly all closed on west side. Narrow passage between houses. Box makers. 6/6 for three rooms plus wash-house. LIGHT BLUE to DARK BLUE, in map LIGHT BLUE.

W along Corliss Place. S & E along **Zoar Street**. 2-st, clean, houses tidy. 4½ ft of cement up the outside walls from the ground, evidently carefully looked after. Many poor. LIGHT BLUE to PURPLE, in map LIGHT BLUE. One woman pays 8/- for four rooms plus wash-house. Another who has been 15 years in her house and 28 years in the street pays 7/6 for four rooms.

Out of the S side is **Hopetown Place**. Twenty-two houses, clean windows, flowers, many doors shut. 2-st. 8/- for four rooms plus wash-house. LIGHT BLUE to PURPLE, in map LIGHT BLUE.

W of Canvey St **Zoar Street** is poorer. 5-st buildings on south side (LIGHT BLUE as map). Children dirty, noisier, more bread lying about, well asphalted. At north west end rough, poor, gas workers. LIGHT BLUE and DARK BLUE as map.

S down **Canvey Street**. Like Zoar St. LIGHT BLUE, in map PURPLE. Where it turns west, more respectable. PURPLE as map.

N & E along **Cashers Grounds**. Very poor backs of Zoar St. DARK BLUE as map. Howards Box Works on north side. Large.

N to Sumner St. N along **Holland Street**. Odd mixture of old sloping tiled roofed houses and modern. A few lived in by foremen and poorish at north east. PURPLE as map.

Out of E side is **Ridler Place**. Broad, asphalt. Cricket being played across it by lads of 16–18. Two houses on north side only. Leading to the Bottle Exchange. PURPLE to PINK, in map LIGHT BLUE.

W & S along **Holland Street**. Epp's large cocoa factory, "are careful about the girls they employ", on south side.

Out of the E side is **Knights Court**. 2-st, clean, quiet, paved. Houses on north and south sides. PURPLE to PINK, in map LIGHT BLUE. The Medical Mission at the north west end is an old house with wrought iron railings.

S of Knights Court are **Hopton's Almshouses**. Pretty, old, rather ill-kept grass.

Walk 6

B363

Tuesday 16th May 1899.
George Duckworth with H Barton.

Starting at the corner of Union Street and Great Suffolk Street.
E along Union St. Out of the S side is **Damon Place**. Clean and tidy. Two 3-st houses on east side only. LIGHT BLUE, in map DARK BLUE.
S down **Risborough Street**. 2-st. Some poor, others fairly comfortable. Poorer south of Orange St than north of it. LIGHT BLUE, in map DARK BLUE, on east side only.
S to **Orange Street**. Factories on north side, DARK BLUE goes. 3-st. Old inhabitants. Cobbled, paved, clean street. Lightermen, waterside labourers. No trouble to the police. LIGHT BLUE, in map DARK BLUE. East of Argent St and on the south side are very pretty Miss Hill-like cottages with green wooden doors and red tiles (Walpole Cottages). These run to the corner of Lemon St. East of Lemon St are others in different style called Winchester Cottages. At the east end on south side are 4-st Winchester Buildings. Poor, LIGHT BLUE to DARK BLUE, not criminal, in map DARK BLUE-barred. Mark the cottages PURPLE and the buildings LIGHT BLUE to DARK BLUE. Many spring flowers in the cottage windows, cowslips, bluebells, etc.
S down **Argent Street** which is the road east of Risborough St, out of the south side of Orange St. Two very poor houses on west side only. DARK BLUE as map.
S to **Loman Street**. 2-st. General labourers and carmen, clean. 9/- for 6-roomed house. Old wooden house still standing but not tenanted at the west end north side. LIGHT BLUE to DARK BLUE, in map DARK BLUE. Also three 2-st houses. PURPLE to LIGHT BLUE.
E along Orange St, S down Southwark Bridge Rd, past the headquarters of the Metropolitan Fire Brigade. On the W side of Southwark Bridge Rd, S of the Fire Station is **Goldsmith's Place**. Fourteen 2-st houses, very poor. Some houses with fair furniture. Court is rather but not very messy. Dirty children. 6/- for two rooms and small yard. DARK BLUE as map.
N to Union St then W. Out of the S side is **Townshend Yard**. Houses on east, north and south. Poor, respectable, quiet, clean. Houses done up outwardly. "I think they ought to do 'em up inside now" said a woman who pays 8/6 for four rooms and yard on the south side. Houses on north side, two rooms for 5/6. LIGHT BLUE as map.
W & S down **Victoria Place**. Entered through iron gates. All Hallows Mission at south end, east side better than west. Quiet. 11/6 for four rooms plus yard and wash-house. Two houses in a passage on east side. East side is PINK to PURPLE, west is LIGHT BLUE. Mark the whole PURPLE, in map LIGHT BLUE.
W & S down **Pepper Street**. Very poor. Houses on both sides. DARK BLUE as map.
E along **Golden Place**. Roman Catholic church on south side. The Place turns abruptly north. Six houses, narrow and dark. 4/6 and 5/- for two rooms, "mere cupboards". DARK BLUE, in map LIGHT BLUE.
E to Southwark Bridge Rd. S past Goldsmiths Place. W at **Lant Place**. Cement-paved court, with zinc dustbin. Doors open, potato parings, basins, plates etc on the tables. Windows cracked. Houses with fair amount of furniture but very poor. Two rooms are 5/- and 5/6. Houses on north and south sides of east end but only on north side of west end. No communication with King's Court or Queen's Court. DARK BLUE to LIGHT BLUE, in map LIGHT BLUE.

Out of N side is **Grotto Place**. 2-st. Very poor, like Lant Place. Costers' barrows. DARK BLUE as map.

N of it is **Lower Grotto Place**. The worst of the lot in appearance, it is a continuation of but is walled off from Goldsmith's Place. 5/6 for two rooms, no wash-house but a yard behind. This bit is known as 'the Grottos'. Many children, all well fed but dirty and with sores on faces, clothes ragged, too large and too small. Windows broken and patched. "There may be a few thieves and prostitutes" but Barton does not know them as such. They make their appearance in the police court for drunks and assaults. Many carmen. DARK BLUE

S down **Sturge Street**. 2-st and 3-st. Four rooms plus wash-house 10/-. Bread about. It looks very poor but Barton says that it is much better than the Grottos. DARK BLUE to LIGHT BLUE, in map LIGHT BLUE.

W & N up **Queen's Court**. Cement paved. 1-st and 2-st. Rather better on the east side than the west. Children clean but plenty of DARK BLUE. DARK BLUE to LIGHT BLUE, in map LIGHT BLUE.

W & N up **King's Court**. One 1-st house. All children well fed. Out of 20 playing in the street, ages from six months to 14 years, about half with clean, five with dirty and five with very dirty faces, clothes sufficient. DARK BLUE, in map LIGHT BLUE. At the south east end are the Victoria Dwellings. LIGHT BLUE, in map PURPLE. Barton said that these courts are poorer but not criminal like the streets off Friar St.

Out of the **SW** end is **Princes Place**. With courts running out of the west side. The southern court is the poorest, rough looking. Windows broken, birdcages at windows, flowers. Southern court is DARK BLUE as map, the rest LIGHT BLUE, in map PURPLE.

S & W & N into **Cafrey Place** (late Thomas Place). Ten houses with 15 ft frontage to each. 2-st, 6/- for two rooms plus wash-house. Cement paved, clean. DARK BLUE to LIGHT BLUE, in map DARK BLUE and uncoloured.

S down **Great Suffolk Street**. East side much poorer than west. PINK to PURPLE on west, LIGHT BLUE on east, in map both are PURPLE. East of Sturge St shops begin. PINK.

N up **Little Suffolk Street**. Houses on east side only. Cable Cottages (Miss Hill), gables, red tiles, 2-st. PURPLE to LIGHT BLUE. Poorer 2-st and 3-st houses north of them. Strong smell of cough lozenges, Rowlands panegoric is made in a factory on the east side. PURPLE and LIGHT BLUE as map.

E along Lant St and S down **Bittern Street** (late William St). 2-st. Bread, paper, bones, etc. "Drunks and assaults." LIGHT BLUE, in map PURPLE.

Out of the E side is **Rodney Street**. 2-st. Sore eyes. LIGHT BLUE, in map PURPLE. There is no LIGHT BLUE court east of the Board School.

S down **Toulmin Street**. LIGHT BLUE, in map PURPLE.

W along **Lant Street**. West end poorer than east. LIGHT BLUE as map. At north west end are Brigade Buildings. PURPLE to PINK, in map LIGHT BLUE.

N up **Lombard Street**. Very low, mixed lodging houses on east side for low men and women, hold about 40. The Evelina Hospital extended absorbs the BLACK on the west side, BLACK on east remains.

The BLACK continues round into **Mint Street** where six houses look more respectable but they are also one lodging house and have the windows trimmed with the same red curtains as in the lodging house in Lombard St. East of these is a mission club room (St Michael's Mission House and Club) with a curate or caretaker living over. Further east are, on the south side, the Douglas Buildings and Ilfracome Buildings on the north. Not so good as Brigade Buildings. Police (about 12), mechanics, warehousemen. PINK to PURPLE, in map PINK.

S down **Harrow Street**. Factories on east, Buildings on west.

E along **Vine Yard**. Houses at east end only. 2-st. Lowest class of prostitute and loafer, men brought home. BLACK as map but less of it.

S across Lant St and down **Aster Place** (late Ann's Place). 2-st. PURPLE to LIGHT BLUE, in map LIGHT BLUE. Four rooms 8/9.

E along **Lant Street**. Factories on either side.

Into the Borough High St and **S**. Out of the **W** side is **Nelson Place**. Flagged court, eight houses. Women rough, children clean, windows bad, window boxes. Scavengers, 'drunks'. LIGHT BLUE to DARK BLUE, in map LIGHT BLUE.

S of it is **Star Yard**. Shoeing forge, stable rats. LIGHT BLUE as map.

General Remarks

In this round there is more poverty in the Grotto area and in Bittern St, Toulmin St and Rodney St off Lant St but there is considerably less in Orange St and the streets off it. The east end of Lant St which was formerly DARK BLUE-barred has now a church and rectory on the north side and Winchester Cottages on the south. The only rough bit remaining there is Winchester Buildings at the south east end of Lant St.

The poor class are carmen, waterside labourers. Rents vary from 4/6 to 10/6 per week for two rooms and a yard or wash-house, old tenants paying rather less than new. The worst spot is Vine Yard, happily only a few houses, difficult of approach and a dangerous place at night.

Walk 7   B363

Wednesday 17th May 1899.
George Duckworth with H Barton.

Starting at the corner of the Marshalsea Road and the Borough High Street.

W along **Marshalsea Road**. Common lodging house on north side east of Harrow St. Rough. DARK BLUE to BLACK, in map BLACK.

N up **Harrow Street**. Very poor and rough, criminal. 2-st. Well asphalted. At the corner of Birdcage Alley are Farmhouse Lodgings, for men only. West of Harrow St on the north side is another common lodging house with a stink coming from the windows that reminded me of Medland Hall. Bread and mess in street. One woman in the cul de sac continuation of Harrow St. pays 7/- for three rooms plus wash-house, "quite enough for these pokey holes".

S along **Birdcage Alley** with Farmhouse lodging house at St George's Buildings on north side and two or three 2-st houses on south. DARK BLUE-barred. St George's Building looks better than the rest, better class of wash hanging out to dry, but Barton gave the whole place the same character.

E along **Mason's Buildings**. Very poor. Houses on north only. The exit into Borough High St is down a passage under a house, not a yard wide. The whole of this bit might be BLACK. The inhabitants of the houses and common lodging houses are prostitutes and ponces and thieves. Those in St George's Building are waterside labourers and market porters (no gutter merchants). Youths and middle-aged men of the lowest casual class loafing; undergrown men; women slouching with draggled skirts, hatless but hidden under long shawls; a deformed boy with naked half-formed leg turned in the wrong direction, made up the scene.

N & W along **Falcon Court**. Houses both sides, old-fashioned, red-tiled, small-paned windows. Buildings at west end south side. Women's common lodging houses on north side.

At the Borough St end there is a public house at the south side and a pawnbrokers at the north. Thieves, prostitutes, bullies standing at the Borough St end – spiders to catch flies. Women sitting on doorsteps. Barton said it was bad but not so bad as Redcross Place. An awkward place for a stranger at night. BLACK rather than LIGHT BLUE of map. At the west end of Falcon Court is New Buildings, 7-st houses, on south and Mowbray Buildings on north. PURPLE and DARK BLUE.

N up Borough High St and W at **Brent Court**. 3-st on north, 2½-st on south. South side better than the north. 7/6 for three rooms and wash-house downstairs. Attention paid to flowers, Virginian creepers in window boxes, fine hydrangea in another window ledge. North side DARK BLUE, south LIGHT BLUE, in map both are DARK BLUE.

N & W along **Eve's Place** (late Adam's Place). Roman Catholic Schools at west end. 2-st plus attic and 2½-st plus attic, palinged fronts to north side. Poor and very poor, a few respectable with brass paraffin lamps as ornaments in the window. DARK BLUE to LIGHT BLUE, in map LIGHT BLUE.

Scenes at Redcross Place.

N up High St, W at **Redcross Place**. 3-st and 2-st on the north side, 3-st on the south. Notorious women's lodging house at the north east end and to its owner belong four houses on the south side of the place. Hardly a whole pane of glass in any window of houses on the south side. A row of stables (1-st, no-one living there) runs down the centre (DARK BLUE in map). Tenanted by one scarecrow horse. Stableyard used as dumping ground for house refuse and full of manure, bread, bones, rotting oranges, brickbats. "Stabling to let" on a notice. Three women sitting on doorstep at east end, one suckling a child, bare breasts, no attempt to cover herself as I passed. All of lowest type, the other two huddling under shawls. Women decoys at entrance to High St. Barton was nervous at my going down here alone, saying the chances were in favour of brickbats or slops upon my head. Many evil faces at the windows but nothing happened. Rough children and lads of 14 or 15, holey, ill clothed, dirty, well fed, playing at wood chopping with a hatchet at west end. "Any man at all the worse for drink has a bad chance if he once gets in here at night; he is sure to be robbed of everything and is lucky to get out of the place without bodily injury." An obvious improvement would be to sweep away the stables and foul stableyard. Mackerel being cried out 1½d each. "Police don't go down here unless they have to and never singly."

N & W at **Maypole Alley**, entered through passage under houses from the High St. 3-st and 2-st, some very poor. One middle-aged woman pulling fur at her open windows, air full of fluff and herself covered with it, spoke in shaky husky voice "must do it to live you know".

Fair amount of furniture in the houses, one with brass timepiece under glass shade. Elaborate wooden carving on one door lintel. Windows bad. Sewing machines at work. LIGHT BLUE to DARK BLUE, in map DARK BLUE. Rents 3/6 for two rooms, 6/6 to 8/3 for three rooms, no wash-house but backyard. Wash hanging across the yard not of the poorest, more poor than bad.

N up High St. W at **Maidstone Buildings**. Only warehouses, uncoloured as map.

N & W at **St Margaret's Court**. 3-st and 2-st. Mixed poor, a few fairly comfortable. A little village by itself. Small paned windows and shops of its own. Brave show of flowers in boxes at west end. The turning north out of it is rather poorer than the rest, it is a flagged passage. LIGHT BLUE as map. Rent, three rooms for 7/-, no yard.

W into **Redcross Street**. Poor at north end. LIGHT BLUE as map.

Out of the E side is **Wood's Yard**. Four 2-st houses, on north only. Overhanging wooden tops, red-tiled roofs. LIGHT BLUE as map but less of it, stables at east end.

S down **Redcross Street**. South of Union St on the east side are first some poor houses, LIGHT BLUE as map, then come blocks of Metropolitan Industrial Dwellings Company houses. The two northern blocks are called Stanhope Buildings, the two southern are Mowbray Buildings. The front blocks are better in both cases than those behind. Rent in the front blocks of Stanhope Buildings: single rooms 3/-; two rooms 4/6 and 5/6; three rooms 7/- and 7/6. In Mowbray Buildings: single rooms 3/-, 3/3 and 3/6; two rooms 4/6, 4/9, 5/- and 5/6; three rooms 7/3 (taken from notice board). Eve's Place is the dividing line between Stanhope and Mowbray Buildings. The windows of the back blocks are very bad. Many thieves but not many prostitutes in them. They are 5-st high, dingy. Bread and meat and mess in the street. Mark fronts LIGHT BLUE and backs DARK BLUE or DARK BLUE-barred, in map both are LIGHT BLUE.

Opposite on the W side of Redcross St is **Redcross Gardens**. Carefully laid out with a pond, rustic bridge, mosaics let into wall on north side. Flanked on north and south by walls of high hop warehouses. Gallery with covered playground under running along south side. Bandstand. Several but not very many old people sitting about on the benches and a few children. Cottages on west side and Redcross Hall. The cottages are well tenanted and PINK.

The SE end of **Redcross Street**, south of Falcon Court, is small shops, a general shop, two small dairies, barber, etc. Not known to the police as receivers. PURPLE, in map LIGHT BLUE. South of Birdcage Alley is all factories, in map BLACK. On the west side south of Glenthorne St is very poor and might be DARK BLUE, in map LIGHT BLUE.

N along **Quilp Street** (late Queen St). 5-st buildings on the triangle on south side. PINK to PURPLE, in map PINK.

N up **Dorrit Street**. Common lodging house at south west, 4d and 6d. BLACK. Very poor on east. Might all be DARK BLUE-barred.

N & W along **Glenhorn Street** (late Peter St). 2-st. Quiet. Gospel Lighthouse at No. 19 on north side. LIGHT BLUE as map.

W up to **Whitecross Street**. 2-st. Clean, well asphalted. Whitecross Cottages and Redcross Hall on east side. PINK, in map PURPLE. Quiet poor on west side. LIGHT BLUE, in map PURPLE. Factories both sides above Henry Place and a common lodging house for men at the north east corner (40 or 50 beds).

N up **Marshalsea Road**. Buildings on west side, PINK to PURPLE, in map PINK. Houses on east, PINK-barred, in map PINK. Occasional servants. The BLACK spots shown in map on north east side of Marshalsea Rd should go, they are mistakes in transference from the big map.

E along Union St, N up **Worcester Street**. One LIGHT BLUE house remains on south west. A Roman Catholic Church takes the place of LIGHT BLUE on east side and the Chocolate works replace the RED at the north end.

W along Southwark St. **Southwark Square** out of the south side is covered by Measures steel joist works. PINK of map goes.

S into Union St. E. On the S side is **Mander Place** (late James Place). One woman pays 7/- for three rooms and another 7/- for two rooms and copper but no yard or wash-house. The second woman has been here five years and said the 1/- a week was added to the rent when the copper was put in six months ago. "The houses swarm with black beetles and bugs...rabbit hutches."

E along **Union Street**. Shops. PINK as map.

E across Borough High St to **Newcomen Street**. Cobbles. 3-st shops. Narrow at west end. PINK to PINK-barred, in map PINK-barred.

N up Borough High St. Out of the E side going N from Newcomen St is **Nags Head Yard**. Only one living at north west end. Not worth marking, in map PURPLE. The rest is Great Western Railway goods yard.

N to **Spur Inn Yard**. Some living in 3-st houses on south side only. Poor. LIGHT BLUE, in map PURPLE. On north are 2-st wooden-topped storehouses, full of hams and margarine tubs. East of the dwelling houses are more stores, old, with long low-hanging roofs as shelter for carts loading and unloading. Also stables.

N to **Three Nunns Court**. None living.

N to **Queens Head Yard**. Remains of old inn with balconies and balustrading on north side. Has been offices, now untenanted and falling to pieces. One house lived in on north and old double-fronted, wooden, red-tiled, dormer-windowed house on south side. Both PINK as map. Leading to extension of Guy's Hospital.

N to **George Yard**. On south side the old inn remains, an old family hotel with small leaded diamond window panes, balustraded balconies. Old four-poster bed seen through upper window. Not so large as formerly since its eastern half is given up to railway officers. Great Northern Railway goods yard at east end. There is no LIGHT BLUE on north as shown in map.

N to **Old White Hart Inn Yard** which leads round to **Kings Head Yard**. Mostly hop factors. Down's Surgical Instrument factory. Wood paved.

W across Borough High St to **Three Crown Square**. Only one house lived in at north west end. Potato salesmen, full of porters carrying sacks and small courts. All PINK as map. There is a passage through to the Borough market at the north west end.

N & E along **St Thomas Street**. RED as map.

N & E up **Denman Street**. Not yet built up.

W along **Railway Approach**. Shops. RED as map.

Into Tooley St. W under London Bridge into **Montague Close**. High warehouses.

S down Church St. W along **Winchester Street**. Clearances for extension of the market. Some PINK of map goes. Poor west of public house, LIGHT BLUE as map.

N up **Winchester Yard**. Two very poor houses on east side, DARK BLUE, in map LIGHT BLUE. North of them is open space on west and warehouses on north.

W & N up **Stoney Street**. All houses on east side cleared. LIGHT BLUE of map goes.

S down **Counter Street**. Market shops on south. PINK as map.

W along **Park Street**. Shops, eating places. Poor on north side. PURPLE to PINK, in map PINK.

S down **Redcross Street**. Fair class Buildings on west and small shops on east. Buildings PINK to PURPLE, in map LIGHT BLUE. East side LIGHT BLUE as map.

W along **Castle Street**. 3-st. PINK as map. On the north side are Buildings belonging to

Barclay's Brewery with cellars underneath them. A strong smell of beer and cellars everywhere. Behind the Buildings is a well cement-paved yard.

W of them out of the N side is **Park Place**. Six 2-st cottages with two rooms in each, 5/3, no conveniences. LIGHT BLUE to PURPLE, in map PURPLE.

N up **Southwark Bridge Road**. Jays large hat factory on west side, some decent houses on east. RED as map.

Out of the E side is **Bridge Place**. Eight houses, 3-st. PURPLE to LIGHT BLUE, in map LIGHT BLUE. Leads to the extension of the Brewery. Now building.

W along **Sumner Street**. Twelve 2-st houses. Quiet, poor. Four rooms 10/6. Children clean, well fed, fairly dressed. PURPLE to LIGHT BLUE, in map LIGHT BLUE.

Out of S side of Sumner St are a large block of **Peabody's Buildings**. PINK to PURPLE, in map PINK.

E & N up **Emerson Street**. Houses on west only. PINK to PURPLE, in map PINK.

Out of the NW is **Lizette Place**. Two houses. 8/6 for three rooms and washhouses. Water from tap in the court. PINK to PURPLE, not shown in map.

S to Park St and E. Out of the N side is **Bear Gardens**. 2-st and 3-st. Beerhouse on west, block of Buildings on east. LIGHT BLUE as map. The passage continues north to the River between factory walls, very untidy and ill kept.

E of it is **Rose Alley**. Only backs of Bear Gardens Dwellings on east side.

Opposite out of S side of Park St is **Hamors Court**. One double-fronted house. PINK to PURPLE, not shown in map.

E along **Park Street**. On north side is a block of 6-st Dwellings. PURPLE as map. On south side are respectable houses (Barclay's foremen probably). PINK as map.

W along Park St and Sumner St and N into **Moss Alley** and attendant courts. 2-st. Marked DARK BLUE and BLACK in map. A little village by itself. Men employed in Phoenix gas works and waterside. Not so bad as it used to be. The west side of White Hand Alley is monopolised by the City Electric Light Works. Some thieves, snatches, van draggers, not many Irish. Women in Epp's Cocoa works etc. LIGHT BLUE-barred rather than DARK BLUE and BLACK of map. Barton "would a deal rather walk here at night than in Redcross Place." This round finishes District 31.

General Remarks

There is in this round a set of courts and small streets which for number, viciousness, poverty and crowding is unrivalled in anything I have hitherto seen in London. Together with the Friar St area adjoining, they make probably the most serious blot on the map for all London (excepting only the Tabard St area). The boundaries of this area are: on the north Union St, on the east High St Borough, on the south Borough Rd on the west Blackfriars Rd. This is a district which has gained little from demolitions within its own borders, though the courts off Kings Bench Walk and Green St are gone, and has suffered appreciably from demolition in other districts. Kings Bench Walk and Green St are better than they were because much has been demolished and some rebuilt. Orange St and Lowman St are better for the same reasons. The BLACK on the west side of Lombard St and the south east end of Redcross St and the north side of Vine Yard has been displaced by the building of factories and a hospital (Evelina Hospital in Lombard St). But all this betterment is more than counter-balanced by the worsement in the streets between Friar St and Borough Rd and Redcross St and Borough High St.

The only street that with the same buildings has nevertheless improved in tenancy is Surrey Row (south of Nelson Square). The new colouring of the map suggests that the old tenants of Kings Bench Walk etc, though dispossessed, have yet found houseroom close to their own haunts and that others displaced by railway extension, eg. in the courts off the north side of Union St and the east side of Great Guildford St, together with former tenants of Duke St, Tower St and Gray St (between Blackfriars Rd and Westminster Bridge Rd) just outside the area, have found their way in. The inhabitants are all South Londoners. None have come from the north side of the Thames. They are the dregs of the population and not scum that has floated off from distant places and infected new areas as in Notting Dale. The worst spot of the police division is Redcross Place and Falcon Court runs it close. As in Notting Dale the worst specimens are found in the common lodging houses. They are prostitutes and bullies, about half the prostitutes are Irish women and their gains are made far more by robbery than by prostitution. Their favourite haunts are Borough High St and Clapham Common. Bullies live on their earnings. They are English or Irish cockneys, not foreigners. The foreign bully has nearly deserted London since the law of last October and foreign women come no further south than Stamford St. The police have tried to run in the English bully from the High St courts but had a failure in their first case and are fearful of trying again. The man they charged was notorious as a ponce but was able to prove that he had earned some money by himself and therefore the charge fell to the ground.

No. 1 Redcross Place is a common lodging house for women and "every woman there is a prostitute". The Superintendent said that out of all the cases at the South London Police Court, more than half came from this area. "Last year there were over 4,000 charges from this block of streets."

The same change is going on in Southwark that in years past took place in the City. As site values rise those who can most afford to pay for them leave, ie. the rich leave first. After them go the fairly comfortable and last of all the poor and very poor. Hence those who properly can the least afford to pay high rents are the last to leave. The rich were the first of the residents to leave the City, the poor have only just left. In Southwark the rich have already left, the fairly comfortable are leaving, the poor and the very poor remain and will remain until they are evicted.

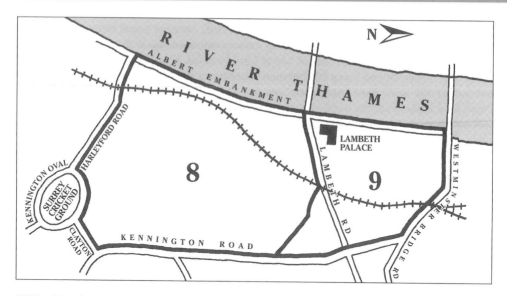

Walk 8

B363

Monday 5th June 1899.
George Duckworth with Reserve Inspector Albert Green.

Starting at the corner of Upper Marsh and Westminster Bridge Road.
S down **Upper Marsh**. Narrow, cobbles. Stage entrance to the Canterbury on south side.
Fields Soap Works on south side. Some very poor houses on north side, south of Waxwell
Place. PURPLE and DARK BLUE, in map PINK. The PINK on either side south of Stangate
St remains.
N up **Finck Street**. 2½-st. Flag-paved passage. Mixed, many poor, children dirty, one
barefoot. PURPLE to LIGHT BLUE, in map PINK. At the north east end are two very poor
DARK BLUE houses.
S along **Boniface Street**. Factory on north side, then poor. Rather better at south east.
LIGHT BLUE, in map PURPLE.
S along **Waxwell Terrace**. 2½-st plus attic. Flagged passage. Poorer than Finck St. Doors
open, barefoot boy, mess of bread and paper, rough women. LIGHT BLUE as map.
W of it **Heathfield Place** is down and **Shrub Place** has only two houses left at south east
end. One woman pays 9/- for four rooms and a kitchen and complained at the demolition of
Heathfield Place and of the building up of Russell Buildings by the South Eastern Railway.
"They do it to take in those they have turned out, but they don't want us in and though they
give us the first choice of coming they turn us out again the moment we are in arrears with
our rent."
W along **Boniface Street**. On the north side are Russell Buildings, built by the South
Eastern Railway to compensate those who were disturbed in Bermondsey. Now largely
tenanted by police and their own men. No poor. 9/- for three rooms. PINK, in place of LIGHT
BLUE of map.
E along **Frederick Street**. At north west end is a fair set of Dwellings but next to them
going east is very poor. LIGHT BLUE as map.
N & E along **Lambeth Palace Road**. Shops. No servants on south side. PINK, not

coloured in map. The north side are new red-brick flats with some servants. PINK-barred, not coloured in map. These flats cover the old site of Astley Theatre.

SE down **Stangate Street**. 2-st and 2½-st. PINK to PURPLE. Mechanics working over the other side of the river. PINK to PURPLE, in map PINK.

S & E down **Crozier Street**. 2½-st on north side, 3-st on south. PINK to PURPLE, in map PINK.

S down **Little Paris Street**. 2½-st. North side better than south. Ladies collecting rents. PURPLE to PINK, in map PINK.

N up **Paris Street**. 3½-st. Some poor. PURPLE to PINK, in map PINK.

E along **Sudbary Street** (late Mary St). 2-st. PINK as map.

S down Crozier St to **Royal Street**. 3-st on west which are markedly better than the old 2-st, 3-st and 3½-st houses on east. Either PINK and PURPLE or PURPLE and LIGHT BLUE, in map PINK. The inhabitants of this block of streets (ie. between Westminster Bridge Rd, London & South Western Railway, Paris St and the Lambeth Palace Rd) are working class, fairly comfortable except for the tenants of Waxwell Terrace, Finck St, Frederick St and Upper Marsh. Most work away north of River. In the new South Eastern Railway Buildings are policemen from the 'A' or Whitehall and 'L' or Lambeth division. Very few Irish, no prostitutes.

S down **Carlisle Street**. Comfortable on east, poor and very poor on west but improves on west south of a block of model Dwellings. PINK on east, uncoloured in map and from PURPLE to LIGHT BLUE on west.

N up **Park Place**. 2-st. Mixed. PURPLE to PINK, in map PURPLE. At the south east end is a turning by the railway arches, 2-st houses with small gardens in front. LIGHT BLUE, in map PURPLE.

E into **Hercules Road**. Wood paved. Old-fashioned houses. East side better than west. No servants. PINK, rather than PINK-barred of map.

Out of the W side is **Homer Street**. Two houses on east side. Less PURPLE than map. The railway arches have been so widened here as to take off a large bit of the ends of these streets.

N & W along **Allen Street**. 2½-st. PURPLE to PINK, in map PINK.

N & W is **Newnham Terrace**. 2½-st. Mixed. Mechanics, betting men, prostitutes. PINK to PURPLE, in map PINK.

S down Kennington Rd and N up **Mead Row**. Comfortable. House stands back off south east end. Houses on east only. PINK as map.

W along **North Street**. Mixed. PURPLE as map.

Out of the SW end is **North Place**. Three houses. LIGHT BLUE both sides, in map only on east.

E & S down **Crow Place**. Six houses, 2-st. Rents 5/- for two rooms, tap in court. Very poor but decent. DARK BLUE to LIGHT BLUE, in map LIGHT BLUE.

S into Colwyn St. W of the public house, with houses on west only is **Wylie Place** (late William Place). Three 2-st houses. LIGHT BLUE to DARK BLUE, in map PURPLE.

E along Colwyn St. E of Crow Place is **Abbey Place** which is a continuation east of Crow Place and separated from it by a house which turns the corner. WCs in front. Flowers. Two rooms 5/- and 5/6. LIGHT BLUE as map.

It is separated by WCs on the E side from **Pennell Place**. Five houses in flagged court like preceding. Poor. LIGHT BLUE to DARK BLUE, in map LIGHT BLUE.

N up **North Place**. Red-brick model houses on east. PINK and PURPLE as map.

Into **North Street**. 3-st. Children well fed and dressed. Many poor. PURPLE as map.

S & W along **Colwyn Street** (late South St). Poor, rough labourers. Doors open, messy street. Improves at south west end. LIGHT BLUE to PURPLE, in map PURPLE.

W to **Hercules Road**. On the east side, south of Colwyn St, are Orient Buildings. 5-st, well tenanted, ugly red brick. PINK, in map PINK-barred.

S of them is **Sidford Place** (late Bucer Place). Quiet, retired, 2-st cottages. Very pretty with trees and well-kept gardens. All comfortable except one house at east end. PINK as map.

E along the **Lambeth Road**. Houses tenanted by two and three families, very few servants. PINK-barred, in map RED.

S down **China Walk**. Built 1776. Irish labourers and some queer characters living over the shops. PURPLE, in map PINK. It is poorer south of Lambeth Walk and LIGHT BLUE rather than PURPLE of map.

Out of the W side going S is **Karl Place**. Houses look very poor but clean. Children clean, well fed and dressed. Kitchens down and living room upstairs. Houses on east side only. Many windows broken and patched. 6/- for two rooms and kitchen. LIGHT BLUE to DARK BLUE, in map LIGHT BLUE.

S of it is **St Alban's Buildings**. 2-st. Poor, dirty, well-fed children. Flagged passage. Looks a bit rougher than Karl Place. 5/- for two rooms and kitchen. LIGHT BLUE to DARK BLUE, in map LIGHT BLUE.

Out of the E side of China Walk is **China Square**. Poor, houses newish. Three rooms and wash-house for 8/- and 8/6. LIGHT BLUE as map. This 'China area' is rough. Inhabitants are chiefly costers and Irish labourers. No prostitutes, a few thieves, many drunks, both men and women.

N & W along **Canterbury Place**. 3-st. A few police and many poor. PURPLE to PINK, in map PINK.

S down **Saville Place**. PURPLE to PINK, in map PINK.

E along **Lambeth Walk**. Many poor shops with poor living over. Wood paved. PURPLE, in map PURPLE-barred.

S down China Walk to St Alban's St. Out of its SE end is **Walnut Tree Place**. 2-st. Well cement-paved, better than the Chinas. 5/- for two rooms to an old tenant. No copper nor kitchen. LIGHT BLUE to PURPLE, in map PURPLE.

W along **St Alban's Street**. 2-st. Broadish street, 29 ft from wall to wall. China pots in windows, mess of paper in street. PINK as map.

S & E along **Richmond Street**. 2-st. Messy. PURPLE, in map PINK.

W into **Walnut Tree Walk**. East side better than west. Old houses south of Board School have long gardens behind. Some converted into builders' yards, others to be built over. South of the Board School is a large block of Dwellings. Has been a brothel on west side. On east side between Richmond St and St Alban's St is a poor court of two double-fronted houses in which a decrepit four wheel cab was standing. LIGHT BLUE. Mark the whole PURPLE instead of PINK of map.

Entered through passage under them is **St Olave's Gardens**. Twelve 2-st houses, look poor, policeman coming out of one. Brickbats from demolished walls in front. PURPLE, not on map.

N up **Kennington Road**. Apartments general, front gardens, very few servants. PINK-barred, in map RED.

Like it is **Lambeth Road**, only rather less respectable. Prostitutes and Music Hall agents and there used to be a brothel or two. PINK-barred, in map RED.

General Remarks

A good deal of light blue has disappeared from the courts between Westminster Bridge Rd and Stangate St and also between Hercules Rd and the Railway. This has been owing

Stangate Street.

to demolition for the sake of railway extension and factory extension (Fields Factory in Upper Marsh) and has not been followed by rebuilding of houses except in the case of the courts off Stangate St. Here the SER put up the Russell Buildings avowedly to accommodate those whom they had turned out in Bermondsey. But Bermondsey would not or could not come to Lambeth and their place has been taken by railwaymen and police of the 'A' (Whitehall), 'E' (Strand) and 'L' (Lambeth) division.

The other poor spots are the courts off Colwyn St, rather poorer now than 10 years ago and the China Walk area which is much the same as 10 years ago.

Many of the mechanics whose work is in the West End live between Westminster Bridge Road and Lambeth Rd, while unskilled workers live further south, ie. anywhere between Lambeth Rd and Upper Kennington Lane. The only rough spot is the China Walk area and here, as always, is the Irish cockney.

Walk 9

B363 continued in B365

Tuesday 6th June 1899.
George Duckworth with Sergeant E Sales.
Sergeant Sales is a man of 41 with 23 years service in the police force which he entered at 18. He is a tall man, fair moustache, blue eyes, with a sad and rather disappointed look. It seems he had expected to be made an inspector two years ago but was told his application

and expectation was useless on the ground of having seen too much service. "They will not make a sergeant of many years standing into an inspector."

Starting at the corner of Lambeth Walk and Walnut Tree Walk.
S down **Lambeth Walk.** Market street. Thursday early closing, about half the shops and half the costers close. Wood paved, narrow, busy. Very few keep servants. Poor north of Walnut Tree Walk. PURPLE and PINK or PINK-barred, instead of PINK-barred and RED of map.
E along **Fitzalan Street** (late Union St). 3-st. West end poorer than east. Very poor women standing about east end and one very poor house at the west corner of Goad Place at north west end. Compositors, cabmen, police, Doulton's men, waiters, postmen. PURPLE to LIGHT BLUE, in map PURPLE.
Out of **NW** is **Goad's Place.** Four 2-st houses on either side. All doors open. Poor costers plying in the Walk, women bare-headed and rough. Six bare-footed girls and boys in this court alone. Drunks. Houses let out by rooms at 2/6 and 3/- per room. DARK BLUE as map.
E & **S** along **Distin Street** (late William St). 2-st. Bread, paper litter, much mess. Houses on east side south of Lollard St are LIGHT BLUE, in map PURPLE and unmarked.
W along Lollard St and **N** up **Gundulf Street** (late John St). 2-st. East side rather better than west and south end than north. Carmen and labourers, poor, "women in public houses all day". LIGHT BLUE, in map PURPLE.
W & **S** down **Saunders Street.** 2-st. Costers, poor, "very drunken". Great mess in street. LIGHT BLUE as map.
Off the **NE** end is **Saunders Place.** Four 2-st houses, very poor but fair furniture inside. Let into the house wall is a stone engraved "Depend on Providence. Res 1823". Rent for two rooms and backyard is 5/- or 5/6. DARK BLUE, not shown in map.
Opposite on the **W** side of Saunders St is **Graves Place.** More space than in Saunders Place but worse homes, fearful mess. Three 2-st houses. Four rooms 9/-, no wash-house. DARK BLUE as map.
At **SE** end of Saunders St is another **Saunders Place.** One very poor house. DARK BLUE to LIGHT BLUE, not shown in map.
S into Lollard St and **E.** On the **N** side is **Mannings Place.** Quiet, tidier, poor. Six houses. LIGHT BLUE, not coloured in map.
W along **Lollard Street** (late East St). 3-st and 2-st. LIGHT BLUE to DARK BLUE from Gundulf St westwards. Very rough. Rather better eastwards. In map LIGHT BLUE and PURPLE.
N up **Topaz Street.** 2-st. Very poor. "Women fight like tigers." Drunkards, pilfering class but not criminal. Birdcages at windows, windows broken and patched. LIGHT BLUE to DARK BLUE, in map LIGHT BLUE.
Out of the **NE** end is **Thrift Place.** Five 2-st houses. Three women who had each been there five years said they pay 5/- for two rooms and a little yard. No change in rent during their tenancy. DARK BLUE to LIGHT BLUE, in map LIGHT BLUE.
W along Fitzalan St. **S** down Lambeth Walk. **E** at **Fountain Gardens.** Houses on north and south, too much colour on map. Mostly police living here but not a very pleasant place to live in because of the awkwardness of getting home at night. So many drunken men about. Fourteen 2-st houses. Decent well-kept front gardens. PINK as map.
S down **Lambeth Walk.** The DARK BLUE courts shown on map on the east side north of Lollard St are shut and demolished.
W along **Paradise Street.** Great mess. 2½-st on south, 3-st on north. South side better than north. LIGHT BLUE, in map PURPLE.

N up Lambeth Walk. W along **Juxon Street** (late Mill St). Only a few houses lived in. Electrical Cab Company's works on the south side with a PINK house west of it. The other houses (very few) are LIGHT BLUE, in map PURPLE.

N up **Berkeley Street**. 2-st, broad road. Price's candleworks. Creepers over houses. PURPLE to PINK, in map PURPLE.

W along Saville Place. **S** down **Sail Street**. Railway arches used as stables on west. 3-st on east. Cab drivers, engineers, many poor. PURPLE as map.

W into **Pratt Street**. 3½-st, old fashioned. Two houses keep servants. Some poor. PINK as map.

S into **Old Paradise Street**. West of railway bridge are very poor but improves at south west and on north west of church curate's house. On south side is the Lambeth School of Arms, a place for boxing matches, rough. Notice of match between Bill Grimes and Bill Dobbs. Some thieves in this street, no prostitutes. LIGHT BLUE and PINK in place of PURPLE of map.

Out of the **NW** end is **Pearson's Place**. Very respectable, old residents, Doulton's moulders. Over one door-way is an elaborate Virgin and Child after Della Robbia, blue background wreath of coloured leaves and fruits surrounding it. Legend underneath "He died that we might be forgiven. He died to make us good." Many poor also. The west side is called Horrands Cottages. PURPLE as map or LIGHT BLUE?

N up **High Street**. Mixed. Doulton's foremen and many poor. Some small shops. PURPLE to LIGHT BLUE, in map PURPLE.

W along **Farry Street**. Nearly all Doulton's. Only one LIGHT BLUE house remains on the north side in what was Bunyan's Place. PURPLE in map. Stacks of earthenware drainpipes being laden onto carts as we passed. Furnaces on south side.

E along Old Paradise St and **N** up **Norfolk Row**. 2-st houses on west side only. Flagged passage, many children playing cricket with centre lamppost as wicket. Doulton's men. LIGHT BLUE, in map PURPLE.

N into Lambeth Road and **W**. On the **S** side is **Norfolk Place**. Houses belong to Doulton's and are inhabited by their men, very poor. "5/- for two rooms, copper and small back yard", from a 12 month's tenant, very poor and rough. DARK BLUE to LIGHT BLUE, in map PURPLE.

W & S down High St. E along Old Paradise St and Lollard St at whose **NE** end is **Little East Place**. 5-st buildings with balconies running round outside, on west side only. No mechanics but poor and cabmen. Great place for pitch and toss. Brick round door posts worn shiny and greasy. LIGHT BLUE, in map PURPLE.

Out of the **S** side of Lollard St, **W** of the Board School is a passage leading to Wake St not shown on map called **Tinman Court** (late Crown Court). 2-st. Low and rough, sore-eyed children, draggled women. Two rooms 4/6, no wash-house. West side rather better than the east. DARK BLUE.

S into **Wake Street**. 2-st. All costers, rows of barrows, great mess of paper etc. Doors open, windows broken, women hatless, children well fed, sore eyes. LIGHT BLUE to DARK BLUE, in map LIGHT BLUE.

Leading from Wake St to Ethelred St is **Globe Court**. 2-st. Flagged passage. Poor. 5/6 for two rooms plus wash-house. LIGHT BLUE to DARK BLUE, not coloured in map.

E along **Ethelred Street**. On the north side just south of Board School is Stones' Buildings. Ten houses, cement yard. PURPLE to PINK, in map PINK.

W along **Ethelred Street**. 2-st and 3-st. Some very poor on north side but mixed. PURPLE as map.

W across Lambeth Walk to **The Parade**. Broad, open, clean, well paved. Mixed class.

PURPLE as map but LIGHT BLUE where the mews begin.

E along Ethelred Street. Out of the S side is **Lambeth Mews**. Delete LIGHT BLUE of map, none there now.

E to **Tracey Street**. 3-st. Dull high houses flush with pavement. Quiet children. Clean, quiet. Machine minders. PURPLE as map.

S down **Hotspur Street**. Like Tracey St. PURPLE as map.

W to **Doris Street**. South of Ethelred St Doris St is PINK rather than PURPLE of map. PINK and PURPLE, in map all PURPLE.

Out of the W side of Doris St is **Burrup Place**. Poor, quiet. LIGHT BLUE to PURPLE, not shown in map.

E along Ethelred St. Out of its W side is a court called 8½B **Ethelred Street**. Poor and quiet. One woman pays 8/6 for three rooms up, large kitchen down and wash-house, all to herself. Five children, making six with herself. LIGHT BLUE, not coloured in map.

W along **Princes Road**. Mixed 2-st and 3-st. Poor west of the workhouse. PURPLE to PINK, in map PINK.

N up **Goda Street**. 2-st. Poor. PURPLE to LIGHT BLUE, in map PURPLE.

W & S down **Hutton Road**. 2-st. Better, doors shut, clean. PINK to PURPLE, in map PURPLE.

Out of the W side by the Chapel is **Grays Place**. Practically a continuation northwards of Over Place but walled off from it. Quiet, flowers. "9/- for four rooms plus wash-house", has been there 16 years, during which time the rent has remained the same. PINK to PURPLE, in map PURPLE.

W along Ethelred St, across Lambeth Walk to **Hamish Street**. 2-st and 3-st. PURPLE to PINK, in map PINK.

Out of the S side is **Sellon Mews**. Some poor dotted about. Large bacon curers at north west, volumes of smoke from the windows, unpleasant smell. LIGHT BLUE, not coloured in map.

W to **Newport Street**. Poorer north than south of Hamish St. 2½-st and 3-st. LIGHT BLUE and PURPLE, in map PURPLE. Stables under railway arches on west side.

E & N up Lambeth Walk and E along **Bolwell Street**. 2½-st. Mechanics working over the water. PINK as map.

Like it are **Wood Street** and **Ward Street** (both PINK as map). 2-st. Built 1830.

E along Princes Rd. N up **Over Place**. Twenty-two 2-st houses. Flagged passage. Poor, mixed. Small fronts. PURPLE to LIGHT BLUE as map.

W along Broad St. Out of the S side is **Wilders Cottages**. Four 2-st houses, on west side only. LIGHT BLUE, not shown in map. 5/- for two rooms plus back yard, no wash-house.

Broad Street itself is poor, old houses and small shops. 3-st. 1776. LIGHT BLUE to PURPLE, in map PURPLE.

W & S down **Shanklin Court** (late Lilac Place and Gardeners Cottages). Quiet, old fashioned, poor. Doulton's men. LIGHT BLUE to PURPLE, in map PINK.

W to Vauxhall Walk and N up **Granby's Buildings**. New. 2-st plus attic flats on east side. Rough, poor, let out in tenements. Drunks. LIGHT BLUE to DARK BLUE on east and the same in Vauxhall Walk, in map DARK BLUE and LIGHT BLUE. On the west side of Granby's Buildings are old red-tiled well-kept houses. One woman had been 33 years in the same house, another 40 and pays 6/- and 7/- for five rooms. One said her husband's family had lived in the same house for well over 100 years. Date on houses 1769. PINK, in map DARK BLUE.

W along Broad St. Out of the S side, W of the railway are **Gunnell's Cottages**. Entered through swing wooden door. DARK BLUE to LIGHT BLUE. Four 2-st cottages, used to be

Gunnell's Cottages.

tenanted by notorious dog stealer. On his death 50 dogs were found concealed in the yard. Not coloured in map.

N up High St and E along **Whitgift Street**. 2-st. Messy, unswept, poor, drunks, Doulton's men. LIGHT BLUE as map.

Out of the N side is **Cotford Place**. 1-st on east, 2-st on west. Poor. LIGHT BLUE as map.

E of it is **Ado Place**. On west side are 1-st. 4-st Buildings on the east side. Poor. LIGHT BLUE as map but more of it on account of the Buildings. There is now an open space between the railway and the Buildings. No-one lives on the east side of the Lambeth Burial Ground (now a recreation ground). In map PURPLE.

W into **High Street**. Mixed. Many poor and some foremen. PURPLE to LIGHT BLUE, in map PURPLE.

E along Broad St and S down **Salamanca Street** and **Salamanca Court**. Rough, poor Irish. Children well fed, dirty, ill dressed. LIGHT BLUE to DARK BLUE. In map DARK BLUE.

S to **Randall Road**. 5-st Albert Buildings on the south west corner. Poor. LIGHT BLUE to PURPLE, in map PURPLE. Crowds of children just out of school. Clean faces and dirty pinafores, some hatless. There are no other houses now in Randalls Rd. Delete PINK of map on north side.

S & E along **Anderson's Walk**. West end is rough. Gas workers from Vauxhall and South Metropolitan, a few of Doulton's men. On north are old-fashioned houses with sloping red-tiled roofs. At north east are seven 2-st houses running north. Uncared for fronts. LIGHT BLUE, in map PINK and PURPLE.

W of the railway it is called **Harts Cottages**. Five 2-st houses. PURPLE, in map PINK.

W to the Albert Embankment and N. Just S of Salamanca St are two courts:

Beet Court (late Lemon Court) has three houses on north, 2-st, very poor. Doulton's works on south. DARK BLUE, in map LIGHT BLUE.

N of it is **Lemon Place**. 2-st. Well asphalted. 7/- for three rooms plus wash-house. DARK

BLUE to LIGHT BLUE, in map LIGHT BLUE. Children dirty. Irish cockneys. "Like Salamanca St." The east end is now Doulton's so that the DARK BLUE of map goes.

S & E along **Tinworth Street**. 2-st. Poor, like Whitgift St. LIGHT BLUE, in map PURPLE. On either side of the road east of railway is Clarkson's dustyard, contractor for several vestries (Holborn etc). Full of rough, dirty women from the surrounding streets, disgusting smell and a disgusting occupation.

E into **Vauxhall Walk**. Poor, mixed, very poor at north west end and majority of poor all through. Dustmen, waterside workers, glass blowers, gas stokers, Doulton's men. LIGHT BLUE to PURPLE, in map PURPLE.

E along **Jonathan Street**. 3-st on north, 2-st on south. Rough and poor. Dock and wharf labourers. LIGHT BLUE, in map PINK.

Out of the **NE** end is **Pleasant Place**. 2-st. Poor but well-kept fronts. Fowls. Children with clean faces but boots and skirts bad. LIGHT BLUE to PURPLE, in map PURPLE.

S down **Wickham Street**. 2-st. Poor and very poor except at south end where there is some PINK. Windows bad, ill-shod dirty children. LIGHT BLUE to DARK BLUE, in map PURPLE.

W & S down **Tyers Street**. Better south than north of Jonathan St. 2-st, 2½-st and 3-st houses. Mark PURPLE north of Wickham St and leave PINK of map south of it.

Out of **W** side is **Glyn Street**. 3-st, all with three and four families. Many poor. Girls work in Pimlico clothing factory. PURPLE to LIGHT BLUE, in map PINK.

W along **Leopold Street**. 2-st, like Glyn St. PURPLE to PINK, in map PINK.

W & S down **Burnett Street**. Poor. Buildings on the west side between Gye St and Vauxhall Walk. Irish cockneys, gas and iron workers, dock labourers. LIGHT BLUE, in map PINK and LIGHT BLUE.

W & S down **Goding Street**. Very rough and poor from Italian Walk to Vauxhall Walk. Doors open, windows dirty, paper peeling off passage walls. Women rough. No houses on west side between Vauxhall Walk and Spring Garden Walk. DARK BLUE and LIGHT BLUE, in map LIGHT BLUE. It is as if the DARK BLUE from the Albert Embankment had come here. At **SE** end is a mews called **Coburg Mews** with one very poor family living over.

E along **Italian Walk**. 3-st. PURPLE to LIGHT BLUE, in map LIGHT BLUE. No houses in Spring Garden Walk. As map.

N & W along **Gye Street**. Buildings on north side. Poor. LIGHT BLUE as map, but more of it.

N up Vauxhall Walk. Out of the **E** side, **S** of Laud St is **Spring Gardens**. Messy, poor and very poor. Children dirty, ragged, well fed. Mess of bread, paper and stones. 2-st. Cricket going on in the court. 10/- for five rooms plus wash-house. DARK BLUE to LIGHT BLUE, in map LIGHT BLUE.

W along **Glasshouse Street**. The south side is all high 5-st, red-brick Guinness Buildings which cover the space called Vauxhall Square. "Their tenants are better than those who live in the surrounding streets." They look PINK but should, I suppose, be LIGHT BLUE. The Buildings run through in five blocks to Vauxhall Walk in blocks built east and west. Their cement yards were full of children, well fed, clean and fairly dressed. Old people sitting on benches. Yards well kept. The north side of Glasshouse St is 2-st. LIGHT BLUE rather than PURPLE of map.

W to the **Albert Embankment**. Mixed, the PINK of map should be PURPLE. Some old wooden houses still left. The blocks of Albert Buildings marked DARK BLUE in map, built by the Prince Consort, have been recently lighted and bettered. Now poor but not very poor. LIGHT BLUE instead of DARK BLUE of map.

W along Upper Kennington Lane to **Vauxhall Bridge Approach**. Bridge shut for rebuilding. Shops with some living over on either side to come down when Bridge is ready.

PINK-barred or RED as map.

Out of the N side is **Marble Hall Place** with one PINK house at its west end, north side. In map RED.

N up Albert Embankment, E along Anderson's Walk, into Vauxhall Walk, out of whose E side is **Vauxhall Gardens**. Now a bedstead factory. Delete PINK of map.

S & E along **Glasshouse Street**. Vauxhall Mansions (3½-st) is working class flats on south, 2-st on north. A few railway porters and shunters but the best part of the railway men live in Vauxhall St. Mark north side LIGHT BLUE, south PURPLE to LIGHT BLUE, in map PURPLE.

Out of N side is **Hunt Street**. Very poor. Five rooms plus wash-house for 10/-. LIGHT BLUE, in map PURPLE.

N up **Catherine Street**. 2-st. Rough, Irish cockneys. Dirty, rough, well-fed, badly-booted children. One woman who had been there six years pays 9/- for four rooms plus wash-house. LIGHT BLUE to PURPLE, in map PINK.

S & W along **Laud Street** (late Cross St). Very poor at the north east end. Filthy children and sodden women. DARK BLUE, in map LIGHT BLUE. At the west end the Vauxhall Mansions come through, LIGHT BLUE as map. The south side is made up of the backs of Pleasant Place.

E & N up **Tyers Street**. 2-st, fairly broad. Railway carmen and labourers. PURPLE to LIGHT BLUE, in map PINK.

N to Princes Rd, E then S down Vauxhall St and E along **Sancroft Street**. 2-st and 3-st. South side better than the north. Good backs. Quiet, poorish, houses seldom empty. Old dark brick. PURPLE as map.

Out of the N side, W of Newburn St, are **Pegwell Cottages** (late Park Cottages). Four cottages covered with vines and Virginia creeper, well-tended fronts. LIGHT BLUE to PURPLE, in map LIGHT BLUE.

E of Newburn St off N side of Sancroft St are **Sewell's Cottages**. Three cottages. LIGHT BLUE to DARK BLUE. One woman who has been there 10 years pays 9/- for four rooms plus wash-house. Another who has been there two years pays 6/- for two rooms plus wash-house.

S down **Cardigan Street**. East side down except at north and south ends. 2-st. Poor, carmen. LIGHT BLUE as map but less of it.

W & N up **Courtenay Street** (late Devonshire St). 2-st. Leases falling in at the north west end and new 2-st flats being built for two families, each with three rooms and a kitchen and letting at 8/- per set. PURPLE as map

Smiths Place at the NW end is now an omnibus depot. DARK BLUE of map goes.

S down **Newburn Street**. Rebuilding at north end. Two cab yards. It is a poor street like Vauxhall Walk. LIGHT BLUE to PURPLE, in map PURPLE.

Out of W side is **Queen's Place**, where new buildings (LIGHT BLUE) are replacing the DARK BLUE of map.

On the E side are **Garden Cottages**. Entered under passage. Five 2-st houses. Poor, tidy garden fronts. 6/6 for four rooms plus wash-house, hardly any yard. LIGHT BLUE, in map DARK BLUE.

Further S out of W side is **Hampshire Street**. Five 2-st cottages on south. LIGHT BLUE, in map DARK BLUE. Two on north, very poor. DARK BLUE, not shown in map.

Further S of Malmsey Place out of W side are **Mancroft Cottages** (in map Andrew's Cottages). Built 1852, ten 2-st houses. Well-cemented yard. Children very dirty and ragged. DARK BLUE to LIGHT BLUE, in map DARK BLUE. 4/6 and 5/6 for two rooms.

Out of the SE end of Newburn St is **Dunmow Place** (late Cottage Place). 2-st. Very poor. Palinged fronts. Barefoot filthy children, vestry scavengers. 7/- for two rooms plus wash-house. DARK BLUE as map.

S down **Dolland Street**. 2-st and 3-st. Poor, cabmen and one or two police. PURPLE to LIGHT BLUE, in map LIGHT BLUE and uncoloured. The south side is small workshops, wood turners and a cab yard.

W across Vauxhall St and up **Tate Street**. Narrow, well paved with cobbles. 2-st, two and three families in each house. Railway carmen and porters. Children dirty and poorly dressed. LIGHT BLUE to PURPLE, in map PINK.

The court N of Tyers Terrace is called **Lapford Place** (late Pleasant Place). Houses on each side only. Twelve 2-st houses, gardens in front, carmen and Doulton's labourers. 8/- for four rooms plus wash-house. The usual 15 ft frontage houses. LIGHT BLUE, in map PURPLE.

W along **Tyers Terrace**. 2-st. Poor. LIGHT BLUE, in map PINK.

N up **Neville Street**. Very poor and very rough on the west side, north of Tyer Terrace. Irish labourers, brick cart carmen. Women half dressed, sack aprons. Children ragged, well fed, clothes ill put on and falling off. At north end are six 2-st cottages with ill-kept fronts. Bread and mess in street. DARK BLUE to LIGHT BLUE, in map PINK. South of Tyer St Neville St improves. Railway carmen. LIGHT BLUE to PURPLE, in map PINK.

E to **Vauxhall Street**. Mixed. PURPLE, in map PINK. Canie Hall at south west end "does good work".

Out of the E side is **Malmesey Place**. 2-st. Labourers. Poor and very poor. LIGHT BLUE as map.

N to **Frank Street**, 2-st. Labourers from Myers bedstead factory. LIGHT BLUE as map.

N to **Orsett Street**. 2-st, new flats for two families. Was very rough, now LIGHT BLUE to PURPLE, in map LIGHT BLUE.

S down Vauxhall St, across Upper Kennington Lane and S down **Farnham Royal**. Twenty 2-st houses. Old tenants, "a rare job to get into these houses". Five pensioned police live here. There are some poor. 9/- and 10/- for four and five rooms. PINK to PURPLE, in map PINK.

W & S down **Henry Street**. 2-st, cul de sac. Compositors, chefs, watchmakers. Fewer poor than formerly. PINK to PURPLE, in map PURPLE.

W & S down **Kennington Grove**. 2-st, broad cul de sac. PINK as map.

N into Upper Kennington Lane and S down **Durham Street**. 2-st, broad. Mechanics. PINK to PURPLE as map.

W & SE along **Harleyford Road**. 2-st and 3-st. Trams and tram lines. A few servants at east end. Houses built 1820-26. PINK, in map PINK-barred.

Round **Kennington Oval**. PINK as map. At the west corner of Vauxhall St is Selina Cottage, old fashioned. Sales said it was the place where the mistresses of Henry VIII lived. At the east corner of Vauxhall St are high Buildings, working class. PINK to PURPLE, in map PINK.

N up **Vauxhall Street**. PINK as map.

E along Upper Kennington Lane and N up **Loughborough Street, Wynyard Street, Esher Street**. 2½-st. Labourers, cabmen, mechanics, police. PINK to PURPLE, in map PINK.

S across Upper Kennington Lane and down **Shepherd's Place**. 2½-st. Postmen and mechanics. PURPLE to PINK, in map PINK.

E & S down Pilgrim Place. Now all called **Montford Place**. 2-st and 3-st. Labourers and mechanics, a glass factory here. Improves at south end. Leave south PINK but mark the part running north and south PURPLE.

E into **Kennington Road**. Fine old houses. RED as map.

N up **Windmill Row**. 3-st and 2-st. Old established shops. PINK as map.

General Remarks

The story of Lambeth in the last ten years is a story of worsement. The fairly comfortable have left and are leaving. The poor remain and additional poor are coming in. The effect of cheap trams and cheap railway fares is most marked in this area. Brixton and Stockwell have claimed the mechanic and artisan while the labourer remains and his ranks are reinforced by displacements in Westminster across the river. Sergeant Sales thought that the increase of poverty was a purely natural increase and is not of opinion that Westminster drifts to Lambeth. Westminster, he says, goes to Battersea, but proximity, similarity of conditions etc make it more than probable that many come to Lambeth.

Between Lambeth Rd and Lollard St are the remains of ancient old established poverty. Newer poverty is found more between Princes Rd and Upper Kennington Lane.

Here, as in other parts of London, the worst name is given to Irish cockney. He drinks the most and is the most difficult to deal with. Here too is the same baleful influence of gas works. Poverty in Lambeth hugs the London Gasworks and those of the South Metropolitan Company. But whether it is in Fulham or Bromley, in West or East, in North or South London, gasworks and poverty always go together.

The poorest spots in the district are:
1. China Walk area
2. Between Fitzalan St and Ethelred St
3. A large area bounded on the north by Princes Rd, on the east by Newburn St, on the south by Upper Kennington Lane and on the west by the Albert Embankment.

Pottery Works

The employments followed by men living in the district are: pottery workers at Doulton's, of whom a small number are skilled workers while the majority are labourers and carmen; a great number of costers round Lambeth Walk; gasworkers at the London gasworks and South Metropolitan works; waterside labourers; a great number of carmen; a few cabmen and railway men; and a large number of builders and other unskilled labourers whose work is in the west end of London.

The houses are for the most part 2-st, built at the end of the last and the beginning of this century. The brick is a dark red, almost black with age. Fifteen feet is the common frontage and rents run from 2/- to 3/- per room. The lowest rental was 6/- for five rooms by a tenant of 40 years standing in Granby's Buildings off the north west end of Vauxhall Walk. The Prince of Wales, according to Sergeant Sales, is the largest ground landlord. As leases fall in, the old houses are being replaced by 2-st houses built in the flat system for two families and letting at 8/- a floor as in Orsett St.

Lambeth Walk is the shopping street of the district – wood-paved, narrow, costers – "almost as busy as the Cut itself". Canterbury lamb was selling at 4½d a pound, fair bacon between 4d and 6d a pound, bread 4lb loaf at 3¾d and 4d. But it was Thursday afternoon when I was there and most were shutting because it is their early closing day.

The lowest women's work is in the dustyard in Tinworth St. A great many young women work across the water in the Pimlico clothing factory.

Sergeant Sales spoke of the poor area between Princes Rd and Upper Kennington Lane as a "Drink and Fried Fish district". He does not see any improvement in drink and says the women are as bad as the men. He would like to see all children prevented from going to fetch beer, though he has only once in 23 years seen a child drunk. "It might prevent them of the habit of going into public houses." He professed ignorance of the values of licensed houses but thinks there has been a considerable drop in their value in the last year.

Note that the Vestry are very careless about cleansing mess of bread and paper in all the poor streets. Roads badly tended and loose stones common. Now and then we came across a group of inefficient old men with brooms but they did not seem to sweep anything.

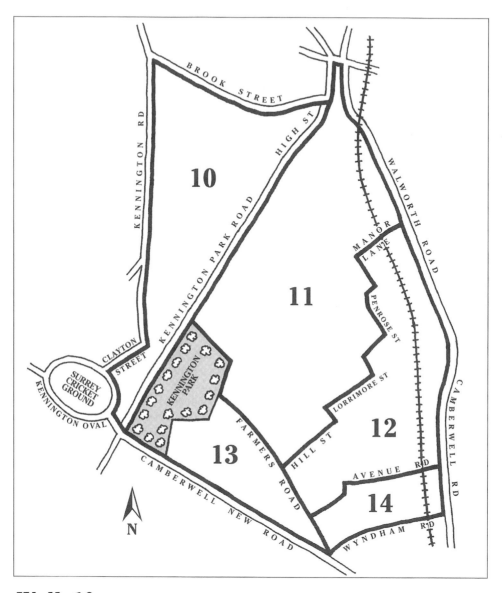

Walk 10

B365

Monday 12th June 1899.
George Duckworth with Sergeant E Sales.

Starting at the corner of Brook Street and Kennington Road.
E along **Brook Street**. 3-st. Dull street. Mostly professional music hall men and women. Two and three families to a house. It is poorer east of Austral St. The division between PINK and PURPLE should be here. The map makes the division further west.
E along **St Gabriel Street**. 3½-st and 4-st. Poor and vicious, thieves and prostitutes. Used to be all brothels at the north east end but cleared out two years ago with the help of the

Vigilance Association. Some prostitutes still remain but no brothels. The infamous 'Girdle' gang came from here. When the brothels were turned out they migrated and were discovered in a coffee house at the east end of Graham St in Hackney. Other prostitutes went to Deptford. Great mess of bread and paper in street. Windows dirty, patched and broken. Sales has had men out dressed as females to convict the brothels but has never succeeded. "They always know." LIGHT BLUE-barred as map.

E into Newington High St. S & N up **Church Yard Row**. Now taken up by the Wilberforce Mission House and by a huge Rowton doss house for 800 men, whose Superintendent came out and spoke of the effect of the house on the neighbourhood. Each has a separate cubicle, men only. All sorts come, good, bad and indifferent, clergymen and clerks, very seldom a row. Only once in the police court in 18 months. About 250 book for the whole week. The effect has been to close a number of filthy lodging houses in Southwark. LIGHT BLUE to PURPLE, in map PINK.

N & W along **Longville Road**. 3½-st and 4-st. Poor. Some prostitutes but not like St Gabriel St. Dead, dismal street. LIGHT BLUE to PURPLE, in map LIGHT BLUE.

S down **Dante Road**. 2½-st and 3½-st. Many poor but a mixture of mechanics. PURPLE to LIGHT BLUE, in map LIGHT BLUE.

N up **Holyoak Street**. 3½-st. Like Dante Rd but improves at north end where many police live. Messy streets. PURPLE to LIGHT BLUE, in map LIGHT BLUE.

Into Brook St. W & S down **Bird Street**. New flats at north east. Poor. PURPLE, in map LIGHT BLUE.

On the E side, going from N to S are: **Trowes Place, Fran Place, Strewant Place**. Each with six 2-st houses, three on north and three on south. All very poor. South side of Fran Place better than north.

On the W side of Bird St going from S to N are **Langhope Place, Bywell Place, Bird Place**. Likewise six 2-st houses in each. All these houses have two rooms and a yard with a copper in the corner. 6/6 per week, 7/- for the corner houses in Bird St. Very poor. Builders' labourers, casuals, prostitutes. Like St Gabriel's St. Barefoot, dirty children. School Board Officer going his rounds after truants. Low and rough. Bread, meat and paper in Bird St. Smell of dirt. All these courts are DARK BLUE, though some are given in map as LIGHT BLUE.

S along **Monkton Street**. Mechanics, postmen, meat salesmen. 2½-st. PINK, in map PURPLE.

Like it are **Oakden Street** (3½ st) and the streets lying between Monkton St and Lower Kennington Lane, namely **Wincott Street, Gilbert Road, Renfrew Road, Hurley Road**. All 2½-st. Favourite habitations for police of the 'E', 'A' and 'L' divisions. Respectable, many mechanics and postmen. Rent 20/- for 10 rooms. In Renfrew Rd are police candidates' section houses.

Kempsford Road, Lucretia Road and **Reedworth Street**. All PINK as map.

E along Kennington Lane. Out of the S side is **Cricketer's Court**. Two houses on east side only. A woman who had been there 12 years pays 4/- for two rooms. She is a widow who does dressmaking. LIGHT BLUE to DARK BLUE, in map LIGHT BLUE on the wrong side.

W along **Orange Court or Cottages**. Poor, quiet. Small perambulator maker or dealer. More LIGHT BLUE than map.

S down **Evin's Cottages**. 2-st, 2-roomed houses with no copper nor wash-house. Rent 4/6. Houses on west side only. DARK BLUE to LIGHT BLUE, in map DARK BLUE.

On the N side leading to workhouse is a cul de sac with one double-fronted house on east side. Numbered in **Lower Kennington Lane**. PINK, not shown in map.

W past **Ebenezer Row**. None living. Uncoloured as map.

W & N up **Fairford Grove**. 2-st. Respectable, police inspectors. West side better than east. PINK as map.

W & N up **Reedworth Street**. 2½-st and 3-st. PINK as map.

At the W end on S side is **Chester Square**. 2-st. Poorer than the rest. A good LIGHT BLUE or poor PINK, in map LIGHT BLUE.

N & E along **Ship Lane**. No houses except where it runs into Walcot Square. Delete RED of map.

S down **St Mary's Square**. 2½-st and 3½-st. Professionals and mechanics. Uncared for plot of grass with iron railings round makes up the Square. PINK as map.

N to **Walcot Square**. 2½-st. Mess in street, some trees in Square. PINK as map.

S to Lower Kennington Lane. Out of its S side runs **Opal Street**. 2-st and 3-st. Poor. West side not so good as east. Was a brothel on south side but now cleared. LIGHT BLUE to PURPLE, in map PURPLE.

Out of N side is **Lyric Place**. 2-st. One good double-fronted house with well-kept garden on south west. The rest is poor, quiet. LIGHT BLUE and PINK, in map LIGHT BLUE.

Out of the SE end of Opal St are **Rood Cottages** (late Garden Place). 2-st. Small, palinged, well cared for fronts. LIGHT BLUE, in map DARK BLUE.

Out of W side is **Garden Cottages**. Very poor. 2-st. 4/- a week. "No yard, copper nor wash-house", this woman had been in the house 1½ years. The houses were at one time all brothels but were cleared out. "The man was getting 20/- a week as rent then, as against 4/- now for each house." In the last house at south west end took place the Kennington murder, a fortnight or three weeks ago. A woman was stabbed in 54 places by her coster husband who then undid a flock mattress and put her into it. He was discovered a day or two afterwards trying to wash the stains from his coat in a public house in Covent Garden. DARK BLUE as map.

S & W along **Mansion House Street**. Mechanics, carmen. A shade better than Opal St. PURPLE to LIGHT BLUE, in map PURPLE.

S down **Regency Place** with **Regency Square** out of its E side. Poor, quiet. 2-st. Labourers. LIGHT BLUE to PURPLE, in map Regency Square is PURPLE. The south west end of Regency Place is LIGHT BLUE, rather than DARK BLUE of map.

Out of the SE end is **Diamond Place**. 2-st houses on south side only. LIGHT BLUE as map.

Into White Hart St. W & N up **Cupar Cottages**. Five 2-st cottages on west side with very neatly-kept fronts, but very poor. 4/3 for two rooms plus wash-house. DARK BLUE to LIGHT BLUE, in map LIGHT BLUE.

N up **White Hart Street**. 2-st and 3-st. Mixed, cabmen and washers from the yards in Princes Rd. South side better than north. PURPLE to LIGHT BLUE, in map PURPLE.

S down **White Hart Square**. 2-st. Poor and very poor. Labourers and carmen. Messy. LIGHT BLUE, in map PURPLE.

N across Lower Kennington Lane. Along **Mart Street** (late Edward St). Poor. 2-st. Labourers. LIGHT BLUE to DARK BLUE, in map DARK BLUE.

Denny Street and **Golden Place**. 2-st. Poor. LIGHT BLUE as map. In these streets are labourers, cab yard men and ironworks labourers for the Wandsworth Rd. Great mess of paper, loose stones, etc.

Into **Chester Street**. South side better than the north. Houses on the north stand back with long, bare, uncared for fronts. Unequal, villagy houses, very poor, next to the public house at east end north side. Cab yard and new houses at north west end. Some new 3-st flats on south side. Mark north LIGHT BLUE and south PURPLE, in map PURPLE.

The court N of Chester St out of the E side of the Kennington Rd is, in reality, a continuation of **Chester Gardens** in Reedworth St but is walled off from them. DARK

BLUE to LIGHT BLUE, not shown in map.

S past Kennington Cross and **E** along **Cleaver Street**. Some shops at west end with flats (working class) over. The north side better than the south, except on the south side west of Bowden St. Cleaver St is like Princes Square. Mark PINK and PURPLE, in map PURPLE.

E into **Princes Square**. 3-st. Mechanics working over the water. The Square in the centre is taken up by a florist and nursery garden. "There may be a servant in three houses in the east corner, north side." PINK as map.

S down **Bowden Street**. 3-st, on east only. Poor. LIGHT BLUE to PURPLE, in map LIGHT BLUE.

Into a group of PINK streets: **Methley Street, Ravensdon Street, Milverton Street, Radcot Street**. 2½-st and 3½-st. All the same, dull and depressing, fair backs. Mechanics, compositors, no poor. Rent 20/- a week.

Out of the **W** side of Milverton St is **Wigton Place**. "Small cab owners, about two horses each." PURPLE to PINK, in map LIGHT BLUE.

E down Ravensdon St and **S** along **Stannary Street**. 2-st and 3-st. West side better than east. PURPLE to LIGHT BLUE, in map PURPLE.

Out of the **W** side is **Aulton Place** (late Grove Place). 2-st and 3-st. Tenements. Poor. LIGHT BLUE to PURPLE, in map LIGHT BLUE.

S of it, still on the **N** side of Stannary St, is **Cottage Place**. Not shown on map. Five 2-st houses. LIGHT BLUE.

S across Kennington Rd, along **Clayton Street**. 2-st and 3-st. Fairly comfortable. Tram drivers and conductors, mechanics, post and policemen, compositors. PINK to PURPLE, in map PINK.

Out of the **N** side going **W** are three cottages (PURPLE, not coloured in map) and **Little Clayton Street**. Quiet, creeper covered, fowl run, pigeons. PINK or LIGHT BLUE, in map LIGHT BLUE.

S down **Dale Street**. Stables. Delete PINK of map.

Into **Bowling Green Street**. 2-st, creeper covered. A few poor on south. PINK as map.

S down **Magee Street** (late William St). 2-st. PINK to PURPLE, in map PINK.

Little William Street exists no more. In map LIGHT BLUE.

Walk 11   B365

Monday 19th June 1899.
George Duckworth with Sergeant Feador Sziemanowicz.
Sergeant Sziemanowicz is the son of a Russian Pole and an English mother. He has been five years in the district and came here from Whitechapel. He never expects to rise higher because of his inability to spell and write compositions. He has attended education classes all the winter but was told it was useless for him to present himself for the examination for Inspector. He is a young man with dark moustache about 35 years of age, rather over middle height. Not very intelligent but willing to take any amount of trouble in order to please.

Starting at the Elephant and Castle.
S down Newington Butts, **E** at **Draper Street**. 3-st, old-fashioned shops with small window panes and box windows. No servants. Almshouses on north side. PINK, in map PINK-barred.

Out of the **S** side is **Roy Place** (late Union Place). Costers. Poor and very poor. Children dirty, healthy, one barefoot. Fine show of flowers at windows. LIGHT BLUE, in map DARK BLUE.

W of it is another court called **Sherston Place**. Ten 2-st houses on east side only. A woman who has been there "12 months come next August" pays 6/- for two rooms and wash-house. Old tenants pay 5/-. LIGHT BLUE, in map PINK.

S down High St. Out of the E side is **Cock Passage**. Only a few poor remaining in the remnants of the passage at the west end. Here very poor on north side, rather better on south. To the east the passage becomes a road with new 3-st flats on the south and almshouses on the north. The east end was pulled down five years ago. A tenant of the poor west pays 9/6 for five rooms plus wash-house, she has been there seven years. LIGHT BLUE and PINK in place of DARK BLUE of map. The north west might be left DARK BLUE as map.

S of it is **Brune Place** (late Rose Court). Built 1708. Seventeen 2-st houses. Quiet, poor. Clean passages and windows and fair furniture. LIGHT BLUE, in map DARK BLUE.

S down Crampton St, E up **Hampton Street**. 3-st. Three families to a house. Comfortable. PINK as map.

S & W along **Steedman Street**. Out of the N side are two courts, one east and the other west of the railway. Both very poor. That east of railway is called Steedman Place and is a 3-st tenement house with basement occupied by iron bedstead works. LIGHT BLUE to DARK BLUE. That west of the railway is still poorer with five 2-st houses, smelly and bare. The corner house pays 12/- for five rooms and shop. One old woman pays 3/- for a roof garret. DARK BLUE to LIGHT BLUE, in map LIGHT BLUE. Steedman St itself is 3-st. PINK to PURPLE, in map PINK.

Along Crampton St and E up **Amelia Street**. 2-st, 3-roomed houses. Poorer. Large coal yard on north side. Drivers from Hodson St. PURPLE as map.

S & W along **Manor Place**. 2½-st and 3-st. Bus drivers, a shoe black. Looks fairly comfortable. PINK to PURPLE, in map PURPLE. West of railway on north are Pullen's Buildings. PINK. On south side is large new Baths and Wash-houses with superintendent living over.

Out of SE end is **Occupation Road** (late Manor Mews). Stables on east with a few over. LIGHT BLUE. At south end is a yard, foreman's house (PINK) and a slaughterhouse and zinc works (LIGHT BLUE and PINK, in map PINK). At this north west end is a mortuary and coroner's court and vestry yards below them on west side.

N up **Penton Place**. 2½-st and 3½-st. Mechanics, labourers, printers, clerks, none really poor. PINK to PURPLE, in map PINK and PURPLE.

Out of the NE is **Thrush Street** and N of it **Amelia Street** and **Iliffe Street**. All Pullen's Buildings. Built of yellow brick, ornamental stone over doors and windows. 4-st, well built but dull. In Iliffe St some are still building and old Mr Pullen in a top hat and fustian suit was on a scaffolding superintending. Walls flush with the pavement but protected with iron railings from the street. Many police from 'E' (Strand), 'A' (Whitehall) and 'L' (Lambeth) divisions living here. "Occupied before the paper is dry on the walls." Some built five years ago. Sergeant 'Simanowix' (it is pronounced like this) lives in one set. Rent 8/- for three rooms, kitchen and scullery. Plus 6d per week which is charged for cleaning the stairs and gas. Each incomer has to make a deposit of 24/- which is an effectual bar to any poor tenants. Two years ago the rent was only 7/- plus 6d for stairs and gas. All these streets are PINK, Amelia St is PURPLE in map.

N & W along **Newington Crescent**. 2½-st. Comfortable, mechanics. PINK as map.

N up Newington High St. Out of the E side is **Arcot Place** (in map Waterloo Place). Poorish working class. Creepers over houses and fronts. PURPLE to LIGHT BLUE, in map PINK.

N of it is **Wesley Place**. Thirteen 2-st houses on south side. Two houses at west end on north side very poor, the rest poor. LIGHT BLUE to PURPLE, in map LIGHT BLUE and DARK BLUE.

N of it is **Horse and Groom Court**. 2-st. Rough poor, costers, windows broken. 7/6 for two rooms plus wash-house or 6/6 without wash-house, there four years. DARK BLUE as map.

N & E along **Peacock Street**. Much already rebuilt at north east and closed for demolition on south. Many poor. PURPLE and PINK or PURPLE all through instead of LIGHT BLUE of map.

N up **Hodson Street**. Poor, remnants of old inhabitants. Horse keepers, carmen of coal yard in Amelia St. 2-st. Some down on west side and all to come down.

W along **Hurlbutt Place**. 2-st new houses until the west extremity. The new are 2-st for two families. PINK and LIGHT BLUE, in map LIGHT BLUE.

N & E into **Crampton Street**. 3-st and 4-st. Respectable. 24/- for houses then let off. PINK as map.

SW along **Manor Place**. The great Sutton & Dudley Buildings on either side. PURPLE, in map PINK-barred.

N up **Berryfield Street, Suffield Road, Tarver Road**. All known as 'Surrey Gardens'. Dismal, dark Buildings. Overcrowded, no backs, all messy streets. 2½-st and 4-st. Mechanics, carmen, labourers. Well built, ugly yellow brick. No yard for light and air, not so good as Pullen's Buildings. Tarver Rd is the poorest, Berryfield St the best. Suffield Rd now continued into Crampton St and Berryfield St built on both sides. Might be PINK, in map PURPLE. Tarver Rd, in map LIGHT BLUE, to LIGHT BLUE or PURPLE. Add PURPLE to Suffield Rd.

W along **Delverton Road**. 2½-st. PINK to PURPLE, in map PINK.

N up **Cavour Street** (late Edward St). 2½-st. Some clerks, mechanics and warehousemen working in the City. PINK as map.

W & S down **Alberta Street** (late Albert St). 2½-st. Good backs but all to come down when leases fall in. These houses are two rooms thick, the new ones are all three rooms thick. PINK as map.

W of Alberta Rd is **Canterbury Mews**. Bus yard, only one LGO foreman living over. PINK if marked.

W along Penton Place to Kennington Park Rd. **S & E** along **New Street**. 2-st and 3-st. 1828. Old-fashioned unequal houses, a few poor. PINK to PURPLE, in map PINK.

Out of the **NW** end is **New Street Mews**. 2-st. Small shops and poor carmen. LIGHT BLUE to PURPLE, in map LIGHT BLUE.

E & S down **Gaza Street** (late Green St). Narrow. Row of cabs down street, cabmen. Poor, drink. Board School has been extended at south east. LIGHT BLUE as map.

E & S down **Doddington Grove**. Broad, pleasant road with old semi-detached houses and trees on pavement. Music hall artistes, clerks, cab proprietors, some servants. PINK-barred as map.

S & W along **Harmsworth Street**. New red-brick flats on south. No servants. PINK, not marked in map.

N up **Faunce Street**. On the Faunce de Laune Estate. 2½-st.

W of it is **Sharsted Street**. 2½-st. PINK as map.

W & N up **De Laune Street**. 2½-st. Stables on west side tenanted by small cab owners with two or three horses. New houses at south east. 2½-st. PINK to PURPLE, in map PINK and PURPLE. "Small cab owners are generally the most decent men, must be steady."

E along New St into Manor Place which has shops at this end. **S** along **St Paul's Road**. 3-st and 2-st. Mixed. PURPLE to PINK, in map PURPLE. Where the road turns to Cooks Rd it might be PINK.

W along Cooks Rd. **S** at **St Agnes Place**. Mixed old and new houses. Servants. RED to PINK-barred, in map RED.

S along **Farmers Road**. 2-st. Bus drivers and conductors, carmen, labourers, milkmen. Birds at windows. "Only fairly quiet". That part shown in map as PURPLE should be LIGHT BLUE and the rest PURPLE instead of PINK. Much drink in this street.

E & W along **Aldred Road**. 2-st. Mixed, mechanics and labourers. Many poor. PURPLE, in map PINK. North of Otto St it remains PINK.

E along **Kennington Park Gardens**. Continued round here from Kennington Park. PINK as map. 3½-st. No servants.

S down Royal Rd. W along **Otto Street**. 2-st. PURPLE to PINK, in map PINK.

S down **Royal Terrace**. Narrow, 2-st, mixed. PURPLE to LIGHT BLUE, in map PURPLE.

E & **N** up **Royal Road**. 2-st, two families. 15/- for six rooms. Mixed. PINK to PURPLE, in map PINK.

E & S down **Cook's Road**. North end rather better than the south. 2-st. PINK as map.

E & N up **Heiron Street**. 2-st. PINK as map.

Out of **SW** is **John's Place** with two 1-st cottages with flowers in front. Two rooms in each. Pay monthly, 7/4 for calendar month.

E along **Lorrimore Street**. Dull, bare street. 2-st. Good outward repair. Not a flower at any window. China pots with evergreen fern in front windows. Small backs, stables behind. Clerks and bus drivers. PINK, in map PURPLE. It has been rebuilt since 10 years ago.

N up **Draco Street**. PINK as map.

Into **Lorrimore Road**. 3½-st, 2-st and 2½-st. 1852. Good PINK but no servants, in map PINK-barred.

W to **Lucas Road**. Small shops at street corners. PINK as map.

E then N up Cooks Road. E along **Finchley Road**. 2-st, two families. Fairly kept, iron-railed fronts. PINK as map.

E into **Lorrimore Square**. Parsonage with rather ill-kept garden and churchyard in the middle. 3½-st. South side better than north or west. A few servants on south. PINK-barred and PINK instead of RED and PINK of map.

N to **Fleming Road**. PINK as map. Like Finchley Rd.

N up St Paul's Rd and W at **Chapter Terrace**. Narrow, 2-st, mixed. PURPLE as map.

E along **Frederick Road**. 2-st and 2½-st plus attic. Better. PINK to PURPLE, in map PURPLE.

E into **Chapter Road**. PURPLE to PINK, in map PINK.

E to **Sturgeon Road**. 3-st and 5-st. PURPLE as map.

Stopford Road, Pasley Road and **Marsland Road** are all PURPLE as map.

Borrett Road (late Dorritt Rd). 5-st Sutton & Dudley Buildings on east side. Rather better than the others. PURPLE to PINK, in map PINK. This is all part of the Sutton & Dudley estate. Dark and dismal, no air space. There is very little space between the two blocks which run north and south between Penton Place and Borrett Rd and what space there is is filled by paper and mess. The mess is so great and so seldom cleared that the owners have put up a wooden palisade at either end so that it may not be seen from the street. Rents on the estate are 6/- for two rooms, 8/- for three, 10/- for four rooms and 5/- is demanded as key money on taking possession. There is so great a demand for space that all the rooms are readily let, though not to so good a class as Pullen's Buildings in Amelia St etc.

E into **Walworth Road**. Shops, public library, vestry, etc. Very few servants. PINK-barred, in map RED.

Out of the **W** side N of Amelia St is **Frant Court**. Five 2-st houses, poor, flowers. LIGHT

BLUE to PURPLE, not shown in map.

General Remarks.

No-one is very poor in this round with the exception of the remnants of old established poverty in the courts off the east side of Newington High St. Only one, namely Horse and Groom Court, still remains DARK BLUE. For the rest it is a quiet, dull district of mechanics, policemen and clerks, with a certain admixture of labourers, horse keepers and cab washers. Sergeant Sziemanowicz said there was a constant stream from 5am to 10am of workers going out and a return between 5 and 6 pm. The majority work out of the district.

As the leases of the small houses fall in their places are taken by blocks of Buildings like Pullen's or Sutton & Dudley's. The new Buildings are both higher and deeper than the old, nothing of a back garden remains. The Sutton & Dudley estate is more crowded and forbidding looking and rather less well tenanted than the more expensive Pullen's, but both are alike in the absence of air space behind and flowers are conspicuous by their absence from the windows.

Flower boxes and windows are brightest in the poorer coster streets. It almost seems as though it were thought more respectable not to have flowers. House room is eagerly sought and Pullen's are full before the wallpaper is dry. This is no exaggeration. Sziemanowicz said that they never had to advertise their empty rooms.

Walk 12   B365

Thursday 22nd June 1899.
George Duckworth with Sergeant Feador Sziemanowicz.

Starting at the corner of Walworth Road and Penrose Street.
W along **Penrose Street**. 3-st. Bus and cabmen. At the south east are large tramway works and opposite is the Newington Electric Light Station. PINK to PURPLE, in map PINK.
Out of the S side is **Cottage Grove**. 2-st. Front gardens, trees. PINK as map.
S down Penrose St. Out of the E side is a passage with three 1-st cottages. LIGHT BLUE, not coloured in map.
On either side of Penrose St runs **Carter Street**. 2½-st on the east, 3½-st on the west. Neat, a few poor at north east. Police subdivisional station at south east. No servants. West better than east. A bookmaker owns many and lives in one of the houses. Two and three families to a house. PINK as map.
S & E along **Sutherland Square**. 2½-st and 3½-st. Tallymen. Very few servants. Bernstein, the sarsaparilla seller, lives in corner house, "sells himself all over London and owns a tidy bit of house property". Next to him is a retired provision merchant who keeps a carriage but the majority of inhabitants don't keep servants. Tie factory employing 50 girls on south side. PINK-barred to PINK, in map RED.
Sutherland Street. North side better than south. Only one servant kept in one house. PINK, in map PINK on north and RED on south.
S & E along **Sutherland Place** (late Charlotte St). East end narrower and poorer than west. PURPLE as map. The west end has no servants. "Bedroom to let furnished." At north east is the Blue House Laundry employing 40 to 50. PINK, in map RED.
Out of the S side is a **nameless court**. Three poor double-fronted houses facing south.

LIGHT BLUE, not shown in map.

S down Walworth Rd and **W** at **Olney Street**. 1856. 2-st. Mixed class, many poor. In Rufus Terrace nearly all poor. Olney St is a continuation of Lorrimore St and used to be better than it but now, since rebuilding of Lorrimore St, it is decidedly poorer. PURPLE, in map PINK.

S down **Montpelier Street**. Poor. PURPLE on west side, in map PINK. On east LIGHT BLUE as map. On west side is a Music Hall, many Benefits, price of places 2d and 6d, the highest price is 1/-. Never very full.

E along **Empress Street** (late Princes St). 2-st and 3-st. Many poor. North poorer than south. On the north side is a poor rough common lodging house, 4d, 6d and 8d. Mark north side LIGHT BLUE, south side LIGHT BLUE to PURPLE, in map PURPLE.

N to **Alpha Square**. 4-st and 5-st buildings. Some poor and others above waterline. Fountain in the yard, windows well kept. PURPLE, in map PINK.

S down Walworth Rd, **W** at **Arthur Street**. 2½-st plus attic. PINK to PURPLE, in map PINK.

S down **Blucher Street**. 2-st and 2½-st. Mixed, cabmen. PURPLE as map.

E & **N** up **Cyril Street**. 2-st, narrow. Poorer. PURPLE to LIGHT BLUE, in map PURPLE.

W along Hillingdon St. Out of the N side is **Jerome Place**. 2-st flagged court. Poor, doors open, dirty children. 6/- for four rooms, copper in back room and nice garden, has been there 12 years. LIGHT BLUE, in map PURPLE.

W of it is **Kettle Place**. Six houses, on east side only. Good fronts. Some very poor. LIGHT BLUE to DARK BLUE, not coloured in map.

W along **Hillingdon Street**. 2-st. A mixed street all through. Many poor, many fairly comfortable. On the south side between Royal Rd and Herion St there are new flats, 2-st, for two families, which remain PINK. The rest from PINK to PURPLE.

S down Thomas St and **E** along **Beresford Street**. 2-st. Broader and better than Hillingdon St. Stedall has a depot for mantle making, gives out a lot of work in the neighbourhood. PINK as map. Two Board Schools in this street, one very large and new at the east end on south side.

S along Walworth Rd, **W** along **Grosvenor Terrace** (late Brunswick Terrace). 3-st and 2-st. North side better than south. PINK-barred and PINK rather than RED of map.

W along **Grosvenor Park**. Tallymen, clerks, very few servants, none on the south side. The east end opposite the church and the south side of the park are the best. Good gardens, majority have no servants. Mark the outer ring of the park PINK-barred and the inner PINK, in map RED. Many lodgers, card with "apartments" or "a bedroom for a gentleman" in many windows.

E along **Grosvenor Street**. Detached and semi-detached, good gardens. 2-st and 3 st. PINK to PINK-barred, in map RED.

S down Walworth Rd. **W** along Avenue Rd and **N** into **Horsman Street** (late Chatham St). 2-st. Poor and very poor, rather rough. LIGHT BLUE, in map PURPLE.

W & **N** up a cul de sac called **Goschen Street**. 3-st and 2-st, rather better. PURPLE as map.

W along Avenue Rd and **S** into **Cambridge Street, Palmerston Street** and **Grosvenor Terrace**. All 2-st, a few poor, but majority fairly comfortable, PINK as map. This finishes all the Carter St subdivision that comes under our District 41.

General remarks

The marked feature in this round is the deterioration of the RED and PINK streets. RED has become PINK or PINK-barred and PINK become PURPLE. The PINK-barred streets might almost be PINK and many of the PINK streets have an admixture of the poor class.

The original 1d tram fare was from Westminster Bridge to Camberwell Gate. Beyond it was 2d. Now the 1d fare runs to Camberwell Green. No doubt this has taken the PINK and

RED class further afield.

The poorest bit in this round is Montpelier St where the influence of the third rate music hall has been felt and also Empress Rd (late Princes Rd) where there is a rough common lodging house.

Walk 13   B365

Thursday 22nd June 1899.
George Duckworth with Sergeant Feador Sziemanowicz.

Starting at the corner of St Agnes Place and Kennington Park.
S down **St Agnes Place** (late Marley Place). 3½-st. Working class south of Warham St, a few servants north of it. PURPLE to PINK, in map PINK.
Out of the E side is **Rutley Gardens**. 2½-st, two families. "Piano taught by a lady." PINK, in map PINK-barred.
N along **Bolton Road**. Small shops at south end. 2-st. PURPLE to LIGHT BLUE, in map PINK.
E into **Warham Street** (late Thomas St). Mixed. Poor at north east. Houses on east side south of Beresford St are 2-st, newly done up and well tenanted. These remain PINK. The rest from PINK to PURPLE.
W along **Smith Street**. 2-st with fair backs. South side rather poorer than north. PURPLE, in map PINK. West of Bolton St it is poorer, especially on south side, but PURPLE as map. Out of the south west end is a passage with two 2-st LIGHT BLUE houses, not shown in map.
S into St Mark's Rd, W along Camberwell New Rd and N up **Kennington Park Terrace**. 2½-st and 3½-st. "Very respectable", all with servants. RED as map.
S & E along **St Mark's Road**. 2½-st and 3½-st. No servants, cabmen. PINK to PURPLE, in map PINK-barred.
S down Warham St. Out of the W side is **Dugdale Street**. 2-st. Ill kept, no thoroughfare for wheels. PURPLE to LIGHT BLUE, in map PINK.
S of it, out of the W side of Warham St, is **Ivins Place**. 2-st. Quiet. 6/- for three rooms with large back, has been there six years. Front gardens. LIGHT BLUE, not shown in map.
S into Camberwell New Rd. N & E at **Dugdale Street** (late Charles St). 2-st. Better this end than the other. Out of the north east are a few houses leading to a nursery garden. PURPLE to PINK, in map PINK and unmarked. Further west out of north side is another turning with two cottages. Poor. LIGHT BLUE. Cart painter's shed in front, not marked in map.

General Remarks
This is the only portion of District 35 that lies in the Lambeth Police Division.
There is here the same deterioration that was noticeable in the streets between Royal Rd and Farmers Lane.

Walk 14   B365

Thursday 22nd June 1899.
George Duckworth with Sergeant Feador Sziemanowicz.

Starting at the corner of Farmers Road and Warrior Road.

E along **Warrior Road**. 3-st. Dingy street, many Irish. About half the houses let in single room tenements. Windows dirty, doorposts shiny, brick walls rubbed, doors open, mess in street. PURPLE to LIGHT BLUE, in map PINK. The east end is poorer than the west and should be LIGHT BLUE.

S down **Elfin Road**. 3-st. Like Warrior Rd. North end better than south. PURPLE and LIGHT BLUE, in map PINK.

E & W out of it is **Westhall Road**. 3-st. The same, many poor. East end LIGHT BLUE, west end perhaps PURPLE, in map PINK.

W & S down **Farmers Road**. 3-st. LIGHT BLUE, in map PINK. Here the houses are of the same character as Warrior Rd.

E along Wyndham Rd and N up **Pitman Street**. 2-st and 3-st. Poorer at south than at north end. Costers, Irish. DARK BLUE to LIGHT BLUE, in map LIGHT BLUE. On the west side is a Roman Catholic school, children coming out, all well fed, but ill dressed, draggled skirts and holey boots, some sore eyes, all in very good spirits.

E & S down **Toulon Street**. Very poor at south east, south west and north west. A little better on north east. The south east is thoroughly bad, windows broken, blinds pinned up, dirty, rough women, children dirty and crying, one pinched face. Doors open, passages quite bare, a child's head through empty pane. Costers' carts stacked along south west, 2-st houses on west side and the north east. DARK BLUE, in map LIGHT BLUE.

E along **Beckett Street**. 2-st. Narrow. All costers and fish curers, in look and smell a reminder of the Donkey Row area. Barefoot children, may not be very poor but are certainly very rough. Costers' carts. New houses at east end on north side which are better than the rest. DARK BLUE and LIGHT BLUE, in map LIGHT BLUE.

N up **Crown Street**. Very poor and very rough, especially at north west and south east. DARK BLUE, in map LIGHT BLUE.

W along **Hollington Street**. 3-st yellow-brick houses. All doors open, some flowers, fearful mess in street, bread, meat, paper, vegetables, old tins. Heavy rain but street full of children, bare heads and bare feet. Most windows broken and blocked with boards, stuff or brown paper. Inhabitants are Irish cockney, general labourers, not the costers of Beckett St. Much overcrowding, 1-roomed or 2-roomed holdings usual. Many turned out when Sanitary Inspector went round 12 months ago but have all and more come back since. Narrow backs, no gardens. Drunk and rough, wife beating, assaults, "but not criminal, no thieves, housebreakers or prostitutes, maybe a few van draggers". DARK BLUE-barred as map.

N of it is **Sultan Street**. 3-st. The same as Hollington St in appearance and character. These two streets are tucked away by themselves. There is a foot passage by the church, out of the west end of Sultan St, but none for carts. Sziemanowicz said it was the worst part of the subdivision but not compared with White's Row or Dorset St out of Commercial St for crime. Nevertheless there are so many charges for assaults and drunkenness that the BLACK line of the map might remain.

N up Crown St out of its W side is **Grange Street**. 2-st, asphalt. Houses on north only. Better than Crown St. LIGHT BLUE, not shown on map.

N & W along Avenue Rd and S down **Laurel Terrace**. 2-st. Messy, asphalt, narrow. DARK BLUE to LIGHT BLUE, in map LIGHT BLUE.

W of it is **Gurney Terrace**. 2-st. DARK BLUE to LIGHT BLUE, in map LIGHT BLUE.

W & S down **Thompson's Avenue**. 2-st, very poor at south end. Houses down on north side. LIGHT BLUE to DARK BLUE, in map DARK BLUE.

N into Avenue Rd. Out of its north side opposite Thompson's Avenue are **Avenue Cottages**. 2-st. LIGHT BLUE. (Note: the LIGHT BLUE of map is placed too far east.)

E along **Avenue Road**. Mixed. Buildings at south east, many police here. These might remain PINK but the rest all PURPLE, in map PURPLE and PINK.

General Remarks

This round finishes the Carter St subdivision of the Lambeth Police Division.

Carter St subdivision is bounded in the east by Walworth Rd and Camberwell New Rd, on the south by Wyndham Rd and Camberwell Rd, on the west by Kennington Park Rd. Speaking of the subdivision as a whole, the good streets are less good and the bad streets as bad. The Sultan St area shows some inclination to extend its DARK BLUE, the increase here being balanced by the disappearance of DARK BLUE from courts at the north east end of Kennington Park Rd.

There are 40 cab yards in this subdivision alone, in Chapter Rd, Gaza St, Amelia St, Penrose St, Hampton St, Newington Crescent, Canterbury Mews, Avenue Rd, etc. The largest yard has 50 cabs and employs about 70 men. The next largest has 40 cabs. Beside these there are many small men owning and driving their own cab in De Laune St.

The casual men such as washers and stablemen still drink and are poor but the drivers are a steadier class now than before the strike. When the strike was over they petitioned the Commissioner to have stricter enquiries as to fitness made before licenses to drivers were granted. In this way they freed themselves of the odium of purging their own ranks and are now a steadier set of men than ever before. Taxameter cabs are not popular in this region though £2 is offered as a regular wage. Sziemanowicz thinks that the life of a taxameter driver is more costly and less pleasant than that of a cabman and that that is why they oppose them. A cabman must change his horse and come home for dinner. One dinner then does for man and wife. The taxameter man has no time off and must buy a separate dinner for himself.

As for the richer parts of the district the RED has gone for ever. A little PINK-barred remains in Lorrimore Square, Sutherland Square and Grosvenor Square but there are more houses in all of them that do not keep servants. The PINK of the centre of the district remains but there is an ever broadening band of PURPLE round it.

The vestry is not remarkable for the care bestowed on street cleaning. The poor districts, especially the Sultan St area, have an undue share of unswept garbage.

There is more drinking as the district becomes poorer. Sergeant Sziemanowicz notices especially an increase among women of the working class. He has never seen a child drunk.

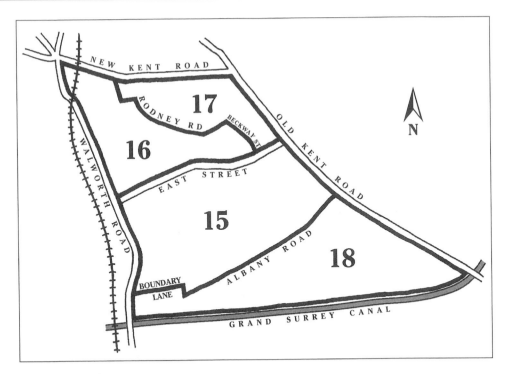

Walk 15

B365

B365

Wednesday 28th June 1899.
George Duckworth with Sergeant Wyatt.
Sergeant Wyatt is a tall, grave man with dark moustache and quiet determined voice. He has been in the force 14 years and, having passed his exam, is waiting for a vacancy to be promoted to the rank of Station Sergeant. Before he came here he was in Clerkenwell.

Starting at the corner of the Walworth Road and Boundary Lane.
E along **Boundary Lane**. 3-st and 2-st. Working class. Three poor houses at the south east end, east of Holmby St. High forbidding Albany St Buildings on the south side. PINK to PURPLE, in map PINK.
N up Providence St into **Boyson Road**. 3½-st. Good class of city worker, a family on each floor, no servants. Leave at 8 or 9 am and come back between 5 and 8 pm. The best houses are between Portland St and Villa St. Here 2-st, yellow brick, comfortable. PINK as map.
W & N up **Red Lion Row**. Houses on east side. LIGHT BLUE to PURPLE, in map PINK.
Out of the E side is **Red Lion Mews**. All costers, fair class, live over, pony and barrow under. The yard used as a common home by the inhabitants. Five of them had kindled a wood fire in front of their stable and were cooking their dinners over it. "Earn good money but spend it quickly." One family that has been there five years pays 8/6 for two rooms and stable. LIGHT BLUE as map.
Into Westmoreland St. N up **Horsley Street**. 2-st. Poor, costers, rather poorer than Mount St. LIGHT BLUE, in map PURPLE.
W along **Mount Street**. 3-st and 2-st. Small shops at south west end. Rag, bone and bottle dealer, fish supper bar and barber "Shaving 1d, hair cutting 3d, *poudre d'amour* for the

complexion." LIGHT BLUE to PURPLE, in map LIGHT BLUE.

S down **Little Mount Street**. Poor and very poor. Flagged passage. Costers' barrows. A man who has been there 13 years pays 7/- for three rooms, two down and one up. LIGHT BLUE to DARK BLUE, in map DARK BLUE.

E & N up **Queens Row**. 3½-st. Old houses, small masters. Home workers, whirr of sewing machines. PINK as map.

N to **Merrow Street**. Mixed. New 2-st houses on north side west of Little Liverpool St remain PINK. The rest from PINK to PURPLE.

Out of the **SE** end is **Grantham Place**. 2-st. Very quiet poor. Wooden palinged front gardens. LIGHT BLUE as map.

S down Portland St. W at **Sondes Street** (late Smith St). 2-st. PINK to PURPLE, in map PINK.

N up **Doctor Street**. Some poor. PURPLE rather than PINK of map. South of Sondes St is better than north.

W along **Cancel Street** and S down **Elizabeth Street**. Both PINK as map.

E & N up **Phelp Street**. 2-st. PINK as map. These are old yellow brick houses, solid, built between 1814 and 1840. One family takes the house and lets off to lodgers. Tenants are workers in the warehouses in Bermondsey and the City. Go to and come back from their work in the tram.

S into **Westmoreland Road**. 2-st, 2½-st and 3-st. Shops at west end. Is a very busy street market on Friday nights and Saturdays but not much on Sundays when East St is the rendezvous of buyers and sellers. PINK as map. East of Boyson Rd some houses are shut for the extension of the workhouse.

S down Thurlow St. E along **Sedan Street**. 2-st. Broad street. Fairly comfortable. 14/- or 15/- for 6-roomed house. Mess in street. Windows whole. A few poor. PINK to PURPLE, in map PINK.

Like it is **Lebanon Street**. 2-st. PINK as map.

N to a block of streets running between Alvey St and Portland St, namely **Faraday Street** (3-st), **Mann Street** (2½-st), **Inville Road** (2-st and 2½-st), and out of the **NE** side of Inville Rd is **Hopwood Street** (2-st). This area is known as Walworth Common. Built on sandy soil and renowned for its healthiness. Houses never empty, some dingy curtains but majority comfortable. No poor now, "such good times that everyone has enough work but they are not a class that save much". All PINK to PURPLE. Children going in large numbers to the public house at the corner of Faraday St and Thurlow St with jugs for the dinner beer. No sipping. Sergeant Wyatt "knows it is not usual to think so but has never been able to see any harm come of it himself". One child looked as though she were sucking a sweet as she came out but the others did not. It was constant come and go, one moment to go in and get the jug filled and out again the next. None of the children waited to talk or play with one another but at once hurried home. A large new School Board now takes up the block between Mann St, Thurlow St, Faraday St and South St. Inville Rd is rather poorer east of South St than west of it.

W & N up **Brettell Street**. 2-st. LIGHT BLUE as map.

Clandon Street. 2-st. LIGHT BLUE to PURPLE, in map LIGHT BLUE and PURPLE.

Burton Street. 2-st. LIGHT BLUE as map.

Wooler Street (late Webb St). LIGHT BLUE as map.

These are all coster streets. Mess in road. Women and men rough. Men buy in the Borough Market and sell all over London, a few buy in Covent Garden. Women for the most part work in R Whites ginger beer and mineral water factory. A rough, poor class with white or sackcloth aprons. They go fruit and hop picking in the summer and autumn. The streets are full of barrows. Open front doors lead to back yards where pony or donkey is kept. Windows broken and dirty, children dirty and ill-dressed but fat and happy. One or two women with black eyes, told the usual tale of coster streets, they make a lot of money but spend so freely that they have to borrow each week to buy their stock for Saturday. They borrow from more careful costers and not from outside lenders.

N up Portland St. E along **Trafalgar Street**. New 2-st houses. PINK as map. Poorer at extreme north east.

S down South St and W along **Thornton Street**. 2-st. Cab yard at south east. Many poor. Vestry workers and builders' labourers. LIGHT BLUE to PURPLE, in map PINK.

From the W end to Wooler St is a flagged passage called **Hope Street**. 2-st on north, 1-st on south. Italians at south west. Poorer than Little Mount St. Casual street hawkers, sell from door to door. DARK BLUE to LIGHT BLUE, in map PURPLE. The south side is poorer than the north.

S to **Shaftesbury Street**. 2-st labourers. PURPLE to LIGHT BLUE, in map PINK.

W & S down Villa St. Out of the E side S of Shaftesbury St is **Ewhurst Street**. Six 2-st houses. Very poor and rough, barefoot children, hardly a pane of glass in any window. DARK BLUE, not coloured in map.

S & E along **Clandon Street**. Costers. Walworth crèche at south east end for use by mother jam and ginger beer workers as the Hammersmith crèches were for mother laundry

Clandon Street.

workers. Many poor. LIGHT BLUE to DARK BLUE, in map LIGHT BLUE and PURPLE. Out of the south east end is a nameless court with two 2-st and one 1-st cottages. Collection of old tins in back garden, tap left running. DARK BLUE, not shown in map.

N up South St, W along Trafalgar St, N up Portland St and E along **Sandford Row**. Poor. LIGHT BLUE, in map PURPLE.

N up **Blewett Street**. 2-st and 3-st. Bricks rubbed. Labourers and costers. Dirty children, rough women. South east worst. Windows broken. West side better than east. LIGHT BLUE, in map PURPLE.

E along **Runham Street**. 3-st on north, 2-st on south. Great mess in street. Children dirty, hatless, ill booted. Windows broken, doors open. Looks and is a grade above Sultan St but belongs to the same order. Chiefly labourers, mixed with a few cabmen and railwaymen. South side better than north. LIGHT BLUE to DARK BLUE, in map PURPLE.

N to **Kingston Street**. Rather better. 2-st. LIGHT BLUE to PURPLE, in map PURPLE.

S down **Portland Street**. Labourers. Many poor. LIGHT BLUE to PURPLE, in map PINK.

W & N up **Richmond Street**. 2-st and 2½-st. Small shops with poor over. Narrow. PURPLE, in map PINK.

W along **Bronti Place**. 2-st and 2½-st semi-detached houses. Coster dealers, buyers of unconsidered trifles, small cabmen, sack collectors, dry cooper, carriage builder, small master men. Some poor but a class above Dale St. PURPLE to PINK, in map PURPLE.

S down Richmond St and W along **Date Street**. 2-st on north, 3-st on south. Many poor. Woman suckling her child on the edge of the curbstone. LIGHT BLUE to PURPLE. North poorer than south side. In map PURPLE.

S into **Trafalgar Street**. 2-st. Broad open street, good backs, some poor. PINK to PURPLE, in map PINK.

W, S & E along **Liverpool Street**. 2-st, 1842. Good PINK as map.

Out of the N side is **Liverpool Terrace**. Six houses, 2-st. LIGHT BLUE to PURPLE, in map PURPLE. Further east are two poor houses standing back by woodyard. LIGHT BLUE, not shown in map. The gardens to Liverpool St have suffered owing to their size. It has been possible to cut off part of them for other purposes and still leave a small bit of garden.

W into Walworth Rd then N & E at **Beckford Place**. 2-st. Poor working class. LIGHT BLUE as map but more of it.

N & E along **East Street**. 2-st and 3-st. Cobble paved. Third rate shops on either side as far as South St going down, not so busy as it used to be. Busiest on Sunday mornings when all the shops are open and the place is filled with hawkers, quack doctors and all sorts. "You could walk on the heads of the people, there is such a crowd." PINK to PURPLE, in map PINK-barred.

E along East St. S down **Etherton Street**. PINK as map.

S & E along **Ann's Row**. Mixed. PURPLE as map.

S down **Ann's Road**. Mixed. PURPLE as map.

S into **Aylesbury Street**. Mixed. PURPLE west of Thurlow St, in map PINK, but PINK as map east of it.

Out of the N side is **William's Grove**. Labourers. 2-st. PURPLE, in map PINK.

S along **High Park Crescent**. Vestry labourers. PURPLE, in map PINK.

N up **Thurlow Street**. PINK as map.

W along East St. Out of the S side is **Jesmond Street** leading to All Saints Schools. 2-st. PINK as map.

E along **East Street** which is purely residential east of South St. Common lodging house for a quiet set of regular waterside labourers at corner of Jesmond St. Wellington College Mission on north side and Pembroke College Mission, also St Bridget's nursing home.

S down Alvey St. Out of W side is **Namur Terrace**. 2-st. Flagged. PURPLE to LIGHT BLUE, in map PURPLE. North side are older houses with cared-for fronts. South side is distinctly poorer and might be LIGHT BLUE.

S into Aylesbury St which has two 1-st cottages at the back of south east end called **Victory Cottages**, not shown on map.

Out of the E side of Alvey St are **Alvey Mews**. Cabs and costers. Neat. PURPLE, in map PINK. A very poor house is at the entry to them in Alvey St.

S of it is **Innis Place**. 2-st. Newly done up. Hearthstone dealers and manufacturers. Hawkers. LIGHT BLUE to PURPLE, in map PURPLE.

S of it is **Brockley Terrace**. 2½-st houses, neat. PINK as map.

S & E to **Surrey Square**. 3½-st on north, 3-st on south. North side better than south. Old houses in square. Two vicarages. PINK to PINK-barred, in map PINK.

N up **Fremantle Street**. PURPLE as map on east. Where it turns west to Exon St PINK as map. Many of better class railwaymen, engine drivers, guards, etc.

N into East St. W & S down **Claremont Terrace**. Houses on west side only 7/6 for four rooms plus wash-house, another who had been there 10 years pays 6/6 and others 7/-. "They always raise the rent on new tenants." LIGHT BLUE to PURPLE, in map PURPLE.

E along East St and S down **Minnow Street**. 2-st. Carmen and railway labourers. At the north east end is a common lodging house which stands back. Riverside labourers. LIGHT BLUE as map.

S down **Madron Street**. 2-st and 2½-st. Many police. More PINK than map.

W along Surrey Square, S down Flinton Rd and W along **Aldbridge**. 3-st. Gates' property. PINK as map.

S down Alvey St and E along **Surrey Grove**. 2-st. Poor, costers. PURPLE and LIGHT BLUE, in map all PURPLE. East end better than west.

Cross Street is also LIGHT BLUE rather than PURPLE of map.

S to Kinglake St and N into **Cooks Cottages** and **Eagle Place**. 2-st. The north side is much better than the south and has well cared for front gardens. PURPLE and LIGHT BLUE, in map PURPLE and PINK. One woman on the south side who has been there four months pays 6/- for two rooms and wash-house.

W along **Kinglake Street**. 2-st. Poor. Some Italians in a house standing back at south west end, been there five years and pay 8/6 for four rooms and wash-house. It is a poor rough drinking street. At the south east end are shops, newish buildings. PINK rather than PURPLE of map.

S down **Bagshot Street**. 2-st. Mixed. PURPLE as map.

W along **Alsace Street** (late Allen St). 2-st. PURPLE to LIGHT BLUE, in map PURPLE.

E along **Mina Road**. PINK as map

N to **Smyrk's Road**. 2-st. PINK as map. Workers in the City, warehousemen and such like in these streets. The east end of Smyrk's Rd is poorer, PURPLE as map.

W along **Amery's Place**. Poor, narrow. 2-st. Bermondsey leather workers. LIGHT BLUE as map. Houses both sides.

General Remarks

A good deal of the old PINK remains, especially in the Walworth Common Estate (ie. Westmoreland Rd, Faraday Rd, Mann Rd and Inville Rd) but west of Portland St and east of South St, north of the Inville Rd there is the same tendency of PINK to become PURPLE that has been noticed so often before. While between South St and Portland St, still north of the Inville Rd there is the further tendency of PURPLE to become LIGHT BLUE. The LIGHT BLUE is caused by the extension of the coster colony for which Walworth is famous.

The fairly comfortable are City workers, warehousemen and a few clerks and customers and the better paid of the railwaymen – guards, foremen and engine drivers. The poor are costers, railway labourers, cab yard men. The majority of the poor are costers, men who make good money but do not bring it home. The older houses belong to the decade before 1820. The majority are of later date in between 1840 and 1860, yellow brick and fairly built.

Walk 16

B365

Friday 30th June 1899.
George Duckworth with Sergeant Wyatt.

Starting at the west end of East Street.
Going E out of the N side are **Manchester Buildings**. Sixteen 2-st houses with careful fronts and flowers. Comfortable, old tenants. One woman of about 50 said she had been in her house 42 years, her mother died there, "I've buried my husband these ten years" and she still lives on there with her children and pays 8/- for four rooms and a wash-house. Other houses let for 10/6 (the same size as hers) and a larger one for 14/-. PURPLE to PINK, in map PURPLE and LIGHT BLUE.
E & N into **North Row**. Well asphalted. 2-st. Costers, strong smell of decaying fish and a load full of rotting cauliflowers in one room. Windows broken and rooms rather bare. 4/6 for two rooms plus wash-house, no copper. "Wants whitewashing badly" said someone who had been 15 years there. LIGHT BLUE to DARK BLUE, in map LIGHT BLUE.
E & N into **Kings Arch Place**. Twenty 2-st houses, all old tenants. Rents 8/- to 10/- for four rooms plus wash-house. Costers, very poor and messy round corner at north east. Marked wrongly in map. DARK BLUE to LIGHT BLUE, in map LIGHT BLUE.
E & N up **Lestock Place**. 2-st houses on east only. Rooms bare, many children hatless, dirty, bad boots. Two Salvation lasses visiting house to house talking to one girl of about 16 and making her look very uncomfortable. DARK BLUE to LIGHT BLUE, in map PURPLE.
E & N up **King & Queen Street**. Very poor costers on west side. 2-st. Board School on east. Rough, many charges for drunkenness and assaults among themselves. "Costers summons one another freely and will often subscribe to help their assailant to pay the fines inflicted." This end of King & Queen St is LIGHT BLUE to DARK BLUE, in map PURPLE.
Out of the E & W sides is **Angel Street**. Costers on east side, vestry men on west. Look very poor. Shoes and clothes bad, all hatless. Houses lately done up. LIGHT BLUE to DARK BLUE, in map LIGHT BLUE.
N & W along **Beddome Street**. 2-st. Poor. Bread. Doors open. General labourers. LIGHT BLUE as map.
W & N up **Revesby Street** (late James St). Cab washers. Hearthstone and sand hawkers and makers. General labourers. LGO bus stables at south east which stretch some way back. It was midday and the fourth *Star* was being cried down the street. LIGHT BLUE, in map PURPLE.
E to **Lock Square**. Poor. LIGHT BLUE on south, better on west side. The space in front is boarded round and used as a yard by a carman and contractor. Used to be Lock's Fields. The west side made by the east side of King & Queen St is better. LIGHT BLUE to PURPLE, in map PURPLE.
W along **York Street**. Robert Browning Hall on south side, much used for political meetings, concerts and lectures (Herbert Stead), and a working men's Mission Hall at north west end of Revesby St. On north side are 3-st houses with bow on ground floor.

Yellow brick, iron rail around narrow front. The regular Building of the Gates' property. PINK as map.

Out of the **N** side of York St are **Colworth Grove**, **Walcombe Avenue**, **Turguard Street**, **Cotham Street**, **Charleston Street** (late Charles St), **Larcom Street** and, out of its **NW** end, **Ethel Street**. All Gates' property. Tenants work in the city. PINK as map.

W into Walworth Rd. N & E into **Wansey Street**, **Vowler Street**, **Heygate Street**, **Hewson Street**, **Bodley Street**. All 2½-st. Good PINK as map. Tradesmen with shops in the main roads, no servants. Surrey congregational chapel on north side of Wansey St is large and ugly but "attracts a large congregation from all parts of the suburbs, people who used to live in the neighbourhood years ago".

N & E along **Deacon Street**. Third rate shops with poor living over. PINK to PURPLE, in map PINK.

Out of NW end is **Winch Place**. Seventeen 2-st houses. Flagged court, narrow. Children dirty, ill dressed, sore eyes, very rough. Some thieves. Dalton the ratcatcher lives here, has been locked up many times, makes a very good living in clearing corn vessels of rats. LIGHT BLUE-barred to DARK BLUE, in map LIGHT BLUE.

E & N up **Gurney Street**. Old red-tiled 2½-st plus attic houses on east, 4-st Buildings on west. A street with a bad name. "Where do you come from? Oh Gurney St, well you can't come in here." The home of Hooligans. Used to be brothels on east side, now all cleared with the help of Sergeant Wyatt and the vestry. The agent and the landlord of the houses got three months hard labour. They appealed to sessions but the sentence was confirmed. It was proved that when they were used as brothels the rent was raised from 13/- to 20/- per week. The street might now be LIGHT BLUE instead of PINK and PURPLE of map. At the north east end fronting New Kent Rd are Sutton & Dudley's Buildings. Some Piccadilly prostitutes but they don't bring men home. PINK, in map PURPLE.

W & **S** down **Chatteris Road**, **Ash Street** and **Lion Street**. 5-st Sutton & Dudley Buildings. Narrow backs separating blocks, mess shot out there. City police and workers in the city. PINK as map.

At **NW** of Lion St are **Lion Buildings**. 1882. "Belong to a private lady." Red brick, lately done up outside and do not look worse than LIGHT BLUE but have a very bad reputation, "an awful place". Drunks and fights, shoeblacks and loafers, women flowersellers, a few thieves. Narrow stair entrance. LIGHT BLUE-barred, in map DARK BLUE-barred.

Like them are Weymouth Buildings in **Sayer Street**. LIGHT BLUE-barred, in map DARK BLUE-barred. The rest of Sayer St is PINK to PURPLE, more PINK than is on map.

N into New Kent Rd. E & S to **Chatteris Square**. 5-st Sutton & Dudley's Buildings. All windows unbroken, a few flowers, respectable, few poor, curtains clean, white tiles to staircase. Police and City workers. PINK to PURPLE, in map PINK.

W along New Kent Rd. S down Sayer St and W along **Elephant Road**. West of the public house are a few poorish 2-st houses. PURPLE, not coloured in map. Then, going south, comes a large public house hotel and below it the almshouses and schools of the Metropolitan Tabernacle.

N to New Kent Rd. W to **Elephant & Castle**. Now being rebuilt and nearly finished.

S down Walworth Rd out of whose E side is **Black Prince Court**. Six 2-st houses on south only. 7/- for three rooms, kitchen and wash-house combined, has been there seven years without having rent raised though a neighbour living two doors off under a different landlord has been raised to 8/-. Less LIGHT BLUE than map.

S & E into **Ostend Place**. 2-st. LIGHT BLUE as map.

S & E into **Ventry Place**. Twenty 2-st houses. Flagged court, wash hanging across. Very poor, windows broken, children barefoot and dirty. Rents 6/- on south side, 5/- on north, two rooms only, one up and one down. Small yard with copper behind. My informant has been here one year last April, no-one here more than three years. Three years ago court was closed and houses done up. Before that time the houses were used as brothels. Sergeant Wyatt has never had any prosecution from here. Children with sore eyes and faces, and dirty. DARK BLUE, in map BLACK. In a stone let into the wall is an inscription: "This court was paved at the sole expense of M D Cook in 1844."

S & E into **Farrell Court**. Leading to railway arches and the yards of the Star Omnibus Company. Poor on north only. LIGHT BLUE, in map PURPLE. Bookies receiving bets under the railway arch, made off in a hurry as I appeared.

S down **Walworth Road** past large Vestry and Public Library and Mission to cabmen, all on east side.

E along East St and N up **Morecambe Street** (late Camden St). 2-st, old fashioned. Poor, nearly all costers. PURPLE to LIGHT BLUE, in map PURPLE.

E along **East Street**. Just east of the chapel is a nameless turning leading to Ellis Bros Richmond Boot factory. Two poor vine-covered cottages on north side and one fairly comfortable on south. LIGHT BLUE, not shown in map. 9/- for four rooms and kitchen and wash-house. Has been there a month.

E & N up **Townley Street**. 2-st. Very poor, improves to north east. LIGHT BLUE and DARK BLUE, in map DARK BLUE. Great mess, costers' carts, all doors open, windows broken, bread about. Constant charges, cockney Irish, children ragged, dirty, well fed. 7/- for four rooms no wash-house. R H Tomkins at the LCM Townley St Mission. DARK BLUE to LIGHT BLUE, in map DARK BLUE.

Like it is **Hard Street**. DARK BLUE as map.

S & E along East St. N up **Blandon Row**. 6-st Victoria Buildings on west side. Rough, poor, a few thieves. Quite as poor as Townley St but do not look worse than LIGHT BLUE of map. Houses on north side down. The centre is now an LCC playground with giant slide, swings, see-saw, for boys and girls. A woman to look after the children and a man for the boys. Square crammed with all sorts, it being a school holiday, the roughest and poorest at play as well as those rather better off. "The finest bit of work the Council has ever done."

E along **East Street**, which is PURPLE between Camden St and South St rather than PINK of map.

N up **South Street** (late North St). 2-st and 3-st. South end rather better than north. PURPLE and LIGHT BLUE, in map PURPLE.

Out of the NE is **Rossett Place** (late Nelson Court). Flagged court. Twelve 2-st houses, clean, quiet, poor. LIGHT BLUE as map.

W & S down **Orb Street**. Poor costers. 2-st. South better than north. LIGHT BLUE to PURPLE, in map PURPLE.

W along **Eltham Street**. Rather better, still costers, hawk all over England. PURPLE as map.

N & E along **Nursery Row**. 2-st. Respectable. Gates' building on north side. City warehousemen. PINK to PURPLE, in map LIGHT BLUE. The open space on the south side is used by gipsy caravans in winter.

N & W along **Bedford Street**. 2-st. Gates'. PINK, in map PURPLE.

Back to Rodney St. S down South St and E along **Northampton Place**. 2-st. Costers, poor. LIGHT BLUE as map. A large RC school is at the south east and beside it a turning with four 2-st houses. LIGHT BLUE as map.

S & W along **Dean's Buildings**. Poor and mixed. East end better than the west. LIGHT BLUE to PURPLE, in map PURPLE.

Out of the S side is **Dean's Court**. Eight 2-st houses. Very poor, dirty children, boots holey, almost dropping off their feet. DARK BLUE on both sides, in map LIGHT BLUE. One pays 5/- for two rooms and kitchen, been there eight years. Windows bad.

S & E along **East Street**. Residential. PINK as map.

N up **Flint Street**. New houses on east side PINK, the rest PINK to PURPLE, in map PURPLE. Out of the south east end are two LIGHT BLUE houses behind a swing door, not shown on map.

E & N up Elsted St, out of whose **SW** side is Larissa St, leading to **Tisdall Place**. Very poor and rough, windows bad, mess. All costers and a few thieves.

Larissa Street rather worse than Tisdall Place. 2-st, narrow. DARK BLUE to DARK BLUE-barred, in map LIGHT BLUE.

N up **Elsted Street**. 2½-st, old red-tiled houses. PURPLE as map.

E along **Osborne Street**. Sawyers and carpenters working in yard on north side. PURPLE as map.

S & W along **Tatum Street**. 2-st and 3-st. Some costers, mixed. PURPLE as map.

S down **Halpin Place**. Well asphalted. Very rough. Some Italians, many complaints for gaffing. Wellington College Mission at south east. DARK BLUE as map.

S into **Huntsman Street**. 2-st. PURPLE to LIGHT BLUE, in map PURPLE.

E into **Barlow Street**. Very much mixed. New 2-st cottages on east are PINK, in map LIGHT BLUE. North of them is PURPLE on both sides. South might remain LIGHT BLUE as map.

E & N up **Backway Street**. 2-st and 3-st. South west better than rest. Poor labourers, scavengers, wood paviours. All doors open. LIGHT BLUE as map.

Out of the E side is **Acre Street**. 3-st. LIGHT BLUE as map.

General Remarks

In this round the Walworth coster is to the fore. Though not poor if his earnings are considered, it is he that is responsible for the band of LIGHT BLUE and DARK BLUE streets and courts lying between East St and the Rodney Rd. Only a small proportion of his money is spent on his home. His numbers increase yearly. Every year the block bounded on the north by the New Kent Rd on the east by the Old Kent Rd on the south by the Albany Rd and on the west by the Walworth Rd becomes more densely populated. Houseroom becomes more precious and rents rise. There is a great demand for school accommodation. The large school in East St takes in the poorest and roughest of the children. This is a district which must have received many of those who were turned out of Southwark for railway extension. But on this point it seems impossible to get any information from the police.

Walk 17   B365

Friday 30th June 1899.
George Duckworth with Sergeant Wyatt.

Starting at the corner of East Street and the Old Kent Road.
W along **East Street**. New red-brick shops on the south side. Mixed small shops with poor over on north. PINK and PURPLE, in map PINK.

Out of N side is **Stanford Place**. 2-st. Very poor. LIGHT BLUE, in map PURPLE.

E & N up Old Kent Rd. W at **Alfreton Street**. 2-st and 3-st. East end has poor labourers but the west is Gates' 2-st. Good class, guards, railwaymen. PINK and LIGHT BLUE, in map PINK and PURPLE.

N up Backway St. E along **Comus Place** (late Swan Place). Old street, cobble paved. Much LIGHT BLUE at west end. 2-st. PURPLE to LIGHT BLUE, in map PURPLE.

Out of the **S** side going **W** is **Malling Place** (late Pleasant Place). Eleven poor 2-st houses with well-kept fronts on east side. LIGHT BLUE, in map PURPLE.

Also **Swan Buildings.** 2-st. Poor. Well asphalted. Dirty fat children, boots very bad. LIGHT BLUE, in map PINK.

S down Old Kent Rd and **W** at **Cornbury Street.** 2-st. Decent. PURPLE to LIGHT BLUE, in map PURPLE.

S to **Massinger Street** (late Clarence St). Decent. 2-st. PINK as map.

W to **Cook's Buildings.** North end better than south. North PURPLE, in map LIGHT BLUE. South west LIGHT BLUE, in map PINK.

N up Old Kent Rd. **W** at **Townsend Street.** 2-st, newish. Railwaymen. PINK to PURPLE, in map PURPLE and LIGHT BLUE.

At **NW** end are two streets enclosing blocks of models called **Mardyke Street** and **Crosslet Street.** Blocks named after Arthur, Grant, Lincoln, Washington, Cavendish, Hartington, etc. 4-st. Dark, dingy, flush with the pavement. Bread and mess in the street. While we were there a brickbat was heaved out of one of the upper windows. Tenants all casuals: paper sellers, whelks, coffee stall men, flower girls. There are many charges and rows, "very badly managed" and as rough as anything in the subdivision. A sprinkling of thieves, worse than Lion Buildings. DARK BLUE-barred, in map PURPLE. Children dirty, hatless with very ragged clothes and bad boots but enough to eat. The west side of Crosslet St is better and might be LIGHT BLUE.

N & E along **Mason Street.** 2-st at east end but poorer at west. PURPLE and PINK, in map LIGHT BLUE. Belongs to Mr Gledhow Builders, as does Townsend St. Built not four years ago.

N into Darwin St. **W, S & W** along **Hillery Road.** PURPLE rather than PINK of map.

N & E at **Darwin Street.** 3-st, Gates'. Workers in Bermondsey. Respectable. Men come home for dinner, wives seldom work. PINK as map.

Out of the **NE** is **William Street.** 2-st. Never to let, can only get into them by being friend of outgoing tenant. PINK as map.

E towards **New Kent Road.** The house on the north side marked RED in map is two old wooden stables and should be LIGHT BLUE.

W along **Chatham Street.** Gates'. PINK as map. It is poorer at the west end and PURPLE as map west of Chatham Place.

S down **Hemp Row** (late Chatham Row). Four poor cottages on west side. LIGHT BLUE, in map PURPLE.

E along **York Place**, which is the continuation of Salisbury Row east of Hemp Row. Two 3-st and two 2-st houses. Poor. LIGHT BLUE instead of wrongly placed PURPLE of map.

W along **Salisbury Row.** Old and poor 2-st houses on north side. Improving from half way westwards. LIGHT BLUE and PURPLE, in map PURPLE. The south side is now 3-st Gates' Buildings. PINK, in map PURPLE.

N up **Little Chatham Place.** 3-st. PINK to PURPLE, in map PURPLE.

W along **Larcom Street** (late Dale St). 2-st. PURPLE to LIGHT BLUE, in map PURPLE.

N & E along **Henshaw Street.** Bread and mess. West end better than east. R Whites has a large mineral water factory at the back of the north side. PURPLE as map.

W along **Paragon Row.** 4-st plus attic. Buildings on the north belong to Fishmongers' Company. Porches, covered with creepers, look much better than most Buildings. Eagerly tenanted. PINK as map. On south side are 3-st, poor but respectable. PURPLE to LIGHT

BLUE, in map DARK BLUE.

N & E along **Victory Place**. At the north east end are three blocks of 4-st Buildings called Salisbury Buildings. Red brick. Poor, tenanted by labourers and carmen, always shifting. "Not quite as bad as Lion Buildings." Built 1886. There were two brothels here. Windows dirty, blinds half down, pinned up. Everything dingy and dirty. LIGHT BLUE, in map PINK. East of Chatham Place there are on the north side only a few poor houses tenanted by horse keepers. Tillings' bus yard is on south side and entry to R Whites factory at south east. LIGHT BLUE, in map PURPLE.

N up **Munton Road**. Salisbury Buildings on west. At north east are Sutton & Dudley's Buildings. Several prostitutes working Piccadilly and West End live here. Dark stairs. Mixed. PURPLE to PINK, not shown in map. Where the road runs east and west there are 5½-st Buildings on south side. High, dark, dismal, rubbish shot out behind. PURPLE, in map PINK.

S down Rodney Rd and **E** into **Little Trafalgar Place**. 3-st houses on north side. Leads to large rag factory. PURPLE, in map PINK.

N to New Kent Rd and **S** down **Pollock Road**. 5-st, Sutton & Dudley. High, dull and dark with rubbish behind. Very narrow space separates the blocks. Those fronting the New Kent Rd are PINK and better than the rest. Those behind are PINK to PURPLE, not so good. In map PINK.

W & S down **Brandon Street**. Guinness Buildings at the corner of Deacon St. Red brick, clean, well built, curtains and windows good. Great competition to get into them, well looked after. Tenants once in never leave. Look PINK but I suppose they must be LIGHT BLUE by reason of the conditions of occupancy. Below them are Warren Buildings, good class. On the whole the street is mixed. PURPLE as map.

E along **Larcom Street** (late Sarah Ann St). 3-st. Poor. PURPLE to LIGHT BLUE, in map PURPLE.

S down **Content Street**. 2-st houses at north west done up and well tenanted. The rest poor and narrow. Costers and horse keepers. LIGHT BLUE as map.

S into **Wadding Street**. Name taken from Wadding factory on north side. Poor. Carmen and workers in the factory and in Dicky Wood's Ironworks. LIGHT BLUE, in map PURPLE.

E into **Rodney Road**. Mixed. East side newer and with better shops than west. Perhaps PINK from Flint St to Eider St (late Short St) then PURPLE. In map the whole is PURPLE except a bit of east side.

N to **New Kent Road**. Old houses. A few old tenants remain and keep servants but the majority have none. Old families have moved further out. Places taken by music hall artistes. PINK-barred, in map RED.

S down **Searles Road**. 3-st. New road, tenanted before the builders have left. Good PINK, not shown in map. This takes the place of the old Paragon whose garden has been turned into a playground by the LCC. YELLOW of map goes.

General Remarks

The remarkable part about this round is the number of model Buildings which, in height and density increase as the New Kent Rd is reached. Houses everywhere increase in height towards the main road and seen from above London would shew a series of ups and downs between the main thoroughfares. This tendency is well illustrated here by the long range of Buildings on the south side of the New Kent Rd which already stretch from Sayer St to the Munton Rd.

In character the Buildings vary very much. Weymouth and Lion Buildings between Sayer St and Lion St are very poor and very rough. Chatteris Square and the various

Sutton & Dudley Buildings are neither very good nor very bad. Well built but without any regard to light or air or amenities of any kind. The narrow yard behind is in every case a rubbish shoot and not a resting place or playground for its inhabitants. They form a marked contrast to the Guinness Buildings in these respects. On a par with Lion and Weymouth Buildings are Salisbury Buildings, lying between Munton Rd and Victory Place, and the blocks with the high-sounding names between Mason St and Townsend St. In these Sergeant Wyatt ascribed badness, owing to the inefficiency of the agents and caretakers in allowing a bad class to come in.

In Chatham St as we passed were three vestry employees – young men between 25 and 35 – who should have been digging up the road but were all drunk and were singing and dancing with one another. Wyatt said they belonged to the St George's Vestry. The east end of Chatham St is just in the parish of St George's.

Walk 18   B 365

Monday 3rd July 1899.
George Duckworth with Sergeant Wyatt.

Sergeant Wyatt is a tall, grave man with dark moustache and quiet determined voice. He has been in the force 14 years and, having passed his exam, is waiting for a vacancy to be promoted to the rank of Station Sergeant.

Starting at the corner of the Old Kent Road and Albany Road.
W along **Albany Road**. Wood paved. Bus route. Old road with RED houses. No poor. PINK, in map the east end is PURPLE.
Out of the NE is **St Thomas' Road**. 2½-st. Comfortable. People work away. PINK to PURPLE, in map PURPLE.
W to **Bagshot Street**. 2-st. Mixed. PURPLE as map.
Out of the NW end of Albany Rd is **Albany Mews**. Runs east and west. Small cab owners. Tidy. PINK as map.
Out of S side of Albany Rd is **Surrey Place**. 2-st houses on east only, poor. LIGHT BLUE as map.
N to a high, dark block of Sutton & Dudley Buildings which cover **Maydwell Street, Millais Street** and **Holmby Street**. High 6-st, dull, dingy, dark, mess behind, very little space between blocks. Music Hall artistes, a few thieves, mixed class. PURPLE as map.
S down **Canal Street**. 2-st. West side better than east. Rather rough. Canal bank men. LIGHT BLUE as map.
E & S down **Harling Street**. 2-st and 3-st. Bath brick and sand factory at south end employs a good many men. LIGHT BLUE as map.
E into **Wells Street**. 2-s. Comfortable. PINK as map.
S on to the **towing path** and west along it. There are some houses at the bottom of Harling St on the bank. LIGHT BLUE, uncoloured in map. West of them are lime works with four 2-st cottages by large uncared for garden, private property. LIGHT BLUE as map.
E into **Cunard Street, Neate Street, Chumleigh Street, Scarsdale Rd, Scarsdale Grove, Jardin Street, Cowan Street**. All PINK as map. Fairly broad and clean streets, tenanted by people who both work and live in the District. Fair backs, built about 1820, better class of White's & Rawlings mineral water traders and foremen live here. R Whites main

factory is in Cunard St and he has another huge place east of Herring St on the north side of Neate St and has absorbed Rawlings' works which take up the whole of Chumleigh St. South of Neate St there is a large Bible binding factory of the north side of Scarsdale St. Out of the S side of Neate St opposite the south end of Jardine St is **Arlington Grove**. Eight 2-st houses, PINK, in map PURPLE. Four rooms and kitchen 9/-, six rooms 14/-. Have been there 19 and 26 years respectively but notwithstanding a year back their rent was raised 1/- a week.

N up **Albany Row**. Mixed. PURPLE as map, as is the east end of Scarsdale Rd.

N into the Albany Estate which lies between Albany Rd and Odell St on north, Calmington St on west, Longcroft Rd on south and Brymer St on east and comprises:

Calmington Road, PINK as map, **Silcote Road**, PINK, in map PURPLE, **Secretan Road**, PINK (north end) in map PURPLE, **Kempshead Road**, (north end is PINK, in map PURPLE), **Odell Street**, PURPLE as map, **Dartnall Road**, PURPLE as map, **Brymer Road**, PURPLE as map.

S of **Sandover Road**, which is PURPLE as map, these roads are poorer:

Pooah Road, LIGHT BLUE (in map PINK), **Dartnall Road**, LIGHT BLUE (in map PURPLE), **Brymer Road**, (LIGHT BLUE (in map PURPLE), **Longcroft Road**, (PURPLE as map and the rest PURPLE as map). The houses are 3-st with very narrow backs, not at all well but not very badly built. The Company that built them has lately sold the lot to different purchasers. They have been re-drained and re-tenanted with the result that some of the property has gone up (eg. the north ends of Silcote Rd, Secretan Rd and Kempshead Rd) while the other streets like Pooah Rd, Dartnall Rd and Brymer Rd have gone down. The LIGHT BLUE has distinguished itself from the PINK. Longcroft Rd has the worst reputation, there are some thieves, no prostitutes and a fair proportion of juvenile criminals. "It's not the parents but the youngsters that get into trouble in streets like these." The women work in Ord & Pink's jam works, the boys as printers' labourers, children are badly looked after. Pooah Rd looks the worst of the lot, windows broken, smell of dirt etc. A month since Odell St was responsible for the Camberwell tragedy – a man fired at his wife and three children with a crowd looking on and it was thought that all were killed but all are recovering.

E along **Longcroft Road**. 2-st new houses, east of Brymer Rd, belong to White's mineral water factory. Should be PINK.

W, S & E into **Herring Street**. 2-st. That part running east and west is poor. A sheepskin factory at north east. PURPLE as map.

E along **Neate Street**. Poorer east than west end. PURPLE as map.

S & E along **Ann's Terrace**. 2-st flush with pavement. Poor. Small paper bag makers, costers, wood choppers. A standing for caravans at north east. LIGHT BLUE as map.

N up **Cobourg Road**. Broad, pleasant. Large collar and cuff factor on east side, very good work and respectable class employed "best in London", pays over £1,000 a week in wages. Well dressed, very respectable young women coming out as we passed. 2-st and 3½-st. A few poor but PINK as map.

N into Old Kent Rd, W down Albany Rd, E into **Danville Grove**. 2-st. PINK to PURPLE, in map PINK.

E into Old Kent Rd. E & S into **Oakley Place**. New 2-st. PINK as map.

Nile Terrace. Older. PINK as map.

S down **Poplar Road**. 2½-st and 3½-st plus attic. A few poor, work away. PINK as map.

S into **Waite Street**. 3-st. PURPLE to LIGHT BLUE, in map PURPLE.

Out of the S side is **Bronte Place**. 2-st. Poor, a bit rough, windows show it. LIGHT BLUE as map. 10/- for five rooms and wash-house, has been there 18 months.

E of it is **Abouker Place**. 2-st. LIGHT BLUE as map.

Victory Place. Doors open, flagged court, bricks rubbed, very rough, a few thieves. 9/- for five rooms and wash-house on the west side and 10/- for the same amount of room on the east. LIGHT BLUE as map.

E across Trafalgar Rd into **Willowbrook Grove.** 2-st. 1847. PURPLE, in map PINK.

N up **Trafalgar Road.** 2½-st and 3-st. A few ministers still living in this and Glengall Rd but most have moved out to Peckham and Dulwich. Fine gardens at the back of the houses. PINK to PINK-barred, in map PINK-barred.

E along **Glengall Terrace.** No houses on north, in map PINK-barred. 2½-st on south. No servants. Comfortable. PINK, in map RED.

N up **Glengall Road.** No servants kept south of Glengall Terrace, like Trafalgar Rd above it. PINK-barred, in map RED and PINK-barred. At the south east are Chubb's large lock and safe works. At the north west end is Ormond Passage. One stable lived over. LIGHT BLUE as map but less of it. At the west end are Glengall Cottages. 2-st on west only. LIGHT BLUE as map.

E along **Ingoldisthorpe Road.** 2-st. PINK as map.

E down Old Kent Rd and **S** down **Ossory Road.** No servants. PINK, in map PINK-barred. Out of the **NE** is Ann's Avenue. 2-st. PINK as map.

S & E along **Olmar Street.** 2-st. PINK as map.

N into **Aulay Street.** PINK as map. Continues at the north west into Ossory Rd.

N up **Malt Street.** PINK as map.

E & S down **Bowles Road**, leading to large LCC tram stables. PURPLE to PINK as map.

Herman Street. PURPLE as map.

E & S down **Mills Street.** 2-st houses on west only. LIGHT BLUE as map.

General Remarks

Those who live in this district, work in it. For men and women there are the large ginger beer, kops ale and mineral water works belonging to the firm of R White in Cunard St, Chumleigh St and Neate St. For men, women and boys there is the bible binding factory in Scarsdale Rd. For artisans there is a large prepayment gas meter factory and Chubb's lock and safe works in the Glengall Rd. For first class labour there is tramway work under the LCC. For poorer labour there is canal work and lime kilns and horse tending and for rough skilled labour there is sheepskin dressing in Herring St and Goldie St and for skilled women's work there is the large collar and cuff works in the Cobourg Rd. Small unskilled labour is represented by paper bag makers and wood choppers in Goldie St and Ann's Terrace.

With the exception that fewer persons keep servants in Trafalgar Rd, Glengall Rd and Glengall Terrace, there is practically no change in the character or status of the inhabitants. The Poor are in Canal St, Harling St, Neate St, Ann's Terrace, Goldie St. The Little Earnings out of the south side of Waite St and Mills Terrace is of old standing and likely to remain until forcibly displaced. The Shadiest Characters are found in the Sutton & Dudley Buildings at the north west end of Albany St and in the block of streets between Albany Rd and Longcroft Rd.

This round finishes the Rodney Rd subdivision and with it the whole of the Lambeth Police Division.

Before Sergeant Wyatt came here he was in Clerkenwell. The main difference between Clerkenwell and Walworth he said was in wealth and viciousness. The poorest earn more money as a class in Clerkenwell than in Walworth but they are much more vicious. In Walworth there is nothing so bad as Verumlam St and Baldwin's Place. As to change in character of the people since he has been in the force, there is less roughness, "everyone is better behaved", but juvenile crime seems to be increasing and, more serious than that he thinks, is the increase of women's drunkenness and women's gambling. Betting among women is an invention as far as he has seen it of the last two years; he thinks it is quite common now. "It comes of their greater freedom and greater earning power. They keep what they earn and try to spend it as men spend their spare cash." Just because of this tendency to drink he would not encourage their fetching their own beer by forbidding the children to go for it. He has never seen a child drunk and sees no harm come to the children by running in and out with an empty and full jug to and from the public house. If it were possible to do without drink altogether he would stop the children but, as it is not possible, the fetching and carrying of the children prevents a greater evil for the women he knows would many of them go with the jug and remain to drink.

The class that is most characteristic of Walworth are the costermongers. As far as he can see they are just as poor in their appearance and homes whether the years are good or bad for trade. They are never very poor. When times are bad they spend less on music hall and drink than when they are good. But whether the season is good or bad the same amount is spent in the home. As a class they never work on Mondays and seldom more than two or three days in the weeks – Fridays, Saturday and Sunday mornings are their busiest times – "Time was when they only sold apples and vegetables. Now they sell any mortal thing." Some of the roughest go in for fish. Others linoleum, crockery, clothes, beds and bedding and any rubbish you can think of. Linoleum and iron bedsteads were a good line two years ago but he hears there is not much to be done in them now.

Bread was steady at 3½d for 4lb loaf in most shops, though there were always a few asking 4½d, and coal at 1/3 the cwt during the whole time I was in Walworth.

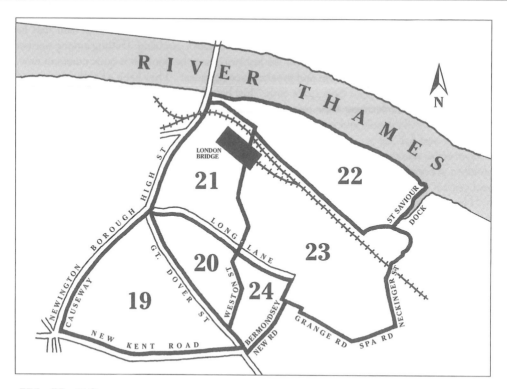

Walk 19

B364

Wednesday 24th May 1899.
Ernest Aves with PC Somersgill.
Sommersgill is a constable of some ten years' standing and is expecting promotion to the rank of sergeant in about six months. He is intelligent, and knew the district well. He did not talk easily or much, but, I think, sincerely. He appeared to be a man of excellent character and the respectability of his get-up was overpowering. He had a clerkly face.

Starting at the Elephant and Castle.
E along the New Kent Rd, we turned N up **Poplar Row** (now part of Tarn St). On west side nothing but Tarn's premises as far as Tarn's Yard. Colour out here. Then 2½-st houses with forecourts. PINK as map. On the east side only three shops. PINK as map. The rest a bus yard. Tarn's Yard (Rockingham Court of the map) is non-residential and is almost entirely taken up by Tarn's premises.
W of Wellington St is **Rockingham Street**. On south side, RED out for warehouses etc. PURPLE as map. On north side are shops and a poor block of Dwellings. PURPLE as map, as also the rest of the street running east and west. On the north side is the Holy Trinity Mission.
Tiverton Street. 2-st houses, flush with pavement. "Rather rough." South side better than the north. Many gossiping women and ill-clad children. Improved but still DARK BLUE. Omit BLACK barring at north west corner.
Behind is **Goode's Court**. Seven 2-st cottages on east side only. DARK BLUE as map.
Wellington Street (now a continuation of Tarn St). 2-st houses with forecourts. A few shops, respectable. Rents 11/- to 13/-, generally six rooms to a house. The occupiers mostly

old tenants, but "a good deal of packing" was the information of an old resident. LIGHT BLUE to PURPLE.

S to **Dorset Street**. 2-st houses, flush with pavement. Untidy. DARK BLUE as map.

Running N is **Linwood Place**. Narrow, paved cul de sac. 2-st houses. Rough, ragged children. Three or four rooms to a house. Rents 6/- to 7/6. DARK BLUE as map.

Uxbridge Street. 2-st houses, flush with pavement. Better than Dorset St. Flowers, blinds, ornaments, etc. North of Uxbridge Place and Dorset St is DARK BLUE to LIGHT BLUE, the rest DARK BLUE as map.

On the SE side is **Foston Place**. 2-st houses. Doors shut, no broken windows. DARK BLUE to LIGHT BLUE.

Also **Uxbridge Place**. 2-st houses. Two and four rooms to each. Terrible women, mostly pregnant. DARK BLUE as map.

To the S is **Arch Street**. Mainly coal, corn, bus yards, etc. Small block of 3-st Dwellings on south side near east corner. Bus men of the lower grades mainly. Uncoloured to LIGHT BLUE.

Meadow Row. 3-st houses with three rooms at 9/6. Gloomy but low-grade PINK as map.

Running N is the rest of **Rockingham Street**. 2-st houses with forecourts. Police and other decent folk living here. Respectable. PURPLE to PINK.

To the S is **Paul's Passage**. Mainly dye-works etc but two cottages on each side. On the south DARK BLUE, on the north PINK, rather than PURPLE.

Along Union Rd into **Bath Terrace**. 3-st houses, others 3-st plus basements. The conspicuous feature on the north side is the Bath Chambers, 5-st and basement. Well built. A good many City police living here. The whole street PINK as map.

To the S lies **Devonshire Street** (now Avonmouth St). 2-st and 3-st houses. LIGHT BLUE as map.

At the SW corner is **Bideford Court**. Not shown on map. Narrow. 2-st houses with three rooms, letting at 6/-. Crowds of babies. DARK BLUE.

Devonshire Street loses its DARK BLUE at the Newington Causeway end, the houses having given place to stables etc. Nearly opposite is a new, small 4-st block. Decent. Uncoloured to PINK.

By the Causeway into **Union Road**. Mainly 2-st houses, a few shops. PINK as map. The recreation ground was crowded with children as we passed.

St George's Road (now part of Falmouth Rd). 2-st houses with forecourts. Opposite the Welsh Church is Falmouth Chambers. A good street but PINK-barred to PINK.

Out to **New Kent Road**. For about half way to Harper St the big forecourts that ought to be gardens are still uncovered but after this point they have met their doom and all are built over. The street PINK-barred as map.

N up **Harper Street**. 3-st houses, shops etc. PINK as map.

W along **County Terrace Street**. 2-st and 3-st houses. LIGHT BLUE as map. At the west end running north are four houses not shown on map. They are 2-st and LIGHT BLUE, like the rest of the street in which they are included.

Brunswick Court. 2-st cottages. Remains DARK BLUE as map.

By **Woodman's Place**. Asphalt. 2-st houses. LIGHT BLUE as map. Went into one occupied by a baker's labourer. Three rooms with a little yard behind. The woman had recently come from Peckham, said the Court was very quiet but Peckham was "pleasanter like". Her rent was 6/-.

Turning left we came to **Union Place**, unnamed on map. 2-st houses fronted with a rather desolate gravel yard. The terrace dated 1827. Three police said to be living here. PURPLE as map.

NE is **Ayliffe Street**. 2-st houses, flush with sidewalk. PURPLE as map.

At NE corner are two courts. **Pitney Place** is 2-st houses. Quiet. Rents are 7/- for three rooms and a wash-house. Was told there were no lodgers here, there was "no room". A pensioned policeman living here. DARK BLUE to PURPLE.

The other court is **Harmers' Buildings**. 2-st houses on south west side only. Like Pitney Place. Gardens, some cared for, and the court a pleasant enough spot. A pensioned policeman here too. DARK BLUE to PINK.

E is **Ripley Street**. 2-st houses, flush, quiet. LIGHT BLUE to PURPLE. The DARK BLUE goes out, the site having been apparently absorbed by the School.

Theobald's Street. 2-st houses, flush. Very much like Ripley St. PURPLE as map

Arnott Street. Like Ripley St. LIGHT BLUE to PURPLE.

Adam Street. 2-st houses. A cul de sac, bus yard etc. LIGHT BLUE as map.

To the NE is **Deverell Street**. 2-st houses with forecourts. Good. All PINK as map.

To the W is **Standard Street**. 2-st houses. PURPLE as map. Of the Ripley St and Theobald's St type.

Continuing on 25th May 1899.

Starting from the N end of Union St, N along the Borough to **King's Place**. A cul de sac of 2-st houses. Quiet. Colour LIGHT BLUE as map but on both sides.

SW into **Trinity Street**. 3-st houses and basements. PINK-barred as map. This, with Merrick Square and Trinity Square, is "the aristocratic part of the Borough".

Near the SW corner is **Trinity Place**. 2-st houses. Very rough, a small court. DARK BLUE as map.

SW down **Swan Street**. 2-st and 3-st houses. PINK as map.

Brockham Street. 3-st and 2-st houses. Very much like Swan St. PINK as map.

Trinity Square. 3-st houses with basements and forecourts. Some private but mostly lodgings. Many Guy's students here and hereabouts. PINK-barred as map.

Merrick Square. 2-st houses with basements. Something like Trinity Square but rather better. Apartments the rule, however. RED to PINK-barred.

Falmouth Road. 2-st and 3-st houses. Rather more stylish than the lower end (the St George's Rd of the map). PINK-barred as map to Circular Rd, then PINK-barred to PINK.

Ralph Street and **Union Square**. 2-st houses. Quiet working class. PINK as map.

To the S is **Circular Road**. 2-st houses, working class. Very much the same all through. PINK and VIOLET to PINK.

Ralph Street (south of Falmouth Rd), **David Street** and **Canterbury Road** (now part of Upper Bland St) are all 2-st houses and PINK as map.

Upper Bland Street (as shown on map). 2-st houses and some queer old cottages on south east side. All from DARK BLUE and LIGHT BLUE to PURPLE.

By **Great Dover Street**. PINK-barred as map with an omission for Dewrance's large engineering works

To **Lawson Street**. 2-st houses, "very much like Great Bland St", and the big block of Britannia Chambers (6-st, stucco, ugly). A police constable among the occupants. A bus yard behind giving an unprepossessing appearance to an unprepossessing block, but it, with the street, from LIGHT BLUE to PURPLE.

Great Bland Street. North of Lower Bland St is 2-st houses with forecourts, many of them gardens. PINK as map here. South of Lower Bland St is a poor 4-st block on the east side. PINK to LIGHT BLUE. On the other side are stables etc. Colour omitted.

S of Lawson St is **Iris Place**, divided only by a fence from **Margaret Place**. Both have 2-st cottages. LIGHT BLUE as map. In Margaret Place and probably in the other, there are three rooms to a cottage. Rents from 7/- to 7/6.

Lower **Bland Street**. 2-st houses. LIGHT BLUE as map. DARK BLUE court at the north east end gone. New cottages at street frontage here. Two or three houses opposite show signs of the demolition of the DARK BLUE court, some of the occupants having moved into them and made certainly one DARK BLUE house. Omit some colour on this south east side for a new warehouse.

SE is **Warner Street**. 2-st houses with forecourts. PINK as map.

Buckenham Street and **Buckenham Square**. 2-st houses, all flush with sidewalks. Poor class, some broken windows and neglected children. PINK to PURPLE. The Square dated 1828.

N up Trinity St to **Cole Place** (now a continuation of Globe St). PURPLE as map.

Running **N** is **Cole Street**. 3-st houses, flush. Some rebuilding, dated "1895". Used to be "very rough" and "rough still but better". Omit colour at north east corner for new bakery. The rest from DARK BLUE to LIGHT BLUE.

Swan Street. 3-st houses plus 4-st Edinburgh Buildings. All PINK as map with an omission of colour for the bakery mentioned in Cole St.

To the **N** running into the High St is **Swan Place** (now Avon Place). Some rebuilding. Asphalted. 2-st houses, flush. Much improved. BLACK to LIGHT BLUE.

By Trinity St into the High St. On the **S** is **Landor Place**. 3-st houses on west side only. Most doors open, untidy, poor casual class. LIGHT BLUE to DARK BLUE.

Hulme Place (Union Place on map). 2-st houses on west side only. Paved. Two offices at north end and four or five houses. Rent (for four or five rooms) 12/-. LIGHT BLUE to PINK. Next is Swan Place. **Swan Yard** belongs to Tillings.

General Remarks

This area includes the best part of the Borough and the tendency is for things to improve. There is no important local employment excepting Tarn's and the other shops of the main streets. It would probably be found on closer analysis that many of the men in regular employment, like the City police living in Bath Place, go to the City for their work. The worst corner is that of which Wellington St is the centre with many costers and casual labourers. Sommersgill appeared to think that many of the men living in these adjacent courts picked up much of their casual livelihood in the crowded neighbourhood of the Elephant and Castle, on the assumption that the immense congestion of trams and buses and people there made work of one kind or another – light-fingered or otherwise. The adjacent bus yard also doubtlessly absorbs a certain amount of low-class labour, with a penchant for drunkenness and disorder. But the area, taken as a whole, is respectable and decent and, as stated, improving.

Walk 20

B364

Thursday 25th May 1899.
Ernest Aves with PC Sommersgill.

Starting from the north end of **Tabard Street**.
On the **W** is **Silvester Street**. Mainly block Dwellings on the north side. In addition, a common lodging house. Better south side than north. Here LIGHT BLUE to PURPLE. North side is LIGHT BLUE for Buildings and BLACK for lodging house. This was described as being occupied by the regular run, "not all thieves" but plenty of them. A policeman mobbed there about six months ago.

Napier Street (now Nebraska St). 2-st and 3-st houses. Uncoloured to PURPLE.

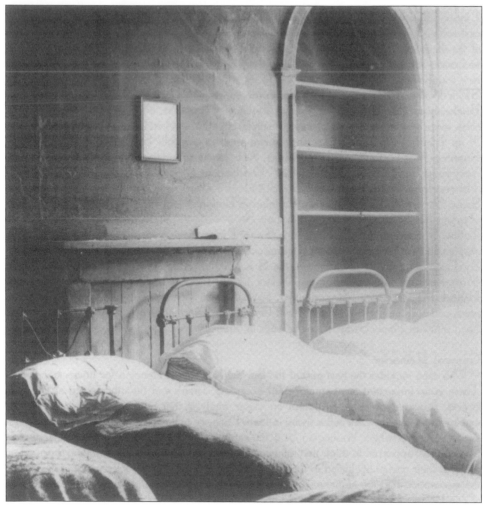

Beds crammed together in a typical common lodging house.

On the S side is **Babel Place** (now Pearl Place). 2-st houses. LIGHT BLUE as map.
Further S is **Globe Street**. 3-st houses and 2-st with attics. Re-fronted on north side, improved. Here from DARK BLUE to LIGHT BLUE. Omit bar on both sides but leave south side DARK BLUE.
On N side is **Violet Place**. Partly rebuilt. Globe Buildings (LIGHT BLUE) are 3-st houses. The rest are 2-st houses as before. DARK BLUE to LIGHT BLUE.
On the S side is **Warren Place**. 2-st houses. Costers, carmen, etc, as everywhere round here. From DARK BLUE to LIGHT BLUE. All these courts very much like Pearl Place.
Blackhorse Court. Public house on south side, two houses and a shop on the other. Here uncoloured to LIGHT BLUE. The Black Horse has recently changed hands, the late landlord having been convicted of selling drink to a drunken person.
Tabard Street. Remains very much as it was. The BLACK-barred line consists mainly of houses owned by a widow living somewhere in the neighbourhood. They are let out in rooms for single nights and short periods and are much used by prostitutes and shady people

generally. The bar remains here and on the opposite side of the street it should be added for a shorter row of houses used very much in the same ways. There are some common lodging houses in the street but nothing special is said against them. Vice, poverty and business jostle as usual in the street, which, with the addition of the barring mentioned, may remain PURPLE and PURPLE-barred as in the map. A portion of colour on the west side should be omitted for Dewrance's place.

Up Great Dover St. On the NE side is **George Court**, a back way to The George. Four 2-st cottages on north side. LIGHT BLUE as map. Omit colour on south side.

Continuing on Friday 26th May 1899.

Starting from the top of Long Lane.

On the S side is **St George's Place** (now Cardoll Place). 3-st buildings. Cul de sac. Some broken windows etc, but "pretty quiet". LIGHT BLUE as map.

Lower down is the entrance to a small network of courts and alleys: **Southall Place, Sarah Place, Henry Place**, where a half-drunken man wished to show me his rent book and prove he was not in arrears.

Sterry Street is a kind of main artery in this little world of 2-st houses with, on the south, Fisher's Buildings and Myers' Place, a tiny court of three houses with a very respectable woman in one mangling linen that looked clean and tidy and, on the north, Providence Place, very small houses white-washed on south side only, ending in a cul de sac. All these courts are coloured LIGHT BLUE except Henry Place which appears to be PURPLE and Providence Place which is DARK BLUE. But there is little or nothing to choose in the whole block. There were very few people about and an air of decent quiet prevailed. From PURPLE, DARK BLUE and LIGHT BLUE, to LIGHT BLUE throughout.

By Tabard St and S to **Fox's Buildings**. Clean. LIGHT BLUE as map.

On S side is **Fox's Court**. Very miserable, 4-roomed cottages. Rent 5/-. DARK BLUE as map.

St Stephen's Square. 3-st houses. PURPLE as map.

St Stephen's Place. Something like Fox's Court. DARK BLUE-barred as map. This court and the Square are a great gambling resort for boys on Sundays.

Wickham Gardens. 2-st houses. Cul de sac. Some broken windows, doors shut. PURPLE to LIGHT BLUE.

On the N is **Wickham Court**. A decent little spot but not PINK, LIGHT BLUE.

Board's Buildings (the passage leading to Amicable Row). DARK BLUE as map.

Castle Street (now Camelot St). LIGHT BLUE as map.

On the N side is **Little Britain**. Small and narrow. Houses on east side only. DARK BLUE as map.

Amicable Row. DARK BLUE as map.

Staple Street. LIGHT BLUE as map.

On the S side are openings with strange names leading into Delph St, the centre of the fish-curing trade just here. The first opening is **Stannage**. LIGHT BLUE as map. The second and third, **Uppermill** and **Dobbs' Cross**, are both poorer and more forlorn. Most of the dwellings appear to consist of two rooms only and in Uppermill the rent of one was 4/6. Both DARK BLUE, the PINK of the map goes out.

To the NE is **Walker Street**. Better. LIGHT BLUE to PURPLE.

Delph Street is the centre of interest here, however, and its fish-curing establishments give character to the little colony round. Many of the houses look miserable to a degree but there is probably a good deal of money going. In one of the establishments that we penetrated a

Fish curing in Delph Street.

buxom woman showed us round and we found fish galore and five or six men working. While in the street a smart pony drove up. Sommersgill had previously mentioned the good cattle that these curers possess. It was significant, too, that the driver of the cart had an evening paper with him and that a small throng at once gathered round him, eager for news as to the latest race or for the latest odds. LIGHT BLUE is still probably the best colour for the street. At the north west corner is a Ragged School. Close by and a considerable centre of employment is Pink's Factory.

A passage under one of their buildings, leads out of Staple St into **Minto Street**. Most of this is now taken up by Pink's extensions. The rest is PURPLE as map.

Chapel Place (leading out of Long Lane). A centre of the Wesleyan Mission, the leader of which, Mr Hopkins, Sommersgill spoke of as having done a deal of good work in the district. The houses in the Place at the south east corner are poorer than the rest but the whole may still remain PINK as map.

Long Lane. Some shops. It is hardly a PINK-barred street. A flourishing local tradesman (Fogden) has a house in which servants are kept but this is exceptional to the street. PINK-barred to PINK.

Weston Street. The boundary street on this side of the Borough subdivision of the police. PINK and PURPLE as map to Wilderness St but from this point the east like the west side becomes PURPLE. Two new small blocks have been built between Wilderness St and Rothsay St on the east side. Add PURPLE for them.

To the **NW** is **Little Hunter Street**. Some rebuilding but LIGHT BLUE as map.

N is **Paul's Cottages**. East side only. Little 2-roomed houses, one occupied by an old woman and her cat. She is a paper-sorter, a decent soul. Rented at 3/9. The Cottages are not coloured separately on the map and should be LIGHT BLUE. They lead nowhere and a large yard and the seclusion of the spot mark it out as a place for Sunday gambling.

By Tabard St into **Falstaff Yard**. 2-st houses with many broken windows. Untidy children, costers etc, but money said not to be scarce. LIGHT BLUE as map.

Clarendon Street (now Law St). A mixed class of people living in it, including some fish-curers, as in Delph St. Many very poor. 2-st houses. Leave LIGHT BLUE as map.

Herbert's Place (now part of Lansdowne Place) has a few miserable houses at the south corner. PURPLE to DARK BLUE here, a corresponding block north, PURPLE to LIGHT BLUE like Law St.

Lansdowne Place. 2-st houses, as in all this block. DARK BLUE as map. Said to be quieter than a few years ago.

Clarendon Place is now part of Westcott Street. Both are DARK BLUE as map.

Wilfrid Street, bisecting Law St, takes no separate colouring.

Henry Street (now Pardoner St). 2-st houses. Colour out on south side for school. Said to be rougher than Lansdowne Place but not so bad as Etham St. Thieves etc. LIGHT BLUE to DARK BLUE-barred. A beer-house here that has lost its license for opening at illegal hours.

Entering at the NE end of Etham Street. 2-st houses. Narrow, cobbled. An evil look about most of the people one saw but quiet and few signs of extreme poverty. Noticeable that the north east end, which is said to have the worst character, looked the best off. The street is "one of the darkest in the Borough". Thieves, prostitutes, ticket-of-leave men, etc. BLACK as map.

Red Cow Alley. The DARK BLUE patch near the Tabard St end is now closed. Omit colour.

General Remarks

Just as the area of the last walk took in the best parts of the Borough, so does this take in some of the worst, the streets lying between Tabard St and Long Lane making up an area than runs hard for notorious degradation, vice and poverty. The darkest streets lie to the west of the High St. The industrial features are the brush-making in and around Tabard St, fish-curing and Pink's big factories. The proximity and growth of such factories in the immediate neighbourhood of much cheap labour is a feature that has been previously noted in the cases of Nicholls and Coombes near Hackney Wick and Machonochie's in the Isle of Dogs. The goods yards off the Borough High St and the Borough Market account for much of the adult unskilled labour, while costers and hawkers abound.

Structurally there is little change in the district. The rebuilding and enlargement of Dewrance's engineering shops, and the extension of Pink's big places being the chief changes. There has been little or no change so far as dwellings are concerned and much of the district will doubtless form part of an "improvement" scheme before many years have gone by. On the whole the colours of the map stand and any improvement that can be shown appears to be that which is generally at work, making on the whole for less violence, intemperance and brutality. But much of all three remain.

Walk 21

B364

Monday 29th May 1899.
Ernest Aves with PC Sommersgill.

Starting from the St George's Church.
Along the High St and N to Angel Place. New buildings on south side and some houses closed on north. PURPLE out, part of PURPLE-barred remains as map.

The E continuation is Colliers' Rents. Very much like Angel Place. 3-st houses. A queer mixture of people, thieves etc. Both said to be somewhat improved. BLACK to PURPLE-barred. Lower down the houses are demolished on the right (PURPLE out). On the left is a Mission Hall and new 3-st buildings with attics. Poor, a queer lot of occupants. Sommersgill speaks of seeing women going home in the small hours of the morning etc. Uncoloured to LIGHT BLUE-barred.

Into Long Lane, to **Wilmott's Buildings**. DARK BLUE as map. Costers etc. Very poor but not shady like Colliers' Rents.

Skirting the churchyard is **Bangor Court**. Very much like Wilmott's Buildings. DARK BLUE as map but colour should be slightly extended on the north.

Through the Churchyard, which was at the moment, and is said to be, well used by the poor of the neighbourhood as a recreation ground, to the High St again. On the **S** is **Layton's Buildings**. 3-st houses with creepers. Respectable. PINK as map, but colouring in a somewhat different position. The opening leads into a large yard not patrolled by the police. Large gates are at the beginning of the private property, and Sommersgill said that these were often 'marked' by the police. In this case, the gates being wide, the 'marking' would be by pinning black cotton from side to side in such a position that if the gates are scaled the cotton gets displaced and a search can be instituted. Marking was, he said, a common practice, as with houses that are empty and in special charge of the police. Bent and interlocked pins, so fixed that the opening of a door or window would remove them and thus show that fastenings had been tampered with and that someone was at his night work, are often used and Sommersgill mentioned a dodge of his own by which a small piece of bent whale-bone was wedged in such a position that tampering or opening would release it and suspicion thus be roused. All these 'marks' when used are said to be removed at dawn. They seem sufficiently primitive and I do not suppose that these devices are very secret. But, as Sommersgill said, "We, of course, don't tell everybody".

A little further **N** is **Layton's Grove**. 2-st houses with three and four rooms. The rent of one of the latter was 8/-. A 3-st house at the end of the Grove is uncoloured on map and this should be LIGHT BLUE with the rest of the Grove (not PURPLE).

Along High St, past the **Half Moon Yard**, with the entrances to the public house of that name on either side and the quaint bridge connecting the building overhead – a bit of Old London.

To **Chapel Place**. 2-st houses and 2-st with attics. At the end is Trinity Buildings. 4-st. A good many broken windows but poverty not the prevailing impression. In two houses on south side about 12 women are said to be living. They are prostitutes but the house are not used as a brothel. Some thieves in the Buildings. DARK BLUE to LIGHT BLUE-barred.

Through a passage archway to **Mermaid Court**. 3-st and 4-st houses. One of the former, which has a small yard, is letting at 13/- a week. Very respectable woman tenant. Part sublet to one other family. The Court PINK and PURPLE as map, extra PINK on south side and LIGHT BLUE for the Trinity Buildings already mentioned, one entrance to which is in Mermaid Court. No barring here, better than the part in Chapel Place.

NE and unnamed on map is **Tennis Court**. Colour on east side only. 3-st houses. PINK to PURPLE.

In **The Ride** there is nothing but the back entrance to the Horse and Groom.

Bowling Green Lane. Schools, warehouses, etc. Houses are mainly 3-st. Respectable. PINK as map with extra at north west corner for a good 2-st house.

S to **Price's Buildings**. 2-st cottages with not forecourts but real gardens. A small oasis. PINK as map.

Newcomen Street. Mainly 3-st houses, some shops. Servants unlikely. PINK-barred to PINK. Down Crosby Row in which on the **W** are:

Surrey Place. Three 2-st houses on north side only, two with three rooms, one with five rooms. A decent woman occupying one of the smaller houses was paying 6/-. The court clean. DARK BLUE to LIGHT BLUE.

Bader Place. Rebuilt. Warehouses. Colour out.

Plantain Court. Unnamed on map. 2-st houses. Very much same class as Surrey Place. PURPLE to LIGHT BLUE. Some colour out for new warehouse.

Dove Place. Again much the same. Clean, flowers in window etc. DARK BLUE to LIGHT BLUE.

Crosby Row itself is 2-st and 3-st houses. PURPLE as map, with colour omitted on site of the Charterhouse Mission Church.

W along Long Lane to **Laxon Court**. 3-st Buildings on the right. LIGHT BLUE. One PINK 2-st house on the left and one built up.

Further W is **George Place** (now Balin Place). 2-st houses with forecourts. Dozens of children, few ragged. LIGHT BLUE as map.

E of Crosby Row is **Laxon Street**, leading to the Board School. 2-st houses. PINK as map. Returning N up Crosby Row to the E is **Trinity Place**. PURPLE to LIGHT BLUE with omission of colour for space occupied by Charterhouse Mission. This is a queerly-shaped building, with church and club-rooms combined. Sommersgill at first assured me it was a Roman Catholic Church but there seemed doubt about it and in Trinity Place I asked again. Two women made a shot, one saying "Puseyan" and the other some further corruption of Carthusian. In another cottage were two other women, one of whom proved to be a strong Protestant from Cornwall, "the same county as he comes from" meaning the missioner in charge. "He ought to know better than to run about to other churches besides his own. He goes as far as he dare and further than he ought. I have no patience with him." The other woman was a Catholic and she listened, saying little to the indignation of her friend. It did not appear that on the whole the Mission was making very great headway in Trinity Place.

Into **Porlock Place** with an outlet south to Kipling St. 2-st houses. PURPLE to LIGHT BLUE.

Careth Place. Not shown on map (late Union Place). Narrow cul de sac. 4-room cottages. One letting at 7/6. DARK BLUE.

Cusack Place (late Cottage Place). Not properly shown on map. 2-st cottages. DARK BLUE or LIGHT BLUE.

Snows Fields. From the west end to Kipling St on the south side is PINK-barred to PINK. Shops etc. On the north side from Great Maze Pond to Weston St are some poor shops and little old houses, many of them with very poor occupants. PINK to PURPLE.

Kipling Street (late Nelson St). PINK for the Buildings and PURPLE as map. The Buildings are an old block of the Metropolitan Association (1855). Good class of tenants, always let, so said the caretaker, a very quiet and capable Scotchman. "I can pick and choose." Three rooms are let for from 5/9 to 7/6, four rooms from 6/3 to 8/6. When he came arrears were £30. This was 14 years ago and now arrears are a few shillings only. Many pay in advance; then the practice was unknown.

Out of Kipling St are:

Edmund Place. 2-st houses, cul de sac. PINK to PURPLE.

Rudyard Place (late Alfred Place). 2-st houses. PURPLE as map. "We've got a fine name now, haven't we?" said a woman living here, "Rudyard" with all the emphasis on the second syllable. I thought at first that the authorities appeared to her to have been guilty of a foolish redundance in calling the spot a place as well as a yard, but she aired her knowledge the next moment by saying "Rudyard Kipling" in a tone half of scorn and half of amusement, mouthing, as it were, some strange thing.

On the W side of Kipling St is **Lockyer Street** (late West St). 2-st houses. LIGHT BLUE as map with some colour out for the school.

Continuing on Tuesday 30th May 1899.

E of Nelson St (now Kipling St) is **Richardson Street**. 2-st houses, flush with sidewalk. PURPLE (good type) as map. A gap in the houses on the west side.

Guy Street. 2-st and 2½-st houses. PINK as map. New recreation ground just opened at north west corner.

Weston Street. Mainly 2-st houses with forecourts. North of the Market the east side is a clearance. Also at other points colour to be omitted for new leather warehouses.

The SW angle is called **Molesworth Square**. 1844. Very respectable. All the street, save omissions, is PINK as map, except two larger houses on west side midway between Guy St and Snows Fields. These have a poor tenement house look. PINK to LIGHT BLUE.

S of Molesworth Square is **Weston Place**. 2-st houses with creepers. Forecourts, no gardens. Paved and no way for vehicles. Respectable. PINK as map to Short St. Below this point on the east side are four 3-st houses, rather unkempt. Some broken windows. Dirty women, have a bad reputation with the police for drinking etc, not crime. PINK to LIGHT BLUE or DARK BLUE. On the west side a new 3-st house (good) has been built (a builder's) and the PINK might be extended somewhat to indicate this.

Round the corner, leading out of Long Lane is **Valentine Place**. Cul de sac. Bread in street. Asphalted, entered by paved archway. 3-st houses. Quiet, some poor looking windows and untidy women. Occupiers a very mixed class. PINK to PURPLE.

NW to Great Maze Pond. On the left is **Holcombe Buildings**. 2-st. Belong to Guys and they are getting their own employees in to a great extent. Others are riverside workers etc. Spoke to one woman who had been there for 30 years. Her rent is 5/9, others now pay 7/- but hers will not be raised. Her husband is 76 and she is 72 and the former is still good for a day's work. He is a sail hand at Hays Wharf. His dinner was cooking ready to be sent – three quarters of a pound of steak and a suet pudding, and he will eat it "every bit...He has a good appetite, and a good digestion, thank God." PINK as map.

After marking the licensed places in the stations (SER and LB & SC) we went down the steps to the end of **Joiners Street**. A good deal of the street runs under the railway arches and turns in the middle making a dark angle. Prostitutes used to give a good deal of trouble here, soliciting etc. Mostly for low class and working men but others for students at Guys'. Much improved of late and these complaints are rather of the past.

E of New St is **Maze Pond Terrace** (Steel Yard on map). A public house and a row of good lodging houses. Students here mainly. RED to PINK-barred.

Maze Pond. 3-st plus attics on north side only. PURPLE as map. No RED which is not intended to indicate any houses in this street.

S is **Great Maze Court**. Cul de sac. Paved. From DARK BLUE and PURPLE to LIGHT BLUE on both sides.

A narrow passage leads to **Maze Court** (not shown separately on map). DARK BLUE to LIGHT BLUE.

An archway leads out into Maze Pond and **Dean Street**, which should go like Maze Pond Terrace from RED to PINK-barred (Customs office etc).

To the S of Great Maze Court is **Sparrick Row**. 3-st houses. PINK as map.

W of Weston St is **St Thomas' Street**. Need have no colour east of Guys, unless the public house at the Dean St corner be shown. The rest of the coloured part is offices etc. West of Guys are some good private houses with doctors etc living there. RED as map. On the uncoloured north side, a little east of the church is one private house, good, a parson's, Sommersgill thought. A spot of RED might be added here.

General Remarks

Conditions have been again fairly stationary in the area covered by this walk, but stationary at a higher level than in the preceding. Neither Guy's Hospital nor the railway termini appear to have any great effect upon the class of people living in the neighbourhood, although the effect of the former is traced in the doctors living in St Thomas St, in the students who lodge in Steel Yard and in the occupants of Holcombe Buildings. There has been little building, less than might have been expected in a district that is so near to London Bridge and to the City. Working class dwellings are still, with few exceptions, 2-st and 3-st houses. Block dwellings are few and far between. This fact, combined with the inclusion of the termini, the Hospital, the carmen and contractors' yards including many belonging to the railways, together with a considerable number of business and non-residential premises, prevents the people from being very thick on the ground.

The general impression left by a survey of this half of the Borough, lying east of the High St, is that it has been too much depreciated in the press and in public opinion and that, in spite of the part lying between Tabard St and Long Lane, it is not an area that presents problems of a social and administrative kind in any peculiar degree. Excessive drinking and the increase of gambling and betting, rather than crime and professional vice, appear to be the most prevalent weaknesses. Sommersgill has known the district well for some 10 years and when we finished the Tabard St area he was emphatic in expressing his opinion that the signs of improvement were undoubted. There was less wife-beating, less fighting, less violence and less drunkenness, although in all these respects there was plenty of room for still further improvement and at one point in the walk he hinted that "one ought to come on Saturday night to see the real character of the people". The police patrol everywhere alone and have done so for some years.

Sommersgill hardly ever condemned the management of any particular public house, although he occasionally mentioned some offence that a previous landlord had committed. The roughness of some of the houses was traced rather to their connexion and surroundings than to their management. But he was clear that there are far too many of them, "too many by three-fourths" as he once said, and he mentioned that at one fixed point on their ground there are 13 houses within a stone's throw.

A chance incident on May 30th threw light on the action of the police in enforcing the law that forbids the serving of a drunken person or allowing him to be on the premises. Just as we came up to the public house in Maze Pond Terrace, late Steel Yard, a man (a navvy) came out, reeling and spewing in abject beastliness up the pavement and making his way to the pub urinal. He was in there a minute or two and I waited to see if he would return to the house. He did and again I waited to see if he would be served. In a minute or so I noticed another man offering him beer and then we moved away. It appeared then that Sommersgill had seen the man who offered beer also order whisky or some spirits for himself and I asked Sommersgill what he would have done in the case had he been on duty. The answer was not quite clear, but it was evident that the course most often pursued is to point out the man who is drunk to the publican and prevent him from being served. When any step at all is taken it appears that in the vast majority of cases the matter begins and ends in this way. If any charge is made against the publican the precaution is always taken of having a witness and every case is apparently defended in the courts by the Legal Protection Society of the Trade. The police are, therefore, uncommonly cautious before taking any serious step. The case that we had seen was, however, so clearly an offence that Sommersgill began to have quickenings of his official conscience, just as I had had of my public one, and he asked me if I wished him to take further action in the matter. This was rather a poser as neither had we time at the moment nor did I want to be mixed up in the affair and called as a witness. Eventually, however, we went back to the house and I expected that Sommersgill would have gone straight in and made his complaint. But not a bit of it. We must, he said, see the man drink, but this at the moment he appeared to have no intention of doing and we again moved on without any step being taken.

This time I had quite decided to give the matter up but as soon as we got away Sommersgill's anxiety returned and I realised how mortally afraid he was lest his superiors should hear anything of what had happened and of his neglect of what, although he was told off for special work with me, he still clearly regarded as his duty. He even feared punishment and loss of his hoped-for promotion. Eventually, as the simplest thing to do, I went in myself and spoke to the barman in charge, the publican being at the moment absent. He was quite alive to the offence of which he was guilty, was a good deal perturbed, extremely grateful and said that the man should be put out at once, shouting for the chucker-out who came from the recesses of the house at the word. A minute later, and the navvy, the man who had offered him the beer and a small boy of about twelve, apparently the son of the latter, came out (the two former quite drunk, although not helplessly so) and reeled out of sight, perhaps to another public house. The incident happened at the dinner hour, we having first seen the man at about 1.10. Our share in it took perhaps ten or fifteen minutes. The house when I entered it was quite full and so far as I could tell, save for the two sots, the trade being done was legitimate.

In talking the matter over with Sommersgill afterwards I suggested that the incident ought to be reported and a black mark registered against the house. Again Sommersgill was on tenterhooks for he appeared to fear that if he made any report and the matter was inquired into he would be considered to have condoned an offence and for that again punishment might be serious. Eventually he said that he would make a report but whether this was done or not I cannot say. He appeared to think that I might let someone in authority know of what had happened, and his fear of consequences, even if he made his own report, seemed to show that if any such incident as that which we had seen does get down in black and white the action taken by the officer who reports is very closely scrutinised. On the other hand, save under the most exceptional and flagrant circumstances when inaction would be almost impossible or, perhaps the more likely case, when it is thought that witnesses would report such inaction, it appears that the police would be very unlikely to take any serious step, other perhaps that of pointing out the man who ought not to be served, should they be on the spot when a man obviously drunk entered licensed premises.

Walk 22   B364

Monday 5th June 1899.
Ernest Aves with PC Watts.
Watts is a thorough-going policeman, heavy in build, in manner and in tread. He has been in the district for about 10 years and knows it intimately. Like Sommersgill he was not talkative but he appeared straightforward. He is one of the many who go through their service without being promoted and, although he perhaps would not have been successful had he done so, he professes not to have "troubled" himself in the matter. He appeared to have a grudge against the Force inasmuch as it is using the best years of his life and if he saw a chance of getting out of it he would. But he not going "to throw his years of service away" and the pension they will ultimately bring him. I liked him and, although perhaps less capable and certainly less ambitious than Sommersgill, he was a sturdier fellow.

S down **Hobman Street** (late William St). Much poorer, some very poor. LIGHT BLUE as map.

W along **Maynard Road**. 2-st. Loose stones, mess, broad street. Poor, houses flush with pavement. LIGHT BLUE to PURPLE, in map PURPLE.

S & E at **Trident Street**. 2-st. Rough, dirty children, out at knees and elbows, boots bad, well fed, smell of dirt. Some flowers at windows. LIGHT BLUE, in map PURPLE.

S into **Plough Road**. Broad road. South side better than the north. One or two master lightermen and a doctor with a general servant but as a whole servantless. PINK rather than PINK-barred of map. There is a new bridge and a new approach to it since ten years ago at the east end.

S down **Yeoman Street**. 2-st. Poor, mixed. PURPLE, in map PINK.

W along **Chilton Street**. 2-st. Few poor, pretty fronts. PINK to PURPLE, in map PURPLE.

S down **Croft Street**. Not so good as Chilton St but PINK as map, except the east end which joins Chilton St and Croft St and should be PURPLE, in map PINK.

W and N up **Lower Road**. Shops fair. PINK-barred as map.

W along New Rd and S down **Oldfield Road**. 3-st, mixed. Laundries. North of Eugenia Rd is PURPLE as map. 2½-st south of Eugenia Rd, better, PINK as map.

W along **Fawcett Street**. 2-st with bow windows on ground floor. PINK to PURPLE, in map PINK.

S down **Alpine Road**. 2-st. Small shops at south west end. PINK as map.

E along **Cornbury Road**. Not so good. Some sore-eyed and dirty children. Mixed. PURPLE to LIGHT BLUE, in map PURPLE.

Like it is **Reculver Road**. 2-st. PURPLE to LIGHT BLUE, in map PURPLE.

And also **Walker Road** and **Rudford Road**.

W to **Goodson Road**. South side down for railway extension. North side remains poor. LIGHT BLUE as map. Only an "off" licence remains on the south side with men drinking outside on the pavement.

St Helena Estate. The above roads from Oldfield Rd to Goodson Rd all belong to the St Helena Estate. The southernmost are worse owing to the turning in of the demolished inhabitants of Goodson Rd and the turning out of the better PINK to the new roads (probably those north of Deptford Park). Cornbury Rd, Reculver Rd, Edale Rd and Rudford Rd are all a bad PURPLE or a good LIGHT BLUE. Always two families to a house and some overcrowding. Very few Irish but many 'drunks' from this area, both men and women. Cockett thinks them a shade worse than Manor Lane and Reed St. "Some would let a family into one room."

General Remarks

The poor parts in this round are: Little Cherry Garden St, Prospect Place, Lillington St, Debnams Rd, Manor Lane and the southern half of the St Helena Estate. Debnam's Rd is and was the worst. The rest are, if anything, better than ten years ago.

Apart from these, which only form small patches, there is decided improvement. PINK prevails between Southwark Park and the LB&SC Railway. Well-built streets with fair gardens, near the park and within reach of the City owing to new buses over the Tower Bridge. Have more than held their own and the tendency is from PURPLE to PINK as against the usual 'London Rule' of PINK to PURPLE.

With the exception of a few shops there are practically no servant-keepers in Rotherhithe. The great feature of the district is the amount of air and space. Streets are broad, houses low, gardens long and Southwark Park within easy reach. Beyond the Park are the open docks.

As compared with the Island it is well above high water and dry.

The main Industry is ships, shipping, wood, wharves, dock work for men. Peak Frean's Biscuit Works for the women. Jamaica Rd and Southwark Park Rd are the shopping streets.

Walk 31   B367

Thursday 27th July 1899.
George Duckworth with PC William Cockett.

Starting in the north west corner at Bush Road.
Bush Road. 2-st. Mixed. PURPLE to PINK, in map PINK.
W along Midway Place. East end less good than west where it turns south by the railway with gardens and is PINK as map.
S & W at Lee Terrace. 2-st. Poor, dock labourers. LIGHT BLUE as map.
E along Bestwood Street (late Bush Rd). 2-st with front gardens. Many poor. PURPLE to LIGHT BLUE, in map PURPLE.
S down Lower Rd and W into Crooke Road. 2-st. PINK to PURPLE, in map PINK.
S under railway bridge to a block of new streets at the north, west and south sides of Deptford Park. All working class. Alloa Road, Crooke Road, Hicks Road on the north side, Scawen Road on the west side, Grinstead Road on the south side. All comfortable, servantless and PINK. Built in 1897. Grinstead Rd is still building. The west end is built for a better class than the east which is too near the noise of Braby's Zinc & Iron Works to attract a good class. The west end is PINK. The east is PINK at present but will soon be PURPLE. Deptford Park in the centre is a broad, open, flat, green space. Full of children this afternoon, hardly anyone there above 12 years of age except the policemen and caretaker. Attempts at flowers and shrubs at the corner and in one place near the centre.
E into the Lower Road. New houses built along the Park on the west side. PINK.
W along Grinstead Road. As yet unmade and full of ridges and furrows.
N up Trundley's Road. A new Board School at south east end. PINK as map. On west side is a bone boiler and animal charcoal maker, smell awful. North of the railway bridge are new houses on east side, PINK, and north of them are some older, PURPLE to PINK, PURPLE in map. The new houses are 2-st, red brick, for two families. The upstairs reach their rooms by a staircase at the end of the passage, the downstairs by a door at bottom of the stairs.
E along Bestwood St. S down Lower Rd. E along Colwick Street (late Albion St). Mixed. PURPLE as map.
S down Clarence Street. Poor. Houses on east side. LIGHT BLUE, in map PURPLE.
S into Windmill Lane. PURPLE as map.
S to Kempslade Street and Stowick Street. 2-st. Mechanics and lightermen. Comfortable. PINK as map.
E over Windmill Bridge along Windmill Lane. Less good here. Rough workers in Scott's tin works in Hanlon St. 2-st. LIGHT BLUE to PURPLE. New houses on north east. PURPLE to PINK.
N up Sayers Street. Poorer. 2-st. Tar and whitening workers. LIGHT BLUE to DARK BLUE, in map LIGHT BLUE.
E & N up Grove Sreet. No houses except occasional publics. At the corner of London St (PURPLE in map) the houses – not the public – are down so PURPLE of map goes.
This is the southern limit of this police division. Further north we re-enter District 33.

Walk 32   B367

Friday 28th July 1899.
George Duckworth with PC William Cockett.

Starting at the west end of Union Road.
E & N up **Prospect Place**. 2-st. Poor, mess, old clothes. Gasworker and dockers. One very
poor double-fronted house at the north west end. LIGHT BLUE to DARK BLUE, in map PURPLE.
E & S down **Staples Rents**. 18 houses. Narrow. Children dirty. One pays 6/- for four
rooms plus wash-house with a small room over wash-house. Was raised 6d three years ago
but not since. On the west side is a 3-roomed house which pays 6/6 but the occupants are
always in and out. LIGHT BLUE, in map PURPLE.
E & N up **Cathay Street** (late Lucas St). 3-st and 2-st. Only one poor house at south
west end. PINK to PURPLE, in map PURPLE.
W along **Paradise Street**. On the south side is a yard opposite Braddon St where
Pickford's have a depot. Only a foreman living over. PINK, in map PURPLE.
S into **Union Road**. Tramway, shops. North side less good than south. PINK and PINK-
barred, in map PINK-barred and RED.
E past Culling Rd and S down **Paradise Place**. Dockers. 3-st, six houses only, on east side.
Poor. Small front gardens, cared for and some full of flowers, others bare. LIGHT BLUE as map.
N up Market Place, E & S down **Rezia Place**. 2-st, eight houses on east side only. Bare
and poor, ill cared for fronts. "Four rooms 5/9, was 4/9 20 years ago", has been there 23
years. Walled off at south end. DARK BLUE to LIGHT BLUE, in map LIGHT BLUE.
N up **Princes Street**. Built 1726. Handsome old Queen Anne houses, used to belong to
ships' captains, carved door posts, panelled passages, 3-st. Cobble-paved street, much mixed.
Lodging house on the west side. PURPLE as map.
S & E along **St Mary Church Street**. Shops. PURPLE to PINK, in map PINK.
N up **Elephant Lane**. 2-st plus attic. Watermen. PURPLE to LIGHT BLUE, in map LIGHT
BLUE.
E along Rotherhithe Lane and S down by **St Mary's Church**. Now shut out from the
river by rumbling flour mills. The churchyard is full of trees and tombstones, greenery and
birds. Square box tomb and headstones crushed together, the legends on them dark and
crumbling, partly illegible, of captains and their relations. One Captain H Wilson
commanded the Hon East India Company's packet the *Antelope*, which was wrecked in the
Pelew Islands in the month of August 1783 and was wonderfully preserved together with all
the ship's company in a land infrequented and unknown. "Reader, Reckon on thy life and the
days that are past and thou will most assuredly…" the rest is blank. On the south side of
Church St is the Rectory and the St Mary watch-house and a school with small figures of
the scholars over the door and a garden full of weeds and flowers. It is a free school founded
in 1613 and removed here in 1797.
S down **St Mary's Place**. Twenty 2-st houses plus attic, red-tiled, each with three rooms
plus kitchen, no wash-house. One pays 7/6 for her house, has been there nine months.
Children poor, many old inhabitants who have been there 20 or 30 years. PURPLE to LIGHT
BLUE, in map PURPLE.
E along Rotherhithe St and S down **Railway Avenue**, which is just E of the Tunnel.
Nine houses, 2-st, on east side only. South end better than the north. Oar and mast maker's
yard occupies west side. LIGHT BLUE to PURPLE, in map LIGHT BLUE.

S into Adam St. W & N up **Hatteraick Street**. Very poor. 2-st. DARK BLUE as map. Out of the **NE** end is **Nolan Place**. 3-st and 2-st. Cement court, all doors open, very rough and dirty. Barefoot children, young wives, hour midday, 11 children in the court. Windows broken and patched. Waterside, gas and dock casuals. DARK BLUE, in map LIGHT BLUE. **W** along **Adams Gardens**. Some stand back at north east end, 2-st. Messy uncared for fronts. A small hall is on the north side whose stone was laid by Field Marshal Sir William Gomm, lord of the manor of Rotherhithe. Adams Gardens is dated 1822. LIGHT BLUE, in map PURPLE.

W & S down **Eve Place**. LIGHT BLUE as map.

W & N up **Oran Place** (late Adam Place). Poorer, 2-st. Back to back with Eve Place. Mess of bread. One pays 4/6 for two rooms plus wash-house, "all different landlords down here, don't know about the others". DARK BLUE, in map LIGHT BLUE.

S into **Adam Street**. Mixed. PURPLE as map.

S down **Neptune Street**. Also mixed and PURPLE as map. Out of the **W** side is **Thetford Place**. North end better than the south. 2-st. Cement road. LIGHT BLUE to DARK BLUE, in map DARK BLUE.

S down Neptune St and W at **Irwell Place**. Narrow, 2-st, with Frederick Court out of its west side. Much DARK BLUE but rooms full of furniture. Gas and dock labourers. 5/- for two rooms plus wash-house, has been there three years. LIGHT BLUE to DARK BLUE, in map DARK BLUE.

Out of the **E** side of Neptune St is **Risdon Street**. New at north west end, 2-st plus attic. The rest is 2-st. Full of children, mess of paper, no bread. Children out at knees and elbow but all well fed, no sore eyes, faces very dirty, boots bad, dancing to a barrel organ. Women with sack or dirty white aprons and bare arms. Struggling pots and tins of flowers at the windows. Built 1821. 12 ft frontage. DARK BLUE as map.

S down **Elton Street** (late Lipton Court). Runs both north-south and east-west. 10/- for four rooms plus two kitchens, has been there five months. All waterside labourers, casual, not poor now because work has been good. Dirty, bandy-legged, hatless children. The east-west bit is rather better. No houses on north side, 2-st houses on south. One pays 7/6 for four rooms plus garret and wash-house, has been there five years. Was raised 1/- four months ago, she came in at 6/6. All waterside labourers. DARK BLUE to LIGHT BLUE, in map DARK BLUE.

E & N up **Renforth Street** which is 2-st and like it. DARK BLUE to LIGHT BLUE, in map DARK BLUE. Improves near Albion St.

N & E along Albion St. **S** down **Hadland Street**. 2-st. Houses on west only. Mixed but a good PURPLE. PURPLE to PINK, in map PURPLE.

E & S down **Clack Street** (late Berkeley St). PURPLE to PINK, in map PURPLE.

N into Albion St. On the **N** side opposite the Board School is **Gooch Place**. 3-st. Very poor. DARK BLUE, in map LIGHT BLUE.

E along **Albion Street** which is a broad cobble-paved, 2-st, yellow-brick street. Mixed. PURPLE as map.

S down **Temeraire Street**. 2-st. PURPLE to PINK, in map PURPLE. At the south end are two 1-st hovels. LIGHT BLUE as map. Ships' masts tower over the dock wall at the end of the street.

E & N up **Swan Lane**. 2-st. Poor. PURPLE to LIGHT BLUE, in map PURPLE. Road broad, metal ill-laid but kept sufficiently clean.

W along **Kenning Place**. Fourteen 2-st houses on south only. Bread lying about and barefoot children. LIGHT BLUE as map.

E along **Ainsty Street**. 2-st. Poor but not very poor. Street well asphalted. One woman pays 6/6 for a house with two rooms up and two down and small wash-house. This, she said, is the usual price on the east side of the street. Houses on the west side with the same amount of room go at 5/6 and two of them at 7/6 (same rooms). She has been there five years, was raised 6d three years ago last May. All waterside and dockers here, she said, only one gas stoker. North end of street better than the south. On the whole LIGHT BLUE as map.

At the S end is **Seth Street**. 2-st. PURPLE to LIGHT BLUE, in map PURPLE.

W across Swan Lane at the SW end of which is **Sarah Place**. LIGHT BLUE to PURPLE, in map PURPLE.

E along Seth St, across Clarence St and E along **Clarence Place**. Now called Loat Place. Decent poor. LIGHT BLUE to PINK, in map LIGHT BLUE.

N up **Oak Place**. 3-st. Flagged passage. Gasworkers, clean faces and well fed. 4/6 for three rooms plus wash-house for old tenants, others go at 5/-. LIGHT BLUE to DARK BLUE, in map DARK BLUE.

N up **Forsyth Street**. 2-st. Broad, like Oak Place. West side better than east. A little PINK but more LIGHT BLUE. Paper, bread and mess in street, all doors open, windows unbroken. LIGHT BLUE to PURPLE, in map PURPLE.

N up **Neston Street**. Like Forsyth St but narrower. LIGHT BLUE as map.

E & S down **Brunel Street** (late Wyndham St). Five 2-st houses facing south. All doors open. PURPLE to LIGHT BLUE, in map PINK.

S down **Kinburn Street**. 2-st houses on west only. Many poor. PURPLE as map.

N into Rotherhithe St, E across the **Lower Entrance** to the Surrey Docks. On the south side are poor houses, LIGHT BLUE, in map PURPLE.

S down **Parnell Place**. 2-st plus attic, old houses, some wooden tile roofs. 7/- for five rooms and wash-house. LIGHT BLUE, in map PURPLE.

Out of the E side is **Charlotte Place**. Poorer. Four 2-st houses. DARK BLUE to LIGHT BLUE, in map LIGHT BLUE.

E along Rotherhithe St past a **closed court** (LIGHT BLUE in map), no name, with a notice over the locked entrance: "Public right of way: keys at Vestry Office."

E & S down **Reid's Place**. Three 2-st houses, very poor. DARK BLUE, not coloured in map.

E & S down **Mistears Buildings**. 3-st houses. Narrow court. Only 13 ft between house walls. Barefoot, dirty children. 6/6 for four rooms and wash-house on west side, has been there five years without a rise. 6/- on east side. LIGHT BLUE as map.

E & S down **St Paul's Lane**. Old wooden house at north west end, a very dilapidated and broken-windowed school on the east side. Mixed. PURPLE rather than PINK of map.

E & S down **Beatson St** (late Globe St). 2-st on west side, 5-st poor Buildings on east. Leads to pleasant gardens. PURPLE to LIGHT BLUE, in map PURPLE.

E & S down **Essex Place**. Seven 2-st creeper-covered houses with front gardens, neat, quiet, many flowers. LIGHT BLUE or PINK, in map PURPLE.

E & S down **Lavender Lane**. Two poor houses at north east, LIGHT BLUE. PINK to PURPLE on south, in map PINK.

N into **Rotherhithe Street**. Old-fashioned, many public houses, not very busy, mixed. PURPLE as map. Rather better at the turn east of the Lavender Dock and might here be PINK. Out of the E side by Cuckold's Point and Stairs are **Horn's Cottages**. Fairly comfortable, used to be a licensed house here but licence has been taken away. PINK, not coloured in map.

W & S down **Silver Street**. North end 3-st, older and poorer than the new 2-st houses at the south west. Houses on west side only. PURPLE and LIGHT BLUE, instead of LIGHT BLUE of map.

E & S down Rotherhithe St. W at **Cow Lane**. Very poor but south side better than north. DARK BLUE, in map PURPLE.

N up **Faustin Place**. 2-st and 3-st. Very poor. South west end down and now a wilderness of brickbat. Mess of bread, children very dirty and many barefoot, doors open, windows broken. Casual waterside labourers. One woman pays 8/- for six rooms and wash-house and has been there nine years without a rise. Another pays 6/- for four rooms. There is a rough Irish look about the inhabitants.

S down Rotherhithe St. N up **Trinity Road**. Small houses stand back on east side. PURPLE to PINK, in map PINK.

Off the E side are courts called **Mariner's Buildings** and **Bryant's Place**. These are an odd collection of 3-st 3-roomed cottages, one room above the other reached by steep wooden staircase. Poor and very poor, all work at the Docks. Mostly barefoot and bare-headed, boots very bad. For the three rooms and wash-house one pays 3/6.

The N end of Trinity Rd turns abruptly W and was called Acorn Place, now **Trinity Road**. New houses at west end. Poor, rough, all casuals. Smell of dirt, 'a few Irish'. Barefoot dirty children. One said "That window was broken by my mother last night". DARK BLUE, in map LIGHT BLUE.

S & E along **Odessa Street** (late Thames St). Poor at south west end, here LIGHT BLUE. Foreman's home on east PINK. As a whole perhaps PURPLE or LIGHT BLUE and PINK. At the extreme south end is a ship captain's or boat builder's house, probably servants, PINK or RED.

W along **Randells Rents**. Houses on south side only. Quiet. PURPLE, in map PINK.

N up **Derrick Street**. 2-st plus attic. Mixed. Old-fashioned, clean, red tiled. Danish names to the shops, a decent Danish restaurant on the west side. Demand from sailors and officers of timber ships. PURPLE to PINK, in map PURPLE.

Out of the SE end are **Sedger's Buildings**. Eight houses, 3-st. Poor, rooms fairly full of furniture, flagged court. LIGHT BLUE to DARK BLUE, in map LIGHT BLUE.

N of it is **Castle's Buildings**. Five houses on south only, 2-st. Poorer than Sedger's. One pays 4/6 for three rooms, one down and two up, no wash-house nor copper. Used to pay 4/- but was raised last Christmas. Another still pays 4/-. DARK BLUE as map.

W along **Elgar Street**. Houses, 3-st, on north side. Poor and very poor. LIGHT BLUE to DARK BLUE, in map DARK BLUE.

N up **Elgar Street**, 2-st. Mixed. PURPLE rather than PINK of map.

S along a passage between walls and across the **Greenland Dock** which is now dry and full of cranes, steam engines and trucks, its depth being increased to admit of larger vessels. Much trade expected to result from it.

S & W along **London Street**. New docks being built on either side, others full of shipping, sailing and steam. A one-horse bus runs down the road. At the corner of Grove St only the public house remains. PURPLE of map goes.

N up **Swing Bridge Road**. Only two houses inhabited. One on west by an old servant-keeping family. RED as map. Another by dock engineer on east.

W over Plough Bridge, along Plough Rd. N up **Lower Road**. Less busy than it used to be, trade left when the barrows were removed at the instance of the shopkeepers. PINK-barred, in map RED.

Out of the E side is **Cottage Place**. Two 2-st cottages. Very poor. DARK BLUE as map.

N & W into **Richard's Place**. PINK as map.

N of it is **Orange Place**. Six 2-st houses on south side only. Built four years ago. PINK, in map LIGHT BLUE.

Off the E side of Lower Rd is **Hothfield Place** (late Portland Place). 2-st. PINK to PURPLE, in map PINK.

N & W into a small block of respectable, no-servants streets:

Gomm Road. PINK, in map PINK-barred.

Rebecca's Place. PINK, in map PINK-barred.

Henwood Street. PINK as map. In all three two families per house is usual.

N & W into **Somerset Place.** LIGHT BLUE to PURPLE, in map PURPLE. Full of flowers growing from uncared for beds.

N & W into **Wells Tenements**, leading to St Olave's Union Infirmary. 2-st. Poor. LIGHT BLUE as map.

N & W into **Claremont Place.** Built 1818. 2-st with well cared for flowered fronts. Fowl house, green house at south west. PINK to PURPLE, in map PURPLE.

N past new large Tewis Theatre which takes up the block of Lower Rd between Culling Rd and Claremont Place. E along **Moodkee Street**. Comfortable. Large town hall takes up west end between Neptune St and Moodkee St. Delete LIGHT BLUE of map. Moodkee St is PINK as map.

N & W up **Culling Road**. 2-st, two bow windows, most with two families. Like the PINK roads off Grove Rd in Bow. 15/- per week. A good PINK rather than PINK-barred of map. This finishes District 33 and with it the eastern limits of the 'M' Police Division.

General Remarks

District 33 is bounded on the north by River Thames, east by River Thames, south by London St, Eugenia Rd, Rotherhithe New Rd, Roles Rd and west by Upper Grange Rd, Grange Rd, Spa Rd, Neckinger St, Gedling St and St Saviour's Dock.

It is poor the whole length of the River boundary, on either side of the Lower Rd at the south west corner of the Docks and on the west side off Dockhead and Spa Rd. The Dockhead and Spa Rd area consists of Bermondsey Poverty, ie. tan yard men and other poor crushed out from inner London. There is distinct worsement in the courts off the south side of the Spa Rd (Parker's Buildings, Vauban St etc).

The Riverside Poverty shows no change. It lies between Jamaica Rd and the River and the Docks and the River. Irish, casual, waterside labourers preponderate between Jamaica Rd and the River and these are mixed with Gasworks Poverty between Albion Rd and the river. The circle of Casual Poverty continues all round the Docks in the courts and streets off Rotherhithe St and off the south west corner of the Docks.

All the remainder is fairly comfortable, strictly working class, and is unlike any other part of London so near the centre in that there is a distinct tendency for the PURPLE of the map to become PINK instead of vice versa. The reasons for this improvement lie in

1. The greater accessibility to the City given by the Tower Bridge.

2. The abundance of small houses with gardens, likely to appeal to the fairly comfortable.

3. Comparatively lower rents.

4. The great open spaces (Southwark Park and the Docks) which, coupled with the lowness of the houses, give Rotherhithe more light and fresh air than any other central district.

East of St Mary Church St and Lower Rd Rotherhithe is very like, both in character and formation, the Island, only turned the other way up. Each is surrounded on three sides by the River, each has a centre of docks and each is bounded by a high street off which are turnings where both very poor and fairly comfortable inhabit. Both are shut off from the rest of the world. They differ in that Rotherhithe is higher and healthier than the Island, sailing ships are more frequent than steam and Rotherhithe boasts fewer factories.

Southwark Park Rd and Jamaica Rd are the two great market streets. Lower Rd lost most of its business on the removal of the costers' barrows. Of the three, Southwark Park Rd is the busiest and the best. There is no recognised Sunday market. Those who wish to buy on Sundays have to go to the Bermondsey New Rd where business is done until 1 or 2 pm.

In Jamaica Rd this day (July 28th) prices ruled per pound: for good chops 6d, scraps 3d, fair bits of meat 2d, steak 10d, cherries 4d, gooseberries 3d, bread 4lb 4½d.

For dock work there is some influx from Deptford. The regular place of engagement is at the corner of the Rotherhithe New Rd and Lower Rd, at the south west corner of the Docks where stevedores take on men every morning between 7 and 9.

Drink and drunkenness is the worst offence. There may be some improvement but not much. The worst streets for roughness and drunkenness are those between Paradise St and the River. As to children fetching beer, Cockett does not like it for respectable children but for the children from the poorer streets they cannot hear or see worse than they do in their own homes.

This has been a most prosperous year for work in Rotherhithe. More work and bigger steam ships are expected as soon as the new dock is deepened at the south east corner of the district.

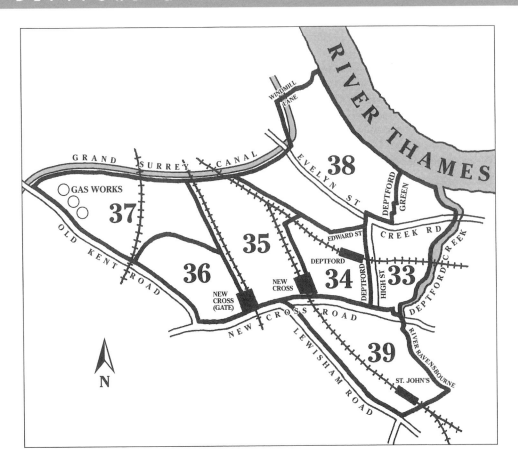

Walk 33

B368

Tuesday 18th July 1899.
George Arkell with Inspector Gummer & Sergeant Goddard.
Inspector Gummer is a smart, well-dressed, portly man. Jacket suit and straw hat. Has over 10 years service at Blackheath Rd and knows the district well. We started about 10am, Sergeant Goddard having instruction to release the Inspector at noon as he was due at Woolwich Police Court.

Started at Deptford Bridge, where Deptford Creek passing under becomes the Ravensbourne.
The north side of **Deptford Bridge** is 3-st shops. Gardiner's large establishment at corner, clothes and general stores. Modern building with clock tower above. Upper floors used as Liberal Club. RED as map.
Deptford Broadway. Triangular open space, paved with cobble stones. Stand for barrows and the meeting place of the neighbourhood. Political and other meetings held here. Men standing about. Good 3-st shops to High St. Slightly poorer near Church St. RED as map.
N up **Church Street** (to Reginald Rd). Poor class of shops near the Broadway, 3-st, and old-fashioned private houses. A few let in tenements but most look comfortable. Poorer as

you go north. PINK as map. Portion of colour on east side gone – houses taken for mineral water factory. Lease for sale.

E along **Creek Street**. With the exception of two, the houses on south side are gone. Taken for business premises. On north side are 2-st houses. People look comfortable, work on the Creek. PINK rather than PURPLE of map. Portion of street going north is poorer. East side is nearly all gone. West side is 2-st houses. PURPLE as map to LIGHT BLUE, prefer latter.

By the **S** side of the railway is a passage eastward leading to the railway bridge across the Creek known as the 'Halfpenny Hatch'. Toll of 1d charged for crossing.

W into **Leonidas Street**. 2-st, four rooms. Flush with pavement. Paint good, clean and well kept. Decent people, mostly one family in a house. PURPLE rather than LIGHT BLUE of map. Colour omitted on south side, LIGHT BLUE.

S down **Hosier Street**. Poorer 3-roomed cottages. Poor labouring class, some broken windows. Part of south east end of street taken for a factory. LIGHT BLUE as map. Colour to come off west side south of entry into Addey St. Ground plan of street wrong at south end. Street runs into Creek St near Addey St. There are several houses between Hosier St and the turn in Creek St.

N along **Addey Street**. Small 2-st houses like Hosier St south of the passage into Hosier St. LIGHT BLUE in character. Between the entry into Hosier St and Leonidas St is a row of old houses on east side. Four rooms and attic in roof. Footway leading to houses is about 2 ft below level of roadway and is protected by iron railing. Some prostitutes and criminals, low rough class. The Inspector reckons this is the worst part of Deptford. He went into a house to arrest a man at 5am and found father, mother and five children in one room. All rooms are small. This piece should be DARK BLUE-barred. Houses opposite are 2-st. DARK BLUE in character. Northern part is 2-st and LIGHT BLUE, except three shops and a public house north of Leonidas St, all comfortable, PINK.

W into **North Street**. Three 2-st cottages. Windows clean. Good white clothing drying in yard. PURPLE to LIGHT BLUE, LIGHT BLUE on map.

S along **Church Street** (Railway to Creek St). On the west side by the railway is a passage leading to High St. Ground on south side is taken for Holloways' Builders Yard. One house occupied by foreman. 2-st and 3-st houses, a few shops. Opposite Giffin St and south of it people are poor. Barefoot girl came out of one house. Group of women talking in doorway near Hales St. Men sitting outside pub with feet stretched across footway. Pony cart standing in road, chalked for sale. A few of the shops are comfortable, German baker etc. PURPLE as map for whole but portion south of Giffin St might be LIGHT BLUE. South of the Addey's School the houses are pulled down and the ground is to let.

W along **Giffin Street**. 3-st, about six rooms. Many of the houses at the east end are dilapidated and boarded up. Slatternly women standing about, some shoeless children. Low class, some prostitutes, hawkers, etc. Some houses let in furnished rooms. Roadway has been made up – covered with tar paving and shingle. Like streets in Notting Dale. Not many charges come to the police, it has improved in that respect. DARK BLUE with BLACK line as map.

S along **Bevill Street**. Deptford Ragged School is in a large square block at west corner of Giffin St. 3-st houses on east side, like Giffin St. DARK BLUE.

E along **Regent Street**. 2-st, broken windows. Some street sellers. Two women talking in roadway as we entered. "Well-known prostitutes" said the Inspector. The women moved off quickly, evidently recognising him.

S & W along **Hale Street**. Narrow crowded street with 2-st houses. Broken windows, sills broken away. Street doors open into rooms. Beds seen through ground floor windows. When visiting in the morning with the Inspector the women were standing about the doors criticising their visitors. At an afternoon visit I found them sitting in groups on the footpath, one on a chair, more on the edge of the kerbstones whilst one woman completed a small circle by sitting in the road with her feet towards the kerb. Costers driving home on their pony carts. Candle factory at west end of street, emitting very evil smells. Not much crime. DARK BLUE as map.

N into **Stanhope Street**. 2-st houses flush with pavement. Broken windows, cemented roadway blocked with barrows. Two men breaking up some gas fittings and putting the metal in a sack. A few Italians, some costers and prostitutes, shoeless children running about and frowsy women gaping at the doors. Board School takes up greater part of north side. Lined BLACK on the map. The west end of the north side is more open and people a little cleaner, approximating to LIGHT BLUE. DARK BLUE lined with BLACK as map.

S along Church St to **Reginald Road**. 2-st and 2½-st houses. A few are modern on the south side near Church St. Some houses covered with creepers, clean curtains. Nice little houses. Only a few near Reginald Place look poor. Two contractors but the remainder are comfortable working people. Mission Church on north side, Girls' Friendly Society Home on south. PINK rather than PURPLE of map. Has improved.

S into **Reginald Place**. Broad street. 2-st houses flush with pavement. Quiet working class. Paper hanger, people in regular work. Two families per house as a rule. Nearly as good as Reginald Rd. PINK to PURPLE, PURPLE on map.

At the end is **Amelia Terrace**. Row of old 2-st cottages with flower gardens in front. On the front of centre house is a full-sized figure of a sailor holding a Union Jack. PINK to PURPLE, PURPLE on map.

N along **Reginald Street**. 2-st, six rooms. Exactly like Reginald Place. PINK to PURPLE, PURPLE on map.

W to **Deptford High Street**. Wide market street. 2-st and 3-st houses. Almost as many styles of building as houses, the only agreement being that all have shop fronts, sometimes a part of the original building but more often an addition thereto. Near the railway station, the Public Hall is being converted – two shops are being improvised, one on each side of the pillars supporting the porch. Most of the shopkeepers live over their shops. The best shops are nearest the Broadway, the decline in character being gradual towards the railway arch. RED as map to archway. North of railway arch to Evelyn St the shops are 3-st. Trade less brisk and shops not so good on the east side. Some assistants living over the drapers. RED as map.

At this point Sergeant Goddard relieved the Inspector.
He is a thin man of about 40. Face mottled, the result of bad digestion or too close application to the worship of Bacchus. Walks slightly lame, owing to rheumatism. Has been over 10 years in the sub-division, but for last 18 months at Blackheath Road.

From the corner of High St a new road has been cut through to Creek Rd, continuous with Evelyn St, involving the demolition of a great part of Wellington St and Queen St. It is named **Creek Road**. Land is cleared and LCC advertise it 'to let' except a plot near east end where a new Deptford Fund House is being erected.

W along **Queen Street**. A few cottages at east end, standing back, are closed and boarded up. 2-st houses. Poor-looking white curtains, broken windows, a few flowers here and there. Narrow street. Rough labouring class. DARK BLUE as map.

S to **Albury Street** (late Union St, given as Creek Rd on map). Deptford Medical Mission at south corner of High St. Old 3-st houses built for middle class and formerly occupied by sea captains etc. Fine panelled doors and carved lintels. Now most are occupied by labouring people, three or more families in the house. Doctor, day nursery, registered lodging house (around 40-50 beds). PURPLE as map.

S along Church St to **Andon Buildings** (late Union Terrace). A few 2-st houses with basement. Two families in each. Narrow paved court. LIGHT BLUE as map.

Back into Church St, then **W** along winding passage to **Mary Ann's Buildings**. At east end is a small cottage, about three rooms, ground floor only, large garden in front filled with vegetables, "new laid eggs for sale". PINK in character. Then come to old 2-st cottages. Roadway has been made up and you descend two steps into the cottages. Salvation Army Barracks at west end. North side modern four-roomed cottages, only east end built. LIGHT BLUE rather than DARK BLUE of map.

S past church to **Crossfield Lane**. On south side 2-st and 3-st old houses, some used as shops. A few pairs of old boots, stays and stockings strung up outside one making a very primitive second hand store. North side 2-st and 3-st modern houses. Very neglected, broken and dirty windows, doors open, children playing about. Costers, wood choppers, etc. Squalid poverty. LIGHT BLUE to DARK BLUE, LIGHT BLUE on map.

On **N** side at **E** end is **Rectory Buildings**. Three blocks of tenements with five floors. Belong to the Industrial Dwellings Co. Labourers but don't look poor. Rough but better than the street. All the tenements are full and place is better than 10 years ago when many were empty including one whole block. PURPLE to LIGHT BLUE, LIGHT BLUE on map.

On the **NW** side of Church St (joining Crossfield Lane with Church St) is **Alfred Place**. Five 2-st houses with small gardens in front filled with broken boxes and other rubbish. Costers. A few broken windows but don't look very poor. LIGHT BLUE to DARK BLUE, DARK BLUE on map.

E along **Alvar Street**. 2-st houses, flush with pavement, two families. LIGHT BLUE as map. The part of Alvar St east of Church St is cleaner than west part but still LIGHT BLUE. Costers etc. Entrance to asphalt works at end of street.

Archway on **N** side leads to **Bronze Square** (late Copperas Square). Three 3-st houses on west and three 2-st on east side. Cemented yards in front with much litter. Dirty ragged children. A murder here some months ago. DARK BLUE. Not marked on map.

N to **Benmore Street, Hamar Place** and **Dugald Street**. These form a block of 2-st cottages together with the **Knott Street** frontage. Streets are narrow. Hamar Place faces wall of works on Creek bank. Costers and street sellers, a few Italians. Dugald St has houses on south side only. DARK BLUE as map.

W along **Bronze Street** (late Copperas St). South side is old dilapidated houses, windows broken, others closely curtained. Low labouring class. On north side houses are more modern, 2-st, with gardens in front near middle of street. Houses very neglected, wood and brickwork damaged at east end. Signs of great and continued neglect. At west end of north side is a pottery (RED). Children amusing themselves by throwing clay pellets at each other. A girl knocks another one over in the middle of road and is at once assailed with a volley of oaths from a woman at first floor window. DARK BLUE as map. Centre of north side might be LIGHT BLUE.

Into **Church Street** (Railway to Creek Rd). 3-st houses and shops on west side. Have been good but look neglected now. Rough men and women at doors. Better near Creek Rd where there are shops. On east side are 2-st and 3-st houses. Registered lodging house near Bronze St – an old double-fronted house. 2-st houses are modern with six rooms and bay windows but neglected and knocked about. Bricks peeling, flagstones broken, woodwork perishing for lack of paint. LIGHT BLUE, except shops on west near Creek Rd, PURPLE as map.

E into **Pender Street**. Six rooms, bay window, fitted for two families. Rent marked on board as 10/6. Same estate as those in Church St and same neglected look. Many children playing in the street. LIGHT BLUE as map.

E into **Berthon Street**. 2-st, six rooms. Better condition. Two families. Some mechanics and others in regular work. PURPLE rather than LIGHT BLUE of map.

Knott Street. On west side are a few 2-st houses with gardens in front near railway arch, LIGHT BLUE. Creek Road Board School has been extended and has an entrance here, LIGHT BLUE to DARK BLUE. Houses on east side are 2-st and small like Benmore St, LIGHT BLUE on west and DARK BLUE on east side. DARK BLUE on map.

E along **Creek Road**. North side is 2½-st with gardens in front, 2-st on south side. Near Copperas Lane is a row of old 2-st cottages, much poorer than rest of Creek Rd. A few shops. PINK as map except near Copperas Lane, LIGHT BLUE to PURPLE.

N into **The Stowage**, a stinking unpaved lane with wharves on north side until the bend in the road is passed. One PINK house in wharf. On south side are 2-st modern houses occupied by a low rough waterside population. Remainder is 2-st and 3-st old houses, still with waterside people but better. Nearly opposite the church the houses are well kept and few are poor. Street grows better as you pass from east to west. DARK BLUE to PURPLE at west.

On **S** side near Cross St is **Maiden Court**. A narrow courtyard reached through archway. Two small cottages, some broken windows. DARK BLUE, not marked on map.

S into **Cross Street**. Three 2-st houses on west side. PURPLE, PINK in map.

W into **The Orchard**. Irregular open space with 2-st cottages on three sides. Labouring people. LIGHT BLUE, except at east end where the houses are painted and better kept, PURPLE.

General Remarks

This walk includes the greater part of poor Deptford. Both officers agree that it is better than it was, not so much crime or violence. To me, little or no improvement is apparent in the poor streets and I have grave doubts as to the knowledge of the police of the social condition of the people. They measure the streets mainly by the proportion of offences against the law and diminution of these is an improvement which they attribute to increasing social position.

The Irish streets – the block between the Railway and Hales St – appear little different to 10 years ago, possibly more congested, except Giffin St where so many houses are closed.

East of Church St the houses belong to the Addey Charity. All are small and poor, Addey St being distinctly poorer than formerly. The Addey Charity has a school in Church St and is now building a large red-brick building in New Cross Rd which will take its place.

North of the railway the streets appear poorer and more neglected. Rectory Buildings and Mary Ann Buildings are better than they were but against these must be set Crossfield Lane which is distinctly poorer.

Most of the people living here work at one of the factories along the Creek. Beside the Chemical works, there are numerous business places employing a large number of 'hands'. The Parish Yard, the Hay Wharf and the Asphalt works employ many hands and numbers also work at Penn's and Humphreys' and the riverbank. The Steam Navigation Co has a large yard in The Stowage. All these works are busy and work is plentiful so that no man need be unemployed.

An Italian colony is growing up near Knott St, ice cream vendors and asphalt workers. Some have also settled in Stanhope St.

Walk 34

B368

Wednesday 19th July 1899.
George Arkell with Sergeant Goddard.

Started at corner of High Street and New Cross Road.
W along **New Cross Road**. On north side are shops, 3-st and 4-st, near High St. Good class private houses near New Cross Station, some used for business purposes. Large Music Hall at corner of Watson St – Empire Theatre of Varieties – just completed. To be opened on July 31st. RED as map.
N along **Amersham Vale**. 3½-st private houses. Well-kept. Two families and occasional lodger. Some railwaymen. PINK as map.
E into **Douglas Street**. Wide airy street. Houses uniform, 2½-st, seven or eight rooms. Clean, well-kept windows. Some trade plates by doors. People rarely move. PINK as map.
S into **Stanley Street**. 2-st, six rooms. East side comfortable, might be PINK. West side smaller and rather poorer, PURPLE as map.
E to Glenville Grove. At entrance of Grove are two blocks of cottages (two rooms) at right angles to roadway. Eight in each block, four back to back with gardens between the blocks. Except the front four all are poor. LIGHT BLUE, only partially marked on map. Further down are some small 4-roomed cottages. Clean white blinds, quiet street. PURPLE rather than LIGHT BLUE of map. East side is taken by Clarke, Burnett & Co. engineering works, over 100 men employed. Glassworks on other side.
Back to **Mornington Road**. 2½-st, small forecourts with shrubs. Family and lodgers or two families. All comfortable. PINK as map.
Along Douglas St to **Watson Street**. Two houses in Douglas St have been pulled down and a wide entrance made to the street. Small, old, 2-st cottages built when every man did what was right in his own eyes, most are flush with footway. Here and there two are placed at right angles to road. A few are back to back with a side passage leading to the pair behind. Ordinary labouring people but not all poor. Nursing Sisters of St John the Divine have a newly-built house on east side. LIGHT BLUE to PURPLE of map.
W into **Baildon Street**. On north side at entrance are three 2-st houses. Doors open, short blinds, rough women. DARK BLUE to LIGHT BLUE, not marked on map. Opposite these are two old wooden cottages and a third looking like a converted stable. Not as bad as opposite side. LIGHT BLUE, not on map. Baildon St itself is 3-st on west side, about seven rooms, two large registered lodging houses. On east side 2-st, five rooms. Some have had small forecourt in front but palisade has gone and the path is so much wider. Costers' barrows, knife-grinder's wheel, ice cream barrows standing in street. Women, frowzy and half-dressed, eye you curiously as you pass; one asked the sergeant whether he had come for her "this time". Children, some shoeless, all dirty and ragged, playing in street. A few men getting ready to go out with their stock. Windows and doors open. Nicknamed Tug-of-War Street because so many fights take place here. "Better than it was", says the sergeant, "fewer cases come from here". Used to have to send 20 men to make arrests. He would hardly call it criminal now. To me the street looks worse than it did ten years ago. If any men and women have the criminal brand on their faces, these seem on my two visits unmistakenly to bear it. DARK BLUE with BLACK line as map.
E through narrow passage into **Charles Street**. A public house at the corner is being rebuilt, a huge 3-st building. The new music hall backs on the passage and the enlargement

must be to catch its patrons. "A failure at present", says the sergeant, "has not taken enough to pay its rates".

At S end of Charles St is **Charles Place**. Six houses on south side, 2-st, built 1884. LIGHT BLUE as map. Opposite side is taken by Mission Room (Shaftesbury Hall).

Charles Street itself is 2-st cottages, some with only two rooms, a few 3-st houses. Poor labouring class, decorators, manglers etc. Becomes poorer at north where Italians are coming in. Costers and ice cream vendors. LIGHT BLUE at south to DARK BLUE at north end, LIGHT BLUE on map.

On W side at N end is **Wybourn's Cottages**, a row of four 2-roomed cottages. Italian ice cream vendors. DARK BLUE, on map LIGHT BLUE. A second row of five, two rooms, small gardens in front.

These back on another row (seven), **Providence Cottages**, which faces the back of Douglas St. Two rooms, WCs and water in front. Flowers and creepers in front garden. LIGHT BLUE as map.

Across Douglas St to **Octavius Street**. 2-st houses with small gardens. Two families as a rule. Saw one servant. Comfortable. PINK rather than PURPLE of map.

W to **Idonia Street**. 2-st. Not quite as good but might be PINK instead of PURPLE of map.

Adolphus Street. Little better than Idonia St. PINK as map.

Into **Payne Street**. 2-st houses with small forecourts. East end of north side is not so good as remainder of street. Some windows broken and holey curtains. Other end is as good as Adolphus St. PINK, except east part of north side, PURPLE on map.

S along **Warwick Street**. New Jerusalem Church at north end. 2-st houses, some with bay windows. Houses near Douglas St have a basement floor. No signs of poverty. PINK as map.

N along **Napier Street**. 2-st houses flush with pavement. Two families or lodgers. Several bills, "furnished room for a gentleman". Four boys playing cricket in roadway with caps and coats for wickets. Policeman appears at corner and paces slowly along the street. "Copper" cries one lad, the four run off with the wickets under their arms. "He hasn't got a badge on" cries one boy. All stop and reconnoitre the enemy for a moment, then continue their retreat when the badge is identified. Policeman continues his beat, amid the smiles of the mothers of these or some of the other children playing in the street, who saw the incident. Poorer than the other streets. PURPLE as map.

S along **Amersham Vale** (to Napier Rd). 2½-st houses and a few shops by Napier Rd. Some windows used for trade purposes – watchmaker etc. Comfortable. PINK as map.

Into **Napier Road**. Three 2-st houses on north side. PURPLE to PINK, PINK on map.

N up **Hereford Place**. Railway has taken west side. 2-st houses. Some poor. PURPLE as map.

Into **Royal Naval Place**. 2-st houses, like Hereford Place. PURPLE as map.

N to **Amersham Grove**. 2-st houses. Portion running west is the better. Double-fronted house on south side recently occupied by an old sailor who built a small museum in the garden at the side and stocked it with curios. Dairyman and many railwaymen. PINK to PURPLE, PURPLE on map.

Atkinson Street (previously Frederick St). 2-st houses, gardens front and back. Like the Grove. PINK to PURPLE, PURPLE on map.

N to **Arklow Road**. 2-st houses, six rooms. Clean and well-kept. At the corner of this road and Kerry Rd is a large Coffee Tavern and Institute used mainly by the men working at Stone's engineering works opposite. Many of the men live in these streets.

Kerry Road. 2-st, six rooms. Not quite so good as Arklow Rd, but PINK rather than PURPLE of map. Many mechanics.

Trim Street. 2-st, six rooms, bay windows. Some own their houses. PINK as map.

S into **Edward Street**. Between the two railway arches is 2-st houses with six rooms, bay windows. Two families in each house. A few shops at east end. South side is smaller and older, 2-st houses. Looks rather poorer. PINK as map.

E of the railway to **High Street** are five old-fashioned houses on north side. 2-st and 3-st, red-tiled roofs. On the south is a row of 2-st houses. Much more modern and uniform. Comfortable working people. A few of the houses near each end have been converted into shops. PINK as map.

S to **Hyde Street**. 2-st houses flush with pavement. A number of poorly-dressed children playing in the street. Curtains and short blinds to windows. No attempt at display. PURPLE to LIGHT BLUE, PURPLE on map.

S along **Edward Place**. Four 2-st houses facing railway. One is occupied by a contractor, the others look poor. PURPLE to LIGHT BLUE, LIGHT BLUE on map. Railway arches facing these houses are used as stables and carts and vans stand on the ground in front.

E into **Hamilton Street**. Old-fashioned 2-st houses, flush with pavement. Well kept. Some of the windows look very nice, flowers etc. Better than Hyde St. Might be PINK, PURPLE on map.

S to **Ffinch Street**. Small 2-st houses flush with path. Rough class of people but not many signs of poverty except at end near railway where a colony of Italians occupy some rooms over stables. Ice-cream barrows stand in the yard. PURPLE as map, except stables on north side, LIGHT BLUE.

General Remarks

This neighbourhood contrasts sharply with that to the east of High St. With the exception of Baildon St and the streets between it and High St, the poor patches are small and stand in marked contrast to their surroundings. Napier St is the only place west of this group that can be termed poor.

The streets are well kept. Nearly all are regularly laid out with the houses having a small garden or forecourt. All have some garden at back and many have quite long piece of ground so that plenty of light and air is secured in back and front.

The people seldom move and there is an air of comfort about the houses. The bulk of the people have incomes sufficient to obtain not only the necessities but many of the luxuries of life. Near New Cross the proportion of railwaymen is large and these men are constantly to be seen on the streets.

Walk 35

B368

Thursday 20th July 1899.
George Arkell with Sergeant Vanstone.
Sergeant Vanstone is a fresh-coloured young man, a native of Deptford and far away the best officer I have met so far as local knowledge is concerned. In nearly every street he knew personally some of the people, the only instance he was in fault was County Grove. He lives in Deptford and has been stationed here over nine years and remembers the district for about 14 years.

Started at New Cross Station.
N up passage to **Railway Grove**. 2-st houses with small gardens in front. South of Walpole Rd are navvies, labourers etc. Two and three families in a house. Some broken windows.

PURPLE to LIGHT BLUE, PURPLE on map. North of Walpole Rd the street is much cleaner, flowers in windows, etc. Railwaymen, guards and others. PINK as map.

W to **Pagnell Street**. 2-st houses, six rooms, bay windows. Two families as a rule, a few large families keep whole house. PINK as map.

N up **Snead Street**. Like Pagnell St. PINK as map.

Angus Street. 2-st houses, bay windows on ground floor. Railwaymen. PINK as map.

S into **Vance Street**. 2-st houses, 15 ft frontage, small windows. Looks poorer than adjacent streets but probably PINK as map.

S into **Walpole Road**. 2-st houses, a few shops on north side. Houses well kept. Passages and stairs carpeted. PINK as map.

S into **Walpole Street**. 2-st plus basement, two families as a rule. Clerks, railwaymen, plasterers, police. Some own their own house. Wide clean street. PINK as map.

W into **Achilles Street**. 2-st houses with little front gardens and flowers. Railway porters and similar men. North side is better than south and might be PINK. Large sheep-skin dressing factory here. PURPLE as map.

N up **Clifton Hill** (to railway). Descends sharply from New Cross Rd. Few shops at top. On west side houses have six rooms, two floors, built for two families. Other side, older houses with gardens in front. A few shops opposite Angus St and at corners. PINK as map.

E into **Edward Street**. 2-st, six rooms. Not so good on north as south side where homes have front gardens, around 10–12 ft long. Mostly railway people. PINK as map.

S into **Liardet Grove**. 6-roomed houses with long gardens like those in Edward St. Well kept. Belong to Railway Company and are occupied by their servants. PINK as map.

N up Milton Court Rd to **Alexandra Street**. 2-st houses. Not quite as good as Edward St. PINK as map.

E along **Vansittart Street**. Like Alexandra St. PINK as map.

Milton Court Road. 2-st houses, old style without bay windows as far as Desmond St. North of there, modern houses with bay windows to ground floor. Does not differ from other streets. Ten years ago many of the houses were empty, now none. PINK, PURPLE on map.

W along **Desmond Street** (late Abinger Rd West). 2-st houses. South side like Alexandra St. North with bay windows. PINK to PURPLE, PINK on map.

N & E along **Liardet Street**. 2-st houses, six rooms, bay windows on ground floor. PINK as map.

Simla Street. Same class of house and people. West Deptford Relief Station on north side. PINK as map.

N through railway arch to **Rolt Street**. Row of 2-st houses. Bay windows with flowers or ornaments, venetian blinds. Clean paint, well kept. PINK as map.

N into **Oareboro Road**. Great improvement here. Road made up and footway paved. 2-st houses, flush with pavement. Wood chopper, labourers. Rougher than others in neighbourhood. Two and sometimes three families in a house. Some are comfortable. PURPLE, DARK BLUE on map.

N up **Trundley's Road**. Houses on west side, Nos. 164–220. 2-st shops near Sanford St. Near the Canal are new bay-windowed houses. PINK, not marked on map.

A turning on W side leading to railway arch is called **Sanford Street**. 2-st private houses with bay windows. Two families. PURPLE to PINK, not marked on map.

The ground on E side of Trundley's Rd is occupied by seven blocks of model dwellings running east and west. Built by the South Eastern Railway Company and called **Folkestone Gardens**. Three floors with drying ground on roof. Wide asphalted yard between the blocks. 231 tenements. Well built. Venetian blinds, walls coloured. Gas laid on, penny in slot. Two southern and largest blocks are full and the third was filling when I went the second time. A few families were in the fourth block. All will be full soon. Sergeant Vanstone says they had some people known to the police at first and they feared the dwellings would become 'warm'. They have gone and the place looks decent. PINK to PURPLE, not on map.

S to **Knoyle Street**. 2-st houses, bay windows. Built for two families with separate entrance to yard from first floor. Street built both sides to mission church. Railway has taken land beyond. PINK as map.

W through railway arch to **Coldblow Farm**. Old farmhouse and two wooden cottages are still occupied. PINK, not marked on map. A roadway has been run northward and the ground behind the houses is being utilised for factories. The Mazawattee Tea Company is erecting a large factory near the canal.

Back and **S** by railway to **Chubworthy Street**. 2-st houses, six rooms. Street entirely built and paved. New houses have two bay windows, others only one. Comfortable working people. Those in old houses are rather poorer than those in the modern houses. A few broken windows, children at doorways. pink. Old house PURPLE to PINK, LIGHT BLUE on map.

W along **Chipley Street**. 2-st houses, bay windows on ground floor. Looks slightly poorer than preceding streets. PINK to PURPLE, PURPLE on map.

S by railway to **Cottesbrook Street**. New 2-st houses are being erected. None ready for occupation yet.

Nynehead Street. South side is fully built, 2-st and some larger. Large dairy near Woodpecker Rd. PINK, partly coloured on map.

Woodpecker Road. 2-st houses, bay windows, small garden in front on east side. A few shops near Chipley St. Nearer New Cross Rd houses are built for two families. People are old inhabitants. Railwaymen and others, some pensioners. PINK instead of PURPLE and PINK as map.

W into **Bawtree Road**, with **Childeric Road**, **Ludwick Road** and **Ruddigore Road**, constitutes Clifton Hill estate. All the houses are alike in structure. Six rooms, 2-st with bay windows. Fitted for two families, the family on first floor having direct access to back yard and in a few cases a separate street door. Estate was built by Hobman & Son, the tar paviours, and the footway and roads are tar paved. Roadway has been neglected and the paving is worn away in large patches. Very mixed set of people: labourers, railwaymen and all classes. Some occupy two tenements. A few shops. PINK as map.

S to **Batavia Road**. 2-st houses fitted for two families. PINK as map. A few old houses nearer North Rd are poorer and might be PURPLE.

North Road. Row of houses on east side, 2-st, bay windows. Better than it was – had six fortune-tellers here, now railwaymen. Houses near New Cross Rd are older. PURPLE to PINK, PURPLE on map.

E along **New Cross Road**. North side of the road between the two railway stations is shops and private houses converted into shops. Three floors. Most seem prosperous. RED as map.

General Remarks

Wedged between two railway stations the railway influence is strong here. District has risen considerably in last 10 years, especially streets in north which were then occupied by inferior tenants and many were empty. Increasing demand for houses has led to the elimination of the more undesirable people.

East of Woodpecker Rd, roads are wide and houses have large gardens, all of 6-roomed type. Older part south of Desmond St are without bay windows characterising the modern houses in the area. West of Woodpecker Rd, gardens are smaller and houses are more diverse. Large amount of open ground by the railway compensates for smaller gardens and on both sides the air is fresh and pure and the dwellings receive plenty of light.

Walk 36

B368

Friday 21st July 1899.
George Arkell with Sergeant Goddard.
I had hoped to have had Sergeant Vanstone but he had a case at the Courts and so Sergeant Goddard came in his place.

Started from New Cross Station.
N & W past entrance of the railway carriage works into **Brighton Grove**, a flagged passage leading into Harts Lane. Nine houses, 2-st, six rooms. Well-kept front gardens. PINK as map. The houses behind coloured PINK have been taken by the railway.
No houses in **Harts Lane**. Backs of Nettleton Rd on west and railway carriage shops on east.
W into **Nettleton Road**. 3½-st, front gardens. Several have cards: "apartments furnished". Keep a girl. Two advertised for sale, said to yield £72 pa. PINK-barred as map.
W along **Hatcham Park Road**. 2-st and 2½-st houses, a few with bay windows. Well-kept front gardens on south side. Railwaymen and clerks. PINK as map.
E along **Billington Road**. 2-st, six rooms. Bay window, Venetian blinds, front gardens with small trees. PINK as map.
N up **Brocklehurst Street**. Houses on east side to Egmont St. Not so good as previous streets. PINK as map.
Egmont Street. Like Billington Rd except houses have cemented forecourt instead of garden and the green, refreshing look of the street is lost. PINK as map.
Casella Road. West part is 2½-st and 2-st with bays. A few near main road are semi-detached. PINK to PINK-barred. Eastern part of Casella Rd, **Leylang Road**, **Camplin Street** and north part of **Brocklehurst Street** are all the same class of property and wear the same look of comfort. 2-st, six rooms. Small gardens in front and a large one behind. Ornamental flower pots in windows. Comfortable people, railwaymen and clerks predominantly. All PINK as map.
Through the railway arch at top of Brocklehurst St is a triangular piece of land still uncovered. Being used as a market garden, rhubarb etc.
Back and along **Hunsden Road**. 2-st houses with two bay windows. Near the hospital windows not quite so well kept. PINK as map.
Along **Hatfield Street**. Same class of houses. Not quite so good between Barlborough St and Old Kent Rd. PINK as map. South of Barlborough St might be PURPLE.
Edric Road. 2-st, six rooms, garden. PINK as map.
Wrigglesworth Road. 2-st, six rooms. Cemented courts. Servant seen here. PINK as map.
Barlborough Street. 2-st, six rooms. Little different from other streets. Poorer on south side near Monson Rd. PINK rather than PURPLE of map.
Monson Road. 2-st houses like rest of estate. A few shops near Eckersley Gardens and at corners. Laundry, baker, grocer, etc. PINK as map.
E into **Eckersley Gardens**. 2-st houses, look squeezed in. Those at entrances are double-fronted, no backs. Not quite such a good class as the other streets. Occasional complaints of fowls missing and the neighbours suspect Eckersley Gardens. A poor or holey curtain the only signs of poverty and these are not frequent. PINK to PURPLE, PURPLE on map.

NW up **Reaston Street**. 2½-st, seven or eight rooms. Like west end of Casella Rd but people not quite so well off. Two families in a house. A few poor windows on upper floor near Hatfield St. PINK rather than PURPLE of map.

Back along to **New Cross Road**. East side is 2-st and 3-st houses with gardens in front as far as All Saints. Some are double-fronted, servants kept. RED as map. South of this point, shops, 2-st and 3-st, doing a good trade in food and clothing as far as New Cross Gate where a row of imposing private houses, 3-st and 4-st, begin. Large gardens in front, well kept and an air of comfort in all. RED as map.

General Remarks

Hatcham Park Estate. Wide streets, long gardens, well-kept houses and general appearance of comfort and respectability. Railwaymen, clerks and others in regular employment live here. The women are well-dressed, the doorsteps are clean and though there are lots of children they do not play about the streets. Only two pubs on the estate but there are four grocers' licenses and several pubs on the main road.

Essentially well-to-do better class of working people, many probably hold leases to their houses. Some houses have two families. Where they don't the family is large or a gentleman lodger is taken. The area has improved over the last ten years. No houses even to let – people don't move so they don't come onto the market.

West from Deptford status rises, culminating in this estate. Houses behind the west side of New Cross Rd are poorer again.

Walk 37

B 368

Saturday 22nd July 1899.
George Arkell with Detective Sergeant Vanstone.

Starting from Old Kent Road Station

Up **White Post Lane**. East side is the wall of the Fever Hospital. The lane leads to Tomlinson & Sons (box makers). On west side are two cottages with well-kept flower gardens. Occupied by carmen. PINK, not marked on map.

NW along **Wagner Street**. 2-st houses. Tram and stable men. LIGHT BLUE, not coloured on map. The portion of the street west of Canterbury Rd is occupied by large bottle merchant and 3-st tenement houses. LIGHT BLUE as map.

N along **Canterbury Road**. On railway side, 2-st houses and a few shops to the Board School. Some look very poor, children without shoes. Others fairly comfortable. West side is 3-st houses, one family on a floor. Some poor. PURPLE as map. North of this is a terrace of 2-st houses, small bay and forecourt. Mostly one family in each. Post office employees and railwaymen. PINK to PURPLE, PINK on map.

E through railway arch into **Hornshay Street**. 2-st houses with bay windows, shops at corners, small gardens in front. PINK as map.

To the S is **Hornshay Place**. 2-st houses, road not made up. A few houses newly built on east side. PURPLE rather than PINK of map, part not coloured.

N into **Lovelinch Street**. 2-st houses, some with bay windows, small forecourts. Street has been extended northward almost to the Canal. Tram, gas and railway workers. Some houses poor. PURPLE rather than PINK of map.

W along **Rollins Street**. New street from Lovelinch St to Canterbury Rd opposite

Penarth St. 2-st houses flush with footway on north side. Road not made up. PURPLE to PINK, not marked on map.

S along **Upcott Street**. 2-st, bay windows. Front garden with small trees. Rather better than Lovelinch St. PINK as map. Add colour for extension north of Sharrett St. Wedding was being celebrated in this street. Women were standing talking in groups, whilst waiting return of the wedding party. Children also gathered, looking thro' window at the feast spread in the parlour: tomatoes, apples, cake, etc.

N up **Blockhouse Street**. Like Upcott St. Very quiet, children have migrated to the next street to view the feast. PINK as map. Newer portion of street north of Sharrett St is poorer, no bays. Might be PURPLE, not marked on map.

Sharratt Street. Two floors. Rather poorer than Blockhouse St. PURPLE to PINK. PURPLE on map.

Canterbury Road (Board School to Canal). East side known as Stolesbury Terrace. 2-st, small forecourt, creepers on walls. North of Rollins St are small shops (unmarked) almost to the Canal. West side 2½-st, painted fronts, well kept. Stokers, labourers, warehousemen etc. PURPLE as map. The Canterbury Rd here forms the boundary between Districts 45 and 44. On the west side of Canterbury Rd, north of Penarth St, is a terrace of small 2-st cottages, below the level of the road which here rises to the Canal Bridge. Cemented fronts. Wood choppers etc. Large wood yard and wharf at end. LIGHT BLUE to PURPLE of map.

W along **Record Street**. Wharves on north and some warehouses on south side. No residents. Street is used as a cricket ground by the *gamins*.

S along Hatcham Rd. Factories and White Lead Works on west side and open ground on east to **Penarth Street**. Pub at corner of Hatcham Rd is the only house on north side. Take off colour between Ormside St and Hatcham Rd – warehouses. South side from Canterbury Rd to Hatcham Rd is small shops of a poor class. Boot repairer has following notice: "The Little Wonder Children's Boots soled and heeled 10d, women's 1/4 and men's 2/4." Women standing about. LIGHT BLUE with traces of DARK BLUE. West of Hatcham Rd are 2-st houses, very dilapidated. Wood choppers, fish curers. DARK BLUE to LIGHT BLUE, PURPLE on map.

S along **Hatcham Road**. "Should not call these respectable" said Sergeant Vanstone. 2-st houses. Some costers' barrows, shoeless child. Some houses look poor but others are well furnished. The criminal record is better than formerly. "People have improved their homes but not their manners." LIGHT BLUE to PURPLE of map.

Manor Grove. 2-st. A few shops. Corpus Christi Mission at corner. Roadway dirty, children playing about. PURPLE to LIGHT BLUE, PURPLE on map.

S along **Tustin Street**. On east side a few little houses like those on Canterbury Rd – very respectable – but opposite to these the people are poor and rough. Pointed out two houses – "the people never work there". Remainder of the street is mixed, some 2½-st, others semi-detached. A few shops with tenements over. Large chemical works on east side. PURPLE, PINK on map.

E into **Bridson Street** (late Stockwell St). Narrow street. 4-roomed cottages. Four of the best are let at 7/- or 7/6 a week. Coarse, fat women standing about, children ragged and dirty with sore faces. Juvenile thieves etc. A few decent people. The houses near the north entrance are better than the rest of the street. LIGHT BLUE with BLACK line as map.

Across Tustin St to **Cambrook Street**. Irregularly built, unpaved entry. 2-st houses. A few broken windows. Gas stokers and chemical labourers. LIGHT BLUE to PURPLE, PINK on map, small portion not marked.

Along Manor Grove to **Ormside Street**. A few 2-st houses north of Penarth St might be PINK but prefer PURPLE. Except four or five houses at the top, the west side of the street (2-

st) looks poor, might be LIGHT BLUE, but becomes better south of Manor Grove. 2½-st on east and 2-st semi-detached on west. Gas stokers and building employees. Used to be rough but better now. Got two policemen to live here. These men are privileged to report themselves to the sergeant on the beat instead of at the station. Always quiets a street if they get a policeman in. PURPLE rather than PINK of map.

On W side N of Manor Grove is **Woodlands Cottages**. 2-roomed dwellings (ground floor only) facing the wall of the gas works. Labourers etc. Flowers planted against wall. Look very poor. Broken windows and furniture. LIGHT BLUE, PURPLE on map. A second block of these cottages (unmarked on map) is entered south from Manor Place. Two rooms let at 4/6 and 5/-, the latter to new tenants. One woman has been here seven years, got £3 back with her rent and now landlord is pressing her, says she is to get out. LIGHT BLUE, not on map.

Along Old Kent Rd to **Sylvan Grove**. 2-st, some with wide frontages. Have been good houses and still a quiet little place. Trees in front of houses. Some new 2-st, bay-windowed cottages on west side. Mostly people working in district, small builders, carpenters, dairymen, laundry, mineral water maker. PINK, PINK-barred in map.

W to **Devonshire Grove**. 2-st, red-brick houses on west. Poorly kept. Mostly gas workers and men employed in timber yard on east side of street. PURPLE rather than PINK of map.

W into **Devonshire Street**. Old houses, 2-st, flush with pavement. Street has been continued into Old Kent Rd with 2-st, bay windows. Better class of people, gas workers etc. Long curtains, ornaments in windows. Old houses. LIGHT BLUE as map. New portion is PINK, unmarked on map.

N up **Alexander Street**. 2-st. Laundry, gas workers, poor-looking children. Houses on north side of portion leading to gas works wall are poorer than the rest. Shoeless children running in front of the houses. PURPLE to LIGHT BLUE (LIGHT BLUE north side), PINK on map and part not coloured.

Ruby Street. 3-st, a few 2-st and 2½-st. Small gardens in front. Mixed class. Some broken windows and dirty curtains. All working people. PURPLE as map.

W into **Hyndman Street**. Only four houses left on north west side. Two floors. LIGHT BLUE to PURPLE, PINK on map.

N into **Hyndman Place**. Two floors, gardens in front, cul de sac. Children well fed and healthy. PURPLE to PINK, PINK on map.

Hyndman Grove. 2-st, cemented fronts. Trees on roadway. PINK to PURPLE, PINK on map.

N to **Bradshaw Street**. Narrow footway with 2-st houses, five or six rooms. Gardens in front. Children dirty. PURPLE, PINK on map.

N to **Vaughan Place**. 2-st. Like Bradshaw St but not in such good condition. Much rougher. Labourers, gas workers, carman and a foreman. Some very ragged children. LIGHT BLUE as map.

N to **Church Place**. 2-st houses, garden in front. Clean. Tar-paved footway. PURPLE to PINK, PURPLE on map. North side absorbed by the gasworks.

W to the **Triangle**. 2-st houses, many with creepers and gardens in front. Two families as a rule. Children playing in the central open space. PURPLE rather than PINK of map.

W into **Caroline Street**. Mostly 2-st. Two large tenement houses, nearly new, let in flats. Poor class, rather better near Old Kent Rd. PURPLE to LIGHT BLUE, PINK on map.

NW to **Canal Grove**. 2½-st houses. Shut off from main road by large wooden gates. Looks PINK as map. Not known to the officer as police do not work it. Probably belongs to the Company as a door thro' wall leads into the works.

Old Kent Road (Canal Bridge to White Post Lane). Very mixed character. Large shops (RED) from Canal to Caroline St. Then private houses to Hyndman St. Decent people,

South Metropolitan Gas Works in the Old Kent Road

some with servants, others in trade. Large house standing back is converted into a laundry (The Alexandria), employs about 300 people. Shops to Devonshire Grove, private houses to Sylvan Grove, then shops and private houses of a rather inferior class to the railway station. A few poor lodgers in some of the houses but in all cases the householders are comfortable and often very well-to-do. PINK-barred to RED, RED on map.

General Remarks

This district is largely dominated by the Gas Works and from almost every point the huge gasometer (the second largest in London) is visible, whilst the workers are found in every street. Near Canterbury Rd the works on the Canal become more important to the people as centres of employment, whilst the proximity of South Bermondsey and Old Kent Rd stations had induced large numbers of warehousemen, post office employees and others engaged in the City to settle here and use the cheap workmen's trains. As a whole the district has deteriorated, chiefly by the removal of the better class workers so that the PINK streets tend to PURPLE and PURPLE to LIGHT BLUE.

Walk 38   B368

Tuesday 25th July 1899.
George Arkell with Detective Sergeant Vanstone.

Started at corner of Wootton Road and Clyde Street.
N up Wootton Road. 2½-st, seven rooms, a few six rooms and wash-house. Windows well curtained, flowers here and there, street clean. Men employed at Victualling Yard, Woolwich Arsenal and meat market. All comfortable. PINK as map.

N & W to **Grove Street** (to Barnes Terrace). Old 2-st and 3-st houses, red-tiled roofs on east side. Coal porters and men in docks. All look comfortable. Board School takes part near Barnes Terrace. West side modern 2-st houses, six rooms, two families. PINK rather than PURPLE of map. Take off part of colour on east side.

On W side is **Bingley Place**. 2-st, one bay window. Costers' barrows standing in the Place. Looks comfortable. PINK rather than PURPLE of map.

N & E to **Barnes Terrace**. Eight 2-st cottages. Five rooms and scullery, garden in front, 7/- a week. Windows small and poorer than Grove St. Entrance to Sayes Court and Gardens. PURPLE as map.

N into **Barnes Walk**. Four 2-st houses, now numbered as part of Grove St. Little better than the Terrace. PURPLE as map.

NW along **Grove Street**. On north side are 2-st houses, modern style with bay windows extending to the high wall of the Victualling Yard. On south side are old 2-st and 3-st red-tiled houses and 2½-st modern houses with two bays. Further west 2-st houses with six rooms. Many Victualling Yard men, also some of Braby's who have large iron barge-building and galvanising works here. Street has greatly improved. Many houses were empty, now filled and street is losing its old rough character. PINK, except few houses near Windmill Lane, PURPLE, PURPLE on map.

W along **Windmill Lane**. North side is better than the south. On south side 2-st houses flush with footway. Poor near Canal. PURPLE rather than LIGHT BLUE of map. A few of the cottages in north side are closed. A light railway from the Docks to the meat market is coming through and will run along Grove St where the rails are already laid along by the kerb.

S along **Hanlon St**. Both sides now built up, the new houses being the better. 2-st. All comfortable – engineers and others employed in the works nearby. A G Scott & Co have large factory at end of street, employing many hands, principally girls. PINK as map.

S to **Junction Road**. Much improved. 2-st houses with six rooms let at 10/- a week. Caretaker, an old soldier, lives in one house. He went over people's occupations, mostly Braby's men, a few Victualling Yard and some labourers. One house looked very poor, the man was described as a 'pot lifter'. Three families in this house, caretaker had just given them notice. Two families in the others. Rents have been allowed to fall into arrears and he is slowly pulling them up, has collected 11/6 backrent this week. Could let the street to good tenants in a fortnight if the houses were empty, but the difficulty is that if these people are turned out, they break the place so much that the repairs become expensive. "It is more difficult to get them out than in." PURPLE, LIGHT BLUE on map.

On N side is an opening, **Sarah's Place**. Two houses on west side. Poor. Small white curtains. Entrance to Braby's Library and Classrooms. LIGHT BLUE, not marked in map.

E to **Hood Street**. 2-st, six rooms. Neat little houses, one bay. East side only. Windows curtained, Venetians, flowers on table. Passages covered with carpet or floor cloth. Labourers, Tennants' men, laundresses. PURPLE, LIGHT BLUE on map.

E into **Boscawen Street** (formerly part of Greenfield Place). 2-st houses, a few old, flush with pavement. Only two or three look poor. Only one house east of Elm's Terrace then Pickford's Yard. PINK to PURPLE, PURPLE on map.

N through **Vincent Place**. No houses, just footway to Grove St.

S to **Elm's Terrace**. Six houses, 2-st. Labouring people. A great change here. Could hear oaths and curses here wherever you went some time ago. Now all quiet. LIGHT BLUE, DARK BLUE on map.

W into **Greenfield Street**. 2-st. A few broken windows. Carmen, cattle market men. PURPLE as map.

E to **Boscawen Street**. On west side 2-st modern houses. East side 2-st cottages. Very narrow frontage. Two families in most. Carmen etc. One independent woman. PURPLE as map. East side might be LIGHT BLUE.

Evelyn Street (north west of Rolt St). Very mixed. Shops and private houses on south west side. Older houses and 3-st shops on north east. Foremen, skilled men and labourers. PINK, PINK-barred on map.

SW along **Blackhorse Road**. 2-st houses, 13 ft frontage. Railings in front. Many broken windows and some houses look very poor but others are neat and clean, flowers in windows etc. Most of the front doors are open and in nearly all the passages some attempt at floor covering is made. Men are dock and waterside labourers, a few wood choppers. Women work in wood yard and laundry, girls in tin factory or as 'gut girls' in the meat market. Not much trouble to the police now. Great improvement in the street; the children are cleaner and one misses the women who used to stand about here in groups. LIGHT BLUE to DARK BLUE, DARK BLUE on map. At the end of the street is a piece of vacant land and a footway leading to Oareboro Rd. Ten years ago it was the rendezvous of the men and boys; pitch and toss and other games were carried on vigorously. Police raided the spot several times and have stopped it. Now only see a few women collecting pieces of wood for fuel from the heaps of refuse.

Passing around the footway to **Gosterwood Street**, a new neighbourhood is reached. 2-st modern houses, with bay windows, forecourts, tiled paths. Houses fitted for two families and have three rooms and scullery on each floor. Everything is clean and eminently respectable. PINK as map.

SE along **Alverton Street** (late Duke St). 2-st, six rooms, one bay. PINK as map.

Etta Street. 2-st, six rooms. Two families as a rule. Some own their own houses. Wide street, front gardens. Rather better than Gosterwood St. PINK as map.

E along **Childers Street** (late James St). Two floors. Houses fitted for two families as far as corner of Rolt St. PINK as map.

Rolt Street. 2-st, one bay, narrow forecourt. Not quite as good as Etta St. Few 2½-st houses between Board School and Evelyn St are poorer. PINK as map.

Alverton Street (Rolt St to Abinger Rd). 2-st, small gardens. Working class. Some widows keeping laundries. PINK as map.

Dorking Road and **Shere Road**. 2-st houses, two families. Most have been here for years. PINK as map.

SE along **Childers St** (late James St). From Rolt St to Abinger Rd are 2-st houses, not so good as above. Policemen, carmen, cattle market men and men working at Tennants. PINK to PURPLE, PURPLE on map. The south east portion has improved (late Henry St). 2-st houses, 15 ft frontage. People all seem comfortable and in regular work. Used to have drunks here nearly every night but gone now. PINK to PURPLE, PURPLE on map.

N along **Gorston Street** (late Arthur St). Two floors, two families, three families in two cases. Dock labourers and working people. Children well fed and dressed. PINK to PURPLE, PURPLE on map.

Into **Abinger Road**. Most 2-st, a few north of Gorston St are 2½-st, six rooms. Some retired people, foremen etc. Several own their houses – five of one block of nine. The sergeant lives here. People don't move. PINK as map.

SE into **Staunton Street** (late William St). 2-st, six rooms. Labouring class. Several broken windows, not so noisy as formerly. Sergeant says the people are comfortable. PINK to PURPLE, PURPLE on map.

S into **Clyde Street**. Two floors, one bay. Houses well kept, clean curtains etc. PINK as map.

Along street into **Wellington Place**. 2½-st, two and three families. Cattle market men etc. On west side are four 2-st bay-windowed houses which might be PINK. PURPLE to PINK, PURPLE on map.

This finished the day's walk.

Continuing on 26th July 1899.

Started at corner of Creek Road.

Creek Road. PINK to corner of Knott St where a large house is used as a women's lodging house.

On either side of the Board School is a cul de sac, **Henrietta Street**. Each side contains seven 2-st houses, facing the school. Dock and riverside labourers. Look poor, dirty white blinds and short curtains. LIGHT BLUE, PINK on map.

N to **Deptford Green**. Old-fashioned houses, 2-st and 3-st. Very mixed in style and also character of occupants. Some red-tiled roofs, others slated, one wooden house. Some look quite comfortable, others LIGHT BLUE and one DARK BLUE in character. A few houses on the east side near church are quite comfortable and should be PINK. West side PURPLE, PURPLE on map. At northern end is Hood & Co's Iron Works and the Dry Dock employing a large number of men.

W into **Butcher Row**. Humphrey & Tennants and Penn's Engineering works on north side extending to Watergate St.

S along **Hughes Fields**. A few 2-st houses north of the Board School. LIGHT BLUE in character. Also small 3-st tenement dwellings facing the school. Remainder of east side is irregular old-fashioned houses like Deptford Green. West side has several clearances by LCC. Houses mostly 2-st. Women standing about and young children playing in roadway. PURPLE as map except north end, LIGHT BLUE.

On W side of Fields near S end is **St Mary's Place**. Four cottages, 2-st, two rooms, one up, one down. Wood choppers working on ground in front of houses. Poor. LIGHT BLUE, not marked in map. Off this is another entry. Four houses on north and three others backing on St Mary's Place. Well-kept gardens in front. Secluded place. Some poor in north row but others look comfortable. PURPLE on north and PINK south row, not on map.

S into **Church Street** (north of Creek Rd). On east side are old-fashioned red-tiled houses. Two double-fronted. Keep servants. A few shops, two are good. Some working people. A few poor shops on west side. PINK to PINK-barred, PURPLE on map.

W into **Wellington Street** (formerly Flagon Row). Old-fashioned shops. Two registered lodging houses. Some are comfortable. PINK to PURPLE, PINK on map.

On N side is **St Nicholas' Garden** which has been extended northward to Benbow St, the northern part being a children's playground. The ground is narrow but well stocked with trees, the shade of which is evidently appreciated by the people. Many men of the riverside type resting here.

Armada Street. Three old dilapidated houses on east side near Wellington St. Old inhabitants. LIGHT BLUE. On west side are five 2-st houses, modern. PINK to PURPLE. Remainder of street is taken by LCC dwellings. 2-st at south end with separate entrance for each floor. Further north four tenements in each block, ground at back divided off to form a separate courtyard for each block. Buildings are well built, everything is good and a refreshing contrast to some other modern buildings. The only fault is the small windows which give a heavy appearance, accentuated by small panes and exceptional solidity of the bars of the window sashes. Costers' barrows standing at top end. Notice of Prudential agent

Watergate Street.

exhibited. PURPLE to LIGHT BLUE, not on map.

E along **Trevithick Street**. North side is open ground. At east end a few 2-st cottages. Doors open into rooms, no back. Labouring people. LIGHT BLUE rather than DARK BLUE of map.

Along Butcher Row past Humphrey & Tennants and Penn's works. S along **Watergate Street**. Cattle market wall on west side and facing it (north of Trevithick St) are 2-st houses, old with red-tiled roofs. Cattle market men and engineer labourers. LIGHT BLUE to PURPLE, DARK BLUE on map.

W & S along **Orchard Place**. Narrow, unpaved roadway by the cattle market wall. On east side are two old wooden houses occupied by costers. Dirty children, filthy blinds. Men used to be decoyed here and robbed. Will soon be taken for the market. DARK BLUE, not marked on map.

Back into **Watergate Street**. North of Prince St is mostly 2-st old houses. Some poor but a few comfortable. PURPLE rather than DARK BLUE. South of Prince St character rapidly deteriorates. Except a few shops on the west all is poor. Old houses, mostly 3-st, let in tenements. Faint foetid smell prevails, overpowered in places by disgusting stench. Rough women, one with head bandaged, others with black eyes. One old harridan sitting on doorstep with dirty clay pipe, shoeless children. Costers, street-sellers, gut cleaners. "Whenever there is beer there they are and the more the better" was the Sergeant's summary of these people. Some of the houses have been good family residences. One row occupied as a tenement house has a fine carved overhanging porch with a fat cherub carved in full relief supporting the pediment on either side. DARK BLUE as map.

On W side is **Barnes Alley**. One house (2-st) left on north side. Widow of a butcher (DARK BLUE, not marked on map). Ground between this alley and Blake St has now been cleared and is waste.

S to **Rowley Street**. 2-st and 2-st plus attic on north. Broken windows. Costers' and fish-hawkers' barrows standing. Rough girls with coarse aprons standing about, others sitting in doorways. Rough and very poor. DARK BLUE as map.

Into **New King Street**. Mixed old and new houses. Row of 2-st bay-windowed houses on west are clean and well kept. Remainder of street mixed. Some shops near Evelyn St. PURPLE as map. At north end on east side a court runs off by tanner's premises. Some of the employees live above the stables at the end. PINK, not on map.

Into the **Cattle Market**. On the east side are two rows of houses partly occupied as offices but also residences of Supt, Assistant and Clerk, Clergyman of St Nicholas' Church. RED, not coloured on map.

Prince Street. 2-st houses flush with pavement east of market. Very poor in a few cases. PURPLE as map. West of market are 2-st houses, some with bays. Some old houses. Dock labourers, cattle market men and engineers. PINK, PURPLE on map.

N into **Sayes Court Street**. 2-st, bay windows. West side only. Comfortable working people. PINK as map. At the end of the street is Sayes Court Gardens, a nice open space with gardens extending to the wall of the cattle market.

E into **Dacca Street**. 2-st, bay windows. Some look poor. PURPLE to PINK, PURPLE on map.

Czar Street. Like Dacca St but people rather better. PINK, PURPLE on map.

Evelyn Street (Rolt St to High St). Shops east of Czar St. West of this on north are old 3-st houses with shops interspersed. A few keep servants but in most of the houses two families are found. More modern 3-st houses on south. Several people in small way of business: tailor, bookbinder, carpenter, ladies' school. Good shops between Rolt St and Abinger Rd. PINK-barred as map.

General Remarks

The district covered in these two walks may be roughly divided into two parts by Evelyn St differing in style of buildings and character of inhabitants. On the riverside is old Deptford with its red-tiled, small-windowed houses which in their decadence retain much of their quaint, picturesque appearance. Deptford Green is the representative of the style which dominates to New King St, although the LCC buildings in the centre show that the old order is passing away. In this area the riverside and cattle market workers form the bulk of the population. A careless hand-to-mouth class of people. One characteristic of this area is the large number of fully licensed houses. Some are large gin palaces but even the little places that in most districts would be beer houses have the full licence. The cattle market and works on the river bank explain this peculiarity but in any case the district has too many licensed houses.

South of Evelyn St is a comfortable neighbourhood. Regular modern streets, wide and airy, occupied by comfortable working people. Very few signs of poverty but many of comfort. The district compares favourably with the streets off Woodpecker Rd.

Throughout the district a distinct improvement is noticeable. South of Evelyn St the LIGHT BLUE element has been practically eliminated, changing PURPLE to PINK. A similar tendency is observable in the streets off Grove St. Houses were easily obtainable here in former years, now the demand is greater than the supply and landlords are weeding out the undesirable tenants. In the district east of New King St the change is working through demolition, the newer buildings being occupied by (outwardly at least) a better class.

A great change has come over the people. Instead of spending so much in the public houses they go for excursions of all kinds and to this change Sergeant Vanstone attributes the improvement.

The value of house property has risen enormously. An old man, who formerly lived at the corner of Grove St and Windmill Lane, bought a house there for £100 some years ago and sold it to the Railway Company for £105. He has recently sold the 40 year lease of a house there for £300, ground rent 50/-.

Walk 39

B368

Friday 28th July 1899.
George Arkell with Sergeant Vagg.

Started at the Marquis of Granby.
SE along **Lewisham High Road** (to Florence Rd). Beyond the pub are a few shops and some small 2½-st houses to corner of Park Rd. PINK-barred instead of RED on map. Between Park Rd and Florence Rd are 3½-st houses with long gardens in front. Keep servants. A few shops near Florence Rd (2-st). RED as map.
E into **Park Road**. Mostly semi-detached, 3½-st, front gardens. Retired publican and City people. Nearly all keep servants. PINK-barred to RED, RED on map.
Into **Amersham Road**. Wide clean road. 3-st and 3½-st terrace houses on east to the bend then semi-detached. On west all semi-detached. RED at upper end where all keep servants. PINK-barred near New Cross Rd where there are two families in each or they are let as apartments. RED on map.
Florence Road. 2-st plus basement on east and 2-st on west. £36 houses. Working class, two families or lodger. Plants in windows. Roadway clean. No servants. PINK, PINK-barred on map.
W into **Alpha Road**. Three double-fronted houses face the railway. Remainder 3½-st. Three families, no servants, have doorstep girls. City people. PINK to PINK-barred, PINK-barred on map.
New Cross Road. From Marquis of Granby to the railway is 3-st shops and private houses used for businesses – dressmakers, milliners, builders, solicitors. Nearly all have plates affixed and most keep a servant. PINK-barred to RED. East of railway to Florence Rd is better class terrace houses, 3½-st, gardens in front. Few near Florence Rd are turned into shops. New Addey & Stanhope School being built to east of Zion Chapel. Few poor class shops with people living over reach to Wilson St. RED as map to Florence Rd, then PINK-barred.
Deptford Broadway. Theatre at corner of Tanners Hill and large shops to Mill Lane. Shopkeepers live over and a few housekeepers. RED as map.
E to Greenwich Rd, known as **Deptford Bridge**. 3-st shops on east side, second rate. No backs, the Quaggy runs behind. On Deptford side is Peppercorn's Depository, a few houses and Hollands Distillery and Norfolk Brewery at corner of Mill Lane. PINK-barred to RED, RED on map.
W to **Wilson Street**. 2-st houses flush with pavement. West side poorer than east. Windows curtained, doorsteps whitened. Lot of Italians, costers. At far end vegetables are heaped on the pavement and a coster is arranging his stock on the barrow before going his round. LIGHT BLUE as map. East side may be PURPLE.
E leading into Tanners Hill is **Pearson's Avenue**. Mission Hall and two 2-st houses on south side. LIGHT BLUE, not on map.
Back across Wilson St into **Florence Grove**. 2-st houses, flush with pavement, three on south side, six on west side. Torn curtains. Flower hawkers, agents. New Addey School has entrance on north side. PURPLE as map.
S into **Florence Cottages**. 2-st houses. 10/- a week. Look comfortable working class. Fancy flower pots and clean white curtains. PINK rather than PURPLE of map.
S into **Florence Street**. 2-st, six rooms, small forecourts. Narrow street, houses face back gardens of Florence Rd. Respectable working people, builders etc. Look comfortable. PINK as map.

E into **Florence Street East**. Seven houses, 2-st, six rooms. 10/- a week. Two families in each. PURPLE as map.

Heston Street. 2-st houses, small bay windows. South of Florence St is the poorer part. People from Mill Lane have come in. Costers. Free fights at night. At extreme south end near railway are four 2½-st houses, DARK BLUE in character. North of Florence St on west side are some respectable families, PURPLE at north. Remainder LIGHT BLUE as map. Add DARK BLUE at south end.

At N end of Heston St are eight cottages known as **Fishers' Rents**. 2-st, cemented fronts, outer door opens into room. Court is below the level of the street. LIGHT BLUE as map.

E into **Heald Street**. Two 3-st tenement houses on north side. PURPLE as map, colour wrong.

Tanners Hill. Near Broadway, old 2-st shops. Between Nelson St and Ship St the houses have been rebuilt, now 2-st private houses. West side is mainly shops, 2-st, irregular. Second rate trade. PINK as map. Broadway to Nelson St is PINK or PINK-barred instead of RED of map. From St John's Rd to the railway the houses are old, very mixed in character. 2½-st and 3½-st on west, 2-st on east. A few small shops. Italian ice cream vendor etc. Mostly old residents. PINK to PURPLE. East side near railway is LIGHT BLUE. From railway to Lewisham High Rd, 2-st houses on south and small shops on north. PINK as map.

On **NW** side leading out into Heston St is **Summer Street**. Old 2-st houses, flush with pavement. Labourers and hawkers. LIGHT BLUE as map.

On W side is **Kentford Place**. Six 2-st cottages, no backs. Wash-houses and two WCs on ground in front. Rough labouring class. Small rooms but people are content and even think themselves fortunate. "Not half the convenience you have here" said one of the women in a disparaging tone of the tenement houses.

Nearer the railway is **Spring Street**. Old 2-st and 3-st houses. Broken windows stuffed with bundles of rags. Dirty and ragged children playing in the unpaved roadway. DARK BLUE, LIGHT BLUE on map. At the end of the street are three houses shut off by fence and gate. These are better, LIGHT BLUE.

Lewisham High Road (Florence Rd to Oscar St). Mostly shops, 2-st and 3-st, some large. One double-fronted house. RED as map.

Between Tanners Hill and Florence Rd, is entrance to **Alexandra Cottages**, a cul de sac of twelve 2-st houses. Clean and well kept. Notice in one window: "mangling done here". PURPLE as map.

E into **Lucas Street**. 2-st houses. All working people, builder, bootmaker. PINK as map.

On N side is **Nicholas Street**. 2-st houses, narrow fronts. Mineral water factor on east side employs some of the people. LIGHT BLUE as map.

Oscar Street. 2-st old houses near St John's Rd. Rather poorer than Lucas St but comfortable working people. PINK as map.

Back to **Thornville Street** (late Hill St). On west side facing railway is Board School, caretaker's and one other house. Marked LIGHT BLUE on map, should be PINK. On east side between Oscar St and Lucas St are five little cottages. Labouring people, PURPLE to LIGHT BLUE, PINK on map. Open space in front of these cottages with railway passing under is used as playground by the children.

Lewisham High Road (Oscar St to Railway Station). Shops extend a little beyond Friendly St. Good class trade. Then 3-st and 4-st terrace houses with large gardens in front and a few detached houses. Stone House is very large, the front being built to represent a Grecian temple. All keep servants. RED to YELLOW, RED on map.

St John's Road. West side is semi-detached houses, 3½-st, three with bays. South of Ashmead Rd is 2½-st. Some servants. PINK-barred, PINK on map.

S into **Cliff Terrace**. 3-st and 2-st houses at south end. Near St John's Rd are 3½-st, double-fronted. Keep servants except a few at south end. RED to PINK-barred, RED on map.
Ashmead Road. 3-st on west, 2-st on east. Wide road and good gardens in front of houses. Comfortable folk, men go to the City. PINK, west side might be PINK-barred, PINK-barred on map.
Friendly Street (to St John's Rd). 2-st shops on south side between Lewisham High Rd and the Mews. Not marked on map, should be PINK. 2-st private houses and the remainder occupied by comfortable working people. PINK as map, colour to be added near High St.
N along **St John's Road**. Immediately round the corner on west side is a yard with house standing back. PINK. 2-st houses, old on west but east side rebuilt and considerably improved. Builder, insurance agents, etc. PINK, PURPLE on map.
W up **Deloraine Street** (late Brunswick St). Small 2-st houses, flush with pavement. Clean and well-kept. Labouring people but don't look poor. PURPLE as map.
On W side is **Knott's Terrace**. 2-st houses in a raised paved court with two other rows reached down a flight of steps. Small crowded rooms. Costers etc. Two houses have notices: "mangling done here". Girl turning mangle and singing one of Sankey's hymns. Women come to doors, stare at you as you walk past and talk to each other from one doorway to another. LIGHT BLUE as map.

Continuing on 29th July 1899

Started from corner of Broadway and Tanners Hill.
SE along **Nelson Street** (late Nile St). Modern houses built for two families. Venetian blinds. Let at 12/-. Mechanics, brewers' men and others, mostly in regular work. PINK, rather than PURPLE and LIGHT BLUE of map. The block between Nelson St and St John's Rd (east side) and Friendly St and Tanners Hill has been rebuilt in this style and is greatly improved.
Friendly Street (Mill Lane to St John's Rd). North side like Nelson St. South is older houses but look comfortable, well-kept windows, fancy flower-pots etc. Except foul houses close to Mill Lane which are very poor. Some prostitutes and other bad characters. PINK except corner of Mill Lane, LIGHT BLUE with BLACK line, PURPLE on map.
N up **Cranbrook Road** (late Victory St). Like Nelson St. Cabinet maker, insurance agent. Tablet: "piano and mandolin taught". PINK, PURPLE on map.
Ship Street. New houses, 2-st but little poorer than other streets. Houses flush with pavement. PURPLE to PINK, LIGHT BLUE on map.
E along **Harton Street** (King St on map). Small old shops left on south side. Tradesmen are old established. North rebuilt partially. Between Nelson St and Ship St, 3-st tenement houses. North side PURPLE, south side PINK. All PINK as map. DARK BLUE patch behind south side of this street has gone.
E into **Mill Lane**. West side to Friendly St has been cleared by the LCC. Other side remaining are 4-roomed houses. Prostitutes and bullies. Two houses south of Friendly St also bad, broken windows. DARK BLUE to BLACK, BLACK and PURPLE on map. Further south are two houses on the Kent Waterworks ground occupied by Secretary and other official. One of these is marked PINK, it should be coloured RED.
S into **Ravensbourne Street**. 2-st houses, some double-fronted where the depth is small. Nearly all on east side. Few shops near Cranbrook Rd, look comfortable. Some police, brush maker, tailor, etc. Entrance to recreation ground near the railway. PINK, PURPLE on map.
N up **Albyn Road**. 2-st houses, bay windows. Good class of people, foremen etc. Street makes a turn and runs north, improves as it approaches St John's Rd. Furnished apartments,

Back yards in Mill Lane

no servants. PINK, PINK-barred on map.

On E is **Bolden Street**. 2-st, bay fronts, covered with creepers. Like Albyn Rd, no servants. PINK, PINK-barred on map.

Lind Street. 2-st, bay windows. Foremen, mechanics, people in the City. Some lodgers, others two families. PINK, PINK-barred on map.

Batsford Road. 2-st and 2½-st. Well kept and comfortable but no servants. PINK, PINK-barred on map.

N up **St John's Road** (to Friendly St). 2½-st on east, 2-st on west. Gardens in front. Comfortable working people. A few trade notices exhibited: two bookmakers etc. PINK as map.

Strickland Street. 2-st, small forecourts. Rather smaller than other houses. Two families as a rule. PINK as map.

S to **Clandon Street**. Cul de sac. 2-st. Clean and well kept. PINK as map.

Cranbrook Road (to Friendly St). Few shops on east, remainder 2-st houses. Working people. Two monthly nurses. PINK as map.

Seymour Street. St John's Schools at corner. Facing school houses are 3-st, remainder 2-st with small forecourt. All working people, a few trade cards and plates: coal and coke merchant, dressmaker, etc. Saw one ragged child leave house on north side but was well nourished. Most of the children are well dressed. PINK as map.

General Remarks

Roughly the South Eastern Railway divides this district into two parts. The western differs entirely from the portion of Deptford on the north. The ground is much higher, overlooks the north, the air is fresher, always a breeze. The people are comfortable, not crowded. East of the railway the land sinks to the Ravensbourne. In the southern portion the people are tending to a PINK level, PINK-barred streets changing to PINK and PURPLE to PINK. Between Friendly St and Tanners Hill the improvement due to rebuilding is immense. Old cottages have been displaced by comfortable working class dwellings. Excepting a few houses near Mill Lane the only poor part is the area between Tanners Hill and Florence Rd and this, compared to the poor streets north of the Broadway, is quite comfortable.

MAP DESCRIPTIVE OF LONDON POVERTY, 1898-9

(IN 12 SHEETS)

THE STREETS ARE COLOURED ACCORDING TO THE GENERAL CONDITION OF THE INHABITANTS, AS UNDER:-

Lowest class.
Vicious, semi-criminal

Mixed. Some comfortable
others poor.

Very poor. casual.
Chronic want.

Fairly comfortable.
Good ordinary earnings.

Poor. 18s. to 21s. a week
for a moderate family

Middle class.
Well-to-do.

Upper-middle and Upper
classes. Wealthy.

A combination of colours–as dark blue and black, or pink and red

indicates that the street contains a fair proportion of each of the classes

represented by the respective colours.

The following sheets have been extracted for interest from the published maps.
They do not cover the whole area and they are at different scales.

Bermondsey

Blackheath

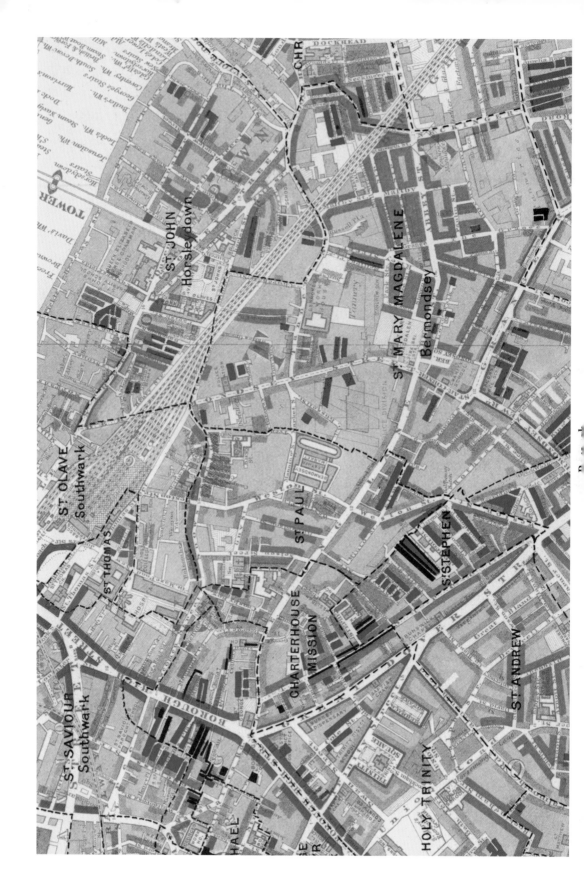

Deptford

Greenwich Riverside

Kennington

Lambeth

New Cross & New Cross Gate

Peckham

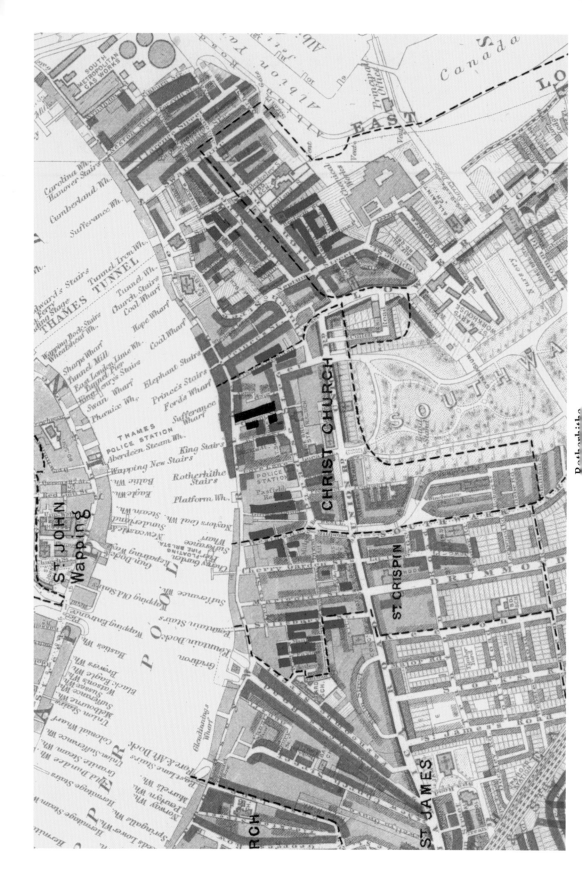

Southwark

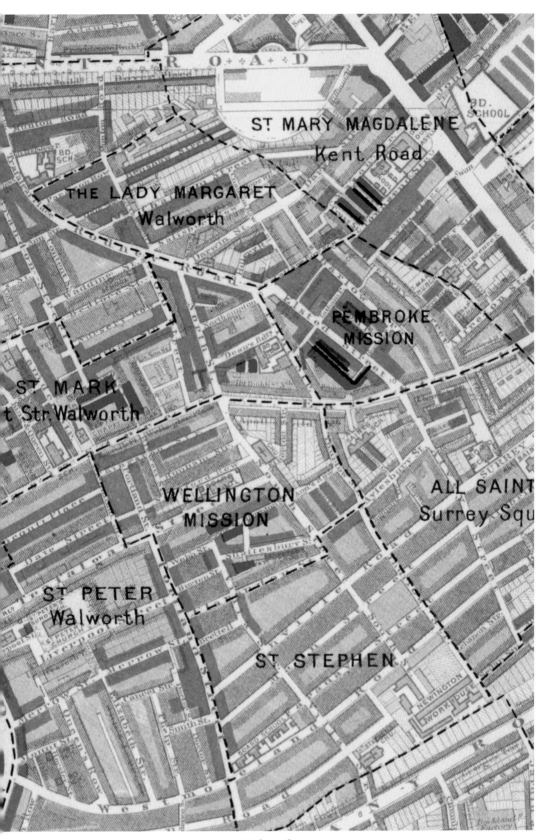

Walworth

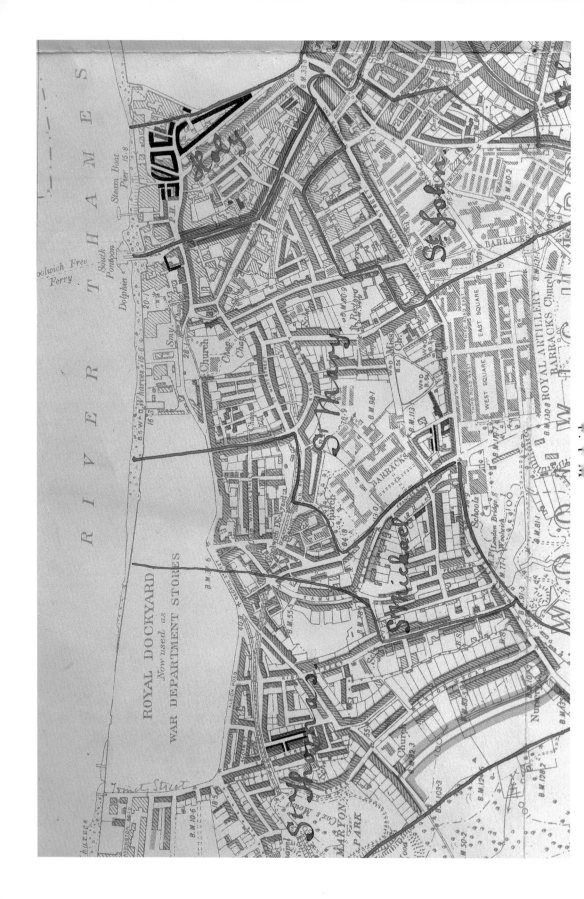

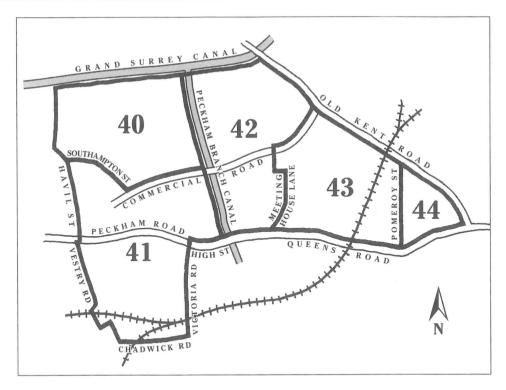

Walk 40

B373

Monday 9th October 1899.
Ernest Aves with PC Dolby.
Dolby has been in the police for about eight years, and has been stationed at Peckham for the whole time. He is one of the men marked out for promotion and is hoping to be made a sergeant in about a year. He is a good fellow, capable and honest. He is one of the few "Cockneys" in the force, having been born in Fore St, City. He knew his district well. It is not one that gives special scope for a constable's energies and Dolby said that, had he been a single man, he might have been glad to get moved into a district where there was more to do. Excepting 'H', whose work lies in such a "dirty" part, there was no Division to which he had any special aversion. On promotion, every man has to sign a form undertaking to serve where the authorities may choose to send him, be it to the East End, to one of the Dockyards or anywhere else.

Starting up Hill Street as far as Commercial Road, and crossing the Canal Bridge. N up Canal Bank. Small cottages with garden fronts. PURPLE as map.
Middle Street. Much the same style of house and class of people. PURPLE as map.
Parallel with the Canal is Sumner Road. Irregularly built street. PINK and PURPLE as map, except at the north corner of St George's Rd where colour has to be omitted for the All Saints' Club.
At the NE corner of Rosemary Rd is Castle Square. Five or six 3- and 4-roomed cottages. The former letting at 7/- and said by an occupier to be "dear at half the price", but not a bad-looking little corner. PURPLE as map.

On the E side of Sumner Rd are **Shields Street** and **Nutt Street**. The latter is a cul de sac. Both poorer. From PINK of map to PURPLE.

On the W side of Sumner Rd are:

Scipio Street. 2-st houses. PINK as map.

Edward Street (now Garnies St). Much like Scipio St. PINK as map.

Daniel Street, Alder Street and **Davey Street**. Three cul de sacs, all with 2-st houses. Mechanic class. PINK as map except that in Alder St the Chapel has given way to extra cottages, for which extra PINK is required, and in Davey St there is now a church on the south side, omit colour.

From here to the N end of Sumner Rd and along the **Canal Bank**. This end has no dwellings and is closed at night at the north entrance. At the south approach there is a police point. The Bank is lonely enough, but the only trouble appears to be from children tumbling in and getting drowned. These Dolby said are nearly always children from a distance. The native-born get wary.

NW up Willowbrook Road. PINK as map, with additional colour for new 2-st, bow window cottages, on east side, occupying part of the site of the School shewn on map.

On the same site and on unoccupied ground, a new street, **Pennick Road**, has been built. Houses like the new ones in Willowbrook Rd, east side only. The street runs from Willowbrook Rd to Sumner Rd. Add PINK.

St George's Road. 2-st houses mostly, some shops. Forecourts. Additional PINK on clear space at corner of Dorton St (grocer's). The rest PINK as map.

Cator Street, East Surrey Grove and **Camden Grove North**. All very much alike with 2-st houses. Little life apparent. Single occupiers the exception. All PURPLE as map.

In **Raglan Passage** one house only, small builder, believed to be entirely occupied by him. Untidy rather. From DARK BLUE of map to PINK.

W of Camden Grove North is **Tilson Street**. One of the streets of low repute on the section. By no means so poor as other parts but a centre of drinking and disorderliness. As we passed two neighbours were jangling, by way of sampling the street. Broken windows and signs of neglect frequent. Houses 2-st, flush with sidewalk, the common, though not invariable, feature of the poorer class of streets. Many doors open. Women and children generally untidy. Leave DARK BLUE as map.

Into St George's Rd again and down **Gloucester Road**. This east end is 2-st houses and 2-st plus basements. Forecourts. Decent. From PURPLE of map to PINK, omitting for Board School. The rest of the road PINK as map.

Albert Road (now part of Castlemain Rd). 2-st houses with forecourts. PINK as map.

Further W is **Eastdene Street**. 2-st houses with forecourts. A cul de sac. PURPLE as map.

Cooden Street. Another cul de sac. Houses flush with sidewalk, some broken windows. LIGHT BLUE as map.

Dorton Street. 5-roomed cottages, flush with sidewalk. One and two families. Have been done up, repointed etc. Piano being played in one of them. From LIGHT BLUE of map to PURPLE.

The five preceding streets have been on the S side of St George's Rd. On the N side, nearly opposite Dorton St, are **Mason's Cottages**. Three of them, backing on Canal. Untidy yard, costers sorting their grapes and getting ready for their rounds. From PINK of map to LIGHT BLUE.

E of Dorton St is **Dragon Road** (now including Victoria Place). Mainly 2-st houses with basements. Two or three families to each. PURPLE as map.

Into **Wells Street**, the boundary street this side of the section and already taken with Young. On the east side, north of the Church, is the towing master's house. Uncoloured to PINK.

S to **Southampton Street** (north side to Commercial Rd) 3-st houses, some shops, a doctor's house quite an exception. The street here mainly good working class. From PINK-barred of map to PINK.

Rainbow Road. 2-st houses with double bow windows and forecourts. PINK as map.

Very much of the same character are **Dowlas Street, Bonsar Street** and **Coleman Road**. All three PINK as map.

Further E is **Peckham Grove**. Many semi-detached houses, good fronts. Trees getting a rather forlorn look. Several laundries. Houses, in some cases, with servants. From RED of map to PINK-barred.

Sanders Rd now forms part of **Blake's Road**. Mainly 2-st houses. Improved. Perhaps from the PURPLE of map to PINK.

Hornby Road. 2-st houses with forecourts. Improved. From LIGHT BLUE of map to PURPLE. At the north end are two cottages. Uncoloured to LIGHT BLUE.

Further N is **Graylands Road**. PURPLE as map.

At its N end is **Fendick Road**. 2-st houses on both sides and not on north only as in map. From PINK and uncoloured of map to PINK or perhaps PURPLE.

Hazelmere Road. PINK as map.

To the S is **Lidgate Road**. LIGHT BLUE as map.

Thence by Rosemary Rd to **Diamond Street**. 2-st houses, a few shops. From DARK BLUE of map to LIGHT BLUE.

On the S side, E end is **Diamond Court**. Stucco buildings with gardens. Pleasant. From DARK BLUE of map to LIGHT BLUE.

To the NE are **Moody's Cottages**. Poorer than either Diamond St or Diamond Court. LIGHT BLUE as map or perhaps DARK BLUE.

By Southampton St to **Riddell Street** (late Regent St). 2-st cottages. Cul de sac. Houses flush with sidewalk. Much improved. From DARK BLUE of map to LIGHT BLUE.

At the NW corner is **Curran Place**. Still as poor and neglected as ever. DARK BLUE as map. Several women came out to see what our business might be and began to complain of the drains. There appeared to be some special grievance at No. 2 inside which was an agitated group. I went in, at their request, and looked at the WC in the little yard behind. Whether from want of flushing or from stoppage, it was hopelessly blocked and in a most filthy condition. One stalwart woman said that things had been as I saw them for months and that complaints to the landlord were met with the reply that if they did not like the houses they could leave them and let someone come in who would pay 7/- instead of 6/-, the present rental. I was told of the numbers who had been made ill by the drains and had one poor thing pointed out to me who had just returned. But the sadness of the scene culminated in a small coffin of a child that stood on a table at one side of the room in which we all were. They showed me the rent book when I asked who the owner was and later in the day I reported the state of things at the Office of the local Medical Officer. I gathered that the name of the Estate (Clement Davis, Surrey Estate, 11 Peckham Rye) was familiar at the Office, but the man I spoke to would not commit himself to any opinion. He was silent. "Davis" happens to be the name of a man who is building largely in Whitechapel and who gives a lot of trouble there.

S of Riddell St is **Camden Square**. 2½-st houses, stucco faced with fronts. Done up, improved. From LIGHT BLUE of map to PURPLE.

Commercial Road (north side to the Canal). At the west end, a new row of flats. Rents about 10/-. Working class. PINK as map.

Thence to **James' Grove**. Mainly 3-st houses. PINK-barred as map. Then mainly 2-st houses and some shops. From PINK-barred and PINK of map to PINK.

Branches Buildings (now the west end of Rosemary Rd). 2-st houses flush with sidewalk. Done up, much improved, quiet. From LIGHT BLUE of map to PURPLE.

Rosemary Road. An irregularly-built street. Mainly 2-st and 3-st houses, some shops. PINK, PURPLE and LIGHT BLUE as map.

S of Rosemary Rd are:

George's Street. 2-st houses. PINK as map.

And Camden Grove. 3-st houses with basements, lodgings etc. Some servants. Perhaps PINK-barred as map or PINK if altered.

Further E is James' Grove. 2½-st houses. From PINK-barred to PINK. Practically no servants, poorer rather than Camden Grove.

At the SE end of Sumner Rd on the sites of a nursery and wood yard a recreation ground is going to be laid out by the Vestry. It will face on the Canal and involve the demolition of some cottages. As yet nothing has been done.

General Remarks

This forms a somewhat monotonous part of Peckham, its redeeming feature being the absence of high dwellings. Except in one or two dark little corners, people may always be conscious of the sky and have plenty of light.

Of local employment there is little to say. A certain number of women give employment to a few of the men, but it is probable that the vast majority of the people living here, as in every part of Peckham and Camberwell except in the immediate neighbourhood of the Gasworks, find their employment in more central London. The solitary line of RED in Peckham Grove disappears and if one had to colour the district as a unit, and not by streets it would be an undeniable PURPLE. There is only one new street, Pennick St, of the prevailing local type of 2-st houses. In the district as a whole, there has been practically no rebuilding, and the general class of occupant appears to have changed as little as the structures during the decade.

Walk 41   B373

Tuesday 10th October 1899.
Ernest Aves with PC Dolby.

Starting along Peckham High Street.

N up Martin's Road. 2-st houses. PURPLE as map.

Into the Melon Ground. Small cottages, "all fronts", large garden fronts. Some conductors said to be living here, a few costers etc. LIGHT BLUE as map.

Salisbury Cottages. Two little cul de sacs near the Canal. 4-roomed cottages. LIGHT BLUE as map. Here and in Canal Place, lying just to the west, is mainly costers, a much larger proportion than in the Melon Ground itself. 4-roomed cottages. LIGHT BLUE as map.

Adelaide Place. Just like the Melon Ground. LIGHT BLUE as map.

E down Lisford Street. East end is like Adelaide Place, the cottages being most of them built up to the backs of those of the latter. LIGHT BLUE as map.

W to Sumner Road. South side is 2-st houses with fronts. PURPLE as map. North side is 2-st houses flush with sidewalk. Doors open into rooms. Poorer. From PURPLE of map to LIGHT BLUE.

NE to Stanton Street. 2-st houses with forecourts. Dull and depressing. The street has an indifferent reputation: "two or three wife-beaters living in it". Some broken windows. Perhaps from PURPLE of map to LIGHT BLUE.

Jocelyn Street. 2-st houses. Better than Stanton St. PURPLE as map.

Sumner Road. The southern light blue part backs on the Melon Ground, and the cottages there are a replica of those in Sumner Rd. LIGHT BLUE as map. The rest 2-st houses, some shops. purple as map. Three beer-houses and one full licensed house in this street, including one at the corner of its southern continuation, Winchester Place.

Winchester Place. 2-st houses. PURPLE as map.

Sumner Avenue. Unnamed on map, just to the south of the Board School. 2-st houses. No thoroughfare for vehicles. Decent, mainly conductors and drivers. PINK as map.

Just to the S of Haslam Place is **Hawker Street** (late Bath St). 2-st houses flush with sidewalk. Mostly no passage entries. Doors shut. "All costers." LIGHT BLUE as map.

Cator Street. 2-st houses with forecourts. Some houses newer than others. A murder in this street two years ago, a house breaker. PURPLE as map.

Further W is **Pitt Street**. Mostly 6-roomed houses letting at 13/-. Some newer letting at 8/6 a flat. "Violin taught" outside one of them. Small fronts to all the houses. PINK as map.

Camden Street. 2-st houses, semi-detached. PINK-barred as map.

A gate on the E side leads by a long path to **Camden Houses** (unnamed on map). A well-built block with a large and pleasant space in front. Built, so a very respectable woman living there informed me, by a Mr Groning who quarrelled with his relatives and left the block to the Armourers' and Braziers' Company. All of the tenants save three are now pensioners put in by the Company. The Houses rank, therefore, as almshouses, and colour should be omitted. The police do not patrol here, and Dolby had never been up.

Camden Grove. Semi-detached and a row of 3-st houses. Well-built. Some servants. From RED of map to PINK-barred. In No.1 a German bully set up his establishment a year or two ago. He was convicted and sentenced to three months.

Commercial Road (south side, from west end to Canal). A few offices and business premises but nearly all the houses east of Camden Grove now let out and in working class occupation. West of the Grove, therefore, leave PINK-barred as map. East of the Grove, from PINK-barred and PINK of map to PINK. Near the west end down the passage just below the "C" of the map, are two cottages, one occupied by a rag dealer and surrounded by a yard full of his unpleasant wares. Uncoloured on map, to LIGHT BLUE.

Southampton Street (from Commercial Rd to Peckham Rd). Mainly 3-st and 4-st houses. Some servants. PINK-barred as map, omitting all colour on space at south west corner for new and very large Board School.

W along the **Peckham Road**. Mainly substantial residential houses. RED as map, omitting 1) at the corner of Southampton St for the Board School and the Divisional Offices, 2) opposite Bushey Hill Rd for the new Fine Art Gallery and Institute, 3) on the south side for two of the large houses east of Vestry Rd now occupied by Dr Stocker for additions to his private Asylum, and 4) west of the Public House at corner of Grummond St for free Library.

N up Havil St to **South Street**. Mostly 2-st houses with good gardens and fronts. Poorer at east end. Irregularly built. PINK as map, omitting colour east of Muscatel Place beyond which there are no dwellings.

On the N side is **Absolom Place** (unnamed on map). East side only has 4-roomed cottages with no passage entries. LIGHT BLUE as map.

Just E of this is **Buck's Mat Factory** with a row of buildings of which only two are now occupied. PINK as map, omitting colour at north end. The yard is private.

N up **Wells Place**. Very like South St in class of people. Small houses with gardens. One family to a house the rule. Some new houses. From PURPLE of map to PINK.

Wells Crescent. 2-st houses, some new, all distinctly lower grade than the Place. PURPLE as map, omitting colour on west side for business premises.

Sedgmoor Place. Most semi-detached, 2-st houses with garden fronts. "Better class mechanics." From PURPLE of map to PINK.

Southampton Street (south side). LIGHT BLUE is the exception. Mainly shops, not very flourishing, but PINK rather than PURPLE of map.

In the afternoon, starting in the High St just to the west of Victoria Place.

Down **Paradise Place**. Unnamed on map. Three cottages, untidy yard. LIGHT BLUE as map. To the W is a passage leading through from the High St to Victoria Rd. Unnamed on map and locally known as **Mad House Passage**. On the east side are four cottages. Improved. LIGHT BLUE as map. The passage said to be unpleasant at night. Women haunt it and it is much used as an urinal.

Victoria Place. No passage for vehicles. Mostly costers. Improved. 2-st houses. Some broken windows, but from DARK BLUE of map to LIGHT BLUE.

Victoria Road. Mostly 2-st houses occupied by mechanical class. Some shops. Improved. VIOLET and PINK of map to PINK. On east side, north of South Grove, add PINK for new row of 3-st houses, shop fronts, and a little extra PINK is wanted on the opposite side, apparently omitted in error.

Lyndhurst Road. South of railway is 2½-st houses. Working class, no servants. From RED of map to PINK. North of railway is 2-st, 3-st and 4-st houses. Servants the rule up to Lyndhurst Square. To this point, RED as map. North of the Square are smaller houses. Extra colour for new row on site of nursery, 2-st red brick, £40 or £50 a year. North of the Square and this new row, RED and uncoloured to PINK-barred. The north west corner is clear, for demolition. Dolby said that the north end of Lyndhurst Rd was an unpleasant beat at night, as it was not an uncommon thing to hear the jabbering and the cries of the inmates of the Asylum.

South Place. Only 2-st houses on the north side. Shops. RED to PINK.

On the W side of Lyndhurst Rd is **Azenby Square**. 2-st and 2-st with basement houses. A great mixture, "mechanics and labouring class". Gone down. Two and three families in most houses. The east end the poorer. Perhaps all from PINK of map to PURPLE.

Hanover Road (now part of Hanover St). 2½-st and 3½-st houses with garden fronts. Trees. PINK-barred as map.

Lyndhurst Square. A leafy corner. Small detached and semi-detached villas, gabled. Linen out to dry in the gardens. Some servants. From RED to PINK-barred.

Sidmouth Place. One house occupied by a mantle-maker. From RED of map to PINK-barred. Into Peckham Rd, turning W and S down **Grummont Road**. 2½-st houses. Respectable artisan and mechanic class. No servants. From PINK-barred of map to PINK.

Note: at the south end of Lyndhurst Grove, Chadwick Rd running west is the boundary of the Peckham section. There are no houses in it on the north side, beyond the Brewery.

Talfourd Road. Good middle-class. red as map.

Talfourd Place. 2-st and 2½-st houses with garden fronts. Small salaried and high waged class. No servants. Three new houses built at end. All red-brick, bow windows. From PINK-barred of map to PINK, with extra colour for the new houses.

Denman Street. In class something betwixt and between Talfourd Rd and Talfourd Place. 2-st, 2½-st and 3½-st houses. The line of colour is broken on the east by the gardens of the Lyndhurst Rd houses. South of this break the houses are smaller and on both sides should go from the PINK-barred of map to PINK. The rest PINK-barred as map.

Lyndhurst Grove. PINK-barred as map.

Bushey Hill Road. Nearly all the detached houses shown on the map have given way to smaller dwellings. Occasional servants. From RED of map to PINK-barred.

Crofton Road. Better and larger houses north of the bend and servants frequently kept here. South of the bend 2-st, 6- or 8-roomed houses with bow windows, ornate. High waged and low salaried classes. Apartments often let. Servants not kept. PINK-barred as map north of the bend, from PINK-barred to PINK south of it.

Shenley Road. No part so good as the north end of Crofton Rd. Otherwise the same class. 2-st and 3-st houses. Mostly two families to a house. Servants the exception. Perhaps from PINK-barred of map to PINK.

The W end of Lyndhurst Grove remains PINK, as map. Dolby considered that exactly the same class of people lived here as in the southern end of Crofton Rd. The houses are 2-st, much the same as those in Crofton Rd, although less ornate.

Of the same class are the houses and people in Gairloch Road and Oswyth Road. Both PINK as map.

Linnell Road is also much the same and goes from PINK-barred of map to PINK.

General Remarks

This area, in as far as it lies north of the High St, differs little from that lying still further north, that is, north of Southampton Rd and Commercial Rd. It is mainly a working class neighbourhood, made up of little 2-st houses. The poorest corner is that lying round about the Melon Ground and here, whatever may be thought of the tiny houses as dwellings, plenty of space and garden ground is found, and there is plenty of air to breathe. It is such an area that might have led the woman whom I came across in a narrow court in the Borough and who had recently moved there from Peckham, say that the latter neighbourhood was "pleasanter like". There has been little fresh building, doubtless because there is little space available for building, and there is no special change to be noted. As the local industries, there are none of importance, unless it be brewing and looking after lunatics. The district includes two very large Private Asylums.

South of the High St the streets are almost exclusively residential, and are mainly occupied by the lower middle class. The greater part of Lyndhurst Rd holds its own as a "RED" street, but the tendency is for the servant-keeping class to decline in numbers. But deterioration is perhaps most marked in Azenby Square, coloured PINK on the map, a feature perhaps partly explained by its nearness to the railway, by the size of many of the houses (which are too large for single families), and by the fact that it leads nowhere. In Bushey Hill Rd, the tendency for large houses to give place to smaller ones is noticeable.

Walk 42   B373

Thursday 12th October 1899.
Ernest Aves with PC Dolby.

Starting up Park Road to Commercial Street,

In Commercial Street we caught sight of the Roman Catholic Church in the distance and it was perhaps not simply a coincidence that led Dolby, who had previously said that we were going to do "the worst part" of his section, to remark that it "was the only Roman Catholic Church in Peckham".

We turned E up Commercial Rd and N up **Cornwell Street**. 2-st, 6-roomed cottages with forecourts. The street "has not a good name". Leave LIGHT BLUE as map.

On the E side is **Victoria Place**. 4-roomed cottages flush with sidewalk. Cul de sac. Dirty, poor. LIGHT BLUE as map.

Back into **Commercial Road**. On south side the larger (8-roomed, 3-st) houses are mainly sublet and in working class occupancy, some business premises. Here from PINK-barred of map to PINK. North side still PINK as map, some of it though of low grade.

Radnor Street. 2-st houses. Better class here by far than in Cornwell St. Forecourts. PINK as map.

Peckham Park Road (to Bird in Bush Rd). West side the better, semi-detached houses here, occasional servants, "business people". Here PINK-barred as map. East side 2-st houses, working class. From PINK-barred of map to PINK.

Hill Street. Irregularly built, mainly 2½-st houses. Better on the Canal side. Here PINK-barred as map. On the east side from PINK-barred of map to PINK.

Willowbrook Road. The little bit east of the Canal is 3-st houses and shops. PINK as map. From there N up **Langdale Road**. Mainly 2½-st houses with attics. "Has a poor reputation" and looks the part, rows etc. PURPLE as map, with less colour on the west side for business premises, in the middle of which, however, there is an undeniable PINK house, probably occupied by a foreman.

Glengall Road. The best part is the row of houses on the west side near the Canal. Here from PURPLE of map to PINK. The rest of the road "only a shade better than Langdale Rd". Leave PURPLE as map.

E down **Reddins Road**. 2-st houses, 6-roomed, letting at 11/6 or 12/-. Nearly all sublet, "very like Glengall Rd". From PINK of map to PURPLE.

Of the same character and style is **Unwins Road**. Also from PINK of map to PURPLE.

Up Glengall Rd and E along **Harriet Lane** and **Bianca Lane**. No dwellings, saw mills, glass blowers, etc.

Into **Latona Road**. Several blocks of buildings, let in sets of from two to four rooms. Quiet. All PURPLE as map.

S down **Haymerle Road**. At the north east end a furniture factory and a fish-curing establishment (Williams, see later). On a first floor, in Williams' occupancy is a boxing saloon and round the corner is "Leo Hart's Painting Rooms", a well-known scene painter from whose studios came nearly all the splendour of Earl's Court. In the row of houses on the east side at the north end, the Mr Williams mentioned above lives. They are coloured LIGHT BLUE and Mr W has a stand at Billingsgate. He employs over 100 men at the adjacent curing establishment and has branches of his business all over the country. He is now buying up public house property and some time ago tried to turn his fish business into a limited company, with a capital of a quarter of a million! The flotation failed but he is evidently a very wealthy man. He is a well-known character, pays his men well and on one occasion when they struck and Dolby was called in on police duty, his way of dealing with them and his speech were forcible and impressive in the extreme. In language and manner generally, he appears to be "Billingsgate" and...he is a teetotaller. A son-in-law is living close by, in the same row, and on the strength of these two plutocrats and the appearance of the houses I think this part of the road might go from LIGHT BLUE to PINK. The rest LIGHT BLUE as map.

Bird in Bush Road. West of Cornwell Rd is 6- or 8-roomed houses. PURPLE and PINK of map to PINK. East of Cornwell Rd to Naylor Rd is PURPLE as map except the row of houses on south side between Ledbury St and Naylor Rd. This is a poor block of 3-st houses. From PURPLE of map to LIGHT BLUE. East of Naylor Rd from PINK-barred of map to PINK, omitting for Board School. On the south side, west of Rodney St are three cottages (not named on map). Garden fronts, chickens. Occupied by pickle-factory employees. PURPLE as map.

On the N side E of St Andrew's Church is **Hereford Place**. Four or five cottages. PINK as map.

Leyton Square. Houses generally eight rooms and scullery, and an occupier I spoke to was paying 15/-. Two families the rule and some extra sub-letting. Improved, the great trouble now being the noise and disorder of larrikins who come and play in the Square. This is soon to be laid out as an open space by the Vestry. PURPLE and LIGHT BLUE of map to PURPLE. PINK of map remains, except the south end of the north east side of the Square. This from the PINK of map to PURPLE. Opposite this bit a small row of houses has been built, very shoddy and rapidly deteriorating. Here from uncoloured to LIGHT BLUE.

Frensham Street (late Surrey Place). 2-st houses with basements. Improved. Several Italians living here, employed at Gatti's Ice Stores close by. From LIGHT BLUE to PURPLE on east side. On west side all but one house unoccupied, this LIGHT BLUE as map.

Round the corner are **Canal Cottages**, three or four of them. A poor class of coster living here, very miserable. From LIGHT BLUE of map to DARK BLUE.

Peckham Park Road. (Upper Park Rd and Park Rd in coloured map). Varied styles, best bit is on west side between Bird in Bush Rd and Commercial Rd. All north of Bird in Bush Rd from PINK-barred of map to PINK. Shops at Old Kent Rd end. Occupants mainly artisan and mechanic and lower clerk class.

At the N end, S is **Shard's Square**. Cul de sac. 4-roomed cottages, fronts. Has a bad name, "low labouring class", drunken. South side worse than north. Here from LIGHT BLUE of map to DARK BLUE, leaving the north side LIGHT BLUE.

Edwin Road. A few houses north east out of Green Hundred St. LIGHT BLUE as map.

On the other side of Green Hundred St is **Bexley Place**. Unnamed on map. Cul de sac. Until four or five years ago it was Irish. Since then almost entirely tenanted by Italians. Little if anything to choose between the two, both a very low lot. The Italians mainly hawkers of ice cream in summer and baked potatoes in winter. When we were there the court was stacked with the potato barrows and a group of men were busy sorting a sack, apparently choosing for the baking – a queer cut-throat looking group. Quaint dark-eyed Italian children running about. The men were asserted by Dolby to be in the employ of an entrepreneur who owns the barrows etc. The dwellings looked horribly poor. Still DARK BLUE as map.

Just above is **Grainger Street**. Locally known as "Go-as-you-please Street". Houses flush with sidewalk. Plenty of rough characters about, coster class and worse. DARK BLUE as map. Off the south west corner is a house that might be shown on the big map, same character as street. DARK BLUE.

Park Street. Houses flush. LIGHT BLUE as map. The time to see this neighbourhood, said Dolby with special reference to Grainger St, is after the hopping, when money is comparatively flush and the debauch is on.

Downes Terrace (south of Downes St, not named on map). 2-st houses, forecourts. From PURPLE to LIGHT BLUE.

Downes Street. 2-st houses. Also from PURPLE to LIGHT BLUE.

Green Hundred Street. Poorer at the north end. From LIGHT BLUE to DARK BLUE from this end to Grainger St, leaving the rest LIGHT BLUE as map.

Lower Park Road. (north of Commercial Rd). PURPLE and PINK as map.

Off the W side is **Sidmouth Grove**. PINK as map.

S of Bird in Bush Rd down **Ledbury Street**. 2-st houses. Quieter than it used to be. LIGHT BLUE as map.

So also **Upper Hall Street**. LIGHT BLUE as map.

To the E is **Naylor Road**. Mainly shops. PINK as map.

Arthur Street. PURPLE as map. All round here, both in the better and in the poorer streets a good many of the South Metropolitan Gas Company's employees are living, the poorer class being their more casual hands. Dolby spoke well of the condition of the employees as a class, saying that it was very difficult to get taken on there as a regular hand and that the competition to get in was keen. Mr Livesey appears to have made his reputation in the district as a man under whom it is an advantage to serve.

Trinby Street. A cul de sac east of Green Hundred St in a line with Shenton St. 2-st houses. LIGHT BLUE to PURPLE.

Thence up Downes St to **Ethnard Street**. 2-st houses, double bow windows. Better class mechanics etc. From PINK-barred of map to PINK with extra colour.

Approached from the Old Kent Rd is **Shenton Street**. A cul de sac. West side 2-st houses, forecourts. PURPLE as map. East side irregularly built, better houses. From PURPLE of map to PINK. At the end are two houses uncoloured on map, PINK or PURPLE.

Commercial Road (east from Cornwell Rd). PINK and PINK-barred of map to PINK, with extra colour for new row, filling in the gap on the south side, west of Lower Park Rd.

In the afternoon working east of Hill St and south of Commercial Rd we started from the High St up **Blue Anchor Lane**. This, with adjacent courts, mainly occupied by a poor coster class. The cottages on the east side have large garden fronts (the line of colour along the line of the lane is an error) and these might perhaps be left LIGHT BLUE as map. All the rest goes from LIGHT BLUE to DARK BLUE including **Carpenter's Place**, which is four old 2-st plus attic houses, tiled, and **Bachelor's Hall Place** (unnamed on map) with a Mission Hall belong to the Ragged School Union. Houses very poor and miserable. Further on in the walk we met Inspector Walsh, who gave a very poor character to the people living in this block and said that there was some talk of the new Borough exercising the powers it will possess and turning the whole of the area into a market.

Further N is **Bell's Gardens**. 2-st houses with basements and forecourts. LIGHT BLUE as map.

Thence into **Hill Street**. PINK as map.

W to **Bonar Road**. A new street with the houses backing on the Canal, the site having been carved out of the gardens of the Hill St houses. 2-st, 6-roomed, ordinary type. Uncoloured to PINK.

Peckham Park Road (west end). Shops. PINK as map, omitting colour on north side.

Close by is **Trafalgar Square**. 2-st houses with basement. Respectable. PINK as map.

S by Fenham Rd to **Garsdale Road**. Mostly 3-st houses. Crowds of children, unpleasant women, broken windows, many doors open, houses crowded. Same class as in Blue Anchor Lane. From LIGHT BLUE of map to DARK BLUE.

Frankton Road. Some houses done up, rough still. From PURPLE and PINK to LIGHT BLUE.

Furley Road. 2-st houses with six rooms and bow windows. PURPLE as map, continuing the colour on the east side to corner and on the west side to the end.

Fenham Road. West of Garsdale Rd is very poor. Here from PURPLE of map to DARK BLUE. The rest PURPLE as map. All the houses 2-st. Omit colour east of Furley Rd, no houses here except one at corner.

N to **Nelson Square**. 2-st houses, good garden fronts. Mechanic class. PINK as map.

W to **Park Row**. 2-st houses, rebuilt, good. Two families to a house the rule. Cul de sac, bad roadway. From LIGHT BLUE of map to PINK.

Lower Park Road (south of Commercial Rd). Irregular style of houses, some rebuilt, improved, some shops. From PURPLE of map to PINK.

Marmont Road. North of Goldsmith Rd is mainly 2-st houses, forecourts. Good working class. PINK as map. South of Goldsmith Rd is larger houses somewhat. On the west side, older, not so bright looking but occupied by same class. PINK as map.

Goldsmith Road. East of the site of Goldsmith's house are 3-st Buildings and three 2-st houses, the Buildings said by Dolby to be "very BLUE", in our terminology. All LIGHT BLUE as map but more of it. The rest of the street also considered very poor and still LIGHT BLUE as map except perhaps the row between Lower Park Rd and Marmont Rd. Here from LIGHT BLUE of map to PURPLE.

Westerfield Gardens. 2-st cottages. LIGHT BLUE as map but on east side only. Omit colour west side.

Hardcastle Street. 2-st houses, double bow windows. Like northern end of Marmont Rd. PINK as map.

Further E and parallel is Stafford Street. 2-st and 3-st houses with forecourts. The 3-st houses were recently bought by Mellins, whose factory is close by, for stabling but the firm is letting them instead, presumably finding that this pays. For the rents are high: for six rooms (small) 15/6. Omit colour at the south west corner for Theatre and at the south east corner for a clearance. The street PURPLE as map.

Walk 43
B373

Monday 16th October 1899.
Ernest Aves with PC Dolby.

Started up Meeting House Lane.
Turning E up Acorn Place. 2-st houses for the most part. In the part running east and west, the south side houses are flush with sidewalk but better than those on north side. The latter have forecourts but are closed in at back. On south side nearly all constables including Dolby. Rents six years ago were 6/6. He now pays 7/6 and newcomers 10/6. This is the rule now in Peckham where demand for houses is very keen. One effect is that the poorer class is being turned out. South side from LIGHT BLUE of map to PINK. On the north side also four rooms and scullery, rents 8/6 and 9/-. Two families the rule. This side from LIGHT BLUE of map to PURPLE. East of the turning on south side are Buildings, 3-st, let in sets of three rooms and scullery. Tenants well-paid class – Mellins' men, tram conductors and drivers, etc. From LIGHT BLUE to PINK. Well managed. On opposite side are two 6-roomed cottages, uncoloured to PINK. Acorn Place running north and south is poorer. LIGHT BLUE as map.

Shard's Road. Mainly 2-st houses with good garden fronts on west half of north side. All PINK as map except the row on south side between Acorn Place and Meeting House Lane. Here from PINK of map to LIGHT BLUE corresponding with the adjoining part of Acorn Place.

Meeting House Lane. At south end are new houses and some quite old, including that used originally as Penn's meeting house (a tablet up records the fact) and a few poor shops. Here PURPLE as map to Shard's Rd. Above this point PINK as map except 1) south side between Carlton Grove and Honiton St, this row poorer, from PINK of map to PURPLE, and 2) south side, east of Montpelier Rd, here 2-st houses, 10 rooms or so, occupied by a well-to-do class, servants often kept, from PINK to PINK-barred. The RED part on the north side is part of a row of small houses similar to those in Asylum Rd with which it is continuous. Said to be in the hands of single occupiers, servants occasional. Perhaps from RED to PINK-barred.

Pennethorne Road. 2-st houses, bow windows. Six rooms and two sculleries. Two families the rule, rents 14/6 to 15/-. Forecourts. All alike and the street occupied by a class of artisans and mechanics, foremen etc, common in the neighbourhood. PINK as map.

Kincaid Road and **Geldart Road** are very much the same. PINK as map.

Also of the same type is **Peckham Park**. From PURPLE of map to PINK. At the north west corner is a new Mission (Baptist). 1894, built apparently on a previously unoccupied site.

Further N is **Elcot Avenue**. Again very like Pennethorne Rd. Rents 15/-. PINK as map.

E along Commercial Rd to **Naylor Road** (south end). Most of it like Pennethorne Rd. PINK as map. Near north east corner down a yard is a house not shown on small map. Uncoloured to LIGHT BLUE.

On the W side is **Lansdown Place**. Poor cottages, "gone down". Garden fronts. Casual labouring class. Broken windows frequent and signs of neglect and poverty. From LIGHT BLUE of map to DARK BLUE.

Nutcroft Road. Very much of the Pennethorne Rd type. Houses not so convenient but same class living here, mostly working in the City, many of the regular and better-off gas workers etc. PINK as map.

Back by Meeting House Lane to **Honiton Street** (Clarkson Place in map). 2½-st houses, stucco. Rents probably about 12/-. Two and three families the rule. Poor and not with a very good reputation, rows etc. But the bad set cleared out when the name was changed. Used to be a nest of disorderly houses. From DARK BLUE-barred of map to LIGHT BLUE.

Thence along Meeting house Lane and N up **Springall Street**. Like Pennethorne Rd except the Vicarage, just north of the church. This from PINK to RED and the rest PINK as map.

Studholme Street. Also PINK as map, same type.

S along **Kings Road**. Generally 10-roomed houses, 2-st and 2½-st. Less well-to-do at south end, managers, foremen etc. Some servants. PINK-barred as map.

Into Queens Rd and up **Montpelier Road**. West side, old-fashioned houses, 3-st, stucco, gabled. East side, very like much of Kings Rd, 2-st and 10-roomed, "business people", a school, piano tanking in one house, "apartments" up at another. A milkman going his rounds and the door opened by a servant. Dolby though thought the people as a class a shade better than those in Kings Rd and had a high opinion of their exclusiveness! "They are the sort of people who will come and make a complaint if a drunken man walks down the street." From pink of map to pink-barred.

Further W is **Carlton Grove**, PINK as map, and **Pennell's Place**, also of the local PINK type. At the south west corner is a yard (wheel-wright's) with a house, PINK, that might be shown in the big map.

In the afternoon we worked east of **Asylum Road**. 2-st to 4-st houses, about 40 or 50 years old, irregular style. Occasional servants. Class compared by Dolby with that living in Clifton Rd (coloured PINK on map). From RED of map to PINK-barred on the west side as far as the Licensed Victuallers' Asylum, on east side as far as the National School. Above the Asylum, from RED of map to PINK. Above the School, and clearance for extension of Board School are some very poor little cottages ("1837") as well as better and newer working class dwellings. Here from PINK of map to PURPLE. At the south east corner of the street new 1-st shops have been put up and the gap round the corner in the Queens Road has been filled up in the same way. No dwelling accommodation, still uncoloured.

On the E side are four cul de sacs:

Newbold Street. 2-st and basements. PINK as map.

Staveley Road, Brimmington Road and Whittington Road. All 2-st houses with six rooms. One and two families. Rents have gone up and Dolby repeated with reference to this group of streets his remark about the elimination of the poorer class in Peckham that cannot afford the present range of rentals. All from PURPLE of map to PINK.

Clifton Road. West of Loder St is very like Asylum Rd. Occasional servants. From PINK of map to PINK-barred. East of Loder St is 3-st houses and small shops. PINK as map.

S is King Arthur Street. 2-st, 5- or 6-roomed houses with forecourts. Improved. From LIGHT BLUE of map to PURPLE.

At the W end is Bland Avenue. Very much the same. From LIGHT BLUE of map to PURPLE.

Loder Street. 2-st and 3-st houses. New, red-brick 3-st houses at north end, better than the rest. Some poor in the 3-st sublet houses, older, on east side north of Clifton Rd, but the whole street may be left PINK as map.

Culmore Road. 2-st and 3-st houses. South side in style like Clifton Rd but the occupiers a somewhat less well-to-do class. Leave PINK as map.

On the N side is Hove Street (unnamed on map). One 2-st house on west side. PINK as map. Leading into Clifton Crescent. 2-st to 3½-st houses. Good garden fronts to part of the Crescent, trees. The rest small houses of local type, double bows. All good PINK as map.

Leo Street. What is left is 2-st houses. Improved, small. Still LIGHT BLUE as map. Omissions of colour for 1) demolitions on north side, north of Clifton Crescent where two or three houses have gone to make way for new tram stabling, leaving only one house on this side, and 2) on south side for new large Board School.

Gervase Street. Also diminished by new Board School and not much left. Houses still up are irregular, 2-st. PINK as map.

Running NE is Back Lane. No dwellings, except one 4-roomed cottage on south side. Uncoloured to LIGHT BLUE.

The Old Kent Road, which is here only a "RED" street by courtesy as being a main thoroughfare, loses its colour between Gervase St and Leo St, the space being taken up by the new tram stabling already mentioned.

Along the New Cross Rd, across the boundary between Peckham and Deptford and thus passing into District 45, S down Pomeroy Street. Mainly 2-st residential houses, but including some big works: Eno's Fruit Salts, two Iron Works etc. Occasional shops and five licensed houses in the street. Several courts leading out of it and it has not a very good name. Occupants a very mixed class. PINK as map north of Mary Ann Place and south of this point from PINK of map to PURPLE.

On the W side is Carlton Square. 2-st houses with basements, "1845." PINK as map.

Just to the SW of this is Clifton Avenue (approached from Clifton Rd). Unnamed and uncoloured on map. 2-st houses with attics and 3-st, stucco, two of them fronting in Clifton Rd. From uncoloured of map to PURPLE.

Mary Ann Place is on the W side of Pomeroy St. Unnamed on map. 2-st cottages, five or six rooms. Gardens. PURPLE as map.

On the same side is Fritton Place (late Alfred Place, west of the "y" of Pomeroy St). Unnamed and uncoloured on map. Six 4-roomed cottages, done up. From uncoloured to PURPLE or LIGHT BLUE.

Thence along Queens Rd back into District 44 and N up York Grove. 2-st houses with basements and 3-st houses. Good, apartments etc. Occasional servants. From RED of map to PINK-barred.

Dayton Grove is of the local type. 2-st, double bay windows. Two families the rule to a house. Rents 7/6 a floor. PINK as map.

Colls Road is much the same. Single bay windows. PINK as map.

Its replica is **Astbury Road**. PINK as map. The last two roads are said by Dolby to have been originally part of the Liberator Estate.

Walk 44

Tuesday 7th November 1899.
Ernest Aves with PC Dolby.

We started by finishing the omitted corner east of Pomeroy St.

Taking first **Kender Street**. Varied style of houses 2-st, 2½-st etc. Not unlike Pomeroy St, mainly "mechanic class". PINK as map. Several courts lie off the street.

On the E side: two cottages to the north of Frederick St, quite poor. Too much colour shown on map and it should go from PURPLE as given to either DARK BLUE or LIGHT BLUE.

Also **Esther Cottages** (south of Faulkner St). PURPLE as map, with extra colour for two others not shown: "Cook's Folly, 1843."

On the W side:

Kender Grove. 2-st houses. PINK as map.

Power's Place. 2-st houses, forecourts. PURPLE as map, placing the colour on the north side, further west.

Dolling Place. Not named on map (east of Rose Cottages). Eight cottages. PURPLE as map on north side. From PURPLE of map to LIGHT BLUE on south side.

Kender Place (south east of Rose Cottages) Not named on map. Gardens. PURPLE as map.

Rose Cottages. Entered from Pomeroy St. Four poor little places. From PURPLE of map to LIGHT BLUE.

Besson Street. 2-st houses, garden fronts. Many railway men living here. Some LIGHT BLUE but still PINK as map.

On the S side:

Mason's Court. 4-roomed cottages. Clean. One family in each, rents 6/-. From DARK BLUE of map to LIGHT BLUE.

Mason's Grove. 2-st houses with basements. Garden fronts. Six rooms, rent 8/6. PURPLE as map.

Martin's Place. 2-st houses. "Better class" here. PINK as map, less colour on the east side where are only two detached pairs of houses.

New Cross Road (east from Kender St). Private houses to a little west of Besson St. Very few servants. The shops when they begin are second rate. Query from RED to PINK-barred?

Briant Street. 2-st houses. PURPLE as map except for clearance at corner of Martha Place and omission for factory on east side.

Martha Place. 2-st houses, garden fronts. Better on north side, all "rough". Two miserable houses in the south west corner. From PURPLE of map to LIGHT BLUE and DARK BLUE, the latter for the two houses mentioned.

Faulkner Place. No thoroughfare, bricked with tiny squares. 2-st houses flush with the sides. "Rough, and low class." A few DARK BLUE houses, most doors shut, on the whole leave LIGHT BLUE as map.

Frederick Street (now Lubbock St). 2-st houses, flush with sidewalk, Done up on north side. PURPLE as map.

General Remarks

A slight shifting of colours is noticeable in this area, but structurally there has been little change. It remains mainly a residential part of London, not of a very desirable kind. The western boundary is a dull Canal, the two other sides of the triangle that the area covers are parts of great London highways but within there is little to break the prevailing monotony. The Licensed Victuallers' Asylum and an occasional Board School impress by their extent, and Penn's little Meeting House and the bare site of Goldsmith's home have considerable historic and literary interest. But there does not appear to be much besides that rises above the commonplace.

The district is too young to have entered upon a period of considerable rebuilding, or even of renovation. On the other hand it is old enough to be full and Bonar Rd is, I think, the solitary instance of an entirely new street – and it was carved out the gardens of the Hill St houses.

It is mainly a small house area and, although there is no great congestion of population, there is only a very limited amount of garden space. Leyton Square is a public garden for the future. Although most of the dwellings are small the area contains all the "models" in Peckham – the very fair block in Acorn Place, the moderately good ones in Latona Rd and the thoroughly bad ones in Goldsmith Rd.

It is not a criminal district and even the BLACK barring of Clarkson Place gives way to the comparative respectability of Honiton St. The only DARK BLUE of ten years ago that remains is that of the Grainger St areas and this has to be slightly extended. Two or three spots of DARK BLUE disappear but on the other hand their place is taken by the courts of Blue Anchor Lane. There is however some reason to expect that the latter are doomed to speedy demolition. Other new ones seem likely to remain.

There is no important local industry, the most important local economic influence being perhaps the South Metropolitan Gasworks, just to the north of the Old Kent Rd. Many indications of the improved conditions of employment there are forthcoming. The poorest and the roughest are by no means the gas workers, nor do they appear to include a casual element now of any considerable size. The poorest and roughest are costers, loafers and the confirmed casual of every trade and no trade. At the lowest level must be added the strange Italian colony in Bexley Place. The area includes the only Roman Catholic Church in Peckham but it does not appear that there is now any numerous Irish element. This class, of the roughest kind, has cleared out of Bexley Place in recent years, and it will be well to find out from the Mission priest whether there has been any other migration, and if so whether this is connected with the changes at the Gasworks.

Asylum Rd and York Grove lose their distinctive badges of RED, but in spite of this – a normal change – the balance of changes as have taken place makes, perhaps, on the whole for a slight improvement.

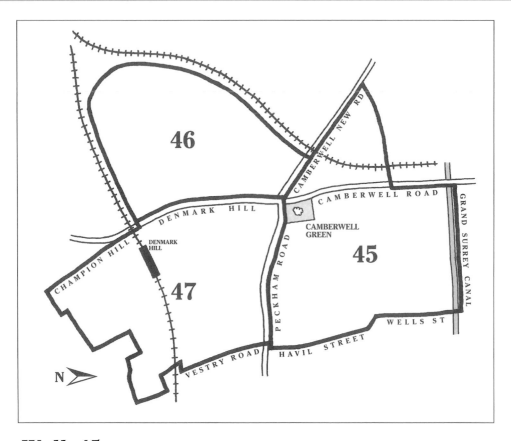

Walk 45

B373

Thursday 28th September 1899.
Ernest Aves with PC Young.
Young is a man of about 38. He has been in the force for 15 years and has been in ths section for six. He is a solid, double-chinned policeman, intelligent and fairly communicative,
in a district about which there was perhaps not very much for him to say. He had been
transferred at his own request from the Pimlico Subdivision, and had worked a good deal in
the neighbourhood of Victoria. He is unmarried, having come to the conclusion that a constable's pay is not suficient to keep a wife and family on. He lives at the section house. He
knew the district well.

Starting up the Camberwell Road.
The first part of the walk is in District 42. E to **Addington Square**. At the west end
Cambridge Hall is on the south side. Some colour omitted here. The rest, with the Square,
PINK-barred and PINK as map. Some servants kept. Middle-class. Lodgings etc. The
Sisters' House connected with the Trinity Mission here. Mostly 3½-st houses of plain brick.
The south east end of the Square, leading to New Church Rd is from PINK-barred and PINK
of map to PINK.
To the N is **Goodyear Place**. 2-st houses. Rents 9/- to 10/6. Men earning about 23/- or
24/- a week. Two families to a house. From PINK of map to PURPLE.

S is **Kitson Street**. 3-st houses. Good working class. From PINK-barred of map to PINK.
Rust Square is very much the same. PINK as map.
To the NE is **Cumberland Place** (now Caldew St). 2-st houses, some new. Respectable. From LIGHT BLUE of map to PURPLE.
Boyton's Place. 2-st houses. LIGHT BLUE as map.
Bath Place. The DARK BLUE line along the Canal has improved. 2-st cottages, mainly occupied by Canal workers. The LIGHT BLUE part of the Place, lying east of Bayton's Rd, (Canal Place on map) looks poorer than the DARK BLUE bit. Said to be rough, much drinking. Very much like the west bit. All should be either DARK BLUE or, better, LIGHT BLUE.
At the W end of Bath Place is **Sugden Street**. 2-st houses. Generally two families in each. Rents 13/- or 14/-. Respectable. From LIGHT BLUE of map to PURPLE.
E of Boyton's Place is **Boyton's Road**. No carriageway, asphalted. Houses and people as in Boyton's Place. West side only. LIGHT BLUE as map.
Into New Church Rd, the S side of which is **Victory Square**. 2-st houses. Some new. Respectable. PINK as map.
New Church Road. Houses various, mainly 2-st and 3-st. Shops at west end and scattered about elsewhere. Trinity Hall, connected with the Mission, a good building, opposite Sampton St. Camberwell Hall a little further west offers "Free Thought Lectures" etc. The poorest part of the street is two rows of 3-st tenement houses east of Sampton St. These quite poor. A clearance west of Edmund St. Leave PURPLE and PINK as map, omitting for clearance and Trinity Hall.
Edmund Street. The main artery of rather a poor block. 2-st houses. LIGHT BLUE as map. Outside a public house we passed a rough group of men drinking in the street and passing the pot round. One of them, a burly coster, was pointed out as a man several times convicted for "drunk and disorderly and for assaults on the police". He saluted Young as we passed. "Always very respectful to me", said my guide, who had himself run the man in a few months ago but had never had serious trouble with him.
On the E side of Edmund St is **Paddock Place** (not named on map). 2-st houses on north side only, with one cottage at end, not shewn on map. A cul de sac. LIGHT BLUE as map.
A little to the S out of E side of Edmund St is **Graycott Place** (also not named on map). Like Paddock Place. LIGHT BLUE as map.
Still working E of Edmund St we have parts of **Westmacott Street** and **Acorn Street**. Both very much alike. 2-st houses, fairly respectable. LIGHT BLUE and PURPLE of map to LIGHT BLUE. A pawn-shop close by here, with its crowds on Monday morning, an index to much of the neighbourhood.
To the SE is **Cottage Green**. 2-st and 3-st houses. Detached on the north side and better here. Leave PINK as map.
Wells Street. 2-st and 3-st houses. Some shops. A good PINK street, leave PINK as map.
Parkhouse Street. A quiet spot with many detached houses. A good many laundries here and in the neighbourhood. Some new 2-st flats called Firle Terrace. Separate entrances for two lettings, about 8/- a floor. The whole street PINK as map.
Southampton Street. 2-st and 3-st houses. An irregular and varied street. Some shops. A new block of 3-st flats north of Parkhouse St. Rents 13/- to 15/-. No servants. The street from PINK and PURPLE of map to PINK.
Into District 43 at **Harris Street**. 2-st houses. Some very poor at south end. From DARK BLUE, PINK and PURPLE of map to LIGHT BLUE.
Behind the school is **Rill Street**. 2-st houses. Poor. Done up. Doors shut. From DARK

BLUE of map to LIGHT BLUE.

Teather Street. 2-st houses. Doors shut. Poor. Coster type, but from DARK BLUE of map to LIGHT BLUE.

Havil Street. Mainly 2-st houses. Some two flats, 4-st, 8/- a flat. Some shops. Good PINK as map.

W is **Ada Road.** 2-st, bow-windowed little houses. Good. PINK as map.

Elmington Road. 2-st, 2½-st and 3-st houses. Some extra colour at east side. Plenty of space round here. Good wage earning and small salaried class. PINK as map with addition noted.

Acorn Street. 2-st. Two families in most houses. Low grade PINK rather than PURPLE of map.

Martha Street (now part of Picton St). 2-st houses. Rather rough, a good deal of drinking. Different class to Acorn St. Respectable folk there, a drinking lot here. Perhaps from PURPLE of map to LIGHT BLUE.

Off Picton St is **Ampfield Cottages.** Three of them. PURPLE as map.

To the **S** is **Cork Street.** 2-st houses. Improves towards south west end. Remains PURPLE as map.

Chiswell Street. Very much like Cork St. PURPLE as map except the block at south east corner of Hampton Avenue which is DARK BLUE.

Hampton Avenue. 3-st Buildings, narrow, gloomy. "Some of the roughest on our ground here", but drinking and roughness rather than crime alleged. Miserable women and neglected children. Broken windows. All the signs of a DARK BLUE street. From LIGHT BLUE of map to DARK BLUE with extra colour on south side.

Waterloo Street. 2-st houses. Irregular outline. Some shops. Perhaps PINK rather than PURPLE of map.

Brisbane Street. South of Picton St it is 2-st houses. PURPLE as map. North of Picton St are 2-st and 3-st houses. Poorer. From PURPLE of map to LIGHT BLUE. Young agreed that, of the last eight streets, Acorn St and Waterloo St were of better grade than the rest.

George Street. Mainly 2-st houses. Irregular. Contains two of the few blocks of model dwellings found in this part of London. A few business premises. Salvation Army Barracks near south east corner. The blocks very fair. The one lying to the north of that called Waterloo Square looking less well looked after but said to be the more expensive. The whole street including the blocks perhaps low-grade PINK rather than the PURPLE of map.

On the **W** side is **Pleasant Place.** Three cottages. Flowers etc. Decent. LIGHT BLUE as map. Entrance marked "private".

Also **Arm's Place** (late South Place). Three poor little cottages. LIGHT BLUE as map. In one was a little chap looking untidy and rather forlorn, aged about seven. But he was not, as I at first thought, quite alone, as a small child of four or five, a clean little girl, came up and presented herself, to be duly introduced as "a little friend, a neighbour". Her home appeared to be quite deserted and we left them in their small companionship.

To the **S** of Westmacott St is **Thornhill Square.** 2-st houses. Dirty children playing about. Date of square "1862". Leave PURPLE as map.

Westmacott Street. 2-st and 3-st houses. PURPLE as map.

N is **Fandon Row.** Costers etc. DARK BLUE as map.

Lying to the **N** of Notley St and much the same as Fandon Row is **Pinnock Terrace.** Here older 2-st houses, with attics. DARK BLUE as map.

Notley Street. 2-st houses. LIGHT BLUE as map.

To the **NE** is **Caspian Street.** 3-st houses. Gloomy and rough. LIGHT BLUE as map.

Entered from New Church Rd is **Sears Street.** A cul de sac of 2½-st houses with six or eight rooms. Generally two families. Respectable working class. PINK as map.

Continuing on 29th September 1899.

Starting up the Camberwell New Road.

Camberwell New Road is mainly 3-st houses with garden fronts. Very few shops. Mixed class, including many good wage earners. Colour PINK-barred, instead of RED of map as far as Wyndham Rd. Beyond this point the road lies in another police division, and beyond Leipsic Rd in our District 35.

Beyond the railway on the N side is Orchard Street (now Medlar St). 2-st houses with bow windows. Tram drivers etc. PINK as map with a little extra colour east of railway.

Badsworth Road is a new street running through to Leipsic Rd. In character very like Medlar St. PINK, uncoloured in map.

Leipsic Road. 2-st houses, mainly semi-detached. Good working class. PINK as map. The small area in the Camberwell Police section lying N of Leipsic Rd is in District 35.

Lying S of Clarendon St is Clarendon Avenue. Bad approach but when reached seven pleasant cottages with four rooms each. Rents are 6/6. Gardens, vines over most of the houses, lots of grapes. PINK as map but more of it. Unnamed on map.

Clarendon Street. 2-st and 2½-st houses. PINK as map.

Clarendon Place. 2-st houses. Rather poorer than the street and perhaps PURPLE rather than PINK as map.

Ulric Street. 2-st houses. One, an exception, let at £20 per year plus rates and taxes. Occupied by a widow who had three women lodging there. Very respectable. She compained bitterly of the noise in the street from the children of the school near, who find it a convenient playground, and the "Curse of the School Board" was mentioned as one of the things that had brought the street down. On the other side, lying just the other side of Wyndham Rd, is the Sultan St area, and this does not make for quiet and decency. Perhaps the street, with Cleveland Street (2-st houses) and Clarendon Place (already mentioned) should all be PURPLE rather than the PINK of the map.

Wyndham Road. Mostly shops. Because of them, remains PINK as map. On the south side, lying back close to the railway, shut in and lonely, is one small cottage. LIGHT BLUE if shewn, uncoloured on map.

On the same side further SW is Pallador Place (late Ebenezer Place). 2-st cottages with gardens. A cul de sac. PURPLE as map.

Also Pinto Place (late Caroline Place). 2-st cottages. Cul de sac. Much poorer. Apparently an Irish population. Six children of school age playing about, said to have been to early Holy Communion and on this account to be having a holiday. This happened about once a month a woman said, but without any sign of disapproval. Colour from PURPLE of map to LIGHT BLUE. The children were playing cards on the flagstones!

In District 43 Camberwell Road has shops. RED as map.

Turning S, on the W side is Castle Street (now forming part of Mansion St). Uniform all through, rather badly-built 2½-st houses. PURPLE as map.

Mansion House Square. With a Chapel used as a mission blocking up the centre and blocking out the light. 3-st houses. PURPLE as map.

Castle Street and Mansion Street. 2½-st. Poor. Much LIGHT BLUE, some PINK. Asphalt paved, cleanly kept. PURPLE to LIGHT BLUE, in map PURPLE. Railway arches form west end and under them is a large gas stove factory whose clerical offices take up the whole of the side opposite.

Mansion House Square. 3-st homes at west end only. Much LIGHT BLUE here. Ashpalt paved and clean. One house at south east corner. PURPLE and LIGHT BLUE.

Blucher Road. 2-st and 3-st houses. PINK as map. On the same side, further south the unnamed LIGHT BLUE goes, stables etc having been built on the site of former dwellings.

On the E side of Camberwell Rd, starting from the S, is **Mazzard Row**. A messy spot. 3-st houses on south side only. LIGHT BLUE as map.

Buff Place. 3-st houses, shoddy buildings. Omit for warehouse and colour LIGHT BLUE to plan.

Guildford Place. On south side old 3-st houses, "1801". On north side, new and shoddy, very much like Buff Place. All LIGHT BLUE as map. In addition, three newer 2-st houses. PURPLE, uncoloured on map.

Out of the S side of Waterloo St by the school, **Haycocks Cottages** is entered by a curious hooked passage. Mark all LIGHT BLUE.

Waterloo Street itself is old 2-st houses. This is a good typical width for a 2-st street. The roadway is 24 ft. The footways on either side are 6 ft. Small wooden rails to small uncared-for forecourts in front of the houses. PURPLE.

On S side is **Waterloo Mews**. Three houses on east side only. PURPLE to PINK.

Lying off from the NE corner of Camberwell Green are **D'Eynsford Road, Harvey Road** and **Kimpton Road**. All 2-st houses and very much alike. Mixed working class. Respectable. Query all from PURPLE of map to PINK?

Sansom Street in which the same sort of people are living, but in which the houses are somewhat newer and larger, 2-st with bow windows. Six rooms letting at 14/6. Generally two families to a house.

On the N side of Waterloo St is **Hopewell Place** (late Providence Place). Five poor cottages on west side only. DARK BLUE, uncoloured on map.

On S side of Waterloo St is **Hearsey Place**. 2-st houses. Poor. Query from PURPLE of map to LIGHT BLUE?

To the E is **Benhill Road**. Mainly 2½-st houses. Almost entirely working class. Young thought no servants. High grade PINK, rather than PINK-barred of map.

Brunswick Square. The garden of the Square in very bad order, but the houses are large and generally in the hands of single occupiers. "City people, etc." Few lodgers. The houses are well built. RED and PINK-barred as map except at south east corner where the houses are closed and coming down for extension of Infirmary.

Brunswick Road. 2½-st and 3½-st houses. PINK as map.

Havil Street. The boundary street of the police section on this side. Houses mostly 2-st. A high grade PINK street, as map. Much of the west side taken up by the Infirmary and Workhouse.

Turn W along **Peckham Road**. Large houses. RED as map.

Behind the gardens runs **Camberwell Glebe**. Only a few stables on the south side. Not many occupied. One a bus proprietor's, others private. PINK and LIGHT BLUE, RED and uncoloured on map. The Glebe patrolled at night only.

Vicarage Road. 3½-st houses. A good many let out to two and three families, especially on west side. Clerks etc. So also north side. East side mainly in single hands. Colour RED here as map but elsewhere PINK-barred.

Belham Street. 2½-st houses. Improved. From LIGHT BLUE of map to PURPLE.

Mosedale Street. Same sized houses as in Belham St. PURPLE as map.

On the N side of Church St is **Datchelor Place**. On west side are 3-st houses. Shops. PINK as map. On east side Gordon Dwellings, "1885", 5-st. Two rooms for 5/- and 5/6, three rooms for 6/6 to 8/-. PURPLE as map.

Artichoke Place. On west side 4-st "mansions". PURPLE as map. Camberwell Baths, "1891", at end.

Artichoke Mews. Also PURPLE as map.

Camberwell Green

General Remarks

The state of things in this area, which takes in parts of Districts 42, 43 and 35, remains very much as it was ten years ago. There is a little less RED and a little more PINK. There is no YELLOW and the centres of great poverty are exceptional. The solitary addition to the DARK BLUE is Hampton Avenue, a squalid block of dwellings off Brisbane St. The poverty here is more depressing and assertive than in the two small courts of Notley St, perhaps because the people are thicker on the ground.

The district as a whole is not densely populated, the houses being for the most part small with a fair amount of ground unbuilt over. Very little, however, is unoccupied, the two or three new streets being found only in the triangle lying west of the Camberwell Rd. The big block dwellings off George St are exceptional, both in this area and in the whole of Camberwell.

There are a certain number of laundries scattered about, but no important local industry. The centre of activity is the Green, on the south and west sides, and Church St. The corner of the Green by the Post Office is the hub of the local world, not only focusing much of the busy trafficking of the place but being also a great starting point and passing place for omnibuses and trams running in many directions. The Green itself is pleasantly laid out.

The Trinity Misson works here and structural and printed signs of its presence come to the surface from time to time. In Camberwell Rd, close by Addington Square, are the two houses with which Trinity Court, now merged in the Cambridge House, was started. Oxford House is the accepted model for the South London Settlement but there is no reason to think that the centre in Camberwell is approaching that in Bethnal Green in the extent of its work. It is not improbable that it will always be somewhat overshadowed by the older and richer Mission. Some think that it will even have difficulty in preserving a real separateness of activity and of life.

Walk 46   B373

Monday 2nd October 1899.
Ernest Aves with PC Young.

Starting up Denmark Hill.
To Bloxham's Buildings. Poor cottages, garden fronts. Costers etc, some loafers, rather rough drinking lot. DARK BLUE as map.
Milkwell Yard (further down on same side). Unnamed on map and uncoloured. On west side three cottages. Laundry employees. LIGHT BLUE. On north side is one house, a carpenter's. PINK.
Cold Harbour Lane. Mainly residential. RED to PINK-barred. Extra colour south of new theatre for new block, "Metropole Parade", flats and shops. PINK-barred like the rest. Omit colour opposite for clearance.
NE to Valmar Road. 3-st houses. PINK-barred as map.
Warner Road. Mainly semi-detached 2-st houses. A very occasional servant. Good working class is the characteristic of the street. PINK as map.
Up Camberwell New Road, passing a milk-yard with one PINK house as shewn on map.
SW to Station Road. Mainly 3-st houses. Poorer at south west end. PURPLE as map here with omission of colour at corner for factory. At the other end good working class. From PINK-barred of map to PINK.
Station Terrace. 3-st houses. Three and sometimes four families to a house, "reckoned a poor corner". From PINK of map to PURPLE.
S of the Terrace is Station Vale. Not shewn or coloured on map. Mews, cabbies, washers etc. Uncoloured to LIGHT BLUE.
Lowth Road. 2-st and 3-st houses. New flats at south east end. All PINK as map.
Crawford Street. 2-st and 3-st houses. Irregularly built. An "occasional servant", decent. From PURPLE of map to PINK.
Morna Road. 3-st houses. PINK as map.
SW to Denmark Road. 2-st and 3-st houses. PINK as map.
Denmark Street. Smaller houses, mainly residential but some shops at south end. Houses mainly 2-st, not uniform. PINK as map.
Dane's Road. 2-st houses, five or six rooms. An occasional broken window. PURPLE and PINK as map.
At the E end is Dane's Cottages. Only three of them. Four rooms, 6/6. Decent. PURPLE as map.
Further S is Roslyn Avenue. PINK as map.
Thence SW to Lilford Road. 2-st and 2½-st houses plus attics. Better east of Flaxman Rd. The west end is rather poor, but still all PINK as map, except the row backing on Redan Terrace. Here from PINK of map to PURPLE.
At the NE corner is Carew Street. 2-st houses. Two families to each the rule. Bow windows. Decent and fresh looking. PINK as map.
SW again to Alma Terrace (now Redan Terrace). 2-st houses. Better on west side. Here from PURPLE of map to PINK. On east side, rougher class, not a good name, drunken, rows. Leave PURPLE as map.
Flaxman Road. 2½-st and 3½-st houses and other sizes. PINK as map.
On the S side are two streets very much of the same type, Eastlake Road and Luxor Street.

Both 3½-st houses, good type of working class, like Flaxman Rd. High grade PINK as map.
Further along on same side is **Pomfret Road**. 3-st houses with basements. Poorer on south
side. Here PINK to PURPLE. Leave north side PINK as map.
From here across Cold Harbour Lane to **Lewis Road**. 2-st and 3-st houses. "Rough."
PURPLE as map.
Padfield Street (running south west). 3-st houses, same class as Lewis Rd. From PINK of
map to PURPLE.
Vaughan Road. 2-st and 3-st houses, some detached. PINK-barred and PINK to PINK-
barred, omitting some colour put in in error round the corner on the east side.
Harbour Road. 2-st houses. PINK as map.
Cambria Road. Irregularly built. 2-st, 2½-st and 3-st houses. PINK as map.
Conderton Road, Bredon Road and **Bengeworth Road**. Uniform in style. Much
shoddy building. Some houses obviously going to the bad, broken windows etc. These the
exception but further deterioration probable. Query all from PINK of map to PURPLE?
Along Cold Harbour Lane to, at the NE corner, **Cold Harbour Place**, including
Denmark Passage, 2-st cottages. PURPLE as map with some colour omitted at corner.
Along Denmark Hill to **Sun Court** (unnamed and uncoloured on map). A most sunless
spot. Three or four cottages. A family of four or five children in one of the houses, quite alone
when we were there, dirty and forlorn to a degree. From uncoloured to DARK BLUE.
Denmark Hill. New flats. 2-st, gabled. Arranged for two families, built out behind giving
lots of room, filling empty space south of new theatre. The Hill RED as map with extra colour
for the new block.

General Remarks

The large amount of open space shewn on the map is open still, being mainly taken up by
the garden of the houses in Denmark Hill and in Cold Harbour Lane, the latter a steadily
declining residential street, and by an Athletic Ground. The only encroachment, so far, has
been in the erection of Electrical Lighting works near the south west corner.

The Theatre and the adjacent blocks are the only important new buildings on any
thoroughfare.

To the DARK BLUE of Bloxham's Buildings the small patch of Sun Court has to be added.
The latter calls for a small clearance, the former for complete restoration and, probably, for
better management. When the colour for Station Vale has been added, this small area will
include all the colours of the map scale, and most of them have remained constant during the
decade. The most important exception will be the change of Cold Harbour Lane from RED
to PINK-barred, and in the south west corner, mainly from the shoddy building of the
Bengeworth Rd triangle, rather more PURPLE will show. But PINK will remain the prevailing
colour.

Walk 47   B373

Tuesday 3rd October 1899.
Ernest Aves with PC Young.

Starting down Grove Lane.
On the W side into **Willoughby Road**. 3-st houses. Cul de sac. More colour required on
north side. PINK as map, with this addition.

Further **S** is **Kerfield Crescent**. 2½-st houses. Cul de sac. Two families to a house the rule. Respectable. PINK as map.

On the **S** side are:

Kerfield Mews (unnamed on map). Three 2½-st houses, like the Crescent. PINK as map.

Love Walk (east end). Small villas. RED as map.

Grove Lane itself is very varied, both in style of house and character of occupant. Mainly residential, including small cottages, rows of large 4-st houses and large detached substantial dwellings. West side is PINK-barred as map. The two rows of houses north of Windsor Rd, YELLOW on map, also PINK-barred. All the YELLOW houses, with these exceptions, to be coloured RED. East side, north of Champion Park, all the RED to PINK-barred except a small block of 2-st houses, small shops, south of Datchelor School. This block from RED of map to PINK. The PINK bit stands for a row of cottages and remains. North of Champion Park, from RED and YELLOW of map to RED. In the space north of the cottages, opposite De Crespigny Park, additional colour for new 2-st, two family, red-brick, gabled houses, good. Uncoloured to PINK-barred.

N of the Railway is **Windsor Road**. Mainly 3-st and 3½-st houses, a few detached. "City People." German Church here. From YELLOW of map to RED. Omit colour at end, outhouses having been coloured YELLOW in error. Add PINK, for stables, close to the road near the Station (west side).

By Denmark Hill Station is **Champion Park**. Large detached houses at east end. Strong, Chairman of LCC, living here. YELLOW and RED as map.

Champion Grove. Mainly detached villas, getting past their best days, but still in single occupancy and RED as map. Along east side a new row has been built. Inferior, for two families. Uncoloured to PINK-barred.

Grove Hill Road. The southern boundary of the Camberwell Police section. Some very large houses. YELLOW as map.

Old stables at Camberwell Grove.

Camberwell Grove. Broad, leafy, declining. Many large houses nearly all in rows. Lodgers coming into many of the smaller houses, especially on the west side. From RED of map to PINK-barred on the west side from Aldover Place to the Chapel and from Chatham Place to the end. On the east side from RED of map to PINK-barred between Edgecombe Rd and Lettsom St and the two last blocks at north end. All the rest of the Grove from RED and YELLOW of map to RED.

Off the W side is **Canning Passage**. Running through to Grove Lane by the public house of this name on the south side are three 2 st cottages (9/- a week) and one older house. Uncoloured in map to PINK. At corner in the Mews, a job-master's house. Uncoloured to PINK. The RED in the Mews further south is an error, omit.

Near NE end of the Grove are **Grove Cottages**. Old, timbered fronts, tiled roofs. Poor. From PINK of map to LIGHT BLUE. New cottages are building on right of passage entry.

Church Street. Shops. RED as map, except for common lodging house opposite Vicarage Rd – 6d, 9d, and 1/-. Colour DARK BLUE. "The usual sort of loafer etc. come here."

E past the Church and S down **Wilson Road**. 3-st houses with basements. Two and three families the rule. Working class. From RED of map to PINK, except for the detached house occupied by one of the local clergy.

Dagmar Road is also like Wilson Rd, even to having its better-to-do detached house. This RED, as map, and the rest to PINK.

Grace's Road. Mainly 2½-st houses. PINK as map.

Maude Road. 3-st houses. Also PINK as map.

Vestry Road (the boundary of this police section). North of Linnell Rd the west side is 2-st houses. Decent working class. From PURPLE of map to PINK. East side has only one house occupied, in the middle of the line of PURPLE, a small job-master's. This PINK and the PURPLE omitted. South of Linnell Rd the houses are larger but occupied by people of very much the same class. From PINK-barred of map to PINK.

Linnell Road (west of Vesty Rd). 2-st and 3-st houses, shops. Working class occupants mainly. From PINK-barred of map to PINK.

McNeil Road. 2-st houses, bow windows, some broken. Bad building. West side the poorer. Here from PINK of map to PURPLE. The street is quiet, both on the poorer west and on the east side. East side let at 7/6 the floor (three rooms and scullery). Here PINK as map.

S to **Lyndhurst Grove**. 2-st, bow windows. Bad building. Rents as in McNeil Rd. Rents, character of building and occupants like much of the neighbourhood. PINK as map.

Rignold Road. Much the same and perhaps from PURPLE of map to PINK. A small area here – apparently this street with McNeil Rd and the Grove – is known as "Bug Island" locally owing to the quantity of vermin in the houses. Perhaps this unpleasant notoriety is not unconnected with the shoddy buildings.

Further W is **Lettsom Street**. 2-st and 2½-st houses. PINK as map with additional colour on the north west side.

S is **Fowler Street**. 2-st houses. Done up and looks better but "BLUE" element still apparent. Untidy children running about. Leave PURPLE as map.

Further W are **Fearnley Road** and **Edgecombe Road**. Both alike. 3-st houses. Generally three families to a house. Decent. PINK as map.

S along Camberwell Grove to **Gillam's Yard** (east side). Three small houses. Uncoloured to PINK. (On map the houses are just under the "S" of "South London".)

Grove Park. For the most part new semi-detached and detached red-brick villas. A few of the old houses still left. On the site of one four new ones have been built, all good, as the ground available was large. Most of the new dwellings, however, cover ground previously clear. Englewood House the only really large one left. This YELLOW, everywhere else RED and uncoloured to RED. "City People", generally fairly well-to-do. A smart lady who passed us with nurse and children was pointed out as the wife of a highly salaried man at some brewery and as a quondam bare-backed rider at Sanger's!

Champion Hill Terrace. Very large houses. Geoghan, the QC, living in one on the Dulwich side. YELLOW as map.

Champion Hill. Also large houses, except the terrace at the north end. This YELLOW to RED, the rest YELLOW as map.

Just to the N of the RED terrace is **Grove Place.** 3-st houses, "1821". RED as map.

Denmark Hill. YELLOW and RED as map on the west side. Shops begin a little north of De Crespigny Park. On the east side one or two very large houses, but most smaller here than on the other side. Here from YELLOW of map to RED. Shops begin at Love Walk.

De Crespigny Park. Substantial houses. From YELLOW of map to RED.

Love Walk (west end). 3-st houses. "Two or three vestry men living here". Servants kept. RED as map.

Further N are four streets, all very much alike: **Selborne Road, Allendale Road, Cuthill Road and Daneville Road.** 2-st houses, six rooms, bow windows, forecourts. Occupied by good working class, small clerks, etc. All PINK as map. In the last-mentioned, omit colour for gap made for new road leading to entrance of new music hall, the main approach to which is from Denmark Hill.

Along Denmark Hill to **Joiners' Yard.** A miserable slum, constant rows, drinking etc. Point given to Young's description by the appearance of a woman to whom I spoke. She had been terribly knocked about about a week before and seemed broken in mind as well as face. The old story –"Me and my husband had a few words" but he had promised to behave better and she had withdrawn her summons, as, according to Young she always had done and

The Terrace in Champion Hill.

always would. Her husband is a brute, well known to the police. The Yard DARK BLUE as map.

A little to the N, Cock Yard has been completely altered and is now occupied by the Star Co. (omnibus) for stabling. Rebuilt, only one house, occupied by foreman. This PINK, the DARK BLUE of map goes out.

Tiger Yard still exists and, with the exception of the house at the west end, is DARK BLUE as map. This house is occupied by a chimney sweep, an old man who "has enough to live on" and is the plutocrat of the Yard. His house-front is strangely and wonderfully decorated with oyster and other shells and before the house, encroaching I imagine on the public land, he has made little grottoes. It is all very barbarous and very effective, and the house might with propriety be honoured with a touch of PINK. The old man is very proud of his handiwork.

After this Wren Road seemed commonplace. 3-st houses. For the most part PINK as map.

General Remarks

This area well illustrates the tendency for what may be called the inner ring of suburban London to be occupied by a less wealthy class than formerly. The YELLOW is driven back to the south of the railway, save for a short strip along Denmark Hill, and even on the south side there will be considerably less of it in the revised map. On the other hand, there will still be some left and this is not surprising for the part lying round Champion Hill Terrace is exceedingly pleasant, with much open ground and splendid views to the north over London and south towards Dulwich. Even in this neighbourhood, however, when there is any alteration, the tendency is for smaller houses to take the place of the old large ones, as for instance, in Grove Park Rd. But the "smaller" ones are not small and for many years it is probable that the greater part of this area will be occupied by a well-to-do middle class, of the type occupying the new houses put up on the Grove Park estate. Thus, south of the railway, RED will be the dominant colour, just as PINK will be north of it.

The two remaining slums are again found in the near neighbourhood of Camberwell Green, a fact probably not unconnected with the fact that every point where traffic congests, buses stop and crowds pass tends to attract and provide for a considerable amount of casual labour – the smaller fry of the hangers-on of the community.

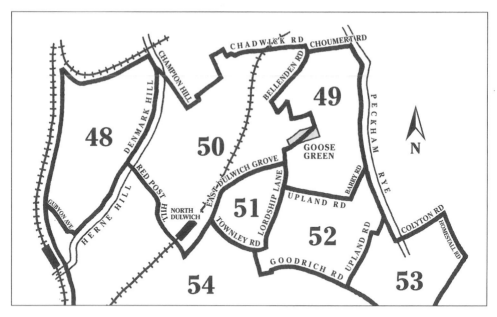

Walk 48

B373

Thursday 5th October 1899
Ernest Aves with PC Young.

Denmark Hill (forming, south of its junction with Champion Hill, the boundary line of the Camberwell and Dulwich Police sections), together with its southern continuation Herne Hill, has nearly all large houses on the Camberwell side, as far as Herne Hill Lodge. Remains YELLOW as map. Stedall the big drapers and the Druce (cricketing) family were mentioned as residents and, in a smaller house, an exception in the road, Marie Lloyd turned up again as a late occupant. "Little Tich" had also been a tenant here. South of Herne Hill Lodge (at the moment empty), both along the main frontage and on the open ground behind, an area of new building begins and several new streets have been laid out or completed since the map was published.

A little to the S of the Lodge is the end of Rolls Court Avenue and south of that a row of new houses in red brick with stone facings. Fairly substantial, very much after the styles of the houses in Grove Park. The row is continued south of Kestral Avenue (wrongly named Hereward in the map) as far as the four older dwellings shown in the map. Colour all RED.

Rolls Court Avenue, Cosbycote Avenue, Kestrel Avenue, Shardcroft Avenue and Gubyon Avenue. All very much alike, houses tending perhaps to be occupied by a somewhat less well-to-do class towards Milkwood Rd. The houses are very similar to those in the new row mentioned as having been put up in Herne Hill. Colour all RED except the small part of Gubyon Avenue to the north of Fawnbrake Avenue. This part PINK-barred.

Fawnbrake Avenue. Still in the making and the haste with which people are getting into the finished houses points to a very keen local demand for dwellings. The houses are of a somewhat less substantial class than those in the other avenues. 2-st with rooms built out at the back, making perhaps 10 or 12 in all. Timber work and supports of those in the builders' hands looked very slight. Intended for single families. Will probably let for from £50 or so per annum.

Colour as occupied (parts being still vacant and parts still under erection) PINK-barred. The Avenue (named Kestrel in the map, in error) now runs through to Poplar Walk Lane.

From there **SW** along **Lowden Road**. The first of the streets of 2-st houses with forecourts and bow windows. Generally six or eight rooms, according to the dignitary that is given to the scullery. Not infrequently occupied by two families. May be described as the local type and will be so referred to. Colour PINK.

Milkwood Road. The south end mainly of the local type but the road includes some 3-st houses and has shops on the east side between the greater part of the space between Jessop Rd and Heron Rd and a little north of the latter point nearer Poplar Walk on both sides. Colour PINK.

Jessop Road, Heron Road and **Poplar Walk**. All of the local type. Colour PINK.

Hinton Road. 2-st and 3-st houses. A few shops at the north west corner bordering on Poplar Walk. All PINK except the houses on the south side of the part running east and west. Here better, some servants. PINK-barred.

Herne Hill Road. 2-st and 3-st houses. PINK-barred from the south end to Wingmore Rd then poorer with some quite inferior houses on the west side just south of the public houses. Here PURPLE and the rest north of Wingmore Rd PINK.

Alderton Road. Local type. Good, with larger forecourts than ordinary. PINK.

To the **N** is **Wingmore Road**. 3-st houses, bare forecourts. Three families to a house as a rule. A bit poorer than Alderton Rd. Low grade PINK.

Wanless Road. On the west side of Herne Hill Rd are houses like those in Wingmore Rd but a poorer class living in them. Colour PURPLE here. East of the Herne Hill Rd on the south side are the Coroner's Court and the Disinfecting Station. Officials live in one of the two houses but colour might be omitted. On the north side is one PINK house.

Part of Wanless Rd and the whole of **Hardess Road** are within the borders again of the published map. The north side of the latter is the poorer. 2-st houses. PURPLE as map. The south side has 2-st and 3-st houses. Better. From PURPLE to PINK.

To the **SW** is **Kemerton Road**. 2-st and 3-st houses, some shops. PINK as map.

Cambria Road. Very much of the local type. PINK as map.

A little to the **S** and just off the map **Anstey Road** is a replica of Alderton Rd. PINK.

At its **SE** end are **Loughbourough Park Buildings**. 2-st, 8- or 10-roomed houses. Very quiet spot. High grade PINK.

Further **N** and again within the map **Dumbleton Road** and **Northway Road** are both of the local type. PINK as map.

General Remarks

Much of this district is rather colourless and but few people, with hardly any men, are about in the daytime. We passed Nevill's Bakery in Milkwood Rd and this gives a certain amount of local employment but the chief field of employment for the people of the neighbourhood was, Young said, Brixton. It is emphatically one of the parts in which one walks and wonders what all the people do for a living, the district itself giving practically no clue.

Walk 49

B375

Thursday 30th November 1899.
George Arkell with PC 'Taffy' Jones.
PC Jones is a big beefy man of 40 with a full, jolly-looking face and a fund of humour and contentment that nothing can disturb. He is a Norfolk man and has had 17 years service in

the East and West Dulwich sections. He was examined for promotion 12 years ago but failed to pass and is now looking forward to his pension. Although not a scholar he is a shrewd sensible man with a good record – only one caution during his service.

We started from the East Dulwich police station at the corner of Upland Road and Crystal Palace Road.

W along **North Cross Road.** Poor class of 2-st shops on the south side. A few 3-st shops and 2-st bay-windowed houses on north side near Archdale Rd. PINK to PINK-barred.

N up **Lacon Street.** 2-st terrace houses on west side and semi-detached houses on east. Two families as a rule. PINK.

S down **Archdale Road.** 2-st houses. 16 ft frontages. 9/- to 12/- a week. Two families. Labouring people, carpenter, milkman, etc. LIGHT BLUE to PURPLE. St John the Evangelist's school at corner of North Cross Rd.

N up **Nutfield Road.** 2-st terrace houses, a few 2½-st. Two families. Something like Archdale Rd but a trifle better. Carpenters, gardeners. PURPLE to LIGHT BLUE.

Frogley Road. 2-st, narrow fronts. Two families. Labouring people, sweep etc. Some broken windows. LIGHT BLUE to PURPLE.

Lordship Lane (North Cross Rd to Goose Green). 3-st shops on east side to a little north of Crawthew Grove, then a few 2½-st houses which are fated to become shops. Other side 3-st shops at north, good class to Matham Grove. South of that point, private houses (2-st) are being turned into shops. RED to PINK-barred. 2½-st houses. PINK.

S along **Spurling Road.** 2-st, one bay. Decent working people. PINK to PURPLE.

Crawthew Grove. 2-st houses. Worst part is near Lordship Lane. Two families in house. Sweep, navvies etc. Small shops at corner. LIGHT BLUE to PURPLE to the bend, rounding which, houses and people are better, bootmaker, mangler, etc. PURPLE to PINK to Worlingham Rd and east of this are new 2-st houses on north and 2-st semi-detached on south. Some keep servants. PINK-barred.

N up **Worlingham Road.** 2-st houses with bay windows mostly occupied by one family. Few 3-st at north end. Private school etc. A few keep servants. PINK to PINK-barred. Better than Spurling Rd.

East Dulwich Road. West of Worlingham Rd is a row of 4-st houses with gardens on front. Two servants as a rule. Doctors etc. RED. To east is Presbyterian Dulwich Reform Church (caretaker only), Batty's Mineral Water Works and the Public Baths with attendant in residence. Near Crystal Palace Rd are four semi-detached houses (3-st). Keep servants. RED.

S along **Crystal Palace Road.** 2-st and 3-st houses, some semi-detached with large gardens. A few servants. One or two families. Better than Worlingham Rd. Good PINK to PINK-barred.

Upland Road (to Barry Rd). 2-st and 3-st shops, mostly 2-st. Best near Barry Rd. Dairy, tailor, etc. A few 2-st houses, one bay on north side. PINK to PINK-barred.

N up **Hindmans Road.** 2-st houses, four and six rooms. A few shops near Upland Rd. Police sergeant, gas fitter etc. Some vacant ground in middle of east side. PINK.

Tyrrell Road. 2½-st and 2-st semi-detached houses with two bays near Barry Rd. A few shops and 3-st houses facing Hindmans Rd and some 2-st houses, known as Percy Villas, at the west. Old inhabitants, a few keep servants. PINK to PINK-barred.

E into **Ferris Road.** 3-st houses. All comfortable, some keep a girl. PINK-barred. At east end are some 2-st houses, which are only PINK.

N into **Oakhurst Grove.** 3-st semi-detached, two bays, good gardens. Many keep servants, Jones says all but I know there are two families in some. PINK-barred to RED.

E into **Kelmore Grove**. 2-st houses, bay windows, some semi-detached. Don't let as a rule and mostly keep a servant. PINK-barred.

S into **The Gardens**. 3-st terraced houses on north side, not so good as the rest. May keep a servant. Remainder is semi-detached, 3½-st houses, bay windows. One or two servants. City people, doctor, etc. RED. Garden in centre is laid out and used by the residents for tennis etc.

Peckham Rye (from Barry Rd to East Dulwich Rd). 4-st semi-detached and detached houses. Going north are some 3½-st and 4-st terrace houses. Nearer East Dulwich Rd the houses are smaller (2½-st). City people, doctor, etc. All keep servants. RED. Some vacant ground at corner of East Dulwich Rd is now occupied by the vans of a travelling cheapjack. The south side of the road is large semi-detached houses with grounds as far as Oakhurst Grove. North side, some private houses near the Rye and a row of 3-st shops near Goose Green. Might be RED. On south side an entrance has been made to Solway Rd, a new turning with Oakhurst Grove, built on the gardens of the East Dulwich Rd houses. 2-st houses, eight rooms, let at £40 a year. Nine houses are occupied on south side only. Road not made up. PINK to PINK-barred.

N to **Hinckley Road**. Good class of house, 2-st with bay windows. Windows are well kept and look as if one family. Some probably keep servants. PINK to PINK-barred.

N up **Keston Road**. 2-st with bays but not so good as Hinckley Rd. PINK to PINK-barred.

N into **Amott Road**. 2-st houses with bay windows. Comfortable working class, turncock etc. Two families in some. Poorest near Fenwick Rd where houses might be PURPLE. PINK.

S along **Gowlett Road**. 2-st, one bay. City people, comfortable. Might be a servant or two. PINK.

N up **Fenwick Road**. 2½-st and a few 3-st houses with gardens in front. About eight rooms. A few keep servants. I think most of the houses have two families but Jones did not know about this. PINK to PINK-barred.

On the W side is **Fenwick Grove**, a cul de sac with four semi-detached houses, 2-st. Jones has seen servants here. PINK-barred.

Round by a few shops (PINK) in Nutbrook St into **Troy Town**. 2-st cottages on east side. Road not made up. Labouring people, carmen etc. LIGHT BLUE.

At S end leading to Fenwick Rd is **Dewar Street**. Three 2-st houses on south and a few small shops on north. PURPLE.

E of this is **Princes Terrace**. 2-st houses facing north. Two families. PURPLE. Ground plan of map is wrong here.

E through archway to **Peckham Rye**. From the Kings Arms northward are private houses, 3-st and 2½-st. Comfortable people, doctors, veterinary surgeon, photographer, etc. North by the pond are small shops (2-st) with a few larger near Nigel Rd. RED to PINK-barred. Down an entry on the west are two 2-st houses known as 40 Peckham Rye. Working people. PINK to PURPLE.

W to **Rye Buildings**. A badly-built straggling block of 3-st and 2-st tenements, with small 2-st and 3-st cottages built in the yard behind, also let in tenements. Colony of Italians here – organ grinders, potato car men, wood choppers. Some rough labouring people. The worst part of Peckham – "people who can't get in anywhere else come here". DARK BLUE. (This is one of the worst blocks in London, I have known it for over ten years and it has always been bad.)

W along **Nigel Road**. 2-st houses, one bay window and small forecourt. Working people. Two families, no poverty. PINK.

Relf Road. Similar class of house. Two families but slightly poorer at north end. PINK.

Through a narrow lane to **Ainstey Road**. 2-st, bay window and forecourt. Looks poorer but Jones says "all are alike, as well off as I am", 30/- a week. PINK to PURPLE. Several do washing.

N into **Choumert Grove**. Little 2-st houses (old). Insurance agent etc. PINK to PURPLE.

E to **Alpha Street**. 2-st old houses. Board School takes part. Stable on east side. Working people. PINK to PURPLE.

S & E into **Sternhall Lane**. 2-st houses. Labourers and others. Used to be very rough but has improved. Near Rye Lane some of the houses are comfortable but poor at other end. LIGHT BLUE to PURPLE, LIGHT BLUE and PURPLE on map.

Rye Lane. Good 3-st shops by Nigel Rd. A few private houses north of Sternhall Lane. The Democratic Club and a large house occupied by Congreve, the man who advertises a cure for consumption. Good shops near Choumert Rd. RED as map.

W along **Choumert Road**. Shops to Board School and private houses (2-st) west of School to Costa St. From this point to Bellenden Rd is shops with a few private houses. Mostly doing a good trade but not at the shop. PINK-barred as map. Colour to come off for the School.

S along **Costa Street**. 2-st houses with small gardens in front. Working people, mostly labourers. LIGHT BLUE to PURPLE.

S along **Waghorn Street**. 2-st, six to eight rooms. Some let at 14/- a week. Two families. Labouring people. Houses badly kept. Trade notices in windows. A few shops at south end. PURPLE, PINK on map.

Nutbrook Street. 2-st houses, two bays on south side, six and seven rooms. Two or three shops near Fenwick Rd (east). Two families. Clerks and working people. PURPLE to PINK. Ground plan of map is wrong at east end.

N to **Howden Street**. 2-st, six rooms, bay windows. Two families. Mostly labouring people. Poorer than Nutbrook St. PURPLE to LIGHT BLUE, PINK on map.

Wingfield Street. 2-st. Like Howden St. PURPLE to LIGHT BLUE, PURPLE on map.

S into **Wingfield Mews**. Rooms over stables. Cabmen and stablemen. Publican's car kept there. PURPLE to LIGHT BLUE, PURPLE on map.

Maxted Road. 2-st houses with bay windows, like Howden St. Poor class except near Bellenden Rd where a few shops are found and some private houses used for business premises north of Soys Rd. These might be PINK, remainder PURPLE, PINK on map.

McDermott Road. No houses on south side. Map is wrong – gardens of Wingfield St go through. On north side about three shops, one a beerhouse near Alpha St. PINK.

Sandison Street. 2-st cottages with little gardens in front. Labourers, plumbers, hawkers, costers. Rather rough. Jones places it next to Rye Buildings. LIGHT BLUE, PURPLE on map.

Reedham Street. Three shops, 3-st, on east side south of the Union Church. Lodgers occupy rooms over shops. PURPLE as map. North of McDermott Rd are 2-st houses (old). Mostly two families. Bootmaker, builder, etc. Don't look very poor. PURPLE, PINK on map. This completed the day's walk.

General Remarks

The area covered in this walk includes two poor patches: 1) In East Dulwich between Crawthew Grove and North Cross Rd and 2) Peckham between Choumert Rd and Nutbrook St. In both areas the labouring element preponderates, the main difference being that whilst the Dulwich area is gradually improving, the Peckham area is as gradually becoming poorer, chiefly owing to the increased rents which are driving the better class workers further afield to find cheaper house room. In both areas the people are decent though often rough working folk, the only really bad spot being Rye Dwellings.

North of Upland Rd to East Dulwich Rd is a lower middle class area. Shoals of silk-hatted people leave these roads every morning for the City. The roads are wide, most of the houses have good gardens and very little change has taken place here during the past ten years except in the filling of empty houses – an unoccupied house is very rare now.

Walk 50   B375

Friday 1st December 1899.
George Arkell with PC 'Taffy' Jones.

Started from corner of Bellenden Road and Choumert Road.
N up **Victoria Road**. 2½-st private houses on west side. Mostly used for some trade: bootmender, photographer, umbrella mender. PINK as map. Other side is 3-st shops. Should be PINK-barred.
W into **Chadwick Road**. 2½-st houses with two families in some. Others keep a servant. Comfortable. Gordon Brewery and open ground on north side. PINK-barred as map.
Back and W along **Choumert Road**. 2-st houses, most with bay window. Houses vary much in style but a gradual improvement toward Copleston Rd. Working class. Building trades etc near Bellenden Rd. Clerk, travellers at upper which might be PINK-barred. PINK instead of PINK-barred of map.
Copleston Road. 2-st, 2½-st and 3½-st houses. West side is the better. Long gardens backing on railway. Meal salesman, private school. Many keep servants on west side but few on the east where the houses are mainly 2-st and often have two families. PINK-barred as map on west, PINK on east.
E along **Danby Street**. 2-st houses, mostly with one bay. Becomes slightly poorer near Bellenden Rd. Very few if any keep a girl. Many leave at 5.30am to catch the early trains and trams. PINK instead of PINK-barred of map.
Bellenden Road. From Choumert Rd to Maxted Rd is shops, 2-st and 3-st, the market of the district. Does a good trade during the week with people who do not care to walk to Rye Lane. PINK-barred as map. From the Chapel to Avondale Rd are some second-rate 3-st shops. Remainder of street is private houses, mostly 2-st. Comfortable people in regular work. PINK to PINK-barred.
W along **Soames Street**. 2-st houses, small. Two families as a rule. Working people in regular work. PINK. Ground plan of map is wrong, street not marked.
N to **Avondale Road**. A row of 3-st houses near Bellenden Rd. Remainder is 2-st houses with the usual bay window. A few shops near Copleston Rd. PINK, PINK-barred on map.
Malfort Road. 2-st houses with two bay windows on west side. Two families in some. All comfortable. PINK, PINK-barred on map.
Grove Hill Road. From the bend to Ivanhoe Rd is 3-st houses, a few 2-st. Mostly occupied by one family but two in some. Clerks, travellers, schoolmaster, solicitor. About half keep servants. PINK-barred, RED on map.
Ivanhoe Road. 2-st houses with bay windows. 3-st shops between Malfort Rd and Bromar Rd. A few servants. All comfortable except houses facing the shops. PINK to PINK-barred, PINK-barred on map.
NW up **Bromar Road**. 3-st houses with two bays on west side, 2-st and 3-st on east. Comfortable people, vicar, minister. About half keep servants. PINK-barred, RED on map.
Along Grove Hill Rd and S along Grove Lane to **The Glebe**. Large detached houses on south side with carriage drives. YELLOW as map. North side is gardens of the large houses in Grove Hill Rd.

W along **Champion Hill**. Large houses with grounds and stables attached. Mostly old houses but on south side an old house has been pulled down and new detached red-brick houses erected. City merchants and other well-to-do. None with less than four servants. Large number of Germans. YELLOW. Lodges and stables. PINK.

Roadway turns N and leads into **Denmark Hill**. The east side has large mansions with grounds but here again the builder has begun to work and a modern house is built at corner of Red Post Hill and a new road – Sunray Avenue – carried through from The Grange to the foot of Red Post Hill. YELLOW.

Sunray Avenue is only partially built. 3-st detached and semi-detached villas. About ten houses, mostly near Denmark Hill. RED to YELLOW.

Red Post Hill. No houses north of the bend. To south on east side is Hill House (YELLOW) and on west side two houses near railway (RED). New roads are being carried through on west side to Half Moon Lane.

S of the railway **High Street Dulwich** begins. Old houses, mostly 2-st on east side. Estate agent and others keeping servants. RED. Ivy Lodge, a large rambling house at corner of East Dulwich Grove, is empty and coming down.

E along **East Dulwich Grove**. 3-st modern villas, mostly detached. Two or more servants. RED to Townley Rd.

N into **Green Lane**. Two houses on east side south of the railway. 2-st and 3-st. Keep servants. Butchers etc. RED. North of the railway are two lodges. PINK. One on the St Olave's Recreation Ground and the other on Sir H Bessemer's estate (west side).

E along **East Dulwich Grove**. Semi-detached or detached houses (2-st plus attic) to corner of Thorncombe Rd. Keep one or two servants. RED. On the north side near the Infirmary is The Parade, a row of 3-st shops, post office etc. RED. South side to Melbourne Grove is 3-st and 2-st with attic. Mostly semi-detached but not so good as west end of Grove. RED to PINK-barred. St Saviour's Infirmary is the most conspicuous building in this district. A large red-brick pile with several wings connected with the central building by corridors, the whole being surmounted with a number of cupolas which catch the eye from many points of view.

N up **Melbourne Grove**. 2-st semi-detached houses with small gardens in front. Houses mostly kept by one family. Tailor etc. A few shops at north end, 3-st. PINK. Shops are PINK-barred.

W into **Jarvis Road**. No houses. On north side is the entrance to some stables with rooms over. One family. PINK.

N to **Dog Kennel Hill**. On the west side is Constance Villas. 2-st houses with one bay window. Look comfortable. PINK. Beyond this is one 2-st cottage. Also PINK, and the open fields to Champion Hill.

W into **Constance Road**. 2-st houses with bay window to ground floor. Poorly built. Entrance to Camberwell Infirmary at end of road used by the Parish Ambulances. Porter at Infirmary and other working folk. Two families. PINK to PURPLE.

S along **Grove Vale**. Adjoining East Dulwich Railway Station are three houses occupied by station master and porters. On the north side are 3-st and 2-st houses, all now occupied for business purposes – laundry, florist, decorator, etc. Further east are 2-st houses with attics. Shops. PINK-barred to PINK.

S along **Derwent Grove**. 2-st and 2½-st semi-detached houses. Some kept by one family, others have two. Very few servants, only one known. PINK to PINK-barred.

East Dulwich Grove (Melbourne Grove to Lordship Lane). 3-st and a few 2½-st houses to west of Matham Grove. Some keep servants. PINK-barred. East of this point the houses are 2-st with bay windows. Milliner etc. PINK to PINK-barred.

W along **Zenoria Street**. 2-st with bays. All comfortable. PINK. A new road is being made from this street north over the nursery.

S along **Oxonian Street**. 2-st with bay windows. Two families in some. PINK.

N up **Elsie Road**. Small detached and semi-detached houses, 2-st. Mostly one family. Several keep servants. Better than Derwent Grove. PINK-barred to PINK.

Grove Vale. East of Elsie Grove the small shops are replaced by more modern 2-st houses with bay window and garden in front. Doctor and a few others keeping servants. PINK to PINK-barred.

E into **Placquett Road**. 2-st houses with bay windows. Houses in bad repair but all look comfortable. PINK.

Wildash Road. 2-st semi-detached. Bay windows, wide hall, garden in front. Some servants. PINK-barred.

N into **Placquett Terrace**. 2-st terrace houses. Smaller than Wildash Rd. Rents about 12/-. Mostly two families. Milkman etc. PINK.

S & E along **St John's Villas**. 3½-st semi-detached houses. Good class of people, keep servants. RED. A row of shops have been built on the west side of Goose Green and will soon be occupied. One is advertised to open before Christmas.

N up **Ady's Road**. On east side, facing the church, are a few 3-st houses and one detached house. Some servants here. PINK-barred. Remainder of road is 2-st terrace houses with bay windows. PINK. A few shops at corner of Amott St.

W into **Ondine Road**. Semi-detached houses. 2-st plus attic, about eight rooms. A few terrace houses near Ady's Rd. All comfortable, some servants. Two families in some houses. PINK-barred to PINK.

N up **Marsden Road**. 2-st with six and seven rooms. Semi-detached near Oglander Rd and look better than south end of street. PINK to PINK-barred.

Oglander Road. South west end is 2-st semi-detached houses to Muschamp Rd. All comfortable. PINK. East end of road is 2-st terrace houses, much smaller than the others and occupied by a poorer class – dressmaker, labourer. A few poor shops to the east of Ady's Rd. PINK west, PURPLE to LIGHT BLUE east end of road.

S along **Muschamp Road**. Semi-detached houses, like Marsden Rd. Two families in some houses. Doorstep girls come round and clean steps etc. PINK to PINK-barred.

General Remarks

Much open ground still remains between Denmark Hill and the railway and, except near Red Post Hill, is likely to be built over soon. Several cricket and tennis clubs use these fields and on Saturdays they are the scene of much activity. In the valley near the railway are the St Saviour's and Camberwell infirmaries, both huge establishments. On Sundays they bring streams of visitors along Grove Lane and an almost equal stream of their occupants going in the opposite directions towards Camberwell.

Grove Hill Rd and the streets to the east of Dog Kennel Hill have deteriorated within recent years and the neighbourhood has become a PINK-barred and PINK district. This will probably be its permanent status. In the roads near East Dulwich Station a similar change has taken place, accompanied by a great rise in rents.

Walk 51

B375

Tuesday 5th December 1899.
George Arkell with PC 'Taffy' Jones.

Started from the corner of Lordship Lane.
W into **Matham Grove**. Well-built 2-st houses with large bay windows. Some occupied by
two families, others kept by one. Music teacher etc. PINK as map.
W to **Tell Grove**. Small 2-st houses, some flush with pavement, others with small forecourt
and bay window. Labouring people. PURPLE as map.
S to **Ashbourne Grove**. 2-st semi-detached houses. Comfortable working people. Clerks,
people on morning papers. Few, if any, servants. PINK as map.
W along **Chesterfield Grove**. 2-st terrace houses, one bay. Narrow frontage. Some have
been done up and are now to let. Mixed working class. PURPLE to PINK.
Melbourne Grove. 2-st semi-detached houses, north of Chesterfield Grove. Gardens with
bushes and shrubs in front. All are comfortable and a few may keep girls. PINK. South of
Chesterfield Grove are a few shops on east side and then some 2-st houses with one bay
window extending to Blackwater St. The Grove gradually becomes poorer towards the south
but is still PINK, RED on map.
On the W side is **Lytcott Grove**. 2-st houses on north side only. PURPLE. Two families in
each. South side is open ground advertised for building purposes, while at the west end
Allsopps are building a bottling store close to the wall of Alleyn's School, which bars any
chance of a road through.
S and along **Blackwater Street**. 2-st houses with square bay windows on north side. South
side houses are smaller and poorer. A large steam laundry has been built on the north side
near Lordship Lane and many of the women live in this street. PURPLE to LIGHT BLUE on
south side, PINK on map.
Lordship Lane (Chesterfield Grove to Melbourne Grove). West side is private houses
which are being converted into shops. Four are already transformed. To south of these is the
Wesleyan Mission, a steam laundry and the RC Church, south of which are a few 2-st shops
and semi-detached houses to Melbourne Grove. PINK-barred. The east side is shops, 3-st
near North Cross Rd and 2-st to Whately Rd. Moderate trade. PINK-barred.
W into **Melbourne Grove**. 2-st houses with bay window on ground floor on south side.
North side to corner of Blackwater St is shops. Rather poor class. PINK.
S into **Colwell Road**. 2-st houses with bay windows. Several policemen, carpenters and
others in building trades. None less than 3/-, says Jones, who lives in this street. PINK. At
angle of street is a Mission Hall now being converted into a shirt-dressing establishment. It
was worked by a Miss Griffin, who has recently died. She was very popular and had more
influence in the district than anybody. Jones pointed to one very respectable house and said it
was occupied by a carpenter whom she had reclaimed. She seems to have devoted most of her
time as well as her income to this place.
Lordship Lane. The east side between Whateley Rd and Pellatt Rd is 3½-st houses with
a few shops at the south corner. Two or three families in each house and more in some. Looks
poor and is the poorest part of the Lane. PURPLE. South of this to Heber Rd are a few 3-st
shops and 2-st and 2½-st houses. Comfortable. Some own their own houses. PINK. On west
side between Melbourne Grove and Colwell Rd are 2-st cottages. All working class,
sweeper etc. PINK. A few shops and then 2-st houses to Townley Rd. Two families.

Comfortable but no servants. PINK.

W into **Townley Road.** A few 3-st semi-detached houses on south side. Two servants as a rule. Solicitors, army officers, etc. One large house on north side, lease expires in two years. RED. Greater part of road abuts on cricket fields and the grounds of Alleyn's School. A new lodge at the entrance (PINK) and a few RED houses near East Dulwich Grove.

E into **Hillsborough Road.** 2-st houses with grounds. Good class, all keep servants. Tradesmen and City people. RED.

Thorncombe Road. 2-st houses. Not quite so good but probably RED with tendency to PINK-barred.

Glengarry Road. Mostly 3-st houses with bay windows. Looks like two families but Jones says all have servants and does not think there are two families. People go to the City – turn out in hundreds in the morning. PINK-barred to RED.

Tarbert Road. 2-st houses, gardens in front. Most keep a servant of some kind. PINK-barred to RED.

Trossachs Road. 2-st houses, large bay window. All keep servants. Mostly City people. The best of this group except Hillsborough Rd. RED.

At this point we were obliged to stop. Rain had fallen off and on all the morning and had now settled into a steady shower.

PC Jones is a cheery fellow, whom even a drizzling rain cannot damp. He talks freely as we walk along. Today the conversation turned on the Drink question. He is not an abstainer, likes an occasional glass. He would like to see the public houses closed on Sunday, also the clubs. It would be no use to close the pubs without the clubs. The men would simply go to the clubs to drink. Now they go to the clubs in the morning and as soon as the public houses are open they are into them. He thinks that 19 out of 20 policemen would like Sunday closing. Prominent amongst the reasons is the fact that they would be able to have two Sundays off a month instead of one as at present.

Walk 52

B375

Wednesday 6th & Thursday 7th December 1899.
George Arkell with PC 'Taffy' Jones.

Started from the corner of Lordship Lane and North Cross Road.

E along **Shawbury Road.** 2-st houses with bay window on ground floor. Fitted for two families. Mechanics and labourers, mixed. PINK to PURPLE. The Salvation Army has a large hall in this road.

S along **Fellbrigg Road.** 2-st houses like Shawbury Rd except at south end where houses are newer and have two bay windows. Two families. Bus drivers, postmen, men in the building trades, etc. PURPLE to PINK.

Hansler Road. 2-st houses with bay windows. Let in flats. 6/9 for first floor, 6/6 for ground floor. Police, postmen, etc. PINK to PURPLE.

S to **Bawdale Road.** Like Hansler Rd in all respects. PINK to PURPLE.

S to **Whateley Road.** On the north side near Lordship Lane are some 2½-st houses, occupied by costers and a very rough set of others. About three families in a house. Street doors open. Almost as bad as Rye Buildings. LIGHT BLUE to DARK BLUE. Nearer Fellbrigg Rd are 2-st houses built for two families. Bay windows. PURPLE. And near Crystal Palace Rd are 3-st shops with lodgers over. PURPLE to LIGHT BLUE. On south side are a few shops near Lordship Lane (3-st) and then some new 2-st flats. Poor class. Three very small rooms and scullery, 8/- for first and 7/- for ground floor. Two street doors in one entrance. PURPLE. Remainder of side is 2-st houses. Mostly two families. PURPLE.

N up **Ulverscroft Road**. 2-st houses with one bay window. A few shops near Whateley Rd on west side. Six rooms. Navvies, labourers, etc. Improves towards north end. LIGHT BLUE to PURPLE, PURPLE on map.

S along **Crystal Palace Road** (to Whateley Rd). 2-st private houses, bay windows, a few semi-detached. Near Whateley Rd are 3-st private houses and shops. Poor class working people. Three houses have been converted into a large laundry. Some of the private houses are used for business purposes and occupied by two or three families. PINK for 2-st houses at north, PURPLE to PINK for remainder.

N up **Darrell Road**. On west side is a row of 2-st houses, flush with pavement. Occupied by a rough lot, costers etc. All poor. LIGHT BLUE to DARK BLUE. Remainder of street is 2-st. Some houses with bay windows and forecourts. Occupied by two families. Labouring class. Some broken windows. Parlours used as bedrooms. Slight improvement at north end. LIGHT BLUE to PURPLE.

At this point the rain which had been threatening, settled into a steady downpour, stopping proceedings for the day.

Taking up the work at the same point on the following morning, we went S down **Hindmans Road**. 2-st houses. Various styles and frontages from 12 ft to 16 ft. Few small shops near Upland Rd. Rents 10/- to 12/- a week. Two families in nearly every house. Two small builders, gardeners, bricklayer, detective, etc. PURPLE to PINK. Poorer than other part of street.

Underhill Road (Whateley Rd to Barry Rd). 2-st shops at east by Barry Rd. Remainder 2-st private houses with two families as a rule. PINK to PURPLE.

S down **Landells Road**. 2-st houses on east side. PINK, not marked on map.

E of Landells Rd is **Silvester Road**. 2-st houses with bay windows. Nice houses. Seven or eight rooms, 15/- a week. Two families. PINK, uncoloured on map.

Into **Barry Road** (Underhill Rd to Lordship Lane). 2-st and 2½-st semi-detached houses with good gardens back and front near Underhill Rd. Public houses broker, sign writer and others. All comfortable. Keep servant or at least a girl. South of Silvester Rd are 2-st double-fronted houses. All keep servants. RED. Then houses become smaller, 2-st semi-detached and terrace houses. PINK. South of Goodrich Rd the houses are larger but still 2-st. Some keep servants. Nearing the church they are much larger and all keep servants. Some open ground on west side and building going on. PINK-barred to RED near Etherow St.

Lordship Lane (to Crystal Palace Rd). 3-st shops. PINK-barred to RED. On west side new 3-st shops known as Townley Park Parade. Shopkeepers live over. RED.

On E side is **Plough Lane**. Two cottages on south side and another detached house. Men work for a milkman, about 25/- a week. PINK.

N up **Landells Road**. 2-st, one bay. Six rooms, 11/6 a week. Working people, bus drivers, gardeners, upholsterer, etc. Road is poorer near the middle. PINK to PURPLE. Just north of Goodrich Rd are some old 2-st houses in Landells Rd occupied by labourers, watchmen and others. The houses on west side are slightly better. LIGHT BLUE with tendency to PURPLE on west side, where the houses were cleared some time ago. North of these are modern double-fronted houses, each side of a house being fitted for a family and letting at 8/6 a week. Many police from the central districts here and one inspector. Dressmaker and insurance agent have plates. All comfortable. PINK.

W into **Silvester Road**. At the corner of Silvester Rd is the East Dulwich Provident Dispensary, the popular medical resort. People pay a weekly subscription. Sometimes the attendance is so large that they have to have a policeman to regulate it. Jones is a member. Four 2-st houses on north side. Look poor. One is occupied by a bricklayer and a foreman on the roads. PURPLE. West of Crystal Palace Rd to Cyrena Rd the houses are like the new houses in Landells Rd. PINK. Nearer Landcroft Rd are 3-st houses with a family on each floor. Cab washer etc. PINK to PURPLE.

N of Pellatt Rd is **Landcroft Road**. 2-st houses on west side and part of east side. 3-st by Silvester Rd. Two and three families in each. Houses in bad condition, walls cracked. Look poor, proximity to Whateley Rd keeps respectable people away. PURPLE to PINK.

Pellatt Road. A few 3-st shops on south side near Lordship Lane. Rag dealer, grocer. PINK. East of Landcroft Rd are 2-st houses. North side is new and much better than south. Some of the people are buying the houses. PINK. Other side is poor and poorest near Crystal Palace Rd. PURPLE to LIGHT BLUE.

Crystal Palace Road. West side is 3-st houses with shops at corners to Pellatt Rd. Family on each floor. PURPLE. Facing these are 2-st houses which have been turned into shops. PINK. South of Pellatt Rd to Jennings Rd the houses are 2-st semi-detached with about seven rooms. Most are owned by the occupiers. Were sold a few years ago at £290 each, ground rent £5. All comfortable. Doctor, builder, laundress. PINK.

W along **Rodwell Road**. A few 2½-st houses near Crystal Palace Rd on south side. Remainder are 2-st. Some semi-detached at the west end which is better than east end of road. Two policemen here. Milliner has a plate up. 6-roomed houses let at 9/6. 2½-st, 8-roomed, 13/-. PURPLE to PINK, PINK on map.

Landcroft Road (Pellatt Rd to Goodrich Rd). From Pellatt Rd southward the road rises and the houses are better on this slope. 2-st with bay windows. Look comfortable. PINK. Some 3-st houses on west near Goodrich Rd with a family on each floor. PINK.

Heber Road. A few houses on north side near Lordship Lane (2-st and 3-st). PINK. Remainder 2-st houses with bay windows. A few shops near the Board School. Houses on north side, west of Cyrena Rd, are better than the rest. People are not allowed to take lodgers. PINK to PURPLE. PINK on north, west of Cyrena Rd, rest PURPLE. PINK on map.

W along **Jennings Road**. 2-st houses with one bay window on south side. Several to let - rents have been raised. PURPLE. A few houses on north near Landcroft Rd. Gardens of Heber Rd come through to Jennings Rd. Ground plan is wrong. PURPLE.

E along **Goodrich Road**. West of Landcroft Rd are two 3-st houses on north and four 2-st on south side. One to let – eight rooms for 15/-. PINK. East of Landcroft Rd on north side is a row of 2-st houses with bay window to lower floor. Poor. LIGHT BLUE to PURPLE. South side is semi-detached. People mostly own their houses. Two very poor houses by public house. PINK to PURPLE.

W along **Thompson Road**. 2-st houses. Poor working people. Something like previous road. PURPLE.

Landcroft Road. (Goodrich Rd to Crystal Palace Rd) Some 2-st with bay window. Rent 12/- on east side. On west 3-st with three families in most of them. PINK to PURPLE.

Crystal Palace Road (south of Jennings Rd). A few shops between Goodrich Rd and Thompson Rd. 2½-st and 2-st houses to Lordship Lane. PINK.

S & W into **Woodwarde Road**. A few shops and good 2-st villas with gardens in front. Two doctors, schoolmasters, surgeon, builder. All keep servants. RED.

N along **Beauval Road**. 2-st good class houses. Tillings have built stables behind the east side and the houses have depreciated in consequence. Some are offered for sale by the occupiers. All keep servants. RED.

E into **Lordship Lane** (Heber Rd to Crystal Palace Rd). On west side are 3-st red-brick villas. RED. East side is 2-st villas, some new. Also some 3½-st houses, near Goodrich Rd. Nearly all keep servants. RED to PINK-barred.

At this point we adjourned for lunch, recommencing in the afternoon at the Peckham Rye corner of **Barry Road**. On the south east side a few 2-st PINK houses have been built on the gardens of the Peckham Rye houses. Also some stables facing Tyrrell Rd (also PINK). On the north side to Tyrrell Rd are 3-st and 2½-st houses. Mostly with servants. PINK-barred. South to Upland Rd are double-fronted houses on both sides, 2-st and 2½-st. All keep servants. A few shops at corner facing chapel. RED. Remainder of Barry Rd is 2½-st and 2-st private houses, semi-detached as a rule. A few 3-st at south. Mostly comfortable people with servant. Doctors etc. PINK-barred.

N along **Henslowe Road**. 2-st houses. Most have two families. Mixed working class. Several policemen. Improves near Upland Rd. PURPLE to PINK.

Upland Road (Barry Rd to Underhill Rd). Facing Henslowe Rd are a few shops, 2-st. PINK. On south side between Henslowe Rd and Friern Rd are two houses occupied by a dairyman and another. PINK. East of Friern Rd are 2-st houses, some semi-detached. West side rather better than the east. Clerks etc. Might be a few girls. One or two houses are RED in character but PINK to PINK-barred.

E into **Piermont Road**. 2-st houses with bay windows, gardens in front. Some new houses have been built on the north side near the Rye and some of these keep servants. PINK to PINK-barred.

N along side of **Peckham Rye** (to Barry Rd). A few detached and semi-detached houses south of the Board School. Formerly good but have gone down and now only PINK-barred. North of the school are four 3-st terrace houses and a large detached house. These have also deteriorated owing to the Board School. RED to PINK-barred. North of Friern Rd are 3-st and 2-st detached and semi-detached houses. Meal salesman etc. All keep servants. RED. On the Rye itself are two 2½-st houses facing north known as Charlton Houses. Keep servants. RED. Near these but facing west are two others. Modena College, a large girls' school, and Sunnyside, 2½-st. RED.

SW to **Friern Road**. Between the Rye and Upland Rd is a row of 2-st houses with bays. Comfortable people, nearly all keeping servants. South side is gardens of Peckham Rye houses. RED to PINK-barred. Between Upland Rd and Underhill Rd are 2-st terrace houses with bay windows and small gardens in front. Good class of people, clerks etc. A servant here and there. PINK. To Goodrich Rd the houses are 2-st but rather larger. Clerks and others going to City by train or bus. Some servants. PINK-barred to RED. South of Goodrich Rd the property is smaller but improves again near Etherow St. Solicitor, retired publican, schoolmaster etc. PINK to PINK-barred.

Back to **Goodrich Road** (Barry Rd to Upland Rd). West towards Barry Rd are some 2-st houses on south side. Builder, bicycle repairer – all comfortable. PINK. On north side are the premises of a sweep and a cabmaster, and a row of 2-st houses with narrow fronts. Poorer than others but still PINK to PURPLE. East of Friern Rd is a row of 2-st houses used for business purposes – dairy, sweep, boot repairer, laundry. Houses in bad repair. PINK to PURPLE.

S into **Upland Road**. 2-st houses. Good class people, schoolmaster etc. A few servants. PINK to PINK-barred. North of Goodrich Rd well-built 2-st houses with square bay, red brick. Completely built, the new houses are fitted for two families. May be a few servants but doorstep girls find employment here. All are comfortable. Good curtains to windows etc.

PINK to PINK-barred.

W into **Underhill Road** (Upland Rd to Barry Rd). 2-st and 2½-st houses. Well kept. One is occupied by a man who made £20,000 in four years by dealing in public houses. A row of houses between Henslowe Rd and Barry Rd not marked on map. Also new houses on south side by Barry Rd. PINK to PINK-barred.

General Remarks

Broadly the district may be divided into two, Barry Rd and the roads east of it being mainly middle class and comfortable. Here the roads are wide and well kept. The houses are in good repair and the long gardens in the rear make the neighbourhood airy and healthy, giving also a rural appearance.

West of Barry Rd a wedge of closely-built and thickly-populated houses are found, the houses of a working population. Not poor in the sense of being in want but just able to live a decent life while trade is good but with little or no reserve for bad times. During the past 10 years this neighbourhood has improved wonderfully and rents have risen rapidly, in some cases nearly doubled. The streets are quieter and the people more orderly.

One feature of the district is the large number of 'off' beer houses.

Walk 53   B375

Friday 8th December 1899.
George Arkell with PC 'Taffy' Jones.

Started from the corner of Piermont Road and Peckham Rye.

There are three houses facing **Peckham Rye** between Piermont Road and St Aidan's Road. Two are modern. PINK-barred.

SW along **St Aidan's Road**. 2-st houses with square bays. Saw one servant but most of the houses have two families. PINK to PINK-barred.

Underhill Road (Upland Rd to cemetery). On the north east side near Upland Rd are two 2-st good class houses (PINK) and then a row of 2½-st houses occupied by labouring people (PURPLE to PINK) and by corner of St Aidan's Rd two large houses – one empty for years. Near Dunstan's Rd are 2-st houses with bay windows. One family as a rule. PINK. Opposite side is 2-st houses with small gardens in front. Crèche, laundry, etc. Improves as hill is ascended towards Dunstan's Rd. PINK. South of Dunstan's Rd on east side are some 2½-st much larger than others. Gardens in front. Most have a servant. PINK-barred. Facing these is Foot's Nursery which takes the unbuilt land at the corner.

SW to **Crebor Street**. 2-st houses, some semi-detached and fitted for two families. Policemen, insurance agents and working men. Small houses are 12/6 a week (six rooms). Others with four rooms and bathroom on each floor let at 9/- to 10/- a floor. PINK to PURPLE.

S along **Dunstan's Road**. 2-st houses with bay windows. Some have separate street door for each floor. Floor lets at 7/9 (three rooms). All working people. PINK.

Goodrich Road (Upland Rd to Underhill Rd). One house facing Board School, PINK. From this point a house built behind Crebor St and reached from that street (PINK) can be seen. Toward the south east the road arises. New 2-st red-brick houses, a few older houses 2½-st on north aside. Two families as a rule. PINK. Turning eastward the road improves. Houses (2-st) are larger and some servants are kept. PINK to PINK-barred.

In **Underhill Road** facing the cemetery are a few 3-st and 2-st houses. PINK, except two at the corner of Overhill Rd which are new. Occupants keep servants.

NE to **Balchier Road**. Small 2-st houses. Road makes a turn. East side is poorer than west side and the houses older. Policeman, baker and working class. PURPLE to PINK.

E along **Dunstan's Road**. 2-st houses, mostly with one or two bay windows and a small garden in front. Two families as a rule but only on west side to a short distance north of the church (PINK). Here the houses are smaller and the people become poorer towards Peckham Rye. On the east side, north of Balchier St, the houses are poorer. Carmen, gardeners. A few small shops and some 2½-st houses near the Rye. PURPLE to PINK.

E into **Cornflower Terrace** (Herne Terrace on map). Small 2-st houses. Porters and men working in the cemetery. PINK to PURPLE.

Herne Grove. 2-st houses with bay window on south side. Two families. No poverty. PINK. North side poorer and smaller houses. PURPLE, uncoloured on map.

Forest Hill Road. Two houses on east side facing Dunstan's Rd. One is occupied by the Park Superintendent and the other by its owner. Detached houses. RED. On the west side, from south of St Aidan's Rd, are 2-st and 3-st shops. Those south of Dunstan's Rd were formerly private houses, four are still unchanged, and then there is a large house (Dunstan's Herne) with grounds. RED to PINK-barred.

Colyton Road. 3-st red-brick semi-detached houses overlooking the Park. One large detached house occupied but the man who did own the Park now owns most of the land hereabouts. All keep two servants. Ladies' School, doctor, etc. RED.

S along **Forest Hill Road**. South of Dunstan's Herne is a row of modern 2-st villas. Some servants. PINK-barred. Facing the Baptist Chapel are smaller houses. PINK in character. Then some private houses used for business purposes, marble mason, artificial flowers (wreaths etc) and shops to the cemetery, the row of buildings being known as Rockell's Terrace. Not much business, several depend on the cemetery for their trade. PINK to PINK-barred.

W into **Royal Oak Place**. Two rows of 2-st cottages, flush with path which is not made up, only a narrow kerb. Cabinet maker, gravediggers, etc. PURPLE.

S to **Rockell's Place**. Eight 2-st houses on each side. Ends at cemetery wall. Footway paved and road made up. Cemetery mason, milkman and men employed in cemetery. PURPLE to LIGHT BLUE. Lodge in cemetery is occupied. PINK.

N to **Mundania Road**. Semi-detached houses, 2-st and attic, with long gardens in front and tiled entrance. One or two servants at least. Minister etc. RED.

Therapia Road. Similar to Mundania Rd but not quite so good. Gardens smaller back and front. RED.

Marmora Road. 2-st plus attic, semi-detached. Trees planted along road. All keep servants but not so good as previous road. Many to be let or sold. One is shored up, brickwork cracked. RED.

Homestall Road has no houses. On the west side are cricket fields while on the east the Southwark and Vauxhall Water Company is extending its works and reservoir accommodation.

General Remarks

This walk completed the East Dulwich section so far as the area included in the Paris map is concerned. As a whole East Dulwich may be described as a working class district with a fringe of middle class on each side. This is emphasised by contrast with West Dulwich which is entirely middle class. All the West Dulwich constables live in East Dulwich said Jones. They cannot get accommodation in their own district.

Very little crime in the district, practically none of a serious character. The number of charges is small and they mostly arise out of drink. Thinks the public houses are fairly well conducted and there is very little, if any, collusion between the police and publicans – certainly not in East Dulwich. He would not like his Inspector to know he drank whilst on duty for £20, nor would he like to be seen entering a public house. The Supt is very sharp upon men for this "and rightly so". One man lost his pension a while ago.

Very little prostitution. Only place where prostitutes live on the ground is Rye Buildings. Some women from the Borough come to Peckham Rye. Very low class but not many of them.

PC Jones has a very good knowledge of East Dulwich and is thoroughly reliable there. Did not know Peckham and Denmark Hill so well and in this district his opinion is not so good.

Walk 54

B375

Tuesday 12th December 1899.
George Duckworth with PC Jones.

Starting at the corner of **Morning Lane and Red Post Hill.**
W along **Half Moon Lane.** Old houses with big gardens on the east side. The north side being gradually broken up by new red-brick houses. YELLOW and RED.
Out of the N side runs **Ardbeg Road.** Houses on east side only. New, red brick, well built. Road unfinished but houses occupied as soon as built.
N into **Red Post Hill.** RED.
S at Beckwith Road. Not so good as Ardbeg Rd but RED. Unfinished. Many Germans. 2-st houses with gabled attic. Small gardens front and back. All keep a servant.
W along Half Moon Lane and N up **Holmdene Avenue.** Good class 3-st houses at south east end, each taking in a lodger. RED. Further north houses are newer. RED.
N into **Denmark Hill.** Many new houses being built in place of the few old ones. The old houses are YELLOW and the new RED. No demand now for suburban palaces.
S down **Hollingbourne Road.** All new 2-st and attic. Comfortable, City-going people. Small fronts. RED.
S into **Warmington Road.** 2-st. Not so good nor so well built. Generally have a girl to do the housework and pay her 2/6 per week with her food. PINK-barred.
W along Half Moon Lane and S down **Burbage Road.** Detached large houses on east side only. RED.
W & N up **Winterbrook Road.** Double-fronted new houses, faced with red brick. All taken. RED.
Like it is **Stradella Road.** RED.
N into **Half Moon Lane.** The Half Moon Hotel – an elaborate, florid, large, newly-decorated public house opposite Herne Hill Stations – was sold a year ago for £64,000. Jones does not think it can pay.
N up **Herne Hill.** Newish, red-brick 4-st flats on the north side. RED to PINK-barred.
N along is **Gubyon Avenue.** Still building at Herne Hill end. Gets less good near Milkwood Rd. RED and PINK-barred.
Out of it on the W side is **Woodquest Avenue** which runs downhill to Milkwood Rd. RED to PINK-barred.
Like it is **Shardcroft Avenue.**
N into **Milkwood Road.** Houses less well tenanted because the position so near station and railway lines is less good. PINK-barred.
SW under the Railway Bridge and S down **Norwood Road.** Comfortable "RED" houses

facing Brockwell Park

E down a slough of ruts and mud called **Croxted Lane**. North better than south side. New houses. Some servants. PINK-barred.

Out of its **S** side is **Guernsey Road**. Still building and untenanted.

Further E is **Harwarden Road**. 2-st, red-brick houses. A good PINK-barred.

S into **Rosendale Road**. The south side west of the railway is PINK, the rest PINK-barred.

E along Turney Rd to Dulwich Village. **S** down **Aysgarth Road**. New but small, pokey, working class houses built by the Dulwich College Estate. Let at 12/- per week. 2-st, yellow brick. Jones spoke ironically of this and Boxall St of having been built by the trustees of the "College of God's gift to the people". PINK to PURPLE.

Parallel with it is **Boxall Street**. Rather poorer houses on south side only, cramped. PURPLE to PINK.

Into **Elms Road**, out of the main road which here has shops and is PINK-barred. Residential with occasional servants. 3-st. PINK-barred, not coloured in map.

Dulwich Village. Mixture of shops, large houses, public house. PINK-barred, PINK and RED. This ends the West Dulwich Section.

General Remarks

Dulwich College and Alleyne's College are the dominant factors in this neighbourhood. The increase in the number of "RED" streets is due to the demand of families who send their children to these schools as day boarders. Comfortable Germans also affect this district.

On general subjects Jones had spoken more particularly to GEA. He had differed with him, he said, only on the question of prostitutes. Jones is convinced that the only remedy lies in recognition of licensed houses. Peckham Rye is much used by the Borough Rd prostitutes.

Speaking generally, Peckham is humdrum and respectable. He spoke of the inhabitants as home-loving, seldom out late at night and not much given to entertainments. He never remembers seeing a child drunk except once when it was a boy of between 16 and 17. The respectable child may suffer he thinks from the language and habits of the public house but the labourer's child will hear worse at home.

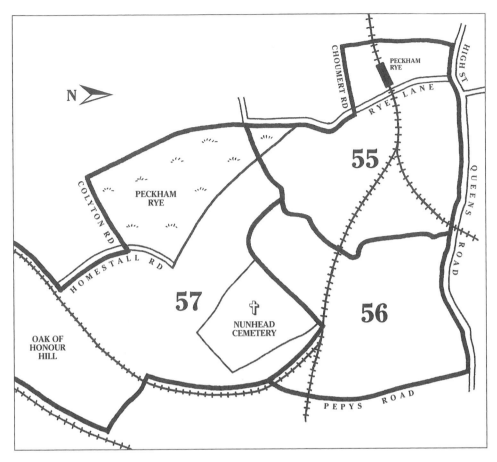

Walk 55

B373

Wednesday 18th October 1899.
Ernest Aves with PC Dolby.

Along High St and **S** down **Collyer Place**. Six 2-st houses, warehouses. Collyer's Hall, unnamed on map. Leave PURPLE.

Basing Road. 2-st houses. "Rather poor class." LIGHT BLUE as map, omitting for Collyer Hall, which flanks on this street.

York Terrace. 2-st, 5-roomed houses just like Basing Rd. LIGHT BLUE as map.

Hanover Street. 2-st houses, generally with eight or ten rooms. Small garden fronts. Often single occupants. "Perhaps half a dozen servants in the road." Perhaps may be left PINK-barred as map.

Elm Grove. On the RED side, trees, shady, but has seen its best days. Lower middle class, occasional servants. Peckham Liberal Club here. From RED of map to PINK-barred. The other (south) side, smaller houses. From PINK and RED on map to PINK and PINK-barred.

South Grove. Very much like Elm Grove. From PINK of map on south side to PINK-barred. North side, only two or three houses, "residential chambers". PINK as map.

S of the railway is **Blenheim Grove**. 2-st and 2½-st houses with garden fronts. The railway

acts against the standard of the road, much more obtrusive than in South Grove. PINK as map.
Chadwick Road (east end). 2-st houses. Decent, trees, quiet. Generally one family to a house. PINK as map.
Choumert Road (east of Victoria Rd) is the boundary road of the section. 2-st, 2½-st and 3-st houses. A few shops at each end. Very few servants. Quiet, trees. Very like Blenheim Grove. From PINK-barred of map to PINK.
Choumert Grove. 2-st houses, six rooms, fronts. PINK as map, with extra colour at north west end for two or three houses of the same style.
Off the E side is **Choumert Square.** North side has 4-roomed cottages. Rents 6/- and 6/6, going up for newcomers. Queer entrances behind out of a covered passageway. Little garden fronts on each side, and "all fronts" as an occupant said, proud, however, of her square. The south side very much the same save that the entrances are in front more after the way of the world. No tenants are taken with children and the whole place appears to be very quiet, select, old fashioned, and quaint. All PINK as map. No traffic for vehicles, private.
This walk had to be cut short as Dolby had to attend the Court in connexion with a summons.

Starting on the 19th along the High Street.
S down **Batten's Place** (just to the W of Albert Rd). Six cottages, four rooms. LIGHT BLUE as map, omitting colour for the two that have gone at the north end.
Further W is **Nungate.** 4-roomed cottages. Costers etc, "poor class". Only one cottage on east side. LIGHT BLUE as map.
Thence, by Clayton Rd, W along **McKerrell Road.** 2-st, 6-roomed houses. PINK as map.
Clayton Road. 2-st houses, a few shops. PINK as map, correcting the line of colour at north west corner, which should be parallel with the street not at right angles to it. The PINK-barred bit at south west corner is 2-st houses, occupied by much the same class as the rest of the road. From PINK-barred of map to PINK. North of this part, extra colour for a new row of houses of much the same style.
Into High St again. W, passing the passsage leading to St Chrysostum School, only one house (caretaker's) into **The Avenue.** Unnamed on map. Mews, costers etc. LIGHT BLUE as map. Avenue House is a Home for Girls (Miss Rye's Home). Inmates emigrated to Canada.
Rye Lane is an increasingly busy street. Jones and Higgins' big premises are at the north east corner and the success of this business has doubtless tended to raise the standard of many of the surrounding shops. The street remains RED as map. In the space on the east side, south of railway, the "Museum" is now Bussey's Games Factory and, south of this on the site of a nursery, Holdron's line of shops, drapery etc, have been built. Extra RED here and the RED behind omitted.
Hanover Park. At the north west corner Jones and Higgins' extension is going up, stabling and additional stores. The only residence the stable-men's houses, PINK. All the rest of this side to corner of McKerrell Rd, excepting one house, the Constitutional Club and Hanover Hall taken by Jones and Higgins for employees. From RED and uncoloured to PINK. East of McKerrell Rd are 2-st houses, like those in McKerrell Rd. RED to PINK. South side is 2-st and 3-st houses. Occasional servants. From RED of map to PINK-barred.
Moncrieff Road. 2-st houses. Two families frequent, apartments etc. From PINK-barred of map to PINK.
Cicely Road. 2-st and 2½-st houses. Good garden fronts, some apartments, servants. From RED of map to PINK-barred.
Raul Road. 2-st houses. Much the same class as in Cicely Rd. From RED of map to PINK-barred.

Cerise Road is more like Moncreiff Rd. From PINK-barred to PINK.

Thence **S** along Rye Lane to **Bournemouth Road**. 3-st houses, plain brick, dull. "Labouring class." PURPLE as map.

Into **Copeland Road**. The PINK part is 2-st houses. Colour as map. The PURPLE part is 2-st, 2½-st and 3-st houses mainly. Two shops at south east end. From PURPLE of map to PINK.

Parkstone Road. 3-st houses. PURPLE as map.

By the Triangle (part of Rye Lane) to **Copeland Avenue** (late Solly Rd). 2-st houses, good, creepers, asphalt, no traffic. PINK as map.

Atwell Street. 4-roomed cottages. LIGHT BLUE as map.

Atwell Road. Like Parkstone Rd and Bournemouth Rd. PURPLE as map.

Along Rye Lane to **Philip Road** (west end). 2-st and 2½-st houses. PINK as map.

Claude Road. 2-st houses. Uncoloured, PINK and PURPLE to PINK and LIGHT BLUE.

Scylla Road. West end is 2-st houses. PINK as map. At the east end (Nunhead Passage on map) the south side is LIGHT BLUE to PURPLE. On north side some houses are new, LIGHT BLUE and PURPLE to PINK.

A new road runs from Scylla Rd to Peckham Rye, **Whorlton Road**. 2-st houses, 8-roomed. Arranged for two families, let at 11/6 a floor, good. Uncoloured to PINK.

Peckham Rye. Two good new houses have been built at north and south of the end of this new street, but the rest of the houses on this east side are old and many of them shabby-genteel including one with a small builder's yard attached. From RED of map to PINK-barred to Nunhead Lane, the boundary here of this section of the police.

In **Nunhead Passage** (east end) are two houses, at north east corner, one of them empty. From uncoloured in map to PINK or PINK-barred.

Nunhead Crescent. South side is 2-st houses. Uncoloured to PINK. North side is 2-st houses and 3-st with basements. Occasional servants. From RED of map to PINK-barred.

Nunhead Lane is said to be better on the Dulwich than on the Peckham side. The west end to Nunhead Crescent is 3-st, a few shops, occupied by good working class. PINK as map. East of the Crescent the style of houses becomes much more varied, 2-st and 2½-st, a school, a Solicitor etc. Some working class, very much like the north side of the Crescent. From PINK of map to PINK-barred.

Old James Street. 2-st houses. All LIGHT BLUE as map including the cul de sac behind, which ranks as part of the street.

A little to the **E** is **New James Street**. 2-st houses. No thoroughfare for vehicles. West side done up but, with the dingier looking east side, perhaps still all LIGHT BLUE as map. This and the last-named street, are just on the border of the published map and the colour, LIGHT BLUE, is cut through in the middle. But apparently it was the intention to colour the whole of the block the same.

Round by Nunhead Grove to **Monk's Cottages** (north of Francis Place). Unnamed on map. 2-st, "1791". PURPLE as map with extra colour to the south for new houses, also PURPLE.

W along **Francis Place** (now part of Scylla Rd). 2-st houses. PURPLE as map with extra for two new houses at south west corner.

Albert Road. PINK as map to the railway, including "The Braid".

Philip Road. East half is 2-st, 2½-st and 3-st houses, the last with shop frontages. All PINK as map.

Vivian Road. 2-st houses, very much like Albert Rd and others of the neighbourhood. No apparent reason for different colour. From PURPLE of map, therefore, to PINK.

Manaton Road and **Wivenhoe Road**. Both alike, 2-st houses. PINK as map.

Heaton Road. South side is 2-st and 2½-st houses, north side is 3-st houses. On south side east of Claude Rd is better and here from PURPLE of map to PINK. The rest PURPLE as map.

Huguenot Street. 2½-st houses. From LIGHT BLUE of map to PURPLE.

Godman Road. 2-st houses. West end is PURPLE as map omitting colour on north side for a laundry. The east end somewhat better, perhaps from PURPLE of map to PINK.

Pilkington Road, Brayards Road (west end) and **Russell Road.** All have 2-st houses and are PINK as map.

N under the railway arch up Albert Rd to **Clifton Square.** 2-st houses. PINK as map.

Albert Road (north of the railway). Most of it much larger and better houses, except on west side where the PINK represents some timbered and stucco cottages, small, and some 3-st houses, let off. Both of these PINK as map. East side north of Harders Rd is detached, substantial houses. RED as map. The rest, various in styles, from RED to PINK-barred.

Along Queen's Rd to **Harders Road.** 2-st, 2½-st and 3½-st houses. On south east side are two or three laundries. PINK as map and from RED of map to PINK-barred. The other side from PINK and RED of map to PINK. The RED house off the west side, due south of the Wesleyan Chapel, is an error, omit.

Mortlock Gardens. 2-st houses. PINK as map.

Gordon Road (to the railway). 2-st houses. PINK as map with extra colour on both sides, north end, for additional houses,

Sunwell Street. In map shown as part of Hook's Rd. PINK as map but Sunwell St as shown in map is 2-st houses with basements. "Labouring class." From LIGHT BLUE to PURPLE.

Hook's Road. West side is 2-st houses, letting 14/- a week. PINK as map. East side is 2-st with basements. Improvement but poorer, done up and doing up. Perhaps from LIGHT BLUE of map to PURPLE.

Woods Road. 2-st houses, rents 13/-. PINK as map.

Thence by **Queen's Road**, south side. Here mainly private houses. RED as map.

To **Burchell Road.** 2-st houses, rents 13/- . "Very respectable." LIGHT BLUE appeared to be very occasional. From PURPLE of map to PINK.

Of the same type are **Cossell Street** and **Bidwell Street.** Both from PURPLE of map rather to PINK, although low grade.

Along Queen's Rd to **Hollydale Road.** 2-st houses, small garden fronts. High waged and low salaried class, servants few and far between. From PINK-barred of map to PINK.

Lugard Road, running south west, is just the same. From PINK-barred of map to PINK.

Caulfield Road. Of much the same type. PINK as map.

E to **Firbank Road.** Still the same, houses said to let at from 14/- to 15/-. PINK as map.

Stanbury Road is a replica of Lugard Rd. PINK-barred of map to PINK.

Brayards Road (east of railway). 2-st houses, a few shops at east end. PINK as map.

Just the same is **Kirkwood Road**, also with a few shops. PINK as map.

Gordon Road (between the railways). 2-st houses. PINK as map. Houses on east side only.

Crewys Road and **Lulworth Road**, with houses of the same type. PINK as map.

Wroxton Road, again of the Lugard Rd type. From PINK-barred of map to PINK.

Lansdowne Grove and **Brabourne Grove** keep their colour, PINK.

SW along **Evelina Road.** More of a business street, especially at the west end. All PINK as map. Just south of the railway on the north side are three or four houses uncoloured on map, additional PINK here. At the house next to the railway, with its passage and boundary running along the bottom of the embankment, the notorious criminal, Peace, lived for some years. Dolby said that he frequently arranged to come home after nightfall from one of his house-breaking expeditions and that his plan was to throw his booty out of the carriage window as the train passed his house. He thus arrived at the stations without luggage and, without exciting suspicion, went home and picked up the booty.

Running **NE** is **Kimberley Road**. 2-st houses. PINK as map.

Kirkwood Road (south end) is just the same.

Grimwade Crescent (off Evelina Rd). 2-st houses. "More of the labouring class", not a good name, brawls etc. LIGHT BLUE as map.

W along Evelina Rd and **N** to **Gordon Road** (to the railway). Mainly 2-st houses. PURPLE and PINK as map.

On the **W** side are:

Ellery Street. 2-st and 3-st houses, PURPLE and PINK as map.

Sturdy Road. 2-st houses. LIGHT BLUE to PURPLE.

Headley Street. 2-st houses. LIGHT BLUE to PURPLE. At the south west corner of Gordon Rd is a branch Free Library, built on land previously unoccupied.

Walk 56   B373

Monday 6th November 1899.
Ernest Aves with PC Dolby.

Started at Nunhead Green.

North side of **Nunhead Green** is a mixed affair with 2-st, 2½-st and 3-st houses, Almshouses, a Salvation Army Citadel and, at the west corner of Gordon Rd, a Chapel. All PURPLE as map omitting for the Chapel. South side is 3-st and 3½-st houses, the former, at the east end, forming a continuation of Evelina Rd, shops. From PURPLE of map to PINK to Banstead Rd. West of this are dwelling houses, "Zetland Terrace". PURPLE as map. The west side is small 2-st dwelling houses. PURPLE as map.

S along **Linden Grove**, the boundary road of the police section. At first on the north side detached, substantial, 3-st houses, servants the rule. Said to be rather a gloomy road, with funerals constantly passing. The Grove to the corner of Nunhead Grove perhaps still RED. Further east along the line parallel with Daniel's Rd are 2-st, 6-roomed houses. Poor. LIGHT BLUE. Next is Daniel's House and large mason's yards, and beyond better 2-st houses. PINK as map to Gibbon Rd, where this police section ends.

Daniel's Road. "1863", 2-st houses, flush with sidewalk. Broken windows occasional, numerous and noisy children, a low standard street. Difficult to say what the peopole do for a living, but some work as labourers in the adjacent cemetery, others as builders' labourers etc. All LIGHT BLUE.

Nunhead Grove. Mainly 2-st houses, the rest 2½-st and 3-st. A short new row on the east side, "Thorne Terrace", arranged for families, 10/- a floor. Near the north east end is "Nunhead Terrace, 1857". All PINK. Near the south west corner is the Cheltenham Mission. A small boys' battle was raging while we were in this street, with stones flying about unpleasantly, but apparently no damage done. One of the common complaints of the section is that of boys who smash a window, instead of cutting an enemy's eye open.

S out of Nunhead Green, is **Marble Arch**, a more than usually inappropriate name. On the west side, near the entrance is one 3-st house, much sublet, and further along on the east side a small row of cottages. Costers etc. All either DARK BLUE or LIGHT BLUE.

Banstead Road. 2-st houses, letting at from 11/- to 13/-. Shoddy building, a few shops, poor. LIGHT BLUE. At the south west end is a row of new houses, "Grove Terrace". Also LIGHT BLUE.

Tappesfield Road. 2-st houses. Done up. Somewhat better than Banstead Rd – "more of the mechanic class". On the east side is Stanley Hall, the headquarters of the Nunhead Christian Band, said to represent a past local split in the Salvation Army. Two houses in the space at the south end, LIGHT BLUE. The road perhaps from the LIGHT BLUE of the map to PURPLE.

Barset Road. Represents a still further improvement. 2-st houses still, forecourts. From LIGHT BLUE of map to PURPLE.

At the **SW** end, running south of the Buchan Rd line, is **Salisbury Terrace**. Poorer. LIGHT BLUE.

Howbury Road. 2-st houses, much like Barset Rd. Better from south end to Machell Rd. Here tiled forecourts and a brighter appearance. Perhaps this part from the PURPLE of the map to PINK, the rest PURPLE as map.

Kimberley Road. South east end has rather larger houses than in the northern bits, bow windows, fronts, 2-st and 2½-st. PINK as map.

Machell Road. 2-st houses, six rooms, forecourts. PURPLE as map

Buchan Road. 2-st houses, good gardens behind on south side. Here from PURPLE of map to PINK. North side PURPLE as map.

Gibbon Road. From south west end to the railway is mainly 2-st houses. Shops east of Kimberley Rd. Beyond the railway to Hollydale Rd is 5-st houses and shops. All PINK as map.

Hollydale Road (south east of Evelina Rd). South side is 2-st houses, forecourts, bow windows. Gone down, poor. From PURPLE of map to LIGHT BLUE. With a little unnecessary severity Dolby remarked that "you generally find houses run down near a school", which would be true of middle class houses and higher grade PINK, but hardly of anything below. At the north east corner, two or three dwellings. From uncoloured of map to PINK.

N to Ansdell Road. 2-st houses, bow windows, eight rooms, houses let on lease. Something like Lugard Rd, perhaps a little better. From PINK-barred of map to high grade PINK.

Dundas Road. Described by Dolby as "just the same". PINK as map.

N into Queen's Rd, passing the entrance to **The Retreat**, "The Marist Convent for Young Ladies", a Roman Catholic Boarding and Middle Class College. Two or three houses appear to be occupied. RED, if coloured, as map.

S down St Mary's Road. Middle class, larger houses north of the church. Here RED as map. South of the church, from RED of map to PINK-barred, omitting at south east corner for St Mary's Church Hall, built 1890.

Evelina Road (east of Hollydale Rd). 2-st and 3-st houses, mainly the former. Shops at north east corner. All PINK as map.

Kitto Road (west end). PURPLE as map.

Hathway Street is a cul de sac between Senate St and Kitto Rd. Not shown on map. 2-st, 5-roomed houses, generally single occupants. From uncoloured of map to PURPLE.

Senate Street. 2-st houses. Poor looking and gloomy, some broken windows. LIGHT BLUE as map.

Selden Road. South of Lindo St is 2-st and 3-st houses. Broken windows, untidy children, poor. From PURPLE of map to LIGHT BLUE. North of Lindo St is 2-st houses, better. PURPLE as map.

Lindo Street. 2-st houses, south side only. LIGHT BLUE as map.

Passing into District 45 at **Arbuthnot Street**. The houses at the west corner are 2-st double-fronted mostly, and might perhaps remain PINK-barred as map. The rest is made up of smaller houses, no servants. From PINK-barred of map to PINK. The road is now continued a long way east to Jerningham Rd but no new houses have been built on the part lying in the police division.

Running S is **Gellatly Road**. 2-st houses. Very occasional servants, but "mostly girls", by which Dolby meant youth and inefficiency, and of such he thought that there were perhaps ten in the whole road. It is of very much the same type as Ansdell Rd. From PINK-barred of map to PINK. It is on the large Haberdashers' Estate of this neighbourhood and contains the only licensed house the Company allows.

Drakefell Road takes one up the higher ground of Telegraph Hill and off the north side part of the new Park lies, finely situated, with splendid views over London. The houses, 2-st and 2-st with basements, small, but generally with well-to-do occupants, middle class. RED as map.

Pepys Road, the boundary of the Peckham Section. Very much the same character as Drakefell Rd. RED as map with additional colour for the Vicarage, built just below the new church, at the corner of Arbuthnot Rd.

W along **Kitto Road** as far as Erlanger Rd. The new Park lies on either side. On the north side, between Erlanger Rd and the new Waller Rd, are new 2-st houses with basements. From uncoloured to RED. Below the Chapel, which has been built lately, the old Chapel becoming schools, the houses are smaller. "Not many servants here." From RED of map to PINK-barred. On the south side are 3-st houses. RED as map.

Bousefield Street. 2-st houses, bow windows. Badly built, many owned by occupiers and bought through Building Societies, said to cost about £400. "Very few servants" of whom however, I saw one! Perhaps from PINK-barred of map to PINK.

Waller Road. Quite a new road of 2-st houses with basements. Narrow and long slips of garden behind, clothes out to dry in many of them. Some servants and a good many "step girls" employed, that is girls who come in a few times a week and do some of the rougher work, including the steps. On the west side a Board School and at the north west corner a Fire Station, a very fine building fronting the Queen's Rd. This PINK, the rest of the road from uncoloured to PINK-barred. The range of roads starting from Bousefield at the bottom of the hill to Pepys at the top, the boundary of the section, tends to improve in standard.

The next, **Erlanger Road**, with houses very much like those of Waller Rd, is a better-off street, differing very little, if at all, from Pepys Rd itself. Two thirds of Erlanger Rd is new and the south end faces the Park. All from RED and uncoloured of map to RED.

Pepys Road on the west side has been built over up to Arbuthnot Rd and all the houses are very much of the same class as those in Erlanger Rd. From YELLOW and uncoloured of map to RED. A few years back much of this site, which is partly built over and partly Park, was taken up by brick-fields.

Queen's Road. RED as map. Residential at this east end, with a few new houses filling in the gap shown on the map.

W of Waller Rd is **Somerville Road**. A cul de sac of 3-st and 2-st houses with small garden fronts. Good. PINK as map.

Dennett's Road. Houses of various styles, 2-st and 3-st. A row of 3-st houses that used to be in very bad repair and occupied by a very low class has been altered and improved, one house alone reminding of the old condition of things. The street from PURPLE of map to PINK. On the W side is **Franklin's Grove**. Houses on south side only, 2-st, 7/-, open in front. Perhaps from PURPLE of map to PINK. One family to a house the rule.

E to **Rutt's Terrace**. 2-st houses, flush with sidewalk. Cul de sac, except for entrance to Waller St Board School. "More of the labouring class than in Dennett's Rd." PURPLE as map.

Dennett's Grove is much like Rutt's Terrace. PURPLE as map.

Washam Road, save that the houses are older and have small forecourts, is again the same. PURPLE as map.

Off the E side of Dennett's Rd is **Mona Road**. 2-st houses with forecourts. PINK as map. In this road is a boundary line between the parishes of Deptford and Camberwell and Dolby mentioned the practice of the police, if they have anyone to arrest who can be shunted along, of getting the offender into the west end of the road prior to the arrest. If this can be managed the case is tried at the Camberwell Court, if not the constable has to go all the way to Greenwich. Doubtless this economy of time and trouble works out in other ways, not perhaps always so harmlessly. For instance, Dolby had previously mentioned that some parts of the Peckham Section are a mile or more from the police station and the trouble it was to get a prisoner from the more distant ground safely into the lock-up. There must be strong temptation in these circumstances to let a man go, if possible, as it so often is in the case of brawlers and of "drunks". Back into District 44 at **Lausanne Road**. Houses of all sorts, 2-st, 2½-st, 3-st and 3½-st. Some servants. PINK-barred as map. On the south side is the very small 'South East London Synagogue', only a sprinkling of Jews said to be in the district, and these mostly Germans. **Edith Road**. Mainly 3½-st, large, "a family comfortable class" but "not many servants". Lodgers. Shops on the west side, south of the Chapel. All from RED of map to PINK-barred. **Wellington Road**. 3-st and 3½-st houses. Compared with Lausanne Rd. From RED and PINK-barred of map to PINK-barred, putting a continuous line of colour on the north side.

General Remarks

As in the last district, the triangle lying north of the Queen's Rd, so here, the changes of the last ten years have been mainly those of colour, not of plan. The important exception to the latter is the part lying to the north west of Telegraph Hill, where a new street or two have been made and where old streets have been filled up. In this neighbourhood also the laying out of the Park on Telegraph Hill is a noteworthy improvement.

The change of colour will, I think, be more noticeable here than in the last district, there being a marked tendency for the diffusion of the colour of the "central" classes. There are patches of PURPLE and touches of LIGHT BLUE that will remain but, excluding these and the few middle class streets such as Pepys Rd, Erlanger Rd, Drakefell Rd and part of St Mary's Rd, together with the important shopping thoroughfare of Rye Lane, it will be found that the area is emphatically one that is occupied by the decently and highly waged and the low salaried classes. This is borne out by the fact that, although still subject to final revision, almost the whole of the changes – 25 or so – that I suggest for lowering the grade of colouring will, if adopted, bring down the RED and PINK-barred streets to a notch below, while almost the whole of the suggestions – some 20 or so – for raising the standard will, if adopted, send LIGHT BLUE and PURPLE streets up. The tendency appears, therefore, to be markedly in the direction of a greater uniformity of colouring, the servant-keeping class tending to move out and the poorer class, as my police guide emphasised several times, tending to be driven out.

A good many laundries are scattered about and the shops of the main streets close by must provide a considerable amount of employment, but the vast majority of the people appear to work at a distance, most travelling daily to the City or Citywards and to Deptford.

Walk 57   B375 (7)

Tuesday 12th December 1899.
George Duckworth with PC Jones.

Starting at the corner of **Manor Lane** and **Peckham Rye**.
Nunhead Lane. The west end the poorest part. 3-st houses on either side. A few poor.

PINK to PURPLE, in map PINK. Further east is poorer. PINK-barred to RED, in map RED. Single men lodgers usual except in the good semi-detached houses which should be RED.

S down **Carden Road**. 2-st, small, comfortable houses, semi-detached. Most with a girl of 15 or 16 as servant. Never to let. Used to be a happy place for house-breakers. Now the former tenants have moved out, less substantial people remain. PINK-barred, in map RED.

E along **Forest Road**. Houses on either side of east end and one small house on south side of west end. PINK as map but more of it. This road is to be run through to Peckham Rye.

N up **Barforth Road**. 2-st. Like Carden Rd. PINK-barred, in map RED.

E & S down **Linden Grove**. Large detached houses on east side, mixture on west. Distinctly less good on west, some apartments. East RED as map, west PINK-barred to RED.

W to **Tresco Road**. Like Carden Rd and Barforth Rd. PINK-barred, in map RED.

E along **Linden Grove**. Opposite the Cemetery, poor gravediggers, somewhat improved. LIGHT BLUE to PURPLE at west end (which is in the Camberwell 'W' Police Division), it improves west of Gibbon Rd. PURPLE to LIGHT BLUE. LIGHT BLUE to PURPLE east of Gibbon Rd. Has always had a bad name for drink and roughness but is not as bad as the streets behind in Daniel's Rd, Tappesfield Rd and Banstead Rd.

E along **Gibbon Road**. A few poor but majority fairly comfortable. 2-st PINK houses with gardens.

S down **Ivydale Road**. Poorish opposite the stations. PURPLE to PINK. Two bow windows to the house and Jones said only one family in each. Further south the road turns west along the south side of the Nunhead Cemetery. The amenity of the road is spoilt by the shooting trial ground of the Army & Navy Stores in the open space at the back of the south side. Road improves as it goes westwards.

W up **Limesford Road**. A few servants. One large house in the centre – Gates' Property. PINK-barred to PINK.

S & W along Ivydale Rd to **Athelney Road**, **Merttins Road**, **Holmesley Road**, **Fernholme Road** and **Rosenthorpe Road**. All 2-st, well-built yellow-brick houses, Rosenthorpe Rd being the best of them. All built by Gates, the South London millionaire who owns property in Walworth and Kennington as well. Small but not very small, small backs. Trees on pavement. Houses let at £28 a year and corner houses at £31. These are low rents for London but conditions are attached that only one family may be in each house and no lodgers may be taken. Foremen, clerks and City people live here, go into their work by train. Some meat salesmen who are off at 4 am. A few servants. PINK-barred to PINK. Perhaps Merttins Rd and Holmesley Rd are a little less good than the others. Jones said that they were all alike. The large field at the west end now used as football and cricket grounds has been lately taken by the Vauxhall and Middlesex Waterworks as a site for a new reservoir.

N up **Hall Road**. Gates' property ceases. Houses 2-st, less well built, much worse tenanted. Two families in each. Rents 7/- per flat. Some shops. PINK to PURPLE.

E along **Surrey Grove**. Still building. PINK to PURPLE.

N up **Rye Road**. Some poor. PURPLE.

W along **Hichisson Road**. PURPLE.

N up **Borland Road** (late Marylebone Rd). Poor at north east, comfortable at south west. PURPLE.

W along **Reynolds Road** (late Pancreas Rd). 2-st. Poor at north west end. PURPLE to PINK.

N & E along **Stuart Road**. Much older houses here, some shops. PURPLE to PINK.

E to **Sartor Road**. One large house still tenanted at the south end, RED. The rest PINK like that part of Borland Rd which faces north. Mostly two families per house.

W along Stuart Rd and N into **Elland Road**. One big "RED" house at the south east corner, the rest PINK.

W along the Rye and N into **Rye Hill Park**. 3-st and 3½-st houses built on the side of a steep slope for good class servant-keeping families. Owing to a scare that the waterworks reservoir at the top might burst the tenants left. Working class have taken their place and many are to let. Good tenants remain only in the houses near the Rye. Colour RED and PINK.

W along **Peckham Rye**. Good class houses with gardens. Retired shopkeepers. RED as map.

N into **Waveney Avenue**. 2-st, two families, rents 11/- per family per week. This and Somerton Rd much sought after by the young married couples of the neighbourhood. Some keep a girl servant. PINK to PINK-barred.

Like it is **Somerton Road** which runs back again to the Rye.

General Remarks

The only noticeable part of this round is the policy of the Gates' Estate in the Ivydale Rd district.

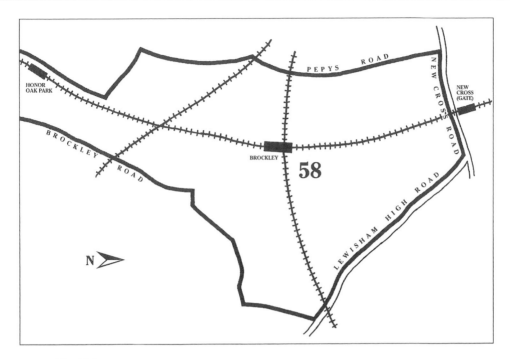

Walk 58

B373

Thursday 9th November 1899.
Ernest Aves with PC Moss.
Moss is still a PC although he has been 17 years in the force. The first year he was in the Lewisham Section and all the rest of the time in Brockley. He was rather bucolic, beefy and provincial but knew the district well.

Starting from the Police Station, we crossed the line at the Brockley Station.
Turning south west to **Arica Road**. 2-st houses, some new. The latter, arranged for two families, let at 10/6 a floor. From LIGHT BLUE of map to PINK, with more of it.
Horsted Road much the same, the newer houses letting at 10/-. The older single houses in both streets, arranged for one family, go at 12/-. Moss lives in Horsted Rd. Uncoloured to PINK. To the south and west the fields are open, and the big Board School looked as though it was waiting for scholars but it was said to be full.
N along **Mantle Road**. Only three houses (on east side). Station master etc. Uncoloured to PINK.
W up **Foxwell Street**. 2-st houses. Poor class, or perhaps a carelessly spending class, coalies etc. LIGHT BLUE as map.
Tolhurst Street, close by on the south side, has dwellings of the same style on west side only. From uncoloured of map to LIGHT BLUE. These two small and poor-looking streets were described by Moss as being "about the worst bit on the ground".
Endwell Road. At south west corner is a 4-st block, largely occupied by men employed by Martin, a local dairyman. PURPLE. At south east corner are shops. The rest is 3-st houses, garden fronts. Some servants, lodgers the rule. From RED of map to PINK-barred.
Sprules Road. 2-st houses, built deep. Same class as Endwell Rd. From PINK of map to

PINK-barred, with extra colour for new houses.

Walbutton Road. West side only, 2-st, 3-st and 3½-st houses of the Endwell Rd type. From RED to PINK-barred.

Penmartin Road. The two east blocks on south side are tenement houses, occupied by Martin's employees for the most part and owned by him. PINK as map with rather more colour. The rest, both north and south, where built, are 2-st and 2-st with basement houses much like those in Sprules Rd. Servants, lodgers. From PINK and RED of map to PINK-barred.

Pepys Road. The boundary on the east, and on the west side RED as map.

Pendrell Road is much the same. From uncoloured on map to RED.

To the **NE** is **Vesta Road.** Of the Sprules Rd type as also is **Reservoir Road.** Both from RED of map to PINK-barred.

Sandbourne Road. 3-st houses. PINK-barred as map.

Jerningham Road. South of Arbuthnot Rd is all new. The "Tennis Ground" of the map is a thing of the past and the only break in the line of houses is to the south of it, for a reservoir. Houses and occupants very much of the Pepys Rd order. From uncoloured of map to RED.

Arbuthnot Road (east of Pepys Rd). 2½-st houses, built deep. New. Fine view from north side. Rents £40 a year or so. From uncoloured of map to RED.

Ommaney Road. New. Between Arbuthnot Rd and Musgrove Rd. Houses very much like those of the former. Well-to-do shopkeepers of the New Cross Rd and Peckham. "Very rarely see a card in any window." Uncoloured in map to RED.

Musgrove Road (which has no houses in it west of Pepys Rd) has not yet been opened through to the east but in the present cul de sac up the Jerningham Rd end a few houses have been built on either side. Uncoloured to RED.

Pepys Road. With new houses east of the Park and on the west side between Musgrove Rd and Arbuthnot Rd, is a good middle class street throughout. On the east side some of the houses are large red-brick erections, but no part should be YELLOW. From YELLOW and uncoloured of map to RED. The road is broad and spacious, with trees, and in a few years time may become a pleasant boulevard.

Much the same is **Jerningham Road.** "One of the best we have." Houses are 2½-st and 3½-st. RED as map. At the north west corner is the Aske School for Girls, an imposing building standing in large grounds. The Boys' School was on Telegraph Hill. Most of this ground is still on the Haberdashers' estate, the Company that manages the Aske Trusts.

The **New Cross Road** east of Pepys Rd is RED as map. A few houses stand in their own grounds – Sir A Kirby, a distiller who went bankrupt, having had one and Miss Gray, "a maiden lady", living in another, etc. East of Jerningham Rd the road is mostly shops.

Crossing the railway, **S** up **St James' Road.** 3-st and 3½-st houses. "Pretty well-to-do". RED as map. At the end is the Church, notorious as a centre of extreme ritualism some 20 years ago.

E along the School Passage to **Laurie Grove.** Mostly 2-st houses, respectable working class. Some of the houses are new. On the west side are the new Baths and Wash-houses and east of them a few small and old cottages, soon coming down. These LIGHT BLUE and the rest, omitting for the Baths, from PINK-barred and PINK of map, to PINK.

Rebecca's Place has gone, some of the new houses in Laurie Grove and a rebuilt public house at the corner having taken its place. Omit DARK BLUE.

Dixon Road. Just like the better part of Laurie Grove. PINK as map.

Lewisham High Road. West side is mainly private houses, except between Malpas Rd and Brockley Rd. All RED as map.

St Donatt's Road. 2-st, 2½-st and 3-st houses from east end to the bend. Salesmen, engineers, etc. Some servants. Here from RED to PINK-barred. From the bend to Malpas

Rebecca's Place, demolished shortly before the researcher's visit.

Rd is smaller houses, 2-st and 2½-st. Few servants here if any and two families to a house often south of Shardeloes Rd. RED to PINK.

Shardeloes Road (north of St Donatt's Rd). Very much the same. From RED of map to PINK-barred.

On the **SE** side is **Brindley Street**. A cul de sac with 2-st houses and 2-st with basements. Garden fronts (small). Railway men etc. PINK as map.

Shardeloes Road (south of St Donatt's Rd). At south east corner some 3-st flats. Working class here. From RED of map to PINK. The rest of the road 2-st and 2-st basement houses, of a kind that in Peckham or Hoxton would be put down as PINK with little hesitation. In Brockley, however, with a much larger proportion of houses taken on lease, with rents paid quarterly and a different class often found in occupation, the right colour becomes more doubtful. Here I am told that the tenancies are yearly and that there are servants in many of the houses. Perhaps from RED of map to PINK-barred; the alternative, PINK.

Thence by Vulcan Rd to **Malpas Road**. Much like the south end of Shardeloes Rd. Query PINK-barred as map, or to PINK?

Luxmore St. 2-st houses. PINK as map.

Rokeby Road. 2-st houses with basements. Good working class and low salaried. Few servants. Much like Malpas Rd. Query PINK-barred as map or PINK?

Brockley Road (from north end to Vulcan Rd). Shops at north west corner. West side 2½-st, 3-st and 2-st houses, RED to PINK-barred. East side 3-st houses of better class, RED as map.

Vulcan Road. 2-st houses, one or two shops. PINK as map.

Vulcan Terrace. 2-st plus attics. PINK as map.

Brockley Road (south of Vulcan Rd to railway). Shops at north east corner. Here RED to PINK-barred. The rest of this side is private houses. RED as map. West side is residential with occasional brass plates. From RED of map to PINK-barred.

Malpas Road (south of St Donatt's Rd). A few shops, but mainly like the north bit, a frequent brass plate street. Query from PINK-barred of map to PINK? The south west corner has 3-st houses with attics. Shops, really part of Brockley Rd. From RED of map to PINK-barred, the colour lengthened a little. Near this end is the old "lock gate house" standing by the banks of where a canal once ran, in well-to-do occupancy. PINK, if coloured in the big scale map.

Brockley Road (south of railway to Harefield Rd). Only two dwellings on west side. On east side 3-st houses and shops in a kind of parade. From RED of map to PINK-barred.

Harefield Road. Mainly 2-st houses, substantial. RED as map.

Cranfield Road (west end). 2½-st houses. Mixed, less well-to-do towards the west end. From RED of map to PINK-barred.

Wickham Road (north of Cranfield Rd). Some good houses – doctors, a master lighterman, a vicar's widow, a Deptford bottle merchant, etc. From YELLOW of map to RED. A very fine broad road.

St Peter's Road. RED as map. Only one house.

The west end of **Manor Road** (on map St Peter's Rd) is like the west end of Cranfield Rd but not so well-to-do. From RED of map to PINK-barred.

Manor Road (as shown in map). RED as map.

Coulgate Street. Close to the Station. 2-st and 3-st houses, shops etc. PINK.

Foxberry Road. Part running north and south is 2-st and 2-st with basement houses. PINK. Part running east and west is mainly 2-st and 2½-st houses. Mixed class. Some with two or three families. "Tinker, sweep, labouring class." PURPLE as map.

Harcourt Road. 2-st houses. PINK as map.

Brockley Road (from Harefield Rd to Wickham Rd). 2½-st and 3-st houses, "apartments" etc. From RED of map to PINK-barred.

Wickham Road (south of Cranfield Rd). Houses rather smaller than in the northern bit. Still a fine wide road with double rows of trees, one in the gardens and the other in the roadway. From YELLOW of map to RED.

Wickham Gardens. Smaller houses, ornate. Middle class, comfortable. RED.

Glensdale Road. 2-st and 3-st houses. Same class of occupants as Wickham Gardens. RED.

Upper Harefield Road (east of Wickham Rd). Like Glensdale Rd. RED.

Cranfield Road (east of Wickham Rd). North side is 3½-st houses. YELLOW to RED. South side no houses, St Peter's Church Hall. Uncoloured.

Breakspears Road. Much like Wickham Rd. From YELLOW of map to RED. Moss pointed out one house, larger than any of the others, just north east of the railway, saying that when he first came into the district, unmarried, he lodged in the house of the mother of the occupier's wife. "They have gone up in the world since those days."

Tyrwhitt Road (running parallel with the lane which forms the boundary of the Lewisham parish – no houses in it). Mainly 3-st and 3½-st houses. Improves towards south end. RED as map with extra colour at south east end for four new houses.

Albert Road. 3-st houses. RED as map.

Tressillian Road (the north and older part). 3-st, 3½-st and 3-st with basement houses. One narrow, semi-detached 3½-st house to let, "£42 a year and free to Xmas". From YELLOW of map to RED.

Clifton Road. Much like Albert Rd. RED as map.

Carlton Road. Again much the same, with slightly larger houses. RED (hand-coloured LIGHT BLUE by mistake).

Tressillian Crescent. 3-st houses, gabled, garden fronts. North east side mostly detached houses. RED as map.

Crescent Road. South side only has 3-st, gabled houses. Semi-detached. RED as map.

Thence by Tyrwhitt Rd into **Hilly Fields Crescent.** New houses, facing the Hilly Fields Park. Brick-fields when the map was made. New villa residences, two or three still in the hands of the builder, the largest occupied by Robinson of the Deptford flour mills. All from uncoloured of map to RED. A breezy, open and healthy corner.

Tressillian Road, now continued south west into St Margaret's Rd. Nearly all the houses occupied although roadway not yet made. 2½-st houses with servants. Uncoloured to RED.

St Margaret's Road. North end is a fine broad road, red-brick substantial houses, "1883." RED as map.

W into **Arabin Road.** 2-st houses, letting at £28 a year or so. Mostly single families, but thinks no servants. From PINK-barred of map to high grade PINK.

Kneller Road. 2-st houses, letting at 10/- or 11/-. Two families not infrequent. At north west end shallow double-fronted houses, crowded up by railway. Poor. This side PURPLE as map. South side from PURPLE of map to PINK. A few houses at west side, round the corner. From uncoloured of map to PINK.

Braxfield Road. Like Arabin Rd. From PINK-barred of map to PINK.

Comerford Road. 2-st houses. Better. "City people, clerks etc." Some servants. Rows of trees planted on the pathway. From RED of map to PINK-barred. Roman Catholic Chapel, new, at north west corner. There is one house west of Howson Rd on north side.

Whitbread Road. Now all built over, much like Comerford Rd. PINK-barred.

Howson Road. Better south of Comerford Rd. All 2-st houses, some servants in the west part – saw one! Here PINK-barred as map. East of Comerford Rd, from PINK-barred of map to PINK.

Dalrymple Road. All built over. PINK-barred.

Beecroft Road. Board School at south east corner takes up the Brockley Rd frontage from here to Dalrymple Rd. South west corner is clear. Elsewhere 2-st houses with back additions like the other new houses of the neighbourhood, all of which have been put up by a single builder, and all of which are of the same type. Uncoloured to PINK-barred, with omissions as noted.

In **Brockley Road** (the boundary of the police section) after four or five shops south of Comerford Rd there is nothing facing the road until the vacant space south of Beecroft Rd is passed. Then new shops, 2-st, north of the railway and past the nursery. Running along the south side of the railway are older shops, these having been added to houses intended originally for private dwellings. All PINK-barred.

Holdenby Road. 2-st houses, including some new ones, arranged for two families. All PINK. The roadway not yet made; it leads nowhere.

It is the same with **Hazeldon Road.** Also both blind and unmade. Very much like Holdenby Rd, with some similar new houses. Asked to compare this road with Dalrymple Rd, Moss answered emphatically that it was "not nearly so good". PINK. In this road and in the preceding the rents of the new little flats are about 10/6.

Eddystone Road. Older houses, letting at 11/- or 12/-. Two families is the rule. PINK as map. West of this there is a bridge over the railway, but it has not yet been properly opened up. On each side of the railway there is a pair of cottages, occupied by railway servants, a platelayer, etc. From uncoloured of map to PINK. The south corners of Eddystone Rd are clear.

Along **Brockley Road** by the "Brockley Jack" (RED) where the name is changed to **Brockley Rise.** South of the Jack is Brockley Green Farm, said to be coming down. Colour PINK. Thence the Rise is clear to the bend, where there are a few houses, some comparatively new but all looking rather forlorn. They will remain so until the drainage system has been continued along this part of the Rise, at present there being nothing but cess pits for these houses, which have to be cleared two or three times a week in the small hours of the morning. There are a few servants and they may perhaps be coloured PINK-barred.

The Stondon Park Estate has not yet been developed and cannot be until the drains have been laid. The only houses lying north of Honor Oak Park, except a few in Stondon Park (called Stondon Rd in map) are two in **Holmesley Road.** From uncoloured to PINK. The whole of the property round here belongs to Christ's Hospital.

Stondon Park has a few houses on both sides north of Honor Oak Park and a longer row on the west side south of the Park. Mainly 2-st red brick, occasional servants. From RED and uncoloured of map to PINK-barred.

Honor Oak Park. South west corner has wine merchants etc. Two or three houses only. RED or PINK-barred.

Brockley Rise (east of Gabriel St). 3-st houses with shops to the Wesleyan Chapel. From RED of map to PINK-barred. South of the Chapel 3-st dwelling houses with attics and basements. From RED of map to PINK-barred as far as Whatman St, the southern boundary of this police section.

On the south side of **Whatman Street**, in the Catford Police Section, are some older, poorly-tenanted houses. On the north side two or three are building, but none are occupied. There is no building yet west of Bovill Rd and south of Agnew St.

Bovill Road itself is still in the hands of the builders. Even where occupied the road is still un-made, the rapid filling of the houses, pointing, even here, to the keen demand for accommodation.

Ackroyd Street and **Agnew Street** are both occupied east of Bovill Rd but, like the latter, neither have their roadways made. The houses here are all of the same type, 2-st, and are advertised as "these conveniently arranged well-built houses, with every modern improve-ment". Rent £32, 99 years leases. The estate belongs to the Leathersellers' Company. All from uncoloured of map to PINK-barred.

Gabriel Street has houses of the same kind on the south side. Here from uncoloured of map to PINK-barred. On north side older and smaller houses. PINK.

Lessing Street. Queer jerry-built houses on east side, with a most extraordinary roof construction, visible from the rears. On the west side newer and smaller houses than the others of the new local type. Not unpleasing, with little toy pillars at the porches. A few servants but this street all PINK.

Wyleu Street has the larger local type of house on west side. Here from uncoloured of map to PINK-barred.

Honor Oak Park. Private houses, 2-st and 2-st with attics, from a little east of Wyleu St to Lessing St. Some of the houses rather larger than those of Bovill Rd etc, but occupants of same class – lower middle mainly. Apartments often let here, as elsewhere in district. West of Lessing St shops, not many yet occupied on north side. The intention is to form a kind of parade here. All from uncoloured of map to PINK-barred, except two cottages on north side west of Grierson St, occupied by railway station-master etc. These PINK.

Ballina Street. East side like the west side of Lessing St with the same little toy houses. Here from uncoloured of map to PINK. The west side is still in the hands of the builders.

Crossing the railway we have the Sydenham Police Section on the left. On the right the ground is open, the first enclosure being dotted with little shanties used for the manufacture of fireworks.

W of this is **One Tree Hill**, with the golf links round it. The road leads by the bank and fence of the Hill round which the attack during the "battles of One Tree Hill" of a year or so ago chiefly waged. Moss was on duty but was stationed at a point where no attack was made. It appears that on the first Sunday the few police on duty were a good deal mauled, but on the second they were in strong force, with a large hidden reserve, and the arrests made, with the subsequent punishments of imprisonment without the option of a fine, speedily put an end to the trouble. Beyond the Church are four good houses and at the corner of Forest Hill Rd, a large house which should be YELLOW (Oaklands).

On **Forest Hill Road** are two more large houses, YELLOW or RED, and at the corner of the Drive, two more smaller houses, one occupied by a doctor, colour RED.

In **The Drive** are three houses, the largest "Bolton Towers" being empty. Colour RED.

Honor Oak Rise has a good house on the south side, "Woodville Priory", which should be YELLOW if any of the houses in this neighbourhood are so coloured. The few other houses are smaller and less well kept up and should be RED. The view from the higher part of the Rise northwards must be a striking one on a clear day. At the east end is a private entrance to the links which, with assumed authority, we had opened and took the short cut across the Hill (passing the stump, all that remains of the "one tree") back to Honor Oak Railway Station. The Hill appears to be of a loose loam and is constantly silting at the steeper slopes. It is said, therefore, to be bad for building purposes and it is so sticky that it can hardly be much better for golf, to which it is still devoted.

General Remarks

Of Brockley it is perhaps enough to say that it contains one beer-house, nine fully licensed public houses and the same number of grocers' licenses; that when a question is asked as to what occupations may be, the most common answer is "The City", either that the people are employed there or that they employ others there; and that whereas in Peckham it is the exception to find streets in which the occupiers are ratepayers and not weekly tenants, in Brockley it is rather the rule.

Socially, Brockley stands something above both Peckham on the west and Lewisham on the east. It is tending to become less well-to-do, but it is still on the whole a very "comfortable" neighbourhood and "social problems", as commonly understood, can hardly be said to exist.

Expansion is at the moment in active progress only in the neighbourhood of Honor Oak Park and the character of this has been sufficiently explained in the notes on the walks. In a short time it is probable that the Stondon Park estate will also be built over. The fate of the still open ground lying between the two railways appears to be unsettled.

Moss said that in the section there was no class of people living who could not have regular work if they wanted it. They had some "boozers" but no "casuals".

The gardens attached to the houses are "one of the good things about Brockley" (Moss).

The charges that come to the Section Police Station amount to something over 100 a year. They are mostly "drunk and disorderly", and it is noticeable that the same people come up time after time. They have a few cases of petty larceny and occasionally one of house-breaking.

Prostitution gives little trouble, solicitation being mainly confined to the Lewisham Road. The women live and have their places of accommodation almost entirely in Deptford. They have a certain number of cases of public indecency and St James' has been already mentioned as a spot that is apt to be used in this way as a place of resort.

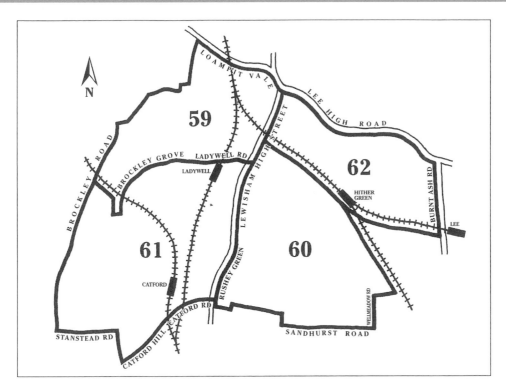

Walk 59

B374

Wednesday 15th November 1899.
Ernest Aves with PC Lloyds.
Lloyds is a man of about 35, married with five children. He has been in the Force for
eleven years, all the time at Lewisham. He is a quiet and capable man and if he were a better scholar would be certain to get promotion. As it is his chance is small. Needless to say,
he was familiar with all the ground, and I think that he told me most that he knew. But, as
in Brockley, there is not very much to tell.

Starting from the Police Station in Ladywell Road.
We crossed the railway close to the Station, into this part of **Ladywell Road**. At the corner,
south side, are shops etc. PINK-barred to the turning to Brockwell Cottages. West of this the
shops end and there are several small cottages. PURPLE. West of this the road is mainly built
along this side to Arthurdon Rd. New 2-st houses, some not yet occupied. Servants.
"Apartments" in many. Uncoloured to PINK-barred. On the north side at the east corner are
new 3-st shops. Uncoloured to PINK-barred. Nothing else on this side until the older 3-st
houses near Ivy Lane are reached. Same class here as in the new houses on the other side;
PINK-barred.
This end of Ladywell Rd is called **Brockley Lane** in map. It is all in a state of undress and
even when fully adorned there will be little to attract in this road of the pretty name.
At the **SW** corner are **Brockwell Cottages**. All closed except four. An insanitary little
nest. Colour those remaining LIGHT BLUE if at all.
Further **S** is the beginning of **Malyons Road**. 2-st houses. Good. Uncoloured to PINK.

Most of the open ground to the south of the **Brockley Lane** of the map (Ladywell Rd at the east and Brockley Grove at the west ends) is being laid out in an estate but, with the exception of three houses, not yet occupied, in Chudleigh Rd, building has not yet begun, save along the main frontage. It is in the stage of having pretty plans shown of it at the local railway station etc. Roughly this is the scheme. Names have already been given to some of the streets destined to run into Chudleigh Rd. It is the intention, I believe, to erect houses much of the same style as those that have been already put up in Ladywell Rd, and, if so, the area will become a "PINK-barred" one.

Passing the ends of the streets-to-be – Phoebeth, Francemary, Arthurdon – we come to **Ivy Lane**. The south end, overlooking the Cemetery has a new row of small 2-st houses. Occupied by clerks etc, no servants. Colour PINK.

Brockley Grove begins just W of Arthurdon St and the PINK-barred new houses reach a little way along on the south side. On the north is the Cemetery, with its Lodge. PINK. Further along is Haddon (now Joy) Farm, coming down. PINK. West of this houses are building until the other end of Chudleigh Rd is reached, then a few more houses are occupied. PINK-barred. Like the new houses in Ladywell Rd. On the north side, east of Merritt Rd, are new 2-st houses. Smaller. Uncoloured to PINK. Between Merritt Rd and Darfield Rd are new 2-st houses with attics. PINK-barred. Then older houses, 2-st. PINK. West of Lindal Rd only one house. PINK. The Grove is continued round the bend facing the open ground of Brockley Hall. 2-st houses. Occasional servants, "a better class than they look". Several cases of afternoon house-breaking; in one recently "a lot of stuff" taken. Uncoloured to PINK-barred. At the extreme corner are two old cottages. Colour LIGHT BLUE. Brockley Hall is occupied by the family of Mr Nokes (deceased), big brewers. Colour YELLOW. From this point in this section there are no houses till those in Ravensbourne Park and Blythe Hill are reached (see later).

The ground is all open fields, except for **Crofton Park Road**, just south west of the railway. New, unnamed on map. 2-st houses, many occupied but road not yet made. Uncoloured to PINK. Further east, south of Brockley Cottages, a large Workhouse is being built, believed by Lloyds to be for the St Olave's Union.

N up **Brockley Road**. New shops. 3-st houses as far as the Cemetery. Uncoloured to PINK-barred. At one shop, occupied by a "wine and spirit merchant" and therefore not marked on our public house map, four children were the customers of the moment as we passed. Two came out with their purchases, one carrying two bottles of Truman Hanbury's Ale and the other a single bottle of the same brew. The children were quite little things and the chance of seeing four crowding at the counter may have been exceptional. But there are many of these small-trade merchants who whether they sell beer or wine or spirits, do mainly a single bottle trade. None will be shown on our map and their existence ought to be noted and emphasised in the text.

Marnock Road. South of railway is new. Houses only on south side. 2-st, gable attics. Mostly with servants and letting lodgings. Uncoloured to PINK-barred.

On the opposite side of the railway is **Lindal Road**. Houses on north side only. 2-st, two families often. Uncoloured to PINK.

Merritt Road and **Darfield Road** are now both "full up". 2-st houses in each and very much alike. In Merritt Rd some of the newer houses are 5-roomed, letting at 9/6 to 11/. Others are built in flats with double fronts and two doors, the alternate doors leading straight up stairs. Rent about 10/- a flat. All PINK as map, with more of it.

Ivy Lane (west end). Little 2-st houses, red brick, garden fronts. Same class as at east end. PINK as map.

St Margaret's Road. 3-st houses, red brick, substantial. RED as map.

Much of the same character are **Adelaide Road** in all the west end part including an extension east along the Hilly Fields front and **St Margaret's Square**.

E of the line of the Cemetery the houses begin again in **Adelaide Road**. Here smaller "maisonettes" for two families, some with and some without servants. This side of the road to the end somewhat poorer class than the west end even when the "maisonettes" cease. From uncoloured of map to PINK-barred. On the north side, east of Eastern Rd, at first good houses then another row of "maisonettes". Uncoloured to PINK-barred.

Eastern Road. New houses on the east side only and only for part of the way. From uncoloured of map to RED.

Facing it on the other side of Hilly Fields is **Montague Avenue**. Again with good houses, 2-st, substantial, 12 rooms or so. With more colour for new houses, RED.

To the **NW** of this, running from Hilly Fields down into St Margaret's Rd, is **Chalsey Road**. Not shown on map. New 2-st houses, very much like the new part of Tressillian Rd, except that parts are taken up with the little "maisonettes" like those in Adelaide Rd. From uncoloured of map to PINK-barred. Perched on the hill, with its playing fields fenced off from the public part, is the West Kent Grammar School, a conspicuous building both from here and from many points of view for miles round.

SE of Ladywell Railway Station is **Railway Cottages**. Two and sometimes three families the rule. Occasionally broken windows and open doors. A poor look but hardly very poor. LIGHT BLUE as map.

To the **N**, unnamed on map, is **Prospect Place**. 2½-st houses, again with two or three families. A shade better than the Cottages. From uncoloured of map to LIGHT BLUE or PURPLE.

On the other side of Ladywell Rd, lying close along the railway, is **Mercy Terrace**, unnamed on map. Much improved, a policeman lives in one of them rent-free and acts as a kind of agent. It was his business to get the houses into good and quiet order and, according to Lloyds, he has succeeded. One house at the north end had a suspicious number of broken windows but I was assured that it was "all right" – "children" he supposed. One or two of the detached houses close by are laundries. All from uncoloured of map to PINK.

At the **S** end of Algernon Rd, **W** side is a nameless road. Houses being built, some occupied on north side, 2-st. Here from uncoloured of map to PINK.

Algiers Road, Vicar's Road, Ermine Road, Embleton Road (south of Ellerdale Rd) and **Algernon Road** are all, except the south end of the last where there are a few shops, taken up with houses, in as far as they are built on at all, of much the same style – 2-st with gable attics. Servants the rule, "City people", occasional lodgers. All from uncoloured and RED of map to RED. The few houses near the top end of Vicar's Rd are the best of the lot, but the estate is very fairly uniform in standard. The south west to north east part of Algiers Rd appears to be an error.

In **Eda Road** there are no houses. North of Ellerdale Rd, now continued, with no houses in it, up the hill till it joins with Vicar's Rd, there are still extensive brick-fields.

Ellerdale Road, the north end of **Algernon Road, Embleton Street** (the north end of Embleton Rd) and **Brookbank Road** are all good working class streets, occasionally with two families to a house, but on the whole high grade PINK. Nothing to choose between Brookbank Rd and the rest although the former has been coloured PINK-barred and the rest PINK. All PINK, therefore, with extra colour in Brookbank Rd on south side, west of Ermine Rd.

N up **Sandrock Road**, leading to another new estate. At this south end there are houses only between Nuding Rd (unnamed on map) and Overcliff Rd. 2-st houses with back additions, some servants. Uncoloured to PINK-barred. At the north end are houses of same description on both sides, same colour.

Nuding Road and **Overcliff Road** are of exactly the same character, the former being occupied on the north and the latter on the south side. Both from uncoloured to PINK-barred. On the south side of Nuding Rd, building in active progress.

Shell Road is vacant except for a tiny lodge at the north east corner – a relic of a not-distant time when much of this ground was taken up by one fair-sized house (still standing) and its gardens.

Halesworth Road. 2-st houses, pretentious, any amount of ornate, machine-worked stone and toy pillars at porticoes. "Good class", servants. Road not finished, houses taken as soon as ready. Uncoloured to RED.

Loampit Hill (from the boundary to Shell Rd). New houses. Uncoloured to RED, leaving opening for the new road (Sandrock Rd).

S of Shell Rd **Loampit Vale** begins. At first only the backs and gardens of the houses in Halesworth Road. Below the public house are irregular, indistinctive, plain brick houses, stabling etc. Lower down, an older world is reached. Small houses, old-fashioned, tiled roofs, little shops, several of them second-hand, like the houses. All PINK as map to Porson St.

Lying **W** of the Church of the Transfiguration is **Dursley Place**. Cottages, one brick row, one timber and others. All perhaps from LIGHT BLUE of map to PURPLE.

Just **N** of the railway are **Hope Cottages**, eight of them with gardens. LIGHT BLUE as map.

By Porson St and **W** under railway arch to **Bertrand Street**. 2-st houses, like Brookbank Rd etc. PINK as map with colour on north side, instead of south.

Off the **NE** side, lying low down, are three cottages, **Hope Cottages (Bertrand St)**. Poor little places. Apparently uncoloured on map, DARK BLUE.

Branscombe Street. Like Bertrand St. PINK as map.

Back into **Porson Street**. 2-st houses. Very mixed class. A good deal of DARK BLUE. A few shops. Gone down. At south east corner beyond the School nothing but a school-master's house. Here from PURPLE to PINK. The rest of the street from PURPLE of map to LIGHT BLUE. Off the west side leading under the railway is the entrance to the East London Industrial School.

Near the **NE** corner, behind the public house, are **Hopewell Cottages**, belonging to the public house, gate closed at night. Tiny, poor, 2-roomed cottages, rent 5/-. LIGHT BLUE as map.

E out of Porson St to **Shrubbery Road**. On east side the school, on west side the Mission etc. Cottages flush with pavement. Respectable, one family the rule, clean. From PURPLE to PINK.

Elmira Street. 2-st houses, varied style, some old. With omission for Gerrard the builder's premises, from LIGHT BLUE of map to PURPLE.

Eureka Place. Five cottages. Costers etc. Uncoloured of map to LIGHT BLUE.

Vian Street. 2-st houses flush with sidewalk. LIGHT BLUE as map with omission for Gerrard's premises.

Loampit Vale. East of Porson St is mainly shops. Better class. From PINK of map to PINK-barred. Between the two beer-houses shown are two tiny cottages, lying behind the frontage line and facing west. LIGHT BLUE if shown on the 25 inch map.

Peartree Cottages (apparently Slough's Buildings of map). Only two or three on east side. Uncoloured of map to LIGHT BLUE.

A little further **E** is **Wilmore Place**. Six or seven cottages. Uncoloured to LIGHT BLUE.

Mill Road. Approached from the Vale under railway arch. A long cul de sac. Ravensbourne River running down the middle and a big mill (Robinson's) towering above everything else. Plenty of room, therefore, between the houses and those at north west have gardens along the side of the river. This is the best part of the road, the east side of which, especially the south end, has a bad reputation for drinking, roughness, etc. "Costers, sweeps, labouring class." Some DARK BLUE but LIGHT BLUE perhaps the better colour for this worst end. The rest from uncoloured and PURPLE of map to PURPLE, omitting colour for the mill.

Loampit Vale (south of railway) and **Lewisham High Street**. Larger shops again to Fuller's Place. Here PINK-barred to RED. Below Fuller's Place, smaller shops etc. PINK-barred, as map, as far as the entrance to Mr Wallis' house (RED). Here a small break in the frontage line and then mostly private houses, good, to the railway. From PINK-barred of map to RED. The Chapel now Unitarian. South of the railway mostly shops again, smaller. From RED of map to PINK-barred on both sides to Ladywell Rd. Some extra colour for new building on east side. Tram lines run down the High Street. Not very much traffic or business, the road perhaps illustrating a name that Lloyds tells me has been given to the parish – "long and lazy Lewisham". The Vicarage at corner of Ladywell Rd and a doctor's house north east of Courthill Rd should be coloured RED.

Molesworth Road (off Loampit Vale). 2½-st houses. Gone down, two or three families to a house as a rule. Some LIGHT BLUE, even DARK BLUE. Perhaps still PURPLE as map.

Rhyme Street. New, three little lots of 2-st houses. From uncoloured of map to PINK.

Rennell Street. Same character as Molesworth St. PURPLE as map.

John's Place. Seven cottages, garden fronts, south side only. PINK as map.

Avenue Road. 2-st and 2½-st houses mainly. All from PINK-barred of map to PINK. The house south of the Chapel (now a Salvation Army Barracks) and the house off the north west end, both uncoloured on map, should be RED.

Off the N side, opposite John St (now Engate St) is **Avenue Cottages**. Four wooden cottages. From uncoloured of map to LIGHT BLUE.

Engate Street. 2-st and 3-st houses with garden fronts. Decent. PINK as map.

Off the **SW** corner is **Avenue Square**. 5-roomed cottages on two sides only. Gardens. From uncoloured of map to LIGHT BLUE.

Romer's Place (called Fuller's Place in map) has 5-roomed cottages with garden fronts on south side. Here LIGHT BLUE of map to PINK. On the north side, tiny cottages. LIGHT BLUE as map.

Behind and backing on these cottages is the real **Fuller's Place**. 3-roomed cottages, south side only. LIGHT BLUE as map.

Whitburn Road. New 2-st red-brick houses. Occasional servants. From uncoloured of map to PINK-barred.

Wearside Road. Also new, smaller houses. Nothing on east side south of Whitburn Rd. The rest, as far as built over, from uncoloured of map to PINK.

Ladywell Road (east of railway). North side is mainly 2-st and 2½-st houses. Occasional servants. From PINK of map to PINK-barred. South side mainly taken up with public buildings: the Parish Hall, Baths, a space and then the Coroner's Court, two cottages (PINK, the only thing to be coloured on this side), a warehouse, finishing off with the Police Station. This side of Ladywell Rd is thus very modern and municipal and round the corner in the High St is a magnificent block belonging to the London Fire Brigade with "London County Council" shining down in golden lettering. If the quiet churchyard is walked through and the back afterwards turned on all the moderness of the Fire Brigade building and Ladywell Rd, the High St, in spite of one or two shops of considerable size, gives the impression of the main street of an old-fashioned small provincial town in which the buildings happen to have run small. Tiled roofs and quaint gables abound and even the tram-line does not destroy the illusion, for the car saunters through only once every six or eight minutes.

Off the **NW** side of Ladywell Rd is **The Avenue**, not named on map. Only two houses. Servants. From uncoloured of map to RED.

Church Grove. Cottages with garden fronts. Two are occupied by an old lady, eccentric, has a "bit of brass" and will have nothing done to the cottages, which are being overgrown like the castle of the Sleeping Beauty. All from PURPLE of map to PINK.

In the High St opposite Ladywell Park is **Reeve's Passage.** Three cottages, one over the archway of the entrance, queer, old. From uncoloured of map to LIGHT BLUE.

Walk 60   B374

Wednesday 15th & Thursday 16th November 1899.
Ernest Aves with PC Lloyds.

Starting along **Courthill Road.** Mainly 3-st and 2-st houses. Improves eastwards. Some new building on the north side. PINK as map at west end. East of the railway bridge, from PINK-barred and uncoloured of map to PINK and PINK-barred. Behind the beer-house, opposite the end of Rycroft Rd, is one cottage. From uncoloured of map to LIGHT BLUE.

Ryecroft Road. North side is 3-st houses. Occasional servants. PINK-barred as map. South side has 2-st houses, some shops. From PINK-barred of map to PINK.

Knowles Hill Crescent. 2-st houses, some with attics, often lodgers and two families. At the east end of the north side of the lower half are two 3-st houses in very drunken occupancy for the most part. These from PINK of map to LIGHT BLUE and the south side of this part of the Crescent from PINK to PURPLE. The rest PINK as map.

Glenview Road has been added to on the north east corner. Here from uncoloured of map to PINK. The older part, also 2-st houses, is a good deal poorer. From PINK of map to PURPLE.

Ennersdale Road takes a better working class. 2-st houses with garden fronts. PINK as map. Off the **S** side is **Lanier Road.** 2-st houses, semi-detached, fronts. Clerks etc, most with servants. From RED of map to PINK-barred.

Hither Green Lane. North from this point, shops on west side, between Radford Rd and Thornford Rd. The rest is private houses, mostly semi-detached, most with servants, a good many taking lodgers. All PINK-barred as map except Camps Hill House, occupied by Mr Gore (tobacco), from uncoloured of map to YELLOW. The lodge below the house is PINK.

Radford Road. Same class as in Lanier Rd and Hither Green Lane but houses rather larger. From RED of map to PINK-barred.

In **Fordyce Hill** there are no houses.

Fordyce Road. 2-st houses with rather shabby-genteel appearance. Perhaps "three or four servants in the 14 houses". Open ground opposite. Perhaps from PINK of map to PINK-barred.

Harvard Road. 2-st houses. Lloyds lives here. Rents are 8/6, 9/- and 11/-. Generally one family to a house. PINK as map.

Thornford Road. 2-st and 3-st houses. "More like Radford Rd". Some servants. PINK-barred as map.

Camps Hill (on map, now part of Hither Green Lane). Mostly small houses, some shops. From uncoloured of map to PINK.

The Retreat. 2-st houses in various styles, some garden fronts. Better at south end. PURPLE as map.

Ladywell Terrace. "1865." At east end of Ladywell Park, not named on map or shown. 2½-st houses. Two families the rule. From uncoloured of map to PINK.

Hither Green Lane (west of The Retreat). Generally 2-st houses, a few shops. From PURPLE of map to PINK.

Ladywell Park. 2-st with basements and attics, 3-st etc. Many semi-detached. Very occasional servants, perhaps four or five in the whole road. Gone down. PINK as map.

High Street (south of Ladywell Park). The old police station, "to let", then small shops for the most part, some antiquated, gabled and picturesque – a bit of old suburban London. All from RED of map to PINK-barred to the Schools. On the opposite side, south of Ladywell Rd, a few shops building at corner, bank etc, then Fire Brigade Station (RED to PINK), then churchyard. The bank block, if coloured, from RED of map to PINK-barred.

On E side of High St is **Park Street**. Not named on map. 4-roomed cottages, cul de sac. LIGHT BLUE as map.

High Street. East side, south of Schools is Lewisham Park and then private houses (good) to Mount Pleasant. South of here a few shops, all RED to George Lane. West side south of churchyard is a bit more of old Lewisham. RED of map to PINK-barred to a cleared space north of Almshouses. Almshouses uncoloured. South of these are four 3-st houses. From uncoloured of map to RED. Then the Workhouse and Infirmary, stretching almost to the corner of Albacore Crescent. Omit RED of map.

Lewisham Park. Some of the best houses in Lewisham. Mainly semi-detached, substantial, middle class. All RED as map except the lodge of Yeddo Grange.

George Lane. Some new houses at west end, both sides, but very few on south side, broken by nursery etc. Here PINK as far as coloured (uncoloured on map). North side, from PINK of map to PINK-barred, from west end to Chestnut Rd. Then the road improves with 2-st semi-detached villas, servants. Either from PINK of map to RED or PINK-barred as far as Fordyce Rd. East of Fordyce Rd certainly from PINK of map to RED.

Chestnut Road. Like better part of George Lane. From uncoloured of map to RED or PINK-barred.

Mount Pleasant. 2-st houses and 2-st with gables, new at east end, most semi-detached. Servants generally, some lodgers. Said to be same class as George Lane but does not look so flourishing. From RED of map to PINK-barred.

Thence E along George Lane with Mountsfield on the right, the home of the late owner of all the fields in the neighbourhood, now occupied only by caretaker and probably coming down. Leave uncoloured.

By the new Theodore Rd (only three houses building in it) into **Hither Green Lane**. On the right Beacon Lodge, a good private house. RED. On west side, south of Beacon Rd, shops, 3-st houses, new, to Laurel Lodge. From uncoloured of map to PINK-barred. North of the Lodge, that has been very pretty and looks unhappy in the middle of its new surroundings, the ground is either vacant or shops are building. On the east side, 2-st houses very much like those further down the Lane. A new Vicarage has been built by the church. Omitting for the latter, from uncoloured and PINK-barred of map to PINK-barred, to Ennersdale Rd.

Continuing on 16th November 1899.

Started from Hither Green Station.

Nightingale Grove contains a few cottages in the station approach. LIGHT BLUE as map. The houses in the main road are scattered, none are new. Some are cottages letting at 6/6. All PURPLE as map.

W along Beacon Road. East of the School are 2-st houses, two families the rule. From PINK of map to PURPLE. Opposite the School are three good houses. RED as map.

The rest of this immediate neighbourhood is made up of bits of streets for the most part and bits of field. The result is a general effect of discomfort and neglect. Such houses as have been built appear to have lost their way. Although little or no building is going on, nothing looks finished. It is a district half-dressed, with no sign that the process will ever be finished.

Ardmere Road. One of the fuller streets. 2-st houses, shoddy building. Two families the rule, more perhaps in some. Signs of the DARK BLUE. From PURPLE of map to LIGHT BLUE.

Maybank Cottages. East of Nightingale Grove, smaller on north side. Here LIGHT BLUE as map. On south side 2-st houses, generally two families. From LIGHT BLUE of map to PURPLE.

Seravia Road. New, four 2-st cottages. From uncoloured of map to PURPLE.

Of just the same character is **Brightside Road.** PURPLE. Lying off the north side is one of the smallest abodes I have seen – a tin 8 ft square shanty, occupied by a coster and donkey owner. LIGHT BLUE if coloured. Further west on the same side is a small corrugated iron chapel, stranded like the houses.

Elthruda Road. Cottages. Poor, two families the rule. From PURPLE of map to LIGHT BLUE with additional PINK for two new little houses on the south side.

Mallet Road. 2-st houses. Two families, separate entrances. Houses now reach to edge of Brightside Rd. From PINK of map to PURPLE with extra colour.

Hither Green Lane at this point has the Park Fever Hospital running along the west side and the little towers of its numerous detached wards are a conspicuous feature of the neighbourhood. The presence of the hospital presumably has a bad effect on the district but Lloyds was unwilling to admit this and it is not from this part that patients come. In the Lane are small villa residences from just north of Brightside Rd to just south of Elthruda Rd. From uncoloured of map to PINK or PINK-barred.

Duncrievie Rd brings us to the beginning of the **St German's Estate** which is being rapidly laid out according to the general plans of a large speculative builder, Corbett. There is much sub-letting of the work and several builders are said to be at work on the estate, but the man just mentioned is the contractor and speculator-in-chief. It is said that when all has been built over, there will be something like 3,000 houses. Most are for a lower middle class and two styles predominate: one a small, single-fronted house letting at about £28, and a somewhat larger double-fronted house letting at from £36 to £38. The larger houses in Brownhill Rd let at about £60. Sandhurst and Glenfarg are, so far, the two working class streets, and the former is the only one in which the houses are uniformly let at a weekly rental. Many of the houses throughout the estate are said to be owned by their occupants. It is a rather weary wilderness of houses and in the day-time hardly anyone is about. The heads of the households go mainly Citywards to work. No licensed house is allowed on the estate and it is, I believe, Mr Corbett who has enforced this provision. My information as to rental was obtained from one of the contracting builders whom we happened to meet and his information corroborated what Lloyds had previously told me. There are two shopping centres on the estate, one in Springbank Rd which has a kind of parade called "The Market" at the north end, and a similar centre is being made in part of Brownhill Rd, with the name of "The Pavement". The latter is rather for the future, but neither are yet very flourishing.

Duncrievie Road has little or nothing in it except an old farmhouse at the south west corner (good, colour RED) and a second house, also somewhat old, occupied by the chief agent for the estate (also RED).

Springbank Road. The Market and south of this, which runs a little north and south of Duncrievie Rd, the double-fronted houses. Several of the shops of The Market have been built on the east side, but besides these almost nothing, and only two or three are as yet occupied anywhere on this side. At the extreme south east corner are two cottages. These PINK, and the rest of the road, west side as far as covered, from uncoloured of map to PINK-barred. At the "PINK" cottages the Board School Visitor was calling to find out about some absent child and his colleague in Whitechapel or Southwark would perhaps envy him in being able to do his work on a bicycle and wearing knickerbockers. Other districts, other manners.

Wellmeadow Road. North of Hither Green Lane, double-fronted. South of Hither Green Lane, single-fronted to Brownhill Rd. All PINK-barred. South of Brownhill Rd, building. Just north of the Lane a large Wesleyan Chapel building.

Hither Green Lane (south of Hospital). North side is shops to above Torridon Rd. South side double-fronted. All, as far as coloured, PINK-barred. Oak Cottage has disappeared.

Brookfield Road. A few occupied at north end. Here PINK-barred. The rest empty or building.

Brownhill Road (east of Laleham Rd). Barring the shops, this is the swell road of the estate. RED as far as covered. The shops, a little to the west of Torridon Rd, north side, PINK-barred. Two detached blocks of smaller dwellings, still further west, one on each side of the road. These also PINK-barred.

Minard Road. Double-fronted to Brownhill Rd. Here PINK-barred. South of Brownhill Rd, vacant or building.

Ardgowan Road. Double-fronted north of Brownhill Rd, single-fronted as far as built south. All PINK-barred.

In **Woodlands** are a few scattered houses, one a nursery and the rest private. All said to have a servant or servants and not to have deteriorated from the Fever Hospital at all. But they are not very bright looking. All RED, except St Mary's Cottage, here only a caretaker, PINK if coloured. The late occupant owned a good deal of property in the neighbourhood.

Torridon Road. No dwellings north of Hither Green Lane, a depot of Wheatley's at corner of Wellmeadow Rd. South of the Lane double fronts to Brownhill Rd. PINK-barred, omitting for site of Congregational Chapel. South of Brownhill Rd, single fronts, east side only, PINK-barred.

Arngask Road and **Fordel Road.** Single fronts. PINK-barred.

Glenfarg Road. Single fronts of a smaller type. A few still unoccupied. PINK.

The total police beats of this Lewisham Section are steadily increasing, and now run to about 58 miles, and from a point in Sandhurst Rd Lloyds was able to point out the considerable southern extension of their ground. It runs along Hither Green Lane to the corner of Whitefoot Lane, west along this lane to Bromley Rd and then north to Cock Shed Lane. Except for the north end of Bromley Rd, I did not walk round this part as it contains only the following dwellings: Oak Cottages (two) near Lee Cemetery, one occupied by an employee of the Cemetery, may be coloured PINK. At the corner of Hither Green Lane and Whitefoot Lane, a farmhouse, occupied by a caretaker. Colour PINK. In Whitefoot Lane are two cottages, one occupied by a gamekeeper and the other by a farm labourer, the wages of the latter being put down by Lloyds at about 28/-. Both may be coloured PINK. At the south east corner of Bromley Rd are two old and two new cottages, all said to be in respectable occupancy – a carpenter, etc – and these too may, I think, be coloured PINK. Park House is a school, RED. White House Farm and Sangley Farm are both said to be in good occupancy with servants, RED. The rest I saw: Sangley Lodge, three good houses (new) and The Priory. All RED.

Sandhurst Road (east of St Fillan's Rd). East of Torridon Rd there are no dwellings. Between Torridon Rd and Ardgowan Rd is a small Recreation Ground, the use of which is, Lloyds said, restricted to subscribers of 10/- a year. It looked very dull, but four or six sets of tennis could be played on it and its existence throws some light on the class of people occupying many of the adjacent streets. East of it, on the other side of Ardgowan Rd, is a temporary Board School. On the south side the site for an English Church has been marked out, and the rest is a chaos of houses half built, a mason's yard, stacks of timber, piles of bricks (of indifferent quality) and unmade roads, with for sounds, the noise, loud or rasping, of hammer and mallet and saw. In a year or two there will be quiet streets and dozens of houses with, doubtlessly, wives in most of them waiting, according to their temperament, bored, gossiping or busy through the long day, for their husbands' return. West of Torridon Rd the houses begin: 2-st, most occupied by a decent class but many on the down-grade. Two families frequent and, even in passing, many signs of deterioration observable. Many living here who are employed on the estate, and many doubtless will therefore leave when the building is finished. The street is not getting a good name and disorder and drunkenness are not uncommon, in spite of the absence of any licensed houses in the immediate neighbourhood. PINK predominates but I think that PURPLE will be the appropriate colour for the street, save for the few shops at the south west corner. The rents are generally 9/-.

Sandhurst Road (west of St Fillan's Rd). Conditions improve, the open ground of Catford Sports behind doing something perhaps to ensure a better class of tenant more uniformly. Here PINK. On each side of the road there is one tiny cottage, of old standing and connected with displaced farm houses. These LIGHT BLUE.

St Fillan's Road. Single fronts. PINK-barred.

Brownhill Road (west of Laleham Rd). Smaller and older houses. PINK-barred except on the south side, east of Bowness Rd, here PINK.

Laleham Road (south end). 2-st houses. One and two families. PINK.

Engleheart Road. North side is newer. One and two families. PINK. South side is poorer, especially east of Bowness Rd. Here LIGHT BLUE and the rest PINK, or perhaps all PURPLE as map.

Cock Shed Lane. 2-st houses, like the preceding but better. One and two families. From uncoloured of map to PINK.

Jutland Road, Bowness Road and **Plassy Road** are all very much of the same class. 2-st houses. Decent working class for the most part. In all there are some new houses, generally arranged for two families. All PINK as map with more colour for additions.

Rushy Green. East side from Cock Shed Lane to Brownhill Rd, as in Lewisham, so here are bits of an older world mixed with the new. Mostly shops. From PINK of map to PINK-barred, with an omission for a clearance. North of Brownhill Rd to Rosenthal Rd is mostly semi-detached, 2-st villas. All still PINK-barred.

Blackshaw Alley. A little south of the Black Horse Inn. Stucco, wooden and brick cottages with gardens. Untidy, with fowl. Rather a low-standard place. LIGHT BLUE.

N to Ringstead Road. 2-st houses, some with gable attic. From RED of map to PINK-barred. Running north is a new road, not named. Two cottages on east side. PINK.

Laleham Road. North end 2-st houses, arranged for two families. Three or four shops. PINK.

Honley Road. The old, west part has small but substantial houses, said to be occupied by as well-to-do a class as those living in Lewisham Park, except on the south side, close to Rushy Green. The new part has 2-st houses, arranged for two families. Here PINK and the rest RED and PINK-barred, the latter for the poorer south side.

Farley Road offers just the same division, save that all the older part may be RED.

Rosenthal Road (no thoroughfare yet at east end). Said to have "the richest people we have in Lewisham". 2-st houses, some with attics. RED.

Davenport Road. Built by two firms. West part has 2-st houses with back additions, letting at £35 or so, PINK-barred. The rest smaller, for two families. PINK.

Rushy Green. North of the Wesleyan Chapel to Davenport Rd are 3-st houses, private.

RED or PINK-barred. Then shops again, new and old to George Lane. All PINK-barred, showing, if possible two little timbered cottages. Poor. LIGHT BLUE.

Walk 61

B374

Friday 17th November 1899.
Ernest Aves with PC Lloyds.

Albacore Crescent. 2-st houses. Clerks etc. Generally one family, some servants. PINK-barred. The Priory Room, used as a chapel. (Note that there is only one house, PINK, on south side west of Felday Rd.)
S to Medusa Road. 2-st houses. Newer but much same class as in Albacore Crescent. PINK-barred.
Felday Road (late Ruthin Rd). 2-st houses. Most arranged for two families on south side. Here PINK. North side is PINK-barred like Medusa Rd.
Blagdon Road. 2-st houses. Generally two families. All PINK (Note only one house north of Felday Rd on east side).
High Street. From Albacore Rd to Felday Rd are good houses. RED. South of the Almshouses are 3-st shops. RED or PINK-barred to Hawstead Rd. South of Hawstead Rd is Lewisham Grammar School for Girls, a large building, plus a lodge belonging to the School and a carriage builders. PINK, if coloured, from the School to Bradgate Rd. South of Bradgate Rd to Patrol Place are six good houses and two or three smaller ones, PINK-barred. S of Medusa Rd is a small collection of streets almost all with 2-st houses, most new, and most of the latter arranged for two families. Some of the older parts are going down, such as the central part of Brookdale Rd, and there are bits of a still lower and poorer grade. But the following may all be coloured PINK: **Hawstead Road** and **Silvermere Road**, including the row of houses at the north end, facing the recreation ground; **Brookdale Road**, north of Bradgate Rd and south of Holbeach Rd; **Nelgarde Road**; **Doggett Road** (north end); **Bradgate Road**; **Holbeach Road** (late The Retreat), west of Brookdale Rd; and **Willow Walk** (west of Brookdale Rd).
Scrooby Road. From LIGHT BLUE of map to PURPLE.
Wildfell Road contains the slum of this area. LIGHT BLUE except for: 1) a row of small cottages at south west corner, PURPLE; 2) two PINK houses a little below them on the same side; and 3) two PINK houses on the opposite side just east of the Chapel.
Patrol Place (off the High St). Wooden cottages. LIGHT BLUE.
A little further up the same entrance but tucked away round the corner is **Waterloo Place.** Tiny brick cottages, garden fronts. Very miserable in appearance. While looking a tram driver came out of one and Lloyds said that he lived there. In spite of this "PINK" man the row should probably be DARK BLUE, the alternative being LIGHT BLUE.
Rushy Green. South of Patrol Place to Holbeach Rd are shops new and old. PINK-barred. South of Holbeach Rd to Willow Grove are smaller shops. PINK. South of the Grove to the Avenue is larger again. PINK-barred.
Off the main thoroughfare are several little courts in addition to the ones already mentioned: **Queen's Bench** (apparently the Gray's Place of map). Cottages with small gardens. LIGHT BLUE.
Crossley Cottages. Two, with two rooms and scullery, rent 5/-. Unnamed on map. LIGHT BLUE. Others just to the north coming down, closed.

Sun Cottages. Four rooms for 6/-. LIGHT BLUE.

Holbeach Road (Elizabeth Place in map). PURPLE east of Brookdale Rd. "Retreat House" standing back in a small garden, being perhaps RED.

Brookdale Road, between Bradgate Rd and Holbeach Rd, is older, more crowded. PURPLE.

Retreat Cottages. South side only, south of Holbeach Rd. LIGHT BLUE.

Willow Grove (east of Brookdale Rd). On south side 2-st houses. PURPLE. On north side a mixture including some tiny 1-st 2-roomed cottages. Went into one of these. The woman is the wife of a carman. Room quite warm but bare of furniture for the most part. In a crib close to the fire a mite of 15 months snugly tucked up, ill with bronchitis, a pale morsel, pale and placid, but breathing heavily. Rent 2/9. In bad repair. All this side of the Grove LIGHT BLUE.

The Avenue. 3-st houses. Shops, not very flourishing. PINK.

W along **Catford Bridge.** Shops etc. PINK.

N up **Doggett Road.** East side to The Retreat, small 2-st houses, going down quickly. Some of the houses were built for small middle class, now with two families and getting in a very bad condition. Others, mainly those in the hands of old occupants, are satisfactory. The road presents the same mixture as Stanstead Rd to some extent, the proportion of the BLUE classes being greater. This side from PURPLE and uncoloured of map to PURPLE. West side at extreme corner, a shop and two 2-st cottages. PINK here. The rest 2½-st houses, poorer than the east side, and more uniformly of a lower grade. Here, from PURPLE of map to LIGHT BLUE.

Across the railway and N up **Ravensbourne Park.** Good middle class houses, some at the top being very large. A late Lord Mayor, Alderman Whitehead, lived in one of them. Two of the largest now empty and the quarter perhaps having a struggle to keep up the plutocratic standard of the past. Four of the houses YELLOW, two (empty) uncoloured, and the rest all RED, from YELLOW and uncoloured of map. The "Cong. Chapel" of map appears to be an error.

Westdown Park Road is much the same as the lower part of Ravensbourne Park. RED as map. North of Blythe Hill is Hillfield House, occupied. From uncoloured of map to RED.

S into **Blythe Hill.** Rather a mixed street, but most of it fair middle class houses. The poorest part is the south east block, which is PINK-barred rather than RED of map. The rest RED. The houses are mostly 3-st, others 2-st. To the north of Blythe Hill are the open fields previously mentioned as stretching to the south from Brockley Grove.

Faversham Road (late Canterbury Rd). Some of it not unlike Blythe Hill, especially at the south and north. In the middle on both sides a certain number of houses in working class tenancy. The whole from PURPLE of map (I think a slip in colouring) to PINK-barred.

Upper Winchester Road. 2-st houses. From PINK-barred of map to PINK, with extra colouring for new houses at east end of north side.

Lower Winchester Road is much the same with extra colour at the east end of the north side and new houses now on south side. All from PINK-barred and uncoloured of map to PINK.

Blythe Hill Lane. This is the boundary of the section, with very few houses in it on the east side, and these (2-st houses, PINK) are south of Blythe Hill, rather than south of Upper Winchester Rd as shown in map. No dwellings south of Lower Winchester Rd.

Stanstead Road. Also the boundary of the section, with new shops east of Blythe Hill Lane to the entrance to Stanstead Grove, not shown on map. From Stanstead Grove to the Chapel, 3-st private houses, To this point, from RED and uncoloured of map to PINK-barred. East of the Chapel a row of 2-st houses. Servants doubtful and improbable. From RED of map to PINK. St Dunstan's College, a big red-brick building, rather new, has the still newer headmaster's house at south west corner and the porter's lodge, as shown, at the south east. Colour RED and PINK.

Stanstead Grove. Not shown on map. "Little middle class people" was Lloyds' comment.

Catford Hill

Servants in two or three of the houses. From uncoloured of map to PINK-barred. (Houses along east side and at north end only. The two houses placed in the map askew to Lower Winchester Rd are really in Stanstead Grove).

Catford Hill, into which Stanstead Rd runs. Shops, new and old, one of the former being really in Stanstead Rd itself. Small dwellings over them, except in the public house, which is of larger build and three cottages at the railway end. All from uncoloured of map to PINK.

Walk 62   B 372

Thursday 16th November 1899.
George Arkell with Detective Sergeant Spencer.
Sergeant Spencer is an upright, athletic man of 35 or so. Fair, keen and more polished than usual.

Starting from the corner of High Road where a Clock Tower commemorating the Diamond Jubilee is just receiving its finishing touches.
S along **Lewis Grove**. East side is 3-st and 2-st shops. PINK-barred. On the other side are old 2-st cottages with shopfronts. Working people. PINK.
E into **Mercia Grove**. 2½-st houses. Six or seven rooms. Two families as a rule. Some broken windows. Mostly labouring people. PURPLE.
S to **Albion Road**. Semi-detached 3-st houses. One and two families. All comfortable. People in City or on railway. Let apartments. PINK-barred.
S into **Bonfield Road**. Semi-detached 2-st houses near Clarendon Rd. Terrace houses near Albion Rd. Many keep servants. Nice little houses. PINK-barred.

High Street, Lewisham (Clock Tower to Limes Grove). Shops from Clock Tower to south of Albion Rd. PINK-barred to RED. Beyond this is a terrace of 3-st houses with two or three families in each. Nearer Limes Grove are newer red-brick 3½-st houses. Dentist, auctioneer, solicitor. RED to PINK-barred.

E into Limes Grove. Mostly 3½-st houses with two families. Some 2-st semi-detached houses on south side. A few servants. About eight houses to let. PINK to PINK-barred.

High Street (to Railway). 3½-st and 3-st houses. All keep servants. Tradesmen in business elsewhere etc. RED

E into Slaithwaite Road. 2-st detached houses with large gardens. All keep servants. Building on vacant ground at east end. RED.

S into Lingards Road. 2-st double-fronted houses. Better than Slaithwaite Rd. All keep servants. Only two houses on west side. RED.

Morley Road. Mostly detached 2-st houses with gardens. Some terrace houses on north side. Not quite so good as Lingards Rd and Slaithwaite Rd. RED.

SE to Hollyhedge Terrace. 3-st houses, a few smaller at east end. Decorator, railwaymen, labourers. About two families. PURPLE.

N into Dermody Gardens. 3-st houses. Comfortable working people. One and two families. Central triangle is open space not houses as map. PINK.

W into Dermody Road. Two terraces: Trinity Terrace on north and Holly Tree Terrace on south. 2½-st houses with two bays. A few shops. Gardeners, railwaymen and policemen. PINK to PURPLE.

N along Clarendon Road. Large detached and semi-detached houses with gardens to St Mark's Church. Solicitor and others. YELLOW to RED. North of the Church the houses are smaller, 2½-st and 3-st. All keep servants. RED. Terrace on east side close to High Rd looks poorer than other parts. Builders etc. All keep servants. RED.

SE along Gilmore Road. 3½-st. East side backs on the Quaggy. Mostly two families but look very comfortable and some keep servants. PINK-barred to St Mark's Church. Further south 2-st on east, 3-st on west, eight rooms. Comfortable working people. Tablets with trade announcements on fronts near Eastdown Park. Decorator, builder, dairy, etc. PINK.

W into Wisteria Road. North side is 3½-st, 2-st modern houses on south. Some with two families. Servants in most houses on north side. PINK-barred to PINK. Portion of Wisteria Rd running south is 2-st on west and 2½-st on east. A few keep the house but mostly two families. No servants. PINK.

S into Pascoe Road. A few old houses on east side and then open ground to the Board School. West side new 2-st houses. Park. One detached house built by an independent man and beyond this smaller 2-st property with 13 ft frontages. Labourers, mechanics and a few police. PURPLE.

Ennersdale Road from Railway to turning is similar property but looks better. Shop at corner. PINK to PURPLE.

A new road continuing Ennersdale Rd in a **SE** direction is being built called **Leahurst Road.** A few houses to the corner of another new road (Longhurst Rd) are built and occupied. PINK. The Quaggy is being straightened at this point and the backs of the houses will go to the brook.

N up Ennersdale Road. New 2-st houses facing Board School. Family plus lodger. Looks PINK. Beyond these, 2-st with one bay window. Mostly labouring people. Sergeant says this is roughest part of the district and like Pascoe Rd. PURPLE to PINK.

N to Dermody Road. On north side semi-detached houses. Keep servants. On south two PINK houses west of Ennersdale Rd and one east, near the Quaggy – a tailor. RED and PINK.

N along Eastdown Park. 3½-st and 2½-st houses with large gardens. Mostly two families and some will have an additional lodger. All comfortable. Some naval pensioners. PINK. The portion of Eastdown Park running east into the High Rd is 2½-st plus attic terrace houses. Several laundry women and lodgers. Comfortable. PINK. South east side only.

S into **Weardale Road**. 2-st little houses, west side only. Mostly family plus lodger, several "rooms to let". Bootmaker etc. Three shops near main road. PURPLE.

E into **Manor Park**. 3-st and 3½-st semi-detached and detached houses. Some good families but lodging house element has entered and road has gone down. Several houses to let. Wide road, gardens with trees. Was one of the best roads in Lee. Are building new villas at south end. 2-st plus attic. RED.

E into **Northbrook Road**. Semi-detached, 3½-st. Wide road. Two servants at least. RED like Manor Park. At the east end new 2-st houses have been built on the north side. PINK-barred. Several houses to let in this road.

S into **Manor Lane**. On the west side is Manor Cottages: three little cottages, one being rooms over stables. In one of these lives Mr Cottell who is building a lot of property here. PINK. These houses are on the Old Manor Farm. From this centre most of the land in this district was farmed. The area under cultivation is now restricted to a few fields south of the farmhouse. The farmhouse and buildings still remain and are occupied. On the east side of Manor Lane 2-st villas are being erected, seven rooms, mostly one family. Keep a girl. PINK-barred.

S into **Abernethy Road**. 2-st with bay windows. Seven rooms plus bathroom. Adapted for two families. Houses are being sold. A nominal sum is paid on entry and balance as rent. PINK. **Murillo Road** running east to west and north into Lee Rd, and **Rembrandt Road** from Murillo Rd to Lee Rd are similar. A few houses on east side of Murillo Rd only just completed and not yet occupied.

E of Abernethy Rd, out of Lee Rd is **Lochaber Road**. Red-brick 2-st houses. Two families. A few keep girls. PINK. On south side of Manor Lane nearly opposite Lochaber Rd are three modern 2-st villas. Keep servants. RED. To the east of this is Wood's Nursery which he terms 'Manor Lane Gardens'. The flower girls of the district buy their stock here. A number are sitting on the ground just outside the nursery, which is surrounded by a high wall, arranging their stock.

E into **Old Road**. On the west side between Manor Lane and High Rd a row of 2-st houses with bay windows are just finished. Will be PINK. On the south side are three good old houses (occupied) and the Manor House (empty). RED to YELLOW. At the east end of this side are a few small 4- or 5-roomed houses. One family in each. PINK. The opposite side is a meadow – sheep grazing and fowls strutting about. Near the main road is a small building erected as an institute. It is now used as Lee Vestry Hall and Offices but still bears the name Lee Institute on the front. On the opposite side is St Margaret's parish room and adjoining it the new Institute erected by the widow of G B Williams.

S into **Aislibie Road**. 2-st houses, some new on west side. Good working class, engineers etc. PINK.

E into **Lampmead Road**. 2-st houses with gardens in front. Large laundry, dairyman, signwriter, postmen, policemen. All comfortable working people. Two families. PINK.

N up Lenham Road. 2-st houses. Comfortable working people. Two families or one and a young man lodger. Pensioned police inspector has built himself a house here. PINK to PINK-barred.

Continuing on Friday 17th November 1899.

Started from the Clock Tower.
E along the **High Road**. North side to Lessington Rd is 3-st shops, very good at west end but becoming poorer eastward. Tradesmen live over shops. RED. South side, a few 3-st shops and

old 2-st cottages with shop fronts – a portion of old Lee. Trade not so good as north side, which is the business part of the road. PINK-barred to RED. East of Blessington Rd to Eastdown Park, private houses mostly detached and double-fronted. Tradesmen and City people keeping servants. RED. A few 2-st houses near Eastdown Park are poorer. PINK to PINK-barred. On north side opposite Eastdown Park is Manor Park Parade, 3-st red-brick shops built on ground of Lee Lodge. Pickford's have large depot built at back. Moderate trade, change frequently. RED to PINK-barred. One large house is left here and then a row of private houses have been converted into shops and named Newton Parade. One of the ugliest blocks of building I have seen, extends to Brandram Rd. RED to PINK-barred. At this corner are the Merchant Taylors' Almshouses, a pretty block with large grounds and east of these to Turners Rd are shops, mostly 2-st but have good fronts and do a brisk trade. RED to PINK-barred. On south side east of Eastdown Park is a row of shops to Weardale Rd, RED, and a few large private houses by Manor Park, also RED. East of this to Lochaber Rd are modern 3-st houses. Mostly two families and an occasional servant. PINK-barred. Modern shops (3-st) known as Furze Parade to Old Rd. PINK-barred to RED. From Turners Rd eastward private houses on both sides (3½-st, RED) to Lampmead Rd where Boone's Almshouses stand. East to Burnt Ash Lane is shops and a few small houses on south side whilst on the north the private houses continue a short way and 2-st cottages and shops to corner. PINK-barred.

Back through Lampmead Rd to **Brightfield Road**. Red-brick, 2-st houses. Small gardens in front. Two families invariably. Lot of laundries. PINK. The portion of the road running east is smaller property, 2-st cottages. Labourers, French polisher and bookmaker. PURPLE. A few shops near the main road. PINK.

S into **Stoneyard Place**. 2-st cottages. Two families. PURPLE.

W along **Hedgley Street** (north side only). 2-st, one bay. Mostly families with a single lodger. One house LIGHT BLUE but rest look comfortable, PINK to PURPLE.

E along Taunton Rd to **Thornhill Cottages**. Three 2-st cottages in a row and two others at right angles. Neat little place. PURPLE to PINK.

W along **Taunton Road**. East end is large 3-st semi-detached houses. Two and three families in each. Further west is 2-st with front gardens. Working people. PINK to PURPLE.

S into **Manor Lane**. 2-st houses on west side. One and two families. PINK. A few houses on east side are poorer. PURPLE.

E into **Effingham Road**. 2-st new houses at west end. Still building. Six rooms plus bath, let at 17/6. East of Wantage Rd the houses are better, older, 2-st semi-detached and a few larger near Burnt Ash Rd. Some keep servants. PINK-barred.

S to **Handen Road**. Detached houses at east end, then semi-detached 2-st plus attic. All keep servants. RED.

Wantage Road (north of Handen Rd). Three villas on west side. People keep servants. RED. Three smaller on east. PINK to PINK-barred. A few houses north of Effingham Rd PINK in character and one RED 2-st double-fronted near Southbrook Rd.

Micheldever Road. Red-brick semi-detached houses. All keep servants. Several to let. RED.

Southbrook Road. At west, 2-st double-fronted semi-detached houses. A few larger terrace houses at east. All keep servants. RED. Near Burnt Ash Rd on south side is Southbrook Mews. Stables with rooms over. Poor class. LIGHT BLUE. On the north side behind the Lord Northbrook are Bungay's Stables. LIGHT BLUE. Two sets of rooms.

Burnt Ash Road. From the railway arch to Congregational Chapel is good 3-st shops on both sides (RED). Going north the west side is 3½-st houses and east is 3-st with long gardens in front. Most are detached or semi-detached. All keep servants. From Taunton Rd to Lee Green is shops. Some have been private houses. Good class business. RED.

General Notes

As a whole the district south of the High Rd is comfortable. The roads are wide and airy. The houses have good-sized gardens back and front and, excepting in a few streets, there is no signs of poverty. It is a middle class district into which wedges of the better class working people are gradually forcing their way. The tendency of the district is downward socially altho" it is from RED to PINK and PINK-barred rather than to PURPLE. The poorer class who cannot pay the rents are being driven further afield. Rents, for a neighbourhood with so much open ground, are high and houses rented under £50 are seldom empty. On the other hand in roads like Manor Park rents have fallen and houses that used to let at £150 to £100 are now difficult to let at greatly-reduced rentals.

Notes on Lewisham

B374

Since 1861 the population of Lewisham has increased fourfold, and building is still in rapid progress. On the new 'estates' houses are being put up rather for the lower middle class than for the working class. The absence of a wealthy section, save in a few isolated houses, and the preponderance of what may be called the £150 to £400 a year class is noticeable. A large proportion of the population of Lewisham probably ought to pay income tax but there would be comparatively few who would not be entitled to abatement.

The slums, such as exist, are nearly all in the older parts of the district and the poor small courts in the near neighbourhood of the old village centres are noticeable. Some of the new building, perhaps much of it, is, however, shoddy – not long for this life, and some of it likely to deteriorate rapidly. Slums of the future are thus not uncommon and an instance in which this undesirable consummation has been reached is seen in part of Wildfell Rd.

The demand for the new accommodation appears to press closely on the supply but rents are not excessive. The "housing problem" of the district is aesthetic in character rather than social. In the older parts there are occasional touches of the picturesque, but in the whole district there is no residential part that charms and no crowded, busy part that stimulates. "Long" and "lazy" seem very good epithets for Lewisham.

In the whole of the section there is practically no DARK BLUE and LIGHT BLUE is the exception. PURPLE is more common and is on the increase, but PINK-barred and PINK are the prevailing colours, both also on the increase. As in Brockley the openness of most of the ground is a feature, but the district has a less finished look and much more of the ground that is still open is destined for building. "Gardens", as one has them in Brockley, are hardly characteristic. Hilly Fields is a high, healthy and well-situationed open space and the Ladywell Recreation Ground is a boon. Lewisham Park is at present reserved for the use of the houses round it.

The daily migration for work, manual or otherwise, must be very large. Inside, apart from building, there seems to be little or nothing for the occupied classes to do. Even large shopping centres hardly exist. As a whole Lewisham appears to be quiet, respectable, rather common-place, and of the district, as of some men, it may perhaps be said that it has no redeeming vices: it hardly smokes.

Charges are mainly for drunkenness and other minor offences. The typical local misdemeanour appears to be afternoon house-breaking, houses being entered while the occupiers are away. In such a district as this, this crime is difficult to prevent or even to detect and Lloyds was amusing in describing the effrontery of the invader – how, having forced the lock, often a very simple operation, he deceives any chance onlooking neighbour by greeting and shaking hands with an imaginary person, entering as he does so and closing the door. On leaving the same thing may be repeated and no suspicions aroused until it is too late.

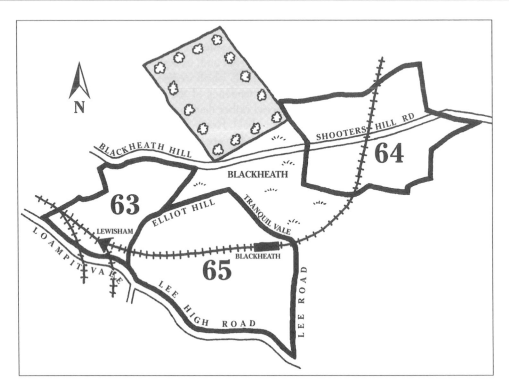

Walk 63

B372

Saturday 5th August 1899.
George Arkell with Sergeant Ashbourne.
Sergeant Ashbourne is a smart officer but has only been in the division a short time and did not know much of the people, his knowledge being mainly general.

Starting from Blackheath Hill Railway Station.
S along **Burling Street**. Narrow unpaved roadway. 2-st cottages with 9 ft frontages. Houses on west side only, plus three at bottom on east. Dirty curtains. Poor, rows sometimes. LIGHT BLUE to DARK BLUE.
Back up **Merton Place**. 2-st houses flush with pavement. One small shop: "Ices ½d and 1d". LIGHT BLUE. Two DARK BLUE houses near Blackheath Hill.
Up Blackheath Hill to **Dartmouth Hill**. Old road leading to the Heath. Modern red-brick houses on east, 2-st plus attic. Old houses and boys' orphanage on west side. PINK-barred.
At end, facing Blackheath is **Lansdowne Place**. Large detached and semi-detached houses, three or four servants. YELLOW.
W to **Dartmouth Row**. Facing the Green Man are some 3-st houses. Keep servants. Going south are a few shops and then some old good houses and some modern 3-st houses. Some very large on Heath side. RED and YELLOW.
W along **Morden Hill**. Nurseryman on north corner. PINK. In Back Lane are a few cottages, formerly occupied by servants but now in ruins. Further west along Morden Hill are a number of very large houses in grounds. YELLOW. On south side is St John's Hospital, the home of the Nursing Sisters of St John the Divine.

NW along **Lewisham Road**. 2-st plus basement private houses. Mostly keep a servant girl to Drysdale Rd. Beyond that point houses become poorer. Shops near the railway arch, rather poor class trade. PINK-barred.

Into **Lethbridge Road**. 6-roomed houses with bay windows to Drysdale Rd, beyond that poorer. Houses flush with pavement. Working people. PINK and PURPLE.

Drysdale Road. South end is the better. Two families. Fronts of houses covered with creepers. Front gardens well kept. People and houses look clean. Five to six rooms. Northern part is poorer, no gardens, houses flush with pavement. Some are LIGHT BLUE in character. PURPLE.

W into **Garden Row**. 5-roomed houses. Paved entry but only a footpath. Houses flush with pavement. Tailor, plumber, etc. PURPLE as map.

E into **Sparta Street** (King St on map). 2-st houses flush with pavement. Poorest at remote end. Many children playing, bad eyes. Entry on south side leads to a cottage, four rooms, like the street. LIGHT BLUE.

N up **Queen Street**. 2-st cottages. Narrow street, houses flush with pavement. Labouring people. LIGHT BLUE.

E into **Essex Place**. 2-st cottages like Queen St but look better off. Laundress etc. Little girl, well dressed in light colours going into one of the houses. PURPLE.

W to **Regent Street**. 2-st cottages like the others. Some broken windows. LIGHT BLUE.

W along **Sparta Street**. Nearing Lewisham Rd the houses improve. Large rooms and wider frontages. Windows look poor but some are comfortable. PURPLE to LIGHT BLUE.

S along Lewisham Rd to **Morden Grove**. Well-built semi-detached houses, 2-st plus basement. Most keep a servant. Only one house on east side. PINK-barred.

At the S end is **Sydney Grove**. Good modern houses near Lewisham Rd on north side. South side older 2-st houses with long front gardens. Near Lewisham Rd the people keep servants. Working class at lower end of road. PINK-barred.

N into **Northam Street** (late Albion Grove). 2-st houses, on one side, with basement floor. Row of trees on one side of street. Some broken windows. Insurance agent, boot repairer, etc. PINK to PURPLE. The portion running north east to south west is better. Little children playing here are clean. Many of Penn's men. PINK.

Turning N towards **Albion St**, a few cottages adjoining the public house and facing on the narrow footpath are reached. LIGHT BLUE in character.

W across the Ravensbourne into **Elverson Road**. 2-st, one bay window. Small gardens in front. All have nicely kept parlours. PINK, except a few houses west of Ravensbourne St where the houses are smaller and look poorer, PURPLE.

Ravensbourne Street between the railway arches is 2-st houses and a few shops. Two families in houses. PINK.

E into **Leathwell Road**. Like the best part of Elverson Rd. PINK

Back across the Ravensbourne to **Conington Road**. New 2-st houses with bay windows. Fitted for two families. PINK.

Back and along **Lewisham Road** to south. Good class houses with long gardens at back. Mostly semi-detached. Keep servants. Row of shops near Railway Bridge. RED.

E up **Blackheath Rise**. Modern villas. All keep servants. RED to YELLOW.

Prince's Road. Similar class. RED to YELLOW.

Lewisham Hill. From Morden Hill to Prince's Rd are large detached houses. YELLOW. South of Prince's Rd are terrace houses (3-st plus basement) occupied by good class tradesmen and retired people. All keep servants. Clergy and doctors. Colfe's Grammar School for Boys on east side. RED.

Through railway arch into **High Street, Lewisham**. Shops built out on gardens of old 2-

st houses. PINK-barred to RED. Around corner by Lewisham Bridge is a row of seven cottages (2-st) facing the Ravensbourne, numbered in Loampit Vale. PINK.

E along **Crathorn Street** (Prince's Row on map). 2-st cottages. Small flower gardens in front. Mostly labouring men. Near the main road a few shops – dairyman, wheelwright, etc. PURPLE.

In **Station Approach** are three 3-st houses. Publican, laundry and one poor-looking house. PINK to PURPLE.

Loampit Vale (between the railway arches). Small 2-st shops doing a fairly good trade. Prosperous people. PINK-barred.

N up **Thurston Road**. 2-st houses with bay window. Comfortable working people with some poor. Much heavy traffic through this street between Deptford and Lewisham via Mill Lane. Come this way to avoid the hill in Lewisham Rd. PINK to PURPLE.

S into **Jerrard Street**. Same class of house on west side and shops on east side. PINK.

Horton Street. Houses like Thurston Rd. Rather poorer. Broken and patched windows. South side of street is taken by School and Jerrard's timber yard. PURPLE to PINK.

NW along **Loampit Vale** (to Sunninghill Rd). Shops, some small, also terrace of 3-st shops. Quieter trade than nearer Lewisham. PINK-barred. 3-st villas just south of the Sunninghill Rd. All keep servants. RED.

N into **Elswick Road**. 2½-st houses. Poor working class. Improves towards north end. PURPLE to PINK.

Sunninghill Road. 2-st villas, a few larger. Some servants kept. Clean, quiet road. PINK-barred.

N of this point **Loampit Hill** is good class villas. Some semi-detached, mostly three floors. Keep servants. RED.

Beaufort Gardens. Cul de sac. Detached houses 2½-st to 3-st. Garden in centre of oval. Comfortable people, a few keep servants. PINK-barred to RED.

General Remarks

The poorest part of this walk is the group of narrow streets in the angle between Lewisham Rd and Blackheath Hill. It has changed little during the past ten years but the poor area tends to become larger. The northern end of Drysdale Rd now differs little from Sparta St and both Drysdale Rd and Lethbridge Rd are poorer than they were. The area east of these streets is much higher and forms a well-to-do residential district. Much of the property is old but the modern villa is supplanting the older 3-st and 4-st houses and filling up the plots of ground that have been left between the houses. Socially Blackheath appears to be declining – well-to-do tradesmen find the neighbourhood convenient and, except in the very large houses (many of which are empty or to let), a large number are occupied by this class.

Walk 64

B371

Sunday 22nd October 1899.
George Arkell with Sergeant Howell.

Started from corner of Westcombe Hill.
E along **Charlton Road**. South side detached double-fronted houses, 3½-st. Major General, merchants, etc. YELLOW to Crangerne Rd. East of this are 2-st houses with bays and a row of 3-st shops between Hassenden Rd and Coulhurst Rd. pink.

S down **Couthurst Road**. 2-st cottages (five rooms). Small gardens in front. Mostly two families. Coachman, gardener, insurance agent. PURPLE to PINK.

Lyveden Road. South side only. Similar class of houses. Florist, tailor. Look a little poorer. PURPLE.

Hassendean Road. Six rooms, one bay. Little better than other roads. PINK to PURPLE.

N up **Furzefield Road**. 2-st, five and six rooms. Dressmaker, watchmakers, manglers. Many gardeners in all these roads. All working people. PURPLE.

S down **Craigerne Road**. On a narrow strip of land on east side four 3-st houses are built. Ground only wide enough for one room, so sides of houses are to the street and with sloping rooms, they resemble the arks seen in toy shops and are known locally as Noah's Arks. PINK. Turning the corner the houses are 2-st, modern with bays. Some have servants, others two families. PINK-barred. Near the main road are large 3-st houses, some detached. All keep one or two servants. RED.

Old Dover Road (west of Banchory Rd). Near Charlton Rd are 2-st bay-windowed houses on south and 3-st on north. Some keep servants. East of Dornberg Rd are shops on both sides. PINK-barred.

Dornberg Road. 2-st houses. Builder and others looking comfortable. Probably a few servants. PINK-barred to PINK.

S down **Banchory Road**. 2-st, six or seven rooms. Carpenter etc. Have girls in to clean up. Rents 13/6. PINK to PINK-barred.

E along **Old Dover Road**. On north side a few private houses and poor class shops to boundary. Five houses east of Russell Place and then open fields. Builder, dairy, etc. PINK. On south side by Sun Lane a row of cottages (five rooms) look poor. PURPLE. East of these are a few scattered cottages with large gardens in front. Contractor, laundry, etc. PINK.

N up **Russell Place**. 2½-st on east side. Other side is 2-st, some semi-detached. Sweep, mangler, etc. PINK to PURPLE.

W to **Lizban Street**. 2½-st, north side only. Entrance to Rectory playing fields here. West end is better than the east. Range from PURPLE to LIGHT BLUE, PURPLE.

Bowater Place. 2-st with short forecourts. Windows look poor, short white curtains. Mixed lot: labourers, carmen, roadmen. West side is better, 2-st semi-detached. St John's working men's club here. PURPLE on west and LIGHT BLUE on east side.

W to **Bedford Place**. 2-st houses with small bay windows. Carmen, sweeps, etc. 2-st cottages on east side. Very narrow roadway. Labouring people, dressmaker. LIGHT BLUE.

N up **Woodlands Road**. 3-st shops, best in the neighbourhood. Mostly managers living over. East side is known as Langton Terrace – private houses converted into shops. RED to PINK-barred.

W along **St John's Park**. 2-st houses on south side with long gardens in front. Most keep a servant. PINK-barred. Near the Avenue the property is larger. Some detached double-fronted houses. All keep servants, some three or four. RED to YELLOW. North side is 3½-st semi-detached. RED.

The Avenue is a fine avenue of trees from Old Dover Rd to Shooters Hill Rd. South Eastern Railway passes below. Part has been enclosed and there is only a footpath left.

E of this point **St John's Park** is 3½-st detached houses with large gardens. Several servants. YELLOW.

St John's Road. Like west end of St John's Park. YELLOW. At south west corner of this road are two sets of stables belonging to St John's Park. PINK. Livery Stable in mews (south side) also PINK.

W to **Vanbrugh Terrace**. 3½-st detached houses with large grounds. YELLOW.

E along **Shooters Hill Road**. Large detached and semi-detached houses. 3½-st on north

side. Three or more servants. South side facing corner of Heath the houses are 2-st double-
fronted. Not quite so good as the rest. RED. East to Woodville Rd the houses are larger
detached and double-fronted. YELLOW to RED. East of Woodlands Rd are a few shops on
north side and then private houses. Not so good as rest of road. RED. Near the corner of
Great Dover Rd are some 2-st cottages. Grainer, florist, etc. PINK. East of Woodville Rd,
south side is detached and semi-detached houses to the Cottage Hospital. YELLOW with
tendency to RED at east end.

S along **Hervey Road**. Six semi-detached houses (3½-st) on east side. One large detached
house and four cement-fronted houses (3½-st). Only one occupied. South side is market

The Paragon, one of Blackheath's wealthiest streets.

gardens. RED.

Eastbrook Road. Four 4-st houses on each side. Mostly keep two servants. Red-brick houses. RED to YELLOW.

Woodville Road. One house on each side. Similar to Eastbrook Rd. RED. South of Hervey Rd a row of houses facing east. Mostly keep two servants. RED.

In **Hervey Road** near Woodville Rd building is proceeding. Some 2-st and 3-st houses with long gardens in front. New houses are 2-st. RED to YELLOW.

Kidbrooke Park Road. Detached and semi-detached 3-st and 4-st houses with grounds. YELLOW to RED.

Westbrook Road. Entrance to Morden Grange. YELLOW.

Kidbrooke Grove. Only a few large houses, detached. East side 3½-st houses in grounds. Three or four servants. YELLOW.

W along **Morden College Walk**, the boundary of the sub-division. A pretty footpath passing Morden College, a fine block of Almshouses for old merchants or wholesale traders with 40 in residence. The path leads on to Blackheath.

N along **St German's Terrace**. Old-fashioned houses standing well back from the Heath. St German's Church and Christ's College here. Kidbrooke Lodge, the largest house, is advertised for sale as a building estate. YELLOW to RED.

General Notes

This area contains very little poverty. The working class is confined almost entirely to a small, closely-built area near the Charlton boundary. The remainder is well-to-do and, near Blackheath, wealthy. Roads are wide, houses have large gardens and trees abound so that the surroundings are pleasant. The neighbourhood has gone down somewhat as a residential place, chiefly I believe owing to the villainous railway services of the South Eastern Railway and London, Chatham & Dover Railway. Trains seldom keep their advertised times and in the winter it is not an infrequent thing for passengers to spend the best part of an hour in accomplishing the journey to or from London. A number of the larger houses are to let, chiefly in the Kidbrooke district but even here there are signs that the decline has reached its limit and that the place will again fill up. There are acres of ground south and west suited for building.

Walk 65 B372

Monday 20th November 1899.
George Arkell with Detective Sergeant Spencer.

Started from the Plough Bridge, Lewisham.
S along **High Street**. Close to the railway arch are a number of 2-st houses. PINK. South of these are terraces of 3½-st houses to Granville Rd. All keep servants. Dentist, dispensary. Two houses are occupied by the assistants of a large draper on the Pavement. RED. The Quaggy runs by the side of the road in front of these houses. From Granville Rd to Belmont Hill is covered by a raised promenade, the approach to some shops, the finest in Lewisham. RED.

E into **Cressingham Road**. 2½-st on south and 2½-st plus attic on north side as far as Belmont Rd. Some keep servants and all are comfortable. PINK-barred. East of this point houses are 2-st some with attic. Comfortable working people. PINK.

S along **Belmont Road**. On the east side are three 3-st houses, Leamington Villas. Comfortable. Rest of side is the grounds of Mr Penn's house. Only gardener's cottage here. PINK.

W into **St Stephen's Road**. 2½-st. All comfortable, mostly two families. Some dress-makers' cards. PINK.

E along **Granville Road**. On south side by Myron Place are a few 2-st houses. Working people, look poor and dirty. PURPLE. Remainder of road is 2½-st like St Stephen's Rd. PINK. Turning **S** into **Belmont Road** there is a row of 2½-st houses on the west side. Look poor. PURPLE.

W & N into **Myron Place** (Ivy Terrace on map which is wrong at this point. The Place makes a turn west before reaching Granville Rd). Row of 2-st cottages on west side. Beyond these round the corner are a few poor houses and stables. One DARK BLUE house. Carman, contractor, hawker, etc. PURPLE to LIGHT BLUE.

E along High Rd to **Marischal Road**. One detached house on north side. RED. Portion of south is taken by the backs of shops in Lee Rd. Remainder is 2½-st and 3-st houses, semi-detached. Mostly lodging houses. PINK-barred.

S down **Douglas Road**. Two pairs of semi-detached villas with gardens at side. Look comfortable. PINK-barred to PINK.

N & SE to **Marlborough Road**. 3½-st detached houses on north and 2-st detached houses on south side. All keep servants, two as a rule. Clergyman etc. RED.

E along **Blessington Road**. 3-st and 4-st detached and semi-detached houses. Large gardens. Two servants at least. Many to let and for sale at west end. Houses are larger and better occupied east of Middleton Rd. RED to YELLOW east of Middleton Rd.

W along **Belmont Park**. Large detached houses, 3½-st. Like Blessington Rd. RED to YELLOW.

E & N up **Glenton Road** (Belgrove Villas on map). 3½-st houses, old style. Private school. Some to let. RED to PINK-barred.

E along **Dacre Road**. 2-st cottages, flush with footpath. Five rooms as a rule, some smaller at east end (four rooms). Labouring people with a few better off. Several houses have fine shows of chrysanthemums in the windows. Mr Penn has a show at which these blooms are exhibited. PURPLE.

S into **Dacre Square**. Narrow paved court with two rows of six 2-st cottages, very small. Some broken windows stopped with paper. Square reached by archway from street. LIGHT BLUE.

N up **Church Passage** (Royal Oak Place on map). Old 2-st cottages with small gardens in front. A few have been turned into shops near Dacre St. On west side are five 2-st plus attic houses. Two families. Respectable working people. PINK to PURPLE.

Along Church Passage to **Kingswood Place**. 2½-st terrace houses. Decorator etc. Comfortable working people. PINK.

S along Turners Rd to **Boone's Road**. Small 6-roomed houses, 2-st and 2½-st. Some of the houses still *pump* their water. Decorator, gardeners, police, etc. All comfortable working people. PINK.

S along **Turner Road**. From Kingswood Place to Dacre St is 2-st cottages, some with additional attic. PINK. A few small shops on east side, then nursery and 2½-st houses. Comfortable, most keep servants. South of these the houses have narrower frontages and are poorer – working people, tailors etc. PINK-barred to PURPLE at south. A few houses on west side near High Rd. PINK.

E along High Rd is **Lee Road**. Good shops near Lee Green and then on west side terrace of 3½-st houses. All keep servants. Large builder. Going north the road gradually improves and at northern part we have large detached houses standing in their own grounds. North of Manor Way all would keep several servants. RED south of Manor Way, YELLOW to north.

S down **Lee Park**. 3-st detached and semi-detached houses with large gardens. Several servants. Like Lee Rd. YELLOW.

W along High Rd to **Church Street**. Small 2-st shops on east side near High Rd and also near Dacre St. Remainder is 2-st cottages, PURPLE to LIGHT BLUE in character. Women standing about chaffed the sergeant, whom they evidently knew. On west side is a small hall with inscription "Soup Kitchen 1856". PURPLE as a whole.

On the W side is **Barrows Place**. Old 2-st cottages with gardens in front. Laundry hands and low class of women. LIGHT BLUE to DARK BLUE.

On E side and only reached by a long passage giving access to the back gardens is **Blows Place**. 2-st houses, four rooms plus scullery. Labouring people. LIGHT BLUE.

S down Boone St. On the east side is **Frant Place**. Two cottages on north side. One LIGHT BLUE and one PINK. PURPLE. Red-brick Mission Hall (The People's Hall) takes the remainder of the place.

Boone Street itself is 2-st private houses, various styles. Turncock, some mechanics but people are mostly labourers. Very little signs of poverty. PURPLE to PINK.

Near High Rd on the W side is **Boone's Place**, a terrace of nine houses facing north. Narrow paved entry. Three or four rooms. LIGHT BLUE to PURPLE.

N up **Brandram Road**. On east side is the Merchant Taylors' Almshouses – three blocks with a central grass plot occupied by old women. Opposite this are 3½-st semi-detached houses. All keep one and some two servants. RED. On east side of road, north of Dacre St, is an Entry with four 3-st houses. Two are double-fronted. "All keep servants" said Spencer but they look a poor RED. PINK-barred to RED. To north of this, Dacre House has been pulled down and new 2-st houses with eight rooms on a floor are built. PINK to PINK-barred. North of Belmont Park, the west side is large detached houses. RED to YELLOW. On opposite side a livery stable keeper has his house and stables. RED.

E along **Lansdowne Road**. On south side 2-st semi-detached houses are being built. Price asked is £620 for freehold. Three are occupied near Brandram Rd. PINK to RED. North side is 3½-st detached houses. RED.

N along **Church Passage (or Love Lane)**. One RED house on east side.

Church Terrace. Two 3-st on east side, rest is 2-st and 3½-st houses. Good gardens, carriage drives. Clergyman etc. RED to YELLOW.

W along **Belmont Hill**. On north side is a very large house (The Cedars) occupied by Penn the engineer. A few other good class houses on the same side. YELLOW.

Then come to **Belmont Grove**. Private road with gates. 3½-st houses. Some are larger whilst at extreme end they are smaller. RED to YELLOW.

Going W along **Belmont Hill**, the north side is mostly detached houses to corner of Belmont Rd. YELLOW. West of Belmont Rd is 2½-st terrace houses. PINK to PINK-barred. On south side the houses are less good as you descend the hill westward near the High Rd. 2-st detached, gardens with trees. RED to YELLOW.

This completed the day's walk.

Started on 22nd November from the Lewisham Railway Bridge.

N up **Lewisham Hill**. Good class houses on east side. RED to the School. North of this point are very large semi-detached. YELLOW.

E up **Eliot Hill**. Steep rise here. 4-st semi-detached houses and then some in their own grounds. RED and YELLOW.

S into **Eliot Park**. 3½-st semi-detached houses. South part is detached houses with grounds. Quiet. All would keep two or more servants. RED to YELLOW.

N into **Walerand Road** (Camden Row on map). 3½-st semi-detached houses. RED to

YELLOW. East side not so good as west.

S to **Granville Park**. Near the railway bridge is All Saint's Orphanage for older lads. A fine red-brick building accommodating 130 lads. Close to it is a small detached house. RED. Remainder is large semi-detached houses (3½-st). Good gardens. Several to let or for sale, one at £55 a year. Houses are larger near the Heath. RED to YELLOW.

Facing the Heath is **Aberdeen Terrace**. Very large semi-detached 3½-st houses. RED to YELLOW. Turning eastward there are several detached houses, also YELLOW. Facing these is the old Orchard House. The ground are now built over. Rows of red-brick modern villas being erected on four of the five sides. The Orchard is the name of those adjoining the old houses. 3-st. RED to YELLOW.

SE into **Eliot Vale**. Similar class of house to The Orchard on east side. 2-st plus attic. YELLOW to RED. Other side is Haddo Villas, 3-st and 2½-st semi-detached houses, older. RED to YELLOW.

S into **Love Lane**. At west corner is West Lodge. YELLOW. Another YELLOW house on east and red-brick stables (PINK) on west.

E along **Eliot Vale**. Modern houses, 2-st, on north side. RED. Older houses on south.

Facing the Heath is **Eliot Place**. Large old houses. 4-st semi-detached as a rule. Two magistrates and others well-to-do. Men servants kept. YELLOW.

The eastern side of The Orchard is known as **Orchard Road**. 3-st modern houses. RED to YELLOW.

Immediately **E** of Eliot Place and behind a detached block of property is **Grotes Buildings**. Old 2-st and 3-st cottages. Working people but don't look poor. PINK. Tillings have built large stables here.

The **W** side of the detached block here is known as **Eliot Cottages**. 3½-st houses. One family plus lodgers or two families. PINK to PINK-barred. Round by the Hare & Billet are two shops and private house. PINK-barred to RED.

Round corner to **S** is **Grotes' Place**. Two detached houses and 3-st terrace houses. Mostly keep servants. Corset-maker uses one for business. PINK-barred to RED.

Across the Heath to **Blackheath Vale**. 2-st houses with one bay. Two families as a rule. Working class but no signs of poverty. PINK. Houses are on north side only of turning on east side of the street. PINK like the rest. Two laundries here. Turning marked Union Vale is now Tillings Stables.

On **E**, facing the Heath, are **Talbot Houses**. Northern part is comparatively modern. 3-st semi-detached and detached houses. Two or more servants. RED.

Talbot Place. Four semi-detached houses, 3-st. Two or more servants. Man servant cleaning windows. RED to YELLOW. Further west is an old detached house. Not well kept but may be YELLOW to RED.

Back across the Heath to **Lloyd's Place**. 3-st and 4-st old houses. Good class lodging houses. Home for Crippled Boys by Tranquil Vale. RED. Much confusion just here as to the names of these places. Grotes' Place said to include part of row marked as Lloyd's Place. Spencer spent three quarters of an hour trying to find a number here whilst making an inquiry.

E into **Camden Row**. A few 3½-st poor-looking houses and then, nearer Tranquil Vale, 2-st cottages with bay windows. Two families. PURPLE and PINK for 2-st houses.

Tranquil Vale. A few private houses on west near the Heath. RED. Some 2-st shops, builder, golf requisites, etc. Fairly good trade. PINK-barred. Remainder of both sides is good class shops to the railway. "Very dear shops" said Spencer. It is a place where ladies come to order their goods. Perhaps this may explain the large proportion of shops for the sale of fancy goods and the grocers and other licences – there are twelve licences in Tranquil Vale and

Montpelier Vale. RED.

S into **South Vale**. 3-st and 2½-st houses. One to let. All working people: tailors, fly proprietor. PINK.

S into **Collins St**. 2-st houses. Look comfortable. PINK. East of these houses the street makes a turn and becomes a narrow paved footway with 3-st houses. PINK to PURPLE.

N into **Montpelier Vale**. Good class busy shops. Houses are old. Some private houses with fronts added, some 3-st shops. RED.

W into **Tranquil Passage**. Mostly small shops: sweets, boots, greengrocery, etc. Some working people. PINK.

N into **Brigade Street**. 2-st houses on west side. Turncock etc. PINK. Turning to the left the Fire Brigade Station is reached, occupies the site of the Methodist Chapel. Men live here. PINK.

Royal Parade. 4-st red-brick shops with rooms over let off. PINK-barred to RED. Going south past Blackheath Station towards Lee Rd (to corner of Lee Terrace). On west side is the Railway Hotel and Blackheath School and on the east a few shops to the corner of Bennett Park with the Alexandra Assembly Rooms on the opposite corner. South of this are new shops (4-st, red-brick) called Beaconsfield Buildings and the Blackheath Conservatoire of Music and Concert Hall – a modern building with a front elaborately ornamented and entirely faced with terra cotta. RED.

W into **Lawn Terrace**. On south side are Seagers' Cottages. 2-st detached. Nearly all gardeners. PINK. Bending southward Lawn Terrace proper is reached. Mostly lodging houses (3-st and basement). The best rooms face to the gardens and the kitchen and offices to the roadway. Something like Colville Square and other places in Bayswater. RED to PINK-barred.

S into **Lee Terrace**. Detached and semi-detached houses. 3-st and 4-st with large gardens, some with grounds and carriage drives. YELLOW.

The Glebe. Detached and semi-detached houses with grounds. YELLOW. New stables being built near western entrance (PINK), belong to large house in Lee Terrace.

S into **Quentin Road**. 3-st houses. Six rooms and no back gardens on east side. Most are empty. Asking £36 a year. People will not have them as they are so dark. Bill in one advertises them "to be let at moderate rent". Belong to a company and people say the directors want to make it bankrupt so that they can buy the houses cheap. Near Dacre Park the houses are 2-st. All occupied. Comfortable working people. PINK. At the corners of Dacre Park are two large blocks of dwellings, 4-st, working class. Poorer than the streets to the south. PURPLE to PINK.

N into **Dacre Park**. Mostly 3½-st terrace houses, a few 3-st and 2-st. Mostly lodging houses. Nearly all keep servants. PINK-barred to RED.

W into **Eton Grove**. 3½-st houses on north and 2½-st on south. Comfortable working class. Dressmaker occupies a house at the end. As we entered the Grove ten girls came out in groups for their dinner. No plate or outward sign of business. One retired man here and Dacre Cottage (RED) at west end. PINK to PINK-barred.

N of Eton Grove, **Dacre Park** improves and might be RED.

On W side is **Victoria Mews**. Only one house now occupied. PINK.

General Remarks

These two walks include portions of Blackheath and Lee, the railway forming roughly the dividing line. The Blackheath portion lies high and is hilly. It is a well-to-do and has been a fashionable district but is gradually losing status socially, many of the large houses are to let and others are occupied by tradesmen. It seems that the decline has reached its limit and possibly the neighbourhood may again improve as the neighbourhood is breezy and healthy, the houses well built, the roads wide with plenty of open ground. The very large houses will probably give way to the modern red-brick villas and the district become a good RED neighbourhood. This change has already taken place at The Orchard and Dacre House.

Blackheath Village has changed wonderfully during the past 10 or 12 years from a sleepy little village to a busy business centre. The few working people living here are persons dependent on the large houses or shops and are a local colony – gardeners etc. Except a couple of laundries in Blackheath Vale and a few livery stables there are few centres of employment.

On the Lee side the character of the population gradually changes from YELLOW to PURPLE and LIGHT BLUE as the high ground by the railway is left and the only poor patch in Lee is included in this walk – the rectangle of streets between Turner Rd, Brandram Rd, Dacre Rd and the High Rd, but even here there is no extreme poverty but rather a rough labouring class, who in the present good times are doing well but to whom a season of bad trade might mean want.

Sergeant Spencer came to Lee from Westminster two years or so ago and has acquired a remarkably good knowledge of the district for so short a time. He misses the life and bustle of Westminster and regards Lee as very dull in the evenings. The nearest places of amusement are at Deptford and Greenwich. This is likely to be soon altered. A new theatre is mooted and an agitation is being carried forward to induce the LCC to run the trams along the High Rd.

The Sergeant is an abstainer and whilst talking over the drunk question he said that when he was on a beat with a good house, it was an understood thing that he kept out of the way when the time for drinks came, one of the other fellows benefiting by his abstention. Very little is down now and the regulations are much more strict now, especially in the central division. He could get more drunk in Lee now than he could in Westminster if he wanted it.

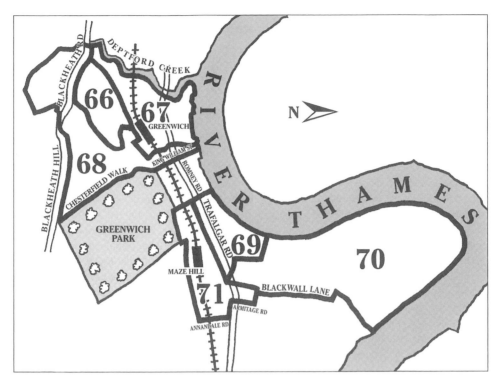

Walk 66

B 368

Tuesday 1st August 1899.
George Arkell with Sergeant Ashbourne.
Detective Mercer was detailed for this duty but having a case in the Court this morning,
Sergeant Ashbourne took his place at short notice.

Starting from the Blackheath Road Station.
E along **Greenwich Road**. On south west side are a coffee shop and a row of poor-looking
private houses, one used as a laundry. PINK in character. Between Burgos Grove and
Devonshire Rd are 4-st private houses with small front gardens. Some two families and most
keep servants. PINK-barred. The Miller Hospital also at corner. From Devonshire Rd to
Egerton Rd are a few 3-st shops and then 2-st and 3-st old houses. Comfortable people. At
corner of Egerton Rd are the Jubilee Almshouses which extend into Egerton Rd where two
blocks of cottages stand – Tranham & Larwell Almshouses. These places have been rebuilt in
red and white brick and are an ornament to this very mixed road. PINK-barred, PURPLE on map.
On S side is **Burgos Grove** (late Wellington Grove). 2-st and basement. Two families as
a rule. Comfortable working class, some police. One poor house. PINK as map.
Next turning is **Devonshire Road**. As far as Egerton Rd the houses are semi-detached, a
few double-fronted on east side. South to South St are terrace houses, 2½-st, and the Roan
Girls' School, a modern red-brick building. West side is better than the terrace houses on
east and near Greenwich Rd most keep servants. Air of comfort and repose characteristic
of place. PINK-barred to RED except terrace on east PINK. RED on map.
W into **Catherine Grove**. 2½-st, eight steps to front door. Nice front gardens, double

avenue of trees, quiet street. Comfortable working people, engineers, police, etc. PINK, PURPLE on map.

Egerton Road. Wide road. Semi-detached, 2-st, some double-fronted. Small front gardens with trees. Well-to-do as a rule: solicitor, inspector of police. Servants in more than half the houses. PINK-barred, RED on map.

E along **Guildford Road**. 2-st and basement, six rooms. Terrace houses £25 to £30 a year. Comfortable working class, engineers etc. Not so good as Egerton Rd. PINK, RED on map.

E to **Ashburnham Grove**. 2½-st houses with large front gardens. Some semi-detached and 3-st at east end. Comfortable working people. PINK, RED on map.

E along **Ashburnham Road**. On east side some 3-st houses built for three families have been recently erected on the erstwhile gardens of Greenwich Rd. A few 2-st old houses on west side, a few good 3-st houses near South St, remainder 2½-st with gardens in front. Good class working people. PINK as map. Add colour on east. Might be PINK-barred at South St end.

E into **Langdale Road**. On east side modern 2-st houses. Working people. Insurance agent's plate on one door. West side is 3½-st semi-detached, bay windows. Comfortable people, some solicitors. East PINK, west PINK-barred to RED. Not coloured on map.

Greenwich Road (Egerton Rd to South St). To Langdale Rd terrace of old-fashioned 3-st and 4-st houses, some double-fronted. Modern bay windows added to some. Contractor, solicitor and professional people. A few take lodgers. PINK-barred in character. Further east are two old 3-st houses, RED, and Queen Elizabeth's almshouses (1576). House built on three sides of a grass flat with chapel and clock in central part. PINK-barred, not coloured on map.

W along **South Street** (to Blissett St.) North side to Devonshire Rd is 3½-st semi-detached and terrace houses. Good gardens in front. Tradesmen and retired people. Keep servants. RED as map. South side is smaller houses, 2-st and basement, a few semi-detached and 3½-st. Poorer than north side. PINK to PINK-barred. Penn's Almshouses, a modern red-brick block with gardens in front, on the south side. All RED on map.

NE up **Blissett Street**. 2-st houses. Shops on south east side near South St and the new private houses to Winforton St not marked on map. Beyond this are old 2-st cottages and north west side are new 2-st houses with gardens in front. PINK except old cottages on south east, PURPLE. PINK on map, part uncoloured.

N down **Royal Hill** (to South St) 2-st houses, modern on south side, others older and look poorer than south side. Narrow fronts, white curtains. PINK (west) to PURPLE (east). PINK on map. On the north side is a narrow court leading to cottages between South St and Brand St. Look poor. LIGHT BLUE, not on map.

N along **Brand Street**. 2-st houses. Comfortable working people, plumber, decorator, etc. Few semi-detached houses. New building at corner of Circus St. PINK as map.

Circus Street. 2-st bay-windowed houses near South St. A few shops and old private houses (3-st). On south side are several large houses. Comfortable people, some let apartments. Bookbinder, builder. PINK to PINK-barred, PINK on map.

S along **Prior Street**. 2½-st. Working class, not quite so good as Brand St. PINK as map. At the top of the street on the west side are three cottages facing north, 2-st with gardens in front, also a new house. PINK to PURPLE, not on map. Between the railway and Royal Hill are a few modern houses facing the railway from Prior St. PINK, not on map.

Royal Hill (Blissett St to Circus St). Near Blissett St are 2½-st and 3-st old tumble-down houses. Some look comfortable and even pretty with creepers on front. Some shops, mostly on west side between Prior St and Circus St. Comfortable and well-to-do even. On opposite side are 2-st houses. Small windows, some look poor. PURPLE except on west side north of Prior St, PINK.

At this time, Sergeant Ashbourne was relieved by Detective Mercer, who was waiting for us at Greenwich Railway Station.

Walk 67   B 368

Tuesday 1st August 1899.
George Arkell with Detective Mercer.

Starting from Greenwich Railway Station (LC&D Railway).
S along **Stockwell Street**. 3-st shops. Good class on east side. Mostly old houses with red-brick facings, two with dormer windows in roof. Shops on west side are not quite so good. RED as map.
W along **Burney Street**. A row of 3-st poor houses near South St. Several families in each house. PURPLE in character. Remainder of street is well-to-do. 3½-st houses. Mostly keep servants. Solicitor etc. Good lodging houses. PINK-barred, PINK on map.
Nearly opposite Burney St in Royal Hill is **Peyton Place**. One 3-st house on north side. PINK. Row of 2-st cottages on opposite side. Coachmen etc. Look comfortable and may be PINK, PINK on map.
Royal Hill (Circus St to London St). Shops, old fashioned and small on east side, a few on the west but greater part of this side is taken by the Public Baths and Literary Institute. PINK. At the south corner of Burney St some 2-st modern houses have been built facing the railway, some entered from Burney St and others from Royal Hill. PINK, not marked on map.
London Street. Principal shopping street of the district. In a state of transition, some newly-built shops, others old and yet others are private houses with shop fronts added. A few semi-detached 3-st houses near Greenwich (SER) Station. Dentists, etc. RED as map. Between the Wesleyan Chapel and Circus St are a few shops in South St. Rather poor class, not so good as London St. One 3-st large tenement house with shops under. Poor working people. PINK-barred to PINK, RED on map.
Two courts run off N side of London St. Near to Roan St end is **Telma Court**. Narrow flagged court, three 2-st cottages on west side and one facing railway. Dirty, old curtains, refuse lying about and children playing on railway wall. DARK BLUE to LIGHT BLUE. On east side are four cottages down little entry – rather better. LIGHT BLUE.
Near the South Eastern Railway Station is **Prince of Orange Lane**. Four houses, 2-st, four rooms, on east side. Gardens at back. Behind these are four other similar cottages, facing west, reached by a narrow passage. Nicely-kept gardens in front. Fowls, flowers, dogs chained up. Labourers. LIGHT BLUE.
Through passageway under Railway Station into a row of houses facing the railway called **Straightsmouth**. Two cottages face north – comfortable. PINK. At west end are 2-st and 2½-st houses. Houses clean and well kept except a few near the Board School. Postmen, many railway men, musician, etc. PINK, PURPLE near the school.
Near the W end is **Glaisher Street**, a cul de sac with 2-st cottages. Doors open into lower rooms. Windows of some look poor. PURPLE to LIGHT BLUE.
NW from Straightsmouth into **Randall Place**. Board School takes south side. North is 2-st houses. Mixed, some coalies. Looks quiet and Mercer says rows twice a week – Saturdays and Sundays. PURPLE. The Place turns north towards Haddo Place. 2-st houses, seven on west and three on east side. Clean but poor. LIGHT BLUE.
N along **Haddo Street**. 3-st and 2-st on east and 2-st on west side. Mixed class. Two or

three families in house. Costers and men employed in the docks and on the Creek. Some just coming home, grimy, to dinner. Some windows well kept, curtains neat. PURPLE.

On W side at N end of street is **Haddo Place**. Two little 2-st cottages. Labourers. One has a fine show of calceolarias in bloom, growing in boxes on the wall. Is very proud of them. LIGHT BLUE to PURPLE.

Into Norman Rd and S along **Pearson Street**. 2-st houses, flush with pavement, six rooms. People working in neighbouring factories, engine cleaner, etc. PURPLE.

NW is **Thornham Street** (late Charlotte St). Houses like Pearson St. A few broken windows the only signs of poverty. All this part has improved. The roads have been made up. PURPLE.

S to **Claremont Street**. 2-st houses. A few houses east of Pearson St might be PINK but street becomes poorer towards the west. Hawkers, wood-choppers, etc. PURPLE to LIGHT BLUE.

S under archway is **Frederick Cottages**. Three 2-st houses, two rooms, with small gardens in front. LIGHT BLUE. The houses in Claremont St have long gardens, beans etc, growing at the back. Tablet on one house gives date "1845".

At end of Claremont St is **Bluckers Building**. Two entries, one on each side of a beer house. 2-st houses, back to back. Two rooms, let at 4/- a week. Caretaker says they average 2/6 a week – charity property and people do not pay. North side used to be very rough but is better now. LIGHT BLUE to DARK BLUE. South side is still rough and is DARK BLUE. Had several cases here.

S along **Cottage Place** (Claremont Place on map). Little 2-st houses. Labouring people, costers and street sellers. Carts waiting in road whilst the men are having dinner. Litter of paper in street. LIGHT BLUE. On the west side is a little court reached through archway, also known as Cottage Place. Four houses, 4-roomed. Poor class, gasworkers etc. Geese waddling about in front of houses. LIGHT BLUE to DARK BLUE.

E into **Roan Street**. On north side is Skinners' Buildings. Ten houses, two rooms, one up and one down. Small gardens in front. 4/6 a week. "Quite enough for these little hovels" said a woman who had been there 2½ years. One house is well kept, children look well fed. Two DARK BLUE houses. LIGHT BLUE. Roan St is wide. A good breeze blowing. 2½-st and 2-st houses to Haddo St. Street sellers, go out with barrows, don't look very poor. LIGHT BLUE. East of Haddo St to the bend of street the houses are old, 3-st. LIGHT BLUE on north. On south side is a lodging house and some houses let in furnished rooms. DARK BLUE in character. East of the bend to London St the houses improve. St Paul's Mission on south side. LIGHT BLUE to PURPLE.

On S side of Roan St, near Haddo St, is **Roan Place**. Two rooms and scullery. Small gardens in front. Windows broken and stopped with paper. DARK BLUE to LIGHT BLUE.

Nearly opposite Roan Place on N side is **St James' Place**. Narrow entry with 3-st houses. Three rooms, one above the other, facing west. Long gardens in front with wash-houses. One garden is well kept, pigeon etc. The others have palings broken and gone. Bricklayers, labourers, street sellers. Women wash and support the men. Eight other houses exactly similar back these and face east but have smaller gardens also numbered in the Place. Both rows are DARK BLUE.

Further E is another entry, **Norris' Buildings**. Four 2-st houses, four rooms, 6/6 a week. LIGHT BLUE to DARK BLUE.

Still further E is another entry, looks like entrance to stables, called **St Alphege Cottages**. Four cottages back to back to four others. Two rooms in each, 3/- a week. One rough man at home and another working as a tailor in one of the wash-houses. LIGHT BLUE to DARK BLUE.

On the S side of the street opposite Norris' Buildings is **another Court** (no name). Three houses facing west. Well-kept little gardens in front, hanging flower pots. Three WCs and one water tap. LIGHT BLUE.

Near the corner of Straightsmouth is a row of cottages running W called **Halford Row**. 2-st with little gardens in front. LIGHT BLUE.

W into **Straightsmouth** (late Gale St). This is the portion between Randall Place and Roan St and has only been recently added to Straightsmouth. Old 3-st houses on south side. On north new houses and a few shops, bakers and three others. Poor. North side is better than south. South LIGHT BLUE and north PURPLE.

This completed the day's walk.

Started on the following day at the SE Railway Station in Greenwich Road.

Greenwich Road (north side). From the Railway Station going west are some old-fashioned 3-st houses, covered with creepers. Behind these is Lovibonds's brewery and the partners live in these houses. Beyond these to Norman Rd is a terrace of 3-st plus basement houses with a few shops at corner. PINK-barred to RED. West of Norman Rd are a few shops, the public house being the only modern building. Then private houses, 2-st and attic in roof. Some are used for business premises. Some of these houses look poor: working people, tailor, dressmaker etc. Some of these houses are to be absorbed by Merryweather's Engineworks which now occupy large premises facing Devonshire Rd. Beyond these works are the tram stables and some shops. PINK to PINK-barred. On map the whole of Greenwich Rd is marked PURPLE.

N out of Greenwich Rd. Just W of Norman Rd is **Capella Place**. 2-roomed houses with scullery behind. Rent 7/-. Dirty windows, patched with paper. Very poor class, some come from Hale St, Deptford. DARK BLUE.

N along **Norman Road**. Near Greenwich Rd are 2-st houses. Doors open into rooms. People about 21/-, carmen etc. Windows look poor. PURPLE to LIGHT BLUE. Open ground west is taken by the waterworks. Just through the railway arch on the west is the entrance to Phoenix Wharf (Eastwood's Lime and Cement Works).

On the N side are two cottages called **Lydia's Cottages**. 2-st. Poor. Small white blinds. LIGHT BLUE.

In **Norman Road** just north of the railway are two rows of 2-st houses facing each other. Merryweather's, brewers and cement workers. Some poor and none look really comfortable. PURPLE. Proceeding north a succession of wharves are passed with an occasional house until near the corner of Thornham St. Men are sitting on the footpath or standing about waiting for work at gasworks or wharves. Houses are 2-st like Thornham St but better kept. Lightermen and others comfortable and a few poor. PURPLE to PINK.

E into **Lamb Lane**. On south side is Drysdale Buildings. 2-st tenement. Separate doors for ground floor and stairs leading to two tenements above. Built 1895. Narrow curtains, blinds drawn. Very poor. Children playing in front – one little thing covered with sores. DARK BLUE. On opposite side of the Lane facing Bardsley St is a block of buildings, Fawn Buildings. 3-st, built in the back premises of the Beehive public house in Bridge St and a back way from the pub passes through (or by) the building. Urinal for the public house is in this passage – no door and full of filth. A most disgusting place and dangerous to health. People are very poor, children dirty, mother swearing at children. DARK BLUE.

S along **Bardsley Street** (late York St). Shops and cottages, 2-st. One old wooden cottage standing alone. Tablet on east side gives date "1810". Look poor. LIGHT BLUE to PURPLE. On west side of street is entry to two cottages, now closed, dilapidated.

On the E side approached by archways from street are **Sexton's Buildings**. Two sets of four cottages, back to back. Two rooms, 4/- a week. Wash-houses in front, cemented courtyards. Women washing and singing, children ragged and dirty, one child in its night-shirt (10.40am). Another three year old is sent with a sister to get beer but objects to be accompanied. Goes alone and presently returns from the Beehive with a pint of porter in a can. DARK BLUE.

S into **Bell Street**. On south side houses are 2-st plus basement kitchen with grating over windows. On north side near Haddo St are 2-st houses with raised footway. East of Bardsley St the cottages have two floors and basement. Here the windows are well kept, sills clean and an air of comfort. PINK. Remainder of street is PURPLE. People are gasworkers and barge labourers.

On the N side of the street near Bardsley St is **Mary Ann Place**. Four 3-st houses with short garden in front. Only three rooms, one above the other. Row of little wash-houses at end and four WCs. Look comfortable – plenty of furniture in the rooms, mirrors. Family in each. PINK to PURPLE.

On S side near Haddo St is **Clyde Place**. Five 2-roomed houses with underground cellars used as kitchens. LIGHT BLUE.

Back and E along **Lamb Lane**. 2-st cottages. Those on south side have basement scullery. Other side is called Providence Place. Men work on barges or in gas works. Back way to Lord Hood pub here also. LIGHT BLUE.

Near Bridge St on E side of the Lane is **Matilda Cottages**. 2-st modern houses. Clean. Stablemen etc. PURPLE.

At the **Lamb Lane** entrance to the Churchyard – now laid out as a recreation ground – are a couple of cottages with outhouses and greenhouses. They are for the use of the keeper of the ground, who lets them and lives in London St tending the gardens. These are quite a picture – masses of nasturtiums, sweet william, calceolarias, dahlias, quite an old-fashioned garden. People living in these cottages are comfortable and should be PINK.

Across churchyard to **Church Passage**. On right near Roan St are three 3-st shops and two 2-st wooden shops. Poor class, broken windows, two families in one house. PURPLE to LIGHT BLUE. Nearer Church St and facing the church are six houses, 2-st with basement forecourt. Windows well kept with flowers etc. PURPLE. At corner of Church St are three 3-st houses, let in rooms. Windows closely curtained with torn cutains. DARK BLUE.

N into Church St. Immediately round the corner on W is **Richardson's Place**. At the entrance is a 3-st house kept by a "chimney cleaner". House well kept, flowers etc. Beyond this are 11 houses, 2-st, two rooms, in courtyard with wash-houses and six WCs near entrance. Everything filthy. Rent 4/6 a week and have to buy key for WC. Three navvies and gas stokers. DARK BLUE. Some girls (about 12 years of age) were playing "school" in the court. It was a singing lesson. Before they noticed us, we were able to hear them sing two pieces – a regio melody and "The Old Folks At Home". They had good voices and sang the pieces well both as to tune and time. The only bright thing about the place, it was a tribute to the value of our Board Schools.

A little further N is a very narrow passage known as **Pennell's Court**, closed by a gate. Entering this alley and after passing the backs of the Church St premises it widens out and on the south are four 3-st wooden houses, each with a scullery in the basement. Houses contain three rooms, one above the other and let at 5/-. Children are better kept and women are cleaner than in the next court. LIGHT BLUE.

Church Street. West side to Bridge St is good shops. 2-st and 3-st, some modern and others old houses. PINK-barred to RED.

W along **Bridge Street**. Shops near Church St then on north side 2-st cottages to Welland St. Some poor opposite Lamb Lane. South side is 3-st houses. Two and three families.

PURPLE in character. Coalies etc. Plenty of money but spend it as they get it and homes are poor. West of Norman Rd are 2-st houses to Bridge. Comfortable working people. PINK. Also on north between Norway St and Horseferry Rd are 2-st houses with gardens in front. One family. Mechanics and others. PINK. Other parts of street are PURPLE.

N into **Norway Street**. Side by the Creek is large coal wharves and two 3-st houses. Look comfortable, PINK. East side is 2-st houses, some with bays, two families. About 30/- people. PINK to PURPLE. At north east corner of street is entrance to a court behind east side. Four 2-roomed houses. Rather poor. PURPLE to LIGHT BLUE.

E into **Thames Street**. West end is entrance to coal wharves and gas works. 2-st houses flush with pavement. Looks poor. LIGHT BLUE to PURPLE.

Two courts off **S** side of this part of the street are: **Lakes' Cottages** (near Norway St). Three 2-st cottages reached through archway. Lady visitor was on her rounds as we entered the court. Rents 6/- (four rooms and wash-house). Have been raised from 5/6 – 6d added two years ago. One family in each but each has a lodger. Nearer Horseferry Rd is **Burlington Buildings**. Four 4-roomed cottages with paved courtway in front. Entered by a narrow passage. Look clean. Both courts are LIGHT BLUE as sheet.

On **N** side near Horseferry Rd is **Bishops Cottages**. Two 3-st houses and two 2-st houses. Labouring people. LIGHT BLUE.

N by **Bishops Buildings** (dated 1825). 2-st houses with basements, facing wharf on west. One double-fronted house. Used to be very rough but people have gone. One man works in the meat market, some widows charring. LIGHT BLUE. Passing under archway at end a narrow entry leading to Horseferry Rd is reached. A house over arch is DARK BLUE. Immediately south is a court with three houses facing north. 3-st. Water and wash-houses in front. LIGHT BLUE.

S along **Horseferry Road**. 2-st houses, five and six rooms. East side poorer than west. Some with half-basement. LIGHT BLUE to PURPLE to Thames St. South of Thames St the houses are better and people look comfortable. Lightermen etc. PINK. A court runs at back of west side of this part of the street. Eight 2-st houses, four rooms, small forecourts with WCs. Poor working people. DARK BLUE.

E into **Little Thames Street**. 2-st houses flush with footway. West end is better than east. Ranging from PINK to LIGHT BLUE. Three barge owners live here. Used to be rough but now better than Thames St. Houses are well kept. Street is narrow. PURPLE.

S side of street is taken by St Peter's Church and Schools and **Nelson Buildings**, 5-st tenement dwelling facing on Bridge St. Belongs to the Improved Industrial Dwellings Co. All look comfortable. Buildings are bright and airy, painted pink and green. Many of the men work on barges. PINK.

Two entries on **N** side of Litttle Thames St lead to **Sarah's Buildings** (built 1821). Three groups of 2-st cottages – three, two and two respectively. Broken windows. Families in single rooms. DARK BLUE.

At **E** is **Welland Street** (Cross St on map). Four 2-st cottages on east and a new 2-st tenement house on west. Working people. LIGHT BLUE.

N into Thames St. On **S** side, **E** of Welland St, is **Towsands' Cottages**. Small court with three 2-st houses, two rooms each,. Mess of all kinds in court. Woman has been here seven years, rent of 3/- a week, raised 6d a week two years ago. Agents Blake & Dennatt. DARK BLUE.

On **N** side nearly opposite is **Rockfield Street**. A cul de sac of 2-st 4-roomed houses. Front doors shut. Clothes drying and airing in street. Poor class. LIGHT BLUE.

Further **W** is **Coltman Street**. South end is 2-st houses (1837). Two families in each. Not very poor. PURPLE. Houses to north are larger and poorer. Poor labouring people. LIGHT BLUE. Entrance to **Coltman Place** on E side. Four 2-st houses. Two rooms, scullery and WC in front. LIGHT BLUE.

Back to back with these and with entrance further N is **Coltman Buildings**. Four houses and two others facing them. Cemented fronts, broken windows. Very poor. Woman washing clothes in the yard. Lot of dirty children playing with a swing fixed in the doorway of the WC. Rents 3/- and 3/6. DARK BLUE.

Out of N side of Thames St, W of Coltman St is **Sherry Court**. Four houses, two rooms and scullery. Have been rebuilt recently. 5/3 and 6/- a week. LIGHT BLUE to DARK BLUE. Further west is another court with one house. LIGHT BLUE.

Nearer Horseferry Rd is **Looney Court**. Five 2-st houses and two facing them. Small lobbies in front. LIGHT BLUE.

On S side of street nearly opposite this court is entry to **Heath's Cottages**, a small yard with one new and two old cottages. LIGHT BLUE.

Nearer Horseferry Rd on S side is **Devonport Place**. Five 2-st houses facing east. Hawkers and others poor. Several hutches of fine rabbits. DARK BLUE. One house a little better than the rest.

Thames Street (Church St to Horseferry St) itself is 2-st houses with poor white curtains. Watermen and people employed in the coal wharves. A large number of men turn into these houses for dinner at one o'clock, nearly all grimy. Most of these houses have good back gardens, though here and there a cottage is built at the back. LIGHT BLUE.

N along Horseferry Rd is **Wood Wharf**. Houses on south side, wharves on north. 2-st houses, "as poor as you like". Pedlars, labourers, out of work half the year. Young woman with baby at front door, girls singing on door step. Houses are old and look dull and dirty. DARK BLUE. Near Coltman St we came to the Sun Public House. Women standing in the bar and baby crawling on floor of bar. Large hay wharf here, Noakes, also Allens Wharf. East of Coltman St are some 3-st houses. Poor labouring people but not worse than LIGHT BLUE.

Walk 68

B368

Thursday 3rd August 1899.
George Arkell with Detective Mercer.

Started from St Alphege's Church.
N up Church St. On the east side is **Fryers' Court**. Very narrow entry, only about 2½ ft across. Four 2-st houses with cellar below. Let at 5/- a week, raised from 4/- about three months ago. Poor working people. Woman scolding children, broken windows, only one water tap. DARK BLUE.

Church Street. 3-st shops, modern to Clarence St. North of Clarence St are old 3-st shops. Poor class of trade, men go to work. A few private houses. The block of buildings near the Thames is the well-known Ship. People stay there in the summer and local balls are held there in winter. RED to Clarence St, PURPLE to PINK on north. On east side of Church St, north of Clarence St is a narrow entry to a Yard. One wooden 2-st cottage on south side and entrance to 3-st tenement house. LIGHT BLUE.

S along **King William Street**. 3-st and basement. Good houses. Most keep a servant. Several "apartments" to let. PINK-barred to RED.

W into **Clarence Street**. 3-st shops. Good class. Shopkeepers live over. On north side is

Greenwich Church Street

a terrace of 3-st houses. A doctor in one but others have two families – not so good as south side. PINK on north and PINK-barred on south side.

S into Greenwich Market. Central part is used for stalls and a stand for market carts. The sides are occupied by tradesmen, mostly in the greengrocery line, but there are other shops – bootmaker, milk vendor, eating houses. Shopkeepers live over. RED to PINK-barred.

W into West Avenue, a narrow passage to Church St. Small 3-st shops. Poor class shops but people are comfortable. PINK. On north side is Entry leading to three 2-st cottages facing north. Paved court. Woman sitting on doorstep with baby. Tanner's workshop facing houses. LIGHT BLUE.

S to **Turnpin Lane** which leads across south end of market to King William St. Shops (two are to let): cutler, hosier, butcher and some refreshment houses. One man has several shops. PINK-barred. The market and adjoining property belong to the Greenwich Hospital Estates.

S to **Nelson Street**. 3-st shops. Houses all alike. Good class trade, main street. RED.

Back to **King William Street**. Clarence St to Nelson St is terrace of 3-st houses with cement fronts – cracked and look bad. Lodging house keepers mainly. PINK-barred. South of Nelson St the houses are nearly all occupied by hotel and eating-house keepers who cater for visitors to the Park. Every class is provided for and the houses rise in the attractiveness of their invitations – "Tea and roll and butter 5d"; "Coffee and roll and butter 4d"; "Tea, shrimps and cake 6d"; "Cut from joint and two vegetables 9d"; "Tea for large parties 4d per head" are some of the notices. Some of the houses have "tea gardens" at back. PINK-barred.

W into **Nevada Street** (Silver St on map). 3-st shops on north side. Large 4-st houses on north and the Parthenon Theatre of Varieties. Latter has been rebuilt and takes half the street. All are refreshment houses. One house (Park Hotel) advertises dancing on Mondays and Tuesdays and holidays, charge 6d. PINK to PINK-barred.

N up **Crooms Hill** (to King George St). Good old red-tiled houses. 4-st plus basement. Professional people: doctors, solicitors, architects, veterinary surgeon. Several have their plates on doors. Houses face Park. All keep two or more servants. RED.

W into **The Circus**. 3-st plus basement. Good class families as a rule, keeping two servants. RED. North side is called Gloucester Place. Terrace houses, 3½-st. Slightly better than The Circus. Garden in centre is well laid out, trees, seats and tennis courts. RED to YELLOW.

Along Crooms Hill to **Crooms Hill Grove** (built 1838). South side is 3½-st double-fronted houses. North side is 2½-st. Two or three families in some, others are boarding houses, all windows alike. Comfortable working people. Quiet retired place. Trees on sidewalk. PINK.

W along **King George Street**. 2-st houses, some with basement. Creepers in front and plants in windows. A few shops. Comfortable working people: carriage builder, decorator, bricklayer, milliner. Many keep the house. PINK. Near Point Hill the houses (2½-st) are slightly poorer. PINK to PURPLE.

On **S** side of street is **Georgette Place**. 2-st and 3-st houses on east side. Comfortable working people. PINK. Large house at end with nice garden and double-fronted house on west side. PINK-barred.

Further **W** is **Luton Place**. Large hall belonging to the Brethren at the corner. 2-st houses, flush with pavement on east and with small forecourt on west side. Look comfortable. PINK.

On **N** side of street is **Royal Place**. East side 3-st and basement, west side 2-st. Working people, some windows look poor. PURPLE to PINK.

On the **W** side is entry to **Rentarn Cottages**, leading through into King George St. Five 2-st houses. Narrow court paved with cobble stones. Honeysuckle growing on houses. LIGHT BLUE.

Back to **Crooms Hill**. Just south of King George St is an entry leading to an old nursery, now being cleared for Electric Light Works. Only one PINK house left. Remainder of Crooms Hill is large detached houses. Ursuline Convent and Roman Catholic Church. Might be YELLOW, RED safer.

Further **S** is **Chesterfield Walk** with a few large mansions – Lord Wolseley and others. YELLOW. Facing these on the Point are a few large detached houses. Also YELLOW in character. Here we are standing on one of the highest points of Blackheath and command a magnificent view of London with Deptford in the foreground.

Immediately below is **Hyde Vale** (Conduit Vale on map). These houses facing the Heath

are good class, a few modern, others the old red-tiled variety. All keep servants. RED. Going towards King George St we come to a row of 2-st cottages with long front gardens. PINK.
Glenmohr Terrace is large houses, 4-st and basement. RED.
Remainder of **Hyde Vale** is 3-st, some semi-detached. Gardens in front. Venetian blinds. A few let apartments but most have only one family, except on west near King George St, where working people have got in – two families. PINK-barred to RED.
W into **Diamond Terrace**. Large semi-detached houses, 3-st and basement. Looks like a narrow country lane. RED. One PINK house at entrance and near Point Hill are a few cottages and stables, also PINK.
Point Hill. Houses on west side only north of Maidenstone Hill. 2-st and 3-st old houses with windows in the red-tiled roofs. Chimney cleaner and other working people. Some shops near Blissett Hill. PINK.
W into **Darnall Place**. Five 2-st houses facing north. Paved court. LIGHT BLUE to PURPLE.
S into **Renbold Place** (Grove Place on map). Blissett St Mission Room at corner. 2½-st houses on west. Doors open on footway. Small shop and working people. On east side houses are smaller and older with very narrow fronts. PURPLE to LIGHT BLUE on east side.
E into **Allas Street**. 2-st little cottages. Old and poor looking. Bricklayers' labourers etc. Back way to Duke of Kent at end. LIGHT BLUE. At end of north side is a Court with five houses, 10 ft frontages. Same class as street. LIGHT BLUE.
Passage leads into **John Street**. East of Renbold Place houses are like Allas St. LIGHT BLUE. Bootmaker etc.
W of Renbold Place street is continued as **Winforton Street**. 2-st houses, some with bay windows. Larger and taller houses than those to eastward. PURPLE.
This completed the day's walk.

Continuing on Friday 4th August 1899.
Started this morning from Blackheath Hill Railway Station.
Along **South Street** (to Blissett Hill). 3-st shops and a few 2-st houses, some semi-detached. Shops are poorer as the cross-roads are left. PINK-barred.
On NW side is narrow entry leading to two cottages, **Laurel Cottages**. 2-st. Old. Poor class. LIGHT BLUE.
SE along **Grove Street**. 2-st cottages. Labouring people. PURPLE.
On E side is **Brigade Place** (Daris Place on map). Narrow paved roadway. 2-st cottages with doors opening on staircase. Cul de sac. Poor class. LIGHT BLUE. Opposite side is taken by the Fire Station, which fronts on Grove St. Large 3-st building. Firemen live on upper floors.
Plumbridge Street. Twenty-five 2-st houses, flush with pavement. A few new cottages. Builder, mangler, turncock. Decent working people. PURPLE, PINK on map.
S to **Orchard Street** (now Lindsell St). Old cottages (built 1812) on south side, a few flush with pavement, others have front gardens with trees. Some are nicely kept. 2-st and 3-st. On north side are 2-st new cottages, back on railway. Poor working class. PURPLE to LIGHT BLUE.
E up **Dutton St** (Trinity St on map). Narrow steep street. On north side are 2-st cottages. Creepers on front. Beer houses. On south side is a row of 3-roomed cottages occupied by costers and street sellers. Barrow laden with salt standing outside one and a lad sawing it into pieces for sale. Vacant ground beyond these cottages. LIGHT BLUE to this point.
N up **Trinity Grove**. Steep slope, narrow roadway. 2-st cottages, 12 ft frontage. Children playing on shady side of street. Labouring people. LIGHT BLUE.
N into **Dutton Street** (which turns corner and is continued to include the Cottage Place of map). This part is better than near the main road. 2-st and 2½-st. Good working people:

carman, laundryman, working at Penn's, roadmen. PURPLE.

Round into **Maidenstone Hill.** South side near Dutton St is called College Place West. 2-st houses. Few are poor near lower end but most are comfortable working people. Row of 2-st houses on north side. Dressmaker, insurance agent. PURPLE to PINK. East of passage leading to the Point the houses are better (2-st). Mostly one family with lodgers. On south side near Point Hill are 2-st and 3-st houses, some new. PINK to PURPLE. On the east side of Point Hill facing Maidenstone Hill is an Entry with two cottages and stables at the end. Three poor children playing. LIGHT BLUE.

S along **Point Hill.** Four houses, 2-st and attic. Nice gardens. Plumber etc. PINK. Facing these at corner of Maidenstone Hill is the Blue Coat Girls' School, a 2-st building. Tablet in front: "To the Glory of God. This house for the board and Christian education of poor girls of the parish of Greenwich (1732)".

West Grove Terrace. 3-st and basement. All keep servants. RED.

Nightingale Lane. Good detached houses with gardens. RED to YELLOW.

At the end facing the Heath is **The Grove.** 4-st and basement. Some modern but most old style. All well-to-do, artist etc. YELLOW. This and the Paragon are the best parts of Blackheath. Across to **Gloucester Terrace.** Five houses, 4-st and basement. Gardens in front. One has very fine display of flowers in window boxes. Good class people. RED to YELLOW. Few houses at corner of Point Hill are also RED.

W down **Blackheath Hill.** Very steep. Footpaths are raised above the level of the carriage way. 3-st new houses on west side to Dartmouth Hill. Remainder is larger houses, some detached, other in terraces. Old and very varied. Towards the church the houses are smaller on the south side and some working people are found. Near the railway station are some good shops. RED near Heath, PINK-barred to RED for remainder.

S along **Lewisham Road** (to railway). Mostly 3-st shops. One double-fronted house occupied by a doctor. Shops are poorer as you go southward. PINK-barred.

W into **John Penn St.** North side is Penn's Engineering Works. South side has 2-st cottage and a couple of small shops. Labouring class. Windows poor. LIGHT BLUE.

S to **Coldbath Street** (to John St). 2-st cottages with short gardens in front. Labourers, Penn's men, some police. LIGHT BLUE to PURPLE.

Through archway on **W** to **Duncan Cottages.** 4-roomed cottages facing the pumping station. Gardens in front. LIGHT BLUE. One double-fronted house with large garden at west might be PINK.

Path leads to **John Street.** 2-st houses. Open breezy street. Houses clean. Mechanics at Penn's etc. PINK to PURPLE.

Passage at **S** leads to **South Crescent** on the west. 2-st houses facing the Ravensbourne. Good gardens at back. Comfortable working people, children look clean and healthy. Entrance to Recreation Ground by bridge across the Brook. PINK.

Back, just through railway arch on left are five cottages in **Ravensbourne Place.** 2-st, little places. Barber etc. PURPLE.

N up **Coldbath Street.** 2-st and 2½-st houses. Rather better than the part north of John St. Few shops near Albion St. PURPLE.

E up **Orchard Hill.** Steep rise toward Lewisham Rd. 2-st houses. Steady working people: policeman, bootmaker, Penn's men. At corner of Bennett St is a large house used as a working men's club and Holy Trinity Working Men's Institute. PURPLE.

N along **Bennett Street.** 2-st houses, small. Labouring people, rather rough. LIGHT BLUE.

Back along **Morden Street.** 2-st houses flush with pavement. Better than Bennett St. Mixed class, some poor. PURPLE.

Orchard Hill. The portion between the railway and Lewisham Rd is better than other part. 3-st old houses facing railway and a few modern houses on north side. Musical instrument maker, insurance agents. Gardens well kept. PINK.

Back and E up **Albion Street.** 2½-st houses. Working folk: plumber, mangler. PURPLE to Board School. Nearer Lewisham Rd is rather better, 2-st modern houses. PINK.

N into **Mount Nod Square.** 2-st houses, some with basement. Centre of Square is gardens, belonging to the houses, vegetables growing. On the west side are two entries, one leads to two cottages and a double-fronted house. Brethren hold services here, notice at entrance: "To Arlington Room". The other entry leads to four cottages, numbered in the Square. The Square has improved greatly during the past three years. People were very poor, better now. PURPLE.

Back along Lewisham Rd to **Blackheath Road.** Shops near Lewisham Rd and also at the other end. Private houses, mostly 3½-st, between. Some good class people: coroner, dentist etc. Keep servants. RED to PINK-barred.

General Remarks

In the whole of the somewhat scattered area included in these two walks, no extreme poverty is noticeable. The poorest parts are the streets in the angle by Penn's Engineering Works and a few streets south of Blissett Hill. Elsewhere the general impression is one of comfort and cleanliness. The houses are mostly old but well cared for. The best part of the district is the high ground between Crooms Hill and Blackheath Hill. It is a nice, open neighbourhood. A good breeze is obtainable, even when the lower streets are quite calm, whilst from many points, fine views of the lower land to the north are obtainable. Originally a good middle class district, the social decay has affected this part and the working class are gradually gaining possession of the better houses. The end of Hyde Vale near King George St is an example of this, whilst at the upper end boarding houses are now superseding the older families.

This walk completes the whole of the Blackheath Road Police sub division except a small portion in Lewisham which is described in Book 13AA [ie.B372].

Walk 69   B368

Wednesday 11th October 1899.
George Arkell with Detective Sergeant Hardy.

Starting from Park Row Police Station.
Facing the Hospital in **Park Row** are 3-st old houses occupied by comfortable people, most of whom keep servants. North of Old Woolwich Rd is a building used as dormitories of the College lads and a house occupied by some of the officers. RED.

E along **Crane Street.** Stable yard (entrance Park Row) takes part of south side. A few poor stablemen live above stables at end of row. LIGHT BLUE. East of stables are 2-st modern houses with two families. Comfortable working people. On north side is the Trafalgar and several old-fashioned shops and houses. Boat builder at one has a lot of property. All comfortably off. The Trafalgar trade is not very good and the owner carries on a large confectionery trade in the basement. South side PINK, north PINK-barred.

E along Highbridge. On S side is **Three Crown Court.** Three houses facing west. Small 2-st wooden-fronted cottages. Paved court. Mostly watermen. Old man sawing wood in

Crane Street, typical of the narrow alleys of Greenwich.

court. LIGHT BLUE.

Highbridge. On north (river) side are a few large houses, one used as Conservative Club. South side has a lodging house by East St, a few old houses, two shops and a tenement house at corner of Queen St. Mixed class. PURPLE.

S along **East Street**. West side is new houses like Crane St but look poorer. PURPLE to

PINK. East side is old 2-st cottages. Labouring people: "dredgermen, watermen and thieves" says Hardy. LIGHT BLUE. South of Exmouth Court (on east side) the street is better and might be PURPLE. Exmouth Court leads to a school and institute. No residents. East St south of Old Woolwich Rd has 3-st old houses, occupied by one and two-room people. All very poor except two pubs. DARK BLUE to LIGHT BLUE. East side is open ground to the Board School. Has been cleaned.

At S end near Trafalgar Rd is **Wyman's Place**. A paved court with a few small 2-st cottages, facing south. LIGHT BLUE to DARK BLUE.

N of this place is **Smith's Rents**. Several blocks of houses built on the former gardens of the street. Paved court. Few have more than one or two rooms. Mostly 2-st houses. Northern part is poorest. Four open WCs, stench is very bad. "You should visit it in the summer" said the Sergeant. "It is the poorest place we have." DARK BLUE to LIGHT BLUE.

N to **Old Woolwich Road** (to Park St). South side to East St is 3-st houses, two or three families in each. Wood merchant and two publicans. Remainder labouring people. East to Board School is cleared. Beyond the school are some 2-st houses, flush with pavement. Coalies – drink, earn good money, but it does not go into the homes. One house is DARK BLUE in character. PURPLE to East St and LIGHT BLUE to Park St. On the north side is the College Buildings and east of East St, St Mary's Institute (policeman caretaker). The cottage occupied by curate. Four poor 2-st shops, two east of Queen St. LIGHT BLUE to PURPLE.

N up **Queen Street**. Old houses, 2-st plus attic. Narrow paved street. Rough dock and riverside labourers. "Wives go out washing and the men loaf about, doing an odd day now and then." North end is better than south. LIGHT BLUE and DARK BLUE.

Queen's Court (on west side of Queen St). Four houses, 2-st plus attic. Only street door and a tiny window to staircase face the court, the front of the houses looking on the gardens. LIGHT BLUE (south side only).

N & E along **Highbridge**, a footway by the river is reached. The entrance to Norfolk College is here, a neat block of almshouses for men belonging to Greenwich. Beyond this is the back of the Tramway Stables (entrance in Old Woolwich Rd), a large public house, the Golden Anchor and a private house occupied by three families. PINK.

S into **Hoskins Street**. On the east side is Crowley's Wharf. Six 3-st houses. Two families in each and some have an additional lodger. Labouring people and a fisherman who catches shrimps at Gravesend and retails them in Greenwich. LIGHT BLUE.

S to **Collington Street** (east side of Hoskins St). Small 2-st houses flush with pavement. Labourers. Small white blinds. LIGHT BLUE.

Near opposite Collington St, out of Hoskins St, is **Alfred Place**. Five 2-st plus basement cottages on south side and five on north side including large tenement house. In one of the long front gardens a waterman keeps his boat and sails. LIGHT BLUE to DARK BLUE.

Further S is **Baxter's Cottages**. Eight 2-st houses facing east and three facing north. Two rooms, 3/6 a week. All conveniences in small front yards. Place full of mess and litter. Costers and labourers. DARK BLUE, BLACK on map.

Hoskins Street (late Bennett St). A few 3-st houses near Alfred Place and from this point houses, 2-st and 3-st, are continuous to Old Woolwich Rd. 3-st houses have five rooms, three in front and two behind. All old property. Labouring people with a few better off. LIGHT BLUE. Court on east side of Hoskins St has four 2-st houses facing north. Poor. Man making boxes in the court. LIGHT BLUE to DARK BLUE. South of Old Woolwich Rd Hoskins St is rather better. 2-st houses. Bootmaker. PURPLE.

Prospect Place (west side of Hoskins St). 3-st houses. A family in each. Engineer, bootmaker. PURPLE to PINK.

Old Woolwich Road (Park St to Hoskins St). South side is 2½-st semi-detached houses. Two families as a rule. On the north side are a few old houses near Hoskins St. The tram stables and some modern 2-st houses attached thereto. PINK, PURPLE on map.

East Greenwich waterfront.

Park St (Lower Park St on map). 3-st on west and 2-st plus basement on east. Long curtains and plants in windows. Police, tram people, etc. Two families or lodgers in each house. PINK.
Old Woolwich Road (to Marlborough St). 2-st cottages on south. One large house and several cottages on the north. LIGHT BLUE to PURPLE.
On N side is **Hampshire Cottages**. Three 4-roomed houses facing west. Sweep and two labourers. LIGHT BLUE.
Marlborough Street. South of Old Woolwich Rd (Gothic Row on map) are four 3-st shops on east, PINK, and 2-st old cottages on west, LIGHT BLUE. North of Old Woolwich Rd on west side are old 2-st and 3-st houses with front gardens as far as Chester St where the street narrows and houses open on footwalk. PURPLE. On east side Marlborough Hall, a handsome red-brick building, occupies corner of Old Woolwich Rd with two houses (PINK) attached. Some vacant land adjoins, courts at back having been cleared. Near Chester St are some 2-st cottages. Poor labouring people. LIGHT BLUE. North of Chester St are little modern 2-st houses with gardens. Mechanics and labourers. PURPLE. This part is clean and well kept. LIGHT BLUE on map.
E into **Ballast Quay**. Three 3-st houses, one a general shop. PINK.
E along **Union Wharf**. Old 3-st houses facing wharves and river. Comfortable people, mechanics and others engaged at the wharves. Harbour master house, a large detached building, is now let in flats, the office having been abolished. PINK, not coloured on map.
Along **Pelton Road**, which is entrance to wharves only here to Newcastle St. South side is 2-st houses, flush with pavement. LIGHT BLUE as map. On north side the houses are modern 2-st. People look better off. Dairyman and men engaged at the wharves. PURPLE, not coloured on map.
S into **Gibson Street**. 2-st houses occupied by poor labouring class. South end of street is not made up and some 3-st houses for family on each floor are built. LIGHT BLUE, PURPLE on map.
S to **Orlop Street** (Marlborough St to King William Lane). A row of modern houses facing south. 2-st plus basement. Venetian blinds, many kept down. Very poor class, one- or two-room people. Labourers who don't work, wives do washing. "They live on fried fish and beer." DARK BLUE, not on map.
King William Lane. Only a rag shop on west side. Man is poor but works hard. LIGHT BLUE.
Old Woolwich Road (Trafalgar Rd to Marlborough St). On north side is a row of 2-st houses. Most of the people keep the house (Hardy lives in one of them). From Northumberland St to Marlborough St the houses are new. Two floors plus attic. Better class people, travellers etc. A few servants here and there. PINK to PINK-barred. The south side is 3-st and 2-st houses. Nearly all are old except a row near Trafalgar Rd. PINK, PURPLE on map.
N up **Braddyll Street**. 2-st houses, new near Old Woolwich Rd. Many police and mechanics. Two families as a rule. New houses, six rooms; others are four rooms plus wash-house. PINK to PURPLE, PURPLE and uncoloured on map
Chester Street (to Pelton Rd). 2-st, five or six rooms, flush with pavement. Mostly two families. Labourers and mechanics. PURPLE, LIGHT BLUE on map.
S into **Caradoc Street**. 2-st, three and four rooms, very small. Street littered. Homes poor. LIGHT BLUE, PURPLE on map.
To W is **Throley Place**. Two old houses on north side, LIGHT BLUE, and two new houses on south, PINK. Like Braddyll St.
S along **Wellington Place** (Marlborough Place on map). East side old 2-st cottages, about three rooms. One family. Long gardens at back. West side is new, 2-st, five rooms. Working people. PURPLE on west to LIGHT BLUE on east side. Hardy thinks west side is nearly as

good as Braddyll St. Had a case in one of them recently. A man took a lodging there and went off with £10 worth of jewellery. Hardy was surprised to find that the man had missed the greater part and the people had about £40 of jewellery in the house.

N up **Northumberland Street**. Greater part of west side is the gardens of Marlborough Place. A few new houses at each end. On east side are 2-st houses. Decent people, mostly keep the houses. Mechanics, labourers and men in the tram service. PURPLE to PINK.

Across Pelton Rd to **Wesslington Street**. 2-st, four rooms. A cul de sac. Mostly a single family. Some respectable people: watermen. Some poor: broken windows. PURPLE, LIGHT BLUE on map.

Pelton Road (west of Christchurch St). 2-st houses with four or five rooms on north and single families. Six rooms and two families on the south side. Clean and comfortable on north side and not so well kept on the south, probably poorer. Houses are poorer north of Chester St. PURPLE to PINK. PINK on south between Chester St and Christchurch St. PURPLE on map.

N along **Lower Chester Street**. 2-st houses. Carmen and others, mixed class. PURPLE. Beyond Paddock Place, the street becomes poorer. 2-st cottages occupied by labourers. A few scattered houses connected with the works. District surveyor lives in one. LIGHT BLUE and PINK.

W into **Paddock Place**. Five 2-st houses facing north. Look comfortable. Work in wharves or telegraph works. PINK.

Across fields at end of Chester St boys are playing football into **Bellot Street**. Four rooms and wash-houses. Poor labouring class. DARK BLUE near the fields but better towards south. Few mechanics but most are labourers. LIGHT BLUE to DARK BLUE.

W to **Derwent Street**. 2-st cottages open on footway. Labouring people, a few may be skilled. South side poorer than the north. LIGHT BLUE to PURPLE, LIGHT BLUE on map.

Christchurch Street. North of Pelton Rd is 2-st houses. People in telegraph works, barge builder, carpenter, etc. Better than Bellot St. LIGHT BLUE to PURPLE, PINK on map. South of Pelton Rd the east side is 3½-st semi-detached houses occupied by two families. West is 2-st with six rooms and a second family or lodger. All are comfortable and those on east very comfortable. Servants in two houses near the main road. Surgeon. PINK to PINK-barred.

[Continued from above in Notebook B371]

N from Trafalgar Rd up **Whitworth Street**. 4-roomed houses. Mostly kept by one family. Men work at telegraph works and factories. Better than Northumberland St. PURPLE to PINK. In Pelton Rd facing Whitworth St is **Lambton Terrace**. 3-st houses. Two families. All comfortable. PINK. On south side to Colomb St are small 2-st houses. PURPLE as map.

S along **Colomb Street**. 2-st houses like Whitworth St. PURPLE to PINK, PURPLE on map.

General Remarks

The area covered includes the greater part of old East Greenwich. West of Marlborough St the streets are narrow, the houses old and most of the people distinctly poor. East of Marlborough St is a mixture of old and modern houses. The streets are more regular and most of the houses have a patch of garden and some have a long strip. The bulk of the people are dependant upon the river or the many factories forming the East Greenwich peninsula. A considerable number of train men are also resident here, the Woolwich and the LCC tramway systems having their terminal near Christ Church.

Walk 70

B371

Thursday 12th October 1899.
George Arkell with Detective Sergeant Hardy.

Starting from the corner of Blackwall Lane and Pelton Road (Tyler St on map)
W up Pelton Road. A few 4- or 5-roomed houses on each side. One family as a rule. Men
employed at cable works. Look comfortable. RC Church and Presbytery on east side. PINK
to PURPLE.
Along **Commerell Street** (Hatley St on map). 2-st, six rooms. Look decent now (10 am).
Women beating mats and cleaning steps. Last night the people were in the street and it looked
as Hardy says it is – rough. Two families as a rule. Men at gas works or cable works. A few
shops near Blackwall Lane. PURPLE, not coloured on map.
Conley Street. Houses and people similar to Commerell St. Slightly poorer at north end,
windows broken and patched. PURPLE to LIGHT BLUE, PURPLE on map.
N into **Blackwall Lane** (late Marsh Lane). West side has been cleared to Commerell St.
Was very poor. East side to this point is small 4-roomed cottages. Coalies, carmen and
labouring people. LIGHT BLUE. A few houses are DARK BLUE as map makes all. North of
this the houses are newer. As far as Davern St is 2-st shops, six rooms. Most are kept by
women, the husband going to work. PINK. North of Davern St also 2-st, 6-roomed houses.
Poor working class, little white blinds, rather rough. LIGHT BLUE to PURPLE. North of this
a small hall used by the Salvation Army and a 3-st block of Buildings belonging to the LCC
called West View Cottages. The ends of the block are tenement dwellings with cottages
between containing four rooms and an attic and letting for 7/6 a week. All comfortable
working people. PINK, not on map. These cottages are really pretty and well built, a
refreshing contrast to the jerry-built rubbish adjoining them.
N into **Azof Street**. On the north side is Rothbury Hall, a very pretty Congregational
Mission Church, red brick with pinnacles. South side is 2-st houses with bay windows. Two
families. Windows are well kept and sheet doors shut. Houses on north side have a narrower
frontage and bay to ground floor window only. Two or three families as a rule. A slow, rough
-looking woman was sweeping the doorstep. Until she came here a short time ago (said Hardy)
she had lived in a tent. The family gained a living by collecting tin from the rubbish shoots and
burning them to obtain the solder, which they sold. North side is LIGHT BLUE to DARK BLUE,
south side is PURPLE. The street is being extended westward, the new houses being like those
on the south side. They are advertised to let in floors: ground floor 7/6 and first floor 8/6 (three
rooms and scullery). Roadway and footwalks are not made up and the centre is a sea of mud,
six to seven inches deep. What it is like in wet weather is difficult to imagine.
N into **Christchurch Street**. A few 2-st houses on west side belonging to a barge builder
who has a yard there. Look comfortable. PINK. At the north end of this street is the entrance
to the Telegraph Construction & Maintenance Company's works.
E into **Mauritius Road**. This road is not made up but is in rather better condition than
Azof St. A footway has been made on the north side. 2-st, 6-roomed houses. Small
forecourts on north side. Men working at Maudsley's, the telegraph works. Mixed. Two
families. PURPLE with strong tendency to LIGHT BLUE on south side.
N along **Blackwall Lane**, now the main road to the Blackwall Tunnel. Market gardens
on both sides, while on the west by the river are seen the shafts of the factories on the bank.
No dwellings until near Morden Wharf Rd when a group of 50 houses belonging to the LCC

is reached – Idenden Cottages. 2-st and attic in roof. Built on three sides of an open space. Look comfortable. Men employed at wood-paving works and earn about 30/-. PINK.

Morden Wharf Rd is now called Sea Witch Lane. On the S is Warwick Place. Six tenement cottages with little gardens in front. Poor. Probably cement workers. Two old houses on east side are closed. LIGHT BLUE.

N of the Lane is Sidmouth Place. Nine 2-st houses. Gardens in front better than Warwick Place. PURPLE.

Along the narrow Sea Witch Lane through clouds of dust which obscure the view 50 yards ahead and the most unpleasant fumes, turning sharply to left and passing under a network of pipes, one is thankful to reach the river bank and breathe the fresh air once more. Here facing the river is the Sea Witch with an erstwhile garden in front, booth and benches sloping down to the river. The garden, however, has been disused for some time and the whole place is covered with dirt and cement dust. Further south about 50 yards is a house occupied by a foreman. River view. Servant cleaning windows. RED. Back along the passage is a house at the north corner of Sea Witch Lane. PINK. Continuing northward we come out on the river bank again. Just beyond Maudsley's Yard are two houses facing south, known as Maudsley's Cottages and occupied by foremen. PINK.

Continuing north round the horseshoe the works of the Greenwich Inlaid Linoleum Company are reached (Steel and Iron works on map). Large houses here occupied by the manager. RED. Continuing along the path which runs along the top of the river embankment until the Asbestos Works are reached (Oil Coke factory on map). Open fields are reached and crossed eastward to main road. On the east side is an open square with buildings on three sides. On the N is Blakeley Cottages. Seventeen houses, 2-st plus attic. Belong to Gas Company and occupied by their work people. One family in each. Comfortable. Foremen. PINK. The east side is the Livesey Mission Hall where a LCM works.

On the S side is Blakeley Buildings. 4-st tenement block with viou gallery in front to each floor. Much poorer than the cottages belonging to the Gas Co. PURPLE. The ground to the east and some distance north and south is occupied by the South Metropolitan Gas Co, their south boundary being only a short distance north of Boord St.

Back to main road, Blackwall Lane. On the west side are two houses on the Asbestos Company's works occupied by foremen. PINK.

S to Ordnance Road. Part of west side, including the Ordnance Arms, has gone for the Tunnel. On the east side is Alpha Place. 2-st cottages. Mostly labourers and wood paving yard. One house has broken windows mended with paper. LIGHT BLUE to PURPLE. Houses on the west side are poor. Labouring men. LIGHT BLUE, PURPLE on map.

W into Teddington Place. 2-st houses on south side with separate entrance for each floor. Four narrow street doors next to each other. Poor. LIGHT BLUE, PURPLE on map. Coming out into the main road we are at the Tunnel entrance. On the west side is a large pub and a small house adjoining it.

Going N on the west side of the Tunnel, Wood Paving Cottages are reached. Nine 2-st cottages with wash-house and other conveniences in front. Men work in the wood paving works. Most would earn about 30/- a week but homes do not look up to this standard. PINK to PURPLE.

S past entrance to the Tunnel – engineer lives in rooms in the archway – to Wheatman Street. Fifteen 2-st houses. Road not made up. All working people. PURPLE.

S along Sigismund Street. West side only, 2-st houses with 13 ft frontages. Narrow street. Roadway not made up. Woman asks when we are going to give them a pathway. Poor labouring class. LIGHT BLUE.

The opening of the Blackwall Tunnel.

N up **Blackwall Lane**. Large coffee tavern on corner of Boord St and then 2½-st houses occupied by poor working people to corner of Greenfell St. North of that 3-st shops and pub to South Metropolitan Gas Company Works. Two families live in the shops. PINK. Houses south of Greenfell St might be PURPLE.

E into **Greenfell Street**. Six houses on south side. Two floors, eight rooms, two families. All windows have long curtains and look comfortable. PINK. The street is overshadowed by a huge gasometer.

Boord Street. St Andrew's iron church is the only building on the south side. On the north side are fifteen 2-st houses built for two families. PURPLE to PINK.

Across the fields to **Marsh Lane**. All east end is Ceylon Place (dated 1801). 2-st houses facing north. On south are two little cubicles leading to nine back-to-back cottages (Ceylon Cottages). These, like the backs of the houses in the Lane, are several feet below the level of the roadway. Further east the houses (24) are called River Terrace. Working people. PURPLE to LIGHT BLUE. At the river end of Marsh Lane is a large house formerly occupied by Mr Hibb, now a caretaker is there. On the north side of the Lane facing the houses are the Electric Light Company works. The Lane terminates in a landing stage (Bugsby's Hole), opposite which Cory's coal derricks are moored.

Back along Marsh Lane. It is just one o'clock and we meet a succession of children – some 40 or 50 – taking dinners to the gas works and other places. Some carry two dinners. After leaving Ceylon Place the Lane crosses open fields, some planted with rhubarb and crossed at intervals with ditches about 3 ft across. Near Blackwall Lane is a large horse slaughterer's place with a dwelling house occupied by the foreman. PINK. Near this is a fireworks factory, with its little huts studded about the field. Away in the fields is a piggery with a tumble-down cottage, the last of the dwellings on the Marsh.

Picking rhubarb in Marsh Lane.

Notes on the District
    The chief interest of this East Greenwich promontory is its numerous manufactories fringing the River bank. These must provide employment for at least 3,000 or 4,000 men, probably more. The dwellings are subsidiary to the works. Some, as Blakeley Cottages, are erected by employers for their work people.
    The northern part is almost entirely absorbed by works, the only large pieces of open ground now available being between Boord St and Tunnel Avenue. This track is mainly market gardens, rhubarb etc. It is below the level of the roads and crossed in various directions by ditches. The most popular diversion of the boys and girls appears to be jumping across, and occasionally into, these channels. Toward the south the land is suited for dwelling houses and I was rather surprised that with the exception of Azof St no houses were being erected. Farther north the ground is lower and marshy and could not be used unless artificially raised. The inhabitants, excepting a few managers and publicans, are all working men and nearly all would find their employment in one or other of the factories or at the River side.

Walk 71   B371

Friday 13th October 1899.
George Arkell with Detective Sergeant Hardy.

Starting from corner of Trafalgar Road.
S down Park Row. Row of 3-st houses with bay windows on east side. All well kept and comfortable. Two families in some, others let apartments. Saw one servant. Police live here. Hardy regards it as like the north end. To me it is distinctly less well-to-do.

E along **Park Place**. 3½-st semi-detached houses facing Park. All keep servants to East St. On opposite side is the Vicarage (Rev Brooke Lambert). East of East St are two comfortable working class houses and a pub, then a row of old-fashioned 3½-st houses. One is a school. Near the Congregational Church, some modern 2-st villas are erected on the site of an old institute. Farther east the old 3½-st houses are continued to Maze Hill. Doctors and others. All keep one or two servants. RED.

By the public house near East St is a small court called **Park Place Cottages**. Four little cottages facing west. One is DARK BLUE, the others LIGHT BLUE. All labourers.

N up **East Street**. On east side near Park Place are a few 2-st and 3-st houses, occupied by comfortable working people. PINK in character. North of these nearly to railway is the Roan Boys' School and, near opposite it and taking the greater part of that end of the street, is the Roan Technical School.

N of this are two LIGHT BLUE cottages and a narrow entry looking north on railway called **Reece's Place**. Three 2-st cottages with small gardens in front. Labouring people. LIGHT BLUE.

Crossing the railway on the E is **Clark's Buildings**. 3-st tenement houses with a piece of waste ground in front. One- and two-room people. Labourers, thieves, field hand,s etc. Women do some laundry work. Several of "our boys" live here. As bad as Smith's Rents. LIGHT BLUE barred with BLACK to DARK BLUE.

N of the railway **East Street** is much poorer. 2-st and 3-st houses with broken windows and dirty blinds. Costers and labourers. DARK BLUE.

Trafalgar Road (Park Row to Park St). Only the Rectory pub and Widow Smith's Almshouses on north side west of East St. A very large coffee tavern on the south corner of Park Row. Remainder of road to Park St is 2-st shops, a few larger. Poor class trade – the pawnbroker is the only one doing a really good business. PINK to PINK-barred, PINK on map.

S into **Trafalgar Grove**. 2½-st houses. Mostly two families or lodgers. Tram, railway and labouring men. PINK to PURPLE. One house is LIGHT BLUE at least.

S along **Park St**. 2½-st and 3-st houses. All look comfortable. A few keep servants. Solicitor, City people and some working folk. PINK-barred.

S up **Maze Hill** (southern part). On the west side are 2-st houses called Hospital Building, looking like barracks and built on the edge of the Park. Most have servants. RED. On the east side are large semi-detached and detached houses. Solicitor, soap boiler merchant. Keep several servants. RED to YELLOW.

Creed Place. 2½-st and 2-st houses with small gardens. Clean and comfortable. Train drivers, mechanics and men working at Arsenal and Telegraph works. North of Woodland Place the houses are older. One garden contains a plaster castle, rockery, etc. PINK.

E to **Woodland Place**. Facing Board School are two detached houses. PINK. Nearer main road and on east side are 2-st cottages. Plumber, school keeper, etc. PINK to PURPLE.

E along **Vale Place** (Fenton Place on map). 2-st cottages. LIGHT BLUE.

To **Ibsen Place** (Mary Ann St on map), a passage leading to Trafalgar Rd. Six 2-st little cottages with small gardens in front, face east. Labourers. LIGHT BLUE.

S into **Fenton Street**. Narrow street with carriageway from south end only. 2-st cottages on east side. Costers and labourers. LIGHT BLUE.

Continuation of **Vale Place** eastward is 2-st cottages. One, occupied by decorator and painted in a conspicuous manner, is comfortable. Remainder LIGHT BLUE. Only one house on south side.

N up **Miles Street**. 2-st cottages on west side. Windows broken. Costers and labourers. LIGHT BLUE to DARK BLUE. South end of east side has been cleared. All the north end is

Miles Street Buildings, a 4-st block with iron balcony in front. Nearly all labourers. LIGHT BLUE to PURPLE.

Trafalgar Road (Park St to Christchurch). West of Creed Place is mostly private houses, some used for business purposes, laundry, doctor, etc. PINK-barred. Further east the line of 2-st shops is continued. A few larger. Character improves near Christchurch where the East Greenwich market begins. PINK-barred.

S into Woodland Street. 2-st houses. Labouring people. LIGHT BLUE to PURPLE. At the south end is a large tenement house and the street turns east. A passage leads to three houses facing south called Pleasant Cottages. Working people. LIGHT BLUE. To the south the ground drops eight feet suddenly and you look down into the yards of other houses from the level of their first floor. Probably standing on the edge of an old gravel pit.

On the W side of the street a passage leads to Woodlands Grove. Cul de sac of 2-st houses. Labouring people and a few better. PURPLE to LIGHT BLUE, PURPLE on map.

S into Earlswood Street (Edward's St on map). 2-st houses with small gardens in front. Wide road with some large 3-st houses. One used as a Radical Club; another, very poor, used as a laundry. Windows broken etc. South of Walnut Tree Rd the street is poorer. PINK to PURPLE.

W along Woodlands Park Road. 2½-st modern houses. Tram conductors and drivers. Might be a few servant girls. PINK.

N along Frobisher Street. 2-st, six rooms, two families. Working class. PINK. At the top of this street is Hatcliff Almshouses for "eight poor women". East of these are five new 2-st houses filling up a gap to Tuskar St.

Tuskar Street is 2-st and 2-st plus basement. West side looks rather poorer than Frobisher St. Many tram men. PURPLE to PINK, west is PURPLE.

Back and N up Tyler Street. 2-st houses with small gardens. North end is the better. PINK.

Trafalgar Road (Christchurch to Vanbrugh Hill). Good shops, the market of the district. Two old private houses at corner of Vanbrugh Hill. Good class. RED.

S down William Street. 2-st cottages facing the backs of Vanbrugh Hill. Labouring people. LIGHT BLUE.

W into Colomb Street (George St on map). 2-st and 2-st plus basement. Working people: milk dealer, undertaker and mechanics. PINK to PURPLE.

Walnut Tree Road. 2-st houses. West end better than east. Working people. PINK.

S to Annandale Road. At west end 3-st and 2½-st semi-detached houses. Doctor, electricians. Some keep servants. Farther east is 2-st houses. Wide road, gardens in front of houses with trees. PINK-barred and PINK. The portion running from south to north is 6-roomed houses. Comfortable artizan class. PINK.

N up Calvert Road. 2-st six-roomed houses with small forecourts. Comfortable working people but not so good as Annandale Rd. A few 3-st near Vanbrugh Hill. Guardians have acquired some houses on north side and workhouse is to be extended. Nurses now occupy some of the houses. PINK.

Vanbrugh Hill (south of railway). West side only, 2½-st near railway and 2-st nearer main road. Signwriter, nurse and other working class. PINK.

Across Woolwich Rd to Hatcliff Street. 2-st cottages, flush with the pavement. Labourers and costers. Two sweeps. LIGHT BLUE.

E along Commerell Street (late Hatcliff St North). 4-st cottages with 12 ft frontages. Labouring people. LIGHT BLUE, PURPLE on map.

Glenister Road (west of Armitage Rd). Two floors, six rooms. Two families as a rule. Mechanics and labourers, mixed. PURPLE.

N up Caletock Street. Same class of house but poorer. Broken windows. Three women standing at one street door. A few houses look comfortable. Bricklayer etc. LIGHT BLUE to PURPLE.

W into **Davern Street**. Same class of house but windows look better. Children are plump and well fed. PURPLE to LIGHT BLUE.

N to **Lenthorpe Road**. 2-st, six rooms. Many broken windows. Few newer houses at east end. LIGHT BLUE to PURPLE.

At N end of Armitage Rd are two small blocks of LCC dwellings called **Armitage Cottages**. Like those in Marsh Lane. PINK to PURPLE.

S along **Armitage Road**. Six rooms, like adjacent roads. North end is poor but improves as the main road is approached and might be PINK south of Glenister Rd. PURPLE to PINK.

General Notes

The district south of Trafalgar Rd is distinctly better than that to the north. This distinction is recognised locally and the people on the south regard those to the north generally as inferior to themselves.

Apart from the small area north of Woolwich Rd, the poor patches included in this walk are East St and Clark's Buildings north of the railway and small groups of old cottages between Creed Place and Woodlands St. These latter neighbourhoods have been improved by the demolition of the courts to the east of Miles St. This has reduced the area and improved Miles St itself, which at the time of our previous inquiry was as bad as East St.

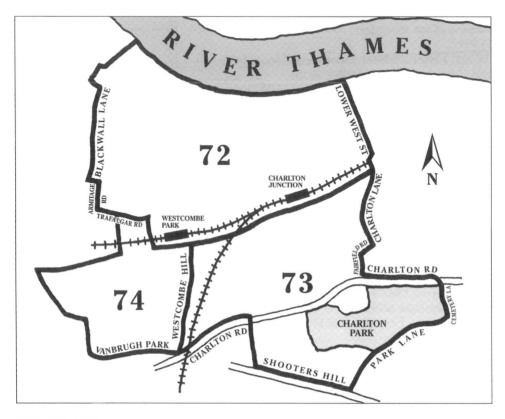

Walk 72

B371

16th October 1899.
George Arkell with Sergeant Howell.

Starting from corner of Woolwich Road.
N up **Collerston Road**. 2-st houses, six rooms. Mixed working class. A little better near main road than at north. PURPLE to LIGHT BLUE.
At N end is **Collerston Cottages**. Two small blocks of LCC Dwellings like those in Armitage Rd. PURPLE to PINK.
Tunnel Avenue at the N, leading to Blackwall Lane from the corner of Horn Lane and Woolwich Rd, is entirely unbuilt. The north east side is market gardens and open fields almost to the river.
S along **Selcroft Road**. 2-st, six rooms. Poor at north end, becoming better near the Woolwich Rd. North of Lenthorpe Rd is LIGHT BLUE. PURPLE to Glenister Rd and PINK south of it. Men working at the factories on the Marsh.
Lower Woolwich Road. On north side from Marsh Lane to Hatcliffe St is 3-st shops. Moderate trade. Lodgers in top floor. PINK-barred. Then 2-st shops, converted private houses, to Selcroft Rd. East of this are a few 3-st new shops and a Wesleyan Mission, the shops ending east of Marlton St. Market gardens then entrance to Horn Lane. PINK to PINK-barred. On the south side the Workhouse and Board School take greater part of frontage to Annandale Rd. PINK. Two small shops by Calvert Rd and four semi-detached

houses and shops by Annandale Rd. Latter comfortable. Market gardeners and others keeping servants. East of this is the Cemetery of Greenwich Hospital and an old farmhouse now occupied by a market gardener. PINK-barred.

N up **Denford Street** (turning leading into Glenforth St). Three 2-st houses on west side. Were rough but have been cleaned up and pointed and now look PINK.

N up **Glenforth Street**. A few 6-roomed houses with bay windows on west side. Remainder of street is modern 6-roomed houses built for two families and let in flats of three rooms plus scullery for 7/6. Automatic gas meters etc. These have already given employment to the police – when people move out, as is frequently the case, the neighbours will rifle the gas meter for the coppers deposited. Street was very rough at first. Took anybody to get them tenanted for sale. Now in the hands of an agent and have improved somewhat. PURPLE.

Glenister Road (east of Armitage Rd). Six rooms. Better than west end of street. PURPLE to PINK.

Fergus Street. Exactly like Glenforth St. Some broken windows. PURPLE.

E to **Marlton Street**. Like Fergus St and Glenforth St. Look a little poorer. Houses have narrow staircase from first floor into back yard which is used jointly. PURPLE to LIGHT BLUE.

E to **Horn Lane**. Roadway not made up. A few 6-roomed houses facing the fields. Look decent. PURPLE to PINK.

E into **Fearson Street**. 2-st, six rooms, bay windows. Street paved. All working people. PURPLE to PINK.

N of Fearson St is a part of **Aldeburgh Street**. 2-st, six rooms, on south side only. Street not made up. Labouring people. PURPLE to LIGHT BLUE. Anglo-American Oil Company's works take the north side of the street and extend to the Thames. Portion of Aldeburgh St running south is better 6-roomed houses with bay windows and small gardens in front. PINK to PURPLE.

Woolwich Road (to Charlton Boundary). North side east of Horn Lane are two shops and 2-st, 6-roomed, private houses to railway. Two families. PINK. South side is unbuilt to Kemsing Rd. Then Baptist Chapel and row of 3-st shops to Combedale Rd on east corner of which is a huge new public house, The Angerstein. Two carmen and contractors, baker and musical instrument dealer here. To railway is 2-st 6-roomed houses with gardens in front. Mostly one family and an occasional servant. PINK to PINK-barred. East of the railway is 2-st houses with six rooms and bay windows. Houses are newer on north than south side and look a little better. Pilots, men employed at the Arsenal and Siemens. Businesses are carried on at a few of the houses, clock maker etc. PINK. East of the Board School are a number of 2-st shops known as Charlton Pavement. Do a good trade but do not appear to have servants. PINK to PINK-barred. South side to Victoria Rd has 2½-st houses, some used for businesses. PINK.

S up **Dupree Road**. 2-st tenement houses. Separate door for each floor on east. West side is 2-st, six rooms. Better than east side which is rougher. East PURPLE, west PINK.

W along **Gurdon Road**. 2-st houses, six rooms. North side is flats with two doors like those in Dupree Rd. Curtains with holes, windows badly glazed. PURPLE to PINK.

S along **Fairthorn Road**. 2-st houses. Some have separate entrance for each floor. Others six rooms, two families. PINK.

S up **Rainton Road**. Same class of house. Small gardens in front. Insurance agent, carmen, etc. Not so good as Fairthorn Rd or Hardman Rd. PURPLE to PINK.

N down **Hardman Road**. 2-st houses with bay windows like Dupree St. Better than Rainton Rd. Electrical workers etc. PINK.

E along Woolwich Rd. On N side is **Morley Road**. 2½-st houses, eleven in all. Roadway not made up. Poor looking, white short curtains. Two and three families. PURPLE to LIGHT BLUE.

E in the Woolwich Rd is **Lombard Terrace**. 3-st shops, pawnbroker etc, doing well. PINK to PINK-barred.

N up **Lombard Road**. On the west side a row of 2½-st houses. Only about eight are occupied. Remainder are condemned and most have been empty for years. Walls are cracked even in the occupied houses. Workman engaged filling up the lower rooms with earth, even the occupied houses being thus treated. Little builder lives in one and does the repairs. Houses nearest the main road are comfortable. One DARK BLUE house. PURPLE to LIGHT BLUE. Remainder of walk is in Charlton parish, the boundary passing along Lombard Rd.

E along **Woolwich Road**. The north side is a succession of little terraces of 2-st 6-roomed houses with entrances left for future streets that will cross the marsh. The road is much higher than the ground to the north which is being filled up with refuse. In places where the process is complete the land has been raised to the level of the tops of the back garden fences of these house. Houses are very poorly built. Some poor. PURPLE to PINK. Some open ground west of Anchor and Hope Lane and a few houses at the corner on north side. PINK. South side is similar class of house but older. Two families as a rule, working people. Large mathematical instrument maker works here, Troughton & Simms. PINK. East of these works are 2-st old cottages with two families. Labourers and mechanics. PURPLE to PINK. Improve again near Church Lane where there are a few shops. PINK.

N up **Anchor & Hope Lane**. Beer house at corner being rebuilt. Just north of it are four cottages on the east side. PURPLE to LIGHT BLUE. On the west side are some parish allotments and on west side at north end three cottages, 2-st. PURPLE to LIGHT BLUE. On the open ground to the west, much of the London slop and other refuse is tipped, the slop being brought by barges. An embankment is made round a portion of the ground with solid material, refuse from gas works mostly. The slop is then tipped from the barges into channels, whence it descends on the land by gravity.

W along **Riverside**. Anchor & Hope pub, several scattered cottages (Atlas Cottages, LIGHT BLUE) and a PINK house and rope walk on south side. The river bank is taken by Cory's and Wood's wharves. Back and along the riverbank past Castle's ship-breaking yard and the Silicate Paint Works until an open piece of land at the top of West St is reached. This is occupied by six travelling vans and a number of gipsy tents – the half-football style. Women, girls and children about the place, some boys playing cards on a tree stump and men repairing a shaft. Some of these people always here. Make a living by selling things and also by other more objectionable methods. Position marked by LIGHT BLUE crosses on map.

W into **North Street**. South side only. Little 2-st cottages. Poor labouring people work at Siemens and on the water side. LIGHT BLUE to DARK BLUE.

S into **Lydenburgh Street**. Exactly like North St. LIGHT BLUE to DARK BLUE.

S into **Lower West Street**. Part to north is like North St. LIGHT BLUE. Block to north of York St is rather better. 2-st, six or five rooms, bay window. Two families at least. Might be PURPLE. Poorer to south. Little cottages. LIGHT BLUE. On west side, pub, shop and house facing York St, PURPLE, and nearer Woolwich Rd 2-st little cottages. Doors open into room. Poor labouring people. LIGHT BLUE to DARK BLUE.

W along Woolwich Rd. On N side is **Coburg Place**. Three shops and two 2-st private houses. Grocer etc. Sawmills and joinery works at west corner. PINK.

Charlton Lane (north of railway). Terrace of 2-st houses on west side. Van proprietor, labouring people, railway porters. PURPLE.

Continuing W along **Woolwich Road** (to Church Lane). On south side several semi-detached and detached houses occupied by doctors and other comfortable people. Long gardens reaching to railway. Some keep servants. PINK-barred. West of these to entrance of Cedar Grove is 2-st 6-roomed houses, with gardens in front. Comfortable working people.

PINK. Except the National Schools, the north side is market gardens to this point, which is known as Ballast Bridge. A railway track passes beneath the road here. It was formerly used to convey sands from the pits on the south to the river. Four semi-detached houses, 2½-st stand here. PINK. Remainder of this side is open ground except a few cottages close to Anchor & Hope Lane. On the south side, west of Ballast Bridge, the houses vary. 2-st, 2½-st and 3-st. Some are comfortable but PINK as a whole. Dressmakers, carmen, etc. Large house stands in ground behind the houses, Lyme Villa. RED.

S & W along **Troughton Road**. 2-st, six rooms, bay windows. Two families. Comfortable working people. Railway yard takes south side. PINK.

Round corner to **N** is **Cambridge Terrace**. Eight 2-st houses. Comfortable working people. PINK.

S & W along **Rathmore Street**. New 2-st houses with bay windows to ground floor. A few at east end are not quite ready for occupation. Look comfortable. PINK.

New street **N** of this is **Bettisfield Road**. Same class of houses. Two families. Shop at corner opposite Troughton Rd. PINK.

In **Victoria Road** between Bettisfield Rd and Rathmore St is Cleveland Terrace. Like Bettisfield Rd. PINK. On the opposite side is Johnston & Philllip's large electrical works, which is encroaching on the houses, a row of which near the railway are used as stores. North of the works are some cottages and four semi-detached houses. Two laundries. Working people, comfortable. PINK.

Notes on District

This completed the day's walk. By far the poorest part is West St, Charlton and the little cluster of streets adjoining it which is really a westerly extension of Woolwich. Much of the ground immediately adjoining the Woolwich Rd has been covered during the past ten years. North of the road little new building has been done, the only noticeable addition being the three new streets near the Tunnel Avenue.

Walk 73

B371

Wednesday 18th October 1899.
George Arkell with Sergeant Howell.

Started from corner of Woolwich Road and Church Lane.
S along **Church Lane**. East side to Railway is terrace of 2½-st houses called Inkermann Terrace. Two laundresses, dressmaker and other working people. PINK. A few shops on west to Troughton Rd. Also PINK.

Through railway arch and **E** into **Cedar Grove**. 2-st and 2½-st modern houses fitted for two families. Comfortable working people. Some Germans – electricians at Siemens. A few shops where the road bends. Beyond the bend the houses are 2-st with two bays, fitted for two families. PINK.

Roadway has been raised about 9 ft above the level of the sand pit across which it is continued to **Charlton Lane**. West side from railway is 2½-st cottages with gardens in front. Family plus lodgers. Like the cottages south of railway but a little better. Extend to the Royal Oak Beerhouse. PINK to PURPLE. Going south up the hill the houses are better. 2-st with exception of a few north of Cedar Grove, 3-st. A few servants here. PINK to PINK-barred. East side is new 2-st houses. Comfortable people, a few keep servants. PINK to PINK-barred.

A roadway gives west immediately south of Lansdowne Rd leading to a large steam laundry. Cottage built on the edge of sand pit here. PINK.

W into **Lansdowne Road**. Near Church Lane are semi-detached 3-st houses. Comfortable middle class. PINK-barred to RED as also large houses on south side. Turning south new 2½-st houses. These and a few houses south are comfortable. One man is large property owner. PINK-barred.

Nearing the Village are two terraces of cottages: **John's Place** and **George's Terrace**. Working people. PINK to PURPLE.

E to **Fairfield Road**. Near the Church is the Vicarage and two detached houses and then, going southward, 2-st and 3-st houses. Mostly keep servants. Some almshouses. RED to PINK-barred.

Back to corner of **the Village**. To the south east is the Deer Park. On south side facing Fairfield Rd are two new 3-st houses. RED. Going west through the Village, the great diversity of the buildings is conspicuous. Between Fairfield Rd and Lansdowne Rd are small old houses and quaint shops. Working people, comfortable. PINK. Remainder of street to the Church is a medley of quaint old gabled shops (3-st) side by side with modern shops with large plate glass windows and a few private houses. Place is in a transitional condition. RED.

Past the Church, a red-brick building with square tower, and N up **Church Lane**. On the west side is a quarry hollow with old wooden house occupied by a postman at the bottom. Beyond this is a row of 2-st houses built on the edge of an old sand pit, known as the Warren. PINK to PINK-barred. A large house here and, between Nadine Rd and Wellington Rd, a row of shops. PINK-barred to RED. On east side near the Church are some Almshouses occupied by old "Dutch or other foreigners". Then 3-st houses. Architect and others keeping servants. RED. Near the railway station, shops on both sides, the east side being modern 3-st houses. RED to PINK-barred.

W along **Delafield Road**. 2-st semi-detached and terrace houses. One for sale is let at 14/6. Contains seven rooms and is fitted for two families. Comfortable working people, foremen etc. A few keep a girl. PINK to PINK-barred.

S into **Invarine Road**. 2-st houses with two bay windows. Two families as a rule. All comfortable. PINK.

W along **Fossdene Road**. Like Invarine Rd. Board School takes all the south side. Insurance agents etc. PINK.

Calydon Road. Board School and school-keeper's house takes north side. On south are 2-st houses for two families. Not quite so good as Fossdene Rd. Road not made up. PINK to PURPLE.

Victoria Road. West side is 2-st houses south of Victoria Works, some with attic. PINK. South of these are a few large houses to the bend. RED. On the east side, south of Calydon Rd, are 2-st houses, a few with basement. Two families. Dressmaker etc. Some broken windows. PINK to PURPLE to Priolo Rd. From this point to Wellington Rd are 2-st new houses with bay windows. PINK.

E into **Swallowfield Road**. 2-st with bay windows, rustic porches and tiled entrances. New houses. Part of east side unbuilt. Dressmaker's plate. Comfortable working people. PINK.

Priolo Road. Exactly like Swallowfield Rd. Same builder. Sells the houses on instalment system – people pay £40 down and balance as rent. City Missionary etc. South east side only. PINK.

Sundorne Road. North side is 2-st houses, a few semi-detached. A few keep girls, several own their houses. PINK to PINK-barred. Near Wellington Rd are four 3-st semi-detached houses on the south side. Rather better. PINK-barred.

At the corner of **Wellington Road** and **Church Lane** is a large building erected as an

Hotel. Dwarfs the other buildings in the neighbourhood. A license has just been granted and a notice in the window says that it will "shortly" be opened for the sale of wines, spirits etc and also several large bills saying that "2415 Charlton Residents have signed in favour of a full license". It was built by a man (James Ellis) who owns a lot of property here and has occasioned a great fight. Ellis threatened that if the license were not granted he would turn the place into a registered lodging house. Over one of the entrances the words "Wellington Temperance Hotel" are inscribed.

SW along **Wellington Road**. 2-st double-fronted houses on north and 3½-st on south. Solicitors and others keeping servants. West end of road is new. 2-st on south, let at £36 and £37 and 3-st with rustic fronts let at £45. RED.

S into **Nadine Street**. 2-st villas. Rustic style: red- and black-tiled roofs. A few keep girls. Ladies' nurse. PINK to PINK-barred.

S along **Elliscombe Road**. 2-st with gardens in front. Tiled entrances. Some keep servants, all comfortable. PINK-barred.

N into **Victoria Road**. Large detached and semi-detached houses with gardens and trees in front. Heavy-looking buildings. People keep two or three servants. Road is deteriorating. RED to YELLOW. Behind the west side of Victoria Rd is a Mews. Five stables with rooms over. Coachmen probably but no carriages can be seen. Flowers in window boxes. PINK to PURPLE.

S into **Charlton Road**. Going toward the village the north side is detached residences with grounds, whilst the south east of Marlborough Lane is taken by Charlton House and Park. YELLOW.

Marlborough Lane is a regular country lane. Fields on both sides and on the west the drive to a large house – Cherry Orchard. YELLOW.

W of Marlborough Lane, **Charlton Road** has old-fashioned detached houses. One is occupied by a market gardener who takes officers as boarders. Remainder are well-to-do people, retired silversmith etc. On north side is Charlton Park Terrace. 4½-st red-brick houses with carriage drives. Doctor and military officers. RED to YELLOW. Then several detached houses and Champion Terrace. 3-st. RED. On the south side of Charlton Rd near the boundary is the Rectory Field, a cricket and football ground. All YELLOW except Champion Terrace. Passing into Greenwich parish the character of Charlton Rd changes. Save one large house (East Cornlee, YELLOW) the north side is a succession of terraces:

Bellevue Terrace. 2½-st. Some keep servants. PINK-barred.

St Clair Villas. Modern 2½-st houses. Good class of house. All keep servants.

Rutland Gardens (to Invicta Rd). 2½-st. Also RED.

Thence to **Westcombe Hill**. 3½-st semi-detached houses with long gardens. Solicitor etc. All keep servants. RED to YELLOW.

N along **Invicta Road**. Mineral Water Manufacturer and two houses on west side and then a new Board School being built. South of this a terrace of 2-st houses for two families. Children playing in roadway. Change frequently. "People cannot get their money here." PINK to PURPLE. Behind this road facing W is **Acorn Terrace**. Six rooms for two families. Labourers and carmen as lodgers. Others better off. PURPLE to PINK.

At the corner of Siebert Rd are two 2½-st houses in **St George's Road**. PINK.

N into **Siebert Road**. Four shops on south east corner. PINK. Remainder of side is taken by the South Eastern Railway which is building workshops here. On west side are 2-st houses. Mechanics and electrical workers as a rule. PINK.

At N end is **Siebert Terrace**. Seven houses. Like the Road. PINK.

General Notes

The greater part of this walk was in Charlton. The Village still retains much of its old quaint appearance but the modern house is springing up on the north west and the bulk of the population is now located in the new streets south of the Woolwich Rd. The people here have their business in London, Greenwich or Woolwich. They market in East Greenwich and all their interests lie in that direction rather than with the Village.

Woolwich has a strong influence on the place. Military officers live in the better roads, whilst the Arsenal workmen live in the streets off the Woolwich Rd. Two large electrical and mathematical instrument makers have their works here and several other large works engaged in this trade are situate just over the border. These and a few laundries are the chief industries of the neighbourhood.

Walk 74   B371

Thursday 19th October 1899.
George Arkell with Sergeant Howell.

Started at corner of **Maze Hill**.
Large house at corner of **Maze Hill**, Vanbrugh Castle. Now empty. YELLOW.
Opposite this are two houses on **Vanbrugh Fields**. Keep servants. RED.
E along **Westcombe Park Road**. North side detached and semi-detached houses, mostly 3½-st. Some with large grounds. All keep two or more servants. Large house on south side, Vanbrugh House, caretaker only. YELLOW to RED to Vanbrugh Rd.
N into **Ulundi Road**. Modern 2-st and 3-st villas. All keep one or two servants. City people. RED.
N down **Vanbrugh Hill**. Very steep. 2-st houses with bay windows. "Mostly keep one or two servants" says Hardy. Very few more than one and some probably none. On west side is a house standing back, reached by a private road. RED to PINK-barred. South of Ulundi Rd houses are double-fronted and detached. Two servants at least. RED.
E along **Westcombe Park Road** (to Coleraine Rd). Detached houses on south side with nice old gardens. North more modern, 3-st. All well-to-do. YELLOW to RED.
N to **Foyle Road**. 2-st and 3-st detached and semi-detached houses. All well-to-do and keep servants. Some parts unbuilt. RED.
Humber Road. Near Vanbrugh Hill are a few houses on north side and four on south side. All comfortable, mostly have a girl. PINK-barred to RED.
Dinsdale Road. 2-st houses. Three old and poor at corner of Vanbrugh Hill, others are modern. Comfortable working people and a few better off. PINK to PINK-barred. Road rises sharply to Humber Rd. Going east on north side are 3-st ugly houses. All keep servants. Several to be sold. South side is 2-st modern houses. Some keep servants. Plate: "Piano Taught". RED on north to PINK-barred on south. East of Coleraine Rd are 3-st semi-detached houses and on north opposite is a row of double-fronted semi-detached houses, 2-st plus attic. Professional people, solicitors etc. RED.
S up **Coleraine Street**. Mostly 2-st modern houses with gardens in front. 3-st near Westcombe Park Rd. All keep servants. Patches of open ground at intervals. Building going on. RED.
E along **Westcombe Park Road** (to Beaconsfield Rd). Detached residences. Those on the north are modern and some very large. YELLOW.

N along **Hardy Road**. On west are two sets of stables with rooms over. Belong to Westcombe Park Rd. PINK. Greater part is unbuilt. A few 3-st semi-detached houses. All keep two servants. RED to YELLOW.

E into **Ingleside Grove**. Four 3-st houses on south side. All keep servants. RED.

In **Beaconsfield Road** the only occupied houses south of Ingleside Grove are two detached houses on west side. RED to YELLOW. Woodlands' stables with rooms over are opposite Ingleside Grove and south of Hardy Rd. Large semi-detached and detached houses. YELLOW. Still building here.

S along **Mycenae Road**. 3-st semi-detached houses. Look as if two families are in some. Plate with "Ladies School". PINK-barred. Improves to the south. On the west side are some double-fronted semi-detached houses. Keep servants. RED.

Westcombe Park Road. East of Beaconsfield Rd is large detached houses. Yarrow, the boat builder, has the Woodlands, the grounds of which extend from Beaconsfield Rd to Mycenae Rd. YELLOW.

S along **Vanbrugh Park Road East**. Large detached houses. One or more servants. Army and professional people. YELLOW to RED.

Vanbrugh Park Road and **Vanbrugh Park Road West** are 3½-st houses. Same class of houses and people as in Vanbrugh Park Rd East. YELLOW to RED.

W to **Vanbrugh Fields**. On the east side are a few houses, well-to-do. RED. Further north is an archway with towers used as a home by one family. PINK. Beyond this is a very large house now unoccupied and falling to ruin and two or three others. RED.

E along **Vanbrugh Park**. Detached houses facing the Heath. Slightly larger and better than those in adjacent roads. East of the Presbyterian Church the houses are smaller and only RED. A few shops near Westcombe Hill. YELLOW and RED. Drill Hall at corner of the Fields is now used as a scene painter's shop.

S along **Westcombe Terrace**. Good 3-st shops face the green. RED.

N along **Glenluce Road**. 3-st semi-detached houses, some double-fronted. Professional and business people. All keep servants. RED to YELLOW.

At S is **St George's Road**. 2½-st and 2-st with bay windows. Some keep servants near Beaconsfield Rd. PINK-barred and PINK. Better near Westcombe Hill.

N into **Ruthin Road**. 2-st houses, six rooms. Road not made up. Working folk, insurance agent, dairyman. PINK to PINK-barred.

At N is **Humber Road**. 2-st terrace houses for two families on south side. On the north a few keep servants. PINK to PINK-barred.

W & N to **Station Road**. Four 3-st shops. Fair trade. PINK-barred to RED. Formerly called Beaconsfield Terrace.

N through Railway Station into **Ormiston Road**. 2-st houses. All comfortable. Factory hands, men from telegraph works and Arsenal. Two families or one and a young man lodger. PINK.

N along **Halstow Road**. 2-st houses, six rooms. Quite new road not made up but all occupied. PINK.

S up **Kemsing Road**. Similar to Halstow Rd. All respectable people. PINK.

E past station entrance **Ormiston Road** is continued. 2-st houses, new, smaller than rest of road. Greenwich Poor Relief station here. PINK to PURPLE.

N into **Milton Road**. Eight 2-st houses on west side. Very small with five rooms. Mostly kept by one family. PINK to PURPLE. Facing these houses is Combedale Farmhouse and all that remains of the Farm. House is occupied. PINK. Adjoining it is Westcombe Park Laundry and an occupied house (PINK).

W into **Combedale Road**. 2½-st and 2-st houses. Two families in a house. Decorator etc.

Police Station here. PINK.

E into **Farmdale Road**. 2-st, six rooms. Police and working people. PINK.

S into Westcombe Hill. On **W** side of Farmdale Rd is **Combe Villas**. 2-st houses with small gardens in front.

S of Farmdale Rd is **Glencythan Villas**. Houses similar to others. All working people, insurance agent, bootmaker. PINK to PURPLE. Glencythan Villas is poorer than Combe Villas in appearance.

Near the Railway Station in **Westcombe Hill** are four shops on west side and on east four others occupied, whilst others are being built. Poor trade. PINK. South of the Railway Arch Westcombe Hill has a few shops on east side to Siebert Rd. PINK-barred. Then 2-st private houses. Six rooms, bay windows. Mostly two families. A few semi-detached on west side (one family) and some 3-st houses to St George's Rd. PINK. Several dressmakers and gasfitter. South of St George's Rd there are houses on east side only. 2½-st with gardens in front. Some keep servants. PINK-barred. Building is still going on, while at the top of the hill are a few RED houses. All keep one or more servants.

General Remarks

Excepting the group of streets north of the railway and a fringe by Westcombe Hill, the district is middle class. The social character of the district improves as the low ground by the railway is left and the hills towards Blackheath ascended, Westcombe Park Rd being the best road. A considerable number of new houses are being built here and are occupied almost as quickly as they are finished. The superior finish and convenience of these newer houses has led people to leave the older houses and the houses to let in this neighbourhood are either the very large houses, as Vanbrugh Castle, or houses that lack modern conveniences.

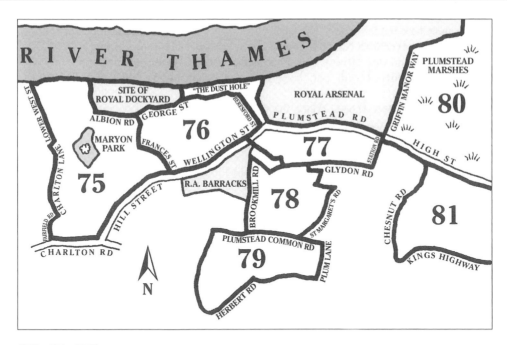

Walk 75

B371

Friday 11th May 1900.
George Duckworth with PC Clyne.

Starting at the corner of West Street and Woolwich Road.
N up West Street. This is on a lower level than the Woolwich Rd. So is the character of the houses and their inhabitants. 2-st. Poor and very poor. A few rather better off near the public house on the west side and on the east side north of York St. Windows dirty and broken, children dirty, blinds dirty and half rolled up and pinned to prevent falling. Waterside labourers. LIGHT BLUE and PURPLE or LIGHT BLUE all through.
N & W at Lydenburgh Street. 2-st, two families. Worse than West St. Dirty, dingy, look and smell of dirt. "But it's not poverty nor want of work that's the matter in these streets, it's drink" said Clyne. LIGHT BLUE to DARK BLUE.
E along North Street. Very poor west of Lower West St, rather better east of it. LIGHT BLUE to PURPLE. Open space on north side opposite the end of Lower West St used as a 'pitch' by gypsies in the winter. Three vans still there, being painted and varnished for the summer season. Dogs, broken crockery and foul language abundant. East of them are a few small gardens rented and worked by the inhabitants of the houses opposite, onions and rhubarb. East of these gardens is the path leading to the landing stage of the truant training-ship *Warspite*.
S down Lower East Street. 2-st, small fronts. Poorer south than north of York St. Maryon Institute on the east side founded by Sir Spencer Maryon Wilson. LIGHT BLUE south of York St and PURPLE north of it.
W along York Street. 2-st. Poorer. Foetid smell of dirt, dirty women and children. LIGHT BLUE.
E into Harden's Manor Way. Better. 2-st. Mixed, one or two small shops at south end. Small palinged fronts. Opposite on east side is large, bare, open space belonging to Siemens

factory, quite bare but fairly tidy. The factory strews its waste ashes here, evenly, not in heaps. At the corner of Woolwich Rd is a Salvation Army Chapel. "The army is strong in Woolwich." N & E along **Bowater Street**. 2-st. Poor as the rest. LIGHT BLUE.

E & N up **Trinity Road**. 2-st. Very poor and rough. LIGHT BLUE to DARK BLUE. Birdcages. Loafers.

W along **Harrington Road**. Along the south side lies Siemens Telegraph Construction Company. Wooden ship-breakers on north side with figureheads as door posts. Two poor cottages, LIGHT BLUE, and one PINK foreman's house on north side.

S down **Trinity Road**. Better. Here PURPLE to the Albion Rd.

W along **Siemens Road**. 2-st, dirty, newish houses. Mess of paper and bread. Some DARK BLUE, especially at east end. All young wives. LIGHT BLUE to DARK BLUE.

S into Woolwich Rd. W & N into **Eden Cottages**. 2-st. Quiet, well-kept fronts, tap in front of each house. PURPLE to LIGHT BLUE.

W & N into **Willis Buildings**. 2-st. Old inhabitants, costers, keep a dog and fowls. LIGHT BLUE to PURPLE.

W past new Board School into old nest of houses called **Charlton Vale**. Gardens to houses. Some PINK, others LIGHT BLUE. Two police living in front houses. Rents 8/- to 8/6. Those just west of Board School are the poorest. Perhaps all PURPLE.

S across Woolwich Rd to **Tamar Street**. 2-st, flush with pavement. Labourers, rather rough. Half belong to one and half to another man, change of ownership shown clearly in change of inhabitants. One rough poor and the other fairly comfortable as tenants. LIGHT BLUE and PURPLE.

E & S down **Sand Street**. 2-st. Poor at north west, better near railway. PURPLE to LIGHT BLUE.

E along **Railway Place**. 2-st. LIGHT BLUE to PURPLE.

N & W along **Acorn Street**. Respectable labourers. 2-st. PURPLE.

E to **Oak Street**. 2-st. PURPLE.

E & S down **Kidd Street**. 2-st. PINK to PURPLE.

W along **Selina Place** (north of railway). 2-st. Clean steps and blinds, one piano. Noisy trains. PURPLE to PINK.

E along **Albion Road**. PINK.

Turning **SW** at **Prospect Row**. Mixed. PURPLE to PINK.

Out of S side is **Prospect Row Cottages**. Very poor. One woman pays 3/9 for two rooms, no wash-house, has been there two years. Flowers. LIGHT BLUE to DARK BLUE.

N into **Harden Street**. 2-st. Mixed. PURPLE. It becomes a passage running uphill at its east end.

Out of its W end is **Morris Street**. 2-st. Thoroughly bad except at south west end. Very poor, some prostitutes and thieves. At the south end a flight of steps leads up into Sand St. Much DARK BLUE of the regular sort. Windows broken, dirty and stopped with paper. Passages bare, walls dirty, paper and bread in street. Bare-armed women. Houses flush with street, one gas lamp sticking out of a bracket from wall to light the street. DARK BLUE-barred to LIGHT BLUE-barred.

W into **Sand Street**. West side better than east. Chapel and Board School at south end. Mixed. PURPLE or PINK on west, LIGHT BLUE on east where it backs on Morris St.

S & W into **Glenalvon Street**. 2-st. PURPLE to PINK.

Leading to **Joseph Street**. Uphill. 2-st. Ebenezer Chapel at north east. PURPLE.

W into **Mount Street**. Artisan, respectable, comfortable. Runs downhill to the north, less good at north end. PINK. Opposite on west side is Maryon Park – shrubs, lilac, laburnum, green grass, attractive, gravel mounts.

S & E along **Prospect Place**. PINK to PURPLE.

N into Kidd St out of whose W side is **Ann Street**. 2-st, old established, quiet. Some labourers. Let off two rooms, rents 10/- to 12/-. PURPLE to PINK.

Leading to **Wick Cottages** which is also PURPLE to PINK.

S down **Kidd Street** which is better south of railway than north of it. 2-st and 2½-st. Two families usual. Some let to single lodgers. Improves to PINK south of Prospect Place.

Lyford Street. PINK.

S down **Maryon Grove**. 2-st. PURPLE to PINK.

S down **Wood Street**. Runs uphill to south. PINK as far as Woodville St.

Woodville Street. 2-st and 2½-st. PINK.

E to **Wood Street**. Here detached and semi-detached. Some officers and families. RED to PINK-barred. Quite at its south end Wood St becomes PINK again.

S into **Hill Street**. Occasional servant west of Pellipar Rd. PINK-barred to PINK.

W & N up **Maryon Road**. 2-st. Good gardens and fronts. South end the best. PINK-barred to RED.

Behind E side is **Lower Maryon Rd**. 2-st. Quiet, gardens. PINK.

W uphill along **Woodland Terrace**. New houses south west of church, apartments. A few servants, one family per house. PINK-barred to PINK. Leads to open timbered fields called Hanging Wood at west end across which is a footpath leading to Charlton Lane.

S down **Heathwood Gardens**. Built and still building. One and two families. Sold as soon as built, £580 for 99 years lease. Apartments. PINK to PINK-barred.

S into **Little Heath**, called Charlton Rd on map. Large old houses on south side, new and smaller on north and building. Red brick, 2-st, with front gardens

E along Hill St and N at **Lower Wood Street**. Mixed. Many comfortable, two very poor at north east. PURPLE.

Leads to **Godfrey Hill**. 2½-st, two families. PINK.

S down **Godfrey Street**. 2-st. Poor, lower rough class. LIGHT BLUE.

S down **Lower Pellipar Street**. 2-st and 2½-st. Rather better. Dockyard workers, PURPLE to LIGHT BLUE.

S to **Pellipar Road**. PINK.

E to **Robert Street**. Steep hill running north. Two and three families to a house. PURPLE to LIGHT BLUE.

E along **St James' Place**. Poor, oldish houses at the top of the hill. LIGHT BLUE to PURPLE.

S down **Back Lane**. Two very rough DARK BLUE houses on west side, the rest LIGHT BLUE. Irish.

Out of W side is a cul de sac called **Dairy Cottages**. Semi-detached cottages with gardens. Poor. One woman pays 6/- for four rooms plus wash-house, there 10 months.

S to **Ogilby Street**. 2-st. Look better but Clyne gives the same character for poverty and drink as Lydenburgh St etc. LIGHT BLUE to PURPLE.

Out of SE end are **Waverly Cottages**. Seven 2-st cottages with long uncared for gardens, two respectable. LIGHT BLUE to PURPLE.

E into **Frances Street**. Noisy. 2-st and 3-st. Shops below poor, above mixed. Opposite barracks, prostitutes. PURPLE.

S & W along **Hill Street**. PINK.

Out of N side is **The Avenue**. Four 2-st cottages. PURPLE.

N along **Frances Street** which becomes better where it begins to run downhill to the north.

Houses on south side are old with good gardens. Some servants. PINK-barred.

W into **Samuel Street**. West side better than east. PINK to PINK-barred.

Out of NE end is Marshall's Grove with cottages running out of it called **St Ives Cottages**. Five 2-st cottages, fronts, quiet, built 1859. PURPLE.

Maria Terrace, Sussex Place, Grove Cottages. Built 1839. All 2-st, four rooms plus wash-house, 6/9 or 7/-, eight years here. Allotments. The easternmost block is the poorest. PURPLE to LIGHT BLUE.

Out of S side of Samuel St opposite Marshall's Grove are **Railway Cottages**. Eight 2-st with six more behind them. Poor, drunks, labourers. LIGHT BLUE.

N up **Bowling Green Row**. Small 2-st shops, leading past the Hardock public house to George St. PINK.

Out of its W side are **Maria Terrace** and **Steer Cottages**. LIGHT BLUE. 1862.

General Remarks

Many poor in this round: 1) Half-skilled telegraph construction workers between Woolwich Rd and River. 2) Poor, vicious and rough in Morris St out of Lower Harden St. 3) Old village poverty in Marshall's Grove and Railway Cottages. Morris St is the worst street of all but the block of streets between Woolwich Rd and the River form the largest area of poverty. If ever these streets could have looked attractive they would have done so today. Fine day, hot sun, cold wind, everything fresh after yesterday's rain. But there is something exceptionally dismal about the low-lying streets north of the Woolwich Rd. The public houses are not flaring or large but there is the mark of drink upon houses and people. All the men, women and children are young. If trouble is to come out of the East in times of unemployment it is from these streets and from those lying north of the railway in Battersea that the worst would come: the admixture of the military would make a crowd from Woolwich more difficult to deal with than other crowds. Men and women are strong and young and unskilled and drunken. If they were hungry they would be a real danger. In a new district like this there is no tradition of orderliness and their dirty piecework, either as soapmakers or cable works, does not encourage sobriety or cleanliness. Bread 4½d quartern, milk 3d quart.

Walk 76   B371

Monday 14th May 1900.
George Duckworth with PC Clyne.

Starting at the corner of George Street and Chapel Street.

S down **Chapel Street**. A mixed street. PINK to PURPLE at north end, north of railway. LIGHT BLUE to PURPLE south of the railway on west side. East side is better than west. The poor courts behind the west side affect the fronts.

Out of the W side is a passage running to George St called **Ship Cottages**. 2-st. Very poor. LIGHT BLUE. North of them are two 3-st. Respectable. PURPLE. Passage is flagged and leads to the Ship Public House.

Out of the E side of Chapel St are **Romford Cottages**. 2-st, new. PINK. Belonging to Ind Coope, the Romford Brewers.

S down **Chapel Street** which takes its name from the large chapel at the corner of Samuel St called Queen Street Baptist Chapel. Rev G Hutchinson. "Popular" said Clyne.

S & E into **Sarah Place**. By the railway (north side) are poor cottages standing back with front gardens. LIGHT BLUE. Leading up steps at east end to two rows of cottages. Both LIGHT BLUE.

The southernmost block is known as **Elgin Terrace**. 2-st, seven houses. Uncared for fronts but rather better than Sarah Place. One woman pays 8/9 for four rooms plus wash-house and a very small back yard. Been there six years and has paid until today 8/6. Just raised, thinks it a grievance.

S & E at **Sims Buildings**. 2-st. Quiet, poor. LIGHT BLUE to PURPLE. The passage at the east end turning into Station Rd is a little better tenanted.

S past the east side of the schools is **Limbrey's Buildings**. Twelve 2-st houses. Poorish. Small fronts, in nearly every one of which was a fowl run. 6/6 for four rooms plus wash-house, has been there seven years. Six years ago the rent was 5/-. Then, when water was put in to the sink and WC, the rent was raised to 5/6, then 6/-, and 12 months ago it was raised to 6/6.

W & S past the west side of the schools into **Eustace Place**. The north block of houses rather larger and better and newer than the southern, but the north block is without front gardens which the south block have. 2-st. North block PURPLE to LIGHT BLUE, south block LIGHT BLUE. One woman in the south block pays 4/9 for two rooms plus wash-house, one room up and one down. Been there 11 years, used to pay 4/6. Some still pay 4/3. Tap has been running for months to waste and a small stream issues from front gate. Landlord and Water Company refuse to move. She hoped that I would speak about it in the proper quarters.

S down **Henry Street**. Built 1831. 2-st. PINK and PURPLE. PINK on west side north of turn. Runs uphill to the south, improves as it rises.

Out of the W side is a court called **Read Buildings**. Cement court. Very poor. DARK BLUE to LIGHT BLUE. Rough drunks.

E along **Station Road**. 2-st and 3-st. Mixed. PURPLE to PINK.

Opposite the Dockyard Station it is called **Cambridge Terrace**. 2½-st. Better. PINK.

W along **Station Road**. A brothel west of the public house, dingy. PURPLE to LIGHT BLUE. East of the railway station Station Rd is 2½-st and very respectable. One family takes a house and lets off. Rent 13/-. PINK.

Behind it is **North Kent Grove** and **North Kent Place**. 4-roomed, 2-st houses. PURPLE to LIGHT BLUE. Rents 8/6 to 10/6.

E into King St. S & W along **Warwick Street**. Long ill-kept, old, 2-st and 2½-st houses with long strips of gardens behind. Some prostitutes. A few fairly comfortable but it is a "rough poor street". A few very poor houses at east end on north side. Red-tiled roofs. LIGHT BLUE to PURPLE.

Out of S side running uphill is **Paradise Place**. Old and poor. Broad, fairly tidy street, cul de sac. Children well fed and fairly dressed. Houses look poor. LIGHT BLUE to PURPLE.

Opposite out of N side of Warwick St is **Martyr's Passage**. Nine 2-st houses. Very poor. 5/6 for three rooms plus wash-house, older tenants pay 5/-. LIGHT BLUE to DARK BLUE.

E into Coleman St which becomes **King Street** south of Warwick St. 2-st and 2½-st old houses with door lintels. Mostly two families per house. PINK to PURPLE. East side better than west.

E along **St Mary Street**. Not quite so good, some prostitutes, mixed. 2-st and 3-st. Runs uphill to the east but character gets rather worse. PURPLE.

N up **Sun Street**. Old chapel used only for children's services on east side in small dilapidated graveyard. New fire station on west. At north end are 2-st quiet cottages, PURPLE to LIGHT BLUE. Out of east side is a nameless place with some cottages. 8/- for four rooms plus attic. PURPLE to LIGHT BLUE.

N into Church St and S down **Orchard Place**. Entered by a crooked passage. 2-st. Clean but poor, windows unbroken. Many children, well fed. Steps whitened but Clyne calls it rough. West side rather better than east. Three rooms 5/6, been there eight years. LIGHT BLUE to PURPLE.

E into **Orchard Street**. Like preceding. All labourers, no skilled mechanics. Some prostitutes in all these streets. They don't bring men home but take a room two together. Householders don't suspect profession of their lodgers. Much drink in these streets but not the degraded appearance of Lydenburgh St, Bowater St and Trinity St. 2-st. Broad like Orchard Place. LIGHT BLUE to PURPLE.

E along St Mary St, going uphill and N down steepish **Parson's Hill**. The churchyard with square-towered brick church and plenty of green trees is on the west side. Next to it is a large chapel, now closed, and opposite on the south side is a very small Welsh chapel which is still used "though very few come". A mixed street. At the bend facing east are three or four houses which keep servants and should be RED, the rest are PINK.

E into **Powis Street**. This is mainly mixed residential west of Hare St. Some poor on north side. PURPLE. At Hare St it becomes the main shopping street of Woolwich. Large drapers, grocers, etc. All the best shops are here and in Hare St. Tram lines down the centre, crowds of people, fashionable parade for soldiers and girls. Should be RED east of Hare St.

S along **Eleanor Road**. 2-st. Artisans. PINK.

W along **Clara Place**. 2½-st by railway. PURPLE.

Monk Street at west end. Also PURPLE.

W & S & E along **William Street**. Much rebuilding, new red-brick 2-st houses with stone mullions. Clerks and artisans. Almost flush with pavement except for low wall with ornamental iron rail around the top. Six rooms plus wash-house for 14/6, only put up in the last 18 months. Old tenants used to pay 8/6 to 10/6. They left when the leases ran out and old houses were pulled down but many have since returned at the higher rent. Clyne knows this is so because many policemen used to and still live here. On the south side is the Polytechnic, Police Court and Police Station and County Court and Town Hall.

Out of the S side is **Lower Market Street**. 2-st old houses on east side. Baths and wash-houses and new Electric Light works on west side. PURPLE to PINK.

W into **Upper Market Street**. Old houses, detached and semi-detached "like William St used to be". Well tenanted. PINK.

W along William St to **Brewer Street**. New 2-st, seven rooms plus wash-house, 14/6. Regular PINK.

Out of W side is **Brewer Place**. Still building, no sooner built than tenanted. The new houses called "5-roomed" are yellow brick, stone above and below windows, bow window on ground floor, flush but for low wall and rail, well built, small back gardens. Two bedrooms and one small room over wash-house (not large enough to put a bed in) upstairs. Downstairs kitchen and front sitting room and wash-house. Now rented at 11/- per week. Clyne goes into one of these houses next week. The old houses (in one of which he used to live) had the same amount of room barring the small room over wash-house and he used to pay 6/- instead of 11/- as rent.

N along **Charles Street**, as the north end of Brewer St is called. Rather less good, especially on east side. PURPLE to PINK.

W along **King Street**. 2-st. Broad, quiet. Mixed, "chiefly labourers" said Clyne. PINK to PURPLE.

S down **Rectory Grove**. 2½-st. Quiet. PINK. Goes uphill to the green aspen poplars round Mulgrave Pond Reservoir which makes a pleasant end to the road. PINK.

E into **Rectory Place**. Better in the centre where there are old detached houses with officers, doctors, solicitors and servants (RED) than at either end where it is PINK. Perhaps PINK-barred all through. The south end is called Mulgrave Place.

E along **Red Lion Street**. New 2-st, PINK, on south side. Less good, old, on north but all are PINK.

S into **Wellington Street**. Broad street, shops, one of the main roads to the Barracks. New theatre being built. Runs uphill to the west. Soldiers' Institute on south side west of church, large red-brick building "much patronised by soldiers".

The continuation to the N is **Artillery Place**. Also shops selling old uniforms, new uniforms, buttons, caps. Games shops, saddlers, tailors, pawnshops, etc. All small outside. Mark both these streets PINK-barred.

Out of the N side is **Back Lane**. Two LIGHT BLUE houses on west side below a row of cottages being dismantled. On the east side is a mission chapel (St Martin's) and two rows of poor cottages. LIGHT BLUE, no name.

W along Artillery Place and N into **Catherine Square**. One of the roughest in the district. Five 3-st houses looking onto broad asphalted court, tap in centre. Built 1843. Irish, fights, a drunken row most nights. Mess of paper, no bread. Children dirty. DARK BLUE to LIGHT BLUE.

W along Artillery Place. Out of N side, W of Rushgrove St, is a court of small 1-st houses called **Lyons Place**. One room in each, 2/3. Old women, lean cats but clean yard. DARK BLUE to LIGHT BLUE.

N up Frances St and E at **Mason Street**. Opposite barracks are old, poor houses. Rooms let to soldiers married "off the strength". Wretched lives led by such wives who take in other soldiers' washing. 2-st. LIGHT BLUE.

S down **Rushgrove Street**. A little better. 2-st. LIGHT BLUE to PURPLE.

E along **Ann Street**. 2-st on south, 3-st on north. Poor, rough, drunken. Boots and windows bad, some thieves and prostitutes, rough and drunken, some prostitutes in each of these three last streets. LIGHT BLUE-barred.

General Remarks

Fine day, strong cold wind. Woolwich is a curious place, remarkable for its broad streets, constant hills and unsuspected turnings. Clyne gives nearly all the streets a bad character. Those marked PURPLE would, according to him, be LIGHT BLUE, those LIGHT BLUE would be LIGHT BLUE-barred or DARK BLUE. "Labourers" predominate but the streets look fairly comfortable and windows and blinds too clean and steps too white for there not to be a good deal of PINK in them. It may be only the extra prosperity of this year, everyone in work and with more work than they can manage, that has lifted these streets but for the moment they are certainly not LIGHT BLUE. There is not here the dirtiness and grime of the streets north of the Woolwich Rd, noticed in the last walk.

Though not so much drunken roughness, there are more prostitutes than in the streets north of the Woolwich Rd. They cling to the neighbourhood of the Barracks, "flies round the honey pot". Clyne says their usual charge to soldiers is 9d or 1/- and soldiers are allowed to go on tick and pay when their money comes in. Coffee shops here as elsewhere have notoriety as brothels but open spaces are more used than houses of accommodation.

Streets fairly well cleaned. Public houses are numerous but not many women seen in them, though today is Monday.

The next round is to take in the notorious 'Dust Hole'.

Walk 77

B371

Wednesday 16th May 1900.
George Duckworth with PC Clyne.

Starting at the corner of Powis Street and High Street.
E along **Powis Street**. Shops east of Hare St. RED to PINK-barred.
N up **Hare Street**, in character a continuation of Powis St. Tram lines. Shops, newly built, not yet numbered. RED to PINK-barred.
N into **High Street**. Very narrow, congested, small shops, tram lines, many common lodging houses. Seaport town street, fair sprinkling of brothels, generally in coffee shops. In the Dockyard and Mitre Chambers, two lodging houses on north side nearly opposite Parsons Hill, beds are at 4d and 6d a night. Hold between 30 and 40 each and are tenanted by loafers, dock and waterside casuals and a few thieves. High St is so mixed it might be PURPLE.
E along High St and N into **Glass Yard** and **Cross Alley**. 2-st. Poor, drunks, some prostitutes. LIGHT BLUE-barred to DARK BLUE. Comes out at east end under an old house in Nile St with a projecting upper storey, now used as a common lodging house and "a rough one".
S down **Nile Street**. Has the Woolwich free ferry at its river end. Has been much cleared by LCC to make a good approach. South of common lodging house it is PINK on the west side.
E along High St and S down **Gough Yard**. Yard of Woolwich District Board of Health on west side.
S into **Union Street**. 2-st, new. Look fairly decent but are not well tenanted. "Used to be a rare place for thieves and prostitutes" and formed part of the Dust Hole in old days. Former inhabitants have been scattered but new houses don't at once give a street a new name and rather a poor lot are getting in. PURPLE.
W into **Myrtle Place**. Old cottages. DARK BLUE to LIGHT BLUE. One woman says she pays 6/-. Her house has been condemned. The only place they can move to is the new houses in Union St where, for the same amount of space, she will have to pay 12/-: "more than a poor working man with family can afford". DARK BLUE to LIGHT BLUE.
E into **Union Buildings**. New on east, old on west side. LIGHT BLUE to PURPLE. Three and four families to a house.
S to Union St. E to **Beresford Street**. 2-st. Trams, cobbles, narrow. Church at south end on east side, above it a theatre, then a large red-brick building known as Wilson's Tabernacle. Some prostitutes living here but houses look fairly comfortable. PINK.
S to Beresford Square Market Place. Broad, booths for market place, busy and crowded on Fridays and Saturdays. One of the main entrances to Woolwich Arsenal on the north side. Great crowd of men coming out at 1 pm dinner hour. The majority were young men. Bowler hats or caps, young men more often caps, middle-aged and old men bowlers. Majority wearing collars. Some labourers making for home in south east and south west directions. Only one man that I saw had his dinner brought to him but Clyne says that a great number bring it with them and cook and eat it in the Arsenal. There is a large coffee house at the corner of Cross St which is much patronised: "Cut from joint & two vegs 6d"; "Roast Beef or Pork 4d and 6d" "Large rasher and two eggs 4d". Shouting among the crowd were six boys selling the 'news', "Sun", ½d papers, not many buyers. Clyne says they buy their papers, discuss it with their dinners and then return and place their bets upon the horses they fancy with the bookies when they come back to work. The bookies are agents of bigger men and wait in the Square.
Out of the W side of the Market Place is **Salutation Alley**. 2-st. Very poor and rough,

Irish, some costers, some thieves, fat loathsome women, barrows. 4/- for two rooms and wash-house. LIGHT BLUE-barred to DARK BLUE.

N up **Rope Yard Rails**. This is the beginning of the Dust Hole. 2-st and 3-st. Sixteen common lodging houses in the street, all on the east side. Some bread and mess but street fairly clean. All the houses practically brothels, used by sailors, loafers, waterside labourers and by the lowest grade soldiers. For soldiers it is out of bounds and patrolled nightly by the military police. On the east side standing back are Council Chambers, late 'Ye Olde Casual Ward' (from a notice at the entrance). Two doors, women on the right and men on the left, no communication between the two. Great many Irish. "Good accommodation for travellers", a common sign here. One woman, poor and dirty, not particularly vicious-looking, pays 5/6 for four rooms plus wash-house, has been there seven years. Her father-inlaw owns the house and has lived in the street 28 or 29 years. He came out, an old man between 60 and 70, above middle height, a yellow white beard, decently dressed as a working man, smoking a pipe, looked like one in the autumn of life enjoying his old age after an honest and industrious youth. Clyne says they make their money by letting out rooms to men and prostitutes. The same room is let out many times the same night. This street is a fair BLACK all through, not for poverty but for vice. In the middle of the road just by Council Chambers is an almshouse for old women.

N into **High Street**. Full of women. One girl of barely 18 with a clean apron, frizzed hair, short skirts, bare head, red, puffy, diseased-looking face, a prostitute. "Has already been in prison 13 or 14 times" said Clyne. Mahoney's Common Lodging Houses frequent. Also BLACK. Road runs uphill to the west. On north side are Stanhope Chambers, model buildings, 5-st. Very rough, poor. LIGHT BLUE to DARK BLUE. West across open market place surrounded by public houses and beerhouse. Small shops, looks poor upstairs. Might be PURPLE.

Out of N side is **Bell Water Gate**. Leading to ferry. A street of five houses Three are public houses, one a beerhouse and one a coffee house, "a noted brothel".

E along a passage called **New Street**. 2-st houses. Asphalt. Six houses on north and two on south. All doors open. Children with holey boots or none at all, all in good health and sufficiently fed. Houses beastly and stink of dirt. Irish and prostitutes. DARK BLUE to BLACK.

E into **Globe Lane**. 2½-st. Runs downhill to the river. Women on doorsteps, sore faces, bare tousled heads, aprons. Some brothels. DARK BLUE to BLACK.

E & S is **Nelson Street**. 2½-st. Rather better. LIGHT BLUE to PURPLE, barred with BLACK.

E along **High Street** which is at this point perhaps the roughest of all the points in the Dust Hole. Women with broken noses, swollen faces, bare dirty unkempt faces and heads, draggled skirts, frayed edges everywhere, coarse Irish faces, bare arms. No men about.

S down **Collingwood Street**. Broad, clean, some bread and broken windows, but noted for bad characters. LIGHT BLUE-barred to BLACK.

Into **Rodney Street**. 2-st. LIGHT BLUE-barred to BLACK.

E & N up **Meeting House Lane**. Rough, poor. Poorer than the rest but less vicious, no brothels. DARK BLUE without the BLACK.

E & S down **Harden's Lane**. Only a foreman's house lived in on west side.

E & S down **Warren Lane**. Two LIGHT BLUE to BLACK houses near High St on west side. East side is Arsenal Wall. The High St where it turns south becomes Warren Lane and is like Rope Yard Rails in character. The almshouses of the Ropeyard come through to this side. The rest is common lodging houses and brothels. BLACK – a vile hole. Bread in the street and beastly women on the pavement.

This is the end of the Dust Hole.

Nile Street, in the notorious Dust Hole.

The Dust Hole

Speaking generally on the character of the Dust Hole, Clyne said it was to the south east of London what Notting Dale is to the west. It forms a house of call for all the tramps from London to Kent and vice versa. There is a regular interchange of tenants between this and Bangor St and Queen, Giffin and Hales Streets in Deptford. Policemen from Notting Dale find old friends in Rope Yard Rails. The casual loafer floats between the two. When 'wanted' in one he is pretty sure to be in the other.

The male inhabitants are bullies, dock and waterside labourers, costers, hawkers and tramps. The women are prostitutes. In the area between the Thames on the North, Warren Lane on the east, Rope Yard Rails, High St and Nile St on the west (ie. the Dust Hole) Clyne reckons between 70 and 80 known prostitutes. Since the Law against bullies of last October year 45 men were run in on this charge and of this number 42 were convicted and sentenced to terms varying between three and fifteen months with hard labour.

The lowest class of woman is of the rough Irish type of the Fenian Barracks in Bromley (Gale St, Box St, etc). The younger prostitute is in appearance the 'Jailor's Wife' of Ratcliffe Highway (Sage St, Albert St). The clean white apron and the frizzed hair and earrings is the mark of this class. Clyne says the majority of young and old, male and female are Irish. No law runs in these streets. The priest is powerless and seldom seen. The police only come when there is a bad row and they are summoned. No man would go alone. When called he waits for at least one other. Missiles are showered on them from every window when they interfere. It is out of bounds for soldiers and the military patrol can capture and confine any soldier found there. But nevertheless the low-class soldier goes there. The police know and see them but have no right to arrest them.

If the man is known to have money or jewels on him he is made to hire a room and robbed, "always cleaned out". If he has only enough to pay the woman then the street is used. There is no regular charge, each man pays as much as the woman can get from him.

The war has had great effect on the district, for the better. The bullies, on coming out of prison, would naturally return to their old games but it is risky work now and there has been a great demand for workers. Neither Dockyard nor private employers have gone strictly into the question of character. In consequence some have found employment and some have gone to the war.

Those who suffer most from the Dust Hole are the recruits. Woolwich is a depot with drafts constantly coming and going. These are the young flies that are caught and may be ruined for life.

The roughest public house in the Hole is that at the corner of Nelson St.

E along the **Plumstead Road**. Blank Arsenal walls on north side. Tram, shops (small) on south side and plenty of public houses. Not better than PINK-barred all along.

S down **New Road**. 2-st and 3-st large shops. PINK-barred to RED north of railway.

E along **Cross Street**. Small shops. PINK.

Out of the W side is **Peake's Place**. Four very poor 2-st cottages, built 1795. DARK BLUE.

N up **Thomas Street**. New 2-st houses and some good shops belonging properly to Greens End. PINK to PINK-barred. South of New Rd, Thomas St is also PINK.

N along **New Road**. Old shops. PINK to PINK-barred.

Into the **Plumstead Road**. A long, dull, straight road with old-fashioned 2-st shops on south side, tramlines down the centre and the blank Arsenal walls on the north. High-pitched red-tiled roofs. Many pubs and beerhouses. PINK-barred to PINK.

S down **Parry Place**. Semi-detached, 2-st. PINK.

W along **Spray Street**. New on south side, east of beerhouse. Old on north and at west end. 2-st. New are PINK, old are PURPLE to LIGHT BLUE.

Out of the **NW** end is **Scotts Passage**. Four 2-st cottages, neatly-kept fronts. Used to be Irish and rough, now quieter. LIGHT BLUE.

Opposite are **Taylor's Buildings**. All poor, look fairly respectable but some brothels. 3-st houses. Are worse than they look. LIGHT BLUE to PURPLE.

S down **Taylor Street**. Newish, built 1885. East side better than west. 2-st on east, 2½-st on west. PINK and PURPLE or LIGHT BLUE.

S into **Wilmount Street**. 2-st. PINK.

N up **Helen Street**. 2-st. PINK to PURPLE.

E & S down **East Street**. East side better than west. 2-st. West side all LIGHT BLUE. PURPLE to LIGHT BLUE.

S & E along **Whitworth Place**. 2-st. Mixed, some rough. Principally two families. PURPLE to LIGHT BLUE.

N up **Armstrong Street**. 2-st. PURPLE.

E & S down **Armstrong Place**. Chiefly labourers. 2-st. LIGHT BLUE to PURPLE.

N into **Eton Road**. Small shops. PINK to PURPLE.

N & E along **Burrage Grove**. 2-st, fronts. Old tenants. PURPLE to PINK.

E into **Maxey Road**. 2-st. PINK.

E & S down **Charlotte Street**. Majority Arsenal workers. Quiet, mixed. Five 2-st houses facing railway at south west end. PURPLE to LIGHT BLUE.

N & S down **Inverness Place**. Narrow, small, poorish shops, 2-st. PURPLE to LIGHT BLUE.

W along **Railway Place**. 2-st. Poor. LIGHT BLUE.

S down **Richmond Place**. 2-st. PURPLE.

Into Pattison Rd where the road runs steeply uphill to the **S**. Out of **W** side of Pattison Rd

is a steep dip into **Oliver Street**, 2-st, PINK, and **Dawson Street**, PINK to PURPLE.
E to Glyndon Rd and W to **Charles Street** and **Arthur Street**. PINK to PURPLE.
Villas Road. PURPLE. Rather better small detached houses north of railway. Small master
builders etc. PINK and PURPLE.
E & S up **Ann Street**. 2-st. PURPLE.
E & N down **Robert Street**. Poorer. LIGHT BLUE to PURPLE. Small 2-st houses with
wooden palinged fronts. Old yellow-brick houses with four rooms and wash-house for from
8/6 to 10/6. Old established tenants.
E & S up **Thomas Street**. Poor. East side better than west. LIGHT BLUE to PURPLE. A
few houses out of east side, PURPLE.
E & S up **Down Street**. Poorer still. Bread and dirty children, doorposts shiny. The
poorest part is opposite the railway out of south east end (LIGHT BLUE) which is called **Down
Place**. One woman here two years, pays 6/- for five rooms plus wash-house. Very poor.
Might almost be DARK BLUE.
E & S down **Station Road**. PURPLE.
E to **Elm Street**. PINK to PURPLE.
Earl Street. PURPLE to PINK.
Robert Street. LIGHT BLUE to PURPLE.
Ann Street. PURPLE. These are all 2-st streets, fairly broad, clean roads. 24 ft between
pavement and pavement and 7 ft of pavement on either side = 38 ft of street, and small fronts
to houses which give additional width to street. Built about 1860.
The street bounding these roads on the S is **Walmer Road** which is PINK to PURPLE
between Station Rd and Villas Rd but LIGHT BLUE between Villas Rd and Vicarage Rd.

General Remarks

This round comprises two distinct areas.
1) The Dust Hole, already treated at length.
2) The streets on either side of the railway between Plumstead Rd and Glyndon Rd. These
latter are tenanted by Arsenal workers, skilled and unskilled, and Dockyard labourers. All
are mixed and bear the impress of drink. Temptations in the shape of public houses abound. It
would seem as though the men here earned too much money and worked too short hours. They
don't yet know how to spend either extra money or leisure hours decently. Clyne said they had
now the eight hours day and higher wages but that it was not usual to give the wife any more
for the home. Just now there is much overtime at the Arsenal. Men come home very tired and
with their pockets more than usual full, with the result that they drink more than usual deep to
refresh themselves. From the Arsenal alone £30,000 is paid weekly in wages (this was told me
by Fred Donaldson, the Director General of Ordnance).

The ground rises steeply in an irregular series of kopjes from the Plumstead Rd
southwards. There are occasional sharp dips to the west as in Dawson St and Oliver St.
Streets broad and well cleaned. The mess of paper, bread etc, where seen, was today's not
yesterday's or last week's as under some vestries.

Coal 1/6 per cwt. Bread 4½d a quartern loaf.

Walk 78

B371

Friday 18th May 1900.
George Duckworth with PC Clyne.

Starting at the corner of Anglesea Road.
Anglesea Road. 2-st, small shops. PINK.
N up Anglesea Avenue. East side better than west. Mixed. PURPLE. Built 1859.
E along Wilmount Street. 2-st. PINK.
S up Mount Pleasant. PINK.
Out of its W side is Mason's Avenue. Six 2-st houses. One has been there "13 years come August", pays 11/- per week for five rooms and wash-house. PINK.
S into Anglesea Road. PINK.
Out of S side is Havelock Place. Three cottages, quiet. Poorish. PINK to LIGHT BLUE. One policeman. Stand on a hill overlooking valley on the west.
Further S are two more cottages with large gardens well filled with vegetables and flowers called Wellington Cottages. Beans, peas, currants, roses, wallflowers. Two policemen live here. PINK.
W into Brookhill Road. Improves southwards. Opposite barracks, some prostitutes. Shops at north end, much mixed. Houses 2-st, 3-st and 3½-st. PURPLE. Might be PINK south of Willenhall Rd.
Out of NE end is Walpole Place. In a hollow. Has had a bad reputation, still drinks. 2-st. Windows shaken by guns being tested at the Arsenal. PURPLE to LIGHT BLUE.
E along Plumstead Common Road. Runs uphill steeply to the east. Old road, improves eastwards near the Common. PINK and PINK-barred.
N up Hanover Road. 2-st and 2½-st. Runs over crest of steep hill to the north, up one side and down the other. Non-commissioned officers and retired pensioners living here. A few poor. PINK to PURPLE.
At the N end is Hanover Terrace. Rather poorer. 2½-st. PURPLE to PINK.
Out of the W side is Willenhall Road. 2-st, newish. PINK.
E along Bignell Road. Broad, clean. Two prostitutes living on south side but don't bring men home. 2-st. PINK to PURPLE.
E into Sandy Hill Road. Runs uphill to the south. East side better than the west. Constant shifting among the tenants of the houses on the west side south of Bignell Rd. PURPLE here, otherwise PINK.
Out of W side is The Avenue. 2-st. Poor. LIGHT BLUE. With a set of cottages running downhill on the north side. LIGHT BLUE.
S into Plumstead Common Rd. E & N up Bloomfield Road. 2-st and 2½-st. May be one or two servants but PINK as a whole.
N to St James' Place. Small fronts, long backs. Comfortable, with generally a lodger. PINK.
N to Frederick Place. Rather poorer west than east of Bloomfield Rd. PINK to PURPLE.
N to Raglan Road. 2-st. PINK.
W to Conduit Road. 2-st and 2½-st. PINK.
Into Crescent Road. PINK to PURPLE. Some poor on north side.
S down Sandy Hill Road. Mixed working class. 2-st, gardens. Road very steep running downhill to Brookhill Road. Admirably paved and clean. PURPLE.

E along Crescent Rd to **Burrage Road**. Runs uphill to the south. Is PURPLE near the Plumstead Rd, PINK to PURPLE south of railway to Crescent Rd, PINK to Raglan Rd, then begin a few servants and PINK-barred to Frederick Place, and RED to PINK-barred from Frederick Place to the Plumstead Common Rd. Officers, retired and active, with their families living or lodging here.

E along **Chester Place**. 2-st. PINK.

E to **Swetenham Place**. 2-st. North side better than south. PINK to PURPLE.

S to **Sandbach Place**. 2-st. PURPLE to PINK.

E to **Pattison Road**. PINK.

E to **Hudson Road**. Poorer. Much LIGHT BLUE. Very poor on west side north of Raglan Rd. PURPLE to LIGHT BLUE.

Out of S end is **Lee Street**, PURPLE to LIGHT BLUE, and **St Margaret's Terrace**, 2-st, PURPLE. Much drink in all these streets.

E to **Vicarage Road**. Steep hill. 2-st. PURPLE to PINK. South end is backs of Hudson Rd.

E to **Vicarage Park**. Deep valley being east side. Servant-keeping house at extreme south end. East of church the road itself is 3-st plus attic on west side. PURPLE to PINK. The east side is much poorer with two and three families. LIGHT BLUE to PURPLE?

N down **Manthorp Road**. PURPLE.

W along **Raglan Road**. Here PURPLE. Some very poor on north side at corner of Hudson Rd. LIGHT BLUE.

W & N up **Copland Terrace**. 2-st. PURPLE.

W to **Church Terrace**. 2-st. PINK. On a rise. Quiet, green, comfortable.

W to **Maxey Road**. PINK all through except south east end, south of public house where it is poorer and might be PURPLE. The crest of the hill is at the Board School, the deep dip is to the north and a lesser one to the south. The garden of 'The Oaks' reaches to end of road, tenanted by Colonel Hughes, MP for Woolwich.

Back again E to **Villas Road**. Poor. LIGHT BLUE at south west. 2-st but PURPLE at east.

E to **Ann Street**. 2-st. PURPLE to LIGHT BLUE.

E to **Robert Street**. Poor on east side south of Glyndon Rd right up to church. PURPLE to LIGHT BLUE.

E to **East Street**. PURPLE to LIGHT BLUE.

Elm Street. PURPLE to LIGHT BLUE.

Station Road. PURPLE to LIGHT BLUE. All these roads are 2-st, clean, fairly broad, built about 40 years ago, poor. Have the look of tenants who earn money but don't spend it well. Clyne gives them all a bad character for drink.

E to **Griffin Road**. New road, new houses, broad, red-brick facings. Arsenal foremen and clerks. PINK.

E to **Orchard Road, Coxwell Road, Ingledew Road, Liffler Road, Miriam Road**. All 2-st newish streets with narrower backs than the roads west of Griffin Rd. Streets broad, clean and well made. Arsenal labourers. PURPLE.

Gallosson Road (Orissa Rd in large map). Newer. PINK.

The **Conway Road**, which is a continuation east of Glyndon Rd, is rather better. 2-st. PINK to PURPLE.

N of the Conway Rd is **Orchard Road**. PURPLE.

E of Orchard Rd are **new roads** covering the old Invicta Athletic Grounds, not yet named. Built and building, tenanted as soon as built. PINK.

E of it is **Bebbington Street**. 2-st, new in last 18 months. Two families, not built in flats but majority built with a view to two families. PINK.

S up steep hill called **Piedmont Road**. PURPLE to PINK.

Out of W side, up another hill rising from Piedmont Rd and descending into Anema Rd, is **Congo Road**. 2-st. PURPLE.

S to **Leghorn Road**. PURPLE to PINK.

S up **Tuscan Road**. 2-st, bow on ground floor. PINK.

W along **Gossage Road**. Older semi-detached houses on south side, gardens. A few servants. PINK-barred on south, PINK on north.

S to Plumstead Common past modern almshouses at south east corner of Heavitree Rd and Park Rd. Along **Old Mill Road**. PINK. 2-st.

N up **Old Mill Cottages**. 2-st. LIGHT BLUE to PURPLE.

E along **Old Mill Road**. Mixed. Old cottages PURPLE, new are PINK.

N down **Chestnut Road**. PINK.

E to **Parkdale Road**. Less good. PURPLE.

N into **Brewery Road**. PINK as far as Griffin Rd but markedly poorer west of Griffin Rd. Old houses. LIGHT BLUE to PURPLE.

S into **Majendie Road**. 1881. Older. PURPLE.

S to **Durham Road**. PURPLE.

S up **Park Road**. PINK.

Into **Heavitree Road**. Large servant-keeping houses at south east end, RED. The rest is PINK.

Out of it down steep hill to the N run **Waverley Road**, PINK, **Burwash Road**, PINK to PURPLE, and **Bramblebury Road**, PINK to PURPLE. All 2-st.

Bounding their N ends is **Durham Road**. PURPLE.

General Remarks

A cold, grey day with a strong north easterly wind. Very hilly district. The houses west of Griffin Rd are old, dating from 1850 to 1860. The usual thing is for a family to take the house and then to let off. Good gardens, long strips at the back and small wooden-railinged fronts. Not much to boast of in the way of flowers but a large number keep fowls or pigeons or rabbits. East of Griffin Rd the new houses are generally 2-st but have less garden. Clyne said people preferred an extra room to a larger garden. In the new houses the extra room is built out behind over the wash-house.

The tenants are Arsenal workers. As labourers they earn 22/- per week and just now are making much overtime. They start at 8 am, relays get home at 6, 8, 9 and 10 pm. Their wives wash and their daughters do homework for Woolwich clothing or games factories. The best part of today's round lies to the west of Pattison Rd, between Pattison Rd and Crescent Rd and the new streets further east, north of the Brewery Rd. These are all PINK except the south end of Burrage Rd where officers with their families live and lodge. The poorer streets lie between Glyndon St and Heavitree Rd. None very poor but all with a considerable admixture of poverty. Clyne says that all round there is a tendency to spend money and evenings in the public houses. There are no counter-attractions in the way of theatres or music halls. The pub is the club. Churches and chapel abound. They seem to be more frequent here than in any other part of London but Clyne says that, except Wilson's Tabernacle, they have very little influence.

Fine views from the hill over Woolwich, over town and Arsenal, across grey river which broadens here, dull red sails of hay and cement barges, dark black chimneys belching volumes of black smoke rising from a bed of white steam, bright green of marshes in the eastern foreground etc. This afternoon there were occasional flashes on the marsh followed by a crash which made even the windows on the hillside shake. These were the guns being tested. Clyne said that windows – sometimes plate glass windows – were broken by the concussion. No redress is obtainable from the Government.

Victoria and Albert Docks on the north side of the river, full of ships, masts, sails, and red and black smoke stacks of the ocean steam boats.

Walk 79

B371

Monday 21st May 1900.
George Duckworth with PC Clyne.

Starting at the corner of Plumstead Common Road.
S down Woolwich Common. 3-st. Lodgings for officers, houses for their wives and families. Some belong to Government and are official residences but are not in any way outwardly distinguished. Mark the whole RED or it might be YELLOW from Rutter St southwards.
E into Jackson Street. 2-st. North side rather better than south. PURPLE.
Manor Street. 2-st. South better than north side. Poor. PURPLE to LIGHT BLUE.
Engineer Road. 2-st. Broader. PURPLE to PINK.
Gildersome Street. 2-st. PURPLE to PINK.
Milward Street. 2-st and 2½-st. These streets are tenanted chiefly by soldiers and their wives and families. The majority are kept by army pensioners who let off to the regiment that happen to be stationed at Woolwich. Tenants always changing houses. Sometimes rough and sometimes respectable depending on the regiment. The Irish Regiments are the roughest. Clyne says that many soldiers live with women unmarried. These temporary wives are accepted in society. Much drink. Some prostitutes in these streets. Their colour as a whole is PURPLE. Rents about 9/- for four rooms plus wash-house.
E into Nightingale Lane which runs downhill to the north and has a dip into a deep valley on its east side. Better. Old houses, some large at south end. Old toll-house on east side by Belmont Place. 2-st, 2½-st and 3-st. A Gospel Hall "not much attended" on west side. PINK.
Out of E side starting at N end are three turnings:
Hables Cottages. 2-st. Three LIGHT BLUE houses. The woman at the east end who has fowls and a bit of a yard has been there with her mother, who died four years ago, in all 76 years. She pays 4/- for three rooms and kitchen.
S to Montague Cottages. Four houses, three have wash-houses at the east end. Front gardens. One woman pays 5/- for two rooms, there four years last December. LIGHT BLUE.
S to Belmont Place. Five 2-st cottages. Not so nice as Montague. Very respectable women. 9/- for six rooms and wash-house. PURPLE to LIGHT BLUE.
S into Dicey Street. In a valley, runs steeply uphill at both north and south ends. 2-st, houses flush with pavement. Some windows broken, rubbed greasy bricks, most doors open. Bread and winkle shells in the street. Rough, Irish, drunken. LIGHT BLUE-barred to DARK BLUE.
S into Delvan Street. Rough dirty class but not so bad as Dicey St. South side better than north. 2-st. LIGHT BLUE.
W uphill to James Street. Broad, clean. Not quite so good as Engineer Rd. Two families usual. PURPLE.
W along Ritter Street. Poor at north west end. 2-st. PURPLE.
S along Keemor Street. Two bow windows to houses on east side. Faced red brick. Broad and clean. PINK to PURPLE.
S down Ordnance Road. 2-st. Broad and clean but a rough street. "Beer for breakfast

here" said Clyne. Good many soldiers, not NCOs, pensioners and labourers. Not so many rows as Dicey St but as poor. 7/6 for four rooms plus wash-house, there five years, raised 6d about a year ago. LIGHT BLUE to PURPLE. Out of the east side are two houses, PURPLE to LIGHT BLUE, and others out of the west side, LIGHT BLUE.

E along **Eglinton Road**. Poor to Llanover Rd, LIGHT BLUE to PURPLE, then improves and goes on improving towards the east. It might be PURPLE between Ordnance Rd and Lower Ripon Rd, then PINK to the turn, PINK-barred on south side, RED for large houses at the bend and PINK-barred at the bend southwards.

W along the **Herbert Road**. Some servants. PINK-barred and PINK between Paget Rd and Whitworth Rd.

Out of **N** side are:

Lower Ripon Road. PINK. 1864. 2-st and 2½-st.

Paget Road. PINK. Terrace stands back on east side.

Whitworth Road. 2-st. PINK. Attendants from RMA.

Llanover Road. PINK to PURPLE.

Out of the **S** side of Herbert Rd is **Upper Ripon Road**. Some servants. Opposite is All Saints Church (Rev Morris). PINK-barred to RED.

Steep hill running up to **S** is **Paget Road**. PINK-barred.

Whitworth Road. PINK. No servants.

S down Paget Rd into **Cantwell Road**. Fine view. Not all built on north side, mixed. Some big houses coming down to make way for smaller. PINK-barred to PINK.

S up **Brent Road**. Steep hill running up to south. Detached houses. RED. Greenery, lilacs and laburnums.

N down **Eglinton Road**. Steep. RED, servant-keeping at south end. PINK-barred from just north of Brent Rd to Herbert Rd.

NE along **Herbert Road**. Shops, fairly comfortable. PINK-barred to RED.

Into **Plumstead Common Road**. Mixed, old. PINK and PINK-barred.

Out of the NE end of Herbert Rd is **Edge Hill Road**. 2½-st. Comfortable working class. PINK.

Leading to Edge Hill, part of **Plumstead Common Road**, which on this side stands on a low cliff well above the rest of the road and is better than the rest of it, ie. PINK-barred.

E along Plumstead Common Rd to **Graydon Street**. Poor, drunken, like Jackson St. PURPLE to LIGHT BLUE.

S up **Westdale Road**. Old semi-detached houses in a valley which rises steeply on the east side. PURPLE.

Back again to **Nightingale Place**. Leads by Barracks to Woolwich Common. Officers' lodgings and apartments. RED, with a row of PINK cottages on both sides in the centre.

Back **E** to Plumstead Common Rd and **S** up **Princes Road**. Old, poor, rough. Built 1845-57. Labourers, prostitutes, children barefoot and dirty. 8-roomed cottages out of west side at north end. LIGHT BLUE to DARK BLUE. The whole street is LIGHT BLUE to LIGHT BLUE-barred. The man keeping the public house on the east side was committed some time ago for murdering his wife.

Opposite pub on **W** side is **Brookhill Row**. Rather better. LIGHT BLUE to PURPLE.

Leading **S** to **Cumberland Place**. 2-st, three houses. LIGHT BLUE.

Turning **E** at **Portland Place**. 2-st. LIGHT BLUE. At the south end of Princes Rd is a brick-built column that looks as though meant for a Jubilee clock but it is only an escape for sewer gas. Behind the **E** side of Princes Rd is **Barnfield Road**. Rather better. PURPLE to LIGHT BLUE. 2-st with bow windows on ground floor.

Leading N to Rocket Row and John's Place. Poorer, Irish, drunks, rows. Poor and very poor. One house standing back is fairly comfortable. LIGHT BLUE to DARK BLUE, and PINK.
E of it is Barnfield Place. Poor. LIGHT BLUE. Lotus Nursery Garden at south end, PINK.
E & S down Wrottesley Road. 2-st, small fronts. Some servants. PINK-barred.
W into Genesta Road. Newish, 2-st, yellow brick, one bow window on ground floor. Life assurance agents. PINK.
S of it is a new unnamed road. 2-st, still building, taken as soon as finished and before dry. The cry of "No room to live" and the series of articles in the *Daily News* has been a godsend to those owners and builders, enabling the first to raise his rents and the second to fill his houses without difficulty. Fine views from east end which is still a hilly waste over the Plumstead marshes. Bricks made from the foundations dug for the houses as for the houses at the north east corner of London in Crouch End.
E along Wrottesley Road. PINK.
Into Plum Lane. PINK.
Out of the N side of Wrottesley Rd is Vernham Road. 2-st. PINK.
And out of it on E are Isla Rd, PINK, and Vambery Road, PINK.
N up Kirk Lane. Older houses. PINK to PURPLE.
E to Plum Lane. PINK-barred at north end and south as far as Clay Farm House. Some detached houses on east side. On the north side of Plumstead Common Rd some poor cottages looking on to the Common and also at the corner of the Blendon Rd. LIGHT BLUE to PURPLE.
Going E out of the S side of Plumstead Common Rd is Hargor Road. In hollow. 2-st and 2½-st. Many poor and windows broken. PURPLE to LIGHT BLUE.
Like it though rather better at S end is Palmerston Road. 2-st. PURPLE to LIGHT BLUE. Between Hargor Rd and Palmerston Rd are two cottages with gardens out of the Plumstead Rd. PURPLE to LIGHT BLUE.
E & S down Ennis Road. New houses on west side, gardens to large house on east. At south end are houses on west side against side of steep hill.
E to Admaston Road. New. PINK.
E along Upton Road. PINK.
S up Olven Road. New. PINK.
Into Hinstock Road. New. PINK. These roads are all 2-st, new and fairly broad. Small fronts surrounded by low wall with a fancy iron rail at the top. Small backs. Six rooms let for 12/- or 13/- per week. These roads are taking away the PINK out of the older streets in Plumstead.
Out of the N side of Plumstead Common are Wernbrook Road, new 12/- houses, PINK, and St John's Road, ending abruptly in a miniature precipe at the west end, also PINK. Opposite is the Plumstead Common laid out in inferior lawn tennis courts. No-one playing this afternoon. Belongs to LCC.

General Remarks

There are three divisions in today's round: 1) the mixed streets east of the Woolwich Common, 2) the PINK to PINK-barred streets between Wrottesley Rd and Eglinton Rd and 3) The new PINK streets built and building which lie south of the Plumstead Common Rd and east of Wrottesley Rd. Each has its own poor. No. 1 has the poorest and roughest in Dicey St, Delvan St and Ordnance Rd, No. 2 poor in Princes Rd and Barnfield Rd. No. 3 poor in Hargor Rd and Palmerston Rd. Irish and drink are the prevailing causes of roughness and poverty. There is no improvement, if anything worsement, by reason of the goodness of the times, the amount of money about and the constant celebration of victories in South Africa.

Speaking about the earnings of the police. The ordinary PC starts at 24/- and rises each year for eight years to 32/-. There he stops. His next rise is to be Sergeant, then to Station Sergeant, then Inspector and the height of his ambition is to be Superintendent. One shilling is paid to the police by publicans for early calling. Not much extra service money. The Theatre is the most regular employer but the job is not much liked as between five and twenty persons have to be put out for disorderly behaviour every week. There are 70 men at the Woolwich station and not more than 10/- is their average yearly sharing of money earned by special service. Out of a man's wages, 1/6 is taken weekly from an unmarried man being 1/- for lodging, 3d for the pension fund, 1d for the band, 1½d for the orphans and widows fund.

Clyne, as special service man, has to visit the pawnbrokers daily with lists of stolen goods. None in Woolwich are Jews. A great deal is put away even for so short a time as a week. The charge for any period of time up to a year is 2d in the 1/-. The boys who pack away the clothes suffer terribly from flea-bites.

Roads as a whole are broad, clean and well kept. Roughness less than it used to be. In the rough streets, police make a point of knowing the men by name and sight. In the new streets, large houses are more valued than large gardens.

Walk 80

B371

Monday 28th May 1900.
George Duckworth with PC Clyne.

Starting at the corner of Plumstead Road and the Arsenal walls
Descending on to the flat along **Griffin Manor Way**. Some cottages at the south east end. Walls of Arsenal on west. Further north is the Arsenal football ground with a grand stand and surrounded by a wooden paling. Crowded in winter. Sometimes 25,000 onlookers of a Saturday, said Clyne. Boys pay 3d, men 6d or 1/-, different gates for each price.
N along road over **Plumstead Marshes**. Like the fen country. Deep ditches of water on either side of the roadway. Broad green grass fields divided by ditches, looking their best now and full of flowers. Horses turned out here, whippet racing round, pigeon shooting clubs come here (Woolwich shopkeepers' shooting club comes on Thursdays and shoots tame pigeons). Fields dry enough now but very marshy in winter. Some thorns, covered with white mayflower, the air heavy with the scent of the flowers. At the north end is the large gun trial ground and the rifle butts of the Arsenal. The first unexpected boom and thud of a big gun makes you jump. You look back to see a great cloud of dust rising from the rubbish heap into which they fire. A little further on is the crack and bang of practice rifles as the bullet leaves the barrel and reaches the target.
The road turns off to the south at the Cross Manor Way which leads to the southern outfall sewage works at Cross Ness. This road running south is called the **Harrow Manor Way** and is one of the boundaries of County Council London. A row of 3-st houses is being built on the Cross Manor Way, untenanted, probably Governmental. Further south there are gipsey camping grounds with groups of ragged, dirty children under tents made of old skirts stretched over hurdles. No school for them!
Further south near Abbey Wood station "freehold lots of this desirable building land" are to be sold and some have been bought – strips of about an acre each, and on them 1-st wooden houses, raised from the ground on a concrete foundation, have been built. The gardens are filled with vegetables and fruit trees. Only one man has ventured on a 2-st yellow-brick house.

It must be very damp in winter. The river is kept out by high banks and the great ships seem to sail by on a level with your chin as you walk upon the road. Crossing the lines of Abbey Wood railway station there are new 2-st PINK houses on the east side and older, poorer houses and a public house on the west. PURPLE to LIGHT BLUE.

Out of the W side are **Dingey Cottages**. One woman pays 4/9 for four rooms plus wash-room and has been there seven years. LIGHT BLUE. Further south the road is PINK to PINK-barred.

W along **Bostall Lane**. A few shops, newish. PINK.

Out of N side is **Grove Road**. 2-st. PURPLE to PINK.

W along **Abbey Grove**. 2-st. PURPLE to PINK. Its continuation to the west is much poorer. LIGHT BLUE to DARK BLUE. Wretched, dirty. The poorest are those who work on the market gardens round about and some builders' labourers. Those next above them are Arsenal workers. But the majority of the dwellers in Abbey Wood are employed locally. The trains are so infrequent and unpunctual that even Woolwich workers are shy of living at Abbey Wood.

W along **Bostall Lane**. Much of the land here on north side belongs to Woolwich Co-operative Society which grows fruit and vegetables and builds houses for its members. At the corner where the Lane turns abruptly south, the secretary was laying the foundation stone of a new row of houses which are to be built on the south side of the Lane. There are poor LIGHT BLUE cottages on the west side of the Lane and behind them two farm houses. Large, comfortable, each keeping a house servant. RED. Bostall Lane turns west at Bostall Heath and has a few houses on its north side. PURPLE. "Boiling water for picnic parties" in windows. The Heath belongs to LCC, wild, hilly, birch trees, gravel soil, green.

W down steep hill along **Bostall Hill Road**. Older house on south side and new on north. PINK.

N into **Church Manor Way**. New. PINK.

W along **Plumstead High Street**. 2-st. PINK.

N into **Kashgar Road, Ceres Road, Benares Road, Brookdene Road**. All new, Brookdene Rd still building. Two bow windows. Two families usual. Iron rails round small front, palinged strips at back. Six rooms plus wash-house for about 12/- per week. PURPLE to PINK. Brookdene Rd is the poorest of them.

W to **Bannockburn Farm Road**. PINK to PURPLE.

W to a block of poorer roads which have the reputation of being the worst in Plumstead – not very poor but noisy and drunken. These are:

Barth Road. 2-st. Very drunken, "the worst". LIGHT BLUE.

Out of it on the W side are **Mabyn Road**. LIGHT BLUE.

Hartville Road. LIGHT BLUE to PURPLE.

Glenside Road. LIGHT BLUE to PURPLE.

Marmadon Road. PURPLE to LIGHT BLUE.

Out of Hartville Rd is **Kentmere Road**. LIGHT BLUE to PURPLE.

W to **White Hart Lane**. LIGHT BLUE to PURPLE.

Garibaldi Street. PURPLE.

Out of it are **Abery Street, Bateson Street** and **Gunning Street**. LIGHT BLUE to PURPLE.

W along **Reidhaven Street**. LIGHT BLUE to PURPLE. Improves west of Stevensons.

Out of its W end is **Heverham Road**. 2-st on east, 2½-st on west. Two or three families. PURPLE to LIGHT BLUE. All labourers in these streets. 2-st yellow-brick houses. Streets fairly broad. Worse class than in the new streets east of Bannockburn Rd. Young wives, dirty children. Some broad but clean streets. Clyne thinks it is unusual for the husband to bring home more than 12/6 per week.

General Remarks

Except for Bostall Woods and the high ground south of Bostall Lane and Plumstead High St this is not a pleasant district. The flats which are bright in summer are damp and dreary in winter. There is plenty of room on good gravelly soil for new houses on either side of Bostall Lane (where it runs north and south). Many would be built and quickly occupied were the train service better. Clyne said that you expected to be 20 minutes late and often 40 minutes late in the 11½ miles journey between here and Charing Cross. The trains are timed to do the journey in 40 minutes (vid A.B.C).

Walk 81
B376

Monday 1st October 1900.
George Duckworth unaccompanied.

Starting at the corner of Lakedale Road and Plumstead High Street.
S down **Lakedale Road** (late Cage Lane). Large building of the Royal Arsenal Co-operative Society on the west side. Tram stables, small shops. PINK right up to Plumstead Common.
E along **Tewson Road**. 2-st. PURPLE at north end. PINK to PURPLE where it turns south and runs uphill, getting better as the ground rises.
S up Lakedale Rd and **W** down **Goldsmid Street** which runs steeply westwards to a valley whose bottom is covered by Roydene Rd. PINK.
W into **Sladedale Road**. Mixed. Not all built on west side. Steep drop behind houses on west side. East side is better than the west. PINK to PURPLE.
W & S along **Roydene Road**. 2-st. PINK. Roydene Rd lies in a steep drop between Parkdale Rd and Lakedale Rd.
Leading **W** by Carling Hill to **Tormount Street**. PINK. Houses on east side only.
W & N down **Chestnut Road**. PINK-barred at top end.
NE down **Parkdale Road**. 2-st. PINK.
S across Common to **Macoma Road**. 2-st, red-fronted. Trees on pavement. Good PINK or PINK-barred.
N along **Tilice Road**. Houses on east side only. PINK to PINK-barred.
E & S along **Garland Street**. 2-st. Poor, old. Field workers in market gardens. LIGHT BLUE.
W along **Pendrell Street**. 2-st. A little better. Long gardens behind. LIGHT BLUE to PURPLE. 6/- to 8/- for four rooms. Old red-tiled houses. The west end of Pendrell St is still open field with the Shooters Hill woods on the south side. Ground rises to south. Field full of bricks and mortar and stacks of ready-made windows and doors.
E to **Garland Street** and south up a steep bit with houses on east side. PURPLE to LIGHT BLUE.
W over a waste of rutted land to a new street called **Alabama Street**. Unmade road. Houses on south side only, 2-st. Open fields on the east side. Part LIGHT BLUE.
N downhill down **St Mary Road**. Road unmade. Houses still building but majority built and occupied. Many look poor. PURPLE to LIGHT BLUE. Here I met the builder and owner of 700 freeholds in these streets who wanted to know whether I was about the LCC tramways extension and of the benefit such a line would do. He said he knew London pretty well but considers this the best-paying district in the Metropolis, steady class coming in – leaseholders. Used to be rough here but the rough'uns are market gardeners, have to follow their work and are moving further out. A great many have taken the 99 years lease – Arsenal workers.

Constant water service, connected with the main sewer. He gets his profit on the cost of
building and on the ground rents. Where houses are let by the week they bring in from 8/6
to 10/6 for four or five rooms plus wash-house. He now gets 4/3 per foot ground-rent. Two
years ago could only get 4/-, but Mr Dawson, who is a very large owner, gets 10/- per foot
ground rent from the houses facing the Common. Dawson and Kersey are the largest
builders and freeholders. Wishes he could get more land: "could sell 100 houses tomorrow if
I had them." Clay soil, has to cart all his gravel. Thinks there would be a rush here if the
Council would start a rope tramway.

Out of the W side of St Mary Rd runs Nyanza Road, whose west end comes out a little
south of Pendrell Rd. PURPLE to LIGHT BLUE.

S & E along Timbercroft Road. Orchards and market gardens on north side with a few
foremen's or farmers' houses. Row of 2-st, new, all tenanted on south. PURPLE. At the west
end by Timbercroft Lane is a set of 1-st red-tiled cottages with neat gardens. LIGHT BLUE.
Just before the Lane meets Garland St is an old beerhouse.

N along The Slade. Old houses. Field workers. PURPLE.

SE along Francis Street. Older and poorer. Gipsy vans, gipsies and Irish. All doors open,
a fine wrangle going on across the street. LIGHT BLUE.

N to Elm Grove and Sutcliffe Road. 2-st, old. PURPLE to LIGHT BLUE. Mission Hall
at north west end of Sutcliffe Rd.

E round The Slade and S into Flaxton Road. A half-tenanted and unmade road. West
side tenanted. East side south end still building. PURPLE. Running east out of its south end
is a nameless road with 2-st houses looking onto a bare waste and running east to Swingate
Lane houses on south side only. PINK.

N along Swingate Lane. Oldish houses. PURPLE. One large house called Heathfield. RED.
E & N along Bassant Road. A deep dip between the south and north ends.

N into Heathfield Terrace. Rather better east than west of Bassant Rd. PURPLE and PINK.

E along the King's Highway. Runs downhill to the east with the Common rising abruptly
to a flat table land on the north side and dipping steeply on the south side to a narrow vale
occupied by strawberry gardens, passing Woolwich cemetery on the south side and a row of
houses on the north. PINK to PURPLE.

E into Wickham Lane which runs along a valley made by Plumstead Common on the south
and Bostall Woods on the north. Some houses on south side, the north side is take by French
beans and rhubarb fields. South past public house along a line of cottages called Cemetery
Cottages. LIGHT BLUE to PURPLE. Active brick-field is opposite.

E & S down Southland Road. More cottages, PURPLE to LIGHT BLUE. Another active
brick-field.

E along Wickham Lane past a large newish cemetery on a hill on the north side of the road.
The Lane rises to the east here. Nearly the top of the hill being where it meets Lodge Lane
which forms the eastern boundary of London. Ground rises here to the north until the level
of Bostall Woods are reached. Raspberry fields on east side and a few old strawberry gardens
on west, now being plotted out for building.

W through Bostall Woods. Mixture of fir woods and rough plantation, birches etc. LCC
police about and a good many people. Wild rose. It is a fine wild country wood.

E down steep hill back to Plumstead High St, turning S into a cul-de-sac. PINK to PURPLE.
Then S down Wickham Lane. Houses on west side only. Some old, some new, beginning
and ending without any particular reason in batches from two to ten. Notices badly written
on boards in front of some inviting the wayfarer to "winkles & watercress, eggs and cake".

Turning W at the King's Highway and across the Common, which is here a sandy gravelly waste on which only the military are allowed to ride or drive, used by artillery as an exercise ground. At the E end with a steep cliff on either side are a set of 2-st detached cottages, PURPLE to PINK. Called **Bleak Hill** on large map.

NW to **Viewland Road**. 2½-st and 2-st. Still building. PINK. Congregational Church at north west end.

E to **Riverdale Road**. 2-st, a few old houses. PINK. Hilly to the south.

E to **Saunders Road**. Old and new houses. 2-st. PINK.

E to **Purrett Road**. Detached and semi-detached. PINK. Good gardens.

S up **Rippolson Road**. 2-st. Poor. Gospel Mission at north east. Poor PURPLE.

W to **Speranza Street**. Many poor at north end. Allotments or market gardens behind the east side. Five rooms and wash-house for 8/-, has been there two years. PURPLE to LIGHT BLUE.

N up **Riverdale Road**. West side rather better than east. PINK to PURPLE.

N into High St. **E & S** into **Hall Place**. By the Infirmary, steep uphill to the infirmary entrance. Poor. LIGHT BLUE.

This ends Plumstead.

General Remarks

Plumstead is dull and ordinary outwardly but it is remarkable in many ways. The houses are ugly, 2-st, yellow brick and for the most part new. The streets are straight and the roads are empty and clean except when the children tumble out of school and leave a litter of small paper bags which once held pennyworths of sweets or fruit. They are also full of a hurrying straggling cord of men on their way to and from home during the dinner hour. Otherwise they are empty, the house doors shut, the windows and blinds clean and everything seems asleep. The women are at home and busy but they are busy in the yards and small gardens behind and not in front. Street life is not amusing. The door slams behind the child when it comes home from school. At night, except on Saturday night in the High St, the roads are dull and dark. More of the doors are open than in the day time for many of the men seem to take their evening pipes in front. Villainous strumming on cheap pianos is also a feature. So is the absence of old people. New houses, newly married couples, young families, wives at home, daughters not yet grown up and expecting marriage and home life not factory work as a career, husbands and sons in full and steady work, earning more money than they really know how to spend. Where in London is there another such place? Almost the only old established poor are in The Slade – Pendrell St, Francis St, Sutcliffe St – gypsies, labourers and market garden workers. But they tend to leave, following their work further into Kent. The new poor lie to the north of the High St in the low ground of the Plumstead marshes or on the south in the clefts made by deep dips in the Chalk as in Roydene Rd and Sladedale Rd. The poorest and nastiest area lies between Reidhaven Rd and Garibaldi Rd. All poverty here due to Irish and drunken labourers.

South of High St the ground rises rapidly to Plumstead Common with sudden dips east and west. Roads broad and clean. Soil gravel and chalk with bits of clay on the high ground. Healthy district.

Splendid park in Bostall Woods and openness in Plumstead marshes and Plumstead Common. Wants better train service, trams up the hill and along Plumstead Common, a music hall or theatre, more working men's clubs. I don't know what would happen if the Arsenal went slack and dismissed many thousand men as it might well do. At present there is no ready means of transferring work to other districts.

A Bicycle Ride at Night

B 371

Saturday night, 27th May 1900.
George Duckworth on a bicycle through the streets of Woolwich between 10 and
12.30 pm.

Leaving Shooters Hill at 9.45 I got to the market place about 10 minutes after 10 – it is
downhill the whole way. Fine night, stars, rather cold but practically no wind.

All dark and quiet until New Rd was reached. There the crowd began. Many soldiers in
uniform. Shops all lighted and open, boots in the west side of the street leading to the Market
Place. All good humoured and well dressed, out for marketing and to see the fun or for a
promenade simply. Men, women and children. All young. Children from babies in arms to 10
years old, husbands between 20 and 35 and women of the same ages, hardly a gray hair or an
old face among them all. A few soldiers almost tipsy opposite the public house at the corner of
the New Rd and Thomas' St, a small crowd watching them and listening to nigger minstrels
playing at the door. The civilians were sober. In the market there was greater seriousness.
Most coming away with their purchases in large brown papers or newspaper wrappers as I
arrived but a good number still buying and the market place full, though not as thickly crammed
as it had been a little earlier. The men never carried the parcels except where the woman had
the child and not always then. Men in caps and bowlers, collars, a few with black coats but most
in ordinary suits. Women in bonnets, cloaks, not quite in their best but like the men evidently
dressed for the occasion. Two or three labourers were in their working clothes but they were
exceptions. The chief interest centred around the butcher's stall: Fair sirloin, 6d per lb;
Canterbury lamb, 4½d per lb. Meat (not joint but not scraps), 3d per lb. All meat looked good.

Flower stalls were doing a good business in bedding out plants, flowers and vegetables.
Other stalls were for tools, fancy goods (purses, braces, cloth caps, oranges, etc), shooting
stall. It was a smaller and less busy market than Lower Marsh (Lambeth) but of the same
character. From the market the flow of the crowd was towards Powis St and Hare St. These
streets contain the best shops in Woolwich. Large drapery stores, grocers, public houses, boot
shops, bacon and cheese shops. Fair small strawberries were on sale at 8d per lb and good
cherries at 6d per lb. Cherries found more buyers than the strawberries. Lipton has a large
new shop at the corner of Hare St and Powis St.

Crowd good tempered, sober, more promenade than business. Such business as was done
was rather inside than outside the shops. After the butchers' shops the boot shops were the
best lighted and made the best show. After them came the public houses.

From Hare St I went through the streets which compose the Dust Hole. Rope Yard Rails
was quiet, dark, the kitchens of the lodging houses as far as could be seen from outside with
only a few persons in them. Not much being done in the beerhouse. One man asleep drunk
on the pavement. Most doors open, smell of dirt, dark stains along the pavement on either
side where men and women had relieved nature. Badly lighted – figures would emerge
suddenly from dark corners and disappear again as mysteriously as they had come. Some old
men and women of the draggled tramp type were laboriously slouching down the street
towards the Canal Ward lodging house as I passed. The first and most obvious improvement
in these streets would be to light them better.

In High St were a few rough women but not many men. Rodney St and the turnings off
it were empty, dark and quiet. Warren Lane also dark and like Rope Yard Rails.

Then I went to the Music Hall in Beresford St. The last piece was already on: a military piece called 'Drummed Out'. The manager said he would not charge me anything as it was so near the end (it was about 10.45) but hoped I would come again. I went to the dress circle (proper price 1/-). Theatre crammed, about 2,000 people, not more than 12 soldiers in uniform and hardly 50 women. The rest all young men and boys. Nearly the whole of the pit (which here includes the stalls) was taken by boys and youths between 14 and 18. The average age of the whole audience would have worked out, I think, at under 25. All quiet and orderly and washed and brushed and dressed for the occasion. The scene showed part of Woolwich barracks and the acting consisted in ordinary military duties being performed on the stage – sentry duty, changing guard, parade, band, etc etc, varied with comic figures (the regimental cook and the Irish grandmother of a drummer boy). The catchwords of the comic characters were well known to the audience. The boys in the pit shouted them out as soon as the actor appeared and were chaffed in return by the actor from the stage. 'Drummed Out' was the set piece and made the 10th and last 'turn' of the evening. The earlier turns had been of the usual Music Hall type. I left about 11.15 and again went round the Dust Hole. All was as before.

Then I bicycled on into Plumstead. The shops were all open though not doing much business. The whole of the Plumstead Rd is a shopping street. No drunkenness or noise, except two women, half drunk. I turned back at the Riverdale Rd. Crowds were then coming from Woolwich to Plumstead, none drunk, all walking fast and disappearing into the dark streets north and south of the Plumstead Rd. Many more men than women and only a few children about.

I got back to the Dust Hole about ten minutes after closing time (ie. 12.10). More life in the streets, but no quarrelling. Women and men had just been turned out of the public houses. The two worst places were opposite Mahoney's lodging house in the High St opposite the south end of Rope Yard Rails and again in the narrow street which rises rather steeply out of Rodney St and is called Globe Lane. There was no noise from these groups of men or women. They were round the open house doors in groups like conspirators; now and then a voice would rise but it never went as far as a street row.

In Rodney St itself the windows were nearly all dark except one on the first floor which was open, through which could be seen bonneted and capped heads and from which came the sounds of a patriotic Music Hall song, evidently a small evening party.

In the market everyone was packing up and going off in barrows and pony carts. One joint of beef which before had been 6d was now 3d per lb; the last few pieces were being sold off at great reductions. Only the poorest buying now, one woman not liking to do more than whisper into the ear of the salesman the price that she was prepared to pay.

Then I went back past the barracks seeing a good number of soldiers who could only just walk and turning into the block of PURPLE to LIGHT BLUE streets off the east side of Woolwich Common. All quiet here, the little general shop at the east end of Manor St still open and a child buying something. South down James St. East and north up Dicey St. Poor and rough. Fewer people in bed, more lighted windows and open doors than in the other streets. No rows but has all the appearance of a rough poor street.

Then west to the Common and south past the RMA to Shooters Hill. In a small patch of wood at the corner of the Common Road and Shooters Hill was a nightingale singing loudly and being answered by another in the Crown Woods on the south side of the Hill. It is thanks to the execrable train service that nightingales still sing and pheasants are still preserved and bluebells carpet the woods within 12 miles of St Paul's.

The south side of Shooters Hill is quite in the country though still in London.

Numbers in brackets refer to chapter areas as shown in the table below. They are followed by the Walk numbers in which the street appears.

Bold type means that at least one street of this name was still surviving in 1996, although it may have changed in definition, eg. from Road to Way.

1 SOUTHWARK	**7 ROTHERHITHE**	**13 BROCKLEY**
2 LAMBETH	**8 DEPTFORD & NEW CROSS**	**14 LEWISHAM**
3 KENNINGTON	**9 PECKHAM**	**15 BLACKHEATH**
4 WALWORTH	**10 CAMBERWELL**	**16 GREENWICH**
5 BOROUGH	**11 DULWICH**	**17 CHARLTON**
6 BERMONDSEY	**12 NUNHEAD**	**18 WOOLWICH**

THE STREETS OF LONDON
The Booth Notebooks –South East

Editors:
Jess Steele
Mike Steele

2019

Deptford Forum Publishing, 2 Osberton Road, London SE12 8AH

The Booth Inquiry archive, of which these notebooks form a part, is held at the British Library of Political and Economic Science at the London School of Economics.

Edited by Jess Steele and Mike Steele
Design and layout by Nixx and Ed Fredenburgh
Cover design and title page graphic by Lionel Openshaw
Sketch maps by Nixx and Community Desktop Publishing
Original illustrations by Godfrey Jones
Original publication printed by Biddles Ltd, Guildford, Surrey

This is not a facsimile edition. We have tried to reproduce the text in a format that can satisfy both academic and general interest. This has meant making some minor changes for the sake of consistency and readability.

Second edition 2019 recreated from original and printed by Short Run Press, Exeter

Second edition dedicated to Peter Hill RIP

ISBN 978-1-898536-31-4
British Library Cataloguing in Publication Data
A catalogue record for this book is available from the British Library

CONTENTS

Special thanks to:

Karen, who sat in the Coal Hole pub in the Strand on a freezing day early in 1994 and first gave me faith that other Londoners would be fascinated by Booth's streets. She followed that up with three years of active involvement. This is a result for her as much as for anyone.

Mike Steele for checking the fate of every Booth street in the modern A to Z to discover what happened to Booth's London.

I am grateful for the help and encouragement of David Englander & Rosemary O'Day from the Charles Booth Centre for Social Investigation at the Open University, Dr Angela Raspin and Sue Donnelly from BLPES Archives, and Carlos and Carl from LSE Photography Unit.

I would also like to thank Richard, Ed, Peter, Lionel and most of all Nïxx for their usual level of hard work, commitment and support.

Photographs courtesy of Lewisham Local Studies Library, Greenwich Local History Centre, Southwark Local Studies Library and Lambeth Local Studies Library.

The Borough of Deptford sponsored by Malcolm Edwards
The Borough of Lewisham sponsored by Lewisham Libraries

Lambeth sponsored by Lambeth College
Bermondsey sponsored by Harry & Edna Bowling
Brockley & Deptford sponsored by Lewisham College
Charlton sponsored by Viscount Gough
Crofton Park sponsored by Rossy and Nancy Bailey and Juliet Desailly
Eastcombe sponsored by Diana Rimel

Amersham Vale sponsored by Chief Superintendant Ken Chapman (Retired)
Blackhorse Road sponsored by Richard White
Breakspears Road sponsored by Roy Bourne
Bronze Street sponsored by Margaret Sandra
Chipley Street sponsored by the Walden Family
Creekside sponsored by Jani Llewellyn
The Cut sponsored by Southwark College
Czar Street sponsored by Tsarevich Paul (The Unsung)
Deptford Green sponsored by Richard Walker
Deptford High Street sponsored by Revival Cafe
Edward Street sponsored by Vincent s Hodgson
Embleton Road sponsored by Julian & Marion Watson
Erlanger Road sponsored by Des Malone
Frankham Street sponsored by Dr Nick McAdoo
Idonia Street sponsored by Nïxx
Laurie Grove sponsored by Centre for Continuing & Community Education, Goldsmiths College
McMillan Street sponsored by Jill Goddard
Mill Lane sponsored by Callum Sheridan Lee
Montford Place sponsored by Laura Hastings-Smith
New Cross Road sponsored by Jess Steele to thank George Hunt
Rolt Street sponsored by Mrs G Braybrook in memory of Charles Braybrook
Rutland Gate sponsored by Mrs W S H Paul
Rye Lane sponsored by Alan Bailey
Selbourne Road sponsored by Adrian Goodall (for Dad)
Strickland Street sponsored by Ray Wheeler
The Stowage sponsored by Ed Fredenburgh
Upland Road sponsored by Karen Bray
Warwick Street sponsored by George Hunt
Woodlands sponsored by Godfrey Smith

We are extremely grateful for the continuing support given to us by the Booth family. They enabled us to publish the original version of the Streets of London: South East in 1998 and now have made this reprint possible.

Jess and Mike Steele
Deptford Forum Publishing

Jess first found the Booth Inquiry archive when researching a local history of Deptford in the early 1990s. Sitting in the chilly archive room she found herself writing out in pencil the full text of the walks from the so-called 'police notebooks'. She knew then that she wanted to publish these fascinating snapshots.

With much help in transcribing we were pleased to publish this volume of South East London walks in 1998 and had at that time high hopes of producing the other volumes in rapid succession. However, constraints of time and money delayed us by a mere 20 years!

In the meantime LSE have digitised the original notebooks and made them available at www.booth.lse.ac.uk. We feel a physical book offers a more useable format. It's certainly much easier to read than the longhand and being organised into chapters, it is possible to browse through these neighbourhoods, aided by sketch maps, contemporary photographs and new illustrations, or to use the index to gain a sense of what your street was like 120 years ago.

There are 392 notebooks in the Booth archive which cover three research collections: Poverty; Industry; and Religious Influences. Around 30 of these are the handwritten notes of 300 walks across the whole of London, while others record over 1,000 interviews with businessmen, workers and trades union representatives, school board visitors, publicans and vicars. The original project had begun by collecting detailed information about individual households. Later they chose to focus on whole streets as it became too time-consuming.

These neighbourhoods were dynamic: "the rich and poor both leave but the middle class are coming in". Since the research aimed to update their own earlier material these notebooks not only describe the neighbourhoods at the end of the century but also how they had changed in the previous ten years.

Despite the impressive scale and fascinating detail of these walks, it has to be said that Booth's researchers and their policemen companions are often obnoxious and patronising. They make outrageous assumptions and blatant generalisations which readers may find disturbing. The notebooks reveal as much about the researchers as they do about the poor of Southwark, Deptford or Woolwich. Their views are, of course not those of myself or Deptford Forum Publishing.

We hope that this volume, and the East London one, will contribute to the debates on London's history and its future, its problems and their solutions. We want it to be used in many different ways: as a source for history and the social sciences, as a resource for school projects, as a guide for Sunday strolling, as a spur to comparison and compassion for those who live in London's poverty 120 years after these walks. Most of all we want readers to enjoy the exploration of their own neighbourhoods, whether out on the streets or from the comfort of an armchair.

Jess Steele, June 2019

POLICE AND SOCIAL INQUIRY IN LATE-VICTORIAN LONDON

Charles Booth has never wanted for an audience. The seventeen-volume survey *Life and Labour of the People in London*, which he published between 1889 and 1903, provided the first scientific estimates of poverty and has been the starting point for all serious discussion of the subject ever since. It is rightly regarded as one of the high points in the British tradition of empirical social research. Employing a subsistence definition of poverty Booth found, contrary to his expectations, that nearly 31 per cent of those surveyed were in poverty. His researches showed too that, apart from inefficient expenditure, the principal sources of poverty were due to low wages, unemployment and old age.

Social inquiry, for Booth, was not an academic pursuit but a guide to social action. His suggestions for the creation of an effective policy on employment ranged from the reform and rationalisation of the labour market to the provision of non-contributory old age pensions. His contribution in respect of the latter, first introduced in 1908, was indeed every bit as important as his work on the conceptualisation and measurement of poverty.

Booth's Life and Motivations

Charles James Booth was born in Liverpool on 30th March 1840 into a public-spirited commercial family that was Liberal in politics and Unitarian in religion. Booth was involved in communal controversies from an early age. Earnest, serious and civic-minded, he combined the development of his shipping line with an active commitment to franchise reform, popular education and social betterment. Booth, though, was no ordinary philanthropist. He rejected charity as a cure and Christianity as a creed. Positivism, the Religion of Humanity, presented a more satisfying foundation for a rational faith. Positive Philosophy offered the young, the intellectually curious and those of unsettled faith a humanist religion and a new ethic of personal social obligation. The crisis of authority had a material as well as a spiritual dimension and Positivists were as much preoccupied with the 'social question' as with any other. Booth, like so many of his generation, was repelled by the crass materialism of the age and the selfishness it encouraged. "The race for wealth is run by a few only and the prizes fall to those who are already rich", he wrote.

"The leaders in this fatal competition, blind to all else, are willing to sacrifice everything to the production of wealth and even talk of the laws which govern this struggle as though they were the only guides to human life...I would not undervalue the motive of this race, or the effect it has had in developing the resources of the world and the power of the workers, nor do I say that it can be dispensed with. But I do say that it now needs checking and that it is only in its subordination to public welfare that we can look for that social improvement which we need."

Positivism had its share of drawing-room radicals, idealists and dreamers. But it also had a hard edge. Booth's close cousin, the able and engaging lawyer Henry Crompton, was among that group of reform-minded intellectuals who enjoyed a special relationship with the trade union movement during the 1860s and '70s. As a large employer of port labour, Booth was hardly unaware of working people and their wants. His attempts to interest trade unionists in arbitration and conciliation procedures, though they proved unavailing, served to enlarge his experience of labour and labour questions as did the Trades Hall which he helped to found. The sectarianism that destroyed his attempts to introduce free secular education into Liverpool's schools convinced him that Humanity could be better served by means other than politics. The social crisis of the 1880s gave a clear focus to his brooding intellect and expanding moral imagination.

By this time Booth had moved from Liverpool to London where family wealth and connections gave ready access to that band of moralists, philanthropists and members of the professional classes who dominated public debate on the social question. As a Positivist believing that social action should be grounded in the scientific study of the laws of society, Booth found himself both moved and fascinated by the lives of the working poor. The fixing of his interest upon the East End of London, however, may well have reflected the influence of his wife Mary.

Mary Booth was the daughter of Charles Zachary Macaulay, a distinguished public servant. Her mother's father established the *Manchester Guardian*. It was Mary Booth who, on a visit to the East End in 1878, told her husband that she was stirred "to help in all this misery". Her cousins Kate, Teresa and Beatrice Potter, who were engaged in voluntary social work in Whitechapel, no doubt contributed to that quickening of interest which led Booth to take lodgings in the East End and to invite workmen to his home in the West End in order to extend his knowledge of working class life.

Mary Booth, wife of Charles, in 1880

The onset of economic depression, mass unemployment, socialism and social unrest gave these interests a new urgency. Such anxieties as he possessed, however, found release in social inquiry rather than in social work. Impatient with the glacial pace of conventional philanthropy, critical of the a priori assumptions of political economy and disturbed by the challenge of socialism, Booth gave primacy to the collection of facts and an accurate description of the condition of the people throughout London as the basis for social diagnosis and public policy. For all the scope, precision and arresting detail of the Life and Labour Inquiry, begun in 1886 and completed 17 years later, it was not a simple compendium or statistical cyclopaedia but a major contribution to social economy and social action. The work of a team of researchers who were co-ordinated and financed by Booth himself, it was probably the largest private inquiry ever undertaken.

Life and Labour and the Poverty Maps

Life and Labour of the People in London was divided into three series. The four-volume Poverty Series related degrees of comfort and wellbeing to the ways in which people lived. The Industry Series examined in five volumes how people worked, what they produced and what they received. The remaining seven volumes were devoted to the Religious Influences Series which, in spite of its title, said little about the spiritual life of the people and much about the distinctive character of the religious life and activities in the various districts of London. A striking feature of the project was the inclusion of a series of thematic maps to show the distribution of degrees of comfort and wellbeing and the spatial relationships between the classes. These maps, reproduced here in full colour, have not received the attention they deserve.

The extent to which Booth's poverty maps consciously belonged to an existing tradition is uncertain. Social mapping developed during the 19th century in response to commercial and municipal requirements and also to satisfy Victorian concerns about the physical and moral health of the urban masses. Gradation shading, developed by the Belgian statistician Adolphe Quetelet in the 1820s to display the distribution of crimes against people and property, had been translated in 1842, making the technique familiar to an English audience. The Census of Ireland in the previous year had also made innovative use of shaded maps to illustrate population density and certain other social characteristics. Colour-coded maps of social conditions to plot the spread of cholera and insanitary housing likewise gave evidence of the growth of a more sociologically-informed cartography around the mid-century. What Booth knew of all of this remains to be established. That he could have worked independently of his predecessors seems improbable but cannot be ruled out. A tendency to re-invent the wheel appears to be a distinctive feature in the history of empirical social research. What is clear is that, from its inception, the diagrammatic representation of poverty was regarded as an integral feature of Booth's Inquiry.

Booth's Descriptive Map of Poverty was first presented to the public in the form of a pilot study of East London delivered to the Royal Statistical Society in 1887. An extended version was included with the first two-volume edition of Life and Labour of the People in London published in 1889-91. The map represented the predominant social class and character of each of the streets of the Metropolis, classified according to a seven-point colour scheme based largely on the impressions of the School Board Visitors (subsequently known as school attendance officers) as told to Booth's research staff. These impressions were then transferred by hand onto a twenty-five inch base map that was subsequently reduced and reprinted by the celebrated map-maker and publisher Edward Stanford. The maps reproduced here have been photographed from the hand-painted 25-inch originals held at BLPES.

The importance of the Descriptive Map of Poverty may be gauged from the considerable resources that Booth invested in its revision in 1897/8 in order to incorporate the changes caused by urban redevelopment and the movement of population in the previous ten years. This time, however, Booth relied upon the impressions of Metropolitan Police officers rather than upon those of the School Board Visitors as his principal source of information. It was a role for which the police were by no means ill prepared.

Police Evidence

Police duties, then as now, extended well beyond the suppression of crime. Britain, though not a police state, often cast the police as a social agency, a kind of substitute civil service, collecting evidence on social problems, asserting a certain expertise in selected areas and offering counsel and advice – sometimes unsolicited – to policy makers. The requirements of public order gave the police considerable latitude in the demarcation of their interests. Questions of poverty, crowding and insanitary conditions, crime, immigration and industrial displacement defined the scope of police observation. Policemen gave evidence to all the principal parliamentary and governmental inquiries of the period: on the housing of the working classes, the sweating system, labour, foreign immigration and the operation of the Sunday Trading laws.

The recognition of police evidence as a significant source of social observation extended beyond the corridors of Whitehall and Westminster. Charles Booth, like Charles Dickens before him, valued the police not only for their protection but also for their opinions and local expertise. With the consent of Police Commissioner Sir Edward Bradford "experienced members of the police force, chosen for their local knowledge" were assigned to the Booth Inquiry in connection with the revision of the Descriptive Map of London Poverty. The Metropolis was parceled out into a number of beats each patrolled together by interviewer and policeman. The bulk of these walks were undertaken by Booth's companionable associate George Herbert Duckworth, the half-brother of Virginia Woolf, who subsequently enjoyed a distinguished career in the public service. Nearly every street in the Metropolitan Police District of London was visited and its social composition recorded. Not only were policemen required to identify the social class and ethnic make-up of individual streets, they also presented much incidental information about the character of the community. "During these walks", wrote Booth, "almost every social influence was discussed, and especially those bearing upon vice and crime, drunkenness and disorder."

How representative are such sources? Bobbies on the beat have left few records. Station records, too, are rare and incomplete. Recent studies of the social composition of the police labour force do, however, suggest that, in terms of class origins, the Metropolitan Police were close to those whom they policed. Policemen were drawn overwhelmingly from the unskilled and semi-skilled working class. With police recruitment (at least up to divisional level) based on a single-tier entry system, lines of authority did not follow social class divisions, as in the military. Serving officers had a close understanding of the everyday experiences and practices – legal and otherwise – of the people in London's streets. Booth's investigators, though sceptical of much that was said, had no grounds for thinking that police observation was rank-related or distorted by social class. And neither have we. The information given to the Booth Inquiry is probably as representative of police attitudes and opinion as we are likely to obtain.

The police were asked to accompany the Booth team on their perambulations and give their views on the changes that had taken place on their 'patch' or 'manor' over the course of the previous ten years but the commentaries to the walks are also a prime source for information about the police themselves, their lifestyle and opinions. Such information varies enormously. The policemen themselves seem to leap from the page as Duckworth and his colleagues sum up their appearance and biography. "Sergeant Vanstone is a fresh-coloured young man; a native of Deptford and far away the best officer I have met so far as local knowledge is concerned. In nearly every street he knew personally some of the people."

Duckworth often noted their attitude to the task at hand. "Sergeant Nunn is a burly, awkward rather heavy man but a good fellow and a very willing guide." Some police were in a better position than others to judge the areas. "O'Dell is a fat man, very fat. He is not now on active outdoor duty but is employed in the clerks' office. He is intelligent and knows a good deal more about the different parts of the Division in their criminal aspects than most of the policemen who have been round with me. All charges from every quarter pass through his hands every day."

It Takes All Sorts

The types of crime and disorder which characterised each area are summarised in a few words by the policemen. In Milan Place near Waterloo Sergeant Saltmarshe explained that "fathers fight their sons of a Saturday night". In nearby Cornwall Road "last Saturday...a woman threw a lighted lamp at her husband and both were burned to death". In Brockley the "bucolic, beefy and provincial" PC Moss told Ernest Aves that the charges were mostly "drunk and disorderly". In Lewisham "the typical local misdemeanour appears to be afternoon house-breaking, houses being entered while the occupiers are away. In such a district as this, this crime is difficult to prevent or even to detect and Lloyds was amusing in describing the effrontery of the invader – how, having forced the lock, often a very simple operation, he deceives any chance onlooking neighbour that there may be, by greeting and shaking hands with an imaginary person, entering as he does so and closing the door. On leaving the same thing may be repeated, and no suspicions are aroused until it is too late."

The police faced some substantial dangers in particular areas. In the notorious Dust Hole in Woolwich Duckworth learnt from his guide that "the police only come when there is a bad row and they are summoned. No man would go alone. When called he waits for at least one other. Missiles are showered on them from every window when they interfere. It is out of bounds for soldiers and the military patrol can capture and confine any soldier found there. But nevertheless the low class soldier goes there. The police know and see them but have no right to arrest them." Another very specific problem was discussed in Brockley when Ernest Aves and PC Moss arrived at One Tree Hill in November 1899. "The road leads by the bank and fence of the Hill round which the attack during the 'battles of One Tree Hill' of a year or so ago chiefly waged. Moss was on duty but was stationed at a point where no attack was made. It appears that on the first Sunday the few police on duty were a good deal mauled, but on the second they were in strong force, with a large hidden reserve, and the arrests made with the subsequent punishments of imprisonment without the option of a fine, speedily put an end to the trouble."

The very respectability of a street might be dependent upon and defined by the fact that police lived upon it. In Mercy Terrace near Ladywell Road, Aves noted that "a policeman lives in one of them rent-free and acts as a kind of agent. It was his business to get the houses into good and quiet order and, according to Lloyds, he has succeeded." Ormside Street in Hatcham "used to be rough but better now. Got two policemen to live here; these men are privileged to report themselves to the sergeant on the beat instead of at the station. Always quiets a street if they get a policeman in."

There were clearly debates within the police force and beyond about the best ways of tackling street crime. No less a mortal than the Metropolitan Police Commissioner debated appropriate policing with George Duckworth. "Met Sir E. Bradford on my way to the station. He on horseback making one of his surprise visits. He stopped & talked for some time in the street – said that he hoped I found the police had a good knowledge of the inhabitants in each street 'for that I believe is the real way in which they should do their work'...In rough streets he liked them to know the names & occupations of every inhabitant. The difficulty, he said, lay in preventing the people feeling they were watched...To be always in the background except when there was real need & then to come down like a thunderbolt was he believed the real policy of the police, ending with 'Don't you think so?'."

Despite all this incidental detail, the purpose of the walks was not to reveal the attitudes of the police nor yet to inform the reader of their working lives and practices. Rather it was to use the policeman's knowledge of the various districts to facilitate an informed revision of the 1889 maps. How well did the police know the community in which they worked? How did the nature of their work determine the help which they were able to offer Duckworth?

On the face of it, they were very knowledgeable and well able to give the researchers the assistance they needed. There were, however, limits to the police knowledge of the streets and their people. They knew most about the people who caused trouble. This had important implications. If a community did not have a high profile in terms of public disorder or criminality, the police knew relatively little about its life. If a street was well known for charges this was reflected in the police estimate of its colour. Booth and his associates were aiming to use the map to describe the levels of poverty and comfort but they used as guides men for whom criminality and disorder, or their absence, were the defining characteristics of the population. George Arkell walked around the poorest parts of Deptford with Inspector Gummer and Sergeant Goddard but "both officers agree that it is better than it was: not so much crime or violence. To me, little or no improvement is apparent in the poor streets and I have grave doubts as to the knowledge of the police of the social condition of the people. They measure the streets mainly by the proportion of offences against the law and diminution of these is an improvement which they attribute to increasing social position."

Black and Blue

'BLACK' and 'DARK BLUE' became associated less with degrees of poverty than with degrees and kinds of criminality, roughness and disorderliness. In the map key BLACK was defined as "vicious and semi-criminal". In two Kennington streets, tucked away by themselves, "there are so many charges for assaults and drunkenness that the BLACK line of the map might remain". The police were excellent barometers in these respects: they proved a less sensitive instrument in others. They accepted that there could be respectable poor but they were generally defined by the absence of criminality. There was little detailed comment about these poor people – other than the fact that their worst excesses were getting drunk on a Saturday night and their greatest virtues working hard and keeping inside their houses.

Duckworth, Arkell, Aves and the police used the external appearance of buildings, streets and people as the criteria by which they measured the accuracy of the map of 1889, so that the reader is oftentimes bemused, wondering precisely what was being assessed. The term 'poverty' is not frequently used (if at all) in the notebooks. Rather the pages are littered with references to 'rough', 'respectable', 'vicious', 'quiet', 'disreputable', 'poor', 'well-to-do' and so on. The BLACK and DARK BLUE areas are defined not by income but by their criminal characteristics. Baildon Street was considered one of the worst streets in Deptford: "'Better than it was' says the sergeant, 'fewer cases come from here'. Used to have to send 20 men to make arrests. He would hardly call it criminal now. To me the street looks worse than it did 10 years ago. If any men and women have the criminal brand on their faces, these seem on my two visits unmistakenly to bear it. DARK BLUE with BLACK line as map."

Often the description was based on the researcher's impression of a whole scene. In Mason's Buildings in Southwark "The exit into Borough High St is down a passage under a house, not a yard wide. The inhabitants of the houses and common lodging houses are prostitutes and ponces and thieves. Youths and middle-aged men of the lowest casual class loafing; undergrown men; women slouching with draggled skirts, hatless but hidden under long shawls; a deformed boy with naked half-formed leg turned in the wrong direction, made up the scene."

Sometimes the researcher would challenge a police description as in Borough's Bell Court, "a dreary well of a place. "'Paint it as BLACK as you can' said my guide, 'it is a little hell upon earth', but when I pressed for a diagnosis it appeared to resolve itself into the common Bermondsey charge of drunkenness and resulting disorders. DARK BLUE as map." In other cases, such as Woolwich's Rope Yard Rails, they accepted the gauge of criminality "This street is a fair BLACK all through, not for poverty but for vice."

The context of the houses could also cause problems with assessing their proper colour. In Shardeloes Road there were some houses "of a kind that in Peckham or Hoxton would be put down as PINK with little hesitation. In Brockley, however, with a much larger proportion of houses taken on lease, with rents paid quarterly and a different class often found in occupation, the right colour becomes more doubtful. Here I am told that the tenancies are yearly and that there are servants in many of the houses. Perhaps from RED of map, to PINK-barred. The alternative, PINK." After a while the colour scheme became so natural a descriptive method for both researcher and policeman that they would talk of "a RED house" or even "a PINK man".

Changing neighbourhoods

The police knowledge of the various districts led Duckworth and the others to an understanding of the changes going on in the capital's various neighbourhoods. Changes in the physical environment accounted for changes in the population. In his general remarks to the walk around St Saviour's near London Bridge, Duckworth concluded: "The same change is going on in Southwark that in years past took place in the City. As site values rise those who can most afford to pay for them leave, ie the rich leave first. After them go the fairly comfortable and last of all the poor and very poor. Hence those who properly can the least afford to pay high rents are the last to leave. The rich were the first of the residents to leave the City, the poor have only just left. In Southwark the rich have already left; the fairly comfortable are leaving; the poor and the very poor remain and will remain until they are evicted."

Changes in rents, extensions to the railways and slum clearance of various types resulted in pushing round London the former inhabitants of BLACK and DARK BLUE areas. Often they did not go far. "The old tenants of Kings Bench Walk etc, though dispossessed, have yet found houseroom close to their own haunts and...others displaced by railway extension...have found their way in. The inhabitants are all South Londoners. None have come from the north side of the Thames. They are the dregs of the population and not scum that has floated off from distant places and infected new areas as in Notting Dale." In Deptford the phrase "people from Mill Lane have come in" was bound to mean costers, prostitutes and nightly fights.

The Researchers

We should remember that the records of the London walks were not kept by the police themselves but by George Duckworth, George Arkell and Ernest Aves. The views of the police are, therefore, mediated and to them are added those of the researcher. Sometimes there is direct quotation from the police, more often there is a summary of the results of the conversation between the two about the neighbourhood. Often we are presented with the researcher's own impressions. In Watergate Street Arkell noted: "Faint foetid smell prevails, overpowered in places by disgusting stench. Rough women, one with head bandaged; others with black eyes; one old harridan sitting on doorstep with dirty clay pipe; shoeless children. Costers, streetsellers, gut cleaners." Risdon Street, Rotherhithe was "full of children, mess of paper, no bread. Children out at knees and elbow but all well fed, no sore eyes, faces very dirty, boots bad, dancing to a barrel organ. Women with sack or dirty white aprons and bare arms. Struggling pots and tins of flowers at the windows." The researchers were learning, with police help, to read the code of the streets.

These walks are not a tourist guide to London. There is much here of local interest so that the modern reader can form a picture of the physical environment, even to the extent of the width of the streets, the height of the buildings, and the existence of courts uncharted on any contemporary map. But the perspective of the walks is heavily influenced by the policeman's working environment. As a result one has to accept that the level of detail is variable and the reliability of the information likewise.

Yet, for Booth's purposes, the police served to underline the purpose of his Inquiry, to describe the lives of Londoners in response to the perceived social crisis of the 1880s. They, like few others, were in a position to pinpoint troublespots and troublemakers. They were prepared to reinforce their assessment of the vicious inhabitants of one neighbourhood by a graphic description of hundreds of rats infesting a cargo of fatty ham. They had views, which they readily recounted to the researchers about the 'problems' of the age – prostitution, gambling, drink, immorality, immigration, marriage, theft, housing, overcrowding, environment. They were always willing to generalise.

"He has never seen a girl brought in drunk under 20 years of age. It is when they get older that women take to gin & ale & become regular soakers." "The worst men as a class for drink are carmen & dockers. They can stand a deal more than ordinary men whose work is not in the open air but even so they take more than they can stand." Coalies were also said to be hard drinkers and easy spenders.

The Drama of the Age

Of all the pre-occupations of the late-Victorian period, prostitution ranks highly. Vigilance committees were trying to clear out the brothels but many police felt it was "better to have them where you can put your finger on them than in places where you don't know of their existence until they are firmly established". St Gabriel Street was defined as "Poor and vicious, thieves and prostitutes. Used to be all brothels at the north east end but cleared out two years ago with the help of the Vigilance Association. Some prostitutes still remain but no brothels. The infamous 'Girdle' gang came from here. When the brothels were turned out they migrated and were discovered in a coffee house at the east end of Graham St in Hackney. Other prostitutes went to Deptford". The researchers sometimes offer us a smile at police methods as when "Sales has had men out dressed as females to convict the brothels but has never succeeded. 'They always know'."

Prostitution was often associated with the common lodging houses such as those in the vicinity of Redcross Place. "Last year there were over 4,000 charges from this block of streets." The Borough prostitutes were mainly Irish women. "Their gains are made far more by robbery than by prostitution...Bullies live on their earnings. They are English or Irish cockneys, not foreigners. The foreign bully has nearly deserted London since the law of last October and foreign women come no further south than Stamford St. The police have tried to run in the English bully from the High St courts but had a failure in their first case and are fearful of trying again. The man they charged was notorious as a ponce but was able to prove that he had earned some money by himself and therefore the charge fell to the ground."

Woolwich was another notorious area. "They cling to the neighbourhood of the Barracks, 'Flies round the honey pot'. Clyne says their usual charge to soldiers is 9d or 1/- and soldiers are allowed to go on tick and pay when their money comes in. The male inhabitants are bullies, dock and waterside labourers, costers, hawkers and tramps. The women are prostitutes...The clean white apron and the frizzed hair and earrings is the mark of this class. Clyne says the majority of young and old, male and female are Irish...If the man is known to have money or jewels on him he is made to hire a room and robbed, 'always cleaned out'. If he has only enough to pay the woman then the street is used. There is no regular charge, each man pays as much as the woman can get from him...Those who suffer most from the Dust Hole are the recruits. Woolwich is a depot with drafts constantly coming and going. These are the young flies that are caught and may be ruined for life."

Engaging and alarming, inexhaustible and compulsive, these Booth Notebooks present a townscape of crowded streets and bustling thoroughfares, of claustrophobic courts and dark back alleys, a fluid, fast-changing environment in which commerce and people vie for space and amenity, industry and identity. They evoke the sight and sounds, indeed almost the smell, of the congested capital a century ago. George Duckworth, with his acute powers of observation and novelist's eye for detail, ushers us into unseemly enclosures and unmapped passageways, through run-down neighbourhoods and the more fashionable quarters, recording land-use changes and population movements with care and precision. Included, too, was much incidental information on house rents and local prices and, where access could be secured, on home work and individual family circumstances.

The streets of London, as presented here, are defined not only by charters and legal regulations, but also by popular culture and popular usage. The information gathered, though selective, is extraordinarily rich. Duckworth was attentive both to the diversity of the built environment and to variations in local architecture. The general condition of the inhabitants, their occupations, dress and bearing, were of equal interest. All were captured by his running pen. The modern reader who wishes to understand Victorian London will find Duckworth an indispensable guide. His observations, for all their absorbing and irresistible qualities, however, are not a simple mirror-image of London at its imperial zenith. Perambulations with the police supplied a stock of knowledge that was shot through with a whole range of personal and professional concerns. It embodied the beliefs, attitudes and opinions of policemen both as public servants and as self-conscious members of the independent working classes.

Apart from the occupational and class biases of police informants, there was the particular viewpoint of the Life and Labour Inquiry itself. The observations, recorded in these Booth Notebooks, were passed through an evaluative filter by which the moral and material were re-combined to create a body of information that was always something more than a descriptive map of poverty. The colour coding of a particular location was a multiple of discrete assessments based on environment, appearance, spatial relationships, trades, dress, clatter and clamour, ethnicity and crime. It also included a large number of surrogate measures of respectability and deviance ranging from clean curtains and a well-scrubbed doorstep to a neat window-box or strategically-placed flower display. These caveats, though, do not diminish the importance of the Booth Notebooks either as source or text. These Notebooks not only impress us by their vividness, immediacy and precision, but also by their idiosyncrasy and humanity. As a guide to the preoccupations of the age they have few rivals.

DAVID ENGLANDER & ROSEMARY O'DAY

David Englander and Rosemary O'Day are Directors of the Charles Booth Centre at the Open University. Their numerous books include *Mr Charles Booth's Inquiry, Life and Labour of the People in London Reconsidered* (Hambledon Press, 1993) and *Retrieved Riches, Social Investigation in Britain, 1840-1914* (Scolar Press, 1995).

Each walk has a reference code (eg. B363). This is the method used at the British Library of Political and Economic Science to archive all the the Booth material. They are reproduced here to enable readers to find the original notebooks.

Both on the colour maps reproduced in this book and within the text each street is colour-coded to indicate the level of poverty or comfort of the people who lived there.

YELLOW	-	Upper-middle and Upper classes. Wealthy
RED	-	Middle class. Well-to-do.
PINK	-	Fairly comfortable. Good ordinary earnings.
PURPLE	-	Mixed. Some comfortable, others poor.
LIGHT BLUE	-	Poor. 18s. to 21s. a week for a moderate family.
DARK BLUE	-	Very poor, casual. Chronic want.
BLACK	-	Lowest class. Vicious, semi-criminal.

A combination of colours – as DARK BLUE and BLACK, or PINK and RED – indicates that the street contains a fair proportion of each of the classes represented by the respective colours. Occasionally a researcher lapses and describes a street as VIOLET!
A bookmark with this colour key is included within this publication.

Booth divided London into 48 numbered districts. The following districts appear in this volume:

31   Lambeth, St Saviour's, Southwark
32   Trinity Newington, St Mary Bermondsey
33   St James' Bermondsey, Rotherhithe
34   Lambeth, Kennington
40   Streatham, Norwood and Dulwich
41   St Peter's Walworth, St Mary Newington
42   St George's Camberwell
43   Camberwell
44   Peckham
45   Deptford
46   Greenwich
47   Sydenham, Lewisham, Eltham, Lee
48   Woolwich

The maps at the start of each area show the boundaries of each walk. They are similar to the rough sketches which the researchers drew in the notebooks at the start of each walk.

The researchers only wrote on the right hand pages and they often used the left hand page for detailed sketches to show the exact layout and colouring of a block of streets. These are sometimes referred to in the text.

The name of each street visited was underlined within the text and an assessment made of its colour according to Booth's code. When all the books were complete one of the secretaries went through them and made a decision whether or not to accept recommended changes in the map colours. These changes were recorded in neat handwriting on the right hand pages. Eventually, the maps were revised in line with these decisions. Charles Booth used the records of the walks when he wrote up his Religious Influences Series.

Compass points given as a single capital letter at the start of each street (ie. N, E, S, W) indicate the direction of the walk. When used descriptively for a part of a street or area the full description is given (ie. north, east, south, west).

The reader should bear in mind that we have transcribed notes written in long hand and cannot guarantee 100% accuracy. Where the handwriting proved impossible to decipher we have tried to make the best guess.

There are some common phrases which may be initially confusing:
"bread in street" – in an age before throw-away packaging, the main litter was bread
"bricks rubbed" – this was a sign of people leaning against them, loafing
"model Buildings or Dwellings" - homes for the Victorian working classes built by companies receiving a competitive return on investment. The principle of philanthropic intention with capitalist return was known as "five per cent philanthropy"
"bullies" – pimps
Gates – the South London millionnaire who built a lot of property, particularly in the Nunhead area. See p211 for his details

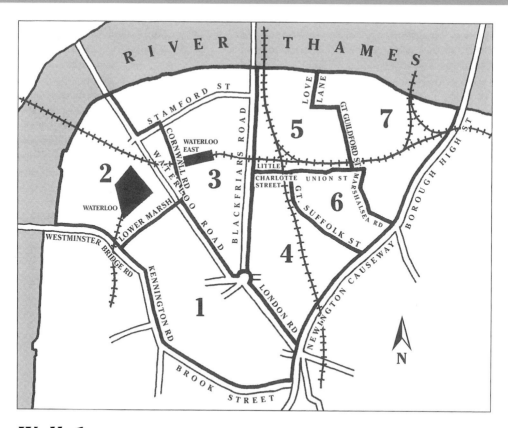

Walk 1

B363

Tuesday 25 April 1899.
George Duckworth with Reserve Inspector Albert Green.
Inspector Green is a fat man rather over middle height, jovial rubicund face, fair moustache, has been 26 years in the Force and seen service in the Drury Lane District and Notting Dale (three years). He has been in this Division over six years.

Starting at St George's Circus.
W along Westminster Bridge Rd. N up **Dodson Street** (late Duke St). 3-st and 2½-st. Some very poor at the south west end and in the centre of the east side. Most of the east side already down and all to come down when leases fall in. Windows and curtains broken, patched, dirty. Bread in street. Costers' barrows and two mattresses lying in the muddy road. A few thieves and prostitutes. "One of the worst places in the Division but not to be compared with Bangor St in the matter of vice." LIGHT BLUE-barred rather than BLACK of the map. At the N corner of Webber St and Dodson St are **Quinn's Buildings**. 6-st. Look poor, well kept inside. LIGHT BLUE to PURPLE, in map PURPLE. On the west side, opposite Quinn's Buildings, Dodson St is very poor.
E along Webber St. N up **Falka Place** (late Ann Place). Houses on east side closed. The west side is Quinn's Buildings. DARK BLUE of map goes.
W along **Tower Street**. 3-st. Many small shops. Better than Duke St. Labouring class above. Many windows broken and patched. Doors open but all with a bit of floor cloth or

matting. Rough-looking, hatless Irishwomen about but many fairly comfortable. Bread in street. 4lb loaf selling in one of the shops for 4d. LIGHT BLUE, in map DARK BLUE.

Out of the E end N side is **Gilbert's Court**. Eight 2-st houses. Very poor costers. DARK BLUE to LIGHT BLUE, not shown in map.

W along Tower St. S down **Gerridge Street** (late Charles St). Jubilee Buildings make the north east side. A large block, courtyard and well-kept trees. That part facing Webber St looks poorer than the rest. Children clean, well dressed. PINK to PURPLE, in map PINK. Gerridge St itself is LIGHT BLUE and 2-st on north west. Unmarked in map. The east side, south of Webber St, is markedly better, 3-st. PURPLE as map. At the corner of the Westminster Bridge Rd are 4½-st buildings, working class. PURPLE to LIGHT BLUE, in map RED. The west side of Webber St is taken up by School except one very poor house. DARK BLUE if marked.

E & W along **Webber Street**. Poor, like Tower St. LIGHT BLUE to PURPLE, in map LIGHT BLUE. Not LIGHT BLUE now east of Jubilee Buildings on north side.

N into Gerridge St. W along Tower St. Out of its NW end is **Short Street**. 3-st. LIGHT BLUE as map but inhabited on east side only.

N into **Pearman Street**. Respectable mechanics. Dull 3-st yellow-brick houses. Many police from 'A' and 'L' Divisions. It is now continued as a street eastwards to the south east of map. The continuation is like the rest and PINK. The south east now better, 2-st, some fairly comfortable at north and one or two still very poor. Altogether LIGHT BLUE.

N up **Mary's Buildings**. 2-st. LIGHT BLUE. Cement paved, clean. One family to a house. LIGHT BLUE to PURPLE, in map PURPLE.

Transwell Street (late Isabella St). 2-st, some with basement. Better than Mary's Buildings. PURPLE as map.

Out of the NW end of Transwell St is **Robert's Place**. Six 2-st houses, flowers at windows, costers. LIGHT BLUE to PURPLE, in map PURPLE.

E along **Thomas' Place**. Four houses on north and two on south. 3-st. Poor. LIGHT BLUE, in map PINK. It is continued east of Coral St with five houses on south side only. LIGHT BLUE, in map PINK.

S down **Little Thomas' Street**. Narrow flagged passage, only 9 ft between house and house. Old inhabitants at north end, very poor at south end. North end is still PURPLE, south is LIGHT BLUE to DARK BLUE. Children clean and well dressed except stockings and knickerbockers of the boys ragged. Mark the whole LIGHT BLUE?

E along Whitinor St and N up **Coral Street**. Built 1820. 2-st and some with basement. PURPLE as map.

W along **Oakley Street**. "Has a bad reputation for roughness and prostitutes" but Green has never been able to understand why. PINK and PURPLE as map. It is a 3-st wood-paved street. There have been brothels in it.

S down **Johanna Street**. Cul de sac. Mud, puddles, children playing in them. 2-st plus attic. Many windows broken but oil cloth in all the passages. Most doors open. LIGHT BLUE to PURPLE, in map PURPLE. North of Oakley St Johanna St is poorer. LIGHT BLUE to DARK BLUE.

W along **Grindal Street** (late Harriet St). Rough, low class, Irish. Like Duke St. All doors open, bread etc. Street full of women and children. Though this is a poor district all the children are remarkable for their clean faces. DARK BLUE, in map LIGHT BLUE.

N into **Lower Marsh**. Very busy shopping street, barrows all along the north side. Groves large clothing establishment on south side. 3-st. PINK-barred to RED, in map PINK-barred.

S down Frazier St. Out of its E side is a small court (north of Gloucester St) called

Corsham Place (late Paved Place). Eight houses, four on north and four on south. Only 4 ft between the houses. Very poor, old people. DARK BLUE, not shown in map.

Frazier Street itself has small, poor shops. LIGHT BLUE, in map PURPLE.

W along **Murphy Street** (late Charles St). Working class. 2-st with 4-st Buildings at north west end. Crowds of children, hatless, clean faces. LIGHT BLUE to DARK BLUE, in map LIGHT BLUE.

Out of the **SW** end is a court called **James' Place**. Seven 2-st houses, only two rooms to a house. Rents 5/- for old tenants and 5/6 for new. LIGHT BLUE to DARK BLUE, in map LIGHT BLUE.

At its **W** end **Murphy Street** turns south. W Hawn's, the great theatrical scene painter's studio, is on the west side and north of it are two houses. LIGHT BLUE, not shown in map.

S into Oakley St, W to Westminster Bridge Rd, N to Lower Marsh. **E & S** into **Lambeth Square**. 3½-st. Small neglected square, grass and trees, no flowers in the centre. One takes the house and lets off. Tallyman going his rounds. PINK as map.

W into Westminster Bridge Rd and **S**, turning **E** at **Burdett Road**. Burdett Buildings on north side, 6-st. PURPLE. Buildings on south side rather poorer. LIGHT BLUE. Both go up to the corner of the Westminster Bridge Rd. On south side of buildings are two very poor and rough houses. DARK BLUE.

S to **Lanfranc Street**. 3-st and 2-st. At the east corner of Burdett Rd and Lanfranc St is a beerhouse for all the world like a dwelling house except for small letters over door. This street is poor. Many women home workers, sound of machines, but LIGHT BLUE rather than DARK BLUE of map.

E along Westminster Bridge Rd and **S** down **King Edward Street**. Quiet, semi-detached on west side, front gardens, apartments. PINK to PINK-barred. One or two servants.

S into **Lambeth Road**. The houses on the north side are called Barkham Terrace. 3½-st, dingy outside, some servants. Superintendent of 'A' Police Division lives here. In the centre is the Upton Baptist Chapel. PINK-barred to RED, in map RED.

N up **St George's Road**. Wood paved. 3½-st on west side. Roman Catholic Cathedral on east with a house for resident priests north of it. PINK-barred to RED.

E & S down **Barbel Street** (late Joiner St). 3-st houses on both sides. The "worst street about here". No common lodging houses but thieves and prostitutes. Windows broken, patched, stuffed, all doors open, no oilcloth or matting in the passages. Irish cockneys the majority. Prostitutes go out to Clapham Common, don't bring men home. "No strong feeling against them in a street like this." Some flowers in windows. Children with dirty faces, sore eyes, torn frocks, hatless. Compares with Bangor St except for the absence of common lodging houses and the rows here are family rows and not against the exercise of authority, police rarely hurt. 6-roomed houses, rents 12/- and 10/-. BLACK as map.

E along **Lambeth Road**. Many without servants. PINK-barred, in map RED.

W along Westminster Bridge Rd. Out of **S** side is **Whitehorse Yard**. Now a private stable yard. Foreman and washers living above on south west side and south east side only. PURPLE, in map DARK BLUE.

E & S down **London Road**. Busy shopping street, costers. PINK-barred to RED, in map RED.

W at **Gladstone Street**. 2½-st. Clerks, no servants, some mechanics, "all go to their work over the water". Six rooms plus scullery, rent £36 to £40 plus rates and takes subletting by one and two rooms. Rents 6/- to 8/- for two rooms. A large family of children would not be allowed in these houses. The schools of Notre Dame have taken in the west end up to the point where the street turns abruptly south. PINK as map.

E & N up **Colnbrook Street** (late Richmond St). Like Gladstone St. PINK as map.

S down **Garden Row**. Many poor. New 3-st flats on west side are PINK, but the whole street is PURPLE to LIGHT BLUE. "A little better than Tower St." In map PINK.

E & N up **Burman Street**. Poor and very poor on east side. New houses but poor on north west. Most of west side taken up by new bus yard which runs through into Garden Row. LIGHT BLUE to DARK BLUE, in map BLACK. It is a 2-st street, inhabited by costers, rough, low, not vicious. The old houses on the east side let four rooms for 10/- to 12/-. The new on the north west let four rooms for 15/-.

E & S down **Marshall Street**. 2-st and 2½-st. Quiet. Labourers working in Maudslays. PURPLE to LIGHT BLUE, in map PINK.

E & N up **Gaywood Street**. 3½-st. Sublet. Dull, dark, rather narrow. A few poor. Rents £36 to £38. Two top floor rooms rent for 6/6, first floor for 7/-, ground floor for 7/- (these are more convenient than the others to get at but the passage has to come out of their size so the rent is the same as for the first floor). The house tenant lives in the basement. Each floor's back room is fitted with a range for cooking. Washing is done in the copper in the basement which is common to all. Washing days are by mutual arrangement by floors. PINK to PURPLE, in map PINK.

E & S down **Princess Street**. Like Gaywood St. Cobble paved. PINK to PURPLE, in map PINK. The passage out of the east side has one poor (LIGHT BLUE) house on north side only.

W along St George's Rd and S down **Ely Place**. A few houses, 2-st, on south side only. PINK, in map PINK-barred.

E into **West Square**. 3½-st and 4½-st. The east side keeps a few servants and is PINK-barred as map. The rest rather PINK. Messy square, great deal of loose paper.

Out of the **S** side is **Austral Street**. Girls' home on west side. PINK, in map PURPLE.

Out of the **SE** side of the Square is **Orient Street**. Rather rough, mixed. Badly-mended road. PURPLE to LIGHT BLUE, in map PINK. That part which runs due east is also PURPLE to LIGHT BLUE, in map PINK. The LIGHT BLUE shown in the passage leading to Hayles St has gone.

N up **West Square**. The houses standing back on the north east side are PINK as map.

N up **West Street**. No houses except one cottage, a public house, on the west side. PINK.

E along St George's Rd and S down **Hayles Street**. 2-st and 3-st. Good proportion of poor. "Some ladies here who work the Elephant." Some new PINK houses on the north east side but the whole is PURPLE, in map PINK.

E along **Lamlash Street** (late John St). Some police. Two very poor houses on north side. These should be DARK BLUE and the rest PINK or the whole PURPLE. Houses on both sides, PINK in map.

N up **Elliott's Row**. LIGHT BLUE to DARK BLUE as map south east but less of it. Above on the east side are new buildings, Hayles' Buildings, 5-st, PINK. The west side is not so good.

E & S down **Oswin Street** (late Temple St). 4-st, quiet, fairly comfortable. PINK to PURPLE, in map PINK. The south east end should be LIGHT BLUE, in map PURPLE. This and the preceding streets belong to a Mr Geats who started life as a labourer and now runs a great deal of property here and in Dulwich.

E along **St George's Road**. The corner is all taken by Rabbit's factory, only a caretaker sleeps. There is no PINK behind.

General Remarks

Green said that the change of the last ten years had been from bad to better and from best to less good. The bad streets are not quite so bad as they were, the good streets are not nearly so good. Thus the BLACK streets (Duke St and Burman St) are LIGHT BLUE or LIGHT BLUE-barred and Tower St, formerly DARK BLUE, is now LIGHT BLUE. But the PINK streets on the west side of the London Rd are fast becoming PURPLE. Green ascribed the change to the effect of neighbouring demolitions. "The fairly comfortable are the first to move, the poor refuse to and have not the money to go far away even if they wished to do so."

Men, women and children seem to live in the street more than they do north of the Thames. Courts swarm with children and the main streets with working men and women going to and from their work. More loafers here at the street corners. Top hats rarely seen; bowlers, soft felt hats and caps the usual head gear.

Walk 2   B363

Friday 28th April 1899.
George Duckworth with Sergeant Saltmarshe.
Sergeant Saltmarshe has a round, fat face and brown moustache, middle height, 21 years service, 11 years in this Division. Inspector Green confessed to not knowing much about the streets east of the Westminster Bridge Rd and Supt Wren accordingly recommended Saltmarshe.

Starting at the corner of Lower Marsh and Waterloo Road.
N up Waterloo Rd and E at **Pear Tree Street**. Cul de sac, quiet. Fourteen 2-st houses. Rents 7/6 to 9/- for four rooms plus scullery. Not coloured in map, PURPLE to PINK.
N & E at **Holmes Terrace**. 3-st houses on north side only. Very poor. Many prostitutes living in the street, work the Strand and Waterloo Rd. All doors open. DARK BLUE, in map PURPLE. West of Chartley Place, Holmes Terrace is 2-st, poor but respectable. LIGHT BLUE. Costers' barrows. The south side is down and the City & Waterloo Electric Railway works take up the west end.
N & W along **Aubin Street**. Mixed, some fairly comfortable. Many railway porters. "Railway porters are known for the amount they drink, earnings not precarious but varying largely in amount from day to day." PURPLE all through rather than PINK and PURPLE of map. The west end is largely stables and a break has been made in the centre leading to Launcelot St.
Out of the **SW** end is **Granby Gardens**. Windows very bad, mess, fowls. Built 1851. The west side is coming down for railway extension. Woman with baby, dirty, bare-armed, bare-headed. Pays 4/- for one room. It is LIGHT BLUE and DARK BLUE, in map LIGHT BLUE.
W into **Granby Place**. North east coming down, one house still occupied. West side and south east are poor, messy, labourers, bad windows. Look rough but Saltmarshe said they were no trouble to the police. DARK BLUE to LIGHT BLUE, in map PURPLE.
E along Aubin St. S into **Launcelot Street**. Mixed, 2-st, many poor. East end taken up by Railway Electric Works. PURPLE to LIGHT BLUE, in map PURPLE.
S into Lower Marsh. E then N up **Chartley Place** and **Grove Place**. LIGHT BLUE. Public library takes up east side south of Holmes Terrace. Well appointed as seen through windows but very few using it (hour 11.30).
E along Lower Marsh, N up Waterloo Rd, under the railway bridge. W along **Vine Street**. PINK to PURPLE, in map PURPLE. Railwaymen. This and the following streets are all PINK to PURPLE.

Out of the **S** side is **Robert Street**. PINK as map. Railway foremen and firemen. Very few living.

N & E along **Francis Street**. 2½-st. Fairly comfortable. PINK as map.

N & W along **James Street**. Like it. PINK as map.

Anne Street. PINK as map. All these streets are alike and PINK to PURPLE in character. 6-roomed houses, letting at 12/- or 14/- per week and sublet. Streets themselves badly kept and want mending.

N up Waterloo Rd, turning W at the York Public House into **York Road**. "Poverty Junction and Out At Elbows Corner", the corner where the poorer Music Hall artistes loaf in hope of a job. York Rd itself is full of Variety Agents. "The demand for 'pros' increases every year."

N to York Rd. W & N up **Tenison Street**. 3½-st, respectable, very few prostitutes. Apartments for musical profession. PINK as map.

E & S down **Howley Place**. 2-st on west, 5-st on east, that is the backs of the houses which face on the much higher level of the Waterloo Rd. The two bottom storeys are used as cellars and stores except a few at north east end which are lived in. Messy. PURPLE as map.

W along Belvedere Rd and S down **Sutton Street**. PINK as map.

E along **Howley Street**. 2-st. Narrow, no thoroughfare for vehicles. PINK as map. Comfortable, quiet.

N to **Belvedere Road**. Mixed street. North side all factories, wharves. Brewery with foremen's houses attached. South side many poor but many fairly comfortable. PURPLE to PINK, in map PINK.

W & S down **Belvedere Crescent**. Rather better east than west. 3-st and 2-st. PURPLE to PINK, in map PINK.

S down **Vine Street**. 2½-st and 3½-st. PINK as map.

Out of the **SE** side is **Manners Street**. 2½-st flush with pavement. Narrow, no thoroughfare for vehicles. PINK as map.

S then W along York Rd and into **Princes Buildings**. 2-st houses. Flagged court crammed with children, clean, well dressed and fed. Four rooms for 9/- and 9/6. Only 9 ft between the housefronts. PURPLE as map.

W along York Rd and N up **Chichely Street** (called in map Edward St). 3-st. Not so many houses lived in on east side as formerly. Mixed. PURPLE as map.

N & W along Belvedere Rd. Out of its S side is **Cox's Buildings**. 3-st. Children well fed and dressed. Cats crowding round cats' meat men, three sticks of meat taken in at one house, 2d a stick. PURPLE to LIGHT BLUE. Houses are on both sides (north and south) of the court and come over the arch under which the court is entered. Map shows houses on south only.

E along Belvedere Rd, N at **College Street**. Mixed. Two houses on the west side given up to prostitutes. Saltmarshe called them prostitutes' "homes" and explained himself to mean that only some houses would board prostitutes and those that did so were called "homes" by the police. "They must live somewhere and don't bring men home to them. Those who work the same road like to live together". PURPLE as map.

S then W along the **York Road**. Variety agents, warehouses, hotels, prostitutes. Many hotels little else than brothels, "girls live there and bring men home". Some servants. PINK-barred as map.

S down **Addington Street**. PINK as map. 3-st.

Out of the **W** side is **Addington Crescent**. Flagged court, clean, comfortable. PINK. Note: That there are one or two houses lived in on the east side, south of the Board School as well as the turning north of it.

S & E & N up **York Street**. Old fashioned. Small 2-st cottages with front gardens. PURPLE as map.

At the back on the **W** side is **Sapphire Place**. 2-st. Five rooms plus scullery for 10/- in the northernmost houses, the rest 7/6 to 9/-. Houses on east side only and at north side of north end. PURPLE as map.

E along York Rd. N then turning E at Bazon St. S down **Commercial Buildings**. Now a cement passage, clean, no-one living. LIGHT BLUE at north west end goes.

E into **Bazon Street** (late Bond St). 2-st plus basement. Flush with pavement. Rough mixture, many prostitutes. PURPLE to LIGHT BLUE, in map PURPLE.

E along **Cage Place** (late Cottage Place). 2-st. Washing hanging across. Some houses very poor. Children fairly clean and well dressed. LIGHT BLUE to DARK BLUE, in map DARK BLUE. Rents: four rooms 7/6 for new tenants, 5/6 for old.

S & E along **Bond Place**. Very poor. 2-st. Children and girls, dirty, boots bad, pink and black toes showing through boots. Mess of paper, cellars with open doors full of mess, pickings from the dustyard in Commercial Rd where most of the women work. Windows patched and broken, bare and untidy rooms seen through open doors. Washing day, washing being done in a tub outside front doors. Redraining to houses at east end. Rents: two rooms 5/6 and four rooms 7/6. It is a flagged court. DARK BLUE as map.

N & E along **Doon Street**. Mixed, many poor. PURPLE as map.

Out of **S** side is **Milan Place**. Eight cottages with a tap in centre to supply houses, defective and water running to waste by gallons. (This is a common sight in the South London courts seen hitherto). Looks quiet and clean, great array of flowers under wire netting at one house, but Saltmarshe said it was noted for family rows, "fathers fight their sons of a Saturday night". Birdcages. Not very poor. Two very dirty well-fed children seen. Two and three rooms for 6/-. LIGHT BLUE to DARK BLUE, in map DARK BLUE.

Opposite on the **N** side of Doon St is **Elizabeth Place**. 2-st. Two rooms plus wash-house 5/6. Geraniums. LIGHT BLUE as map.

E to Cornwall Rd and N. On the **W** side is **Henry Place**. Four 2-st cottages. Two rooms 5/6, four rooms 9/-. DARK BLUE to LIGHT BLUE, in map LIGHT BLUE.

Opposite on **E** side of Cornwall Rd is **Druce's Place**. Two 2-st houses, one DARK BLUE, the other LIGHT BLUE, in map PINK.

Opposite on **W** side of Cornwall Rd, **S** of Doon St is **Perry's Place**. Houses on east and west sides. Children dirty with bad boots, well fed. DARK BLUE to LIGHT BLUE, in map LIGHT BLUE.

Into the **Cornwall Road**. 3-st. Many poor and rough at this north end. "Last Saturday in one of these houses a woman threw a lighted lamp at her husband and both were burnt to death." LIGHT BLUE to PURPLE, in map PURPLE.

General Remarks

The demolitions in the neighbourhood of Lower Marsh owing to railway extension (London & South Western Railway) and the Waterloo and City Electric Railway engine station; the fairly comfortable round Waterloo Station; prostitutes and brothels in the York Rd and the very poor and rough off the north east corner of the Waterloo Rd; are the features of this round. Railway disturbance has only displaced some 'PURPLE' and not much of that. Otherwise the district is much as it was ten years ago. Prostitutes crowd round Waterloo as they do round St Pancras and King's Cross and the York Rd has much the same reputation as the Euston Rd. Rents run between 2/- and 3/- per room.

Walk 3

B363

Monday 1st May 1899.
George Duckworth with Sergeant P S Waters.

Starting at the corner of Exton Street and the Waterloo Road.
E along **Exton Street**. 3½-st. Two and three families to a house. PINK as map.
N up **Secker Street**. 3-st. Rather poorer. St Patrick's Catholic schools on south east side. PINK to PURPLE, in map PINK.
N & W at **Cornwall Place**. Flagged, fairly clean court. Front gardens now cemented over, "but they used to be fine some years ago". Used to be Irish but fewer of them now. Windows and curtains fairly clean. Doors open, fairly well-furnished rooms to be seen inside. Many old tenants, since 18 and 20 years. Waterside labourers. The extreme west end is the poorest. At the back of the north side is a large woodyard with piles of wood stacked alongside of the chimneys, nearly overlapping. There has never been a fire but it is hard to imagine anything that looks more dangerous. Rents 6/- for two rooms, no copper, kettle has to be boiled and washing done in tub in front yard. WCs in front. LIGHT BLUE, leave DARK BLUE at west end, in map all is DARK BLUE.
N past **Cornwall Mews**. A woodyard, no-one living. The thoroughfare into Waterloo Rd has been closed.
On the E side of Cornwall Rd is **Salutation Place**. 3-st houses. Rents for three rooms 7/-, 7/6 and 8/-. No wash-house nor copper. WCs in black wooden sheds in front. Houses on north side only. "He should give us coppers. It lays us all up with bronchitis being without them." GEA says that the Prince of Wales is landlord. At the east end Salutation Place turns abruptly southward, becomes 2-st and much poorer. East end not shown in map, DARK BLUE. West end DARK BLUE in map, to LIGHT BLUE. Costers' streets, hawkers, old inhabitants.
S of Salutation Place out of Cornwall Rd is **Peer's Cooperage**. 3-st. Poor, flowers in windows, costers. LIGHT BLUE, in map DARK BLUE.
N into Stamford St, E, then N up **Coin Street** (late Princes St). 3½-st. Clean, comfortable, some prostitutes. PINK as map.
E along Commercial Rd. S down **Duke Street**. 3-st, old-fashioned. Small panes to occasional small shops. PURPLE as map.
E & S into **Cory Square** (late Princes Square). 3-st houses. Court in course of being well laid with cement. Children very dirty but well fed. Poor and very poor and a few fairly comfortable. All doors open. Some bread about. A few Irish. West side poorer than the east. five-roomed houses let at 10/-, all the east side at this price. Small glass bottle factory out of the east side. Old tenants, one had been 26 years in the court and another boy of about 16 had lived at various times with his family in every one of the various houses in the court. DARK BLUE as map.
E & S down **Broad Wall**. 3-st buildings called 'Parish Garden Dwellings' on the west side. Rough, poor and very poor. LIGHT BLUE to DARK BLUE. The 2-st houses on the east side are in good repair, also poor. LIGHT BLUE as map.
E along **Old Barge House**. Warehouses on south side.
S down **Hatfield Street**. Working class. PINK as map.
E & S down **Boddy's Bridge**. East side is warehouse (or school?) wall. LIGHT BLUE in map. Very poor on west side. DARK BLUE to LIGHT BLUE, in map LIGHT BLUE. The southern court (**called Upper Ground Place**) is more respectable (in map PURPLE). East

side not so good as west, rather LIGHT BLUE than PURPLE. One woman who had been there 16 years pays 14/- for her house of six rooms (three floors) and wash-house. She lets off at 6/- per floor or 4/- for a single room.

E & S down **Bennett Street**. 3½-st on east side. Old, built for a servant-keeping class. Poor. LIGHT BLUE, in map PINK. Cooks, the draper in St Paul's Churchyard, has the whole of the west side as a residence for his employees. PINK as map. The houses at the north east end of Bennett St are smaller, poorer, should be DARK BLUE.

E & S down **King's Arms Court**. Twelve 3-st houses. Six on east and west sides. Ropes across for hanging clothes. Windows broken and patched. Lowest class of prostitutes and thieves. One barefoot child. Rough women with hair in metal curlers, men with faces of criminal type at the windows. Rows on Saturday nights. Children, boys and girls, playing tipcat; dirty, ragged but all well fed and of good colour. "Like Joiner St." BLACK, in map DARK BLUE.

S down Blackfriars Rd and W along **Stamford Street**. 3½-st plus attic. "Great many prostitutes living here. The hotels are places of accommodation, some are little else than brothels. The girls live in them, walk out and bring men home to them. There have not been so many foreign prostitutes since the passing of the Act against bullies." The most disreputable hotels are west of the Waterloo Rd but there are some almost as bad east of it. PINK as map but PINK-barred as map west of Cornwall Rd where there is a greater proportion of servant-keeping hotels.

W & S down Cornwall Rd. E at **Palmer Street**. North side is factories, south side is back gardens of the houses in Whittlesey St.

S down **Theed Street**. Railwaymen. PINK as map.

W along **Whittlesey Street** (late Richard St). 2-st, clean. Railwaymen. PINK as map.

W across Cornwall Rd. Along **Alaska Street**. West end blocked by operations for widening railway bridge. 2-st. PINK to PURPLE, in map PINK.

S down Cornwall Rd. W along **Sandell Road**. Houses on south only. PINK, not coloured in map.

W into Waterloo Rd. S past a beer stores which used to be a Wesleyan Chapel. E along **Morpeth Place**. 2-st. "Four rooms plus wash-house let for 10/-, let off rooms at 4/- each" said one man. Windows bad, children hatless. LIGHT BLUE as map.

S & E at **Peartree Street**. 3-st and 2-st. Small shops, sweep etc. PURPLE, in map PINK.

N up Cornwall Rd. On the W side is **Hammond Place**. Five houses. Quiet, poor. One house at the west end is double-fronted. Four rooms upstairs let at 6/6, three rooms down at 6/9. The other houses are 2-roomed, let at 6/6, "you pay a little more to have the place to yourself" said one woman. LIGHT BLUE to DARK BLUE, in map DARK BLUE.

N up Cornwall Rd. E along **Roupell Street**. Quiet, comfortable, like Whittlesey St and Theed St except at the south east end which is markedly poorer and should be LIGHT BLUE. There are no houses in the court at the back which only leads to the backs of the Brad St houses.

N up **Broad Wall**. Poor. 3-st and 2½-st. Some old red tile-roofed and wooden-sided houses. The block of LIGHT BLUE which was common lodging houses at the south east end is now all warehouses. The rest LIGHT BLUE as map.

W & S down **Duke Street**. Some small shops mixed with poor and very poor. LIGHT BLUE, in map PURPLE. The main entrance to the Peabody Dwellings is here, many poor. PURPLE to PINK, in map PINK.

W along **Aquinas Street**. 2½-st. Flush with pavement, quiet. PURPLE as map.

Off the N side is a small court of two houses called **Thomas' Cottages**. Entered down steps.

Two rooms in each let for 5/6 a week.

W into **Coin Street** (late Prince St). Very poor at south west. LIGHT BLUE. The rest is PINK as map.

Out of the **NE** side is **Prince's Mews**. Cabyard, carts etc. Only one tenanted. In map PURPLE, now not worth marking but it is either PINK or LIGHT BLUE.

W along Stamford St, S down Cornwall Rd, E along **Brad Street**. Houses at east end only. Those (eight) on south side to come down for the railway. Notices to quit when wanted being served. One woman on taking hers said "well, I shan't quit till they come to turn us out". Poor, scavengers, costers and labourers. LIGHT BLUE as map, but less of it on south side.

S down Eaton St and W along **Wootton Street**. North side (in map PURPLE with two courts, LIGHT BLUE and DARK BLUE off it) down for railway extension. South side is mixed, poor and comfortable. 2-st. Many windows broken. PURPLE as map.

Out of the **SW** end is **Wootton Court**. Eighteen 3-st houses. Flagged passage. One room up and one down plus small back yard. Very poor, curtains dirty and windows bad. DARK BLUE as map. Two landlords and one landlady to this block. The landlady lives in one of the houses herself. Rents 6/- and 7/- for two rooms plus kitchen. 7/- for new tenants.

E into Windmill St and E & W along **Ethelm Street**. Poorer east than west of Windmill St. 2½-st. Two or three very poor at extreme north west. PURPLE as map west of Windmill St, LIGHT BLUE east of it. The east corner of Windmill St also LIGHT BLUE. It looks as though the poorer of those off the north side of Wootton St had come in here.

S down **Eaton Street**. LIGHT BLUE to DARK BLUE, in map DARK BLUE.

W along **Little Windmill Street**. 5-st Waldeck Buildings on the north side. PINK as map. Stables on south side not lived in (LIGHT BLUE in map) except a few houses, very poor, at south west end. These should be DARK BLUE. The DARK BLUE court on the west side of Windmill St is closed and seems to have moved across the road. "Waldeck Buildings are rather better than the Peabody's."

N & W along **St Andrew's Place**. Twelve houses, 2-st, on south side only. Clean flagged passage. Very poor. Dustyard scavengers. Young wives, dirty children but all enough to eat, ragged. Houses let for 5/9 for two rooms and a very small yard behind.

E along Ethelm St. S down Eaton St and E at **Victoria Place**. Six houses on north side, three on south and three on the east side of turning south out of it. Bare passage, flagged. Fretful, dirty children, hair matted, hatless, dirty faces. Windows dirty and broken and stuffed. Women rough, bare-armed. All doors open. Half-witted loafer standing at corner. Bare passages seen through open doors. Children and girls throwing bread at one another. Plaster peeling off the house walls. Inhabitants thieves and prostitutes. There seemed to be one respectable family at the west end house north side. "Like Kings Arms Court and Joiner St." BLACK as map but less of it because there are no houses on the west side of the cul de sac which runs south out of the Place.

N up Broad Wall. Out of **W** side is **Sidwell Place**. Twelve houses on north, south and west sides. Newly cement paved. All doors open. Poor, women with sack aprons. Houses 2-st, four-roomed, letting at 10/6 and 11/- for the whole house. When sublet they fetch 4/- for upstairs front, 3/6 for downstairs front, back rooms 3/- each. There is to each a kitchen and copper. DARK BLUE as map.

N past **Mitre Place**. A private yard, none living. In map LIGHT BLUE.

N up **Hatfield Street**. 2½-st and 3½-st mixed. North better than south. Asphalt paved, well-kept road. Some poor. PURPLE to PINK, in map PINK.

Along Stamford St. **S** down **Bennett Street**. Sainsbury the provision merchants' warehouses take up all east side (in map PINK). On the west is a public house, some dwelling houses and Cooksey's (the hat makers) offices. PINK as map.

W along **Stamford Street**. Common lodging house on the south side between Bennett St and Brunswick St. PURPLE rather than PINK of map.

S down **Brunswick Street**. Mixed, asphalted, clean, birdcages at windows. PURPLE as map.

E into **Brunswick Place**. Fourteen 2-st houses, clean flagged passage. Poor. LIGHT BLUE to PURPLE, in map PINK.

E along **Collingwood Street**. Old-fashioned 2-st wooden houses with dormer windows and red-tiled roofs on south side. PINK as map but it should be PURPLE where it runs north and south, many poor, instead of PINK of map.

Off the W side of Brunswick St is **Brunswick Court**. 2-st, very poor. In map it is PURPLE and LIGHT BLUE. The houses at the north east rather less poor than the rest, 2-st. DARK BLUE.

S down **Hatfield Place** which is a flagged passage. Nineteen 2-st houses on the east side, five at south west side. Hatless children, most doors open. A few fairly comfortable families remaining but they are the exceptions, the majority are poor and very poor. LIGHT BLUE to DARK BLUE, in map PURPLE.

E along **Meymott Street** (late Cross Street). Wood-paved, narrow shopping street, not very busy but much wheel traffic as it is the short cut from Blackfriars Rd to Waterloo Station. PINK as map.

E into Blackfriars Rd. On the W side N of Meymott St is **Runninghorse Yard**. Only two still occupied at west end. "Used to be very rough when the houses on the south side were tenanted, now they are stable lofts", said a fat man who had lived there 46 years. Mark LIGHT BLUE, all the DARK BLUE shown in the map has gone.

W & S down Collingwood St. W along **Jane Street**. 2-st. South side not so good as north. Street up for cement paving. PURPLE to PINK, in map PINK.

S down Broad Wall and E at **Isabella Street**. 2-st. North side down for railway extension. Many poor. PURPLE, in map PINK.

Out of the S side is **Norfolk Street**. 2-st. PURPLE to PINK, in map PURPLE. Elwood's hat and helmet factory is at the south east corner.

S into **Great Charlotte Street**. Broad. Shops on north side. Large common lodging house on the south side, Great Surrey Chambers, 5½-st. Separate rooms 8d a night or 3/- a week. Good accommodation 6d a night or 2/6 a week. PINK on north, PURPLE on south, as map.

S down Marlborough St. E along **John Street West**. 2-st. Houses on south side. PURPLE as map.

N up **Burrows Mews**. A few living above stables on north east, south east and south west. In map LIGHT BLUE but in the wrong places.

W to **Gray Street**. 2-st. Many poor. PURPLE to LIGHT BLUE, in map LIGHT BLUE.

N up Short St, out of whose W side run **Ufford Street** (late Queen St), **Mitre Street** and **Caffyn Street** (late New St). All 2-st. Poorer than they used to be, a few fairly comfortable remaining but the majority poor and very poor. Caffyn St is the poorest. Map marks Ufford St and Mitre St PURPLE and Caffyn St DARK BLUE, now there is more of a dead level of LIGHT BLUE. A boy in a fit in Caffyn St with the whole neighbourhood out of window and in the street to look at him.

W to **Webber Street**. Poor. The best parts are the small shops south of the Victoria at the north west end and again between Webber Row and Barons' Place (both sides of street). These might remain PINK, all the rest is LIGHT BLUE to PURPLE. Marshall's Buildings out of the east side north of Valentine Place distinctly LIGHT BLUE. In map the whole is PINK.

Out of the W side N of Gray St is **Asa Place**. Six houses. Small court but 12 children playing in it. Very poor and very rough, the children's clothes all holes. There is a copper in

the court common to all the houses. Two rooms 5/- and 5/6. DARK BLUE, not shown in map.
W along **Gray Street**. Common lodging house on south side, beds 4d and 6d, but not near
so bad as it used to be. Some prostitutes but majority have been cleared out. LIGHT BLUE to
DARK BLUE, in map DARK BLUE.

S down Waterloo Rd and E at **Baron's Place**. 2-st. Very poor costers living here. DARK
BLUE to LIGHT BLUE, in map DARK BLUE and on north side only.

E along **Valentine Place**. Pascall's sweet factory takes up a large part of the north side east
end. LIGHT BLUE as map.

S down **Angel Place**. Passage with 2-st houses on either side. Labourers. "Like Caffyn,
Mitre and Ufford Streets." Not rough. LIGHT BLUE as map.

Into **Valentine Row**. 2-st. Old inhabitants. Rents 9/- for four rooms plus kitchen. Single
rooms let off for 3/6 and 4/-.

W into **Webber Row**. North side down except a few houses. "They propose building model
dwellings here." The south side is poor. LIGHT BLUE not PURPLE.

Out of the **SE** end is **William's Place**. Poor 2-st cottages, shored up to prevent falling in.
Children clean and well fed. Stable yard at south end. One woman who had been there two
years pays 4/6 for two rooms plus wash-house. DARK BLUE as map.

W of it out of Webber Row is **Bennett's Yard**. Two 2½-st houses. LIGHT BLUE to
PURPLE, not shown in map. The DARK BLUE shown in map now disappears. It is merely a
rambling ramshackle stable yard with no-one living over.

E into Blackfriars Rd and S. On the E side are Peabody Dwellings, **Blackfriars Square**.
Large prison-like buildings, asphalt square in centre, fair open space planted with trees.
Eagerly tenanted. Some poor but as a whole PINK as map.

General Remarks

The poorest places in the wedge between the Thames on the north, Blackfriars Rd on the
east and Waterloo Rd on the west are: Bond Place out of Bazon St; Perry's Place out of
Cornwall Rd; Cornwall Place out of Cornwall Rd; Salutation Place out of Cornwall Rd;
Cory Square out of Commercial Rd; Regent's Court out of Ground St; Brunswick Court
out of Brunswick St; Hatfield Place, Meymott St; Wootton Court out of Wootton St; St
Andrew's Place out of Windmill St; Sidwell Place out of Broad Wall; Little Windmill St
south west end; Asa Place out of Webber St; Baron's Place out of Webber St; William's
Place out of Webber Row. All these are DARK BLUE or between DARK BLUE and LIGHT
BLUE. Two of them are BLACK in Regent's Court and Victoria Place. Victoria Place was
BLACK 10 years ago and is still BLACK. Regent's Court now becomes BLACK and was
DARK BLUE. As a whole there has been no increase of the DARK BLUE in this district but
at the same time no decrease. But there has been a large increase in the amount of LIGHT
BLUE and a marked decrease in the amount of PINK. The tone of the whole is today more of
a uniform LIGHT BLUE though a LIGHT BLUE dotted with patches of DARK BLUE.

Railway clearances and increased facilities have driven out the DARK BLUE and carried
off the PINK. The DARK BLUE has sought refuge in the streets nearest to those from which
they were driven while the PINK has found house-room further afield. The district therefore
is getting poorer. It is probable that the streets as marked this year show their minimum of
poverty owing to the goodness of the times and trade and the mildness of the winter.

Except in the few streets north of Stamford St the bulk of the inhabitants both work and
sleep in the district. In this respect the place differs from most of the districts already seen
north of the Thames. The inhabitants make one vast, poor family whose lives are well known
to one another. There is more street life than even in the East End, more children in the

street and more women gossiping at the doors.

The New Cut and Lambeth Lower Marsh is the common meeting place and market street, always busy though busiest on Friday and Saturday nights and Sunday mornings. The prices as I passed were 4d for a 4lb loaf. Meat-scraps from 2d to 3½lb, pork chops (first rate) 6½d each, half a cooked chicken 8d and 9d (not appetising to look at). Sheep heads, uncooked, 5d each. Best eggs, three for 2½d. Eggs 'special line' 24 for 1/-. Four duck's eggs 3d. Whole skinned rabbit 6½d, three bunches of radishes 1d, lemons three a penny. Good cucumbers in the shops 2d and 4d and the same in appearance on the barrows 1d and 1½d. The largest crowd was round a fish barrow where cod or whiting pollock and plaice were being sold, the buyers all women. No excitement, Dutch auction, each fish was cut in half and shown, the seller fixed the price and lowered it until it was bought. Most of it went at the price he first named. A large plaice was to be bought for 4d, cod's head and perhaps 1½lbs of meat cut off with it for 3d, the rest of the fish (4 or 5 lbs at a guess) went for 4d, a whole fish for 6d. Only once had he to lower his outset price; a plaice, fair size, offered for 3½d found no buyer until 2½d was reached. The flesh of all the fish was white and looked fairly fresh. Rump steaks, good, ran from 9d to 11d in the shops and mutton chops 8d and 9d.

The costers' barrows are on the north side only – by arrangement with the Vestry? Besides fish and fruit there are barrows of flowers, fuschias, geraniums and small bedding plants in wooden boxes, barrows of old keys and ironwork, haberdashery etc, but the glory of the Lower Marsh is by night. It is shy and quiet by day.

Walk 4

B363

Thursday 11th May 1899.
George Duckworth with Sergeant F J O'Dell.
O'Dell is a fat man, very fat. He is not now on active outdoor duty but is employed in the clerks' office. He is intelligent and knows a good deal more about the different parts of the Division in their criminal aspects than most of the policemen who have been round with me. All charges, from every quarter, pass through his hands every day.

Starting at the corner of Earl Street and London Street.
E along Earl Street. 2-st. Poor, quiet, careful. Many rag pickers at Joseph's great warehouse. LIGHT BLUE to PURPLE, in map PURPLE and LIGHT BLUE.
N up Mansfield Street. A few 2-st 6-roomed houses on west side only, letting at 14/- a week. PURPLE as map. Hoe's large printing machine works take up the whole of the east side.
E & S down Kell Street. Houses at north east and south west only. The rest on the west side are down and the east closed. "No good doing up property of this kind. Owners find it better worth their while to pull the whole thing down and rebuild for a different class." A drunken and disorderly class here, some ex-convicts. Windows very bad. DARK BLUE to LIGHT BLUE-barred as map but less of it.
W & N up Dantzig Street (late Market St). Houses on east only, Hoe's printing machine work on west. Drunks, like Kell St. 2-st, windows and curtains bad, all doors open. "A class that has money enough for drink and amusement but nothing for their homes." DARK BLUE to LIGHT BLUE-barred, in map LIGHT BLUE. It would seem as though the inhabitants of demolished Kell St had turned in here.
E & S down Kell St, across Earl's St. Out of the S side is Earl's Place. Six 2-st houses. Children dirty, well fed, fairly clothed. 5/6 for two rooms. Women very rough, "very poor

and very bad". DARK BLUE-barred to BLACK, in map LIGHT BLUE and DARK BLUE.

S to St George's Place. 2-st, well asphalted. One fairly comfortable house, the rest very poor. DARK BLUE to LIGHT BLUE-barred, in map LIGHT BLUE.

W across Dantzig St and along **Butcher Row**. Cement passage. Small 1-st houses on the south side which once were the booths of a busy market. The market consists now of stables and a few orange and potato merchants. The houses on the north side are poor, rough, 3-st or 4-st. Windows broken, patched, all doors open. Ice cream vendors. Children dirty and ragged, sore eyes but well fed. Costers' barrows in evidence. DARK BLUE to LIGHT BLUE, in map LIGHT BLUE. The cul de sac turning north looks less poor, LIGHT BLUE. The block opposite the mews also less poor, LIGHT BLUE to DARK BLUE, and behind this are a few tack cottages apparently tenanted, DARK BLUE. The Mews has only one family living over at the north east. All the tenants here are rough poor, plenty of money at times and none at others. Women sitting about on doorsteps. A few thieves and prostitutes and betting roughs, men who regularly snatch the tickets from those who come with their slips after a race to be paid. They are in league with the smaller bookmakers. Perhaps the colouring of the whole should be LIGHT BLUE-barred.

S along W end of the market and E along **Parliament Street**. 3-st. Same class as Butcher Row. LIGHT BLUE-barred or DARK BLUE. The market has gone to the east side of London Rd which every day of the week is lined with barrows.

SW down **Ontario Street** (late London St). 3-st and 2-st. "Rather better than Earl St, nearly on a par with Mansfield St." Shirt and tailoring homeworkers. Some evident effort at cleanliness in the matter of windows and curtains. Rather poorer west than east of Dantzig St. Bread and potato parings in the street. PURPLE to LIGHT BLUE, in map PURPLE.

A row of butchers shops, one slaughtering on the premises, in London Road.

S & N up **Skipton Street** (late York St). "Like Ontario St." Tenement houses above shops. Built to be a shopping street but is a business failure, shops of struggling class, barely make ends meet. PURPLE, in map PINK.

S to Newington Causeway. S & N up **London Road**. Very busy. The market part of the street stretches from Newington Causeway to a little north of Ontario St. Many Jews from the Lane sell here with "women's finery". Trams, omnibuses and cabs crowd in here from Waterloo Rd, Blackfriars Rd and Westminster Bridge Rd – the neck of a bottle.

E along **Bath Street**. Poor at north west end. Rents 12/- to 14/-. 2-st. Peculiar "People's Chapel" on south side, "not much favoured, 12 to 15 on Sunday morning". Most doors open. PURPLE to LIGHT BLUE, in map PURPLE.

N & E along Earl St to **Lancaster Street**. Broad, formerly a tram route, now discontinued, lines remain. PINK as map.

S & N up **Southwark Bridge Road**. Hardly a servant. PINK, in map PINK-barred.

Out of the W side is **Stanhope Place**. On south side only. PURPLE, in map PINK.

N & W to **Borough Road**. The north side is RED in map but now very few shopkeepers live over and the shops are of a poor class. PINK rather than RED. The LIGHT BLUE of map west of Warwick St is now down and a new public library in its place.

The street immediately W of the library is called **Library Street** (late New St). 2-st. Quiet, poor labourers. Public library takes up the east side. LIGHT BLUE, in map PINK. Round the corner at No.8 lives a London City Missionary. On the north side are new buildings of Faulkner's tobacco works (PINK in map). "Do a large public house trade in cheap tobaccos, cigars and cigarettes", employ 400 to 500.

S down **Warwick Street**. 3-st on east side north of King James St. PURPLE to LIGHT BLUE, but LIGHT BLUE on both sides south of King James St and 2-st. In map PINK.

E along **King James Street** (late James St). Houses on north side only, until east of Minor Place. Rebuilding at south west end. St Alphege's on south side. Father Edwardes, "the costers' parson", women flock to him. Windows of street bad, bread and mess. Borough market porters and costers. LIGHT BLUE as map.

At SE end is **Minor Place** (in map Mina Place). 3-st tenement houses, seven rooms to a house. Two rooms 6/-. Great mess of paper, children dirty. LIGHT BLUE to PURPLE, in map LIGHT BLUE.

Out of the N side of King James St starting at the east end runs **Upper Green Street**. Asphalted passage, washing across. 2-st. Very poor. DARK BLUE to LIGHT BLUE, in map LIGHT BLUE.

W & S down **Bean Street**. 2-st. Cement paved, every door open, washing across. Noisy rough class, "do a good deal of singing before they go to bed". Children well fed and a little cleaner than in the other streets but houses poorer, less furniture to be seen through the doors. DARK BLUE, in map LIGHT BLUE.

W & N up **Tupman Place** (late Francis Place). Labourers, poor, mess, doors open. LIGHT BLUE to DARK BLUE, in map PURPLE.

W & S down **Flint Street**. Has only a few very poor houses of its own at the north west end. The lower blocks are the backs of the Gun St dwellings. DARK BLUE at north west, not shown in map.

W & S down **Gun Street**. The southern half of the road up for redraining. The northern half has been up and very badly re-laid. Loose stones and brickbats lying about the dwellings. On either side at the south end are very rough crowds of children, girls and women and hooligan boys loafing about. North of the dwellings are County Council buildings, Clandon Buildings etc. 3-st, less poor but poor, LIGHT BLUE. Gun St should be LIGHT BLUE and

DARK BLUE and the whole should have a line of BLACK.

W & N up **Miniver Street** (late Martain St). Road up, strong smell of gas. LCC Dwellings. Gun St buildings run through at south east. Children very dirty and inhabitants very poor looking. LIGHT BLUE to DARK BLUE, in map LIGHT BLUE.

W & S down **Lancaster Street**. 3-st and 2-st. 15/- for 3-st houses. Mixture of factory labourers, mechanics and city warehousemen, many poor. St Alphege's Mission at north east. PURPLE as map.

W & N up **Little Surrey Street**. 2-st. Very poor, nearly every door open. Heavy bloated-faced women, middle aged and old, not young mothers. Birdcages at windows. Houses in fair outward repair. Fearful mess of bread, meat, paper and sacking in the street. "Same class as Joiner St." Gas lamps from wall brackets. Children sore-eyed, hatless, some clean. Many cats. Organ playing but only one child dancing. DARK BLUE-barred rather than LIGHT BLUE-barred of map.

E along **Friar Place**. Houses on north side only. DARK BLUE as map.

W & S down **Warwick Street**. 3-st. Narrow dark street. Tenements, family to each floor. Many builder's labourers. Small turning off west side rather poorer. Bread, paper, mess. Mark the street PURPLE and the turning LIGHT BLUE, all in map is PINK.

N to **Friar Street**. The Hope Mission Hall has taken place of DARK BLUE court shown in map on north east side. Wicks rotary type machine factory on north side, only a few now living on north side. North side between Green St and Board School down. South side is shops with poor living over. PURPLE as map but less of it.

W & N up **Great Suffolk Street**. East side poor, fairly comfortable on west. Old inhabitants. Should be PINK and PURPLE and LIGHT BLUE, in map PURPLE.

W & S down **Hill Street**. Drapers Almshouses still remain but Rowland Hill's Almshouses are now Parnwell's Cooperage. The LIGHT BLUE on south west of map is now down.

W & S down **Belvedere Buildings**. Houses on west only. PURPLE as map. 3-st and 3½-st. Factories on east.

N up **Green Street**. Some DARK BLUE remains but there are some fairly comfortable on either side north of Kings Bench Walk and wedged close by some very poor. On the east side are Merrow and Ripley Buildings, LCC red-brick, which run through to Kings Bench Walk. North of them there are some very poor. In the west side all the courts are down and replaced by Salsbury's lamp works and Harrison & Barkers' horse slaughtering establishment (the same people have a large place in Belle Isle).

Bird Court. Remains. Houses on north side. Cardboard box homework. DARK BLUE.

E along **Kings Bench Walk**. "Used to be a nest of criminals", now few remain but the old houses are still very poor. DARK BLUE, LIGHT BLUE where the LCC building come through from Green St. In map DARK BLUE-barred.

N & W along **Pocock Street**. East end north side is PINK but some poor in the street. PURPLE as a whole as map.

W & S down **Wellington Place**. 2-st. Very poor, criminal. Tops of cardboard hatboxes drying at the windows. Children well fed. DARK BLUE to LIGHT BLUE, perhaps LIGHT BLUE-barred, in map LIGHT BLUE.

N up Blackfriars Rd and E at **Surrey Row**. Better than it used to be, very poor only at the north east and north west. Some PINK on the south side. Many printing office labs. LIGHT BLUE, in map DARK BLUE (leave DARK BLUE at the north east and north west) and take off the RED from the south side.

Out of the NE end is **Caran Terrace**. Nine houses. 2-st. 5/- for two rooms, no wash-house. LIGHT BLUE to DARK BLUE, in map DARK BLUE.